Austria-Hungary
& the Successor States

EUROPEAN  NATIONS

AUSTRIA-HUNGARY
& THE SUCCESSOR STATES
A REFERENCE GUIDE
FROM THE RENAISSANCE TO THE PRESENT

Eric Roman

✓®
Facts On File, Inc.

Austria-Hungary and the Successor States: A Reference Guide from the Renaissance to the Present

Facts On File, Inc.
132 West 31st Street
New York NY 10001

Library of Congress Cataloging-in-Publication Data
Roman, Eric
　　Austria-Hungary and the successor states : a reference guide from the Renaissance to the present / by Eric Roman.
　　　　p. cm. — (European nations series)
　　Includes bibliographical references and index.
　　　ISBN 0-8160-4537-2
　　1. Austria—Ethnic relations—Dictionaries. 2. Austria—History—1519–1740—Dictionaries. 3. Austria—History—1740–1789—Dictionaries. 4. Austria—History—1789–1900—Dictionaries. 5. Nationalism—Austria—History—Dictionaries. 6. Austria—History—20th century—Dictionaries. 7. Nationalism—Hungary—History—Dictionaries. 8. Nationalism—Czechoslovakia—History—Dictionaries. 9. Nationalism—Yugoslavia—History—Dictionaries. I. Title. II. Series.
　　DB33.R66 2003
　　943'.003—dc21   2002192842

Facts On File books are available at special discounts when purchased in bulk quantities for businesses, associations, institutions, or sales promotions. Please call our Special Sales Department in New York at (212) 967-8800 or (800) 322-8755.

You can find Facts On File on the World Wide Web at http://www.factsonfile.com

Text design by David C. Strelecky
Cover design by Semadar Megged
Maps by Jeremy Eagle © Facts On File, Inc.

Printed in the United States of America

VB FOF 10 9 8 7 6 5 4 3 2 1

This book is printed on acid-free paper.

CONTENTS

FOREWORD

This series was inspired by the need of high school and college students to have a concise and readily available history series focusing on the evolution of the major European powers and other influential European states in the modern age—from the age of the Renaissance to the present. Written in accessible language, the projected volumes include all of the major European countries: France, Germany, Great Britain, Italy, and Russia, as well as other states such as Spain, Portugal, Austria, and Hungary that have made important intellectual, political, cultural, and religious contributions to Europe and the world. The format has been designed to facilitate usage and includes a short introduction by the author of each volume, a specialist in its history, providing an overview of the importance of the particular country in the modern period. This is followed by a narrative history of each nation from the time of the Renaissance to the present. The core of the volume consists of an A–Z dictionary of people, events, and places, providing coverage of intellectual, political, diplomatic, cultural, social, religious, and economic developments. Next, a chronology details key events in each nation's development over the past several centuries. Finally, the end matter includes a selected bibliography of readily available works, maps, and an index to the material within the volume.

—Frank J. Coppa, General Editor
St. John's University

INTRODUCTION

The history of Europe, until the dawn of the 20th century, could conveniently and reliably be told through the history of its empires. In ancient times, as the Roman Empire rose to a commanding position unequaled ever since, political Europe was largely confined to the Mediterranean regions, and Roman power extended only as far north as the Rhine, the Danube, and to southern Britain. By some accounts it was the almost hypnotic memory of the Roman Empire, bridging differences of language, customs, religion, and tradition, that inclined Europeans of later centuries to submerge national aspirations in a larger political framework to which the name "empire" was, at times arbitrarily, applied. While such a framework proved useful in promoting economic integration and a uniform legal structure, it was vulnerable to tensions produced by the great diversity of European populations.

Until the 19th century "submerged nationalities" generally submitted without serious protest to the authority of the dominant nation and of the ruling house. But after the French Revolution and the Napoleonic Wars, both powerful agents of nationalism (as well as of progressive ideals hostile to tyrannical rule), cracks began to appear in the fabric of empires. The Napoleonic empire itself had to yield to the pressures it had helped to bring about, and within a short time the spirit it had fostered afflicted the eastern empires—the Russian, the Ottoman, and the Austrian—which for centuries had held congeries of diverse nationalities and religions together. In retrospect it was the tragedy of late 19th century Europe that the three empires declined simultaneously, not at the same rate but with the same consistency, the Russian due to its inability to master the changes produced by the emancipation of the serfs, the Ottoman and Austrian due to the growing self-assertion of their subject nationalities. In part to resist these forces of dissolution, and in part because territorial expansion was a hallmark of great power status, the three empires were also in an almost permanent state of hostility with one another, deepening their internal crises.

A historian of empires is always challenged to explain by virtue of what particular gift one nation is able to impose its will on several others and turn an initial conquest or acquisition into dominion. In the case of Russia the answer lies in the very peculiar geographic conditions that had enabled first the Varangians (Vikings) and later the Mongolians to exert a disproportionate invigorating influence on one part of the Slavic host that populated what is now known as European Russia at the expense of others; in the case of the Ottoman it lies in a superior military system, whose efficacy, however, always far outstripped that of the political configuration and in the end succumbed to the weakness of the latter; Austria is, in more than one respect, a case apart.

❋ ❋ ❋

The Austrian Habsburg Empire, whose history is the subject of this volume, was assembled over centuries in a haphazard manner into a political entity so vast that it proved impossible to govern from a single center by a single member of the ruling family. Territorial conquest was assuredly not the chief instrument of its construction; most lands were added to the core area of alpine Austria by marriage, inheritance, great power consensus, voluntary submission or, as in the case of Galicia, the partition of a sovereign state whose remaining parts were added to other empires. In a legal sense the Austrian was not a unitary empire as the monarch ruled not over a single political entity but over individual parts separately, bore different titles in each and, at least theoretically, was obliged to take an oath to the constitution of each. With the exception of one brief period during the French Revolution, the Habsburgs made no serious attempt to imbue the constituent populations with a sense of unity; the empire remained a collection of diverse political units in which languages like German, Hungarian, Czech, Italian, Flemish, French, Serbian, and a number of lesser ones were spoken; the attempt of one ruler, Joseph II, to make German the language of official intercourse within the bulk of the empire proved a sorry failure. Administratively, as well as militarily, Austria never achieved a truly workable system; it bungled from one misbegotten attempt at uniformity to another; even after the Austrian Empire was transformed into the Austro-Hungarian Dual Monarchy based on a carefully crafted written constitution, it only partially succeeded in governing itself with any degree of efficiency. Of this empire one of its subjects, a Czech, nevertheless wrote that if it did not exist, it would have to be invented. His rationale was that ultimately the stubborn, if unimaginative, rule of the Habsburgs alone brought some measure of unity to a region where no other cohesive force existed.

With the progressive weakening of the Ottoman Empire it also fell to the struggling monarchy of Austria-Hungary to bring a manner of political unity, as well as modernity, to backward Balkan regions resistant to both. The endeavor was by and large successful, but it also awakened the hostility of Slavic populations native to the region; that in turn made the Balkans the most unstable and turbulent region in Europe. When the attempt of the South Slavs, spearheaded by a Serbia supported by Russia, to carve out a state of their own clashed with Austrian determination, supported by Germany, to preserve the Dual Monarchy, the Great War of 1914 erupted. It spelled the end of empires and in a region between the White Sea and the Balkan foothills eight new states emerged in an area previously ruled by empires. The struggle of these "successor states" to work out an equilibrium along a political fault line underlying the region proved no more successful than had the previous struggle of the empires to keep national separatism and rivalry in check.

❊ ❊ ❊

The present work traces the history of the Austrian Empire from its beginnings to its dissolution and then the histories of the successor states of a separate Austria and Hungary, as well as of the new states of Czechoslovakia and Yugoslavia, to the present day. It provides a study in both the construction and administration of empires and in the arduous struggles of nation-making. The three-part division into chronology, lexicon, and history will serve as a prism to view this momentous history from different angles; the perusal of each part will afford the reader a useful and informative survey, though only the three in conjunction will provide a full sweep of the complex histories of Austria, Hungary, and the nations that emerged from under their rule after the Great War.

In the course of time a great deal of controversy had grown up over the history of this makeshift empire. Between British prime minister William Gladstone, who said, "Austria has been the unflinching foe of freedom in every country of Europe. . . . There is not one instance, there is not a spot upon the whole map where you can lay your finger and say, 'There Austria did good,'" and the Czech nationalist František Palacký, who opined that if the Austrian Empire did not exist, it would have to be invented, almost every historian, politician, and statesman had a sharp positive or negative but seldom neutral view of the Habsburg Empire's historic mission. The fact that under the stresses of the Great War it disintegrated beyond repair is a weighty commentary in itself. Today Austria and Hungary, once proud to be the homes of "master races," are small, neutral states, and their successor states had on the whole proved to be manifest failures. As the ancient Romans said, *Sic transit gloria mundi.*

—Eric Roman
Western Connecticut State
University

HISTORIES

AUSTRIA

CHAPTER ONE

Although there had been sporadic settlements in the area we know as Austria today as far back as 1800 B.C. and later, in the period between the last two ice ages, organized societies date from about 500 B.C., after Venetian and Illyric tribes had established themselves in the southeastern regions. Around 400 B.C. the Celtic tribes made their appearance, and in the second century B.C. Celts and Illyrians merged to create the kingdom of Noricum, which then entered into an alliance with Rome.

Toward the end of the first century B.C. the Romans pushed northward to the Danube and eventually organized three provinces, Raetia in the west, Noricum in the middle, and Pannonia in the east. These were connected by high roads with castles at key locations; the Danube already served as the main avenue for commerce. At the dawn of the Middle Ages castles around which merchants and tradesmen settled for protection grew into commercial centers: from east to west Vindobona (Vienna), Juvavum (Salzburg), Lauriacum (Lorsch), Brigantium (Bregenz). During the great folk-wanderings in the Middle Ages, Goths, Huns, Lombards, Avars, and other tribes seeking greener pastures made their way westward, mainly along the valley of the Danube. From the sixth century A.D. onward, Germanic Bavarians settled northwest from present-day Austria, while in the south and east Slavic peoples spread from the southern foothills of the Alps into the northern Balkans. This was the time when feudalism struck firm roots in the region and Christianity gradually replaced tribal systems of belief. The nobility, allying itself with the church that alone was able to impose discipline and order upon an often unruly peasantry, readily supported missionary activities; by the eighth and ninth centuries Christianity was making great strides among the Slavs as well. When in 798 Salzburg was elevated to a bishopric, it became the religious center of Austrian lands.

The southern Slavs in the Alpine region, called the Slovenes, at first had their own princedom with Kornburg as its capital, but in 743 they were reduced to tributary status by the Bavarians; in 788 both were engulfed in Charlemagne's sweeping annexations and became provinces of his Frankish empire. The eastern reaches of that empire became *marks*, frontier regions protecting against unceasing onslaughts from the east, especially by the Avars; in 803 Charlemagne established the Ostmark in Pannonia (western Hungary) and the archduchy of Carinthia in the south. At the end of the ninth century the ferocious Magyars (Hungarians) took possession of the Carpathian Basin, including much of Pannonia, and, after defeating the Bavarians near Pressburg in

907, they continued their westward march well beyond the Enns River in Lower Austria. Only their defeat in 955 at Lechfeld near Augsburg by united German forces under Emperor Otto I put an end to their uncoordinated conquests in the west. Otto I then reestablished the Carolingian frontier posts, the Ostmark (which in 996 was first referred to as *Ostarrichi* (Austria in Latin). In 976 the emperor assigned this eastern region of Austria to a member of the Babenberg dynasty. Carinthia in the south separated itself from Bavaria and became an independent princedom. In the fluid political conditions of the age, in 1192 the Babenbergs also acquired Styria as an archduchy.

Although feudalism was the dominant system of landholding, its conditions were not uniform through the land. In Austria, Styria, and Carinthia the great majority of the peasantry was reduced to bonded serfdom, in Tyrol they were more or less free subjects of the *Landesherr* (lord of the land) and participated in the political life of the province. Meanwhile urban centers developed significantly as Austria's central position in the east-west as well as north-south commercial axes stimulated the enlargement of existing towns and the founding of new ones. Among the former, Vienna, first referred to as a city in 1137, became the outstanding one.

The Babenberg family died out in 1250; in the ensuing struggle for the possession of Austria the Czech king Ottokar Přemysl emerged victorious. In 1261 he added the archduchy of Styria, and in 1269 Carinthia, to his possessions. But in 1278 Ottokar was in his turn defeated by the Habsburg king Rudolf, who incorporated the conquered provinces as feudal fiefs in his holdings. In 1282 Rudolf donated Austria and Styria to his sons, Albert and Rudolf, respectively; thus began the long rule of the Habsburgs over Austrian lands. In part through purchase, in part through inheritance, and more seldom through conquest, other lands were later added: Carinthia in 1335, Tyrol in 1363; parts of Vorarlberg in 1375. When in 1382 Istria and the Windische Mark were gained, and Trieste surrendered itself, the Habsburg lands acquired an outlet to the Adriatic Sea.

Yet ability, statesmanship, and intelligence were seldom virtues of which Habsburg princes could boast. It might be cynical to attribute their good fortune over the centuries to luck, perhaps fortified by a gift for scheming and, when necessary, for outright brutality, but, given the mediocrity of most of the princes of their line, that conclusion is hard to escape. The extent of Habsburg lands waxed and waned but in the long run it always grew. As rulers of Austrian hereditary lands the Habsburgs were archdukes, but subsequent titles bore witness to the motley nature of their acquisitions: margrave of Styria, duke of Carinthia and Carniola, count of Tyrol, king of Bohemia, margrave of Moravia, duke of Silesia, king of Hungary, Croatia, Slavonia, and Dalmatia, prince of Transylvania; their imperial title from the mid-14th century on derived from their elective office as Holy Roman Emperor.

It was by dint of that last title that the Austrian Habsburgs assumed a commanding position in all-German affairs. Although the Holy Roman Empire is often cited as one of the oddities of European history, it was also the political entity that perpetuated the ideals and practices of the Middle Ages well into modern times. It was a crossbreed of the feudal principle of particularism, on the one hand, and of the Christian dream of uniting the peoples of Europe, regardless of ethnic and cultural differences, in one empire under Christ on the other. To be sure, of the two impulses the former proved more powerful and enduring: the more than 300 political units in the empire jealously guarded their separateness and privileges, resisting all attempts at centralization. The ideal of Christian unity failed to attract countries beyond central Europe; almost from its proclamation in 962 (as a continuation, or resurrection, of the Carolingian Empire) the Holy Roman Empire's geographic boundaries made it in effect an enlarged Germany. Well over half of the entities within it were church estates governed by archbishops or abbots, a smaller number were governed by princes; one, Bohemia, curiously the only one where Czech rather than German was the native language, by a king; there were some 50 free cities ruled by the wealthy merchant class, and an indeterminate number of small knightly holdings. The rulers resisted the trend of the new monarchies, as they were developing in France, Spain, England, and elsewhere, in which the entrenched nobility gradually yielded to central royal authority and where succession followed established bloodlines. Holy Roman Emperors were elected; from 1356 on by seven electors, three ecclesiastical and four secular, who chose the new emperor upon the death of the old one, and the coronation was an occasion for confirming local liberties. The first Habsburg to serve as Holy Roman Emperor was Rudolf I, elected in 1273, but it was from 1438 on, when the electors chose Albert V emperor as Albert II that the Habsburgs, by means honorable or otherwise and with one brief exception, had themselves elected continuously until 1740, when Charles VI died without a male heir and his daughter's husband, Francis of Lorraine, ascended the imperial throne. Properly speaking the line was from then on not purely Habsburg, but the Habsburg-Lorraine designation is somewhat pedantic; the Austrian Empire continued to be known, until its demise in 1918, as the Habsburg Empire.

The arch maxim, *bella gerant alii; to felix Austria nube* (let others wage war, you happy Austria marry) hints at a long series of felicitous marriages; actually there were only two of significance in succession, but they bestowed upon the Habsburgs the largest empire ever ruled by a single family. The first acquisition of noncontiguous land was the princedom of Burgundy. Its core area (for it was a patchwork of scattered holdings) was then part of the Holy Roman Empire, but its prince, Charles the Bold, held several of its holdings as a vassal of the French king, Louis XI. The question of his primary allegiance would in the end be resolved by marriage. Charles the Bold had but a daughter, Mary; the man she married would inherit not only Burgundy but other possessions of Charles along the key Rhine waterway, including the Netherlands. Louis XI designated his 10-year-old son as Mary's future husband, but he had nothing to offer in return for her hand; Frederick III of Habsburg however, as Holy Roman Emperor, could bestow upon Charles the title of king he coveted, and Ferdinand had a 17-year-old son, Maximilian. He sent him with a large entourage to Burgundy to declare for Mary's hand. Mary, 18, not surprisingly chose the handsome young Habsburg over the prospective 10-year-old French bridegroom; the great expansion of the Habsburg Empire began.

Holy Roman Emperor Charles V *(Hulton/Archive)*

Maximilian and Mary of Burgundy had a son, Philip; he in time married the oldest daughter of Ferdinand of Aragon and Isabella of Castile, Joanna, while Philip's sister Margaret married Joanna's brother, Juan, the crown prince, thus establishing a dual Habsburg claim to the crown of what by the union of Castile and Aragon became the kingdom of Spain. All this occurred in the closing years of the 1400s, when the possessions of Spain were immensely enriched by the discovery of the New World. The Spanish crown prince died while his parents were still alive and the Habsburgs became the expectant heirs to an empire spanning the Atlantic and a stretch of the Pacific. Philip himself died early, but not before he had fathered two sons, Charles and Ferdinand, and a number of daughters. The young man who in the end fell heir to all the wealth that the Habsburgs had married was Charles, 15 years of age when he became king of the Netherlands, and still hardly more than a boy when other possessions devolved upon him (not Burgundy though; to that province the French king was able to make good his claim). He was 19 years old when he was elected Holy Roman Emperor as Charles V.

Charles treated his younger brother Ferdinand, whom he first met only when he was 15 and Ferdinand 13, with less than respect and affection, but when he found the governance of his vast inheritance too burdensome, in 1522, at Brussels, he assigned his Austrian possessions to Ferdinand's regency. Thus began the division of the Habsburg line into an eastern and a western branch, a division that would become definitive when Charles abdicated the Spanish throne in 1556.

Maximilian, who had started the process that made the Habsburgs the wealthiest dynasty in the world, lived until January 1519, long enough to hear about an audacious Augustinian monk, one Martin Luther, who had taken issue with the very church he served as a humble foot soldier, thus beginning the movement Protestants would call the Reformation and Catholics the Protestant Revolt.

The Austrian lands, which now fell to Ferdinand to govern, were modest and backward compared with the western empire; as to territorial expansion, Ferdinand's only prospect was that his sister, Maria, was married to the young Jagiellonian king of Hungary and of Bohemia, Lajos II. Ferdinand's own wife Anna also had some obscure claim to the Bohemian throne. But Lajos was still in his teens and there was no realistic chance that he would vacate his throne any time soon. His kingdom, however, lay athwart the broad path along which the Ottoman Turks were advancing toward the heart of Europe; opening up unforeseeable opportunities, as well as perils, if and when Hungary should be engulfed in the advance.

Sultan Selim died in 1520 and was succeeded by his son Suleiman, during whose 46-year reign the Ottoman Empire reached the height of its power and glory. After some initial thrusts into Hungary, in the course of which he took a few border fortresses, Suleiman's huge army in 1526 invaded Hungary. Near the town of Mohács his forces encircled and annihilated the Hungarian army; Lajos himself drowned in a swollen creek as he tried to flee the scene of battle. At one stroke the thrones of both Hungary and Bohemia fell vacant. To the Bohemian throne there were other claimants besides the Habsburgs, notably the powerful Wittelsbach dynasty of Bavaria, but Ferdinand's clever and financially generous agents secured the consent of the Bohemian estates to his coronation, which took place on October 23, 1526, in Prague. The subordinate provinces of Moravia, Silesia, and Lausitz duly followed Bohemia's lead.

Hungary proved to be a different case. Back in 1505, on the field of Rákos, the powerful nobles, who were the effective ruling caste in the kingdom, resolved that henceforth only a Hungarian could occupy the throne. As it happened, there was an eminently suitable native candidate at hand to succeed to the kingship. János Szapolyai, a high noble from Transylvania, had recently put down a widespread peasant revolt with draconian severity and earned the gratitude and respect of his fellow nobles. In November 1526, less than three months after the death of Lajos II, Szapolyai's followers elected him king. There was, however, a strong rival faction gathered around the widow Maria that favored Ferdinand's election. Certain earlier written agreements between Hungarian kings and the House of Habsburg served as a legal basis for the claim; the more practical reason was that the defeat at Mohács had so decimated the Hungarian army as to render it helpless in face of the Turkish threat, and the Habsburgs alone possessed the means of halting, and possibly reversing, the advance. Thus on December 17, at Pressburg, this faction bestowed upon Ferdinand the royal title.

The new king certainly was not widely popular, even in Austria. Although from a family that had its roots in German Austria, he was a Spaniard, born and raised in Iberia; he spoke German poorly and surrounded himself with a foreign entourage. He was decidedly of limited intelligence but hard-working and conscientious. He early realized that the meager administrative apparatus he inherited no longer served the needs of his enlarged empire and, on January 1, 1527, he issued a rescript outlining the governance of his realms; the system he established would remain in effect until 1848. The highest authority was the

Secret Council, composed originally of six members, later enlarged, consisting of councillors of his own choosing and of family dignitaries. It dealt with dynastic and foreign policy matters. A separate Court Council acted as the supreme court, at first for the whole eastern empire, and later, because of repeated complaints from Hungary and Bohemia, only for Austria. After his brother Charles abdicated as emperor, the competence of the Court Council was extended to the Holy Roman Empire as well. The court chancellery that dealt with purely administrative matters was of old standing; Ferdinand enlarged it from three to seven sections, three dealing with Austrian, two each with Hungarian and Bohemian affairs. Starting in 1559 the latter provinces had their own chanceries. Finally the Court Chamber, with subordinate offices in the diverse provinces, was responsible for financial affairs.

Yet in a figurative sense, with grave practical consequences, the crown was still divided. Ferdinand, fearing that every day Szapolyai's claim remained unchallenged his own would be weakened, early in 1527 sent his armies, fortified with Czech and imperial troops, to invade Hungary. They routed Szapolyai's forces, confining the land he ruled essentially to Transylvania. On November 3, 1527, Ferdinand was crowned king of Hungary a second time.

Although Szapolyai had for years been a vocal advocate of the struggle against the Turks, in his hard-pressed position he turned to the Porte, the Ottoman government, for support against his royal rival. Suleiman welcomed any opportunity to weaken Habsburg power and threw in his lot with Szapolyai, thus in a way posing as a champion of an independent Hungary. But direct military help was not forthcoming and Szapolyai's position continued so precarious that he was forced to leave Hungary altogether and seek refuge in Poland. It was here that he was joined by a gifted Paulist monk, György Martinuzzi, who for the rest of János's life and beyond proved to be a trusted friend and adviser of the Szapolyais. The ousted king collected an army in Poland and invaded Hungary; in a dramatic change of fortunes it was Ferdinand who found himself in a tenuous position.

Suleiman did not wait long before he took advantage of Ferdinand's predicament. After the Battle of Mohács, he had retreated to Constantinople but in 1529 resumed his offensive in the direction of Hungary on his way to Austria. He laid siege to Vienna in September; the early onset of cold weather found his troops, who were used to the Mediterranean climate, unprepared, and in October the siege was lifted. Suleiman made another thrust, this time from the south, against Vienna, in 1532, but was puzzlingly halted in the siege of the small and insignificant fortress of Kőszeg. Most likely he had second thoughts about engaging the Habsburgs who by now had help from many other Christian countries, and once again he retreated.

Ferdinand and Szapolyai did not come to terms until 1538, when both had reason to end the draining struggle. Szapolyai had proposed to a Polish princess and could gain her hand only if he validated his claim as king; Ferdinand was urged by his brother Charles to make peace lest Szapolyai yield Hungary to the Turks. In the Peace of Várad, Ferdinand and Szapolyai pronounced each other brothers and they agreed that each would keep the land he held at present,

Szapolyai essentially Transylvania, Ferdinand the western strip and the northern province. Should Szapolyai die first, Ferdinand would inherit his realm, but if Ferdinand predeceased him, his own son, or that of Charles V, would inherit the entire country.

In July 1540 Szapolyai's wife bore a son, János Zsigmond; Szapolyai renounced the agreement and on his death bed instructed Martinuzzi to preserve his land in favor of the infant. Thus the peace of Várad lasted only a year.

The war with the Turks was stalemated, but a new offensive from Constantinople could come any time; still, in the century that followed the most crucial and divisive question in Austrian, as well as all-German, affairs centered on the religious issue. The struggle between Catholics and Lutherans defied accommodation, and, when an uneasy peace was finally reached at Augsburg in 1555, it proved to be a peace of exhaustion rather than of reconciliation and religious enmity continued unabated.

CHAPTER TWO

Ever since Roman emperor Valentinian V had decreed in A.D. 444 that the bishop of Rome was superior to all the bishops in the empire, the institution of the papacy, and by extension of the Christian clergy, had been so firmly built into the religious, social, and political structure of Europe that any challenge to its authority was considered blasphemous and potentially suicidal. Yet it was precisely such a challenge that Martin Luther offered when he proposed that the efficacy of the sacraments, and indeed salvation itself, depended not on priestly ministrations but on individual faith. Taken literally, that meant that in the absence of true faith on the part of the supplicant the priest was helpless. He could not perform the miracle of the Mass and final rites were empty rituals. Put in a more direct way, the clergy became superfluous. Luther sought to give moral authority to this dictum in his pamphlet, *The Babylonian Captivity of the Christian Church,* in which he argued that just as the Jews of antiquity had been held captive in Babylonia, Christianity had for a thousand years been captive to a corrupt clergy. He went a step further when he claimed to discover that the clergy, to advance its own position, had sanctioned sacraments unsupported by the Scriptures. Luther insisted that final authority rested not with the pope but in the Scriptures, which every Christian was both free and duty-bound to read and interpret for himself.

Little wonder that the priestly establishment from the pope down took immediate issue with Luther's arrogant presumptions. Holy Roman Emperor Charles V, then 21 years old, gave Luther a chance at the Diet of Worms in April 1521 to renounce his teachings; when Luther refused, the struggle between Catholics and Lutherans assumed epic proportions. Would the Catholic clergy, its own presumptions and corruptions having been exposed, be able to assert its authority, as well as its efficacy in granting salvation, among skeptical believers dismayed by the worldly and unseemly conduct of so many priests and friars? The challenge was formidable indeed.

In Austria, where Catholicism had deep roots, yet where the peasantry lived in exceptionally dire conditions which the clergy seemed to condone on the argument that resolute suffering paved the way to heaven, the exposure of the clergy as cynical timeservers was particularly fraught with danger. Ferdinand's authority was not firm enough to impose his Catholic convictions over all of his provinces. Upper and Lower Austria, Carinthia, Carniola, and Styria had their own estates, which possessed primary authority over local matters, including the religious. A number of high nobles, either out of defiance of the Habsburgs or out of genuine conviction, quickly embraced Lutheran teachings; many of those who retained their Catholic faith showed enough interest in reformist ideas to send their sons to universities in Germany proper, to Wittenberg, Tübingen, and later, when Calvin had established himself in Switzerland, to Geneva. These young men, upon returning home, often succeeded in converting their families to the new learning. Lutheranism also made many converts among the peasantry, but in that downtrodden stratum Anabaptism (re-baptisement) became more popular. The putative founder of Anabaptism was the Swiss Conrad Grebel, and nothing in his early teachings suggested a radical social message. He was a religious reformer; he differed from most other reformers in his rejection of the very idea of an *established* church, a *Volkskirche,* into which one was born and whose beliefs and commitments were imposed on him. Religious belief in Grebel's view was a matter of free choice. For this reason he also rejected infant baptism; baptism had to be voluntary, accompanied by a pledge to live a holy life. He could not reconcile holiness with the pomp and ostentation of the Roman Catholic Church, with its failure to promote equality and its acceptance of a social elite, which made its condemnation of wealth as a product of usury hypocritical. He advocated joint ownership of property and extreme simplicity of religious worship, but it was his egalitarianism that appealed to the lower classes—though there were a number of converts to Anabaptism among the nobility too. Because of the radicalism of the sect and its insistence on biblical authority exclusively, Anabaptists suffered persecution by Catholics and Lutherans alike; their refusal to resort to physical resistance produced more martyrs than any other faith. Grebel himself was burned at the stake at age 28.

In Austria the foremost Anabaptist was Jakob Huter, who, to escape persecutions, transported his "brotherhood" to Moravia, where members lived a communal life in sharing all material possessions. When Huter made a return trip to his native Tyrol, he was seized, condemned, and burned at the stake in Innsbruck in 1536. But, as is usually the case with religious persecutions, far from shaking the faith of the believers, such acts only fortified it; both Lutheranism and Anabaptism continued to make significant gains in German lands. Ferdinand could not leave the difficult task of dealing with religious dissent to the Catholic establishment alone; in Austria, according to ancient tradition, not the church but the secular ruler as *advocatus ecclasiae* had to lead the fight against all forms of heresy. When Ferdinand made his periodic visitations, the testimony of his own eyes confirmed the rapid spread of Protestant teachings. By the 1550s these teachings reached the southern Slav regions of the Habsburg lands; a Slovenian theologian, Primus Trubert, translated the New Testament into Slovenian and received generous support from a high Styrian noble, Hans Ungnad. Even after Ungnad was forced to give up his official position and transfer himself to Württemberg, he continued to show helpful interest in Trubert's work.

Ferdinand labored mightily to overcome the many difficulties that beset his empire. He was not a fanatic but he realized the danger of adding to the diverse elements in his lands that of religious dissent. The Turks, always on the alert for signs of weakness in Austria, remained a constant threat. Ferdinand was king of Hungary but controlled only the narrow western part of the country and the northern highlands; the central portion was under Turkish occupation, and the princes of the eastern province of Transylvania acted independently, at times fighting against the Turks, at other times cooperating with them against the Habsburgs. Most of them were champions of Protestantism. Even the German-speaking lands were rent by discord. Ferdinand's eldest son, Maximilian, destined to inherit his crowns, showed distinct Protestant leanings. The Holy Roman Empire, from the mid-1540s was a battleground between the Catholic League and the Protestant Union and the outcome of the struggle carried the potential for changing the entire equilibrium in the German lands.

On the religious front Ferdinand benefited from two separate but complementary developments: the Protestant camp was plagued by doctrinal disagreements, which effectively prevented united opposition to the Catholic Church, whereas the latter, realizing that if it wanted to put an end to doubt and dispute, it would have to state its position on all contested theological issues unequivocally, assembled a great council at the city of Trent for just that purpose. This council convened, disbanded, convened again, was visited by an outbreak of the plague, and finally finished its work in 1562. While it instituted firm disciplinary measures against questionable practices by the clergy, in doctrinal matters it made no concession to Protestantism; all the dogmas of the church were stated and reaffirmed in majestic language. No Catholic had any reason to wonder whether his prayers, rituals, and beliefs were pleasing to God or whether salvation was attainable by alternate means. A militant order, the Society of Jesus, commonly known as the Jesuits, was active in many lands, its agents targeting first and foremost renegade Catholics associated with one or another Protestant denomination. In the 1550s, at Ferdinand's invitation, the Jesuits established themselves in Vienna and Prague, later in Innsbruck as well. The first missionaries were not German, but their work in parts of the empire proved successful.

The religious question remained of special importance as the Muslim threat from the south showed no sign of abating. In 1562 Suleiman the Magnificent offered peace on condition that Ferdinand pay a heavy yearly tribute in exchange for remaining safe from attack; although Ferdinand agreed, no one expected that the peace would last long. Indeed, in 1566 the aging sultan launched still another attack against Hungary. He invested the fort of Sziget but died in the midst of the siege; his death was kept secret even from his own soldiers; Vienna did not learn of it until two years later. In 1588 another peace was negotiated and the obligation to pay tribute was extended.

Ferdinand himself died in 1564. Either because he did not trust his oldest son's Catholicism, or because he wanted to preclude a fratricidal struggle over the inheritance, or possibly because he deemed separate smaller provinces easier to control and govern than a heterogenous empire, 10 years earlier he had provided that the eastern Habsburg inheritance should be divided among his three sons. The oldest, Maximilian (who in 1548 had married his cousin Maria, daughter of Charles V), received Upper and Lower Austria, and in 1562, with Ferdinand still alive, he was also crowned king of Hungary and of Bohemia. The second son, Ferdinand, inherited the Tyrol and the Vorlände, small principalities in the northwestern corner of the empire; the youngest, Charles, came into possession of Styria, Carinthia, Carniola, and the Adriatic provinces.

Maximilian was crowned Holy Roman Emperor in 1564. He had promised his father before the latter's death that he would remain a faithful Catholic, and he kept his promise, but not to the extent of continuing the persecution of Protestants. Unlike his father, he had no love for the Spanish branch of the family; he had been in Spain between 1548 and 1550 and had developed an antipathy for the rigid protocol of the court and for the unrelenting and uncompromising Catholicism of his Spanish relatives. The same feelings motivated him in his dealings with Jesuits. He knew Luther's teachings well; his papers discovered after his death contained many Lutheran writings. Those around him knew that it required of him great self-control to sit through the long Catholic services; to one of the papal legates he once declared that he was neither a Papist nor a Lutheran but a Christian. In 1568 he proclaimed religious toleration in his realms; in 1571 he allowed his nobles freedom to choose their religion (though by the terms of the Augsburg Peace of 1555 the subjects of each state in the Holy Roman Empire had to adopt the religion of the ruler). However, he bestowed no such freedom on the cities.

In the provinces ruled by Maximilian's brother Ferdinand, Catholicism had much sturdier roots, especially in the Tyrol; the great majority of the nobility remained Catholic, as did most of the peasantry. Only in the cities and in the mine districts did Lutheranism make significant gains; Anabaptists were either expelled or forced to leave. In the central and southern provinces, however, where Charles ruled, the religious conflict remained sharp and divisive. Both Charles and his wife, Maria of Wittelsbach, were firmly Catholic, and they faced a formidable challenge from the estates; the latter, encouraged by Maximilian's concessions within his own realms, were as determined to defend their privilege to choose their own religion as their ruler was in trying to extinguish it. Charles was forced to opt for the path that so many Catholic rulers, who at first resolved not to yield on the religious question, eventually chose; in February 1572 he proclaimed "religious pacification." To a provincial assembly meeting in Graz he stressed his own unbroken loyalty to Catholicism but granted religious freedom to the noble and knightly estates, as well as to their serfs, knowing full well that serfs had little choice in the matter. Protestants were even allowed to found missionary schools until such time as a "comprehensive Christian peaceful compromise" had been reached. Here too, however, the cities, with their independent-minded bourgeoisies and their pockets of Jewish congregations, did not enjoy the same rights.

These compromises elicited the scorn of the Spanish Habsburgs who looked on their Austrian kin as poor and feckless relatives, though by now the mighty Spanish ruler Philip II was involved in his own consuming religious strife in the Netherlands, and his unyielding and unforgiving Catholicism in time cost him the northern Dutch provinces. The Spanish branch ruled over Spain, parts of Burgundy, northern Italy, the Netherlands, and most of the New World; the Austrians ruled only over their hereditary German provinces in addition to

Bohemia and Hungary; their hold over Hungary was insecure as Turkish power could strike at any moment, as it repeatedly had in the past. The eastern Habsburgs scoured the landscape for opportunities to conclude another felicitous marriage that would yield a territorial dowry.

In 1572 the opportunity presented itself: the last Jagiellonian king of Poland-Lithuania died. Although governing that country was a near impossibility because of the assertions of an unruly, contentious nobility, the crown was still a great prize. Protestantism had not found a home there, the bulk of the nobility remained Catholic, and the Counter Reformation vigorously suppressed religious dissent. The future king, naturally, would have to be a Catholic. Maximilian himself, as Holy Roman Emperor, did not qualify. His son Ernst was, however, a possibility. The Polish estates were divided but the majority in the end chose Prince Henry of the French house of Valois. Henry's older brother Charles IX died, however, in 1574, and Henry chose to be king of France rather than of Poland-Lithuania. Prince Ernst's name was once again put in nomination; the Polish estates, distrustful of the Habsburgs, turned him down and chose instead the prince of Transylvania, István Báthori. He was by far a safer ruler than the imperious Habsburg.

Maximilian II died on October 12, 1576. He was followed by his oldest son Rudolf, a man of undeniable intelligence and artistic taste, but stubbornly Catholic, mentally unstable, far more interested in esoteric pursuits like clock-making and astronomy than in governing his complex empire. He had been brought up at the Spanish court, totally isolated from all non-Catholic influences; his father in his own lifetime had had him crowned king of Hungary and Bohemia, in 1572 and 1575, respectively; Rudolf was also elected Holy Roman Emperor in 1575. He had four younger brothers, each of whom hoped to be given some part of the inheritance, but Rudolf, bowing to the demands of the estates in the diverse realms, agreed in 1578 that there would be no further territorial divisions. His two uncles, Ferdinand in the Tyrol and Charles in Styria and Inner Austria, were in full agreement with the main thrust of his policy, which was to bring the Counter Reformation to a victorious issue. In Hungary and Bohemia, where Protestantism was well entrenched, Rudolf did not press the matter, but in Austria he was unrelenting. Enforcement was strictest in his brother Charles's realm: Protestant clergymen were summarily expelled from churches and replaced by priests. Catholicism became the established religion and those who refused to convert to it were exiled. Charles and Maximilian were aware of the shallowness of religious conviction imposed by force and allowed Catholic religious orders wide latitude in pursuing their missionary activities; the Jesuits were generally active among the noble classes, the Capuchins among the commoners. Meanwhile in Upper and Lower Austria Melchior Klesl, son of a baker, a quondam Protestant, now a Catholic elevated to the bishopric of Passau, was in charge of returning the population to the "one true faith." When he converted a noble, the serfs followed their master as a matter of course. Those of any station who clung to the Protestant faith (except serfs, who had no choice either in the matter of religion or in the matter of leaving the land) were forced out of Austria.

The entire era was marked by repeated peasant uprisings, sparked by religious dissent, but deeper resentments fueled their fury throughout. Such risings were the nightmare of the landowning classes, Catholic and Protestant alike. One broke out in Upper Austria in May 1594. The peasants at first demanded freedom of worship, but they soon voiced grievances of a more practical kind, protesting their steadily increasing monetary and labor obligations, forced recruitment into military service, uncontrolled plunder by mercenaries who often victimized the peasants when they failed to receive their pay from the royal coffers. It took nearly three years to overcome the uprising, but no lesson was learned; meanwhile, the brutal conditions of serfdom persisted.

And now the Turks were on the warpath again. In 1571 they had suffered a disastrous naval defeat at Lepanto in a battle against a combined Spanish and Venetian fleet, in which most of their 280 galleys had been destroyed; although they rebuilt their navy in a short time, they preferred to fight their battles on land. The war, waged with changing fortunes, lasted 15 years. It demonstrated that the Habsburgs were now able, if not to defeat Ottoman power, to hold it off. Even in the course of the war the religious question complicated the political picture; Transylvania, if it had chosen to accept Habsburg sovereignty at the expense of embracing Catholicism, could have caught the Turks in the center of the country in a vise and possibly expelled them from Hungary altogether, especially as just then the Turks were hard-pressed by their Persian and Anatolian subjects. However, the nobles of Transylvania preferred to put up with the Turkish menace rather than bow to the Catholic Habsburgs.

For its part, the royal house gave no sign of any willingness to live side by side with Protestants. It lacked the means to impose religious uniformity in its distant provinces but served notice on them by demonstrating its resolve in Austria itself. In 1595, after the death of the fanatical Archduke Charles, his son Ferdinand was crowned to rule central and southern Austria. He dispatched reforming commissions accompanied by soldiers along the length and width of his holdings with orders to destroy the material presence of Protestant worship. Churches were closed or razed, Protestant books were burned, and preachers expelled. The turn of the Hungarians, ever rebellious subjects, would come once the Turkish buffer had been removed. But for now, in Transylvania, Protestantism throve, and the prince, István Bocskai, commanding a ragtag force of *hajduk,* shiftless peasants and shepherds, held off Habsburg armies until 1606, when Ferdinand had finally to surrender to a physical and ideological resistance he could not conquer. In the Peace of Vienna he granted freedom of worship to Protestants, a freedom that tacitly extended even to Calvinists.

Negotiations with the Turks had been in progress for some time, and in November 1606 they bore fruit in the Peace of Zsitvatorok. Annual tributes were redeemed by the payment of a lump sum and the sultan (Suleiman the Magnificent's son Selim) recognized Austria as a power of equal standing with his empire. Lines of demarcation were drawn according to the present position of the respective armies. It appeared that the long war between Turks and Habsburgs, Muslims and Christians, had definitively ended.

But Rudolf II, archduke of the larger part of Austria and Holy Roman Emperor, was not inclined to accept the peace with the Turks, or even with the Hungarian estates, judging the concessions made to both excessive. His stubbornness, as his brothers and others at court realized, was due not to sound political considerations but to his growing insanity: periods of apathy were followed by outbursts of rage. His paranoia prompted him to dismiss long trusted counsellors; he ensconced himself in Hradčany Castle in Prague and tinkered with locks and clocks, taking scant interest in affairs of state. At the urging of Melchior Klesl, the militant in service to the Counter Reformation, who took time out from his religious missions, the so-called Secret Council met in Vienna on April 25, 1607, declared Rudolf deposed, and his younger brother Matthias installed as archduke of the Austrian realm. The decision was welcomed by the Austrian and Hungarian estates. The Bohemians alone stuck with Rudolf, hoping to gain freedom of worship in exchange for their loyalty.

In the event Rudolf, still Holy Roman Emperor, did not stand aside meekly, and he managed to retain part of his realm. After a year of negotiations, on June 25, 1608, an uneasy peace was reached in the Habsburg family squabble: Matthias was confirmed in his possession of Upper and Lower Austria, Hungary, and Moravia; Rudolf retained the crown of Bohemia and of the Holy Roman Empire. However, Matthias was 55 years old and tired; he never had much interest in governing and the protracted squabble further discouraged him. He allowed Melchior Klesl, now the leading figure on the Secret Council, to do the actual governing. Klesl was the most unlikely person to mediate between irreconcilable religious beliefs, but he proved his statesmanship by rising above doctrinal debates in working out a compromise with the Protestants, not only in Habsburg lands but in the Holy Roman Empire as well. The Peace of Augsburg was by now half a century old, but it had never carried much conviction and was now in danger of breaking down. Religious questions had acquired such forbidding political and territorial dimensions that conflict in one isolated sphere had the potential of rapidly escalating to general hostilities. Klesl's most sincere and arduous labors proved in vain; in the Holy Roman Empire both the Catholic League and the Protestant Union had its foreign supporters and each side felt confident of victory in case the dispute ended in war.

The question of succession in Austria, and consequently in the Holy Roman Empire, also hung in the balance. Rudolf died in June 1612 and Matthias succeeded him, but because of his advanced age and his insouciance his accession proved a stop-gap solution; his two brothers, barely younger than he, were not viable candidates. Ferdinand, who had destroyed Protestantism in the southern Austrian provinces, made sundry promises should he be elected archduke of all of Austria and Holy Roman Emperor, but he had long forfeited his credibility. Now the Spanish Habsburg, Philip III, put in a bid for restoring the Austrian Habsburg holdings to a state of tranquillity. But Spanish intervention raised the prospect of a restoration of Charles V's monster empire and that distressed everybody. To the non-German countries of the Habsburg Empire Ferdinand appeared the lesser of two evils, especially when he pledged to respect the laws and traditions of Czechs and Hungarians.

Mathias died on March 20, 1619, already an irrelevant figure. Two years before his death the Czech estates had elected Ferdinand as their king; in 1618, the Hungarian estates did likewise. Ferdinand took an oath to respect the privileges granted by his brother to these estates. However, by the time he took the throne the whole political and religious equation had changed; the war that had been brewing for the past two decades, and indeed since the Peace of Augsburg, had broken out, in Bohemia first, and it quickly spread to other parts of the Holy Roman Empire and beyond. Christian Europe was at war with itself, waging the battle with all the fury and intolerance that characterizes civil wars.

CHAPTER THREE

No Habsburg ruler after the start of the Reformation could look forward to a tranquil and politically stable reign. It remains a matter for debate whether the religious cleavage was primarily responsible for the periods of upheaval, both in Austrian lands and in the Holy Roman Empire (even such a staunchly Catholic ruler as Charles V had a number of Protestants in his camp and his brother Ferdinand was tireless in trying to reconcile religious differences), or whether doctrinal quarrels merely raised existing controversies over territory and sovereignty to critical levels. The war that began in 1618 and rapidly escalated to a full-fledged confrontation between Catholic and Protestant forces is generally cited as the culmination of the passions and conflicts that grew out of the Protestant revolt, but, while religious furor no doubt accounted for the ferocity with which it was waged, political rivalries in the end superseded the religious. Catholic powers had fought other Catholic powers long before the war; Austria and France had been adversaries for over a century, competing for land in Italy and along the Rhine; Styria in Inner Austria had, in the early 1600s, warred to secure the Adriatic coast with Venetia, another Catholic state. Even within Austria the dominant question was not so much uniformity of worship but whether portions of the empire, notably Bohemia and Transylvania, with the latter's position legally still undefined, would accept Habsburg domination. In German Austria questions as to whether Protestants were allowed to worship publicly or whether a Protestant church could legally be erected on court property, camouflaged the larger issue of how much independence the estates, divided along religious lines, really had.

Habsburg rulers, as Holy Roman Emperors, had to deal with similar problems in a dangerously enlarged version within the empire. Religious alignments in that sprawling realm were confused and contradictory. By the Peace of Augsburg subjects in each of the more than 300 states were obliged to adopt the religion of their ruler, but this provision was violated wholesale (in Austria first and foremost), as was the so-called ecclesiastical reservation, whereby a Catholic prince-bishop, who converted to Protestantism had to abdicate his princely office and return his estate to the church; the failure to do so placed many more states under Protestant jurisdiction than the Augsburg settlement envisioned. Overriding these irritants was the question of how much power the Holy Roman Emperor really possessed, whether and to what extent individual rulers could defy him and be masters in their own domains. This in turn begged the question of whether the Holy Roman Empire was an entity governed by a single political will or whether it was a loose collection of states that granted the emperor ceremonial rights while each pursued its own political agenda. There was no forum, secular or religious, that could answer these questions and they were too contentious to be resolved by peaceful means.

The Thirty Years' War has a large and complex history of which only an outline can be presented here. When tensions are high a small incident often suffices to light the fuse, and this is what occurred in Prague on May 23, 1618; two Catholic representatives whom Ferdinand had sent from Vienna, Martinico and Slavata, in the course of a debate over the Protestant liberties the Bohemians had taken, were unceremoniously thrown out of a window of the Hradčany palace. Falling on a dung heap, both survived and went on to busy careers in the service of the Habsburgs, but this so-called defenestration gave heart and courage to the perpetrators. They assumed that they had removed Habsburg authority from Bohemia altogether. The province's Protestant estates, after considering several candidates to replace Ferdinand, chose the Calvinist elector of the Rhenish Palatinate, Frederick V. The young man was the son-in-law of English king James I, and the Bohemian nobles expected that James would involve himself in continental affairs on his behalf; further encouragement came in October of that year when the prince of Transylvania, Gábor Bethlen, met with Bohemian nobles in Pressburg to discuss the help he could offer against the Habsburgs. In August 1619 Ferdinand was elected Holy Roman Emperor and acquired, if nothing else, a psychological advantage in dealing with the rebellious Bohemian estates. No help for the latter was forthcoming from the Protestant princes of the Holy Roman Empire. These rulers, as well as their Catholic counterparts, remained neutral, which enabled Ferdinand to raise in Austria forces large enough to prevail. In the historic battle at White Mountain near Prague, on November 8, 1620, his army routed the disorganized, poorly led forces of Frederick V. The defeat marked the effective extinction of Bohemia as a political entity; separatist Czechs and Protestants were now hunted down, killed, or expelled. Many fled of their own accord, and in the decades that followed the population of the province was reduced from over 4 million to 800,000.

Despite the victory, or possibly in consequence of it, the position of the Habsburgs remained grave. They were becoming too powerful to suit either the Catholic or the Protestant states, especially as the peace they had recently (in 1606) concluded with the Turks freed Austrian military forces for employment elsewhere. Yet even in its hereditary provinces the royal house faced a challenge: in 1625 Calvinist peasants in Upper Austria, when attempts were made to replace their clergymen with ousted Catholic priests, rose in protest and earned several victories. It took over a year to put down the revolt, and, in the armistice of 1626, Ferdinand was compelled to promise the lightening of material burdens placed on the peasantry. Meanwhile the Transylvanian prince Gábor Bethlen thrice led campaigns—first for a three-year period between 1619 and 1621, in 1623, and again in 1626—against the Habsburgs on behalf of the Hungarian estates, which chafed under royal control. However, the success of each incursion depended on the support of Bohemian forces that no longer existed, and each resulted in a humiliating retreat.

The Battle of White Mountain resolved Austria's conflict with the subject state of Bohemia, but in the Holy Roman Empire the struggle was just beginning. With Frederick V, the ephemeral king of Bohemia, a fugitive, his native land, the Rhenish Palatinate, became the object of ambitions of the rulers of Bavaria and Spain, both dependable allies of Ferdinand; these two demanded that Austria follow up her victory and occupy the province for their benefit. Ferdinand complied; with armies of the Catholic League joining his forces, he struck against the mercenary armies of the Protestant Union in northern Germany. It was a campaign that promised a quick end to the war. In previous engagements the general of the Catholic League, Count Johannes Tilly, had earned a string of victories against the ill-led and ill-paid Protestant armies. In the summer of 1624 he destroyed their remaining forces and it appeared that the Catholic side faced no more challenges within the Holy Roman Empire.

The Empire had indeed been pacified, by the sword, but now Denmark's Lutheran king, Christian IV, alarmed at the seemingly fatal weakening of the Protestant position, took the field against the Catholic League. The latter entrusted its cause to the prince of the German state of Friedland, Albrecht Wallenstein, who, assuming the rank of marshal, recruited a mercenary army of 30,000. In July 1626 he earned a great victory at the bridge of Dessau; the following month Tilly, commanding his own forces, inflicted another major defeat on the Danish forces. In the course of the next year and a half Wallenstein's Catholic army proceeded to occupy practically all of northern Germany as well as the mainland portion of Denmark. In a peace with Christian IV, on May 22, 1629, the latter pledged never to involve himself in German affairs again.

A general peace on Catholic terms was now a distinct possibility; but Ferdinand of Austria compromised it when, in the flush of victory, he issued an edict demanding that all ecclesiastical estates that had been retained by former archbishops who had converted to Protestantism be returned to Catholic sovereignty. Of course, it was one thing to issue such a sweeping order and another to enforce it. Even Catholic princes were growing uneasy because the edict assumed such plenary powers in the hands of the emperor as even they were not willing to grant. They feared with good reason that Ferdinand would not stop by imposing his will in the matter of misappropriated princely estates but would claim power of decision in the internal affairs of the states as well. Still, the chief object of their discontent was not Ferdinand but rather Wallenstein; the marshal had immensely enriched himself in the process of fighting Protestant forces and it was he who was held responsible for the decree concerning the former ecclesiastical states. In July 1630, at a great meeting at Regensburg of Catholic rulers (with Protestants represented by ambassadors), Wallenstein found himself the target of concentrated verbal attacks. He resigned on August 12 and his mercenary army was disbanded.

Already a new protagonist stood ready to enter the conflict. Gustavus Adolfus of Sweden, who had one of the best trained and disciplined armies in Europe under his command, had been promised material support from France, always ready and anxious to see Habsburg power weakened. The Swedish king, although a devoted Lutheran, had scant interest in the religious issue; his long-standing ambition was to establish a *Dominium maris Baltici* and rule as the master of the Baltic shore. Entering the war, he earned significant early victories. The northern German Protestant princes, however, sobered by their defeat at the hands of Catholic generals, hesitated to join him. This enabled Tilly to capture the Protestant city of Magdeburg, which he proceeded to raze and burn to the ground, in the process perpetrating some of the worst atrocities of the war: some 50,000 of the inhabitants lost their lives. In September of that year, 1631, Swedish forces inflicted two disastrous defeats on Tilly, invaded Bavaria, and pushed to the very gates of Tyrol. The tide of the war had turned.

Ferdinand, hard-pressed, recalled Wallenstein to active service. The latter, endowed with almost unlimited power, managed to recruit another army, but in November 1632 he suffered defeat at the Battle of Lützen, in which, however, Gustavus Adolfus himself fell. Following this defeat Wallenstein's conduct became erratic, even mystifying. All kinds of rumors circulated regarding his plans: to overthrow the Habsburgs, have himself crowned king of Bohemia, reorganize the political structure of Central Europe. Most ominously, he demanded oaths of loyalty to himself personally from his troops. Vienna issued an order to have him delivered dead or alive; on the night of February 25, 1634, with several of his followers, he was assassinated.

The war continued, almost out of habit, one could say; there simply was no basis—religious, political, or territorial—upon which a peace could be constructed. In April 1635 France and the United Provinces of the Netherlands entered into an alliance; in April, France declared war on Spain; in October, Austria and Spain became formal allies. The religious question receded into irrelevancy. The Spanish faced secessionist movements in Portugal and Catalonia; the French eagerly supported the insurrectionists. On the battlefield the Spanish suffered a great defeat in the Netherlands, the southern portions of which they had reconquered, and the Austrian Habsburgs could no longer expect any help from their Spanish cousins.

On February 15, 1637, Ferdinand II died, unbroken in his Catholic convictions to the end. He was followed by his son, Ferdinand III, also a staunch Catholic but more of a realist than his father was. The fortunes of the Catholic forces were in decline. Spain suffered one defeat after another, both internally and on distant battlefields, and in Germany French forces, under the young commander Condé, inflicted several defeats on the armies of the Catholic League. But the alignment, or misalignment, of forces was too complicated ever to produce a clear-cut victory for either side, if indeed it was possible to speak of only two sides, as had been the case in the beginning. In the closing phases of the war the Swedes, fighting after the death of their ambitious king for undefined objectives, in 1643 allied themselves with a Transylvanian prince; in the summer of 1645 they advanced to the Danube, occupied a part of Lower Austria, then moved against Prague and took its fort after a three-month siege. In that year peace negotiations began in a leisurely fashion. They were conducted in two towns, Münster and Osnabrück, because the delegations representing the two religions would not directly face each other. Even composing the agenda took months.

The final instrument was signed on October 24, 1648, in Westphalia, but it could not possibly put an end to all the conflicts that had erupted in the course of the past 30 years. Territorially, Sweden and France were the greatest gainers; Austria received no new lands. Perhaps most significantly, the superiority of the individual rulers in the Holy Roman Empire in relation to the emperor was acknowledged; each was master over his own realm and had the right to conclude alliances with the others in the empire, or with foreign powers as long as these were not directed against the empire or the emperor. The provisions of the Peace of Augsburg were reaffirmed; the reservation that only Catholicism and Lutheranism would be tolerated was extended to Calvinists as well. In point of fact, toleration was no longer the operative term; Protestants had complete equality with Catholic states in the empire.

Austria had survived. The Counter Reformation, even though it made no significant inroads in Germany, was victorious in Austrian lands. Nobles had failed to take advantage of the troubles of the ruling house effectively to challenge royal authority. The peace with the Ottoman Empire held. However, about one-third of Hungary remained under Turkish occupation and the princes of Transylvania bowed neither to the Ottomans nor to the Habsburgs. The future was clouded.

CHAPTER FOUR

The Habsburgs combined proverbial luck with wise matrimonial choices in assembling their empire without striking a blow, but then engaged in an unbroken series of wars over centuries to defend it. They were acquisitive but not aggressive, fought only to defend the unity of their holdings, and even so conceded a good part of Hungary to the Turks and fielded an army only when Vienna itself was threatened. Their military was in a chronic state of disarray; the several provinces contributed to the armed forces as much manpower as they saw fit and it was often inadequate; central control over the armed forces was whimsical; regimental commanders sold commissions and even noncommissioned ranks at their discretion. For long stretches in the Thirty Years' War battles had been fought with mercenaries, and Austria paid a price for doing so in giving Wallenstein, the chief procurer of paid soldiery, the opportunity to acquire vast wealth and let his soldiers ravage conquered lands. The lessons had been learned, however. Shortly after the war the emperor of Austria (though his actual title was still archduke) claimed for himself supreme command over the military, and a more orderly system was introduced, regulating enlistment and procurement. It came about none too early because, after many years during which Christian powers fought against one another, the Turks were making ready for a new assault on Vienna. Austria was still trying to recover from the losses suffered in the Thirty Years' War, but Ottoman power had also diminished. The Turks' efforts to control and police their sprawling conquests proved a logistical nightmare. Turkish weaponry had not kept pace with technological advancements (although they had been the first ones to use firepower in the 14th century) and they had never mastered the art of synchronizing the operations of infantry, cavalry, and artillery. Only their conquering zeal remained undiminished.

Austria was by now in a better strategic position. Leopold I, after the Treaty of Westphalia, had concluded a 20-year truce with Louis XIV of France, thus obviating the necessity of keeping forces in the west. Early in 1683 he secured an alliance with Polish king John III Sobieski; a year later, at the behest of Pope Innocent IX, Venice joined the compact, which grandiosely came to be called the Holy League. Even Peter I of Russia, in a draining conflict with the Turks, appended his signature. The Bavarian, Saxon, and Prussian princes promised mercenaries, and the pope underwrote expenses.

Early in 1684 Sultan Mehmed IV began a new northward advance from his Balkan bases. The Austrian army, under the command of Charles of Lorraine, resorted to its usual strategy of giving up as much of Hungary as it could without fatally jeopardizing its position, and forces were concentrated for the defense of Vienna. The Turks, commanded by vizier Kara Mustafa, after taking a number of fortresses in Hungary, laid siege to Vienna in July 1684 with a force of 120,000 men. The situation was so critical that Leopold and his court transferred themselves to Linz. However, the Turks were unable to breach the capital's sturdy defenses and autumn was rapidly approaching; in September Sobieski's army arrived, descending unexpectedly from the forested slopes of Kahlenberg north of Vienna, and putting the Turkish forces to flight.

It was the Christians' turn to press the offensive. Fort after fort in Hungary fell to them during their slow but steady southward advance. In September 1688 Belgrade was taken and the liberation of Hungary seemed complete. The Turks, however, still had fight left in them and just now Louis XIV, taking advantage of Austria's preoccupation in the east, sought to make good his old project of pushing the borders of France to their "natural" limits on the Rhine; he assaulted the Rhenish possessions of the Holy Roman Empire. The Turks on their part found a new vigorous commander in Köprülü Mustafa and unleashed a series of counterattacks. In 1697 the Austrians too placed a new general, the brilliant Eugene of Savoy, in command. In September of that year he surprised the bulk of the Turkish host as it sought to cross the Tisza River at Zenta and annihilated it. The conditions for a definitive peace were finally at hand.

An armistice in 1698 was followed by a peace treaty signed on January 26, 1699, in Karlowitz. The Habsburgs regained all their Hungarian possessions with the exception of the Bánát of Temesvár, and Turkish suzerainty retreated to the line of the Danube-Sava Rivers.

Scarcely had the centuries-old war against the Turks been concluded than the outlines of still another European conflict emerged from the tangled affairs of the Habsburg family, centering on the ever-critical question of succession. The genetic stock of the Spanish branch had become enfeebled by repeated inbreeding; the current king, Charles II, born in 1661, had seemed unlikely from an early age to live a full life or to have children. Yet few imperial possessions in the world were richer and more complex than his; without an heir to bequeath them to, pretenders were likely to step forward and there was no authority to determine the relative merits of each claim. Both Leopold I of Austria and Louis XIV of France had a good case to present as each had married a sister of Charles of Spain. Louis had married the older one, with promises of a rich dowry in exchange for which he renounced any claim to the throne of Spain. However, the dowry was never paid, putting the validity of the renunciation in question. Leopold had married the younger sister but, because the Spanish and the Austrian Habsburg branches were permanently separated, he could not inherit the throne himself; he could, however, claim it for his son Charles, just as Louis XIV claimed it for his grandson Philip. As things subsequently developed, the right of succession was bestowed on neither of these claimants but on a third person, Joseph Ferdinand, son of Maximilian Emanuel, elector of Bavaria, who had married the daughter of Leopold I from his first marriage. The choice was made not by parties to the quarrel in Paris and Vienna but by the "maritime powers," England and the Netherlands, both of which were loath to face the inordinate increase in the power of either France or Austria that the Spanish inheritance would entail, an increase that would drastically upset the European balance and, on the part of France, pose a powerful challenge on the seas. In October 1698, as the death of Spain's king Charles was expected momentarily, the English king William III worked out with Louis XIV, who was willing to compromise to avoid a war, a plan for the territorial division of the Spanish Habsburg lands. Bavaria's Joseph Ferdinand, then six years old, would receive Spain, the southern Netherlands, and the overseas colonies; France would get Italy south of the Papal States; Austria, given a crumb in compensation, would get Milan. However, Charles II still had enough power of decision to nullify this agreement and assign *all* his possessions to the young Bavarian prince. According to dispositions he made on his deathbed, Joseph Ferdinand was to be brought to Madrid and given a Spanish education to be worthy in the eyes of Spaniards to wear their crown. But the heir apparent unexpectedly died before he reached his seventh birthday, and in the spring of 1700 England, the Netherlands, and France worked out a new treaty of partition, by the terms of which Spain itself, the southern Netherlands, and the colonies would remain with the Habsburgs in the person of Archduke Charles of Austria while France would receive southern Italy, Sicily, Sardinia, and Milan, the very provinces over the possession of which Habsburgs and the French Valois had been bitterly feuding since the early 16th century. England would be confirmed in her recent conquests on the seas.

The court at Vienna, however, would not hear of such a division of spoils; it would sooner sacrifice Spain than Italy, seeing that Italian provinces were contiguous to its eastern empire. For his part Charles II of Spain, persuaded by advisers that the unity of his holdings would best be ensured by a French king, willed them to Louis XIV's grandson Philip. Louis XIV, barely recovered from his last war along the Rhine, knew only too well that accepting Charles's will would lead to a new war as Vienna would never concede the immense holdings of the Spanish Habsburgs to the rival Bourbon house. However, the temptation was too great to resist. Louis was still willing to compromise on the basis of the previously completed partition plan, but his offer to this effect met a stiff refusal by Vienna. Meanwhile the Spanish court expressed its willingness to accept Philip of Anjou, Louis's grandson, as the new Spanish king, and at first a number of other states, including England and the Netherlands, signaled their assent. Leopold of Austria had to act quickly, before the Bourbon position solidified. His agents spread rumors that Charles was diseased in body and mind when he wrote his will and that the throne of Spain belonged to Leopold by virtue of his mother's *and* wife's unrenounced claims to it. But Louis XIV had been carried away by the prospect of his family owning Spain and the Americas, even if it meant a division of the Bourbon line into a Spanish and a French branch, just as Habsburgs had ruled over widely separated realms for over two centuries. The powers, including England, realized that the partition plan they had worked out had come to naught and that France would be in full possession of the immense Spanish inheritance; the Netherlands was alarmed by the advance of French troops into Flanders, which it viewed as a possible preliminary move in a new reach for the Rhine frontier. The result was a treaty, concluded September 7, 1701, at the Hague among England, the Netherlands, and the Holy Roman Empire; by its terms, the Empire obtained rights to the Spanish inheritance, and England and Holland secured rights to free navigation and trade. Louis XIV could not accept the great prize being snatched away from him, and a new war was in the offing.

The year of the outbreak of this so-called War of the Spanish Succession is variously given as 1701 and 1702. The reason is that five months before the conclusion of his alliance with England and the Netherlands, Leopold of Austria dispatched a modest force under Eugene of Savoy into Italy to secure Habsburg possessions there, and Eugene earned a succession of victories over the French. England and the Netherlands, however, did not declare war on France until May 15, 1702. In short order a number of other states, alarmed by the prospect of French predominance on the European continent, joined this "Grand Alliance." Louis XIV had only Spain and Bavaria, the latter in nearly permanent competition with Austria, on his side. Leopold, by promising the Prussian elector Frederick his imperial assent of Frederick's promotion from elector to king, secured Prussia's participation on the allied side.

Much of Europe west of Russia was at war. Discounting the diplomatic maneuvers on both sides in response to the changing fortunes on the battlefields, what we have is an extended military history that reflects a distribution of power so finely balanced that it makes it understandable why both sides fought long and hard in the hope of victory. The most significant battle in the early part of the war was at Blenheim on the Danube in which the British commander, the duke of Marlborough, led his forces to a great victory, enabling Austria to bring much of the Holy Roman Empire under her direct rule. The Austrians also seized the opportunity to occupy and ruthlessly exploit Bavaria, raising fears in German lands of a renewed attempt by the Habsburgs to reassert the right of governance in the empire, a right they had lost in the Treaty of Westphalia. Indeed, that was the intention of Joseph I, who occupied the imperial throne after the death on May 5, 1705, of Leopold I. Joseph was far more able and energetic than most Habsburgs, but he did not venture to go so far as to actually annex defeated Bavaria. As Holy Roman Emperor he only placed the Bavarian elector Maximilian Emanuel, as well as his brother, under a high ban, stripping them of their princely rank. Portions of Bavaria were detached, though Austria took only a narrow province called the "Inn Quarters." For the rest, the Habsburgs were determined to nullify the last will of Charles II and reassert their claim to the Spanish throne. Assisted by England, which, in 1704, had taken firm possession of Gibraltar, Joseph's brother Charles, the Habsburg claimant to the throne, journeyed to Spain and proclaimed himself king as Charles III. The Spanish made it amply clear that he was not welcome; his two attempts to establish himself in Madrid were unsuccessful, and he took up residence in Barcelona.

Military skirmishes and battles continued on the peripheries of France; the joint forces of the duke of Marlborough and Eugene of Savoy earned some spectacular victories, although always at high cost, and their invasions of France were repeatedly repulsed. In the battle of Oudenarde in July 1708 they were able to capture Lille, which had only recently passed into French possession and which offered a good base for an advance on Paris, but that project had to be abandoned in the face of stiff French resistance. Louis XIV was nevertheless fighting a losing battle. In talks at the Hague in the spring of 1709 he offered to renounce his grandson's claim to the Spanish throne and compensate him with possession of southern Italy and Sicily; however, when the allies demanded that he help them drive his grandson, Philip of Anjou, out of Spain by force of arms, he demurred and the war was renewed.

What in the end brought the allies to settle for a compromise peace was not so much military considerations as a change of government in England from Whigs to Tories. The latter had always been doubtful about the wisdom of fighting a war over a purely continental affair; as landowners they bore the burden of increased taxes, whereas those who gained were the merchants and entrepreneurs, who supported the Whigs. In October 1711 direct talks between the English and French governments led to a preliminary agreement, according to which Philip V, already in effective possession of the Spanish throne, was allowed to keep it, with the proviso that the crowns of Spain and France would never be united. Louis XIV accepted the colonial gains England had made in the course of the war, notably Gibraltar, as well as Hudson's Bay and Newfoundland in America. A more general settlement was facilitated by the unexpected death, in April 1711, of Joseph I of Austria; he had two daughters but no son and thus his crown was to pass to his brother Charles, who still maintained a hollow claim to the crown of Spain. Charles now departed from Barcelona, to be crowned ruler of the Austrian possessions as well as Holy Roman Emperor.

In January 1712 a general peace congress opened in Utrecht in the Netherlands. It involved lengthy negotiations and did not close until April 1713. The major point of contention was the future of Bavaria. Its anathemized Wittelsbach rulers were willing to cede their province to Austria if they would receive the Spanish Netherlands (Belgium) in exchange. As this could be done only with French consent (Bavaria had been on the French side throughout the war), the allies, especially England and the Netherlands, would not hear of it. For Austria the absorption of Bavaria was of special importance because, after the expulsion of the Turks from Hungary and the reattachment of Transylvania to that kingdom, the great bulk of the Habsburg Empire consisted of non-German provinces, and the possession of Bavaria would nearly double the population of the German core of the empire. But the non-German powers vetoed the scheme. Besides, Charles was still obsessed with gaining the Spanish inheritance, an ambition completely outside of the realm of possibility, as none of those who had any say in the matter, least of all the Spanish, were willing to yield on that question. In the end what Austria was offered instead of Bavaria was the former Spanish Netherlands (Belgium), and even that by the involved formula that it was to be given to the Netherlands, which would then cede it to the Habsburgs. This solution Austria rejected. A general settlement seemed without a prospect of realization; nevertheless, Philip of Anjou was confirmed as king of Spain, and England was allowed to keep Gibraltar and Minorca, as well as her overseas conquests, and London was granted a monopoly of the slave trade. As for Belgium, the Dutch were to remain in control of it (with the exception of Lille, which they returned to France) until Austria too agreed to the peace, at which point the province would pass to the Habsburgs.

Charles of Austria remained unwilling to accept peace on these terms. Eugene of Savoy fought on with an ever diminishing force, abandoned by all his former allies. It was not until March 1714 that Charles finally accepted the terms of Utrecht by the Treaty of Rastatt. Alsace and Strasbourg were lost to the Empire but all other French conquests along the Rhine were returned. Belgium became the Austrian Netherlands. That was Austria's only gain and Charles had to be content with the crowns of Austria, Hungary, Bohemia, and the Holy Roman Empire.

While Charles had spent time in Spain as a young man, pretending to reign over a people that did not want him, he had, in 1703, prepared a "mutual concession pact," providing that if the male line of either the Spanish or the Austrian Habsburgs died out, the male descendant of the other branch would inherit the throne. If neither side had a male heir, a female could exercise the right of inheritance. The provision was prompted by the fact that Charles's older brother, Joseph, archduke of Austria at the time the pact was made, had three daughters but no son. According to the compact, seeing that there had never been a female on the Habsburg throne, if Charles had a surviving son, the crowns of both realms would be his.

Joseph died in 1711 and Charles inherited the crown of Austria. He now changed the family compact, giving his own daughter precedence over Joseph's, although Joseph, as the older of the two brothers, should have enjoyed that privilege. The matter was not of great urgency because in the same year, 1713, when Charles issued this instrument, which he called *Pragmatica Sanctio,* a son was born to him. But the child died three years later; Charles had two daughters but no more boys were born. The older daughter, Maria Theresa, was now to inherit the throne.

As far as the Habsburgs were concerned the Pragmatic Sanction settled the matter of succession within the family, but its recognition by foreign rulers was necessary for it to have international sanction. When in 1718 the *Sanctio* was made public, it carried an additional article, providing that the method of succession should be the same in all Habsburg possessions and should proceed along the lines of the amended family compact. In practice this meant that if Austria accepted the female succession, so would all the other provinces, and the Austrian empire would remain undivided. It took four years for the estates in the Habsburg lands to subscribe to the document, the Hungarians being the last ones to do so, all with the proviso that it would not infringe on their several rights and privileges. By 1832 Russia, Prussia, Spain, the Netherlands, and England had signaled their assent. The consent of Prussian king Frederick

William I was particularly important as his family had certain, admittedly ill-defined, claims to parts of the Austrian province of Silesia. The matter of succession to Habsburg possessions was apparently finalized.

In 1733 another succession question carried Austria into war again; this time it concerned Poland. In that year the Polish king Augustus, ruler also of the German state of Saxony, died. The kingship was elective and, given the fact that Poland was the third-largest state in Europe and fourth in size of population, the election invariably attracted foreign interest. The Habsburgs' choice, as well as that of the Romanovs of Russia, was Augustus's son, but France championed the father-in-law of her king Louis XV, Stanislaus Leszczynski. The French had no land access to Poland and could only send a fleet to support their choice; the Russians invaded Poland and installed their candidate as Augustus III. Larger issues than that of the Polish throne were at stake, however. Maria Theresa's future husband had been selected in the person of Francis Charles, duke of Lorraine; inasmuch as Maria Theresa would inherit the Habsburg throne, once the marriage was concluded, Francis Stephen would, in the absence of a Habsburg male heir, be the primary candidate to be Holy Roman Emperor. The French chancellor Cardinal Fleury wanted to break the by now established Habsburg succession to the imperial throne; he intended to annex Lorraine to France and thus become the arbiter in the election of the emperor when the election came due. To give force to the French choice for the throne of Poland, France declared war on Austria and was joined by Spain, eager to annex Austrian possessions in Italy. Although Austria rallied the Holy Roman Empire to her cause, only a small German force took the field, and when the war ended in 1736, the province of Lorraine went to France, and Naples and Sicily, hitherto Habsburg, went to the Spanish Bourbons.

An immediate opportunity for Austria to make gains elsewhere offered itself in the same year. Russia, at war with Turkey to conquer the north shore of the Black Sea, called on Vienna to honor an alliance dating back to 1726. That alliance had its own history. Austria had barely emerged from the Spanish succession conflict when she had to face, in 1715, a new assault from the Turks who sought to wrest territory from Venetia and, to ensure their northern flank, sent a major army against Hungary. Thanks largely to the exploits of Eugene of Savoy, the attack was defeated, Austrians pushed into the Balkans, even took Belgrade, and in the east, with Russian help, the Romanian province of Moldova. Although the conquests proved short-lived, a community of interest between Austria and Russia was established, producing a loose alliance against further Turkish encroachments. In 1736, when the Russian call came, the Austrian army, exhausted and depleted, and suffering from poor organization and logistics, endured a series of defeats. Austria was fortunate that when the war ended in 1739 the previous borderline with the Ottoman Empire, along the Danube and Sava Rivers, was confirmed.

Charles VI's rule was certainly neither one of glory nor of governmental efficiency. If the army fell to a low state, so did the agencies that directed and supplied it. Seldom was the mediocrity and the lack of progressive spirit in Habsburg rulers more in evidence. Indeed the acceptance of his Pragmatic Sanction at home and abroad was Charles's only visible accomplishment. Even that, given the Machiavellian temper of European diplomacy, was little more than a piece of paper. France remained an unremitting threat to the Austrian position and kept chipping away at lands of the Holy Roman Empire along the Rhine. Spain was no longer Habsburg, and, in foreign policy, Madrid supported the French. Bavarian princes, who had married the daughters of Joseph I, were voicing claims to the Austrian throne after Charles's death. Yet when the time came for the Pragmatic Sanction to go into effect, it was neither France nor Spain nor Bavaria that sought to sabotage it, but another German state, one which during the war of the Polish Succession had actually fielded an army on Austria's side, namely, Prussia.

Charles VI died on October 20, 1740, and his daughter, Maria Theresa, 23 years of age, the wife of Francis of Lorraine since 1736 and already the mother of three daughters, ascended the throne. She had not occupied it for two months before the new Prussian king, Frederick II, long impatient to put the army his father had so assiduously collected and trained to use, moved into Silesia on the flimsiest legal pretext. It marked the beginning of the War of the Austrian Succession.

Whether it was hurt pride or solid political and economic consideration that led Maria Theresa to defend Silesia is irrelevant. To cite the political rationale may be arguing after the fact, but the queen seemed fully to realize that this challenge to the Pragmatic Sanction, if successful, could cause the whole construct to collapse. She also realized that after the recent defeats in the Polish and Turkish wars Austria was precariously close to ceasing to be a great power, and this would be particularly true if she bowed before an upstart German state, Prussia. Victory in the first battle, fought on April 10, 1741, went to Frederick only by a hair and there was no reason to believe that in future battles Austria could not bring her superior position to bear. However, two months later France joined the war against Austria, in return for a promise that Frederick of Prussia, as elector, would vote for the French choice, Bavarian Charles Albert, instead of Maria Theresa's husband, to be Holy Roman Emperor. Spain, hoping to gain more territory in Italy from Austria, joined France. Charles Albert moved into Bohemia, occupied Prague, and declared himself king of the province; in January 1742 he was elected Holy Roman Emperor.

In that year, on July 28, in Berlin, thanks to English mediation, Maria Theresa made her peace with Frederick, ceding Lower Silesia except for two localities. The Austrians then proceeded to reconquer Bohemia from the adventurous but slow-witted Charles Albert; subsequently, their armies entered Alsace and stood poised to retake Lorraine, the home of Maria Theresa's consort. England had entered the picture out of her traditional fear of seeing the European power balance upset by the rising Bourbon power; very soon the original issue that precipitated the war became of cursory interest to all but Austria and Prussia. Frederick, fearing that, if the combination of French defeats and the accretion of Austria's allies continued, his possession of Silesia would be in jeopardy, decided to reenter the war before his position deteriorated beyond repair. It was a hasty decision that did not take account of the odds

turning rapidly against him. Even some brilliant military victories did not suffice to place him in a dominant position. Austrian forces were commanded by
the brother-in-law of Maria Theresa, Charles of Lorraine, who entered
Bohemia. The Bavarian king, elected Holy Roman Emperor in 1742, died in
January 1745, and his Habsburg wife persuaded her son, Max Joseph, to make
peace with Austria. Not only did it take an ally of Frederick out of the war, but
the new Bavarian elector abdicated any claim to the imperial crown and, in
September of that year, the electors returned to tradition and elected Francis of
Lorraine, husband of a Habsburg woman, Holy Roman Emperor. In the end,
however, no political moves could counteract military defeats: Maria Theresa
tried to wean France from the Prussian alliance, then, failing in that, to prevail
on Louis XV to press Frederick to limit his claims to Silesia. Louis would not be
moved, and Frederick's victories in battle in 1745 discouraged Russia, whose
czarina contemplated joining the front against Prussia, from actually doing so.
On December 25, 1745, Maria Theresa with an aching heart agreed to a
renewal of the Peace of Berlin, which signaled her cession of all of Silesia.

Austria's war with France and Spain continued for another three years. On
October 18, 1748, the Peace of Aachen was finally concluded. The validity of
the Pragmatic Sanction, insofar as it pertained to Maria Theresa's position as
ruler of Austrian lands, was generally recognized and so was her husband's title
as Holy Roman Emperor. But Silesia was lost, as were some possessions in Italy.
Austria held on only to the southern Netherlands. In the course of the crisis
Maria Theresa had, through charm and pluck, gained the loyalty of her Hungarian subjects, or rather that of the great nobility who still held a monopoly
over political affairs. That was a greater victory than she could have earned on
the battlefield because the Hungarian estates had been notoriously difficult to
handle, let alone control. It proved to be the one good omen early in the young
queen's reign.

CHAPTER FIVE

Even in the darkest periods of the war against Frederick of Prussia, Maria Theresa's faith that her empire was protected by divine providence never wavered. From her father she inherited a group of superannuated advisers; her husband, despite his intellectual understanding of the art of governing, did not have the temperament and energy to deal with public affairs. He was comfort-loving, even-tempered, devoted to family and the pleasures of home life. It was left to the queen to keep the empire together.

The many misfortunes of war made it clear that military reform was the most urgent task. The existing method of raising an army above the peacetime establishment, the hiring of mercenaries whenever war threatened, was out-dated, as was the system of keeping small military units scattered in towns and villages, billeted in private houses, making their upkeep the responsibility of the locality. New regulations were issued; they provided for units as large as regiments to be kept in battle readiness, fed and housed by the central government. Methods of training and the types of weaponry were made uniform, as were the military garments and the insignia of rank. As a further measure of centralization, in 1752 a military academy, the Theresianum, was established in Wiener Neustadt; at first, only military personnel were trained there, but in time civil servants were too.

Taxation was also in urgent need of reform. In fiscal as well as other administrative affairs, the queen was fortunate to have the services of an extraordinary man, Friedrich Wilhelm Haugwitz, caretaker in the tiny portion of Silesia that had remained with Austria after the two wars with Prussia. Haugwitz recognized the weakness of a system in which the estates in each province assessed the taxes and provided the means for their collection; it was the Achilles' heel of a decentralized administration. Haugwitz prevailed on the Austrian and Bohemian estates to accept a uniform method of taxation and place collection and enforcement in the hands of the central government; this latter office was named *Directorium in publicis et camerabilus*. Outside of these two provinces however, notably in Hungary and Italy, tax matters remained in the hands of the estates, a fact that epitomized the failure of the Habsburg dynasty fully to integrate Hungary into its empire; the Italian provinces, where Habsburg legitimacy was never fully established, were in a permanent state of flux and their position was a source of lasting insecurity.

In 1742, at a time of intensive negotiations with Frederick II of Prussia to end the war over Silesia, a state chancellery for the conduct of foreign affairs had been set up to ensure greater efficiency in dealing with foreign powers; however, the main problems of the monarchy rested with internal affairs, and Haugwitz could claim credit for successfully addressing the most pressing one besides taxation, namely, the separation of the judicial process from the administrative one. In 1749, the same year in which Montesquieu's *Spirit of the Laws*, dealing with just this question, appeared, Haugwitz set up the Highest Court of Justice, which oversaw the judicial system and which was entirely independent of political institutions. His reform drastically breached manorial justice, which had made the landlord the ultimate judge over his serfs; it also did away with medieval methods of ascertaining the guilt or innocence of the accused. The measure constituted the first great step toward bringing the ideals of the Enlightenment to the administration of justice in the empire. However, even here reform was limited to the Austrian lands and to Bohemia; in Hungary the noble landlords remained the arbiters of justice over the serfs on their estates.

Reform of the financial administration followed; it was made particularly urgent by the loss of Silesia, the richest and economically most advanced province. A Universal Commerce Directory was established to supervise the separate commercial institutions, regulate foreign trade, and undertake road building and the improvement of rivers.

Predictably, the religious question proved to be the most sensitive one and most resistant to reform. Maria Theresa was a devout Catholic but, being also an energetic reformer of state government, she would not countenance the Catholic Church as the unassailable institution that in many respects it aspired to be. She forbade papal encyclicals to be read to congregations or otherwise be made public without her permission, she did not allow the heads of religious orders that had their central institutions abroad to visit the empire, and she limited the authority of ecclesiastical courts strictly to religious affairs. There were altogether too many religious holidays at the expense of working days; Maria Theresa reduced their numbers by royal edict, thus reserving to the crown the right to decide which saints or religious events deserved solemn remembrance. She scheduled the hours of religious processions at which she was present for late afternoon because she did not tolerate daytime heat and sunlight well. She did please the church by showing little patience for "heretics," but her attempts to rid the hereditary lands, as well as the Austrian Netherlands, of Protestants had very limited success. In Hungary, especially in Transylvania, it was in any case a hopeless undertaking and she did not even try. She disliked Jews, at one point ordered their expulsion from Austrian lands, but the economic consequences were so severe that she withdrew the edict.

Herself spottily educated, she recognized the importance of a highly trained civil service. Her court physician, Gerhard van Swieten, was her chief adviser in her efforts to upgrade existing universities and to found new ones. In this endeavor too the year of 1749 was the most active and creative one, when van Swieten placed his comprehensive plan for a broad-based educational system before the queen. However, the autonomy of universities remained limited—the state appointed professors and approved curricula and the faculties were subject to the supervision of directors appointed by the state.

In 1749 the final peace with Prussia was one year old, and Maria Theresa had still not reconciled herself to the loss of Silesia. Her gloom was somewhat relieved and her hope revived when the man who had argued the Habsburg case at peace talks in Aachen, Count Wenzel Anton Kaunitz-Rietber, was first introduced to her. Kaunitz presented to the queen his foreign policy assessment, arguing that the Turkish threat had largely passed and Bourbon hostility too was abating; the only dangerous enemy of Austria was Prussia. The chief goal of the empire's foreign policy therefore had to be to undermine Prussia's position. That could best be achieved if Austria managed to range her traditional enemy, France, to her side. Once that was accomplished, a number of other states that had fought against Austria in the previous war would follow France's lead. The queen, partly under the influence of her husband, whose home province, Lorraine, had been a pawn in so many of France's skirmishes with the Holy Roman Emperor, at first treated the idea with skepticism; she nevertheless appointed Kaunitz ambassador to Paris and allowed him wide latitude in pursuing his plan. During his assignment Kaunitz never really passed beyond sounding out several of the king's favorites, male and female; however, upon his appointment to state chancellor (foreign minister) in 1753, he gave his successor in Paris, Starhemberg, instructions to further promote his own initiatives. His main argument was that France's alliance with Prussia, concluded in the first year of the War of the Austrian Succession, was insincere because Frederick II was at the same time actively seeking an alignment with France's arch enemy, England. Proof of this came in January 1756, when England and Prussia agreed on mutually advantageous terms should they fight

Empress Maria Theresa and her minister of state Count Wenzel Anton Kaunitz, engraved by John Sartain; the original by Hanfstaengl *(Library of Congress)*

as allies in a new war. When Starhemberg saw to it that the news was conveyed to Versailles, it at last persuaded the French to switch alliances. Since Austro-French antagonism over Italian possessions had been largely resolved, the decision was easier to take. On May 1, 1756, the two countries signed at Versailles a preliminary agreement, and in August the specifics were worked out: in case of an Austrian war against Prussia, France would provide mercenaries, would not object to the drastic truncation of Prussia, and would receive territorial rewards in Italy or the Netherlands. Meanwhile, Kaunitz ensured Russian cooperation: the czarina Elizabeth nursed as deep an antipathy for Frederick II as did Maria Theresa. All was ready for a war of revanche.

Prussia was actually the first state to assume belligerency as Frederick sought to overcome material odds by taking quick and forceful action. Soon all the states that had undertaken obligations were involved in battle. The Prussian king faced a formidable coalition in what against all expectations became a seven-year-long conflict; with sheer persistence, astounding military skills, and some good luck, he avoided the worst. He was able to extricate his armies from the most perilous situations. Once, for a three-day period, even his capital Berlin was occupied by Russian armies, but they could not maintain themselves in the face of Prussian counterattacks. The decisive stroke of good luck came with the death of Elizabeth of Russia on December 25, 1761. Her successor, Peter III, a German by birth and an admirer of Frederick II, had neither the stomach nor the inclination to continue the struggle. By the time he had withdrawn his troops from battle, a palace revolution unconnected with the shameful change of sides had overthrown him, but Catherine II, his wife who succeeded him on the throne, was herself German and had no more enthusiasm than Peter had for the war against Prussia. Throughout the conflict England and France fought on opposite sides, mainly in America, and, as in the first Silesian war, the original cause was nearly lost from sight. In November 1762 England and France concluded a preliminary peace, which they finalized the following February in Paris. By now Maria Theresa realized that the recovery of Silesia was no longer a viable project and, on February 15, she made peace with Frederick at Hubertusburg, with all territorial arrangements returning to the status quo ante.

Internal reforms had continued even during the war under the guiding concept of centralization, ending what the queen regarded as the ruinous fragmentation of her realms. In the Austrian and Bohemian lands, largely through the creation of the Staatsrat, a six-member council of state, of which three members came from the ranks of the high aristocracy and the other three from the lesser nobility, this goal was at least superficially accomplished. However, Hungary once again proved intractable, even though it benefited most from Maria Theresa's efforts to settle the areas that the long Turkish occupation had left depopulated. Food production had fallen sharply and the sparse population provided consistently low tax revenues. Already Maria Theresa's father had begun a program inviting foreigners into the country to establish themselves, mainly in the regions east of the Tisza River and in the broad strip of land between the Tisza and the Danube. Here Hungary possessed some of the richest agricultural land anywhere in Europe, but methods of production practiced by the indigenous population were still primitive and the yield was well below that derived from soil of the same quality in western Europe; many of the newcomers brought modern agrarian skills, as well as manufacturing expertise, with them. The queen's consort, Francis, showed particular interest in industrial enterprise and his investments proved most felicitous. They were by no means limited to Hungary and by the end of Maria Theresa's reign in the suburbs of Vienna alone 75 manufacturing concerns were active. The greatest industrial growth occurred in Bohemia, where the loss of Silesia created new opportunities for start-ups and where the necessary raw materials were present in adequate quantities.

The paucity of international commerce had long constituted the great weakness of the Austrian economy. A number of treaties for exchange of goods had been concluded with the Ottoman Empire, but they resulted in a continuously negative trade balance. Maria Theresa ordered that Turkish merchants doing business in her empire had to settle permanently and be subject to its taxation and laws. The upswing in the Austrian economy after the Seven Years' War, however, had much broader and more complex causes. There was an increased market for a variety of goods and a more sophisticated monetary policy facilitated their exchange. In 1769 the Vienna stock market opened (there already was one in Trieste), and in 1771 paper money supplemented the silver thalers that acquired a solid reputation in European money markets. Growing prosperity was not equally evident in all provinces of the empire, but the general indicators pointed upward.

Although the queen's concern with the welfare of her subjects was spotty and inconstant, she undeniably felt a religious obligation to protect those who could not fend for themselves, and among these the peasants were in greatest need of royal attention. The core of their problem was that their holdings were not clearly defined in extent and they could never regard the land they worked as their own; their obligations to the landlord were also ill-defined, leading to endless disputes. The queen issued a series of urbariums, first in Croatia and then in other provinces, regulating the relationship between landlord and peasant and firmly separating the former's landholding from the latter's. The system had a negative aspect, too; as the peasant family grew, its landholding did not. However, knowing the land was permanently his inspired the peasant to cultivate it with much greater care. Production increased, as did the taxes paid, and peasant boys inducted into the army were consequently better fed, stronger, and healthier.

This last consideration was of particular importance because an empire located in so many areas of Europe always faced the possibility of war. Alliances were shifting, and there was no overriding issue, no ideological bond, that tied Austria to any of the powers, every new crisis necessitated an opportunistic alignment of forces. This became amply evident when the question of Polish succession, temporarily solved by the war of 1733, which had placed the Saxon Augustus III on the Polish throne with Russian-Austrian backing, still left open the question of who had legitimate claim to that throne. The result was a weakness of royal power which could not stand up to noble pretensions; this in turn fatally undermined the power position of Poland itself.

Augustus III died in 1763. He had spent little time in Poland and in any case would have been powerless to counteract growing Russian influence there. Maria Theresa would have preferred the continuation of the Saxon line, but Catherine II of Russia promoted her favorite, Stanislaus Poniatowski, and by now there was little that other powers could do to limit Russia's dominant influence in Poland. In 1764 Stanislaus was duly elected. By then religious questions with ulterior political motives complicated the picture. Poland was a Catholic country with small Protestant and Greek Orthodox minorities. Catherine and Frederick II of Prussia, having their eyes on Polish lands adjoining their own, decided to demand equal rights with Catholics for the two minorities. Expectably, this raised a storm of protest in Poland and an association, the Confederation of Bar, was formed, determined to lessen or exclude Russian influence. The resulting civil war of extraordinary ferocity practically invited foreign intervention. The first intervention occurred on the part of Turkey, which, encouraged by France, declared war on Russia, ostensibly in defense of "Polish liberties" but really because of Russian incursions into her Moldavian provinces in pursuit of Polish insurrectionists who had fled there. In the war the Russians earned several victories, causing acute concern in Austria that Russia rather than Turkey was the main menace to the Habsburgs' Balkan position. For his part, Frederick II of Prussia perceived the opportunity to preserve the balance among the powers at Poland's expense. He proposed a partition of Polish lands. An agreement to this effect was worked out by Austria, Prussia, and Russia on August 5, 1772. Russia received White Russia to the Dvina and Dnieper Rivers with 1.8 million inhabitants, Austria got Galicia and western Posolia, with 2.7 million people, and Prussia the land separating Brandenburg from East Prussia, with 416,000 inhabitants. In the closing years of her reign Maria Theresa had the satisfaction of seeing her empire, which had been diminished by the loss of Silesia, enlarged by extensive Polish territories. Nor was this the only accretion of land. Although the queen had resisted the arguments of her son Joseph and her chancellor Kaunitz, who had urged her to enter the war Russia fought against Turkey, she took advantage of the loss of Turkish control over Moldavia when that war ended in 1774, and in 1775 made a deal with the prince of that province for the cession of one part of it, Bukovina. Thus a new province was added to the Danubian monarchy.

Two years before her death Maria Theresa faced another war scare; her restless son and designated successor, Joseph, Holy Roman Emperor since his father's death in 1765, wished to realize an old ambition: he proposed that the Austrian Netherlands be joined to Bavaria, and these united provinces be added to the Habsburg Empire. The opportunity came with the death of the Bavarian elector in 1778. Joseph was ready to risk war over the issue, because he knew that Frederick of Prussia would never consent to such an augmentation of Habsburg power. Maria Theresa, no longer confident of decisive influence over her son, turned directly to Frederick to prevent the emerging conflict. She was able to conclude, with French and Russian mediation, the Peace of Teschen, which left Bavaria in its current position, with a small border region going to Austria.

Maria Theresa died on November 29, 1790. She left a legacy of political realism and secured a hitherto unaccomplished unity for her multinational realm. While by no means a champion of the Enlightenment, which was suspect in her eyes because of its pronounced antireligious bias, many of her policies reflected a shrewd understanding of the fact that medieval notions of social relations and principles of governance had seen their day and, even in religious matters, had to be modernized. Under her rule, politics in the empire became truly the art of the possible; even though she introduced many startling innovations, she did not find herself forced to retract any of them. Although she marched in step with the progress of history, she had reason to fear in her last years that the virtue of restraint would cease when her son and successor, Joseph II, took the throne.

CHAPTER SIX

Maria Theresa's reforms reflected a levelheaded pragmatism; no ideology underpinned them; utility was their sole criterion of success. Conservative by temperament, she realized, in part under her son's influence, that stubborn conservatism would lead to a social and political ossification of the empire. Her devout Catholicism did not prevent her from realizing the perils that the privileged position of the clergy, and its often wholesale involvement in civic affairs, posed to the authority of the central government. The confiscation of the riches of the Jesuit order swelled state wealth; her ban on church participation in drawing up wills placed inherited wealth into the hands of lay people who in time fed it into the economy rather than let it flow into church coffers. The reforms were gradual, spread out over four decades, and none was attended by a nervous hurry that would make its implementation hazardous.

By contrast, the reforms inaugurated and carried out in the decade after her death by her son Joseph were informed by ideology. The Enlightenment had a commanding influence on Joseph's restless mind and he never paused to wonder whether the peoples of the empire, high or low, were ready to embrace those ideals.

One of the features of Enlightenment thinking was an optimistic belief in social progress, even in the possibility of a utopia, and the ancillary belief that it was the state's responsibility to set progress in motion and direct it until the desired end was reached. Joseph's primary concern thus was to strengthen state authority and make it equal to the demands of reform. It was with zeal that he declared himself, emulating Frederick II of Prussia, to be the first servant of the state. Aware that a formal coronation would require him to take an oath to respect the privileges of nobility and clergy, a pledge he did not intend to honor, he refused to have himself crowned in either Austria or Hungary, and, in time he earned the nickname "King with a hat." His sense of duty blinded him to the fact that tradition can be an obstacle to even the most enlightened measures, and that aristocratic privileges, especially in Hungary, were too firmly embedded to yield to the royal will. As each part of the empire cherished its own traditions, culture, and language, centralizing measures faced a formidable challenge. Joseph had no patience with an empire of disparate provinces to which no unitary law code applied; he thought in terms of a single political unit directed by a single and supreme ruler. This demanded in the first place that the means of oral and written communication be uniform; in 1784, he issued an edict making German the sole language of official intercourse. He exempted from this rule only his subjects in Italy and the Netherlands, partly because they stood geographically apart but also because he deemed Italian and French suitable for legal texts. Other languages in the empire were in the process of modernizing themselves, eliminating anachronistic phrases and finding native equivalents for Latin terms in wide use—in Joseph's eyes this amounted to an admission that they had not matured to the level at which they could serve as effective instruments for official communication.

His mother, wary of hostile reactions in countries such as Hungary and Italy, had limited her administrative reforms to the hereditary lands; Joseph, after merging several institutions (the Court Chancellery, the Court Chamber and the Bankodeputation, which dealt with financial matters) in Austria, Bohemia, and Galicia, and placing them under one imperial chancellor in order to streamline the bureaucracy, in 1785 introduced what he regarded as long overdue reforms in Hungary too. In that country the legislative estates had their primary strength in the counties, the historical governmental units. Joseph abolished these and divided the country into 10 administrative districts placed under the direct authority of the government in Vienna.

In economic matters he shared his mother's mercantilist views: he valued the prosperity of the state above that of individual enterprise and strove for a positive trade balance. Such a balance necessitated a vigorous industry that he hoped in time to achieve by loosening the strictures of the guilds, which stunted competition. He hoped in time to abolish them altogether. To discourage the outflow of capital he forbade the importation of certain goods while on others he placed a 60 percent customs duty.

A hard and conscientious worker himself, he valued productive work by others. He demonstratively favored and supported individuals whose labor brought income to the state, whether they were tradesmen, manufacturers, bankers, or even monks and nuns engaged in educational, medical, or social work. He had no respect for unearned wealth; aristocrats living off the sweat of their peasants could not count on his sympathy or support. He regarded the problem of the bonded peasantry as the most urgent one, for feudalism lay like a physical weight on the empire; however, in this sphere he did give tradition its due and displayed some caution in proclaiming his reforms. While he protested vigorously against the contempt in which many landlords held their serfs, exemplified in the phrase common among Hungarian aristocrats, *"A paraszt nem ember"* (the peasant is not a human being), when, in November 1781, he issued his decrees for the alleviation of their lot, first in the hereditary lands and later extended to the others, he refrained from making a clean sweep of feudalism; it might shake the entire economic foundation of the empire. He did grant serfs their personal freedom, their right to choose a trade, and the right to register a grievance against their landlords with state authorities. While he did not decrease the amount a landlord could demand of his peasants' ordinary income, he limited the former's right to squeeze money from extra incomes, such as from cottage industries or small trade. Toward the end of his reign he contemplated a more stringent measure, whereby the peasant retained a full 70 percent of his income, while landlord and state divided the remainder between themselves, but he did not live long enough to enact it and ensure its enforcement.

While the term "Josephinism" generally refers to the spirit and letter of the entire body of Joseph II's reform legislation, contemporaries and historians more specifically applied it to the acts pertaining to the Catholic Church. Joseph was a practicing Catholic, but that was more likely due to his respect for Habsburg traditions than to conviction. As a man of the Enlightenment he had a general distrust of religion. This distrust was unconnected to the theological disputes that rent the church since the start of the Reformation; Catholics and Protestants may have quarreled over the correct interpretation of the scriptures and dogma, but not over the saving function of the Christian faith. Both held the fundamentals of the Christian religion to be inviolable. The *illuminati* of the 18th century on the other hand, while they made their peace with the clergy on the premise that the great mass of downtrodden people needed the spiritual guidance that only the men of the cloth could provide, they rejected most of what the clergy preached. They regarded religion as obscurantist and superstitious; it clouded reason, which alone could find a way out of man's deplorable condition. Joseph II was intellectually of this view, but as a ruler he contented himself with ending the monopoly of the Catholic Church over the religious establishment and blunting the impact of the Counter Reformation. That latter movement had by now reached its natural limits within the empire. It had never made much progress in Hungary, especially Transylvania, where Protestantism had become firmly established. Eastern Orthodoxy prevailed in the Serbian parts; in Galicia and the Romanian-inhabited regions the Uniate version of Orthodoxy held sway, which recognized the supremacy of the pope and was thus a sister church to that of the Catholics. Joseph, like his mother, deplored any intolerance on religious grounds; even his intense dislike of Jews did not shake that attitude. On October 13, 1781, he issued his Toleration Patent. It applied primarily to Christian Protestants. The Patent stated that, as royal subjects, Protestants had equal rights with Catholics, they could be appointed to public office and could not be discriminated against on the basis of their religion. While Jews constituted an exception to the general rule of toleration, many of the restrictions affecting them were removed, most notably the requirement that they wear distinguishing garments; they were also encouraged to enter the trades and even to join the army. Such broad-based measures in themselves would have sufficed to reduce the influence of the Catholic Church in public affairs, but Joseph went further. He intended to finish the process of subordinating the church to the state. By no means did this mean elimination of the clergy or doing away with religious services; he in fact attached great importance to the activities of the secular clergy and of some religious orders. He founded a number of new dioceses, though his chief purpose in this was to remove some Austrian churches from the authority of bishoprics in the Holy Roman Empire. The new sees were not materially endowed and their personnel were treated as civil servants. Furthermore, Joseph wanted to limit papal influence to the absolute minimum. To achieve this, he decreed that every written communication by Austrian churchmen with the Vatican had to have royal sanction. As to monasteries and convents, he allowed only those that were engaged in education and in the care of the indigent and the sick to continue their activities. Altogether 700 institutions were closed down and the number of Christian brothers and nuns was reduced from 65,000 to 27,000. Their properties and art works were sold off and the money so realized was added to the treasury.

Pope Pius VI was so deeply concerned about the intent and effect of these edicts that in 1782 he paid a personal visit to Vienna to prevail on Joseph to retract them. When Joseph would not be moved, the pope condemned him and predicted his early death; Joseph, who spurned superstition, replied by issuing further decrees: he banned processions and religious societies and placed seminaries under civil authority to ensure that future generations of priests would be loyal to the state. As for public education, he would have preferred taking it out of the hands of the clergy altogether but could not find enough qualified teachers to replace them, so he had to be satisfied with close supervision over academic faculties. Not a particularly learned man himself, he realized the importance of education for good citizenship and regarded school attendance as much of a duty for youngsters as he did work for adults. Indeed, by the end of his reign a greater proportion of school-age children attended classes in the Austrian Empire than in any other European state.

In the judicial field he could not and did not seriously try to abolish manorial jurisdiction at the lowest level, except that he sanctioned the serf's right of appeal from the landlord's sentencing. Even when he issued his civil code in 1786, he left this crude form of manorial administration of justice in place. His penal code, published a year later, however, represented a great step forward by introducing enlightened criminal procedure. It banned the use of torture to extract confession, forbade corporal truncation as punishment, and ended any class distinction in the application of the law. However, criminal trials continued to be held in secret, and defendants were not allowed to have attorneys. Death penalties were replaced by life imprisonment.

A Catholic in ritual, Joseph's work ethic was Protestant. He seemed to agree with at least that part of Calvin's teaching that pronounced work (apart from prayer) as the one legitimate activity of life. He labored long hours and traveled a great deal, visiting many provinces of the empire. He eschewed royal remoteness and readily engaged in conversation with subjects of any station. Peasants knew him as a benevolent ruler who readily listened to their grievances against unjust or exploitative landlords. Intellectuals too thought of him with respect because they knew only the abstract principles of his policies, not his dictatorial temper.

Whether Joseph II's internal measures were wise and well taken, whether their ultimate failure was due to his own shortsightedness or to the benighted conditions in which he ruled can endlessly be debated, but that his foreign policy was mistaken is beyond argument. He anticipated Clausewitz by regarding war as politics by other means. None of his wars brought the results he expected of them and their failure may have contributed to the rapid decline in the fortunes of the empire, as well as in his health. Always concerned with trade issues, he demanded from the Netherlands, the northern neighbor of his

Belgian possessions, free navigation on the Scheldt River, which emptied into the North Sea and which the Dutch controlled. When he met with refusal, he went to war. The Dutch put up a tough fight and, although they in the end brought peace (in 1785) by paying 10 million thalers, the mouth of the Scheldt remained under their control.

The French had supported the Dutch in the war and the outcome cost Joseph the close and felicitous cooperation with France dating from the time of the Seven Years' War. He had no allies in the Holy Roman Empire, which he nominally ruled, and he chose to rely on his Russian connection. In 1781 he had met Catherine II in Mogilev and had agreed with her on joint action against both the truncated Polish state, which was making strenuous efforts to put its political house in order, and Turkey, which, he reckoned, could not for long defend her Balkan possessions in her weakened state. No benefit to Austria accrued from this agreement, but it encouraged Catherine to move against the Tartars, who, under Turkish overlordship, controlled the Crimea; she wrested that strategic peninsula from them, extending Russian rule all the way to the shores of the Black Sea. Four years later Joseph visited the czarina again; she took him on a grand tour of her recently acquired southern possessions. The Turks took a dim view of her showing off a land that they regarded as their own and made hostile moves in the direction of the Crimea. Joseph conceived the notion (whose time would come only a century later) of partitioning the European portion of the Ottoman Empire in partnership with Russia. When in 1787 the Porte, still harking back to the humiliation of Catherine's and Joseph's Ukrainian tour, declared war on Russia, Joseph entered on Russia's side. Fancying himself a great general, he went to the front, where, after an initial victory in the field, he suffered a series of defeats. He returned home gravely ill, afflicted with tuberculosis.

Nothing but failures attended the closing years of his reign. Hard-pressed to pay his civil servants in both Austria and the rest of the empire, he tried to tax the church estates in the non-German parts in order to meet the payroll; those estates, largely at Frederick II's behest, refused his demand. The Austrian Netherlands were equally obstreperous in the matter of taxation. Joseph's proposal to place a General Council above the estates there to ensure the payment of taxes, a measure that had proved successful in his hereditary domains, met with firm resistance in the Netherlands, as the estates, one after another, simply refused to approve the mandated taxes. Joseph demanded submission by issuing a royal edict; in 1788, he closed down the university in Louvain when the student body joined the resistance; in the next year he threatened the destruction of Brussels. An entirely new situation arose, however, with the outbreak of the French Revolution. In 1789 a French army detachment invaded the Austrian Netherlands; in December of that year, hard-pressed, Joseph evacuated his troops from Belgium.

The spirit of the revolution in France called for the rejection of royal absolutism; ironically, many of Joseph's reforms were popular with the confident and intellectually mature bourgeoisie that made up the bulk of the French Third Estate; but this same estate could not condone his absolutist methods.

Within his realms even those who had benefited from the reforms began to suspect ulterior motives—peasants feared that the "freedom" Joseph offered them would end the landlord's responsibility for their sustenance; Jews interpreted his encouragement of their assimilation as an attempt to wean them from their faith; nobles feared an end of their control over their serfs.

Dying a slow and painful death, and realizing that his best intentions had produced disappointment and resistance, Joseph retracted all his reforms except those affecting religious orders, measures easing the lot of the serfs, and the Patent of Toleration. He ordered that the Hungarian crown, which he had had taken to Vienna, perhaps to remain there and never be placed on a royal head, be returned to the Hungarian nation.

As if he had sensed that he would not live long (maybe he took the papal prophecy more seriously than he cared to show) his reforms from the start bore the stamp of extreme impatience. Frederick the Great's reforms in Prussia had taken 40 years to accomplish; Joseph attempted to put his in place in 10. Frederick's kingdom (except for the Poles coming in with the successive partitions) was homogeneous, whereas Joseph's realm was patched together from a dozen nations, and given the wide differences in their cultures, each demanded a different approach to the acceptance of reforms. Even under the impact of the French Revolution Europe was not quite ready for the thorough transformation that Joseph II envisioned.

⁂ ⁂ ⁂

Joseph was no more successful in matrimony than in statecraft. His two marriages, one to Isabella of Parma, whom he passionately loved but who, tormented by dark premonitions at a young age, died early, the other to Josefa, princess of Bavaria, whom he married for purely political reasons and would have nothing to do with, produced no children. Upon Joseph's death, his brother Leopold took the throne. The fact that Leopold ruled only for two years and that his edicts gave no clear indication of his political leanings have made him something of an enigma that historians still try to unravel. Before taking the throne of the Austrian Empire, he had been ruler of the Italian province of Tuscany for 25 years and had been a model of the enlightened despot. Arriving in Vienna, he found that the Hungarian component of the empire was sullen, especially over Joseph's administrative reforms that deprived the estates of so much of their cherished independence. He recalled the Hungarian Diet and had himself crowned with the crown of St. Stephen, a ceremony that involved an oath to the constitution; and by this act he brought about a measure of reconciliation with the noble estates. In December 1790 Austrian army units reoccupied the Belgian provinces that had fallen to Belgian rebels who sought to secure independence; at a congress in the Hague in that same month European powers guaranteed Austria's right to Belgium. On August 4, 1791 Leopold ended another conflict, with Turkey, in the Peace of Sistova, and although Austria had fared poorly in the war, the old borders were reestablished, even with minor rectifications in Austria's favor.

Internally, Leopold made no substantial changes in the system Joseph II had installed. He too was an absolutist ruler, as he had been in Tuscany, but his actions were prompted by a less visionary nature. He continued the social and religious policies of his brother but allowed the estates much greater scope. At the same time, however, he spread propaganda among the peasantry by way of leaflets, encouraging them to rise against the arbitrariness of landlords, hoping to put the nobles in the legislatures on the defensive. Joseph had already begun building up a secret police to ferret out sources of discontent; Leopold accelerated the process. While definitely in favor of modernizing the state, he possessed the traditional Habsburg mistrust of political dissent, and during his brief reign the distrust was enhanced by the stream of unsettling news from France.

King Louis XVI of France, Leopold's brother-in-law, had had to yield to popular clamor and allow the venerable institution of the Estates General, dominated by the privileged estates, to be transformed into a National Assembly in which commoners formed the majority; violence in Paris and disorders in the countryside had frightened the king's two brothers into fleeing France and becoming émigrés; the royal family had been compelled by a revolutionary mob to abandon its majestic palace in Versailles and move to Paris where they were held virtually hostage by bands of sansculottes seething with hatred of royalty. Nothing that happened in France could leave the rest of Europe unaffected for any length of time. The revolution had to be brought down before oppressed populations in other parts of Europe took their cue. This sentiment was shared by the Prussian king, successor to Frederick the Great, Frederick William II and the rather unexpected outcome was an Austro-Prussian rapprochement. This was particularly welcome to Leopold because there was much pro-Prussian sentiment in the Habsburg monarchy, especially among the Hungarian and Galician nobility, as well as in the Netherlands. There was also the fact that Leopold, once crowned Holy Roman Emperor, became the superior of the Prussian king. He first met Frederick William at the end of August 1791; they discussed the danger represented by the revolution in France in general terms. At home, Leopold's position was firmed up when the noble estates softened their opposition to surviving features of the Josephine reorganization. A foreign war no longer threatened to upset the internal order and in February 1792 Leopold concluded a formal alliance with Prussia.

Hostilities were inevitable given the intolerably provocative attitude of the French Legislative Assembly, dominated by a faction dubbed the Girondins, overconfident hawks in the Assembly who hoped to break both royal power and their leftist political opponents in a victorious war and who deliberately provoked Austria by overweening demands. Leopold did not live long enough to witness its outbreak. Days after making his alliance with Prussia he fell ill, as best could be judged from his symptoms, with peritonitis, for which medical science at the time had no cure. He died on March 1, 1792, leaving the throne to his first-born son Francis. Seven weeks later, on April 20, King Louis XVI of France went to the Legislative Assembly with a declaration of war on "the King of Hungary and Bohemia." (Properly the declaration should have been addressed to the Holy Roman Emperor, for the issue that had brought matters to this point was the failure of the Holy Roman Empire to expel the band of French émigrés gathered in German lands who were maintaining a barrage of propaganda against their revolutionary homeland, but Francis had not yet been crowned emperor, thus war had to be waged against him officially in a sphere narrower than the one in which his power truly rested.

It is historic experience that those wars usually last longest that are planned for a short duration. Although the Girondin hotheads in France painted glorious pictures for their fellow legislators of French revolutionary armies carrying their cherished ideals far into foreign lands, the truth was that the French, that is, royal, army had disintegrated, most of its noble officers had emigrated, desertions were endemic, and morale was sinking fast, whereas Austria and Prussia put a first-rate army under a Prussian general, the duke of Brunswick, into the field. There was little reason to doubt that, with the road to Paris practically open, the invaders would soon be in a position to overthrow the chaotic regime in Paris and restore the king to his ancient position, thus putting a summary end to the revolutionary experiment.

Yet the war that ostensibly grew out of an undignified petty quarrel between the Austrian king and a boastful assembly in Paris proved to be one of the most extended and destructive ones in European history, with Austria bearing the brunt of the fighting through most of its course.

CHAPTER SEVEN

Francis I was 24 years old when he assumed the onerous duties of ruler of the Austrian lands. Had times been more tranquil, had powerful political and military forces not threatened the internal and international status quo, his character and his political convictions would no doubt have emerged in clearer terms. That his rule came to be characterized as one of stubborn reaction was almost exclusively due to the threat that the revolution in France posed to Europe's monarchies and to all the values that divine-right monarchs cherished—against that threat only the most forceful defense of the old order could prevail. Personally Francis was hard-working and dutiful, as his uncle Joseph II had been, and he never sought a return to pre-Enlightenment days. The first change he made was in the administrative sphere: he raised the cabinet, hitherto essentially an advisory body, to ministerial rank, with its members responsible for the diverse affairs of the empire. His second reform was to restore the national police, indispensable in the face of so much potential subversion, to an independent agency answerable only to the king. In foreign affairs, the aged Kaunitz remained in charge, though after March 1793 the actual conduct of diplomacy was in the hands of a remarkable man, Baron Johann Thugut. Born a commoner and ennobled by Maria Theresa, Thugut was the only man of common birth ever to serve the state as chancellor for foreign affairs.

So far as domestic matters were concerned, Francis left Maria Theresa's and Joseph's reforms in place; whether he did so out of indolence or because he agreed with their spirit is impossible to determine.

The new king's rule extended over 43 years and for nearly half that time the empire was at war as a partner in successive coalitions ranged against revolutionary, then Napoleonic, France. It is customary to date the first of those multistate coalitions from February 1793, but its nucleus was the Austro-Prussian alliance entered into on February 7, 1792. When Great Britain, the Netherlands, and Spain, in addition to the Holy Roman Empire, joined those two a true coalition against France was formed. The battles in this early phase were fought along the Rhine and in northern Italy, and hostilities ended in October 1797 with the Peace of Campo Formio, imposed on Austria by the young Corsican-French general Napoleon Bonaparte. In previous encounters French attempts to push into the Austrian Netherlands had been beaten back, French armies deployed against the heart of the Holy Roman Empire and against Austria fought positional battles without making much headway, and the French

Army of the South, facing northern Italy, was in a state of neglect and demor-
alization. The tide of battle flowed this way and that. In the Netherlands, at
Jemappes, on November 6, 1792, the French defeated the Austrians, took Brussels, and occupied Belgium; four months later the Austrians triumphed at Neer-
winden and retook Brussels. There were similar changes of fortune in German
lands. In general, as the revolution in France deepened, the raw armies of what
was now the French Republic became infused with a sense of mission and
marched from one victory to another; only after the demise of the Reign of
Terror in the summer of 1794 did enthusiasm in France for the war flag again.
In this latter phase, on the Austrian side, Francis's younger brother, Archduke
Charles, proved more than an equal to the young, gifted generals the revolution in France had produced, and he forced two of them, Jourdan and Moreau,
to retreat from their conquests in southern Germany. Austria's Italian possessions appeared secure, if only because the French southern army, facing them,
was in a downtrodden condition and seemed to pose no threat. But then, in the
spring of 1796, that army under Bonaparte's command unexpectedly bestirred
itself, and, in barely more than a month, knocked Austria's ally, Piedmont, out
of the war, annexed to France Nice and Savoy, defeated the Austrians in a series
of battles, and took the province of Lombardy. The dukes of small Italian states
paid tribute to avoid being drawn into the war, and the flow of gold and silver
rescued the French treasury from near bankruptcy. During the winter of
1796–97 Napoleon cleared the way to the Papal States and the pope had to
purchase a truce with a major payment of his own. Napoleon then crossed the
Alps and entered the Tyrol, which had been mobilized to oppose his forces. In
his rear, Venetia was in revolt. Napoleon avoided giving battle to Archduke
Charles and concluded the Preliminaries of Leoben, followed by the Peace of
Campo Formio, in which Austria was forced to cede her Netherlandish possessions (Belgium) to France and allowed Lombardy to became part of a new state,
the Cisalpine Republic, which Napoleon had formed from defunct Italian duke-
doms south of the Alps. Austria received Venetia together with Istria and Dalmatia as compensation. In secret articles of the Treaty of Campo Formio Francis
also agreed to support French acquisitions on the left bank of the Rhine from
the Holy Roman Empire. At this price peace was finally purchased, though few
expected that it would last.

Within Austria, Thugut remained an irreconcilable foe of France and argued
for a resumption of the war; by the end of 1798, while Bonaparte was campaigning in Egypt and Syria, Austria joined with Britain, Russia, Naples, and
Portugal in the Second Coalition, and in March 1799 declared war on France
again. Austrian and Russian armies earned some remarkable though inconclusive victories; in the autumn of 1799 Napoleon returned to France, in
November he carried out a coup d'état, making himself master of France as
first among the equals in the three-men consulate that, by a new constitution
promulgated in February 1800, was to rule France. The Russian emperor, Paul,
made a separate peace with France, and, in the course of 1800, Austrian armies
suffered a new series of defeats in northern Italy, parts of which they had
retaken; they also faced two French armies in the north, one advancing along

the Danube, the other from South Tyrol, toward Vienna. Francis, lacking the forces to defend his capital, concluded on February 2, 1801, the Peace of Lunéville, which essentially reinstated the terms of Campo Formio.

Austria had now been at war for nine years and had suffered great losses in territory and human life. Francis forced Thugut to resign, then set about rebuilding his exhausted realms, as well as the morale in the diverse provinces that by this time had lost all enthusiasm for war. However, he had to contend with the danger of revolutionary ideals rapidly spreading among the under-privileged strata of society. As early as 1794 the police had reported discovering Jacobin plots, in Hungary, Vienna, and Graz. None of these posed any true danger to the regime or to the unity of the empire, but the events in France had struck fear into royal hearts, especially as the conditions that had unleashed the revolution in France also existed, often in a more distressing form, in their lands. Only in Hungary did the Jacobin movement assume a concrete form. Although insurrection schemes were isolated and amateurish, Habsburg rulers had distrusted their Hungarian subjects from the very time they acquired that troublesome land in 1526. The leading figure in the movement was a Catholic priest, Ignaz Martinovics, who harbored a deep animosity toward the high nobility. He had been one of the agents of Leopold I when the latter sought to undermine the dominant position of that class in Hungary. Martinovics's circle of coconspirators remained small and never exerted any influence over the general population. He planned an uprising in the interest of the lower gentry by which the monarchy would be abolished and a republic established, the power of the aristocracy would be broken, church lands would be secularized, and the serfs set free, with only their feudal dues to the gentry preserved. This comprehensive scheme, as so many similar ones growing out of the chronic discontent in the empire, never passed beyond the stage of feverish but feck-less planning. The conspirators were hunted down before they were organized for any kind of action; they were tortured or pilloried, several of them exe-cuted, others sentenced to long periods at forced labor. Still, Francis's fear of a revolutionary conspiracy did not abate.

Inaction rather than reform was in any case more suited to his tempera-ment—in his mind bureaucracy and government were synonymous terms. Only in the military, under the direction of Archduke Charles, was there some movement toward reform: the length of service was reduced from life to 10 years in the infantry and to 12 in the artillery, living conditions of enlisted men were improved, the brutal methods in their training were ameliorated, and technical innovations in weaponry were introduced. The peasants' lot, as Joseph's reforms had not had time to take effect, was not eased and even the little progress that had been made was halted in its tracks. An example was Joseph's initiative to allow the peasant to redeem his service and rent obliga-tions in cash; the matter was unresolved when Joseph died. In truth even the peasants did not favor a system that would bind them to cash payments in per-petuity. The landlords saw in it a means for the peasant eventually to buy his freedom and begin competing with them. Francis in 1798 authorized cash com-mutation *if* both sides agreed, but in each instance the district office under noble control had to authorize it, and it would do so only if it had assurance that payments would duly be made. This was a prescription for continued stagnation. Manorial jurisdiction also remained in place, largely because, if ended, the state would have to take over the administration of justice and that involved expenses the precariously low treasury could not afford.

Lack of money was probably the chief cause of the inertia, and as long as the war lasted, the armies and the police would consume much of royal revenue. The respites in the fighting were short and fragile because of the general perception that as long as Napoleon ruled France lasting peace was impossible. When war was resumed in May 1803 with the violation (by whom is a question historians still debate) of the Peace of Amiens between Britain and France, Austria at first remained neutral. Francis was engaged in a competition of a different kind. Napoleon's docile senate had recommended on May 18, 1804, that the first consul's title be changed to emperor. A national referendum overwhelmingly approved the change. The coronation was to take place in December, but Napoleon's imperial dignity was a fact before that, and Francis was still "only" archduke of Austria and king of Hungary and Bohemia. The contrast was all the more striking as Napoleon was an upstart and Francis the scion of one of the oldest dynastic families in Europe. On August 10 of that year Francis proclaimed himself hereditary emperor of Austria. The change in title was desirable in any case because the Holy Roman Empire, which hitherto had assured him the title emperor, was in an advanced state of dissolution. Once it had become extinct, Habsburgs would hold an inferior title to the Bonapartes. Thus, properly speaking, the term Austrian Empire can be applied to Habsburg holdings only from this time onward.

Possibly to give his rivalry with Napoleon more tangible expression, Francis joined Great Britain and Russia in the Third Coalition in August 1805. Napoleon had collected a large army for a planned invasion of Britain; he now turned it against Austria, defeated an army at Ulm on October 20, then marched on and occupied Vienna. The main Austrian force under Archduke Charles was in Italy where Napoleon's next thrust had been expected. A northern force now joined a Russian army in Moravia and on December 2 fought a withering battle against a smaller French army near the town of Austerlitz. The defeat was so complete that on the second day of Christmas 1805 Francis was impelled to sign the Peace of Pressburg that deprived his empire of sundry provinces, such as Venice, Tyrol, and the Vorarlberg; the first of these was joined to the Kingdom of Italy, and the latter two to Bavaria. In addition, Austria was forced to pay an indemnity of 40 million francs. The crowning humiliation came in August 1806, when Napoleon organized most of the west German states into the Confederation of the Rhine and prevailed on Francis to declare the Holy Roman Empire at an end.

More was at stake than the loss of a dignity that, although it had been hollow since the Thirty Years' War, still carried an aura of imperial glory. With the loss of an organic connection to Greater Germany, Austria became a nondescript state of geographically and linguistically disparate units, with no bond to give its people a sense of common destiny. A national character, such as that glorified by the revolution in France, would have been artificial and poisonous; some dozen ethnic groups would be tempted to take pride in their own identity over the Austrian with which they had nothing in common. The new chancellor since 1805, Philip Stadion, supported by the king's younger brother John, favored a mystic popular patriotism, a devotion to an Austrian homeland in which ethnic and religious differences were buried out of sight. Francis was suspicious—to him the very word patriotism had the smell of revolution. He preferred to depend on the commonality of the Germans in Austria only. In this he was largely successful, especially after a Prussian defeat by French arms in 1807 that awakened powerful German nationalistic feelings, abetted by the brilliant pen of men like the philosopher and pamphleteer Johann Gottfried Fichte. In the short term such a resurgence of German national pride could serve Austria, too; once French power was overthrown, the national bond could be abandoned and tested methods of oppression and manipulation be employed for endowing the Austrian Empire with a sense of unity.

More was needed, however, than a sentimental nationalism to break the French stranglehold over German lands. In 1809 Britain prevailed on Austria to join still another, the fourth, coalition against France. Archduke Charles, aware of the catastrophic condition of the Austrian treasury, opposed the resumption of war, but Francis decided to heed the British plea and ordered Charles to assume the command of his armies. Charles had a creditable record as a field commander, though against lesser generals than Napoleon, but now he suffered two consecutive defeats, at Regensburg and Wagram. When he agreed to an armistice, he was relieved of his command and the chancellor, Stadion, too resigned. In October Francis had to sign still another humiliating peace. There was not much territory apart from the hereditary Habsburg lands that he could lose; in the event, he had to give up Croatia south of the Sava River and parts of Carinthia and Carniola, which Napoleon joined to the French Empire as the Illyrian Provinces. Austria was cut off from the sea. A good part of Galicia also was lost; one portion Napoleon attached to the Archduchy of Warsaw, a small resurrected part of the old Polish Kingdom, another portion, Tarnopol and environs, to Russia. Austria was in addition forced to join the Continental System, Napoleon's invention of 1807, seeking to defeat Britain by forbidding all continental trade with her. Austria agreed to abide by these conditions.

Francis attributed these misfortunes in part to poor diplomacy. He appointed a son-in-law of the one-time state chancellor Kaunitz, the Rhenish aristocrat Clemens Lothar Wenzel Metternich, formerly ambassador in Paris, as chancellor. In his first diplomatic move Metternich arranged the marriage of the young daughter of his emperor, Marie Louise, to Napoleon, who had divorced his first wife, Josephine Beauharnais, and was anxious for a male heir of royal blood. The marriage took place in April 1810, and in May 1811 the eagerly awaited heir was born. For Austria the marriage brought a badly needed breathing spell. Metternich had by now familiarized himself with the sorry internal condition of the empire and its inability to continue the war. The treasury was so depleted that in 1811 the government had to order a devaluation of the currency by 80 percent, a measure that struck against every social class.

Given the general situation in Europe, one was by now either with Napoleon or against Napoleon; joining forces with the French emperor was the only viable opportunity to place Austria's economic house in some kind of order.

Napoleon had no enemies left on the continent—with Russia he had a haphazardly concluded partition agreement dating from 1807, assigning the eastern part of Europe, including the Ottoman Empire and Finland to Russia, the rest to France. Napoleon had by now grievances against the Russian czar, Alexander I. He had intended to marry Alexander's sister and was refused, and Alexander also kept up lively trade with England, thus violating the Continental System. On his part, the czar was vexed by Napoleon's refusal to give him a free hand in Constantinople, and also by his alliance with Austria that was the one positive outcome of Napoleon's marriage to Francis's daughter. The most likely cause of Napoleon's decision to go to war against Russia, however, was that he had over 200,000 bayonets at his disposal and war had become for him a natural condition.

For the campaign Napoleon collected the famed Grande Armée, the largest army that ever marched in Europe, of some 650,000 troops. Few doubted that it would be victorious against the much smaller and poorly equipped Russian forces, and Metternich had to play his hand very cautiously. Refusing to participate in the campaign could have cost Austria dearly after a victorious outcome; to offer full support and then see the campaign fail would be catastrophic, as Austria, with the last of her military forces destroyed, would have no bargaining power left. Thus Metternich committed 30,000 troops to the Russian campaign; Prussia sent 20,000.

A combination of terrain, weather, and Alexander's stubborn refusal to negotiate brought Napoleon's invasion to a disastrous end. Less than 40,000 soldiers of the Grande Armée recrossed the border into Poland. Alexander, not satisfied with ridding his country of the invader, decided to pursue him into the heart of Europe, to the very heart of France if it became necessary. He called on Francis to head the new coalition. It was a tempting offer because the national fervor in German lands was at its height and most of the rest of Europe was ready to shake off the French yoke. Metternich still hesitated. There was always the possibility that Napoleon, who had hurried home to recruit still another army, would recover his position and there was no telling how he would then punish Austria for betraying their alliance. More important, Metternich was a great advocate of the balance of power and knew that if France was defeated, a power vacuum would occur that Austria would be unable to fill, and Russia might become dominant on a continent ravaged by war. His policy was to remain neutral and seek to act as a mediator. If Napoleon forswore further conquests and confined his reign to an enlarged France, a healthy balance between France and Russia could be established. But Napoleon, who not long ago had been the master of Europe, wanted not peace but victory. Victory, however, was ever harder to come by. The campaigns of the summer of 1813 were fluctuating affairs. When Napoleon lost a battle, he was inclined to moderate his demands only long enough to rally his forces; if in a next clash he was victorious, he stiffened his terms again. Metternich knew that a decisive battle was bound to come and that Austria by then would have to assume a clear-cut position. At court, the war party was gaining the upper hand. If Austria opted out of the last great battle against Napoleon, her power position would be shaken, and possibly lost.

Napoleon was aware of the gathering forces against him and arranged a meeting with Metternich in Dresden, trying to persuade him to continue the policy of neutrality. Metternich temporized and favored a congress to sort matters out. It met for over five weeks in Prague, in July and early August; at the meeting Metternich continued his policy of mediation. No agreement resulted, the congress broke up on August 11, and on the very next day Austria declared war on France.

Throughout August and September the battles continued with changing fortunes, but by now, time and the reservoir of manpower favored the allies. On September 9, Austria, Prussia, and Russia concluded a formal treaty, guaranteeing each other's territory and each pledging 60,000 men to fight a common war against France. They also pledged not to conclude a separate peace. Between October 16 and 19 the great Battle of Nations near Leipzig took place, and Napoleon suffered a definitive defeat. From this time on, probably he alone had any faith in an ultimate victory. During the winter he continued to skirmish

The Congress of Vienna, painting by J. B. Isabey *(Library of Congress)*

for position, already on French soil, but the great numerical superiority of the allies was more than a match for his tactical brilliance. While campaigning in Lorraine, the news reached him that Paris had, on March 31, 1814, surrendered to an invading allied army. With nothing left to fight with, he concluded with the allies the personal treaty of Fontainebleau, abdicating, and agreeing to withdraw to the island of Elba as his sovereign principality. The revolutionary nightmare had at last come to an end.

In recognition of Austria's belligerence against France, of longer duration than of any other power, as well as of the crucial part Metternich played in the diplomatic game during the closing phases of the war, the allies agreed that a congress called to sort out the tangled affairs of Europe should meet in Vienna. It was an affair of contrasts. Austria was deep in the economic doldrums and Hungary was in stubborn opposition to the devaluation of currency that Francis had decreed without consulting the Diet. At the same time the congress met amid ostentatious pomp and circumstance in September 1814. It sat for some 14 months, during which it was interrupted by Napoleon's dramatic return from Elba to reclaim his ruling position in France and his final defeat at Waterloo in Belgium on June 18, 1815. By then the congress had finished its work, Austria regained all of her lost territories except for the Belgian provinces, which she willingly surrendered to a united kingdom of the Netherlands, was allowed to retain Lombardy, and received in compensation Venetia, as well as the Illyrian provinces. She also joined a Quadruple Alliance with Russia, Prussia, and Britain, pledging joint resistance to any French revival and mutual consultations to deal with such problems as might arise in the wake of the revolution.

Although the principle of legitimacy guided the peacemakers in deciding who should occupy which vacant throne, this principle was not applied to the many defunct entities of the old Holy Roman Empire. Its place was taken by a German Confederation of 39 states, territorially corresponding roughly to the old empire, but with many small entities merged into larger units; by common agreement, representatives from each were to meet annually in the city of Frankfurt, under the presidency of the Austrian delegate. Thus Austria's leading position in German affairs was confirmed and perpetuated. Metternich, the informal chairman of the Congress of Vienna, was at the height of his influence and power.

CHAPTER EIGHT

It is convenient, though inaccurate, to refer to the period between the Congress of Vienna and the revolutions of 1848 as the Age of Metternich. The direction in which Europe moved, politically, economically, and even spiritually was almost opposite to the course Metternich charted, and the upheavals that swept him from power were conclusive proof of that. He was probably right when, in response to people who referred to his "system," he said that he had no system, only principles. In the end, the principles amounted to a system. It was one of absolute, though enlightened, monarchy, because that alone, as he saw it, could ensure social order. He supported absolutism with the argument that most people did not wish to participate in politics; rather, their interest was in their economic welfare.

Representative assemblies were anathema to him, not only because they did not possess a unity of will but also because they represented the pernicious doctrine of popular sovereignty. He mistrusted not so much the lower, as the educated middle classes; they were a novelty to him, he called them the "agitated classes," and regarded them as the chief cause of all the mischief the government encountered. Puffed up by their importance and driven by greed, they saw revolution as a means to gain power and, incidentally, to get hold of other people's wealth. Another source of his animus was that, in his view, constructive intellects were most likely to be found in the middle class, and Metternich distrusted all intellects except his own. His constant self-praise and cynical insistence that he alone understood political necessities in time became tiresome and even ludicrous. In truth, his understanding was limited only to the importance of state institutions to control social unrest and to diplomacy—he complacently turned away from the many vital problems of the day, such as the growing impact of industrialism and the vitality of nationalism.

Austria emerged from the revolutionary wars somewhat diminished in size but more compact and more governable. She lost the Netherlands but became the dominant force in northern Italy. The "Lombard-Venetian Kingdom" became an integral part of the empire; in Tuscany Francis's younger brother Ferdinand was prince, in Modena his nephew Francis IV, in Parma his daughter Marie Louise, the former empress of France as Napoleon's wife. Marie Louise's son, the "eaglet," half Bonaparte and half Habsburg, was brought up in Vienna. Although the court made strenuous efforts to instill in him Habsburg pride, his father, even in exile, cast a long shadow. He was never made a Habsburg archduke—his title was prince of Reichstadt.

Metternich was not blind to the many changes the revolution and rapid economic development had brought about, but he took the position that, if the changes themselves could not be controlled, perhaps their effect could. He understood also that ideas were potentially more dangerous than material forces. His most conspicuous attempt to silence inconvenient voices came in 1819, after a conservative playwright in Germany was assassinated by a misguided youth. Metternich called a meeting of the delegates from the German Confederation to Karlsbad in Bohemia and prevailed on the assembly to pass a number of laws, which provided for strict censorship and placed universities in Austria and Germany under the tightest control. Student societies, the so-called Burschenschaften, were banned; students and writers suspected of subversive activities were blacklisted. These measures were routinely renewed after their expiration.

Metternich classified as subversive not only ideas that had survived the fall of the French Revolution but also those that asserted the right of a people cherishing a common historic tradition to coalesce into a nation. Italy seethed with a passionate desire for national unification. The Young Italy ideal, and the *carbonari* movement in particular, attracted thousands of, mostly young, people to its ranks. Metternich judged it to be Austria's duty to subdue such romantic endeavors. He perceived nationalism as a dangerously disruptive force. When in 1821 uprisings broke out in Naples (a Bourbon principality in which Austria had no direct interest) and Piedmont (the one Italian state ruled by a native dynasty, the Savoys) for a united Italy, Austrian troops were sent in to restore order. Similar uprisings in Modena, Parma, and the Papal States a decade later were also suppressed. What Metternich *was* willing to concede was a need for *social* reform. Even while providing troops to control political unrest, he urged the governments in Italy to alleviate economic and social conditions. More often than not his urgings went unheeded, most particularly in the Papal States.

In Austria, Metternich had a valid reason for holding nationalist assertions on a very short rein. If it was impossible to create a supranational bond to which the various ethnic groups would have been willing to subscribe (the futility of it had been apparent during the Napoleonic Wars), in the absence of such a bond it at least had to be shown that nationalist aspirations were vain and went against the law of God. Joseph II had attempted to create at least a semblance of unity by imposing the use of German in official matters on all his subjects; it accomplished the opposite. The Germans of Austria regarded themselves as culturally (and in certain instances racially) superior to all the other nationalities; some even argued for two separate states within the empire, the western, German, and the eastern, non-German parts. This display of hubris was more than matched by the Hungarians, who felt that their domination for nearly a millennium over Romanians, Slovaks, Ruthenians, and certain other "lesser breeds" was proof and justification of their superior status. Such overweening attitudes had been present for a long time, and the ardent nationalism born in the French Revolution and soon spreading to distant parts of Europe infused new strength into them. However, it also bred resentful self-assertions by smaller national groups hitherto held in contempt. Literary products appeared in the Czech, Slovak, and Ruthenian languages, and there was a genuine linguistic revival in Croatia and Slavonia. Each of these carried the seeds, however immature, of future separatism from Austrian domination; Metternich cynically encouraged the fledgling voices of the smaller ethnic groups as a counterweight to the nationalisms he feared most: the German and Hungarian.

A balance had to be struck, however. Germans and Hungarians could not be allowed to feel victimized or be dissuaded from their conviction that they formed the backbone of Austrian society. When all was said and done, the Germans contributed most of the entrepreneurs, civil servants, and professionals in the empire; the Hungarians paid most of the taxes and supplied most of the military conscripts. In the last resort the German element was the only one the monarchy could depend on to hold the empire together. From Hungary, the money amounts so necessary for the strapped treasury would continue only if the magnates were allowed to retain their feudal rights, because without serfs whom they could exploit at their pleasure they could not make their estates profitable, let alone pay taxes; consequently, many of the rights that Joseph II's reforms had secured for the peasantry were quietly shelved. The magnates were satisfied when their Diet, dissolved in 1811 because it would not support the emperor's inflationary monetary policy, was reconvened in 1825. The other social classes had not yet gained political weight; no expression of discontent would issue from Hungary until the lesser gentry and the middle classes found their voice.

In concert with clever politicians in other parts of Europe, Metternich supported the Catholic Church to the extent that it served his political goals. There was no institution that more resolutely condemned revolutions or assaults on the monarchical order than the Catholic Church. Jesuits, expelled by Maria Theresa, were readmitted, in good part because they alone could supply the pool of teachers the educational system required. That system was placed exclusively in church hands; university students of every discipline were required to attend lectures on Catholic theology. The pervasive censorship banned all writings hostile to or critical of Catholicism. Persons who had converted from Protestantism back to Catholicism were given special preference in appointments to civil service positions.

Despite tentative early signs of the Industrial Revolution gaining a foothold, in the 1830s the great majority of the population still was constituted of the peasantry, and only a small portion of that class was free. In Hungary and Bohemia the serfs were subject to the *robot,* obligatory labor on the landlord's estate, and they had to make money payments to the lord, the church, and the state. In Bohemia one-half of their work week was taken up by the *robot,* and in Hungary, in high season, even more. In lieu of the rent for the land they used for their own purposes, they had to deliver to the landlord a part of their crop, usually between a 10th and a 20th, depending on the region and the landlord's disposition. Taxes to the government paid in money and kind were even more onerous. In addition, on the pattern of the French *corvée,* serfs had to supply carts and horses for the transport of soldiers and government officials when necessary; often they had to billet and feed soldiers in their houses.

While in western Europe governments encouraged and supported industrial enterprise, as well as the building of railroads that made the large-scale transportation of goods possible, Metternich did all he could to suppress such development. (Interestingly though, the first transportation system running on tracks in Europe was built in Austria, a horse-drawn conveyance between Linz and Budweis; the steam-powered engine appeared in the 1840s, hauling trains north of Vienna; by 1848, 1,000 miles of track had been laid.) There had been promising beginnings in the industrial field during the Napoleonic period; the Continental System, excluding English products, largely finished goods, from Europe, led to the establishment of industrial concerns in many countries, including Austria. Metternich distrusted enterprises that brought a number of workingmen together in one place; they could become hotbeds for agitation. Only cottage industries carried out in small peasant homesteads had his approval. Many long hours of draining labor were invested in such production, which, so far as Metternich was concerned, was all for the best. He wrote to Czar Alexander: "The labours to which this class—the real people—are obliged to devote themselves are too continuous and too positive to allow them to throw themselves into vague abstractions and ambitions."

Still, the absolutism he cherished was not powerful enough to retard natural economic forces. In the quarter century after the Congress of Vienna coal production in Austria increased ninefold, textile production sixfold. Metternich's restraining policies were swept away by a groundswell of economic boom. Simultaneously, his political influence began to decline. As early as 1826 Francis I appointed Franz Anton Kolowrat "minister of state," and Metternich had to reconcile himself to sharing power with a man he considered to be of lesser abilities than himself. Then, as the emperor entered old age, the question of succession became timely. Francis's oldest son, Ferdinand, was mentally defective and would obviously never be more than a figurehead ruler. Francis considered placing one of his own brothers on the throne. Metternich, firmly devoted to the principle of legitimacy, dissuaded him. Thus a five-man "state conference" was to act as a regency. When Francis died in March 1835 of a sudden fever, this council assumed charge of state affairs. Francis had admonished his simple-minded son in two separate letters to govern the empire as it had been governed heretofore and to change nothing; in the letter, which was obviously written, or dictated, by Metternich, he begged Ferdinand to accept the old chancellor's guidance. The state conference was formally chaired by Francis's younger brother Ludwig, the one brother of whom he was not jealous because he had the same modest intellectual gifts as himself. Other brothers had conspicuously made their mark in governing one province or another and Francis had always kept them at arm's length. Metternich's and Kolowrat's presence on the state conference assured a permanent impasse. Kolowrat, a Czech aristocrat, in charge of internal and financial matters, held political persuasions not much different from those of Metternich; if anything, he was perhaps more conservative, but because his antipathy for the great chancellor was well known, the public thought of him as something of a liberal. Thus the state conference, far from being a dynamic governing body, became a battleground between two men of monumental egos. Of the enlightened absolutism of half a century earlier absolutism alone survived. Bureaucracy became stifling. In one typical case, involving a claim by one person on another amounting to six florins, the decision was in the end referred to the emperor, and before the final disposition was made it had passed through 48 authorities.

In 1846 a peasant uprising, with all the violence and irrational mob fury that such outbreaks displayed, occurred in Galicia. As it developed in the aftermath (though the details were never fully clarified), Austrian occupation officials, realizing that some Polish nobles planned an uprising against the partition of their country among Austria, Prussia, and Russia, decided to incite their peasants against them; they encouraged the peasants to turn to the emperor for the rectification of the wrongs the nobles had inflicted on them. The poor toilers, needing little encouragement, chose a more direct way; they invaded manors, slew landlords, and flung their dead bodies in front of the Austrian governmental house in Krakow. The affair, which attracted attention across Europe, ended as such bloody risings usually did; the military was called out, troops drowned the revolt in blood, and the customary severe punishments followed.

Despite such local outbreaks, however, there was no overt evidence of a revolutionary mood in the empire. Metternich's oversized police force ensured minute supervision over all civil and governmental affairs (even the mail of some members of the imperial family was being opened and read) and yet—except perhaps in the Italian provinces—there were no plots to discover; if there was discontent, it was mainly with the paranoid preoccupation of the government with threats to its security.

Still, to say that there were no *overt* evidences of discontent is not the same as to say that the general public, not only in Austria but in much of Europe, was not growing impatient with the bureaucratic quagmire that in many places passed for government, with its petty concerns and its insistence on silencing protest of every kind. As was perhaps to be expected, the first stirrings occurred in France. A ludicrously minor incident in Paris, the canceling by the government of a banquet scheduled to be held in a working-class district of the city, escalated into street battles that within days brought down the government and forced the king into exile; that this flare-up, which incidentally was confined to Paris and left the French provinces indifferent, lit fires of discontent in other parts of Europe showed that a deep malaise had afflicted the politically conscious and temperamentally progressive elements of society. The eyes of Europe were on France, as they had been since the years of Louis XVI's reign—when the French rid themselves of king and monarchy, people in other countries took notice.

The economic factor was a weighty one. The potato blight had spread from Ireland to continental Europe, harvests were ruined; the peasants, with little to sell, had no money to spend, and the balance between rural and urban economy was upset. Unemployment rose sharply. In the Austrian Empire a number of interlocking problems magnified the general hardship. While in the German Confederation most states had joined in a customs union that made their goods more affordable abroad, Austria had opted to stay aloof and now began to suffer from price competition. In Hungary the fiery statesman, Lajos Kossuth, launched a "Buy Hungarian!" campaign; soon in that proud country buying Austrian was regarded as unpatriotic, even though there were many essential items Hungary could not produce and had to import from her neighbor. Starting in 1845 a series of floods in Galicia, Hungary, and even in the Italian provinces ruined the harvests; the entire Silesian potato crop succumbed to the blight. In many rural areas people had to browse in the fields; even in cities flour was mixed with maize (in Salzburg with clover) and bread that made up some 70 percent of the diet was of poor quality. In Bohemia cotton mills, unable to sell their products to the indigenous populace, went bankrupt. Public works, which until then had kept thousands of workers employed, were shut down for lack of funds. None of this, to be sure, was the result of government inefficiency or indifference. Nowhere in Europe, or for that matter in the Americas, were governments inclined to step in when the economy began to malfunction. We have noted that in Austria, despite Metternich's distrust of industrial enterprise and its concentration of workers in small areas, mining and manufacturing, as well as railroad building, developed fairly rapidly, fueled by the iron law of supply and demand. Now these very laws were thrown out of kilter as the agricultural sphere failed to supply the goods in demand. The question was only whether these hardships and the despair they engendered would overcome Austrians' traditional respect for authority and lead to an eruption the government could not control.

The ground first began to shake in Italy, and not even in the provinces controlled by the Habsburgs, but in the Kingdom of the Two Sicilies (Naples), ruled by the Bourbon Ferdinand. Following a revolt in Sicily in January 1848, Ferdinand promised a constitution; this promise was, for good reason, regarded by the populace as a sign of weakness and disturbances spread to the mainland. Piedmont, in the northwestern corner of the peninsula, the only principality in which an Italian house reigned, began moving troops to the border with the Austrian province of Lombardy, obviously with the intention of enlarging Piedmontese land at Austria's expense. There was as yet no violence, only a tense expectation of a major upheaval that would shake the complacent governments of Europe, and the societies they ruled, to their foundation.

Then came the electrifying news from Paris of the abdication of King Louis-Philippe, and reports that crowds in the streets were clamoring for a republic. Conservative rulers shuddered. Nicholas I, czar of Russia, strode into a crowded ballroom at his court, stopped the music, and cried out to the officers in their fine uniforms: "Gentlemen, saddle your horses. France is a republic."

This was a far less elemental revolution than the one that had shaken France and Europe half a century earlier. The sansculotte element was not there; in many places the very classes on which the government most depended were in revolt, and they could be put down only at great cost to the stability of the system and to national welfare. Two weeks after the events in Paris the citizenry of Berlin took to the streets; King Frederick William IV, mortified by the sight of Prussian soldiery firing at Prussian subjects, withdrew the military from the city and was then forced to bare his head as the bodies of those killed in the disturbances were paraded before him while officers of his bodyguard wept with humiliation.

How long before other cities erupted into revolt, too?

CHAPTER NINE

Of the year 1848 the British historian Trevelyan remarked that it was the great turning point at which history failed to turn. Given the accumulation of tensions and conflicts since the Congress of Vienna, nationalistic passions, the miserable condition of the peasantry, entrepreneurs chafing under restrictions placed on them, intellectuals stifled by censorship and other restrictions on freedom of expression, it was nearly a miracle that a dynasty that was known for its mediocrity more than for anything else was able to survive the upheavals of 1848–49 and reestablish itself with its powers undiminished. The lack of creative leadership among revolutionary forces, except in Hungary, was no doubt a factor in the failure but there was also the almost mystical staying power of the Habsburgs in face of all adversity, it gave them reason to trust divine providence to which, more than to their subjects, they felt responsible.

The first reaction to the news from Paris erupted in Hungary, where Lajos Kossuth early in March demanded a democratic constitution providing for popular representation. Vienna liberals quickly took their cue; ad hoc assemblies composed mainly of staid bourgeois began drafting petitions to the throne almost identical to the one issued by Kossuth. On March 13, demonstrations, heretofore peaceful, erupted into armed clashes in the Austrian capital when a crowd of students surrounded the parliament building in the Herrengasse and police fired on them; a number of demonstrators died. Soon violence spread to other parts of the city. The two ranking archdukes on the state conference decided to offer up to the crowd the aged Metternich, the most resented figure in the empire. That evening Metternich, after a feeble attempt to display his steadfastness, resigned and took the long road into exile. As had happened in France, the disorders were largely confined to the capital; apart from some minor outbreaks in Graz, the countryside remained quiet. But outside the German lands, in Hungary, Italy, Bohemia, Galicia, even in Croatia, the ferment was unmistakable. The Vienna court hesitated between making concessions and applying force. The latter was the customary course of action but tempers were too explosive to employ it without grave risk. Mere personnel changes in the government after the flight of Metternich were not likely to satisfy the demonstrators. The mention of a constitution, on the other hand, even if insincerely meant, still carried magic. Accordingly, on April 25 the new interior minister, Baron Pillersdorf, proclaimed one, though only for the hereditary lands. It provided for a bicameral legislature, the lower house elected by adult male

Clemens Wenzel
Lothar Metternich
(Library of Congress)

taxpayers, the upper named by the emperor from among landed magnates and trusted aristocrats. The emperor, according to this forlorn document, had an absolute veto over measures passed by either house.

The draft did not calm revolutionary passions; crowds invaded the royal palace, demanding the withdrawal of Pillersdorf's proposed constitution. Ferdinand and his court, insofar as they had any policy at all, geared their reaction to the disorders to the degree of danger they represented. By May passions seemed to have cooled and the emperor attempted to dissolve the national guard, which had made itself responsible for maintaining order in the capital. This occasioned another uprising and, reluctantly, the royal court decided that Vienna was no longer a safe city in which to reside. Ferdinand fled to the town of Innsbruck in the loyal Tyrol, where he was received with thunderous enthusiasm. However, Vienna was still the functional nerve center of a sprawling empire, and the streets there were ruled by a bourgeois national guard, well-to-do men of progressive views, whose aspirations did not go further than royal assurances for the protection of, first and foremost, private property. They were joined by "academic legions," composed largely of university youth. In June the government at last convoked the parliament provided for in Pillersdorf's draft, the Reichstag as it was called, but that body, made up of a majority of Slavs, rejected the very constitution on which its authority rested. Discussions of proposed reforms continued but the only one of import that emerged, on September 5, was one calling for the emancipation of the serfs.

Meanwhile in Hungary, at the urging of Lajos Kossuth, a national constitution was drawn up; known as the April Laws, it provided for a Hungarian kingdom tied to Austria only by a personal union. The emperor, having no alternative under the circumstances, approved the document. But the court, with the obvious intent of undermining Hungary's separatist moves, enlisted the support of a Croatian nobleman, staunchly pro-Habsburg and anti-Hungarian, Josip Jelačić, who was appointed governor of Croatia. Jelačić at once removed his country from Hungarian sovereignty and, collecting an army, invaded Hungary. However, his advance was halted and Hungarian resistance began in earnest.

In August the emperor and his entourage, satisfied that responsible elements were once again in charge in Vienna, returned to the capital from Innsbruck. By now, however, events in Hungary rather than developments in Austria determined the course of events. Kossuth asked the help of first the court and then the newly elected Reichstag in curbing Croatian ambitions, but he met with refusal. There was no single political will left in Vienna. The court, stubbornly conservative, granted only such concessions as it could not avoid if it wanted to maintain itself, always in the hope that once order was reestablished it could withdraw them. The popular mood in Vienna, however, was still revolutionary and favored any action that defied the Habsburgs; in the matter of Jelačić's defiance, it sided with the brave Hungarians. When an Austrian artillery company under orders to march against Hungary crossed the city, crowds prevented its passage and bloody street battles erupted. Vienna once again became unsafe for the royal house, and Ferdinand and his court moved, this time to the Moravian city of Olmütz. A few days later the Reichstag too left Vienna and reconvened in another Moravian town, Kremsier. Obviously though, these were temporary expedients. The displaced court made preparations to reconquer Vienna by military means. On October 31 Marshal Windischgrätz, having reduced to rubble the Bohemian capital of Prague, where a disorderly pan-Slavic conference was meeting, took his artillery to the walls of Vienna and inflicted a similar fate on the capital. Royal authority was finally reestablished, and even though the price was high, the court was willing to pay it. The time for concessions had passed. They had led to nothing but demands for further reforms, and terror became the order of the day. Active and suspected revolutionaries in the Austrian capital, among them lawmakers and respectable citizens, including a number of journalists, were rounded up, summarily tried, and often shot. Military force and military justice accomplished what months of political maneuvering could not; Vienna was secure as the Habsburg capital and reform was off the agenda.

Emperor Ferdinand had been a pathetic figurehead since his accession to the throne; he was unable to carry out his duties as ruler and failed even to attend the sessions of the state conference that had governed in his name. The conditions created by the revolution dramatized the need for a new emperor. As early as November 1847, months before the outbreak, Ferdinand's wife, seeing how the strains of ruling even in the most perfunctory manner overtaxed her husband's energies, had suggested to Metternich that Ferdinand should abdicate, not, however, in favor of the next person in line, his younger brother Francis Charles, but rather of the latter's son, Francis Joseph, as soon as the latter reached age 18. Several times during the revolutionary events Ferdinand had been asked by his wife and others to stand aside, not so much because of his incapacity but because he had made promises for constitutions, to Bohemians and Hungarians, which other members of the royal house and those around them did not intend to keep. Both Windischgrätz and the new prime minister, Felix von Schwarzenberg, pressed for the abdication; Ferdinand held out until he supposedly had a dream in which his late father Francis begged him to yield. On December 2, in Olmütz, young Francis Joseph kneeled before his uncle and allowed the imperial dignity to be bestowed upon himself. From then on the initiative irretrievably passed into conservative hands.

Decisions had to be made almost daily—how much to concede, how much to deny—and some of these decisions concerned Austria as head of the German Confederation. Since May 1848 a German national assembly had been meeting in Frankfurt with a mandate from the electorate to write a constitution for all of Germany. In recognition of the prominent and indeed dominant role Austria had played in German affairs for centuries, the Frankfurt Assembly intended to offer the crown of a united Germany to the Habsburg monarch; the large non-German population of Austria, however, posed a problem. The parliament leaned toward the *kleindeutsch* view, which would leave Austria out rather than bring some 30 million non-Germans into a German empire. At the end of September it resolved that only German states could be part of the union; if any of them possessed non-German territories, these could be tied to the state only by a purely personal union (a position that the Hungarian part of the Austrian Empire heartily embraced). The Vienna court expressed firm opposition to this view, and to the whole work of the Frankfurt parliament, aware that a united Germany would mean Austria's total exclusion from German affairs. Fortunately for the Habsburgs, by the time the parliament settled the question in favor of excluding Austria and offered the crown to Prussian king Frederick William IV, the revolutions in Germany had been brought under control and Frederick William contemptuously refused to accept a crown "from the dust." The German Confederation was revived and, at its yearly meetings, the Austrian delegate was once again the permanent president.

In the end, the armies saved the monarchies everywhere, and this was where the revolutions in central and eastern Europe most dramatically differed from that in France half a century earlier. In the latter, the *royal* armies largely disintegrated within a year of the start of the revolution and a new fighting force, proudly calling itself "a nation in arms" rose up and in time swept everything before it. In Prussia and Austria, as in the lesser German principalities, the armies stood steadfastly by their king. In Austria's Italian provinces, the forces of Marshal Radetzky, after being on the defensive for a year, in early March 1849 crushed the Piedmontese armies of Charles Albert, and, by August, rebellious Venetia met a similar fate. The imperial armies under Windischgrätz's command fought bravely in Hungary too, but Hungarian resistance proved a harder nut to crack than the Italian; under Lajos Kossuth's leadership and Artur Görgey's generalship, Hungarian forces halted the imperial armies and then forced them to retreat. Even Serbian and Croatian uprisings against Hungarian rule proved unavailing. For now Vienna had to leave the Hungarian problem unresolved and concentrate on restoring constitutional order by its own lights in the rest of the empire.

The Kremsier parliament, its days predictably numbered since the royal house regained military control, labored in all seriousness on writing a constitution for the empire; by February, it produced one from the pen of a Silesian German, Kajetan Mayery. The document preserved the historic delimitations of the various provinces in the empire but subdivided them into units of compact ethnic groups for administration on the district level; as to the central legislative body, it enshrined the democratic principle, allowing the emperor only a limited veto right and making provincial governments responsible to the Reichstag.

The time for such wishful scenarios has passed, however. On March 7, 1849, the assembly was broken up by the military and the newly appointed minister of interior, Count Franz Stadion, proclaimed in the name of Francis Joseph a constitution much more to Vienna's liking. It provided for an absolute veto by the emperor and his right to proclaim a national emergency in which he would have absolute power. This "constitution" still featured a parliament, but it was in fact never convoked. The system this document inaugurated came to be referred to as neoabsolutist, because while in practice it differed little from the old one, the memory of the revolution was never erased and even in the most soulless periods of oppression it held out hope for meaningful change.

The Hungarian problem continued to fester. The so-called Kremsier constitution had restored Hungary's ancient rights—its own constitution—but with the weighty qualification that those rights were valid only insofar as they did not negate the provisions of the larger constitution. This dashed any hope of a peaceful resolution of the issue and the armed struggle continued. Windisch-grätz's successor had no more luck against the resourceful Görgey than the old marshal had had. Hungarian forces not only stopped the Austrian advance but threw it back on a wide front. If Hungary's bid for independence succeeded, with Italian provinces still in a state of revolt, the empire might be in mortal peril. It was time to invoke the provisions of a solemn international agreement that had been the subject of so much scorn when it was first put forth in 1815, at the close of the Congress of Vienna. The Holy Alliance, apart from binding its signatories to Christian virtues in governing their subjects and in dealing with one another, promised mutual help to rulers facing revolutionary challenges. Perhaps the author of that document, Alexander I of Russia, would not have judged the challenge offered to Vienna by the Hungarians as one he was duty-bound to meet, but his brother and successor, Nicholas I, was a fanatical champion of the monarchical status quo. It was to him that Francis Joseph, only six months after taking his oath as emperor, turned when the Hungarian uprising appeared beyond the imperial army's capability to conquer. The two sovereigns met in Poland in May, Francis Joseph proffered his plea, and Nicholas promised an army of 200,000 against the Habsburgs' rebellious subjects. With the Croatian army pushing north, Austrians, under the gifted but brutal general Julius Haynau, invading from the west, and a Russian army descending from the Carpathians, Görgey's resources proved inadequate. On August 13, 1849, he surrendered to the Russians at the town of Világos. It is a convenient date for marking the beginning of the postrevolutionary system, an administrative stagnation of nearly two decades.

The period is associated with the name of the man, Alexander Bach, who as interior minister replaced the more malleable and liberal Count Stadion when the latter fell ill in 1849. In the very early phase of the revolution, Bach had been among those who demanded reforms but then, displaying the zeal of the converted, he took his place in the established order, first as minister of justice in late 1848, then as minister of the interior. The post of chief minister at the same time fell to the brother-in-law of Windischgrätz, Count Felix Schwarzenberg, The latter's introductory speech to the Kremsier assembly on November 27, 1848, brimmed with promises of freedom, equality, security for the common man, and the equality of rights for the nations within the empire. In the three years left to him before his untimely death in 1852 due to boisterous living, Schwarzentberg worked diligently to fulfill his promises, *as he interpreted them.* The key promise, and also the least unpopular, was that of security, because fear and weariness with revolution became common in European societies that had witnessed too much upheaval with too little to show for it. In an empire that had, as Schwarzenberg saw it, so many conflicting interests at every level, stability and security could be achieved only if all authority stemmed from a single source. According to the New Year's Eve Patent he issued on the last day of 1851, elected officials, even in towns and villages, were replaced by imperial officials. Civil service in the empire, vertically and horizontally, became one immense bureaucracy. Its chief and governing task was to prevent change. Hardly an inspiring assignment but this much can be said in favor of that bureaucracy, that it was hard-working, honest, and incorruptible. In order to extend police power beyond cities to every corner of the countryside, the gendarmerie was organized in 1849.

Stagnation in the Bach era was by no means universal. Business benefited from the elimination of customs duties in commerce between Austria and Hungary, and the state assisted large landowners with compensation for the loss of their bonded peasantry. The educational system was also reorganized, admission to secondary schools was made more egalitarian, and state supervision over curricula made less tight and imperious. At the same time, however, church influence in the educational system became more pervasive. Even if the young emperor had not been a devout Catholic, the system over which he presided, dedicated as it was to conservative values and hostility to innovation, would have demanded a rapprochement with the Catholic Church after Joseph II's many disabling dispositions. Bishops were once again allowed freely to communicate with the Vatican and the emperor relinquished his right to approve papal pronouncements before they were read to congregations. The new bishop of Vienna, Josef von Rauscher, received a plenary right from the emperor to negotiate with Rome regarding the terms under which harmonious relations between church and state were reestablished in the empire. The outcome of Rauscher's efforts led to the Concordat of November 1855, a document that essentially restored the privileged position the Catholic Church had formerly enjoyed in Austria.

The emperor saw nothing contradictory in promoting a Christian spirit, on the one hand, and, on the other, giving his royal approval to a long series of reprisals, complete with executions or long prison sentences, against all those who by the judgment of investigative authorities had participated in the revolution. In Hungary 12 generals were hanged for commanding armies against imperial forces; the premier of the revolutionary government was saved from the gallows only by a self-inflicted wound to his throat—he was shot. Francis

Joseph, who during an exceptionally long reign earned the respect if not nec-essarily the affection of many of his subjects, was hardly a man of tender emo-tions (except for his love of his adored wife Elisabeth) or of humanitarian inclinations; his mother, the imperious Sophie, had early inculcated in him the hard virtues a king must possess in order to rule effectively. By the time Schwarzenberg died in 1852, Francis Joseph had enough self-confidence to take the reins of government himself. Internal government did not pose a great problem in the postrevolutionary years of apathy; foreign affairs were another matter. While the new emperor achieved a limited success in 1851, when he prevented some German princes from offering their crowns to the Prussian king in a feeble effort to bring about German unification "from above," in sub-sequent developments he was less fortunate. There would have been conflict between Austria and Russia in any case because both powers sought expansion in the Balkans at the expense of a progressively weakening Ottoman Empire, and there was no delimitation of spheres of influence. In 1853–54 a crisis arose. Nicholas I, in a southward move that tested the opposition not only of the Turks but of the other powers as well, sent an army to occupy Turkey's northernmost principalities, Moldavia and Wallachia. His churchmen in Jerusalem were meanwhile engaged in a tug-of-war with Catholic authorities over who should possess the keys to the Church of the Holy Sepulchre. Britain grew increas-ingly nervous about the presence of a large Russian fleet in Sevastopol harbor, a fleet that could force its way through the Straits and pose a threat to British commerce with India that passed through the Port Said–Suez caravan route. Austria had no immediate interests in the developing conflict, but, being a great power closest to the contested areas, could hardly stand aside. The situation would have been complex even for a statesman more seasoned than Francis Joseph, and he, at the age of 23, was befuddled as to what course to take. Sid-ing with Britain, France, and Turkey against Russia might be profitable because Austria could demand the principalities as a reward; on the other hand, turn-ing against Russia after the help Nicholas had given Austria in putting down the Hungarian revolt would be less than honorable. Still, siding with Russia would involve Austria in a war from which she could expect little gain. Hostilities began in October 1853, when Turkey declared war on Russia to dislodge the lat-ter from occupation of their principalities. In April 1854 France and Britain joined Turkey in the war with Russia. Francis Joseph took steps toward bel-ligerency—he mobilized several army corps and, after Russia evacuated the principalities, sent his own forces to occupy them. In December 1854 he con-cluded an alliance with France and Britain, but he shrank from taking the final step of entering the war and relieving the pressure on the Anglo-French armies in the Crimea. Restraint, even of such ambivalent nature, might be wise in times of peace, but in war it is likely to antagonize both sides. Austria's hostile measures infuriated Alexander while her failure to take the field elicited a sim-ilar response from Napoleon III of France. It would be farfetched to contend that when in 1859 Napoleon decided to join Piedmont in the latter's war against Austria it was a deferred payback for Austria's failure to support France in 1855, but it certainly made the decision morally more justified.

We have noted the preponderant influence Austria had in northern Italy; we should also mention that during the revolutions of 1848 Italian patriots invaded the Papal States, occupying Rome itself and forcing Pope Pius IX to flee and watch helplessly as his cherished states, bestowed upon the Holy See a thousand years earlier by the Frankish king Pepin, were being ravaged by street mobs and turned into the Roman Republic. After the revolutions were finally put down, it was Austrian troops who recovered the Papal States and restored the pope to his throne. The retributions that military tribunals inflicted on rebels (on one occasion they sent a mother a bill for the price of the rope used in hanging her son) deepened the hostility Italians nursed for their Austrian taskmasters. Consequently, although the Austrian military had prevailed in the streets of Budapest and Vienna and over ragtag revolutionary armies in battle, they were daily losing the battle for the hearts and minds of the peoples they ruled.

In Hungary passive resistance to Austrian rule in the Bach era reached almost ludicrous proportions. Bach dispatched thousands of Czech officials, the so-called Bach Hussars, in addition to Austrians, to rule that kingdom. Hungarians pretended not to understand either of the two languages spoken to them and met all instructions with blank incomprehension. As one popular novelist later presented the prevailing attitude: "'Cogito ergo sum'. Therefore, 'Si non cogito, non sum.'" Most Hungarians preferred not to think. Consequently, by Descartes's definition at any rate, they did not exist. And no power could rule a person who did not exist.

CHAPTER TEN

Austria avoided war in 1854, out of irresolution rather than timidity, but she got involved in a more pointless conflict in 1859 and lost a precious Italian province in consequence.

"It was unfortunately unavoidable," Francis Joseph's proclamation to his people on July 15, 1859, began, "that the larger part of Lombardy should separate itself from the empire. On the other hand it is a joy to my heart to know that I can once again secure for my beloved people the blessings of peace . . . and that I can from now on devote all my attention and care to the successful completion of my task: lastingly to ensure Austria's internal well-being and external power with the purposeful development of her rich spiritual and material forces, as well as with timely improvement of her legislative and administrative apparatus."

The proclamation was woefully short on specifics, yet the omission was only natural in the stalemated condition of the imperial government. Absolutism, whether in its traditional or its postrevolutionary variety, had proved a failure; Schwarzenberg had chosen to depend on the efficacy of raw force, but Schwarzenberg was dead and so was the theory that loyalty could be bought with coercion. Yet, a wavering but cultivable goodwill toward the ruling house was still present in most of the empire, even in Bohemia, which of all constituent parts had had the most shattering experience with the Habsburgs; there the great Czech writer Palacký declared that the Austrian monarchy was indispensable for a peaceful Europe. The memory of 1848 was still vividly alive, the promised and then rescinded constitution, the destruction of Prague, but the spirit of rebellion had abated. Hungary alone remained irreconcilable. By now the entire crisis of Austrian absolutism was centered in Hungary—nothing less than the laws the hastily convoked Pressburg parliament had passed in the spring of 1848 would satisfy the Hungarians, in any case those classes of the nation who were in active possession of political power, the noble estates. By now these estates included not only the great aristocracy but the numerous and extravagantly patriotic squirearchy as well. Schwarzenberg had tried to reduce both to submission and had failed, or rather he succeeded too well; submission was so total that it turned Hungary into dead wood; it had to be carried and had nothing to give.

Interestingly there *was* one point on which the Habsburgs and the Hungarian estates agreed: the need to keep the minorities—the non-German and non-

Hungarian ethnic groups—in check. In the absolutist system, old or new, Hungary was but a province of Austria, but "historic Hungary" as it was often referred to was itself a mixed nation; it had its Slovak, Ruthenian, Romanian, and Croatian minorities, and kept them under more stringent control than Austria kept hers. The two ruling nations shared a concern that the national awakening that had begun with the French Revolution would lead to ever more vigorous self-assertions by the minorities. This common fear did not suffice, however, to overcome the fundamental difference in conception as to what the Habsburg Empire should be. Francis Joseph and his court envisioned a state governed by a single central authority, a state in which provincial diets, grudgingly tolerated, would serve more to satisfy the particularism some parts of the empire demanded than as substantive, veto-proof legislative bodies.

The defeat in Italy, the uninspired generalship that had produced ad hoc battles with great loss of life, the downright defeatism of the Hungarians, Francis Joseph's self-confident and bungling diplomacy that was no match for the subtle maneuvers of the Piedmontese premier Camilo di Cavour, highlighted the crisis of absolutism. There was nothing beyond terror to hold the nations of the empire together, and terror, no matter how effective, always had its limits. In time the voices rising from the diverse parts of the empire had to be listened to.

The first victim of this realization was the interior minister, Alexander Bach; his dismissal signified the emperor's conviction that a falsely confident business-as-usual type of government would no longer do. What passed for government under the postrevolutionary system was the council of state, the Reichsrat, sitting in Vienna, a purely advisory body in which none of the nationalities were represented. In March 1860 it was enlarged by 38 representatives from the provinces and given the task of assisting the emperor in drawing up a constitutional charter. There was no unity of purpose on this council. The German element, favoring a central parliament, wanted to leave only residual powers to provincial assemblies, whereas the rest of the council, made up largely of Czech, Hungarian, and Polish representatives, demanded genuine legislative powers for those assemblies. What emerged was the so-called October Diploma, issued by the emperor that same year. It provided for a 100-member parliament, which, however, would still have only advisory functions, and then only in matters of finance, industry, and commerce; all other matters were to be handled by the provincial diets. Military and foreign affairs remained the exclusive provinces of the head of state.

The October Diploma, as it turned out, was a mere declaration of intention, and it had a life span of four months; the nationalities looked on it as too little while the German liberals, aiming for a united empire under German domination, as too generous. The Hungarians would not even consider it and once again demanded the reinstatement of their April Laws of 1848. With the absolutism so near his heart a lost cause, the emperor had to consider constitutionalism, though he had never learned its laws and did not understand its functioning. Faced with general opposition to his October Diploma and lacking the experience to provide an alternative, he entrusted the task to his new minister of the interior, Anton von Schmerling, a German-Austrian, who envisioned a liberal program stemming from a strong central authority and administered by a central executive. Animated by these principles he drafted the February Patent of 1861, which called for a bicameral imperial parliament, the lower house composed of elected representatives from the whole empire, the upper of men appointed from the adult male members of the ruling dynasty and from such men as had earned special honors in serving the empire. While this scheme was acceptable to most circles, the Hungarians, whose own Diet had been dismissed as superfluous, again firmly rejected it. Even others who believed in the viability of the new "Imperial Council," as the parliament would be named, soon saw the true intentions of the emperor. It was clear to them that he had nothing but contempt for the concept of parliamentarianism, and his only interest was in the orderly assessment of taxes and the consequent restoration of Austria's international credit. His attitude toward the projected council became palpable when he assigned to it a makeshift wooden building as a meeting place, even though there were literally dozens of decorous stone structures in Vienna that would have lent the assembly the requisite dignity. Still it was due largely to Hungarian opposition (the Hungarian representatives elected to it did not take their seats; the Bohemians at first did but later walked out) that the February Patent never entered into force; in 1865 it was abandoned. The imperial court at last faced the plain truth that only a mutual comprehensive agreement with the Hungarians would bring a constitutional framework to Austrian lands. Until such an agreement was reached, a bureaucracy guided by existing laws would govern the empire.

An account of how the final compromise with the Hungarians was worked out to create the Dual Monarchy properly belongs within the framework of Hungarian history and will be dealt with there. At this point it is useful to point out that the chief Hungarian figure in the prolonged discussions leading to the compromise, Ferenc Deák, as early as May 1861 advanced the argument that the Pragmatic Sanction, dating back to 1713, providing a uniform system of succession in *all* Habsburg lands, gave Hungary equal status with Austria (though he did not claim such status for the other nationalities), and therefore any suggestion of an inferior position was unwarranted. He also pointed out what Francis Joseph could not help being aware of, namely, that without Hungary's active participation the empire could not function in the long run and that any scheme which would relegate his country to an unequal status would meet with the determined opposition of the people.

Schmerling was still in charge of internal affairs when, with the emperor's knowledge and encouragement, a series of unofficial talks were undertaken between imperial officials and Deák. Patience was the latter's greatest virtue, and, regardless of how weak or strong the Vienna court's position appeared, he never increased or softened his demands; in time, they formed a firm platform, that, however objectionable to the emperor and his circle, was the only one upon which a compromise with the Hungarians could be erected.

Deák's voice might have been a cry in the wilderness and the emperor might have been inclined to continue a somewhat updated version of the Bach system indefinitely had it not been for untoward developments in the field of foreign and military affairs. Once the bankruptcy of the February Patent became evident, Francis Joseph dismissed Schmerling and appointed in his stead a former viceroy of Bohemia, Richard Belcredi, though just what his intention was in making this appointment was by no means clear. Belcredi, himself a high noble, was opposed to representative government in any variety; he trusted only the large landowning nobility, with its ingrained political sense and organic connection to the House of Habsburg, to be in charge of national affairs. The emperor revealed his own, somewhat obscure, intention in a proclamation of September 20, 1865. In it he lamented the failure of his attempt to ensure the unity of the empire in a constitutional manner. He blamed the failure on the unyielding attitude of some components of the empire (Hungarians, Czechs, Poles) and asserted that he would have submitted the October Diploma and the February Patent to them for acceptance, except for the absurdity of negotiating with one section of the empire about a document that was already law in the other; he therefore suspended the operation of those documents. Here was the first open hint that Hungarian cooperation was indispensable; the rocky road toward a compromise was opened.

As a first step the emperor summoned for December 5, 1865, the Hungarian Diet and at the same time, in a significant gesture, moved the royal court to the Hungarian capital of Buda for four months. In his speech from the throne to the Diet he promised recognition of Hungary's separate status while asserting, however, that that country with her subordinate provinces was part of the totality of states within the Austrian Empire. It was rather evident that the emperor preferred to keep the whole debate on a theoretical plane, injecting phrases about the Pragmatic Sanction and its legal implications, without committing his government to any concrete course of action.

The actual resolution of Hungary's proper place in the empire may have remained in abeyance for many years longer had the Greater German question not entered a new, sudden, and deliberate phase. Austria had until now, the mid-1860s, been able to maintain a delicate balance between both her dominant status in her own empire, with its majority of non-Germans, and her leading position in the German Confederation. But the Prussian prime minister Otto von Bismarck, who in the early 1850s had taken the position that for Germany to be united Austria had to be expelled from it, did not intend that Austria's special position within Germany should continue indefinitely. In 1864, the Danish king, also prince of the "inseparable provinces" of Schleswig and Holstein (the latter a part of the German Confederation, the former not), had decided to incorporate Schleswig into Denmark while casting its twin adrift. Bismarck urged Austria, as pro forma president of the German Confederation, to spearhead opposition to this move. Francis Joseph reluctantly answered the challenge, and throughout the latter half of 1864 Austria and Prussia, with several other German states, fought together against Denmark (whose hopes of great power intervention proved illusory), and, after defeating her, placed the sister provinces under military occupation, Prussia policing Schleswig and Austria Holstein. The simple fact that provisioning Prussian forces in the northern province required passing through the Austrian-occupied southern province provided ample opportunity for a conflict between the two states, a conflict that Bismarck desired and Austria hoped to avoid. If Francis Joseph had proved a diplomatic novice in his battle of wits with Piedmont's Count di Cavour in 1859, he proved a grossly unequal partner in Bismarck's diplomatic chess game. He was unable to prevent the Prussian chancellor from gaining assurance that France would remain neutral (enabling Prussia to concentrate all her forces against Austria) or from enlisting Italy as Prussia's ally in exchange for the promise that she would be rewarded with the last Italian province still in Austrian hands, Venetia. That alliance forced Austria to divide her forces. Even so, the distribution of military power was fairly equal and the Austrians earned two victories against the Italians. Against the Prussians, commanded by the brilliant general Helmuth von Moltke, the Austrian army, under the inept and defeatist Hungarian commander Ludwik Benedek, proved totally inadequate. In the so-called Seven Weeks' War, which was actually decided in the single battle of Königgrätz (Czech name, Sadowa), the Prussian army decisively defeated the Austrian, and at a single stroke dominance in all-German affairs passed from Austria to Prussia.

The question of whether active Hungarian participation on the Austrian side would have changed the outcome remains a moot one; nonparticipation was the very essence of the passive resistance by which Hungarians sought to win their case against Austria. As early as May 1861 Deák, speaking to the Hungarian Diet, made the dichotomy between the German and the Hungarian half of the empire explicit. "Germany," he had said, "could wage war in her own interest, and in such a war Austria [as head of the German Confederation] would be duty-bound to participate, and to defend the borders under attack. But their war is not our war and their interests are not our interests. . . . Any closer relationship [with Austria] would subordinate us to the German majority [in the empire], what is more, it would subordinate us to the politics of the German Confederation [which is] totally foreign to us, and we could expect from it nothing in return."

At the time he spoke, Austria was indeed an organic part of the Confederation, just as she was master of her own empire; that empire was of course a hereditary possession whereas her position in the Confederation was a formal connection, fortified to be sure by centuries of Habsburg predominance in German affairs. Now, in the wake of Königgrätz, the German connection was, by Bismarck's fiat, terminated. With the all-German Confederation dissolved, Prussia was free to construct a new grouping, the North German Confederation, under her own leadership; Austria, and four Catholic south German states, became unconnected. If the Seven Weeks' War left any doubt as to the relative power position of Austria and Prussia, the latter crowned her military victory by annexing the German states of Hanover, Kurhessen, Nassau, Frankfurt-am-Main, and Schleswig-Holstein, with the result that territorially and in population Prussia possessed some four-fifths of the newly formed North German Confederation. It was an ethnically homogeneous unit, with no fractious minorities, no historic claims of particularism, whereas Austria was still fighting off claims of just such a nature with the Hungarians. Bismarck had taken note of this; he understood that if Austria transformed herself into a dual state, only one-half of which was German, any future claim for leadership of Germany would from the start be compromised. On July 9, 1866, he wrote to his ambassador in Paris: "In the interest of our future position vis-à-vis Austria, we will ask for the fulfillment of Hungary's national demands and the restoration of the Hungarian constitution."

It is unlikely that anything would change between Austria and Prussia whether Francis Joseph complied with this request or not, but the necessity was obvious even without Bismarck's demands. To Belcredi, still premier, the prospect of an exclusively Austro-Hungarian union was distasteful. He immediately developed plans for a federal union in which the Slavs enjoyed equal status with the other two. The Hungarians were spared the task of refusing Slavic inclusion; the German liberals in Austria, already dismayed by the developing multinational trend, would not hear of Slavs posing as equals of Germans. They were not overjoyed by Hungarians making such a claim either, but concessions to them were politically unavoidable, whereas pressure from the Slavs was manageable. Belcredi had to go; he was replaced with the Saxon foreign minister Baron Ferdinand Beust, not so much because of the latter's great political acumen but because he was firmly anti-Prussian and the emperor hoped to succeed in forming an alliance that would enable him to gain revanche for his recent defeat.

To work out an agreement with the Hungarians was still a momentous task and it involved many concessions displeasing to the emperor, but Beust moved in a straight line and knew when to yield and when to be firm. He solidified the informal alliance between the Hungarians and the German liberals. The emperor, once he realized that Hungarian demands were not increased because of his country's recent defeat and were not subject to fluctuating fortunes but rested on historical grounds, gradually reconciled himself to what he had for nearly two decades passionately opposed. On February 17, 1867, he reinstated the Hungarian constitution and named a responsible Hungarian government, one that was charged with negotiating the terms of what became known as the *Ausgleich*, or the Great Compromise. By the time the Imperial Council met on May 22, the basic conditions of the compromise had been worked out. The essential point was that Hungary was an organic part of the Habsburg Empire, but only her direct relation to the emperor and the conditions of the compromise obligated her to share a part of her sovereignty with the Austrians. Constitutionally and in domestic matters Hungary constituted a separate state. Her security was tied up with that of Austria's, a fact that demanded joint defense—from this flowed the need for a joint foreign policy. As both the military and the diplomatic establishment involved financial expenditures, their administration also had to be joint. These exigencies, and the personal union with the Habsburg emperor, who under the compromise would be king of Hungary, were the ties that bound Austria and Hungary together. For the rest, each part governed itself, even in matters such as the recruitment and billeting of soldiers and the assessment and collection of taxes. The legal side of the joint affairs was to be dealt with by delegations from either unit, meeting alternately in Vienna and Budapest, not as a joint deliberative body but as separate entities; all contacts between the two would be in writing to prevent the development of any kind of joint legislature. In case of disagreement, the final word was the emperor's.

What had been the Austrian Empire became the Austro-Hungarian Dual Monarchy. Centuries of hostility and conflict seemed to have come to an end. With internal peace assured, the monarchy could devote itself to restoring its badly frayed power position.

CHAPTER ELEVEN

The Great Compromise undoubtedly amounted to a major sacrifice on the part of Vienna and was accepted in order to remove the worst source of internal discord; whether it accomplished that or the opposite, of affording comfort to Hungarian aspirations for ultimate separation from the Austrian lands, remained an open question. The Czechs of Bohemia were resentful over their exclusion from the partnership and their discontent, which in time spread to other Slavs within the Dual Monarchy, proved a perennially disruptive factor. It was one of the reasons that persuaded the emperor to accept, after the conclusion of the compromise, a liberal ministry opposed to multinational federalism, even though other items on their political agenda were disagreeable to him. The first major action of the new ministry, under the high aristocrat Prince "Carlos" von Auersperg, was to update the moribund February Patent in a series of Fundamental Laws, adopted in December 1867. Known as the December Constitution, this collection of constitutional principles remained in effect until the dissolution of the Dual Monarchy in 1918. Its general provisions were the by now familiar ones: equality before the law, freedom of the press and expression, freedom of assembly. As if to lessen the impact of the dualist character of the Great Compromise in which Hungarians and Germans were privileged units, it provided that "all nationalities in the state enjoy equal rights, and each one has an inalienable right to the preservation and cultivation of its nationality and language." The constitution also confirmed the rights of the Imperial Council, or Reichsrat, but that provision, given that Hungary had her own parliament, pertained to Austria only and assurances of its competence were hollow because the legislature remained without any real authority; laws, at least until 1907, were effectively made by the executive branch and carried out, in general with honesty and efficiency, by a large bureaucracy.

The Auersperg ministry next addressed the item that surfaced with distressing frequency every time a new political direction was embarked on in Vienna: the regulation of the influence of the Catholic Church in state affairs. The Concordat of 1855, concluded at a time when the emperor and his circle hoped to extirpate revolutionary sentiments root and branch by reaffirming the alliance between throne and altar, was anathema to the liberals; the Vienna town council termed it "a baleful agreement" by which Austrians were subjected to "the arbitrary pleasure of a foreign power." The fact that the Vatican had expressed displeasure with the 1867 laws that flowed from the Great Compromise added fuel to the fire. As a first step in defying the church, the new ministry legalized civil marriages; all matters of matrimonial jurisdiction were transferred to ordinary law courts. Although Catholic clergymen in the upper house of the Reichsrat argued that the law constituted a breach of faith with the Vatican, it was passed by a great majority; thereupon, the clergymen withdrew, facilitating the enactment of follow-up legislation.

Most important among the latter was another antichurch measure: the separation of public education from ecclesiastical control and its transfer to state authority in which only expressly religious schools remained within the purview of the Catholic Church. Still another measure aimed at ending the privileged position of Catholicism among Christian creeds, declaring that all religions were equal before the law. Nor were children born from the marriage of a Catholic and a non-Catholic necessarily to be brought up in the Catholic faith; it was for the parents to decide, and if they died without having done so, the son followed the father's religion and the daughter the mother's. If a community had only a Catholic cleric, he could not legally deny religious interment to a member of a different Christian faith. In vain did Pope Pius IX term these laws "destructive, abominable and damnable," and in vain did some Austrian clerics seek to absolve their parishioners from obeying them. They remained laws of the realm.

Conflict between church and state was further sharpened when, at the call of the pope, a general church council met in Rome in December 1869. After prolonged discussions, on July 18, 1870, it proclaimed the dogma of papal infallibility. After the manifold assaults on church authority during the French Revolution, and after the challenges offered by bishops to papal authority in the 18th century, Pius IX felt the need to reaffirm papal privileges not merely in an informal manner but also as a dogma of the church. The resolution of the council stated that all pronouncements of the pope made from the pulpit on matters of faith and morals were infallible. There was to be no further talk about councils of bishops being superior to papal authority.

In Austria enough antichurch sentiment had built up, not only in liberal circles but even within the clergy, to receive the new dogma with open hostility. For Auersperg's government it provided the pretext to renounce the Concordat of 1855; the foreign minister, Beust, in the forefront of the struggle against papal pretensions, diplomatically asserted that the abrogation of the concordat was not a hostile act against the Catholic Church but rather a reminder that it should limit itself to the religious sphere.

Reforms were also enacted in the military. These included, by a law passed in 1868, universal military service (following the example of Prussia whose army had greatly increased its efficiency and prestige since the introduction of universal service), raising the level of competence of officers, a thorough upgrading of weaponry, and a revision of battlefield tactics. For the rest, in the military as well as in civilian life and in criminal proceedings, a general liberalizing trend was evident, as though the doctrine of inalienable natural rights had at last replaced religious doctrines often unrelated to human needs. In the army, corporal punishment was abolished and the civilian penal code, still providing for some medieval procedures, was modernized; a number of remaining restrictions on Jews were revoked. An 1869 law mandated free elementary education for all children, although it was difficult to enforce because educational matters remained within the jurisdiction of provincial estates.

Beust's appointment to the foreign ministry had been made with the distinct intention that he shape a policy, possibly through a system of alliances as Kaunitz had done a century earlier, that would halt the precipitate rise of Prussia and regain an active place for Austria in the German commonwealth. But Bismarck, now that the chief impediment to unity, Austria, had been removed from German affairs, devoted his considerable energies and diplomatic skills to bringing that unity about. North German states were for all intents and purposes Prussia's vassals; four Catholic south German states still existed as independent entities. Napoleon III of France, after the Prussian victory over Austria, demanded compensation for having remained neutral. Bismarck wangled from him specifics as to the desired compensation, and they involved claims to various south German territories along the Rhine. Napoleon's "demands," as it turned out, amounted to little more than a wish-list, but they served Bismarck's purpose of convincing the south German states that France had acquisitive designs on them. They did place themselves, by way of mutual defense arrangements, under Prussia's protection should a war with an external enemy ensue. The external enemy, as it developed, was France, though in a matter unrelated to Napoleon's foiled attempts to gain land along the Rhine. When the throne of Spain fell vacant and the Spanish Cortes surveyed the European scene for an eligible prince, Bismarck eagerly entered the candidacy of a nephew of his king, Leopold von Hohenzollern-Sigmaringen. The French badly mishandled the situation; not satisfied with Prussian king William's withdrawal of his nephew's candidacy, they brusquely demanded promises of future good behavior, specifically that the king would never again endorse the candidacy of a German prince should the throne of Spain be in need of an occupant. The king, with perfect courtesy, gave a negative reply, but Bismarck removed from a report of the interview the courteous phrases and made the rejection appear to be a crass insult. With *honneur* at stake, the overconfident French declared war. Once again the Prussian army proved its mettle; French armies, one of them with Napoleon himself on its staff, were encircled and forced to surrender. North and South Germans fought shoulder to shoulder and the ecstasy of the joint victory accomplished what solemn parliamentary resolutions in 1848 could not: south German states agreed to join their northern brethren in a unitary empire: *das Deutsches Reich* was born. Prussia was its largest and dominant member and Austrian hopes of having a say in German affairs were dashed.

Even within Austria affairs were untidy. Dualism remained an insult to all the smaller nationalities, especially the Slavs. It is not clear whether the appointment in February 1871 of the feudalist-conservative Karl Sigmund Hohenwart to the premiership was an error on the emperor's part or a sincere if mistaken attempt to restore some balance; Hohenwart championed a broader federalism and, as a first step, equal status for the Slavs. He expanded the franchise in Bohemia and on October 10 allowed the Czech Diet to proclaim a "Fundamental Article" with the avowed intention of establishing parity between Hungary and Bohemia in the empire. Soon other provinces, including Tyrol, Slovenia, and Galicia, proffered similar demands. Francis Joseph, whatever his original intention had been, beat a hasty retreat. He had always cherished the idea, also embraced by other Habsburgs before him, that their dynasty had a sanctity that rendered nationalistic aspirations trivial and disruptive. He had not been able to bind Hungary to the rest of his possessions in this manner. Now others were becoming assertive. On October 30 he forced Hohenwart to resign and replaced him with the younger brother of "Carlos" Auersperg, Adolf. The new premier, perhaps because he shunned controversial measures, was able to head a government for seven years.

Meanwhile Austria's international position had to be firmed up. Her exclusion from Germany had restricted her sphere of influence, yet expansion had become an indispensable obligation of a great power. The outlines of a new ambitious foreign policy, made more credible by improvements in the armed forces, which, together with Hungarian contingents, now amounted to over a quarter million, began to take shape at the Ballplatz*. The narrow northern coastline of the Adriatic Sea, and the choke-point at the heel of the Italian boot, made overseas expansion requiring a substantial naval force unthinkable. The Balkans, controlled by a decaying Ottoman Empire and practically crying out for modernization, was Austria's natural sphere of expansion. It was, however, also the traditional focus of Russian foreign policy. Whether Austria would work hand-in-hand with Russia or be pitted against her, given the new power configuration in Europe, each would have to consult a third power: Germany.

With plans of revanche for Königgrätz abandoned, and Germany predictably a crucial player in every diplomatic situation, Francis Joseph, never sentimental about his appointments and dismissals, dropped Beust, whose anti-Prussian credentials became a distinct disadvantage and, on November 14, 1871, appointed the Hungarian aristocrat, Count Julius Andrássy, joint foreign minister. Andrássy, after the failure of the revolution of 1848, had been under a death sentence, was later amnestied, and now, in a new demonstration of unsentimental choices of men to serve him, the emperor called upon him to chart a new course for Austrian foreign policy.

There remained entrenched at the Ballplatz a strong anti-Prussian circle that regarded the new Germany as Austria's greatest enemy. Andrássy, first and foremost a Hungarian, was not so much pro-German as he was anti-Russian, and he saw in a pro-German orientation the best assurance in securing a counterweight to Russian ambitions. Hungary had her own Slovak, Ruthenian, Croatian, and Serbian minorities, and an independent Serbia south of the Bačka-Bánát with its mainly Serbian population, had become a center of South Slav agitation. Russia's larger Pan-Slavism now had its more defined and vigorous counterpart in Serbia's Balkan aspirations.

Both the broader and the narrower would, however, become active only in case of a major upheaval that demanded intervention. In such a case, according to the provisions of the Dreikaiserbund, a loose association of Germany, Austria, and Russia concluded in a somewhat disjointed fashion in 1873, the latter two were to consult with each other in case of international complications

---

*The location and the commonly used name of the joint foreign ministry.

as to their respective courses of action; Serbia was not bound by any formal undertaking.

The disruption that activated the Pan-Slavic program in the Balkans arose in the summer of 1875, when a peasant uprising broke out in Hercegovina and quickly spread to Bosnia. The immediate cause was brutal oppression by land-lords who had converted to Islam to be able to keep their lands, but Pan-Slav-ist agitators were also active in the provinces. The inability of the Ottoman government to deal with the uprising clearly showed its rapid loss of control over its Balkan possessions. Andrássy saw both the need for urgent reforms in that empire, and the opportunity to bring restive Slavic provinces under Aus-trian rule. As far back as 1873 he had proposed to the emperor that Austria annex Bosnia-Hercegovina; strategically this was necessary to make the narrow Dalmatian coast Austria had gained at the Congress of Vienna more defensible, but it would also preempt a Serbian move in that direction. Andrássy even had his eyes on the strip of land thrusting south of the provinces, the Sanjak of Novibazar, again for a dual purpose: to place an Austrian-controlled wedge between Serbia and Montenegro, and to provide Austria with a springboard (*Ausfalltor*) in the direction of Salonika, a projected Austrian naval base on the open Mediterranean.

The revolt of 1875 revealed the bewildering complexity of the Balkan prob-lem. Unrest spread to Bulgaria, and although there it was speedily crushed by the Turks, in the larger setting it could no longer be contained. In June 1876 Serbia declared war on the Ottoman Empire. It was a hasty move without diplomatic preparation and the Serbs quickly learned that Turkish military power was still a factor to reckon with. The Russians, eager to join the fray to pursue their own objectives, seized on their perceived obligation to aid their small Slavic brother. Before they went to war against Turkey, however, they had to consult with Austria regarding dispositions following their expected vic-tory. Russian foreign minister Gorchakov traveled to Budapest and there, in January 1877, concluded with Andrássy the strictly secret Budapest Conven-tion, by which Austria-Hungary would receive Bosnia-Hercegovina as a reward for remaining neutral in a Russo-Turkish war.

The Russians did not have an easy time with the Turks, but numbers and persistence in the end prevailed. When the Porte sued for an armistice the Rus-sians, in a puzzling attempt to circumvent the Budapest Convention, imposed their own terms on the Turks. Protests from the great powers compelled them to attend an international congress that met in Berlin to sort out the pieces. Every power except Italy gained something in the ensuing give-and-take; Aus-tria was allowed to occupy and administer Bosnia-Hercegovina, as well as its territorial extension, the Sanjak of Novibazar, until such time as an outright annexation became timely; other powers, with the exception of Germany and Italy, also made substantial gains at Turkey's expense. Actually Russia, who had made the greatest sacrifices, had to be satisfied with the most modest rewards.

Satisfied she was not, and her disappointment with the outcome of the Berlin Congress led to the dissolution of the Dreikaiserbund. Bismarck's hope of keep-ing Germany on good terms with both Austria and Russia foundered. In any case, he saw the need to replace the loose and ad hoc arrangements of the Dreikaiserbund with a firm military alliance. Its main purpose was not so much to increase German military prowess, which was in any case overwhelming, but to prevent other great powers from allying themselves with France, which, since the war of 1870, was Germany's principal enemy. Bismarck chose Austria as Germany's ally. The Dual Alliance between the two, concluded after long negotiations on October 17, 1879, was first and foremost directed against Russia. Even though Bismarck later voiced his fear that Germany, in backing her Austrian ally, might be drawn into a Balkan confrontation in which Germany had no direct interest, it is unlikely that at the time he foresaw the numberless possibilities of conflict between Austria and Russia. In the short term he was correct in assuming that Russia would not want to remain diplomatically isolated. Indeed the Russians, reconciling themselves to a German-Austrian military connection, entered into a second Dreikaiserbund with those two states in June 1881. Each power promised neutrality if either of the other two was at war with a fourth power; however, if that fourth power was Turkey, prior arrangements had to be made for the outcome. More important, the Balkans were divided into a Russian and an Austrian sphere, not to be breached by either.

For Austria the net gain was that in a new Balkan confrontation she could now count on Germany's help; this would discourage Russia from taking a strong stand and would put Austria in a dominant position when a dispute arose.

That same year, 1881, as the vagaries of European diplomacy would have it, Italy's relations with France, long tense over the papal question and over French annexation of the provinces of Nice and Savoy in the course of Italy's unification, hit a new low after France snatched the Ottoman province of Tunis from under the very nose of Italy; the Italians, fearing warlike complications, sought a military ally. Germany was the natural and only credible choice. However, Bismarck made it clear to Rome that "the road to Berlin leads through Vienna." Although the Italians resented that the alpine province of Alto Adige, heavily Italian, remained Austrian territory, they agreed to obtaining a German alliance not in a bilateral fashion but by joining the Dual Alliance of Germany and Austria, on May 20, 1882. This Triple Alliance would be renewed several times, as late as 1912, but Italy's commitment to it was always doubtful, and it ended after the outbreak of World War I.

CHAPTER TWELVE

The occupation of Bosnia-Hercegovina, though it greatly enhanced Austria's power position in the Balkans, was by no means universally popular. German liberals, long concerned over the declining proportion of the German population in the empire, saw in the addition of two Slavic provinces another unwelcome step in that direction. When the vote for ratifying the occupation came up in parliament, they withdrew their support and Auersperg's ministry fell. After a brief interval the emperor named as premier a childhood friend of Irish roots, long a diligent and capable servant of the Habsburgs, Count Eduard Taaffe. With the liberals on the resentful defensive, there was no possibility of any one group dominating the political spectrum in parliament and Taaffe constructed a coalition of conservatives, composed of German aristocrats, clericals, and Slavs of a moderate persuasion; rather fancifully the coalition called itself the Iron Ring. Slavic representatives, who for the past 10 years had refused to take their seats in parliament, now returned. Taaffe's policy was to conciliate the Czechs in as many ways as was practicable without conceding their chief demand of parity with Germans and Hungarians within the Dual Monarchy. A language decree passed in 1880 placed the Czech and German languages in Bohemia and Moravia on equal status in the public sphere. Two years later, by an additional step in this direction, the University of Prague was divided into a German and a Czech section and soon the enrollment in the latter far exceeded that in the former. Electoral reform reducing the requirements for voting drew a large number of hitherto disenfranchised Czechs into political life.

The 14 years of the Taaffe cabinet witnessed the rise of more extremist political groupings, which drew their strength from the spirit of restlessness that infected the European scene in the half century before the outbreak of the Great War. The reforms in the Czech lands, far from bringing tranquillity, sharpened the differences between the "Old Czechs" who sought to accommodate themselves as a national group within the Habsburg Empire and the "Young Czechs," militantly conscious of their national identity and in general separatist. Within the liberal camp, an incipient racist predilection matured into full-fledged separatism, and found its most cogent expression in the so-called Linz Program, which advocated the creation of an unequivocally German-dominated Austria, closely allied to Germany, and an effective, though not total, separation from the non-German elements in the monarchy. On the opposite end, the most significant political development was the aggressive rise of the workers' parties. As far back as 1848 a General Workers' Union had been formed in Vienna, and at the end of 1867 the Viennese Workers' Cultural Union was founded, with the purpose of elevating the lamentably low cultural standard of industrial workers to a respectable level. A congress in the town of Neudörfl in 1874 resolved differences in organizing the Social Democratic Party of Austria (SPÖ). Although the party, like others, struggled with overcoming a breach between more moderate and more radical elements, at a new congress in Hainfeld in 1888, the two merged to found a united workers' party, based on a Marxist platform. In 1890 the first May Day celebrations in Austria took place. But the party was unable to overcome the difficulties posed by the multinational character of the state. A new congress in Brno, Moravia, in 1899 accepted these ethnic divisions; although in subsequent years the party performed fairly well at the polls, the abandonment by the leaders of the internationalist ideal inherent in Marxist teaching weakened it for the remainder of the life of the Dual Monarchy. The Taaffe government was moderately successful in weakening the party's appeal by its own social legislation: in 1884 the maximum length of the working day was by law set at 11 hours; the same law barred the employment of children under age 12; it made Sunday a compulsory day of rest and introduced a workers' compensation system with insurance against sickness and accidents. These measures were not parts, however, of a comprehensive social reform program. Taaffe in general eschewed long-term solutions; just as his parliamentary coalition was opportunistic, so were his legislative initiatives, intended to meet what appeared most pressing at the moment; possibly, it was precisely this fact that accounted for the longevity of his cabinet.

During his tenure a new tragedy befell the royal family. The emperor had already been deeply shaken when in 1867 his brother Maximilian, two years younger than himself, had been captured and shot by Mexican revolutionaries. Previously viceroy of Lombardy-Venetia, Maximilian gained a reputation for political views distinctly more liberal than those of his brother. Napoleon III of France, seeking to gain a foothold in the Americas, in 1863 prevailed on him to assume the emperorship of Mexico under the protection of French troops. The Civil War in America had rendered the Monroe Doctrine temporarily inoperative, and Maximilian was allowed to occupy his shaky throne. By 1866 the situation had changed and under American pressure Napoleon was compelled to withdraw his troops, leaving Maximilian to his fate. Taking refuge in the fort of Quarétaro, he was betrayed, captured, and, after a short trial by a military tribunal, shot on June 19, 1867, as a traitor. Francis Joseph had reason to reproach himself, as head of the dynasty, for not preventing his brother from taking the throne of so distant a nation.

In January 1889 tragedy struck again. In retrospect it was not entirely unexpected. The emperor's only son, Rudolf, had inherited his mother's free spirits and liberal inclinations and, possibly for that very reason, was early removed from her tender care and placed under a strict, military, regimen. Elisabeth had to put her foot down to ensure for him a more permissive upbringing that gave scope to his gentler nature. At age 23 he had, again under pressure, married Belgian princess Stephanie, and it proved an unhappy union. Rudolf's clashes with his father over his own independent notions and often scandalous conduct

Francis Joseph I,
emperor of Austria
and king of Hungary
(Hulton/Archive)

became more frequent and more tempestuous. Rudolf had nothing but contempt for Francis Joseph's mania for uniforms, military display, and parades; politically, like his mother, he sympathized with the liberals and had a particular fondness for Hungarians. In foreign policy he was opposed to a close pro-German orientation, especially after the accession to the German throne, in 1888, of William II, of whom he had a rather poor opinion. On January 30, 1889, in the hunting lodge at Meyerling, he committed suicide together with his paramour, Baroness Maria Vetsera. The exact particulars of the tragedy have never been discovered, or they have not been made public. With Rudolf's death his uncle, his father's younger brother, Charles Louis, became heir to the throne, although this was never made official. When Charles Louis died in 1896, his son Francis Ferdinand became the heir apparent.

The 1880s witnessed a quickening of diplomatic initiatives, especially in the Balkans, and it was there that the cycle that would lead to an international catastrophe three decades later began. Austro-Russian discord from which, thanks to her German alliance, Austria usually emerged the winner, and a corresponding rise in ill feelings, not only on the part of Russia but of Slavic nations in the Balkans as well, would play out repeatedly. To be sure, after Serbian disillusionment with Russia following the Berlin Congress, the Austrophile Obrenović dynasty in Belgrade concluded with Austria a surprising alliance, in which Serbia pledged to abstain from anti-Austrian agitation and to remain a friendly neutral in case Austria was at war. In exchange the Serbian prince Milan was given Austrian recognition of his assumption of the title of king. But the treaty was not popular in Serbia and could be depended on to last only as long as an Obrenović ruler occupied the throne. For the rest, the second Dreikaiserbund had provided for the division of the peninsula between an eastern—Russian—and a western—Austrian—sphere of influence, in the hope of avoiding confrontations between the two powers. This promising arrangement was upset in the second Balkan crisis of 1883. The affair was fraught with all the complexities and incalculable shifts for which Balkan politics were noted. The king of Bulgaria had been chosen by the Russian czar, but proved an ingrate by ridding himself of his Russian advisers and preferring the support of the Bulgarian parliament, the Sobranje. On instructions from Petersburg, pro-Russian officers literally kidnapped the young king and took him to Russia. There he was made to see the need to comply with Russian instructions; shortly after his return to Sofia he abdicated. A defiant Sobranje, however, insisted on its right to choose the king's successor regardless of Russian wishes and their choice fell on a German prince who had served as an officer in the Austrian army, Ferdinand of Saxe-Coburg. Although he assured Petersburg of his friendly and peaceful intentions, the czar was deeply chagrined. Adding to his chagrin was the fact that in the process of defying Russia, Bulgaria had gained the province of Eastern Rumelia denied her by the Berlin Congress; now, in Russian eyes, a fractious satellite was rewarded rather than punished. To add insult to injury, Serbia, unhappy over the territorial enlargement of her neighbor, declared war on Bulgaria to gain her own share. But Serbian armies were defeated, and Bulgarians were about to carry the war into Serbia. The Austrians warned them off, trying to protect their only Balkan ally. Once again Russia had been unable to exert even a minimum of influence in her own sphere of interest. Resentments began to bite deep.

Complicating the picture was the renewal of the Triple Alliance (Austria, Germany, Italy) in 1887: the Italians, taking advantage of the inexperience of the new Austrian foreign minister, Gustav Kálnoky, inserted a paragraph in the updated treaty, whereby Italy would have to be consulted if any changes in the status quo were to be made "in the Balkans, on the Turkish littoral, or on the Mediterranean and Aegean islands." Thus a new element was injected into the already muddled Balkan affairs. It did not take Kálnoky's successor, Count

Goluchowski, long to realize that the concession to Italy, however theoretical, could not be fitted into the painfully constructed bipolar power balance in the Balkans. When he accompanied the emperor on a state visit to St. Petersburg in April 1897 he worked out with the Russian foreign office a new arrangement, whereby all contentious questions in the Balkans were to be settled by Austria and Russia only; while strictly speaking this did not violate the letter, it certainly violated the spirit of the agreement with Italy.

Internally the compromise with Hungary, although it had averted an immediate crisis in the empire, did not get to the root of the nationality problem, which, in an age of rising expectation, was the very bane of that polyglot state. Even the Hungarians were not at peace with it. While Francis Joseph was personally not unpopular in Hungary, the partnership with German Austria was. A substantial number of oppositionist delegates sat in the Hungarian parliament and their opposition invariably crystallized in grievances concerning dualism: Hungary had to pay too large a proportion of the "joint" expenditures, she had to send too many recruits into the army—and what could not escape the emperor's notice—behind the superficial complaints was the evident unhappiness with a system that deprived Hungary of national independence. The voices of the mature elements, who knew that Hungary could be a power factor only as part of the Dual Monarchy, were drowned out by shrill nationalistic, not to say chauvinistic, protests. Neither was Hungary the only discordant element in the Dual Monarchy. Taaffe's cautious concessions to the Czechs whetted the appetite, if not of the conservatives who felt comfortable with rule by Vienna, then of the radical Young Czechs who kept agitating, with support from the electorate, for goals they never cared clearly to define. In Austria itself the Linz Program, meager though its actual support was, energized Pan-German sentiments, and these, thanks largely to the utterances of Georg von Schönerer, a deputy from Vienna, acquired a distinct anti-Semitic character. The sentiment was heartily shared by another public figure of the day, Karl Lueger. Lueger had initially campaigned as a Christian Socialist. That program in its pure version had been introduced into Austrian politics by Baron von Vogelsang. It sought to sweeten the poison tooth of Marxist socialism with a gentler version that appealed to Christian virtues. Men of this persuasion declared themselves hostile to capitalism, certainly in its crass exploitative stage, and by a bold leap of association blamed that brand of capitalism on Jews. Lueger, in part because of his anti-Semitism, but chiefly because, as a self-made man, he contributed a great deal to the expansion and beautification of Vienna, drew many votes when he ran for mayor of that city. He twice won the election but each time the emperor refused to validate the results, both because of Lueger's anti-Semitism and because of his outspoken hostility to Hungarians. When he finally gave his agreement after a third election, Lueger remained mayor of Vienna until his death in 1910.

Meanwhile on the national scene, Taaffe, a tactician rather than a strategist, sought to address each problem as it reached a disruptive level; in 1890, German liberals in Bohemia became embroiled in a dispute with Old Czechs over the ever vexing language question. The liberals, unable to stifle demands that Czech be made the official language in Bohemia, proposed to divide the province into two parts, with German the official language in one part and Czech in the other. Although this may have been acceptable to the two parties at quarrel, it brought the radical Young Czechs, who had not been invited to participate in the talks, into the fray. Taaffe, or rather his interior minister Emil Steinbach, with the lukewarm support of the emperor, then proposed a new election law that for practical purposes would have made the franchise universal, granting it to all male taxpayers 24 years or older who could read and write their native language. It was Steinbach's contention that the lower classes, enfranchised for the first time, were loyal to the dynasty, were concerned with social rather than national issues, and would thus vote for politicians of a moderate stance. Such a bold extension of the franchise was, however, unacceptable to conservatives, not only in Austria but in Hungary too, and, on November 11, 1893, Taaffe resigned. A brief ministry headed by the grandson of the great Windischgrätz came to grief over so trivial a question as whether the German language could be replaced by the Slovene in a grammar school in the province of Styria. On October 2, 1895, Count Cazimir Badeni, a Polish nobleman and former governor of Galicia, assumed the premiership. For the first time in Austrian history key cabinet positions were occupied by non-Germans: Agenor Goluchowski at the Ballplatz and Leo Bilinski, another Pole, heading the ministry of finance. Interestingly, this shift in ethnic emphasis hardly attracted any attention; the principle of multinationalism gradually struck root in the Habsburg Empire.

Badeni succeeded in carrying out a limited suffrage reform, politically useful but without any significance, because voting in the Reichsrat was still by states (curiae) previously four in number, now raised to five, and although the fifth curia represented the majority of voters, it had only 72 of a total of 425 votes in five estates. With this questionable success behind him, Badeni addressed the festering language question in Bohemia by mandating the use of *both* German and Czech in public offices and allowing officials one year to learn the language that was not their own. The debate in parliament led to vehement arguments and even physical confrontations, finally drowning in filibuster. Badeni then outlawed filibusters and ordered unruly delegates to be removed by police. This provoked disturbances in the streets of Vienna; on November 18, 1897, Badeni, in turn, tendered his resignation.

Two other governments, neither of which lasted a year, followed; in January 1900 the emperor finally asked a former minister of the interior, Ernest von Koerber, to form a cabinet. Koerber, whose ministry lasted four years, gave telling evidence that a bureaucratic administration with no momentous items on its agenda could achieve quite as much as an activist ministry, with less fanfare and controversy. Yet the political atmosphere was not conducive to positive change. Nationalist passions were on the increase. Koerber's proposals to create "national universities" with instruction in the German language ran into stiff opposition from Italians and Slavs. Meanwhile, the emperor and the Hungarian government argued over the unity of the imperial army, a unity many Hungarians wanted to sever by calling for separate Austrian and Hungarian armies. Koerber worked patiently and with the help of the press whose importance in a world of rapidly expanding communication he fully recognized and utilized, in the process freeing it from government control. His other reforms were mainly economic, reflecting his belief that improved material conditions would cool nationalistic passions. He announced plans for the building of a second railway to Trieste, the Dual Monarchy's only fully operational port, and also an extension of its harbor facilities. His program of placing private railway lines in state ownership intended to exclude profitability as a factor in the smooth operation of the railways. Although with the lower rates charged by the state these lines operated at a deficit, increased harbor fees and more voluminous trade made up for the losses.

However, Koerber's hope that greater prosperity would lead to a calmer domestic scene was disappointed. Such was the political climate in the early years of the 20th century, so many were the sources of dissatisfaction and protest, that even the least contentious political leader was likely to incur the displeasure of one or more groups in the long run. It was mostly the emperor's displeasure with Koerber's conciliatory Hungarian policies (as well as his unending parliamentary struggles over finances) that caused the premier to resign in December 1904, but in the absence of these reasons some other controversial item would surely have led to his downfall.

Hungarian separatism became the most critical challenge to the emperor. He had learned not to treat his Magyar subjects lightly, to respect their nationalist sensitivity, but the principle and practice of a joint army was too close to his heart for him to yield. In 1903 army maneuvers were held in Galicia, and in an order of the day Francis Joseph brusquely rejected demands by Hungarian oppositionists for a separate army, reminding them that military matters were the emperor's exclusive province, and that the army was the sole guarantee of the empire's great power rank. That rank could not be preserved unless all nations of the empire labored together toward that end.

The concept of a unified army—and the fact that the emperor lumped them together with other nationalities in the empire—enraged many Hungarians. Was this the true meaning of dualism, they wondered, an association of nearly a dozen nations, all contributing toward the same end? Of course the Budapest government, at least in official pronouncements, did not share this attitude of defiant nationalism, but it was rendered nearly helpless by oppositionist clamor.

And now, early in 1905, word came from St. Petersburg of disorders following the defeat of the Russian army at the hands of the Japanese, disorders that spread to the countryside and led to familiar ugly scenes of peasants attacking and burning manors and chasing landlords away; the whole social order in Russia seemed on the verge of collapse. Uprisings on such a massive scale had proved infectious in the past. To Austrian politicians the only way to prevent them from occurring in the Dual Monarchy seemed to be to make the franchise truly universal and thus take the electorate of the empire into the leaders' confidence. The revolt in Russia was tamed only after the czar issued his October Manifesto promising a national Duma. The Russian premier, Stolypin, in a fit of later regretted generosity, made the franchise universal. Surely Austria could not lag behind the notoriously reactionary Russian government. Francis Joseph appointed as premier Baron Paul Gautsch, a protégé of Francis Ferdinand, charging him with pushing the universal adult male vote through the Reichsrat. His expectation, as Taaffe's had been, was that the great number of working men who would for the first time have the vote would show little interest in disruptive nationality questions and thus break the back of these movements that proved most ruinous for the cohesion of the empire. When Gautsch first presented the bill to parliament in February 1906, it was rejected. But, after a transitional government, a new cabinet headed by Baron Max von Beck succeeded in securing passage of the law for universal male suffrage at the end of the year and the emperor gave it his blessing. Every male 24 years old or more received the vote and voting by curiae was abolished. The debate was vehement; Germans and Italians argued for weighted voting in their favor on the reasoning that they paid the majority of taxes; the Slavs wanted their numerical majority to be the decisive factor. An awkward compromise resolved the issue: the Germans, who made up 35 percent of the population in Austrian lands but paid over 63 percent of the taxes were entitled to 43 percent of the seats in parliament; the rest of the seats were divided among Czechs, Poles, Bukovinian, and Italians. The first elections conducted with the universal, equal, secret ballot took place in May 1907. The hope that the new system of voting would redound to the benefit of the "mass" parties at the expense of the narrow chauvinistic forces was by and large fulfilled. The Young Czechs and Pan-Germans received only marginal representation; the great winners were the Social Democrats and Christian Socialists. The emperor was still free to choose his cabinet, ignoring if he wished the outcome of the parliamentary elections, and the socialist parties were not able to translate their legislative majority into executive prominence. Beck continued as premier. He took up negotiations with the Hungarians over the distribution of government expenses and managed to somewhat reduce Austria's obligation to 63.6 percent of the total; he also won approval of the entire budget by both parliaments. But as so often happened in the Dual Monarchy, minor contentious issues undermined his position. Francis Ferdinand turned against him for alleged concessions he had made to the Hungarians in the talks about quotas; Beck was also hurt by the outcome of the so-called Wahrmund case. Wahrmund, a professor of religious law at the University of Innsbruck, had committed the indiscretion of making antichurch pronouncements; several Catholic dignitaries, including the papal nuncio, demanded his resignation. Others, unfriendly to the church, saw in these demands a breach of academic freedom. In the end Wahrmund was transferred to Prague. This led to new outbursts of protest. The emperor, who most likely agreed with the clerical forces hostile to Wahrmund, yielded to the general protest and requested Beck's resignation.

Increasingly it was the person of the emperor, now 78 years old, who provided the sole bond uniting the nations of the empire. Few dared to contemplate how that already ramshackle structure would hold up once Francis Joseph departed the scene. In European affairs the Dual Monarchy's only ally, Germany, found itself in a gradually weakening position as its vaunted Triple

Alliance, with Italy an unreliable member, was opposed by an alignment of France, Russia, and Britain. Although Britain was not bound by formal treaty to either of her partners, she was engaged in an ill-tempered naval race with Germany and her military conversations with France, although they did not ensure her entering a war on France's side, made it a practical certainty that she would not enter it on Germany's side. In Germany the fear, first expressed by Bismarck, that the Reich would be dragged by Austria into a war over a Balkan complication grew by the day. Only the recent defeat of Russia in the Far Eastern war and her consequent inability to engage in major hostilities in the foreseeable future somewhat allayed that fear. But in Serbia the Austrophile Obrenović dynasty had been overthrown by the Austrophobe Karageorgević dynasty and relations were drifting toward a state of conflict.

Chapter Thirteen

Starting in 1908, the year of a new crisis in the Balkans, foreign policy issues took precedence over the undignified internal squabbles that marked the increasingly muddled history of the Dual Monarchy. Not that there was any diminution of domestic conflicts or their vehemence, but they began to suffer from the weariness of repetition. Hungarian separatism was on the increase, as was Slavic agitation for equal rights. Intensity of emotions magnified issues that in a quieter atmosphere could have been resolved without controversy. In Hungary, to cite but one example, the familiar debate over the right of the Catholic Church to determine the religion of a child born from marriages between Catholic and non-Catholic Christian parents produced parliamentary debates of such venom that the emperor, although much in favor of the Catholic position, was compelled to add enough dignitaries to the upper house, which had twice voted down a bill depriving the church of that right, to obtain passage. No one in a responsible position believed that these recurring disputes were settled with finality; however, their political interest diminished with time. In the end only foreign policy brought novelty to the daily news.

Under Goluchowski's long tenure at the Ballplatz, quietism characterized Austrian foreign policy. The main reason may have been the minister's temperamental pacifism and indolence, but it was also true that European diplomacy, especially in the Balkans, had become so fraught with uncertainty that any daring move was likely to upset the equilibrium. Such was the case with what is known in history as the Bosnian Crisis. The Berlin Congress of 1878 had acknowledged Austria's right to annex the sister provinces of Bosnia-Hercegovina at a suitable time, although it failed to specify what or who would determine the time suitable. At the Ballplatz the tacit assumption was that Austria alone, holding the provinces under military occupation, would make that decision. But much had changed since 1878. At that time Serbia was a minor presence in the Balkans and even Russia exposed herself in her interest in only a cursory way; powers like Germany, Britain, and France favored Austrian predominance in the peninsula, at any rate in the western part of it, as an assurance against social turmoil and insurrections that the Ottoman Empire was unable to control. By 1908, however, Serbia could no longer be ignored and the southern Pan-Slavic idea she sponsored had gained wide currency among Balkan nations. In Turkey, in 1908, the notoriously corrupt and feeble government under Sultan Murad V had fallen and was replaced by vigorous reform-minded elements who called themselves the Young Turks. It was only a matter of time before this new government advanced the entirely credible claim that it was able to do what the government of 1878 had not been able, namely, to govern effectively, and demand that the Austrian occupation of Bosnia-Hercegovina, as well as of the Sanjak of Novibazar, be ended.

The new Austrian foreign minister, Aloys von Aerenthal, a man of much broader conceptions than Goluchowski had been, but also more ambitious and devious, was well aware of all this. What played into his hand was that the newly appointed Russian foreign minister, Alexander Izvolsky, after the disaster Russia had suffered in her war against Japan, turned to the Balkans as a sphere of expansion, and his first objective was gaining permission for Russian warships, bottled up in the Black Sea, to enter the Straits on their way to the Mediterranean Sea. He offered Aerenthal a quid pro quo: Russia would not object to Austria's annexation of Bosnia-Hercegovina if Austria did not object to Russian warships sailing through the Straits. The agreement was oral and apparently based on good faith and the assumption of reciprocity. When Austria announced the annexations prematurely, that is, before the great powers consented to the Russian request, Izvolsky was outraged. The Young Turks on their part felt robbed of two Ottoman provinces, and the Serbs objected to Austria taking insupportable liberties in the South Slav sphere. Even the Germans were offended at not having been given prior notice; they could not, however, afford to deny support to their only reliable ally. Aerenthal spurned the protests and it became a question of what power or combination of powers would oppose Austria, which had a military alliance with formidable imperial Germany. None, as it turned out, ventured to do so. Russia's ally, France, saw no *casus foederis* in the situation, and the government of the Young Turks declared itself ready to abandon its claim to Bosnia-Hercegovina in exchange for a cash payment. Izvolsky's attempt to save face by calling a congress to sanction the annexation so that Russia could bow to a general European concert rather than to a Teutonic combination failed when German chancellor von Bölow brusquely demanded that he withdraw his demand or face the consequences of a refusal.

Historians are at odds over the question of whether this crisis hardened resolutions in the two opposing camps or whether the diplomatic situation still remained fluid with many opportunities for realignments. One relevant fact is that in Serbia a militant organization, the Narodna Odbrana was quickly formed and, three years later, in 1911, it spun off a secret, terroristic, group, the Black Hand; it was this group that unleashed the Great War by assassinating the heir to the Austrian throne, Francis Ferdinand, in 1914.

In Austria, during the Bosnian crisis, the chief of the general staff, Franz Conrad von Hötzendorf, strenuously argued for war against Serbia, predicting that that nation would remain an irreconcilable foe of Austria, and no diplomatic victories would bring it down; it was Aerenthal, awakening a trifle too late to the seriousness of the crisis he had brought on, who vetoed the proposed mobilization.

During succeeding years, even as a series of international complications, largely over colonial issues in Africa, led to repeated war scares, the Balkans remained the chief area of contention. Owing to Russia's alliance with France and Austria's alliance with Germany, every real or perceived threat to the status quo was prone to produce a crisis. Italy had been excluded from Balkan affairs by the 1897 Austro-Russian agreement referred to earlier, yet it was Italy that, after three years of relative calm in the Balkans, in 1911 initiated the sequence of events that led to a new imbroglio, the First Balkan War. Italy had become an increasingly unreliable partner in the Triple Alliance; in 1901 she had made a secret agreement with France, whereby Italy would not object to France's turning the Ottoman province of Morocco into a protectorate if, in return, France accepted Italy's annexation of Libya when it became timely. A French attempt in 1905 to advance into Morocco failed because of German objections; but another attempt in 1911, resulting in the so-called Second Moroccan Crisis, succeeded, as German resentment was disarmed by the cession of some French-held African territory. Italy now felt free to make her own move. On September 23, 1911, she handed the Porte a one-day ultimatum for the cession of Libya; when the deadline passed without an answer, she declared war. Having contracted the colonial fever, the Italians did not appreciate the extreme volatility of what had become known as the Eastern Question. Their early quick victories in the field revealed the terminal weakness of the Ottoman Empire and immediately the territorial ambitions of the small Balkan states, especially of Serbia and Bulgaria, were awakened. Without consulting the Russians (although the Russian envoys in Belgrade and Sofia were fanning the flames) these two states, on March 13, 1913, concluded an alliance expressly against Ottoman power. Soon Greece joined in. Russian czar Nicholas II, when he heard of the compact, was uneasy but did not object; he could not bring himself, after his past humiliations, to restrain the Balkan Slavs. Yet when his foreign minister Sazonov showed the text of the treaty to visiting French premier Poincaré, the latter warned that if put in action it meant war, not only against Turkey but against Austria as well.

The warning had no effect and, just as Chief of Staff Conrad had predicted, Serbia was not contained by diplomatic means. In October 1912 the so-called Balkan League went to war against Turkey and quickly won a series of victories. In Austria Conrad had been replaced by the far less experienced Schemua; the latter urged intervention while the Serbs were tied down in their war with Turkey. The new foreign minister, Leopold Berchtold, overruled him, hoping the Turks would win in the end. When they did not and the war ended with the victory of the Balkan states, it was too late to undo the outcome.

Vienna tried to put a good face on it, but its ephemeral tolerance ended when Serbia demanded as one of the spoils of war a port city on the Adriatic. This Austria could not tolerate. In case of war the Serbian navy could play havoc with Austrian attempts to sail out of the Adriatic. The Russians backed Serbia and suddenly Austrian-Russian tension rose to new highs. An ambassadorial conference met in London to sort matters out. Austria demanded in ultimative terms that a separate state be carved out in the area Serbia aspired to acquire. This demand the conference in London duly granted and once again Serbia and her Russian mentor suffered a major diplomatic defeat. However, Austrians still felt that the outcome of the war constituted a blow to their power position. Serbian territory had been greatly enlarged and Pan-Slavism was on the rise everywhere.

The Second Balkan War erupted at the end of June 1913 due to the disproportionate gains made by Bulgaria in the first war, while Serbia had been prevented from incorporating the newly created state of Albania, and Greece had received only pieces of Macedonia. These two states were joined by Romania, which wanted to wrest Dobruja from Bulgaria, and also by Turkey, which hoped to recover as much of her losses as she could. Bulgaria was rapidly defeated, but when Serbia took possession of the part of Macedonia assigned to her, a local uprising erupted. The Serbians tried to put it down, but in the process chased the rebels into Albania where the Macedonians had taken sanctuary. Immediately Austrian fears over a Serbian presence in Albania were awakened. Demands for the withdrawal of Serbian forces went unheeded and Austria made military preparations. This time the Russians warned Serbia off. Sazonov told Serbian premier Pašić that it would be foolish to pick a quarrel over an issue in which Austria would have the sympathy of most of the powers. In the end the Serbs backed down, but deep resentments remained.

⁂ ⁂ ⁂

The coming of the Great War, the defining event of early 20h-century history, an event that among other results overthrew four empires and redrew the map of Europe, is generally examined in terms of responsibility. Nothing approximating a consensus has been reached among historians on that question, though there is a measure of agreement that, while Austria and Germany were most responsible for precipitating the hostilities, it was Russia that turned what might have been a local conflict into a general European war. This latter charge is somewhat mitigated by the reminder that Russia, having suffered so many reverses in the Balkans since Germany had allied herself with Austria, could not afford to remain dishonorably neutral in the presence of a major international crisis.

Austria on her part, in justifying her bellicose course of action against Serbia, could point to the fact that, despite several adverse decisions in international councils, the Serbian state was growing larger (in the Balkan Wars alone it had gained a population of one and a half million), more assertive, more provoking and, if allowed to pursue her South Slav policies unchecked, would in the end pose a mortal threat to the already beleaguered Dual Monarchy. When Conrad was reappointed in place of Schemua as chief of the general staff, he resumed urgings for military action against Serbia, and possibly against Italy, too.

Then, on June 28, 1914, the heir to the Austrian throne, Francis Ferdinand, having attended military maneuvers in Bosnia, paid a ceremonial visit to Sarajevo, and there he was assassinated, together with his wife, by a young Serbian of Austrian nationality, Gavrilo Princip. Princip had entered Bosnia from Serbia and for that, the Austrians reasoned, he had to have had the active help of Serbian officials.

achieved full battle readiness. On the evening of that day Berlin declared "threatening war danger" and gave Russia 12 hours to demobilize. When the deadline passed without compliance, on August 1 Germany ordered general mobilization and on the same day declared war on Russia. Further declarations of war, by Germany on France, and by Britain on Germany, duly followed. By August 4 all the powers of Europe were at war. The final, death agony of the Dual Monarchy began.

CHAPTER FOURTEEN

Although there was as much prayer as prophecy in Francis Joseph's assurance to his subjects that by the grace of God early victory would come to the Dual Monarchy's forces, the European experience of the past century gave the promise some credibility. All the wars since the collapse of the Napoleonic Empire had been short and localized; the Crimean War, the longest, although it dragged on for nearly two years, had been limited to a promontory of a small peninsula; the Franco-Prussian War, the most consequential one, had settled, after the initial battles, into a prolonged denouement. Still, given military realities, a similar promise of a quick end to the new war came from the German emperor, assuring his soldiers that by the time the leaves had fallen, they would be home, victorious. Germany had an ironclad plan for avoiding a two-front war; the former chief of the general staff, General Alfred von Schlieffen, had projected the rapid defeat of France by concentrating the bulk of German forces in the west, then transferring them to the east against the slow-moving Russian army. But Germany lost some precious days before ordering full mobilization on August 1, then lost more days when Belgium refused to surrender and her formidable fortresses held out longer than German military chiefs had anticipated. Once, however, these fortifications were subdued or bypassed, the German army poured into France in a giant wheeling movement intended to envelop the French armies and proceed to move behind Paris. Meanwhile, the boldly conceived French plan of sending armies into Lorraine in a continuous drive that would carry them into the heart of Germany, failed miserably within a week. After only three weeks of fighting Schlieffen's plan of conquering France in one great offensive seemed close to realization.

But the eastern front could not be ignored altogether. It will be remembered that in the closing days of peace Conrad von Hötzendorf had opted for Plan B, a full and rapid concentration of Austro-Hungarian forces against Serbia. That offensive, for all the preparation, failed. It failed either because the Germans, who had held their own cards very close to their chest (although the essentials of the Schlieffen Plan had been revealed to Conrad by the German chief of staff Moltke), insisted that Austria concentrate her forces against Russia in order to give the German armies more time to conquer France, thus throwing Austrian plans into disarray, or it failed because of tactical errors, a lack of resolute fighting spirit in the Austro-Hungarian army, and the stiff resistance of the Serbians under the inspired leadership of General Radomir Putnik. In time a major Austro-Hungarian army *was* deployed on the Russian front, but from this time on it was under effective German command. What happened in late August and early September of 1914 foreshadowed military events on the eastern front for the duration of the war. In the battle of Tannenberg between August 26 and 30, the Germans inflicted a major defeat on Russian forces under General Samsonov. They then proceeded to drive the army of Russian general Rennenkampf into the treacherous terrain around the Masurian Lakes and in that battle alone took 125,000 prisoners. German losses were moderate, but the Dual Monarchy, in the first four weeks of war, lost a quarter million dead or wounded while another hundred thousand were taken prisoner, and, in the next few months, the Russians conquered nearly all of Galicia. In April 1915 Czar Nicholas personally appeared in Lemberg to annex Galicia (Red Russia as it was traditionally called) to his empire. The preceding winter Russian forces had actually breached the Carpathians and entered Hungarian territory in force.

By now the western front had settled into a grim pattern of trench warfare and there was no longer a possibility of Germany fighting two consecutive wars on two separate fronts as Schlieffen had envisaged; the fronts both in the east and in the west had to be manned. Realizing that the Austro-Hungarian army could not hold its own, in May 1915 the Germans committed a major force to a counteroffensive in the east, near the town of Gorlice. With the Dual Monarchy's forces reduced to a secondary role, the Germans broke through the Russian lines and forced a general retreat from Galicia. The feared Austro-Hungarian collapse was prevented, but how many times could the hard-pressed Germans be depended on to bail out their ill-starred ally?

Internally the war, like an irritant acting on half-healed wounds, brought into the open conflicts that had plagued the Dual Monarchy for the last half century. The Austrian parliament was not in session and Prime Minister Stürgkh thought it best not to convene it. While there had been enthusiasm for the war in the German provinces, most of the rest of the empire remained sullen. In Hungary, the failure of Vienna to authorize a separate Hungarian army under its own command still rankled. Growing scarcities due to the enormous needs of the army and to declining production caused a rapid fall in morale.

Until now the article in the constitution providing that in case of war any act that jeopardized the progress of mobilization or military operations belonged under army jurisdiction had seemed innocuous and in fact necessary. Now it became an object of contention. The army high command (Armeeoberkommando—AOK) placed ever larger areas under military governance and claimed authority not only over legal matters but over raw materials and labor discipline as well; this led to predictable confrontations and protests, not only among the affected populations but even within the Vienna government, which refused to yield its peacetime powers to the military command. When, for instance, in September 1914 the AOK proposed that persons found guilty of treason (by whatever definition) should be subject to confiscation of property, the government strenuously objected to such violation of the sanctity of private property, and the army had to defer.

In September 1915 the AOK advanced the demand that all aliens and "unrealiables" should be expelled from a 25-kilometer-wide area along the Dual

Monarchy's borders and replaced with disabled veterans. Stürgkh vetoed the proposal. By now the monarchy was at war with Italy too, and carrying out the AOK demand would have meant removing hundreds of thousands of Italians from the Trentino and, incidentally, appropriating their extensive timber interests—it was not farfetched to perceive behind the AOK proposal just such an intent. The army high command also tried to use war conditions to introduce other "reforms" close to its heart: the nationalization of schools (the ulterior motive being to make the German tongue universal in the empire), closer supervision of the clergy (especially of the non-German clergy, a great part of which was not loyal to the Dual Monarchy), and the introduction of quasi-military training for school-age youngsters. None of these proposals were in the end enacted, but there occurred a noticeable cooling of relations between army and government. The AOK blamed Stürgkh for frustrating its initiatives and tried to have him removed; only the opposition of the aged emperor prevented his fall. It could not save his life though. On October 21, 1916, a young socialist, Friedrich Adler, son of Victor Adler, one of the founders of the Austrian Social Democratic Party, fired three shots at the premier in a hotel restaurant and killed him. Adler was allegedly distressed over the suffering of the masses and Stürgkh's failure to stop a war from which no gain could be expected.

Francis Joseph lived only long enough to name Stürgkh's successor: the same Karl Koerber who had served him so well at the turn of the century. One month later the emperor himself succumbed, in his 86th year. He was succeeded by a grand nephew, son of the late younger brother of Francis Ferdinand, Charles. Francis Joseph, who had had little love for his previously designated successors, including his own son Rudolf, harbored a distinct affection for the 29-year-old Charles, and for his wife, a princess of the Italian province of Parma, and their children.

The new king had the formidable task of stepping into the shoes, not of a man but an institution, the very embodiment of the Dual Monarchy, the longest ruling Habsburg. Charles inherited a realm whose morale was ravaged by the war, and where supranationalism, championed and promoted by the Habsburgs, had become a sad anachronism. Two distinguished Czechs, Tomáš Garrigue Masaryk, and Edvard Beneš, and an energetic Slovak, Milan Štefanik, were busy abroad gaining supporters for an independent Czechoslovakia to be carved out of the body of the Dual Monarchy. The South Slavs were similarly active and only disagreements within their groups made their aspirations at the moment less potent. Hungarian separatism continued as the most disruptive force. In August 1916 Romania had declared war on the Dual Monarchy, her forces invaded Transylvania, and once again German units had to come to the rescue and hurl the invaders back into the trans-Carpathian province of Wallachia. Charles, aware of the impending catastrophe, aimed, as a first priority, at pulling the monarchy out of the war; only in that way, he felt, could the Habsburg dynasty and its possessions be saved.

Koerber's cabinet lasted only a short time and was replaced by one headed by a Czech aristocrat, Count Heinrich Clam Martinic. His assurance to the Austrian Germans that, although he himself was not a German, he had always been a good Austrian sounded less than convincing and in the circumstances it was in any case irrelevant. Martinic had only enough time to convoke, after a three-year absence, the Austrian parliament before he resigned in June 1917.

By now the momentous events in Russia had raised hopes in the Central Powers of that empire's early military collapse but also fears of a rising tide of revolutionary sentiment in Europe. Czar Nicholas II had been forced to abdicate and a temporary committee formed from members of the legislative body, the Duma, had taken charge of the government. The committee informed its allies in the west that it intended to continue the war, but that decision proved most unpopular because, of all the belligerents, Russia was the most war-weary. A futile offensive against the Germans in July led to widespread antiwar demonstrations, spearheaded—against the convictions of their leaders—by Bolsheviks. Lenin had returned from his exile in Switzerland after a long journey arranged by the Germans who recognized his leadership qualities and knew that he was dedicated to peace. Lenin at once plunged into the political turmoil with a radical program that attracted attention only because no viable competing program emerged from any quarter.

Russia's drift toward chaos was matched in almost its every phase by Austria's own disintegration. There was a growing conviction in ruling circles in

These dead soldiers were part of the Austro-Hungarian troops fighting in the Balkans, 1916 *(Library of Congress)*

Germany that the Dual Monarchy's difficulties could be overcome only if Austrian Germans firmly and unambiguously took charge of the government. After Martinic's resignation in June 1917, Ernst von Seidler, a man of pronounced Greater German sentiments, was named premier. Loyal to Germany to the point of subservience, he labored to rekindle the early enthusiasm for the war. Emperor Charles, who had definite liberal leanings, had wanted to entrust the government to Heinrich Lammasch, one of those who believed in the possibility of transforming the monarchy into a genuine multinational federal state, and who, incidentally, had pro-Entente sympathies, but Berlin had vetoed the choice and Seidler became premier. Lammasch, as candidate, had prepared a broad amnesty plan providing that civilians convicted by military tribunals be set free—the plan was close to the new emperor's heart. No sooner had Seidler become premier than Charles made him append his signature to the amnesty decree, without consulting or involving parliament. Seidler, whose political strength came entirely from Berlin, in any case had no use for parliament with its fractious minorities. On July 15 he prorogued it until September 26; soon after it met on that date he prorogued it again until January 22, 1918.

Parliamentarians could be silenced; the people they represented could not. The Czechs of Bohemia, vocal enough at home and in parliament, had powerful support from abroad. The peripatetic Masaryk, during a visit to Russia in May 1917, had created, within an already existing Czecho-Slovak Alliance, a National Council devoted to propagating the cause of an independent Czecho-Slovak state. President Wilson, in his address to Congress in January 1918, cited as one of his Fourteen Points the "autonomous development" of the peoples of the Dual Monarchy, and, although that fell short of a call for their full independence, it was a clear acknowledgment that the Dual Monarchy had to be radically updated. Seidler proved helpless against these nationalistic ambitions; on July 22, 1918, he resigned. He was succeeded by Max Hussarek, as German in his perception of what the monarchy should be as Seidler was and as far removed from the realities of the hour. He developed a new plan for a federation of four national groups, Austrians, Hungarians, Galicians, and Croats, on the naive assumption that the inclusion of the two Slavic nationalities would satisfy the Czechs. It was a foregone conclusion, probably in everybody's mind except in Hussarek's, that the plan would never get off the ground.

Meanwhile Charles sought peace. A Habsburg, he had through his wife and her Bourbon relatives valuable connections with the western powers. In March 1918 he met with two of his wife's brothers and gave one, Sixtus, a secret letter addressed to French president Poincaré, asserting that he, Charles, would press Germany to honor France's "rightful" claim to Alsace-Lorraine and would also insist on the full restoration of Belgian and Serbian independence. In a follow-up message Charles cited as his chief condition for Austria's capitulation the preservation of the Dual Monarchy—that was a promise Poincaré, even if he had been inclined to do so, could not give, and the overture led nowhere.

The time was in any case ill-chosen. Russia had made peace with the Central Powers; the two-front war had been narrowed to one, in the west, and

Germany had no critical need for Austrian forces, forces whose striking capacity had in any case diminished to the vanishing point. Indeed, it was just at the time Sixtus carried Charles's message to France that the Germans opened on the western front the Emperor's Battle, a great offensive fortified by the transfer of nearly a million men from the Russian front, intended to deliver the knock-out blow to the allied position in France. To suggest to Germany at this point the re-cession of Alsace-Lorraine was totally unrealistic.

On April 3 French premier Clemenceau made the contents of the Sixtus letter public. The Austro-Hungarian foreign minister of the day, Czernin, issued a disclaimer two weeks later, saying that the peace moves had originated with Clemenceau, and denying any knowledge of a letter from his emperor to Poincaré. The most likely guess as to why Clemenceau had revealed a highly secret communication was to make further Austrian-German cooperation not only troublesome but nearly impossible.

Not that diplomatic embarrassments made much of a difference by now. The Dual Monarchy was fighting for its very survival. During January a widespread strike movement had swept through parts of the empire; in early February units of the naval fleet in the port of Cattaro mutinied and were put down only by the harshest measures. The high command, in a vain attempt to restore morale in the armed forces, launched a massive offensive on the Piave front in Italy; a hundred thousand soldiers lost their lives without any major territorial gains to show for it. Meanwhile, the internal disintegration was accelerated from abroad. Only a few months earlier both President Wilson and British prime minister David Lloyd George had disclaimed any intention of breaking up the Austro-Hungarian Monarchy, the latter expressly stating that that was not one of the Entente's war aims. By the end of the summer the internal breakup of the monarchy had progressed so far that the western powers could not lag behind actual developments. On August 9 British foreign secretary Balfour stated in parliament that His Majesty's Government regarded Czechoslovakia as an allied nation, and her "Czech Legion" as an allied army that would wage regular war against Austria and Germany. On September 3 the British government recognized the Czecho-Slovak National Council as the future government of Czechoslovakia. The day before, the United States had recognized the Czech forces as regular belligerents. And on September 28 the French government obligated itself to "restore" the Czechoslovak state within its historic frontiers. On October 24 Edvard Beneš, the prospective foreign minister of the new state, named his ambassadors to several friendly countries.

On that day the mainstay of the Central Powers in the Balkans, the Bulgarian front, collapsed, greatly relieving pressure on Serbia and on South Slav nations seeking union with her. At this late stage the Vienna government decided to try to save the monarchy by a new set of reforms. Czernin had resigned as foreign minister and was replaced by the Hungarian István Burián. Burián, aware that intensive negotiations were being conducted abroad for the creation of an independent Yugoslav state, suggested to the cabinet that the merging of Slavonia, Croatia, Dalmatia, and Bosnia-Hercegovina into one federal state within the Dual Monarchy would, for the time being anyhow, solve the South Slav problem. This position was to be made public in an imperial manifesto. The Hungarian premier, Wekerle, also present at the meeting, objected to issuing such a manifesto; what he apparently had in mind, knowing that the separation of his own country from Austria was a nearly accomplished fact, was that the South Slav provinces, unable to fend for themselves, should join Hungary.

The manifesto was nevertheless issued, in the emperor's name, on October 16. It announced the federal reorganization of the Dual Monarchy and called upon the constituent units freely to choose their national councils, which would then establish contact with the central government in Vienna. No response to this call was forthcoming. Federalism, attractive only a year earlier, had lost its appeal. Even dualism had been eroded. The Hungarians, apart from their long-standing desire to sever all ties with Austria, hoped that as a separate country they could get more lenient peace terms from the Entente if they posed as a state subjected to Habsburg rule against its will. The other nationalities too chose the road of separatism. On October 28 the Czech National Council proclaimed the union of the Czech parts with Slovakia and the formation of a Czechoslovak state; a day later the Yugoslav National Council announced in Zagreb the formation of an independent Yugoslav state. Galicia declared itself part of a resurrected Poland. The Hungarian parliament had, on October 17, voted for complete separation from Austria, though it still maintained the personal union with the House of Habsburg. Two weeks later, in what came to be called the Chrysanthemum Revolution (returning soldiers fired by revolutionary ideas wore chrysanthemums in their buttonholes), a high aristocrat of liberal and pacifist views, Mihály Károlyi, was named premier. On November 16 a newly elected National Council declared Hungary a republic. It then announced the liquidation of the dualist system. Austria had shrunk to a small all-German state without any established constitutional form.

On October 21 the German deputies in the former Reichsrat, the parliament for the Austrian half of the monarchy, constituting themselves as the Provisional National Assembly of German Austria, met to determine the structure of their diminished state. Politically the assembly was divided among Social Democrats, Christian Socialists, and the Greater German party advocating union with Germany; but also present were other groupings, notably Sudeten Germans from the border regions of the newly proclaimed Czechoslovak Republic. The majority favored the continuation of the Habsburg monarchy with constitutional limitations; the Social Democrats alone argued for a republic. Their leader, Victor Adler, soberly opined that either the Austrian republic could gain the consent of its parts for a federal state structure or, failing that, Austria itself (minus the Tyrol, Styria, Carinthia, Carniola, Slovenia), being economically unviable, would have no alternative to joining Germany. This pronouncement marked the beginning of the *Anschluss* movement in its active political form (although the idea, as we have seen, had been a part of the Linz Program of the 1880s).

Whether this National Assembly had any legitimacy and whether it spoke authoritatively for Austria was an unsettled question. The Hussarek government was still in place; its new "joint" foreign minister, the Hungarian Count Gyula Andrássy the Younger, on October 27 turned to the Entente powers for terms of peace. Undeterred by the presumptions of the incumbent government, the National Assembly named a State Council as the executive body, headed by Karl Renner of the Socialists. The conduct of foreign affairs was entrusted to Victor Adler. For 12 days, from October 30 to November 11, two governments sat and spoke for Austria.

The appeal for a separate peace (laborious negotiations with Germany were in progress) produced no response from the Entente powers. The war continued. On October 30, Entente naval units seized the Adriatic fleet of the Dual Monarchy and in northern Italy British and French forces launched an offensive against decimated and demoralized Austro-Hungarian units. Peace could no longer be negotiated; on November 3 in a villa near the Italian city of Padua, military leaders of the Austro-Hungarian forces signed an instrument of unconditional surrender. On November 9, in Berlin, the German republic was proclaimed; the next day the kaiser, who heard the news of his abdication on the radio at military headquarters in Belgium, took the long road into exile.

On November 11, the same day that German delegates signed armistice terms with Entente representatives at Compiègne near Paris, Charles I of the House of Habsburg issued his own manifesto, stating that "I recognize in advance the decisions that the Austrian people will make about its form of government. Through its elected representatives, the people had assumed governance. I hereby resign from any further participation in matters of state." The manifesto had been composed by the emperor's father confessor, Ignaz Seipel, and it was noted that, although Charles had pledged to take no further part in the conduct of state affairs, he had not abdicated his throne.

The next day, as hundreds of thousands cheered, a spokesman for the Provisional National Assembly announced: "German Austria is transformed into a democratic republic." He added, in an ominous postscript, "German Austria, as part of the German Republic, wishes to unite with Germany."

How many of his listeners agreed with that last statement could scarcely be answered at the time. Only one thing was certain: imperial Austria, with or without its multinational empire, was no more.

CHAPTER FIFTEEN

When the Great War ended, the Bolshevik regime in Russia was a year old and the threat of a general revolutionary collapse hung over Europe. In the Dual Monarchy even the process of dissolution reflected the powerful forces that had been unleashed by the passions of the war. Workers' parties, until then immature dabblers in politics, became the dominant presence. The leadership of the Social Democratic Party had since its foundation been made up of bourgeois intellectuals who, while formally endorsing the Marxist prescription for social transformation, in practice eschewed the idea of an armed revolution. Yet, if the lot of the working class had been hard before the war, its misery, as indeed that of the bulk of the population, became nearly unbearable in the aftermath of the Dual Monarchy's collapse. Food and coal shortages were critical and unemployment was rampant. As representatives of the victorious powers gathered in Paris in January 1919 to frame the peace treaties, there was every reason to believe that their dispositions concerning Austria would make things, if anything, even worse. In these conditions the more extremist workers' party, the Communist, was able to gain support, mainly among the lower classes. Unlike in Germany and Hungary, where Communists sprang from the radical wing of the Social Democratic Party from which they eventually split off, in Austria they emerged from the grass roots, the membership made up of returned soldiers, disaffected workers, and a few intellectuals. Significantly, the rural population remained unaffected; the party's strength remained concentrated in the cities.

The first postwar parliamentary elections were held in February 1919. The Communists knew that they did not yet have the strength to make a decent showing, and they did not participate. The Social Democratic Party gained a narrow plurality with 1,211,814 votes (69 representatives), the Christian Socialists garnered 1,068,382 votes (63 representatives), and the Greater German bloc 454,935 votes (25 representatives). Karl Renner, until now provisional head of the government, formed a cabinet. There was little this government could do at the moment to ameliorate economic conditions; its social program was nevertheless so impressive that, if fully implemented, it would have made Austria one of the most progressive countries in Europe. It introduced unemployment insurance, the eight-hour workday, and paid vacations; a special law provided for collective bargaining and the mediation of disputes; working conditions for women and children were regulated, as were those of miners and bakers. The program also provided state aid for the disabled and health insurance for public employees. These measures for now took the wind out of the sails of revolutionary elements and, by the fall of 1919, social peace had returned to the republic.

Yet by then the disastrous Treaty of St. Germain had in essence confirmed the territorial losses Austria had suffered in the closing phase of the war; matters were made worse by many formerly Austrian Germans finding themselves under foreign rule. At first these territorial losses had no great-power sanction and were regarded as a temporary condition. When the fighting ended the Provisional National Assembly announced its claim to the following territories: a number of Sudeten districts occupied by Czechoslovak troops; the Burgenland, which, although largely German-speaking, was part of Hungary; the part of the South Tyrol where German was spoken; and the northern region of Carinthia in which Yugoslav armed units had made themselves at home, although the large majority of the population was German. There was no practical way at the time to make these claims effective. Final decisions were the exclusive province of the peace conference, and prospects were not promising. The Czechs, Yugoslavs, and Italians, if only by virtue of having been liberated from Austro-Hungarian rule, counted as victor powers, whereas Austria was on the losing side and would surely have to bear some responsibility for igniting the world conflagration. While the Czechs were generally restrained in their conduct in the contested areas and did their best to avoid bloodshed, the Yugoslavs, on the dubious claim that much of the population of Carinthia spoke German not because it was their native language but because of the vigorous Germanizing efforts of the Austrian government, occupied a good part of Slovenia south of the Drava River. Still, President Wilson had proclaimed the principle of national self-determination, the armistices had been granted on the basis of his Fourteen Points, and it was not unreasonable to hope that areas with a heavy German population would be awarded to Austria, or at least subjected to plebiscites that would assuredly go in Austria's favor.

In the meantime the idea of the *Anschluss* with Germany remained a live option; apart from emotional reasons it was hard to see how German Austria as a separate state, cut off from most of its resources, could become economically viable. The foreign minister in the Renner cabinet, Otto Bauer, was an avid champion of union with Germany and held the idea that, if it was effected before the peace conference made its decisions and met with popular support, the great powers would not venture to oppose it. On March 2, 1919, he concluded with German foreign minister Brockdorf-Rantzau a secret agreement, not for an actual union but for increased efforts on the part of both states to make it possible. By the plan, the union would not be total, for Bauer reserved the right for Austria to have separate diplomatic relations with the Vatican and the successor states and to be autonomous in religious and educational matters.

Although the Austrian parliament on March 12 gave its blessing, the agreement never had a chance of becoming a reality. Public opinion was not uniformly in favor of it, and the peace conference, mainly at French insistence, absolutely refused to sanction an *Anschluss*. The French wanted a diminished, not a greatly enlarged, Germany, and as they saw it, union with Austria would reward the loser rather than punish it. Georges Clemenceau, French premier and president of the peace conference, told the Austrian delegation on March 27: "We only demand of you that you remain independent; you can do with your independence what you please, but you cannot join a German bloc and you cannot participate in a war of revanche on the side of Germany." He even suggested to the Austrians, albeit not officially, that if they abandoned the idea of a union with Germany, their territorial claims would receive sympathetic consideration. Meanwhile Wilson admitted feeling uncomfortable about, on the one hand, championing self-determination, and on the other, denying it to a nation because it lost the war. In the end the Treaty of Versailles provided that Germany recognize Austria's unalterable independence, unless the League of Nations Council (each of whose members, including France, had a veto right) decided otherwise.

When the Austrian delegation received the draft of its own treaty on June 2, there was no evidence of its territorial claims receiving any consideration. The Sudeten German regions and their population were awarded to Czechoslovakia and South Tyrol to Italy. Southern Styria was to become part of Yugoslavia, and the matter of southern Carinthia was left in abeyance. No mention was made of any change in the status of the Burgenland, which meant in effect that it would stay with Hungary. (This last provision was subsequently altered, presumably to punish Hungary for its experiment with a Bolshevik government; only in the northern region around the city of Sopron was there to be a plebiscite; when held, the populace voted heavily in favor of Hungary. Thus the chief city of Burgenland and with it a good part of its population remained with Hungary.)

Yielding to Austrian demands, plebiscites were also ordered in southern Carinthia, over vigorous Yugoslav objections. Most likely Italy, already at loggerheads with Yugoslavia over Fiume and Dalmatia, had used her influence in Austria's favor, or rather against Yugoslavia. The plebiscite produced a substantial majority in favor of Carinthia staying with Austria, and this was what the peace conference decided.

On September 10 the Austrian delegation signed the treaty at St. Germain. However, peace, though welcome after over four years of fighting, did nothing to solve an economic crisis that, far from improving, worsened by the day.

❊ ❊ ❊

New parliamentary elections were due to be held in October 1920; in late June the major parties agreed that until that time a provisional government headed by Michael Mayr of the Christian Socialists would govern. The Provisional National Assembly was charged with the task of accepting and ratifying the constitution. When it did so, Austria constituted a federal republic of nine provinces of equal rights (Burgenland, Lower Austria, Vienna, Upper Austria, Styria, Kärnten, Salzburg, Tyrol, and Vorarlberg). There was to be a lower house, the National Council, elected by the general population, and an upper house, the Federal Council, elected by the provinces. The cabinet was responsible to the lower house, which was also the source of all legislation; the upper house could only delay implementation by way of a suspensive veto. The president, whose powers were largely ceremonial, would be elected by a joint session of the two houses.

The Mayr cabinet remained in office until June 1921, vainly struggling to overcome the assorted crises the young republic had to face. Healthy trade relations were essential for a state that for so long had encompassed an ideally integrated economic system, but in the rancorous climate of the postwar years such relations were impossible to establish. Austria suffered serious shortages in oil, coal, timber, and food products. She had retained 30 percent of the prewar industrial plant but only 1 percent of the coal reserves. As a result, industrial production dwindled to a critically low level, electric power had to be rationed, railroads could transport only the most essential items, and passenger traffic was often halted altogether.

In June 1921 the Mayr cabinet resigned, and, as none of the major parties was ready to form a cabinet, a nonparty man, the former police chief of Vienna, Johannes Schober, was entrusted with doing so. During his tenure of less than a year, Schober, after much controversy and bickering, settled the Burgenland question with Hungary and attended the Genoa economic conference convened at the initiative of British prime minister Lloyd George to find a solution for the economic crisis afflicting Europe. In Genoa Schober called attention to Austria's nearly bankrupt condition (a plea that did not produce immediate remedial measures but proved the beginning of League of Nations interest in Austria's plight and of subsequent loans). At home, the chancellor managed to overcome the intense antipathy of Austrians to Czechoslovakia, which many held primarily responsible for the breakup of the empire, and concluded with Czechoslovak foreign minister Edvard Beneš the so-called Lana Agreement, by the terms of which the Austrian government would accept the border between the two countries as final and cease and desist from supporting the Sudeten irredentist movement, very active in the German-speaking provinces of Bohemia, and in return Czechoslovakia would extend credit worth $16 million to Austria for the purchase of coal and sugar. Although this agreement eliminated a damaging friction with a neighbor state and brought Austria badly needed economic relief, it was denounced in many circles as treasonous. It did enhance Schober's prestige, though, at home and abroad, and the Christian Socialist Party viewed the time as being ripe to take the business of government into its own hands, lest the appointment of an above-party man as chancellor became standard practice. In cooperation with the Greater German party, the Christian Socialists brought about Schober's resignation in May 1922. Having had a plurality in the latest elections, they were allowed to choose the new chancellor, a Jesuit clergyman, Ignaz Seipel.

Seipel was known for his ascetic habits and rigid personal discipline. Monarchist in sentiment, he served the republic well, although he never gave up hope of a Habsburg restoration. It was for this reason that he opposed an *Anschluss* with Germany. On becoming chancellor, he publicly foreswore any long-term objectives; Austria's position was too precarious to accommodate programs of extended duration, he said.

The Austrian currency at the time of Seipel's appointment was being swallowed up by escalating shortages and vertiginous inflation. During the summer of 1922 it lost one-half of its value every month, and the banknotes in circulation increased in volume at the same rate. By September one peacetime golden krone was worth over 15,000 paper krone. Salaries and wages were paid twice a week and even then could not keep pace with the steadily rising prices. The state had ceased supporting the prices of staple items at the end of 1921, and nothing stood in the way of the inflationary spiral. As usual, the workers, who had always lived from hand to mouth, and the speculators and entrepreneurs, many of whom turned misery to their advantage, suffered least; the real victim was the middle class, traditionally the backbone of society.

The means of rehabilitating the economy by its own resources simply were not available and Seipel decided to seek outside help. Now that the empire had broken up, competition had begun among the western powers for seeking influence in the successor states. Seipel hoped that in their efforts to outbid one another those powers might be more than ready to come to Austria's aid. At the end of August 1922 he undertook a major European tour of personal diplomacy. At his first stop, in Prague, he reviewed with Foreign Minister Beneš the various alternatives for economic help to Austria. They agreed that given the fact that most states, for political reasons or because they themselves were economically strapped, were unlikely to be of much help, the best hope was for a League of Nations loan, a project Beneš promised to support and to guarantee his country's share of the loan.

In Berlin Seipel found Chancellor Wirth skeptical about Austria's Czechoslovak orientation; he would have much preferred an agreement with Italy. German aid at the time was out of the question because reparations payments, mainly to France, had put a heavy burden on the German economy; a money loan would surely be impounded by France in lieu of tardy reparation payments. Wirth also emphatically rejected any plan for an *Anschluss.* It would do little more than heighten Germany's already tense relations with France. The one solution for Austria's woes was intervention by the league.

Seipel's last stop in Italy was more spectacular than useful. Here too, however, in his talks with the foreign minister, the appeal to the league showed itself as the most promising path to follow. Because this foreign tour was regarded in Vienna as a great success, parliament decided that Seipel should travel to Geneva personally to make the case for a loan. When he did attend the league meeting, the chancellor made a moving speech, depicting conditions of starvation and pointing out that Austria's collapse would produce a power vacuum in the center of Europe no responsible power could fill. That indeed was a frightening prospect at a time when the Bolshevik danger still loomed large. It might be cynical to ascribe the speed with which the loan was approved to this fact, but it undoubtedly played an important role. Four states—Britain, France, Italy, and Czechoslovakia—guaranteed a loan of 650 million gold kronen, of which, however, 130 million were deducted for repayment of previous loans. The remainder was assigned exclusively to cover the budget deficit for the next two years. Austria furthermore had to obligate herself to preserve her independence for at least 20 years, accept league supervision over the manner of disbursement of the loan, and drastically reduce the number of state employees to achieve a more balanced budget. At the same time Austria was exempted from payments of war reparations until at least the year 1967. The so-called Geneva Protocol, containing all these provisions, was signed on October 4, 1922.

Despite the humiliating experience of having a foreign "expert"—the Dutchman Alfred Zimmermann, onetime mayor of Rotterdam—acting as a virtual czar of the Austrian economy and finances, league intervention produced some beneficial results. By the end of 1924 inflation had been brought under control and a new currency, the schilling, was introduced—10,000 paper kronen were exchanged for one schilling. There was also a substantial increase in the gross national product—19 percent between 1924 and 1929—and within that figure industrial production rose by 40 percent. Unemployment, however, remained a critical problem and the number of those without jobs rose from 90,000 in 1924 to 200,000 in 1929.

The straitened conditions led to repeated strikes and protest meetings and these once again served to demonstrate the cleavages existing within postwar Austrian society. "Red" Vienna was the center of most of the labor unrest, often organized by the leftist parties, the Social Democrats, and the Communists; much of the countryside looked on these as harbingers of a Bolshevik revolutionary movement, and the clergy added fuel to the fire. Right-wing organizations proliferated; some were spin-offs from the Greater Germany movement, others autonomous. The so-called Heimwehr (home defense) had originally been organized as an irregular militia guarding the borders of Styria and Carinthia against Yugoslav incursions; it soon began to play a more prominent part in domestic affairs, especially in intimidating, or putting down, socialist initiatives. There was even afoot a plan to create a separate Catholic state under the Bavarian Wittelsbach dynasty, which would have comprised a part of south Germany and western Austria. Amid economic recovery, the political situation continued to be chaotic; even in the rest of Europe leftist initiatives often produced panicky reactions. In Austria these were heightened by the fact that in neighboring Hungary, in March 1919, a soviet government seized power and in the course of the summer earned some significant military victories against invading Czechoslovak armies. Even after that government's collapse in August of that year, the revolutionary danger seemed very much alive and threatening.

In November 1924 Seipel resigned as chancellor and retreated behind the walls of a monastery; he still kept a controlling hand on political developments, however. His successor, Rudolf Ramek, faithfully followed his policies, with only this difference, that he gave a much greater role in his cabinet to provincial representatives. That further sharpened the tension between "Red" Vienna and the "Black" countryside. The two years of Ramek's chancellorship were marked by repeated scandalous bank failures. On the whole, the economic situation, after some initial improvement, took another turn for the worse. In the summer of 1925 the league felt impelled to send two experts to Austria to report on the prospects for recovery. While these experts answered the key question of whether postwar Austria was economically viable in the affirmative, and illustrated that contention with impressive statistics, they also concluded that the country's foreign trade position was untenable. Very high tariff walls erected by neighbor states made exports forbiddingly difficult, yet at the same time Austria was forced to import essentials. Her exports covered only 60 percent of her import needs and thus there was a constant and growing trade deficit. Income from tourism eased the shortfall somewhat, but nowhere enough. Utopian schemes, like a Pan-European union, had wide currency, but there were hardly two people who understood the same thing under that wide concept. The *Anschluss* was only one among the many plans that were being bandied about and that was, if only for political reasons, unacceptable.

The *Anschluss* plan, it should be noted, was by no means exclusively a rightist endeavor. The Social Democrats in both countries had for years favored it on the premise that if the powerful leftist parties in the two countries joined forces, they could form an unconquerable bloc in opposition to capitalist interests and also to those who wanted a union strictly for nationalistic, not to say racist, reasons.

For now, the decision rested entirely with foreign powers, and, given France's commanding position in international councils, prospects were virtually nil. Yet in 1923 France under the premiership of Raymond Poincaré, in a precipitate move to ruin the German economy, undertook military action by invading Germany's most productive region, the Ruhr. The act demonstrated France's military superiority, but it also began a process that led, within a decade, to the rise of a German dictator for whom *Anschluss* with Austria formed one of his central political priorities.

CHAPTER SIXTEEN

Following Seipel's temporary retirement from office, and a brief tenure by a moderate member of the Christian Socialist Party, Johannes Schober once again assumed the chancellorship. It fell to him to deal with two successive emergencies, the first one engineered by the Heimwehr in an attempt to neutralize the electoral strength of Social Democrats by bringing about constitutional change, the other the economic crisis following the crash at the New York Stock Exchange that quickly engulfed much of Europe.

Although known as a "strong man," Schober sought to amend the constitution through patient negotiations with the major parties in order to avoid further polarization in the country's political life. However, the temper of the times militated against gradualism and compromise. Seipel, from his retirement, demanded deeds instead of words in dealing with waxing socialist strength, and two of Austria's neighbors, Italy and Hungary, applied discreet pressure for a more activist course in that direction. Coping with workers' unrest, as the political right saw it, required the strengthening of presidential powers, because as long as legislative authority rested entirely with parliament, every major proposal for change got mired in endless debates. What emerged first was an amendment that provided for the direct popular election of the president every seven years; he would then appoint a cabinet, summon and dismiss parliament, and serve as commander in chief of the armed forces. He could also, with certain limitations, issue emergency decrees. What the Heimwehr, in the forefront of the struggle, was not able to implement were three demands central to the rightist agenda: the replacement of the Vienna city police, permeated with leftist elements, with a national police, the abolition of the provincial status of Vienna, the center of socialist strength, and financial compensation for the Habsburgs.

The serious tenor of the constitutional debate showed how little Austrians understood that the economic downturn and its consequences would soon render these enactments irrelevant. The Great Depression, which hit the United States and Germany with immediate impact, at first seemed to spare Austria. A major bank failed soon after the stock market crash in New York, but that crisis was weathered. Chancellor Schober, on a visit to Germany early in 1930, in fact had reason to boast about the economic strides his country had made since 1922, especially in the industrial sector. Within a few months, however, possibly for no other than psychological reasons, Austria too found itself deep in economic difficulties. Unemployment had been the Achilles' heel of the young republic since its formation, and it had grown dramatically worse when the conditions of the League of Nations loan demanded the dismissal of over one-half of the nation's civil service employees; it now experienced another sharp rise due to the lagging economy. Schober's cabinet proved incapable of dealing with the problem of joblessness. On September 25, 1930, he was forced to resign. His successor was a former minister of war, Karl Vaugoin, an outspoken rightist. Seipel, leaving his monk's cell, became foreign minister. At the same time in Germany too a shift to the right occurred when Heinrich Brüning, a member of the Catholic Center Party, was named chancellor by President Hindenburg. A certain affinity of views between the German and Austrian governments quickly developed. In their economic policies, aiming at a balanced budget at a time of drastic reductions in tax revenues, both tried to curb social services. In the political sphere the time seemed finally to have arrived for a customs union between the two countries.

The plan seemed to receive a boost when French foreign minister Aristide Briand proposed as a partial remedy for the economic crisis the gradual reduction of tariff barriers, which had been the bane of the European economy since the war. In Austria, in this instance, economic and political views were not in consonance. The great majority of the population understood that a customs union with Germany would strengthen the hand of the champions of the Greater Germany idea, and for that reason they were opposed to it. Among foreign powers, not only France but also Italy deemed it unacceptable if the balance of power in Europe was to be preserved. Hungary, hardly a weighty voice in European affairs, but not without influence in Austria, opposed it for fear that her only reliable export item, grain, would be excluded from the German market. The Little Entente states (Czechoslovakia, Romania, Yugoslavia) also spoke unanimously against the Austro-German economic combination. The matter was finally referred to the International Tribunal at the Hague, which, on September 6, 1931, ruled by a single vote that the union was not in harmony with the provisions of the peace treaties. The ruling was more of a blow to the Brüning government in Berlin than to Vaugoin's in Vienna. In the former, Nazi propaganda, emboldened by recent electoral successes, found it easy to denounce Brüning for his impotence in foreign affairs.

When in May 1932 the largest Austrian bank, the Kreditanstalt, with a 70 percent interest in Austrian large industries, failed, the bottom fell out of the financial structure. The government accepted responsibility for the bank's foreign debts, but it could do so only by taking a large foreign loan. To prevent financial collapse from developing into a political crisis, Vaugoin invited the Social Democrats to enter his coalition. The leaders of the party, Karl Renner and Otto Bauer, refused the invitation. They feared with good reason that in a future election they would suffer for making common cause with rightist parties, especially those that were heavily supported by capitalist interests.

By now a new political force had entered the arena and its long-term effect could not be calculated. National Socialism, with a simplistic program that rejected the Versailles peace and declared war on Jews as a people it alternately identified with both rapacious capitalism and revolutionary marxism, captured the imagination of many extreme rightist elements. Its glorification of the Aryan race, of which Germans were presumably the purest representatives, had an appeal to many Austrians who could not understand why they were separated from their German brethren when the mission of making the German race master of Europe beckoned to them. The party leader, Adolf Hitler, wielded a hypnotic personality and incendiary oratory that also played a part. The rapid rise of a militant Nazi party in Austria placed before the political right a difficult choice. The central, Catholic, core of it did not favor the *Anschluss* because it did not wish to see Austria become a province of a Prussian-dominated Greater Germany. The anti-Catholic bias of the Nazis was also a weighty factor. In these circumstances, and with the economic situation showing no sign of improvement, after the brief tenure by a stop-gap cabinet, on May 30, 1932, Engelbert Dollfuss, minister of agriculture in the previous government, was named premier. A shrewd and socially well-placed politician, he entered office without a clear program. He had risen to political maturity in circles that cherished the Greater German idea, but he was personally opposed to an *Anschluss.* Between the alternatives of excluding from his cabinet all partisans of a union with Germany or including them in the hope of controlling them, he chose the latter. In the given situation, opportunism seemed in fact the safest course to follow. The catastrophic financial situation made another League of Nations bailout imperative and Dollfuss did not want to jeopardize its chances by internal political disorder. A special committee in the league was at the time of his appointment discussing the conditions under which a new loan would be made. The British and French wished to demand another 20-year commitment by Austria to honor her obligations under the peace treaty, that is, to preserve her independence. This demand was incorporated in the final set of conditions for granting Austria a loan of 300 million schillings.

Dollfuss was ready to accept that condition (which happened to coincide with his own preference) but Austrian (as well as German) Nazis conducted vehement propaganda against it, branding its acceptance treason. The Heimwehr was of two minds: by no means unanimously pro-*Anschluss,* it also realized that the badly needed league loan would be forthcoming only if any plan for union with Germany was taken off the agenda; at the same time, it hoped that if it tipped the balance in favor of rejecting the loan, the government would fall and, in alliance with the Nazis, the Heimwehr could earn a great electoral victory. In the end it was Seipel who prevailed on the government to ratify the loan agreement.

It did, but this did not resolve the political crisis. The shift to the right was becoming so pronounced that there could be no question of a coalition government, containing diverse, let alone opposing, political forces. Any pro-German orientation would give Austrian Nazis, and the *Anschluss* movement, a powerful boost. Cooperation with the left was unthinkable. The situation became even more perilous, although also better defined, when, on January 30, 1933, President Hindenburg named Adolf Hitler, leader of the German National Socialist Party, chancellor.

Austrian Nazis greeted the appointment with explosive enthusiasm, organized torch parades and demanded immediate elections. Dollfuss was aware that while the Nazis could not win in the elections outright, they could, as the Heimwehr did at present, upset the balance in parliament and the Christian Socialists, who had been the mainstay of the political right, would have to contend with a powerful competitor.

In order to ingratiate himself with the Heimwehr, Dollfuss periodically allowed it to raid socialist strongholds; its units would come to the capital by train for just such a purpose. Much as he feared the Nazis, the Social Democrats remained for Dollfuss the main enemy. In a radio address early in March 1933 he declared that National Socialism must not be opposed with help from the left; his party had to adopt such features of the Nazi program as were compatible with Austrian interests. Parliamentarianism, with its endless rhetorical debates, became an impediment to the course Dollfuss proposed to follow. When on March 4, during one of these debates, the president of parliament and two of his deputies resigned in exhaustion and disgust, Dollfuss declared that parliament had proved its incapacity for action, and, referring to a law dating from Habsburg times, announced its dissolution. He subsequently attempted to emasculate the Socialists by proposing to place their militia, the Schutzbund, the leftist counterpart of the Heimwehr, outside the law. In this he failed, but at the end of April he had the entire leadership of the other workers' party, the Communist, and several hundred of its members, arrested.

Domestic measures alone could not neutralize Nazi influence, however. At Easter in 1933, Dollfuss traveled to Rome and there extracted a promise from Mussolini that Italy would vouch with all its national strength for the preservation of Austrian independence (i.e., would prevent an *Anschluss*). Dollfuss on his part pledged to introduce, unless leftist forces raised insurmountable difficulties, a fascist type of corporative state into Austria.

Proceeding against leftist forces was not an easy matter though and could be accomplished only by forging closer ties with the Nazis, the lesser of the two evils. The Nazis, aware of this, placed an ever higher price on their cooperation. One of their representatives, sent from the Saarland on a special mission, came to Vienna demanding that some key portfolios in the cabinet be given to Austrian Nazis. Dollfuss was only too well aware that such appointments would produce a steady drift toward an *Anschluss,* and he refused. With no agreement in sight, Nazi terror and acts of sabotage directed from Germany multiplied; a breakdown of internal order became more threatening with each passing day. In consultation with Mussolini, whom he visited again in August at Il Duce's summer home in Riccione, Dollfuss finally decided on a three-step program: a reform of the constitution to replace parliamentarianism with a virtual dictatorship, the merging of all political parties into a single Fatherland Front, and the destruction of socialist strength.

The political right was less than enthusiastic about this plan and the alliance between the ruling Christian Socialists and the Heimwehr became strained. The former cherished traditional bourgeois values and a respect for constitutional forms; the latter was by now little more than a collection of rowdies, prepared to take any step to advance its program. Dollfuss had to move fast before the cleavage opened too wide, and so he did. On September 21 he reorganized his cabinet, making a Heimwehr stalwart deputy chancellor, in defiance of the practice that the party with a majority in parliament controlled the government. At the same time, in a bid for foreign support, he conducted intensive negotiations with Italian and Hungarian statesmen. The resulting Rome Protocols (signed on March 18, 1934) provided for close cooperation among the three states, intensifying trade relations, but above all the preservation of Austrian independence. That last undertaking, however, held any chance of success only if the German Nazis discontinued their subversive activities and allowed Austria to follow its own, pronouncedly rightist, course. Dollfuss still hoped such restraint was possible and he sent his minister of education, Kurt Schuschnigg, to Germany to extract a promise to this effect from the führer. Schuschnigg was seen only by Hitler's deputy, Rudolf Hess, who voiced the familiar, unacceptable demands. The approach led nowhere but it showed that Dollfuss felt less than secure in the Italian guarantee and would have preferred a modus vivendi with Germany if only Austrian independence could be preserved.

Action against the Social Democrats could not be delayed indefinitely, however. The Heimwehr was increasing its provocations, illegal searches of socialist premises multiplied. The showdown came on February 12, 1934. The first clash between the Social Democrats and official authorities occurred in Linz. At dawn police carried out a "surprise" raid on party headquarters; the Socialists had had advance warning and fired on the police. When news reached Vienna of the siege of the headquarters in Linz, the workers in the central electrical power plant went on strike in protest. By noon there was no electrical power in the capital and streetcars stopped running.

If it came to an armed struggle, the Social Democrats had numbers on their side; the authorities weaponry and organization. Socialist leaders, frightened by the prospect of wholesale violence, decided against ordering masses of workers into the streets and chose to concentrate on purely defensive action in workers' residential quarters on the peripheries of the city. Here blocs of buildings were surrounded by government forces who cared little whether resistance was offensive or defensive; they deployed artillery and concentrated their fire against isolated foci of socialist strength while in the center of Vienna life flowed peacefully in its accustomed manner. By nightfall most bastions of resistance were overcome (although in some spots resistance continued for days longer), and the Social Democrats as a political force ceased to exist.

Dollfuss lost no time in giving the quasi-military victory a political dimension. The Social Democratic Party was dissolved, as were trade unions, and the party's deputies were deprived of their mandates. Nine leaders of the Schutzbund were placed before a military tribunal, condemned, and hanged.

Three months later the Dollfuss government proclaimed a new constitution for Austria. Couched in religious phraseology, it piously declared that sovereignty stemmed from "the will of an all-powerful God"; and instead of the Republic of Austria, the country was titled the "Austrian Federal State." The constitution liquidated political parties and parliament and foreswore parliamentary elections.

The sole authorized "party" was the Fatherland Front. The new constitution also provided that presidents would henceforth be chosen by the heads of the provinces; for the time being the mandate of President Wilhelm Miklas, elected in 1928, remained in effect.

Although the destruction of the political left pleased Mussolini and Hitler alike, the two men were poles apart on the question of Austria's position as an independent state. On June 14, 1934 they met in Venice for frank discussions. They touched on several issues, but Austria stood at the center of the talks. Hitler objected to the repressive measures Vienna was adopting toward Austrian Nazis and demanded immediate elections. Mussolini categorically rejected this request and called for an end to outside pressures on internal Austrian politics. He warned that continued Nazi interference would fatally vitiate German-Italian relations.

Austrian Nazis held their hand while these talks were in progress, but the news of their failure prompted new terrorist acts on their part. An elaborate though hastily prepared plan for a coup envisioned the forcible removal of the current government and the installation of Anton Rintelen, one-time provincial head of Styria and currently Austrian ambassador in Rome, as the new chancellor. In the German federal state of Bavaria an Austrian Legion stood ready for armed intervention. According to the original plan, a specially selected detachment of the Austrian SS would invade the chancellor's palace when the cabinet was in session, arrest all those present, and force Dollfuss to sign his office over to Rintelen. The conspirators chose for their action the noon hour when the change of the guard took place and both wings of the gate stood open. As it happened, by that time the cabinet session had ended and Dollfuss was alone in his office. The special detachment, finding the cabinet room empty, betook itself to the chancellor's office. Dollfuss, hearing the commotion, tried to slip away but was intercepted and one member of the detachment, despite orders against the use of force, shot him twice. The wounds were not fatal; they were bandaged. Dollfuss regained consciousness, but when confronted with the demand that he name Rintelen his successor, he refused. For three and a half hours he bled and at 3:45 P.M. he expired.

The coup was doomed, however. Pro-Nazi sympathies, sporadically present throughout the bureaucracy, were not shared in the higher echelons, let alone by the police. When news of the deed reached the offices of the ministers, who only a short time earlier had been conferring with Dollfuss, the education minister, Schuschnigg, took matters into his own hands. President Miklas forbade any concessions to the Nazis. Police surrounded the chancellor's palace and by evening the army joined the police units. The perpetrators were all arrested.

Miklas named Schuschnigg, only 34 years old at the time, chancellor. Where the Nazi threat was concerned, Schuschnigg was in a strong position because the assassination had produced an outrage both in Austria and abroad, and the recognition that the true villains were to be found in Germany placed Hitler in an awkward, defensive position. Austrian Nazis on their part could hope for little internal support. And so Hitler switched from the existing plan, which envisioned a violent overthrow of the Austrian regime, to one aiming at slow, patient infiltration. This plan had a strong advocate in Franz von Papen, a former chancellor of Germany, who, at Hitler's almost humble entreaties, had accepted appointment as the Third Reich's ambassador to Vienna. He tied his acceptance to the condition that the German Nazi Party terminate all ties to Austrian Nazis. Indeed in the next year the White Stockings, as the latter were called were a practically invisible presence on the Austrian political scene.

Still, during the four years in which Schuschnigg was chancellor, all domestic issues and all constitutional questions were in effect subordinated to the question of how, if at all, Austria could escape the compelling political pull of Nazi Germany. Schuschnigg was criticized in hindsight for not availing himself of the opportunity of restoring genuine parliamentary democracy, but, also in hindsight, it may be said that doing so would almost certainly have weakened rather than strengthened Austria's position vis-à-vis her powerful neighbor. It would have fragmented political forces and given advantage to Nazi propaganda, which was much more powerful and incendiary that those of other parties. The one hope was that foreign powers would at last gird up their loins and serve notice on Hitler that the extinction of a sovereign European state (an event that had not taken place since the time of Napoleon) would invite vigorous countermeasures. Indeed in January 1935 Mussolini and French foreign minister Pierre Laval agreed in Rome on several vital points, the key one being that they would resist any outside attempt to vitiate Austrian independence. In March France concluded a defensive alliance with the Soviet Union, to which Czechoslovakia, bordering on Austria, added her signature.

But earlier in the year, in January, the plebiscite in the Saar region provided for by the Treaty of Versailles, had taken place and produced a resounding vote for union with Germany. This gave heart to Germans who hoped and campaigned for a union of all those of German blood. Hitler nevertheless decided to bide his time. Papen had ever since his appointment been working on a draft treaty between Austria and Germany; he kept in touch with Schuschnigg, who set as an essential condition an official German renunciation of any intention of extinguishing Austria's independence. Hitler, confident that time was on his side, agreed. The result was a bilateral agreement concluded in July 1936, which stated that the role and activities of the Nazi Party in each state were an internal matter. Both states abjured any interference in the internal affairs of the other and recognized each other's independence. To this last provision Italy and Hungary also adhered, and, together with Austria, committed themselves to peaceful relations in the Danubian region. Austrian independence for now seemed assured.

CHAPTER SEVENTEEN

In the course of 1937 Austria's economic condition showed marked improvement, unemployment fell significantly and political affairs benefited from the practical demobilization of the Heimwehr, until then a constant source of trouble. Other circumstances however boded ill for the future. Despite official assurances that Austria would remain a sovereign state, the forces in the service of Nazi Germany grew stronger and more assertive. In the 1936 treaty with Germany Schuschnigg had undertaken to ease sanctions against Austrian Nazis and to amnesty many who had been imprisoned; he kept some of these promises but violated others and his hostility to National Socialists wherever they were found was unmistakable. He was playing with fire because international support for Austrian independence had dwindled to the vanishing point. The western powers showed little interest, and Mussolini had, in November 1936, soon after the victorious conclusion of his Ethiopian campaign in which Germany alone among the great powers maintained a correct attitude, sent his foreign minister Galeazzo Ciano to Berlin to conclude with Germany an agreement pledging to coordinate the foreign policies of the two powers. (Il Duce proudly proclaimed that the agreement would serve as the axis around which European diplomacy turned; the parties to it were thenceforth referred to as the Axis Powers.) There remained little hope that Mussolini would oppose, as he did in 1934, a German move against Austria. Hitler had scored another foreign policy triumph in March 1936, when he sent troops into the Rhineland, which by the provisions of the Versailles treaty was to remain demilitarized forever. Gestures of disapproval by league members were so feeble, they convinced Hitler that none of the great powers was able, or willing, to preserve the status quo. In November 1937 Lord Halifax, as Prime Minister Chamberlain's personal emissary, visited Hitler at his mountain retreat in Berchtesgaden. He made it quite explicit that Great Britain would not oppose territorial changes in east Europe as long as these were accomplished without resort to force. If this was Britain's position, the French could scarcely assume a different one.

Within Germany Field Marshal Göring, in charge of the four-year economic plan, resolutely argued for the *Anschluss*. A secret memorandum prepared by his office pointed out that the annexation of Austria would increase Germany's population by 10 percent, making it, outside of Russia, the most populous country in Europe with 75 million inhabitants. In territory it would outstrip France and be the largest country in Europe west of Russia. Austria's mineral resources and timber would add badly needed raw materials to the German economy.

However, there were others in high position, both in government and the military in Germany, who opposed Hitler's adventurous foreign policy, especially his plans for a war of conquest, which he had laid before a select audience at a secret conference in November 1937. Hitler had little patience with such opposition; within four months he removed the nay-sayers and installed men who were either totally subservient to him or shared his exalted vision of German destiny. His ambassador in Vienna, Franz von Papen, was a level-headed man, but no less ready to promote the plan for a Greater Germany than Hitler's domestic followers were. Within Austria a so-called Committee of Seven, authorized by Schuschnigg and headed by the pro-Nazi attorney Arthur Seyss-Inquart, instead of carrying out its assigned task of integrating the Nazi Party of Austria into the Fatherland Front, the only authorized political grouping, labored to fortify the position of the Nazis and prepare the ground for annexation by Germany.

Hitler was growing impatient with the slow progress of these efforts. He blamed Papen for not being forceful enough and dismissed him. Papen made a last attempt to salvage his reputation and arranged a personal meeting between the führer and Schuschnigg, with a view of removing misunderstandings and finding common ground. The meeting took place at Hitler's retreat in Berchtesgaden in February 1938 and resulted in Schuschnigg's total humiliation and submission. The terms of the "draft agreement" handed to him went far beyond the provisions of the 1936 agreement, demanding that the Austrian government recognize National Socialism as compatible with Austrian conditions and that measures directed against its members would accordingly cease and that Seyss-Inquart be named interior minister in charge of internal security and three other Nazi sympathizers be appointed ministers of defense, press chief, and minister of finance, respectively.

Schuschnigg could not help knowing that acceptance of these terms would mean turning the instruments of power over to men who would receive their instructions from Berlin and would make Austria into a Nazi state. But when Hitler crudely intimated that in case of refusal he would take military measures, Schuschnigg caved in. Upon his return home he pondered the means of frustrating Hitler's designs. The führer was fairly explicit concerning those designs in a speech on February 20, celebrating with a three-week delay the anniversary of his assumption of the chancellorship, when he emotionally reminded his audience that 10 million Germans living in countries bordering the Reich were deprived of the opportunity of joining the body of Germandom. Nazis inside Austria responded with turbulent demonstrations, which Seyss-Inquart as interior minister did nothing to stop. Schuschnigg in the vain hope that the voice of the majority, when pitted against the extremists, would discourage Hitler from carrying out his plan, scheduled a national referendum for February 13. The question put to the voters practically demanded the answer Schuschnigg wanted: "Are you for a free and German, independent and social, Christian and united Austria, for peace and work, for the equality of all those who affirm themselves for the people and for the Fatherland?" There was space for only a "yes" answer on the ballot.

It was the last straw for Hitler. He would not, as he knew he could not, afford to let the election produce its predictable result. There was no need for him to consult the western powers, but he sent a special emissary to Mussolini, begging him not to interfere. Il Duce, obviously reluctant, nevertheless gave his consent to the extinction of Austrian independence. Hitler through Göring then sent a demand to Vienna that Schuschnigg resign and Seyss-Inquart be appointed chancellor. Schuschnigg did resign but President Miklas refused the other demand. When he finally yielded, at 11 o'clock in the evening of the 12th, German troops had already crossed the Austrian border. Göring instructed Seyss-Inquart to send him a telegram asking for such intervention to restore internal order in Austria. When no such telegram arrived, Göring made one up himself.

The news of the invasion was accompanied by assurances that German troops would be withdrawn as soon as Seyss-Inquart was installed as chancellor, and there is evidence that Hitler did not in fact intend an immediate annexation. But the ecstatic reception accorded to the troops and then to him, and the lack of any countermeasures on the part of the great powers convinced him that an outright *Anschluss* entailed no risks. In an almost ludicrous bow to democratic procedure, he staged a referendum of his own on April 10; 99 percent of those who went to the polls approved Austria's absorption in Germany.

By now forceful measures had been taken to eliminate all opposition to union with Germany and render harmless those who were likely to cling to the Austrian ideal, or who opposed Nazism on political or religious grounds. A delegation headed by Gestapo chief Heinrich Himmler arrived soon after the *Anschluss* to direct the purges; the adherents of Dollfuss and Schuschnigg were removed, Communists, Socialists, and trade union representatives were arrested wholesale; altogether about 65,000 persons were sent to concentration camps. The persecution of Jews began at once and reached new heights in November when, after the assassination by a Polish Jew of a German embassy official in Paris, pogroms swept Germany, synagogues were vandalized, and thousands of Jews were arrested on trumped-up charges or no charges at all.

Administratively, Austria was now the Ostmark of Germany, without a federal status, divided into Gaus, organizational units of the National Socialist Party. Ancient constituent provinces, like Vorarlberg and Burgenland, lost their autonomy and were absorbed into the Reich. The entire thrust of the reorganization was to extinguish traditional Austrian loyalties and instill in the population a sense of Germanness founded on racial concepts. Superficially the effort met with general approval and most Austrians were ready to think of themselves as members of the German blood community. But a secret Gestapo report issued for internal consumption presented a less favorable picture. By its estimations only about 15 percent of the population could be depended on actively to support the Nazis; another 30 percent were opportunistic adherents for political or economic reasons; 35 to 40 percent were leftists, or active Catholics, regarded as enemies of the system.

These numbers were, however, without practical significance. In 1938 Nazism in German lands appeared to be the wave of the future and it swept everything before it. The racial argument had a strong appeal, and the union with Germany ended the postwar position of Austria as a small "remnant" of a once powerful empire. Even the Catholic Church, deeply entrenched in the Austrian countryside, was unable to counteract the appeal of Nazism. Hitler, himself a Catholic, would not tolerate the spiritual appeal of a mystery religion to supersede Nazi ideology. Pope Pius XI demonstrated his unfriendliness to the new German regime when he pointedly left Rome during a visit by Hitler in May 1938, so as not to have to accord to him the reception usually given to visiting heads of state.

In Austria itself, Cardinal Innitzer had at first shown himself friendly to Nazis and sought to facilitate their acceptance; but when the Reich regime proved hos-

Adolf Hitler standing by Dr. Seyss-Inquart, the last chancellor of Austria after Hitler's speech in the Heldenplatz, Vienna, which announced that Germany would be taking over Austria *(Hulton/Archive)*

tile to Catholics and Catholic institutions, he abruptly discontinued negotiations aimed at a conciliation between church and government, and condemned the loyalty declaration the Nazi government demanded, which a number of bishops were ready to sign. Discriminatory measures against the church soon followed: the theological faculties of the Salzburg and Innsbruck universities were closed down, as were lower level schools, day care centers, and similar institutions run by the Catholic Church; many of these were transformed into National Socialist student centers. While Nazism exerted its strongest appeal to youth, many young people remained loyal to their church. On October 7, 1938, the Catholic Church held its traditional commemoration of the 1751 naval victory over the Turks. Over 9,000 youths of school age responded, some carrying signs reading, "Our Führer Is Christ," an apparent defiance of Hitler; when Nazi sympathizers who had planted themselves in the crowd tried to disrupt the celebration, they were chased away. In a counterdemonstration that evening about a hundred members of the Hitler Jugend marched to Cardinal Innitzer's palace and smashed most of its windows. The Nazi Party branded Innitzer a traitor and organized a mass protest against his renunciation of his earlier statements of loyalty to the Nazis. From then on the persecution and arrest of Catholic priests and functionaries became commonplace. In the long run, however, most Catholic institutions, even convents and monasteries, found accommodation with the system and some even proved willing participators in Nazism's campaign against the Jews.

After the *Anschluss,* Seyss-Inquart's title changed from chancellor to Reich commissioner; on May 1, 1939, even that title was abolished. After a stint in occupied Poland in the fall of 1939, Seyss-Inquart was named, following the conquest of the Netherlands in the spring of 1940, Reich commissioner for Holland. As such he earned the sincere hatred of Dutchmen, though it could be argued that given the oppressive nature of the Nazi regime in occupied territories, anyone holding that title would have elicited similar emotions. (Seyss-Inquart was tried as a major war criminal at Nuremberg after the war, condemned, and hanged.)

The incorporation of Austria with all her material and financial assets proved a boon for German national wealth. The 78,000 kilograms of gold that formed the backing for the nation's currency passed into the possession of the Reichsbank, as did an additional 12,000 kilos owned by individuals. Private financial institutions that held major stakes in industrial complexes were absorbed into the German banking system. Factories, plants, department stores, and other assets owned by Jews, their value estimated at 10 billion marks, were simply confiscated, with no compensation offered. Also confiscated were Austria's historic art treasures, including the crown of the Holy Roman Emperor, which was transferred to Nuremberg. From the Vienna Museum of Fine Arts, 55,000 paintings of world fame ended up in Germany.

All this wealth temporarily relieved the problem of the chronic deficits with which the German treasury had been burdened since the introduction of the four-year plan. The chief task of that plan, with Göring at its helm, was to gear up the economy to the requirements of war. In the führer's estimation, as explained at the secret conference in November 1937, that war had to come not later than 1943, the time when German rearmament would be at its peak. This plan, as we have seen, met with critical opposition by a number of men in Hitler's entourage who harkened back to the anti-German coalition in the Great War and feared that a similar coalition would be formed and inflict upon Germany another devastating defeat.

In the event, war came four years *before* Hitler's putative deadline, and it is still being argued whether this was due to his pathological impatience (he never ceased lamenting the fact that he came to power only in his middle years, thus leaving him insufficient time to accomplish his momentous plans for Germany), to the craven appeasement of the western powers, especially Great Britain, or to objective historical circumstances to which Hitler contributed only a hysterical mood that soon gripped Germans inside and outside the Reich. It was ironic that the war eventually broke out over a quarrel with Poland, the country with which Hitler actually desired friendly relations, though he deemed such relations impossible until his minimal demands, the reintegration of the all-German city of Danzig into the Reich and the granting of a "corridor across the Corridor," had been met. The Poles, feeling protected by a guarantee of their "independence," issued by Britain and France, refused *any* concession, and Hitler, feeling confident that the effete democracies would not fight, launched his campaign against Poland on September 1, 1939.

With the outbreak of war Austria was caught up in a broad European struggle that lasted nearly six years. Intentionally or otherwise, Austrians of military age were called up not into native units but haphazardly into companies, divisions, and armies composed of German-speaking soldiers from all over the Third Reich, including the Sudetenland, annexed in October 1938, the Memel territory wrested from Lithuania in April 1939, and Danzig, joined to the Reich the day war broke out. There were no celebrations, as there had been in 1914, to greet this new struggle; too many Austrians alive still remembered the horrors of the first war; only after the rapid conquest of France in the summer of 1940 were there signs of genuine enthusiasm for the triumph of German arms.

Italy had an offensive-defensive military alliance with Germany (dating from May 1939) but failed to honor it. Hitler did not press the matter and in fact exhibited goodwill toward Italy when, on October 21 of that year, he entered into a convention aimed at solving, at least temporarily, the vexing question of South Tyrol. According to the terms of the agreement German speakers in the province had to declare within a stated period whether they wished to be considered Italian or German citizens. If they opted for the latter, they had to move from the South Tyrol to Germany and become citizens of the Reich; if they opted for Italy, they had to assume Italian citizenship, and as such lose their minority rights. Although choosing Germany involved pulling up stakes and starting a new existence in a foreign land, as well as being subject to the military draft, 83 percent of the voters made that choice. In actual numbers that meant 247,000; the resettlement of that many proved impracticable, and by 1943 only 75,000 had made the move.

Meanwhile the territory of what used to be Austria was enlarged when, after Yugoslavia's defeat by Germany in April 1941, large parts of Slovenia, Austrian until 1918, were rejoined to the provinces of Styria and Carinthia. Two months later the Wehrmacht disgorged its battle-hardened divisions into the vast spaces of Russia in an attempt to subdue the last continental power still free of German domination. By the sober calculation of experts on the German and the Allied side the Soviet forces would collapse under the weight of the assault in weeks or perhaps months. The predictions appeared accurate in the opening phases of the battle, but after Soviet forces recovered from the first shock of the assault, the rugged terrain, the extremes of temperature, the distances without boundaries, and the terror Stalin imposed on his fighting forces proved obstacles that the German soldier, to whom, as Hitler proudly boasted, nothing was impossible, could not overcome. The first winter of the campaign sapped the Wehrmacht of its preponderant strength, and, although it resumed the offensive the following summer, by then the Red Army had become a formidable foe. After the epic battle of Stalingrad in the winter of 1942–43 prospects of a German victory faded to near zero. The initiative passed to the Allied powers and German armies found themselves in steady retreat.

Stalin took the position early on that all of Hitler's conquests were illegal and had to be restored to their rightful owners after the war; this position applied to Austria, too. When the foreign ministers of the three powers in the Grand Alliance met in late October 1943, they issued a declaration stating, among other things, that the position of Austria as an independent state must be restored. They added at the same time that the Austrian people had to take responsibility for the enormities inflicted on Europe by Nazi Germany, though they could partially redeem themselves by taking an active part in their own liberation. When the leaders of the three Allied powers—the United States, Soviet Union, and Great Britain—met at Yalta in February 1945, they decided that Austria, as well as Germany, from whom the former would be separated, should be placed under military occupation by the Allied powers, to whose numbers France was now added.

By the time the advancing Red Army reached the Austrian border in April 1945, an effective resistance to Nazi rule in that country had been organized and it frustrated German plans to defend Vienna, street by street, building by building, to the end. The rapid enveloping advance of Soviet forces even prevented the mass withdrawal of the Nazi defenders and 130,000 German troops were taken prisoner. By April 14 Vienna was liberated; three weeks later German resistance on all fronts collapsed and the most devastating war in human history came to an end.

CHAPTER EIGHTEEN

At the end of the Second World War the Allied powers held all of Austria under military occupation. As to its political future, apart from the position taken earlier that Austria was a liberated country, they had no clearly stated program. In the last phases of the war Churchill and Stalin mooted the possibility of combining Austria and Bavaria into a separate state, with Catholicism the bond but, assuming even that this was not one of Churchill's fanciful plans, there was such evident lack of enthusiasm in either state for such a union, and political solutions based on religion were so out of vogue, that the plan never received serious consideration. What the victorious powers did decide was that, although Austria would remain an occupied country (assumedly to liquidate the remnants of nazism), unlike Germany, she would be allowed to hold free elections and choose her own government. These provisions were incorporated in a four-power agreement of July 1945 (signed by the United States, Britain, France, and the Soviet Union); a follow-up compact of July 1946 finalized the boundaries of the zones of occupation. The French zone included the Vorarlberg and western Tyrol, the British eastern Tyrol, Styria, and Carinthia, the American Salzburg and Upper Austria except for the Mühlviertel, the latter being added to the Soviet zone of Lower Austria and the Burgenland. Each power also had an occupation zone in the capital city of Vienna, inside the Soviet zone. Until the country's political life was organized, it would be governed by a four-power council; that council held its first session on September 11, 1945.

Even while the war was still in progress but Austria was already liberated, political parties began to be formed. During the past seven year the monopoly of the National Socialist Party had silenced all competing political voices and leftist parties had been decimated seemingly beyond recovery. The most politically weighty party in the first republic, the Christian Socialist, had retained much of its personnel and appeal, but again, its designation as a party of religious orientation was a handicap. It reemerged as the Österreichische Volkspartei (ÖVP), the Austrian People's Party; some of its mainly elderly leaders attempted to shape the party program according to Christian principles, but this elicited little support from the rank and file. Vying in popularity with the ÖVP was the Socialistische Partei Österreichs (SPÖ). Thus the split so disastrously evident in the first republic, between the political left, well-entrenched in Vienna and other cities, and Catholic conservatism, dominant in the countryside, continued, though in a much more muted version; the horrors of the long war had tamed political passions. There emerged also a tiny Communist Party. Realizing its minuscule size, it proposed to merge with the SPÖ, but it was rebuffed. The Socialists on their part sought to find some manner of cooperation with the Catholic Church; these attempts were met, not with outright rejection, but with a ban by the church on any political activity by the clergy.

As early as April 1945 the first government was formed with Karl Renner of the SPÖ as chancellor; the SPÖ and the ÖVP each held nine portfolios, the Communist Party (KPÖ) seven, and there were three ministers with no party affiliation. In its first pronouncement the government announced the restoration of the Austrian republic in the spirit of the constitution of 1920. The cabinet's composition received the approval of the Soviet government; the Western powers however had serious reservations. They questioned the rationale for the large Communist representation, and especially the fact that the crucial interior ministry was held by a Communist (Franz Henner) who was thus in charge of the police forces. Communists also had great and often aggressive influence in cultural matters. Given the fact that in Communist practice information often took the form of indoctrination, such dominance provided strong propagandistic opportunities.

The new government maintained its seat in the Soviet zone of Vienna, which made it uncertain whether it would be able to extend its authority over the parts of the country occupied by the Western powers. The latter provinces were not inimical to the Renner government, but they demanded a broadening of its base. In response, at a conference in Vienna on September 25, 1945, the government was enlarged and reorganized. Although the Communists still held a disproportionate number of portfolios (10 against 13 for the ÖVP, 12 for the SPÖ, and four without party affiliation), no major protest was registered. On November 25 general elections took place for both a national parliament and provincial legislatures. (Former members of the National Socialist Party, and of the SS and the SD, were excluded from the voting rolls). The ÖVP, with 85 seats, gained an absolute majority. The Socialists had 76 and the Communists four. The chancellorship passed from Renner to the People's Party's Leopold Figl. Although the constitution required national elections for choosing the president of the republic, in order to save the expenses of still another election, the parliament on December 20 chose Karl Renner for the post.

Austria thus had a distinctly favorable position compared with Germany. In the latter country the four-power Kommandatura of the occupying powers was the source of all authority and Germans had no voice in making the laws that governed them. Austrians could legislate for themselves and, although the occupying powers had the right to veto specific pieces of legislation, they could do so only unanimously, something which, given the growing tension between the Soviet Union and the Western powers, was an unlikely prospect.

In the internal political sphere a sensitive yet pressing question was the treatment accorded to former National Socialists. Austria had been classified as a victim of Germany, yet several hundred thousand Austrians had been members of the Nazi Party, many had served the Berlin regime loyally and often beyond the call of duty. Two Austrians, Seyss-Inquart and Gestapo chief Ernst Kaltenbrunner, had been among the major war criminals tried at Nuremberg; both were found guilty of crimes against humanity and hanged. On July 25, 1946, parliament passed a comprehensive "National Socialism Act," one that the government accepted only after it had been made more stringent. Over half a million persons were affected by the law, most of them in losing their jobs or being forced into early retirement. The government then softened its stand by resolving that membership in the Nazi Party did not in itself constitute a criminal act; categories were set up as to the degree to which the person was compromised. No entirely fair enforcement of the law was possible. Several amnesties followed, each exempting more and more persons from the provisions of the law. (It should also be noted that a number of persons guilty of outright war crimes, independently of whether or not they were members of the party, such as the perpetrators of the horrific Eisenerz massacre in April 1945, were tried by Allied military tribunals and many death sentences were handed down.)

A question of international character left over from the First World War was raised again after the second: the fate of South Tyrol. The majority of its population was German and Austrians were unreconciled to its loss. It will be remembered that Hitler had sought to mitigate the problem by an interstate agreement whereby inhabitants of the province could opt for German citizenship, in which case they eventually had to move to Germany. Some 180,000 persons who had made that choice were still in Italy when the war ended. With Austria a victim state and Italy a defeated state, Austrian desiderata were supposed to be the preferred ones. They were negated, however, by the fact that the Yugoslavs, unequivocally victims and victors, took possession of territories in northeastern Italy, and additional cessions at the expense of Italy were not viewed sympathetically by the Allies. It must also be considered that whereas Germans in the areas joined to Yugoslavia suffered persecutions, discriminations, expulsions, and worse, Germans in the South Tyrol were treated with respect, could use their native tongue in official intercourse, and could educate their children in German. And so, by a consensus among the allies, South Tyrol remained with Italy.

Internally, while the coalition government established in 1945 at first worked smoothly, growing strains appeared in time between the Communists on the one hand and the two major parties, the ÖVP and the SPÖ, on the other. It was a common feature in the internal politics of Soviet satellite countries in which Communists were (with the one exception of Czechoslovakia) a small minority party that they enjoyed the active support of Soviet occupying forces, and oppositionist politicians understood the risks of challenging that alliance. In Austria the situation was rendered more complex by the fact that while the country was under four-power occupation, the government sat in the Soviet zone and was subject at the very least to psychological pressure. The ÖVP and the SPÖ did not intend that such pressure should prove decisive in major matters. The legislation of July 1947, which nationalized major banks and industries, although part of the Communist program, generally had the support of all parties. The last act of cooperation among the major parties occurred shortly after the nationalization, when all three agreed on the acceptance of Marshall aid. The offer by the United

States to render economic help to the war-torn countries of Europe with practically no strings attached was a revolutionary novelty; notwithstanding its political motive of depriving the Communists of the opportunity of benefiting from the conditions of misery and want produced by the war, it was nevertheless an act of generous and farsighted statesmanship. Austrians well remembered the humiliating process of obtaining a *loan* from the League of Nations after the First World War, and how foreign appointees supervised every step of fulfillment. Now they were being offered a *grant,* and from a country with which they had been at war only two years earlier. The Marshall Plan, however, also demonstrated the commanding economic position of the United States, and it was precisely for that reason that Stalin rejected it, not only for the Soviet Union but for East European satellites as well. His veto apparently did not apply to Austria, because the KPÖ, which routinely got its political directives from Moscow, joined the other parties in voting for acceptance. But afterward a growing rift developed between the KPÖ and the other two and, in November 1947, the Communists left the coalition over a minor disagreement.

The four-power military occupation weighed heavily on Austria, both in an economic and a psychological sense. It could be ended only by concluding a peace treaty with the victorious Allies, and the Western powers were not opposed to one, but Stalin took the position that an Austrian and a German treaty must be made simultaneously. While this position was by no means inflexible, every time the question of a separate peace with Austria came up, especially at successive meetings of the foreign ministers' council, new difficulties arose. The principal and most abiding one was the disposition of German assets within Austria. The Soviets, in compensation for the staggering losses they had suffered in the war, had gained the right to German assets in countries that Germany had occupied, and they proved rapacious in validating these claims in Hungary, Romania, Poland, and even in the part of Germany under their control. Austria, under four-power occupation, was a special case. Until 1948 Yugoslav territorial demands on Austria, supported by the Soviet Union, also proved a stumbling block to a peace treaty. After the rift between the Soviet Union and Yugoslavia in 1948, this difficulty seemed to be cleared away, but differences between East and West, especially about the future of Germany, continued to hamper any substantive agreement. Finally, a Brazilian motion in the United Nations in December 1952, prompted by the United States, called for an end to the four-power occupation of Austria. In order to allay Soviet concern that, as an independent state, Austria might join a hostile military bloc, Moscow was assured by an Indian intercession of Austria's determination to be permanently neutral. With Germany's future still clouded, however, and efforts under way to integrate West Germany into NATO, the connection between the German and the Austrian peace treaties again became crucial in the Soviet view. Also, Stalin needed a pretext to maintain a large military force in Hungary to ensure political control there, and his only superficially credible pretext was the need to maintain liaison between forces in the Soviet Union and occupying troops in Austria. Once troops from Austria were withdrawn under a peace settlement, this claim would fall away.

Meanwhile, Allied control over Austrian internal affairs had by and large ceased. In the parliamentary elections of October 1949, there appeared besides the two major and two minor parties, a new one, which called itself the Electoral Party of Independents. Without a clearly defined platform, it sought to appeal to those who found neither of the major parties to his or her political taste. The Independents had their chief strength in Salzburg and the west, with scant appeal in the east and in and around Vienna. In the elections the People's Party gained 77 seats, the Socialists 67, and the Independents 16. A so-called Left Bloc, separate from both Socialists and Communists, gained five mandates.

The civility in political life that obtained after the Second World War stood in stark contrast to the electoral struggles and the violence that had polluted the political scene between the wars. There was no equivalent of a Heimwehr or a Schutzbund, and raw force was almost entirely absent. The presidency and the chancellorship generally fell to different parties, not by design but by the vagaries of the electoral process. When the first president of the Second Austrian Republic, Karl Renner, died on December 31, 1950, the new president was chosen by direct national elections in May 1951. The first round did not produce the constitutionally mandated majority; in the second, Theodor Körner of the SPÖ gained a majority. Thus the distribution of powers remained unchanged: the president was a Socialist and the chancellor a member of the Volkspartei. Elections held in February 1953 produced only minor changes in the voting pattern. The expectation that the Independents would make an impressive showing did not materialize; another prediction, that the "people's opposition" (Communists and the left wing of the Social Democrats) would fare poorly was, however, confirmed. Thus, after some halfhearted attempts to include the Independents in the government, the coalition of the two leading parties, the ÖVP and the SPÖ, continued, with the former's leader, Julius Raab, as chancellor.

The situation was increasingly ambivalent and it was difficult to say whether Austria was her own master or whether her apparent control over internal affairs was subject to the occupying powers' sufferance and could be ended at any time. The cold war, which left its stamp on the entire European scene, showed no sign of abating; in fact, it escalated and, to many, it seemed that Austria would remain an occupied country for decades to come. But Stalin's tyrannical leadership, which had reached its apogee during the Second World War, was in sharp decline, and he more than anyone else stood in the way of a general reconciliation in Europe. Undoubtedly the United States pursued her drive for economic domination aggressively and resourcefully, and her creation of a North Atlantic alliance threw down the gauntlet to the Soviet Union; it did not, however, stand in the way of peaceful democratic development in Europe. Since 1948 Stalin had bungled from one fiasco to another—his Berlin blockade failed to squeeze the Western allies from the former German capital, his ostracism of the Yugoslav party and his denunciatory campaign against Marshal Tito proved a disastrous failure, and Stalin badly miscalculated when he sent North Korean forces into a war of conquest against the south. In the fall of 1949 the western part of Germany, combining the British, French, and American occupation zones, had become a separate democratic state, firmly in the Western camp. Stalin thereupon constituted the eastern part into the German Democratic Republic, an entity that could never approach the economic sturdiness and political credentials of its western counterpart. However, it did bring Soviet influence into the center of Europe.

Stalin died on March 5, 1953, and, after the obligatory eulogies and accolades, his name and portrait practically disappeared from the public scene. His successors, while abstaining at first from direct criticism of the dictator, allowed the media to denounce such exaggerations of Stalinist rule as the cult of personality and the irrational stress on heavy industry at the expense of consumer goods. Moscow, which until now had proclaimed that a clash between socialist and capitalist countries was inevitable, now advertised the theme of peaceful coexistence. The West, especially the United States under Eisenhower's presidency, responded skeptically, insisting on deeds rather than words to make the new direction credible.

Soviet foreign minister Vyacheslav Molotov for the first time declared his country's willingness to make peace with Austria at a foreign ministers' meeting in January 1954, but added the unacceptable condition that occupying troops remain until a German peace treaty was concluded as well. This demand the Austrian foreign minister, the former chancellor Leopold Figl, rejected, though he was willing to pledge his country's permanent neutrality. After renewed diplomatic feelers the new Soviet leadership in the spring of 1955 finally resolved to offer the "deed" the Western powers demanded to prove peaceful Soviet intentions; it announced its willingness to conclude a peace treaty with a neutral Austria. The Soviet Union, along with Britain and France (the United States had done so eight years earlier) withdrew its claim that the costs of their occupation be defrayed by Austria. In April of that year a three-member delegation of the Vienna government journeyed to the Soviet Union; after three days of negotiations a memorandum emerged in which the Soviets renounced their currently existing rights to oil concessions and mineral explorations in exchange for Austrian deliveries and cash payments over 10 years. The foreign ministers of the four occupying powers assembled in Vienna, and on May 15 signed the long delayed peace treaty. The preamble omitted any reference to Austria's war guilt, which had been a part of the original draft. One article expressly forbade union with Germany. Another one provided minority rights for Slovenian and Croatian populations in Carinthia. Still another validated Soviet claims to German property located in Austria.

When the treaty was brought before the Austrian parliament on June 7, 1955, it was unanimously ratified. It also declared Austria's eternal neutrality, and a special law was passed to that effect. By October 15 of that year the last occupying troops had left Austrian soil. The occasion was celebrated with a great cultural display; the Vienna Burg Theatre reopened that very night with a performance of Austrian playwright Franz Grillparzer's *König Ottokars Glück und Ende,* and on November 5 the State Opera gave a gala performance of Beethoven's *Fidelio,* as hundreds of prominent foreigners attended, as much to express sympathy for the new Austria as for love of music.

In the political field, Julius Raab of the Volkspartei, first appointed chancellor in April 1953, continued in that position until April 1961. At the same time the electorate's choice for president was always a member of the Socialist Party—Theodor Körner, who stayed in office until 1957, was followed by two consecutive terms of Adolf Schärf (1957–65) and of Franz Jonas (1965–74).

In the elections of March 1966 the ÖVP gained an absolute majority and government by coalition was over. Four years later the SPÖ scored a similar triumph, and in April 1970 Bruno Kreisky formed his own all-Socialist cabinet; he presided over a number of subsequent cabinets with occasional personnel changes until 1983.

The foreign policy of the republic moved within the modest boundaries of a small and neutral state. The one contentious item remained the status of South Tyrol. Between 1959 and 1964 a number of terroristic acts in the province perpetrated by both Austrians and Italians kept tempers at a fever pitch and there was the danger of its becoming a much broader international issue. It was thanks largely to the wise policy of Bruno Kreisky, at the time foreign minister in Dr. Josef Klaus's cabinet, that the conflict was ushered into diplomatic channels. In December 1964, by an agreement signed in Rome, the border remained intact and the German population in the province was given additional minority rights and assurances for the preservation of their language.

In the economic sphere the question of nationalization of private enterprises, and of "German assets" that remained within Austrian jurisdiction led to some parliamentary fireworks, which, however, were peacefully resolved. Minor issues achieved headline status by the absence of major ones. In 1956 there was a lively debate over which political party should be in charge of which mass medium. Chancellor Raab of the ÖVP, who had no faith in the future of television, insisted on his party controlling the radio. The SPÖ was actually surly about having to be content with control over television, but time was to prove that it had fortuitously made the good choice. In 1956 there were but 4,000 television sets registered in all of Austria; by 1958, the number grew to 53,000 and in 1959 to 100,000. It gave the Socialists the opportunity to bring their program and agenda to the living rooms of Austrians, which certainly contributed to their electoral victory in 1970.

The question of Habsburg succession also remained alive. The heir apparent, Otto, had attempted to settle with his family in Tyrol as early as 1945 and to become involved in national politics, but the Socialist government of Karl Renner politely asked him to leave. Otto and his family then moved to France.

Only in 1960, after Austria had become fully independent again, did Otto make a second attempt to be allowed to return to Austria. In the course of the Eucharistic World Congress in Germany, he dined with Austrian chancellor Raab at Chancellor Adenauer's home and voiced his desire to return to his native land. Raab referred to the peace treaty of 1955, which obligated Austria to remain a republic; he saw a possibility of Otto's return only if he formally abdicated the throne. Otto delayed until the following May, when he declared himself a loyal subject of the Austrian republic, claiming at the same time all rights and privileges due to a citizen. Parliament subsequently refused to give its consent to Otto's return, but in May 1963 a law court declared Otto's application valid. In a strictly constitutional state that should have settled the matter, but it became a test of strength among the major coalition parties. The ÖVP supported Otto's request; the Socialists opposed it but were able to defeat the move only with the support of the successor to the Independent Party. Otto, denied the opportunity to be a citizen of a republic, remained a king in exile.

Although a two-party system is by no means either traditional or particularly compatible with Austrian political conditions, by coincidence rather than design the Socialist Party of Austria and the National Party of Austria had essentially governed the country since the end of the Second World War, either alternately or in coalition. Until 1970 the former was the stronger of the two due to the appeal of its platform and its more active concern with public welfare. From that year on the party's electoral success was due mainly to the broad popularity of its leaders, notably Bruno Kreisky, who served as chancellor until 1983. After a three-year interval he was followed by another popular leader of the party, Franz Vranitzky. That it was the personal appeal of these men rather than the party's political agenda that accounted for its continued success at the polls was shown by the fact that during these years the size of the vote steadily declined. In 1990 the joint share of the vote of the two large parties for the first time fell under 80 percent. In the election of 1994 it constituted only 62.6 percent of the total vote.

Meanwhile in the late 1980s the vote for president produced an unexpected and deeply embarrassing incident that for a few years cast its shadow over the republic's political life. In 1986 four men vied for the presidency, but only the candidates of the ÖVP, Kurt Waldheim, and of the SPÖ, Kurt Steyrer, had a realistic chance of obtaining a majority. The former had the great advantage of name recognition as, in the 1970s he had served two terms as secretary-general of the United Nations.

A few months before the elections Waldheim had published an autobiography, which had much to say about his life before the war and his political career after it but glossed over his activities during the war, leaving the impression that he had spent most of the war years engaged in law studies in Vienna. Thanks to some investigative reporting within Austria, later joined by foreign newspapers and the World Jewish Council, it was brought to light that Waldheim had served a considerable length of time on active service in the Balkans, a region that served as the scene of the most appalling atrocities perpetrated by the occupying Wehrmacht. These reports, whose substance Waldheim never denied, opened up the painful question that had been at the heart of the Nuremberg trials and the entire persecution of war crimes, namely, to what extent a military man was responsible for the criminal acts he committed under orders that it was his duty as a soldier to obey. While the most thorough investigation could not find evidence that Waldheim personally participated in any of the outrages, his claim that he was unaware of them was met with derision and disbelief. Soon Austria's electorate was split into two over the affair. In the elections on May 4, 1986, Waldheim, with 49.7 percent of the vote, fell only a few thousand votes short of an absolute majority. In the runoff with Steyrer, he received 54 percent of the total vote.

The world outside was not impressed by the choice of the Austrian electorate. The United States placed Waldheim on a "watch list" in branding him an undesirable alien. Other governments followed, and in the end he enjoyed the support only of the Soviet Union, East European socialist states, and the Arab countries.

An international panel investigated Waldheim's wartime record and subsequently concluded that while there was no evidence of his participating in criminal acts, his claim that he had no knowledge that such acts were being carried out was not credible.

What the affair showed was that the horror of the Second World War would continue to haunt the political precincts of European nations. Waldheim subsequently gave a television address in which he denounced the Holocaust as a great tragedy of history and stated that it was time for Austria to acknowledge that it had played a part in it.

In 1995, Austria joined the European Union, and its membership has spawned one significant controversy. The nationalist, anti-immigrant politician Jörg Haider became head of a coalition between the conservative People's Party and his own far-right Freedom Party in February 2000. The European Union, having labeled Haider a racist, xenophobe, and Nazi sympathizer, denounced the coalition and ceased all diplomatic contact. Although Austria accused the EU of having acted against a democratic government, Haider noted the polemic and resigned from the Freedom Party in May 2000. By September, the EU had rescinded its sanctions against Austria, and, two years later, the coalition broke up altogether following a decline in the Freedom Party's popularity.

After the First World War many had argued that Austria in its reduced state could not possibly survive; crudely put, that, separated from Germany, she made no economic or even political sense. As it subsequently developed, the seven-year-long union with Germany proved to be one of the most traumatic experiences in Austrian history, not, to be sure, because of any incompatibility of Austrian and German national life (though the temperaments of the two peoples are markedly different), but because Austrians were compelled to associate themselves with an ideology and a program of stupendous magnitude and appalling inhumanity. There had been no plan or intent worthy of mention for Austria's participation in another adventure in greatness since. Austria found that modesty, and the most delightful physical environment in Europe, held their own rewards.

HUNGARY

CHAPTER ONE

The origin of the Hungarian people is lost in conjecture and legend. What has been established beyond reasonable doubt is that linguistically they belong to the Finno-Ugrian family, but racially the Mongolian strain was most likely the dominant one, of the same branch to which the Huns also belonged. Assuming even that at the time of their origin the Magyar tribes did have an identifiable racial character, in the course of their wanderings, and even during their settled period, they met and mingled with such a variety of peoples that the incipient purity was in time manifoldly corrupted. The most authoritative Hungarian encyclopedia, the *Great Révai Lexicon,* states: "From the anthropological point of view, the Hungarian is one of the most composite nations of Europe, and thus there can be no talk about a singular Hungarian type." This fact is all the more important because throughout their history the Magyars (as Hungarians call themselves), or a certain portion of them, were intensely preoccupied with their racial distinctness and were apt to regard minorities who shared the Carpathian Basin with them as inferior, or at any rate as racially less respectable.

As part of the search for a pristine Hungarian tribe, much time and effort has been expended to locate the "ancient home" of that tribe. With a nomadic people, constantly on the move, under pressure from other tribes or to find more verdant pastures, such a search was doomed to failure. What *can* be stated with fair accuracy is that in the first millennium B.C. tribes from whom the Magyar people evolved dwelt, together with or in physical closeness to Finno-Ugrian tribes, in the region of the elbow of the Volga River, delimited by the Kama and Bielaia Rivers and the Ural Mountains. To be sure, such ethnic affinity with "Finno-Ugrians reeking of fish" for many centuries displeased race-conscious Magyar historians and they concocted theories of a nobler ancestry, particularly the Sumerian, based on a superficial similarity of certain words in the two languages; these theories have, on closer inspection, all been discarded. Words dating from earliest times, referring to edible vegetation or to means of catching fish and killing game from a distance as well as the domestication of animals, suggest that these early tribes lived a hunting, fishing, and gathering existence. As they gradually moved from forested regions to the open steppes (or as the landscape under climatic influences changed around them) they made animal husbandry their main source of livelihood. Horses were tamed and mounted and movement became easier; it also became necessary because with the herds rapidly increasing, pastures were quickly exhausted. It was to all evidences because of this that the Magyar tribes, about the middle of the fifth century A.D., separated themselves from their Finnish and Ugrian kinsmen. The latter moved northwestward, into the Baltic region, where the Estonians, Finns, and some lesser tribes settled; the Magyars, joined by Khabars, wandered across the southern Russian steppe, paused in the vicinity of the Sea of Azov, then between the Don and Dnieper Rivers, and, subsequently, in the eighth century, in their penultimate "home" between the Dnieper and the Dniester, an area whose name was corrupted from its original pronunciation into the Hungarian Etelköz. By now a portion of the wandering host had chosen not to proceed farther and it eventually returned to the original home along the Volga. A Christian friar found them there in the 13th century; they were eventually swept away by the great Mongolian invasion in that century.

In the course of their westward trek Magyar tribes repeatedly encountered Turkic peoples and on occasion accepted their mastery; intermarriage was common and many Turkish words entered the Hungarian language. Summing up the variety and often conflicting influences on the Magyar tribes, the *Révai Lexicon* writes: "The Hungarian people is composed of Finno-Ugrian and Turkish strains; it is in its character, morality, mentality and customs closer to the nomadic Turks [originating] in Central Asia than to the Finno-Ugrians; its language, however, despite strong Turkic influences, is of Finno-Ugrian origins."

The pattern of migrations during these chaotic times when Asia disgorged its masses of humanity into Europe was that a tribe or a collection of tribes united by a common language or by self-interest established itself in a region that promised to provide rich grazing land for their flocks, only to be displaced by another wave of migrants whose land hunger and nomadic ways made them tougher warriors than the settled population; the latter in turn would press tribes farther to the south or west until those gave way. The area immediately to the west of the Magyars, who were settled in the Etelköz, was the Carpathian Basin, so named from the broad arc of mountains surrounding it from the north, west, and parts of the south. That basin had three main components: Transylvania in the east, forming a geographic unit by dint of its hydrographic unity; the Great Plain, east and west of the Tisza River, stretching to the Danube that majestically marked its western boundary; and Transdanubia, west of the Danube to the Leitha River. The basin had first been the home to a political unit during the Hunnish conquest under Attila in the fifth century; after the latter's death in 453 the Hunnish host broke up and returned to its former home on the Volga. Assumedly a remnant of it ensconced itself in eastern Transylvania; they called themselves Székelys and claimed close kinship with the Hungarians. Following the departure of the Huns, inside the Carpathians there were German tribes, the Gepids in the east, and Ostrogoths, later displaced by the Lombards, in Transdanubia. These in turn fell to the conquering Avar host, which extended its rule over the entire basin, but was in time, in the late 700s, subdued by the armies of Charlemagne.

The Magyar tribes, accompanied by some Khabar units, while still in the Etelköz, waged a series of wars against the Bulgarians, along, and south of, the Lower Danube. Those who remained east of the Dniester were fallen upon by the marauding Petchenegs and were forced to move into the shelter of the

Carpathians. This "conquest of the homeland," *honfoglalás* in the Magyar tongue, was the opening drama and defining moment in Hungarian history. The deed was traditionally attributed to the leader Árpád, the founding father of Hungary, but more exacting scholarship found that he was leader only of the fighting force, and there were two other dignitaries of equal or higher rank responsible for political leadership. The details of the conquest remain sketchy. The only extant account of it is by a nameless historian of a later era, and it speaks of epic struggles; but most likely the only resistance of major scope was offered by the Moravians in the northwest, and that was overcome. The actual settlement of the basin proceeded by stages and, in the meantime, fierce Magyar horsemen terrorized much of central Europe; finally, a shattering defeat suffered at the hands of the Germans in 955 on Lechfeld near the city of Augsburg put an end to those adventurous forays.

The Hungarian tribes, still heathen and uncouth, were, except for the Petchenegs in the east, surrounded by Christian peoples. Conversion to Christianity in the central and northern regions of Europe was by no means a gentle process; it was accomplished more often by the sword than by the cross. In the south, Romans and their allies, rendered overweening by their immoderate greatness, in time embraced the humble and purifying values of Christianity; the barbarians to their north had no such impulses. Charlemagne of the Frankish lands in the west, himself a halfhearted if militant Christian, waged unremitting battles against Germans who, no sooner baptized, reverted to their pagan ways. However, when a prince or king, usually for political reasons, did embrace the faith, his people had no choice but to follow him. In Hungary the prince Géza (970–97) of the House of Árpád was the first one to

Árpád, considered to be the founder of the state of Hungary, is shown here mounted on a white horse *(Hulton/Archive)*

adopt Christianity; he asked the German emperor Otto to send Christian missionaries to his land. When they came, they were accompanied by armed knights whose task it was to deal with any possible resistance. Géza on his part exerted most of his energies not on bringing the one true faith to his land but on breaking down tribal particularism that constituted a challenge to his central rule. He accomplished this with fair success by attracting the military retinue of tribal chiefs to his own forts and camps, thus depriving them of means of resistance.

The wholesale conversion of Hungarians was left to Géza's son Vajk, who, upon being baptized, took on the Christian name of István (Stephen), and in time was sainted. His methods of conversion were often brutal and with many of his subjects the adoption of the new faith lacked religious content, but the Holy See saw only the end result, namely, that despite a series of armed uprisings against enforced conversion, Christianity conquered and the defeated rebels could choose only between conversion and death. In the year 1000 Pope Sylvester sent a crown to place on István's head and thereby elevate him from prince to king. Hungary became a member of the European family of Christian nations.

István laid the foundations of a modern state by establishing counties headed by lord lieutenants (főispánok) for a more efficient assessment and collection of taxes; such taxes were periodically voted by the estates, with the ecclesiastical at the top, the free landowners forming the second estate, followed by town-dwelling commoners (the equivalent of the French Third Estate), with a fourth one for courtiers and servants. This last one in time fell into disuse.

István's successors were engaged in a seemingly endless series of internal and external conflicts, the former centering on the system of royal succession (as both the dead king's oldest male relative and his first-born son claimed the throne), the latter in resisting feudal claims alternately by the papacy and or by powerful German kings. Christianity was slow in taking firm root among the common people and it was not until the reign of László (1077–95), who in time was sainted, that Hungarians became definitively reconciled to the new religion. László garnered other merits. He took advantage of the preoccupation of the Byzantine Empire with the menace posed by advancing Seljuq Turks and conquered Croatia, where he established a bishopric at Zagreb; his successor, Kálmán, successfully battled the powerful Venetians for possession of the northern Adriatic coast, and in time added the Dalmatian littoral and the offshore islands to his kingdom. All the while kings had to fight off claims by the German (Holy Roman) Emperor to ultimate sovereignty over Hungary; László went so far as to take sides in the momentous investiture debate between the German emperor Henry IV and Pope Gregory VII; he supported Gregory, hoping thereby to weaken German pressure on Hungary.

Lying at the crossroads between east and west, north and south, and often appearing easy prey to outsiders because of her internal rifts, Hungary, more specifically her strongwilled and unbending high nobility, also had to fend off repeated attempts by neighbors, either to conquer the country or to force it into some manner of dependency. When in one instance the son of a Hungarian princess married to the Byzantine emperor became emperor in his turn in

Constantinople and tried, on the claim of being half Hungarian, to incorporate the country, or parts of it, in his empire, he proved no more successful than other would-be conquerors.

In the 12th century Hungary was still sparsely settled and only in parts cultivated; the original conquerors had made themselves at home in river valleys, on the plains and in the hills, and much good land lay fallow. The west of Europe at the same time experienced a population explosion and many landless peasants were attracted to Hungary's open spaces. Germans, French, and others came in growing numbers. They brought with them knowledge of technological novelties such as the compound plow, the horseshoe, and the stirrup, and they introduced vine growing on mountain- and hillsides. Culturally the Christian faith enjoyed a monopoly—its language, Latin, well-nigh replaced Hungarian vernacular, the latter remaining alive only among the lower classes.

Contested claims to the throne repeatedly threw the country into political turmoil. Factions of high nobles supported different candidates, and the church was also a frequent player. When István, still of the House of Árpád, became king in 1162, for two years he had to contend with rivals who proclaimed themselves "counter-kings"; when his son Béla III died in 1196, a ruinous strife ensued between Béla's own two sons, Imre and András; it was not resolved until 1205, when András II finally took the throne.

András's reign was an eventful one. Pretenders to the throne often could obtain noble support only by making generous grants of land from royal estates; the result was a constant diminution of royal authority and a reduction in royal income. Governance at the county level gradually slipped from the king's hand and passed into the hands of powerful nobles, thus fortifying feudal enserfment and oppression. Taxation, mainly in kind, no longer provided sufficient income for the royal house, whose expenses had greatly increased, in part because of constant warfare and in part because ostentatious knightly customs replaced the austere practices at court with costly luxury and display. Kings devised avenues to additional revenue by debasing the (largely silver) currency, and by selling or dispensing royal estates. "The measure of royal donations is measureless," wrote one observer at court. Many of the donations went to foreigners, especially Germans who had accompanied King András's German wife to Hungary. Not only the peasantry but even the lesser nobility felt victimized by the inordinate rise of the wealth and political power of domestic and foreign great lords.

In the spring of 1222, when the king appeared at the traditional issuance of new laws, a huge multitude awaited him and compelled him to issue the so-called Golden Bull. This Hungarian Magna Carta primarily favored the lesser nobility, by assuring its members personal freedom, exemption from taxation, and the right to participate in the making of laws. It also promised good currency, reined in the high and mighty lord lieutenants who ruled the counties, and forbade bishops to collect tithes in coin rather than in kind. The high nobility was appeased by the promise that no land grants would be made to foreigners and that no person could hold more than one office. The Bull also gave them the right to defy a king if he stood in violation of the document.

András's son and successor, Béla IV, made strenuous efforts to reduce the presumptions and hauteur of great nobles, going so far as to burn the chairs in the royal council so that the nobles could not sit in his presence; he even sought, with little success, to reclaim frivolously donated royal estates. He granted refuge to some 40,000 Cuman families, heathen nomads who had replaced the Petchenegs across the Carpathians and who were fleeing from the momentous Mongolian advance that had already conquered most of Kievan Rus (present-day Ukraine) and continued toward the center of Europe.

Confusion and panic soon reigned in Hungary itself. The Carpathian region lay athwart the broad swath that the Mongolian host (known as Tartars in Hungary and other places) cut along their route of advance. Appeals to the pope and the Holy Roman Emperor for help went unheeded. The Hungarian military was slow in gathering and in any case had neither the numbers nor the weapons to resist the Tartars, who by some accounts numbered in the hundreds of thousands. The Cumans were accused of spying; many, including their prince, were murdered. Thereupon most of them left the country. In the spring of 1241 the Tartars breached the Carpathians and poured into Transylvania. The one major battle was fought near the town of Mohi by the Sajó River and ended in the catastrophic defeat of the Hungarians. The whole country lay open to conquest and pillage. In the winter the Mongols crossed the Danube and broke into Transdanubia, forcing King Béla to flee abroad.

However, at this point the invaders decided not to continue their westward march. The Great Khan back home in Karakorum had died and the election of a new one required the presence of the commanding general in Europe; also, their hold on the vast territories they had conquered was by no means secure. As they withdrew, they left a devastated, literally burned-out country behind them. The population by contemporary estimates was reduced from 2 million to 1 million; the loss of lives was greatest in the Great Plains, the breadbasket of the country. King Béla, returning from Dalmatia, made further donations of land in the depopulated regions, and sundry inducements brought hosts of foreign settlers who then took deserted lands under cultivation. Even the Cumans returned in large numbers, but they proved so troublesome and recalcitrant that King Béla sought to quiet them by marrying his son, Stephen, to one of their princesses. The couple had a son and, because Stephen died very shortly after his father, an infant was king, with a crude, sensuous woman who had little love for Hungarians as regent. His wayward ways as he grew into a young adult were so scandalous and un-Christian that Pope Nicholas IV preached a crusade against him. The young king was assassinated without leaving an issue and the Árpád line seemed to have come to an end. A blood relation, a grandson of András II, then surfaced in Italy. Brought to his native land, he was crowned king in 1290 as András III. He proved a wise and patient ruler; he died young, in 1301, and the House of Árpád reached a definitive end.

During an interregnum of seven years several foreign ruling families related to the Árpáds aspired to the Hungarian throne. In these years, with central authority absent, a small number of high lords ruled as sovereigns in parts of the country. One, Máté Csák, made much of the northwestern highlands his domain, where he minted money, dealt with foreign potentates, and conducted his own foreign policy. Other nobles acted in similar ways in other provinces. Meanwhile several aspirants to the throne jockeyed for position. The nobles elected a son of Bohemia's Přemysl king, but the pope favored the Naples candidate, Charles Robert of the House of Anjou, and threatened with excommunication any rival; a Bavarian candidate of the House of Wittelsbach was also crowned but encountered such resistance that he had to flee for his life; in the end, in 1307, the Hungarian lords and nobles swore allegiance to Charles Robert, who ruled until 1342.

Many nobles, accustomed to acting as kings on their own vast estates, did not accept the Anjou heir, and he had to fight several open battles to subdue them. Once king without further challenge, Charles Robert devoted his most serious efforts to fiscal stability; royal income was greatly increased by production from the silver and gold mines, among the richest in Europe, and a good part of the debased currency was replaced by coins of precious metal. Exports (mainly of agricultural products) and imports (of manufactured goods), alike were taxed. Income was never large enough, though, to complement the greatly reduced royal army with mercenaries; thus it was necessary, and also desirable, to enlist the large private armies of the great lords into royal service.

The turbulent times through which the country had passed in the 13th century had cost it much of the southern territories conquered under St. László and Kálmán. Although the north Adriatic littoral—Slovenia, Croatia, and Dalmatia—were formally still parts of the kingdom, they were effectively ruled by their governors, as was the area populated by the Cumans in the east. Charles Robert was too preoccupied with his internal reforms to counteract this tendency, but his son Lajos, during his long reign of 40 years (1342–82), made strenuous efforts to extend his rule over the Balkan provinces; he also laid dynastic claim to the Kingdom of the Two Sicilies in the hope of founding an empire "riding on the Adriatic." In 1370 he inherited the Polish throne as sole heir of a childless uncle. His Italian ambitions remained unfulfilled, however, and even his reacquisition of Croatia and Dalmatia was jeopardized by the steady Turkish advance from the south.

Lajos was followed by his son-in-law, Sigmund of Luxembourg, who had another long reign (1385–1437) that was encumbered by rival claims for the throne by the Anjous of Naples and by prolonged warfare with Venice in the defense of Dalmatia. However, Venice was no longer the main threat to Hungary's Balkan possessions. The Turkish advance, which not long ago had seemed too ponderous to threaten the country's security, assumed ever more ominous proportions. Sigmund attempted a crusade against them; in 1396 his forces suffered a disastrous defeat and were compelled to retreat to the relative security of the homeland. The forward positions of the kingdom were so weakened that in the early 1420s Sigmund was forced to finally cede Dalmatia to Venice. All plans for a southward advance had to be abandoned; the question was now whether Hungary could defend what she still possessed in the face of the looming Turkish danger.

Many Hungarians blamed this misfortune on Sigmund's frequent absences from home and his cursory attention to national affairs. In 1411 he was elected Holy Roman Emperor, later also king of Bohemia, and he treated his position as king of Hungary as a mere appendage to his more illustrious titles. If he could point to any accomplishment at all, it was this, that largely in consequence of the Great Schism that rent the papacy, with a pope in Rome and a pope in Avignon in France, and for a short while a third pope elected by a council that had met after the refusal of the other two popes to abdicate, Sigmund was able to issue the *placentum regis,* providing that papal rescripts could be published in Hungary only with royal assent. At the same time, however, the church in Hungary faced a serious challenge from the Hussite movement that spread to Hungarian lands from Bohemia and became particularly popular among the oppressed peasantry. The most forceful repressive measures were employed to halt its advance.

In the middle 1400s, with some minor and short-lived kings occupying the throne, the outstanding figure was a dashing and gifted general, János Hunyadi, who, as the Turks kept pressing against the southern frontiers of the country, earned several brilliant victories against them. He even recaptured the key city of Belgrade in a decisive battle that halted the Turkish advance in its tracks for almost a century. (It was in celebration of this feat that the pope ordered that church bells should toll at noon.) Hunyadi died shortly after his great victory, in 1456. The ruling king, László V, childless and unmarried, died a year later. The country had grown tired of the unsavory struggles among claimants to the throne and a succession of foreign kings. A great assembly of nobles congregated in January 1458 and elected as king Hunyadi's younger son, Mátyás (the older had been murdered to prevent *him* from taking the throne). The news brought Mátyás back from Prague where he was staying, and Hungary was at last blest with a humane, enlightened, wise, militarily adroit king, who was in addition a true Renaissance man. Although a despot, he was a benevolent one.

Personal ambition as well as real or imagined danger from Bohemian and Austrian rivals drew Mátyás into a series of conflicts, which he fought with a large mercenary army composed mainly of former Hussite rebels. Although victorious in most encounters, his gains were ephemeral and his claim that he could not take forceful action against the Turks while his northern and western frontiers were insecure was not a valid one. He was involved in complicated negotiations with Holy Roman Emperor Maximilian I about marrying his own illegitimate son to Maximilian's daughter, but he died unexpectedly on May 6, 1490, before the marriage was concluded.

The high nobles who had elected him 32 years earlier had grown restive under his iron rule and wanted a king they could control. Their choice fell on the king of Bohemia, Vladislav II. Unknown to the lords who claimed for themselves the right to elect the country's kings, Vladislav had entered into a marriage contract of his own, agreeing to marry his son Lajos to Maximilian's granddaughter, and his daughter to Maximilian's grandson, Ferdinand. By the agreement the latter was to inherit the throne of Hungary should Lajos, then still a child, die without a son. At the time this seemed just another in a long series of royal maneuvers in which infants barely out of the crib were used to establish later claims to the throne, but in retrospect it turned out to be the most significant arrangement in Hungarian history. The great nobles, faced with the prospect of another foreigner on the throne, met in a field in 1505 and vowed to accept in future only a Hungarian king.

However, he would have to be one who displayed military prowess and an iron determination to keep the ever contentious high nobles in check because the Turks, quiescent since their great defeat at Belgrade, were on the move again.

CHAPTER TWO

The year 1514 left haunting memories in Hungarian hearts and minds, which to this day have not died. The nation, facing a mortal threat from approaching Turkish armies, turned against itself. A Transylvanian nobleman, György Dózsa, placed himself in charge of a motley army of malcontents, mainly serfs, who had answered a call for a crusade by the recently elected pope Leo X. Landowning nobles tried to prevent their peasants from leaving during the season of plowing and planting, but many volunteer soldiers who regarded their masters rather than the Turks their true enemies defied them and congregated in an unruly horde. They lost sight of the larger task to which they had been called and besieged a stronghold of the nobility in southern Hungary. By now, however, another noble, János Szapolyai, had assembled a smaller but more disciplined force, lifted the siege, and took most of the rebels prisoner. Terrible reprisals followed, to which Dózsa himself fell victim, according to some accounts in a hideous fashion. The uprising, which foreshadowed many others to follow, was an object lesson in the devastations that peasants incensed with all the fury of patience too long repressed could visit on a whole nation when a sense of power liberated them from their ingrained subservience.

King Lajos II of Hungary was eight years old at the time of the upheaval. His father Vladislav, ailing, had him crowned king before his own death and a regency council ruled in the young king's stead. It is a moot question whether the dire destiny that loomed on the southern horizon could have been averted had Lajos been a man of character and purpose; what paralyzed his power was not so much personal weakness as the pretentions and the greed of the great nobles whom even a king of Mátyás's stature had been unable to rein in. Court nobles played on the young king's love of luxury and idle amusements while the defense of the country was neglected. A political bargain with the Turks was still possible because the prize the great sultan Suleiman II had his eyes on was Vienna, and he merely asked for passage through Hungary. When refused, he entered the country with hostile intent. Hungarian preparations were plagued by delay, disorganization, and an epidemic; when a defensive force finally met the Turks in battle near the town of Mohács, it was outnumbered, outmatched in weaponry, and suffered a terrible defeat. The fleeing king drowned in a swollen brook and the throne fell vacant once again.

Succession to the kingship was seldom if ever a simple affair in Hungary. Blood relation to the former king, compacts made on the occasion of princely marriages, the will of the great magnates, all played their part in choosing a new ruler. In 1526 an additional consideration involved which king could bring with him a military force capable of confronting the Turks, who were already wreaking havoc as they pushed northward to the nation's capital, Buda. János Szapolyai, probably the richest landlord in the country and the man who had liquidated György Dózsa's revolt, was brother-in-law of the powerful Polish king Sigmund I, and he was the choice of the lesser nobles who remembered their 1505 pledge that only a Hungarian would be allowed to sit on the throne. Szapolyai was duly elected. With the high nobles, however, dynastic considerations had greater weight than nationality; they also judged Austria to be a more potent guarantee of military help than the distant Poles. They chose Ferdinand I, recently appointed by his older brother, Charles V, the senior member of the House of Habsburg, archduke of Austria. The Turks had by now (the winter of 1526–27) pulled out of Hungary, temporarily abandoning the siege of Vienna, and the country became the battleground between two rival kings. Neither of them had sufficient force to prevail over the other; Szapolyai offered to marry the widow of the fallen king but was refused. With his domestic support inadequate, he fled to Poland and from there appealed to Suleiman to support his claim. The latter installed him in Buda, mainly in order to have a loyal vassal along his route of advance when he launched a new assault against Vienna. This he did in 1529; his forces pushed to the very gates of the Austrian capital but were unable to pierce its defenses and had to retreat before the onset of bad weather. In 1532 Suleiman made a third attempt; on that occasion a small Hungarian fort, Köszeg, with an insignificant defensive force, delayed him so long that by the time it fell, the campaigning season was over and Suleiman once again turned to go home. (There is speculation among historians that the resistance of Köszeg was the excuse rather than the reason for Suleiman tarrying so long; he was discouraged by the size of Austrian and imperial armies gathered for the defense of Vienna and chose not to give battle after all.)

The 1530s passed in fruitless wrangling between the two men, Ferdinand and Szapolyai, each of whom claimed to be king, and the contention was intensified by the rapid spread of the Reformation that had found its way into Hungary and further divided the stricken nation. Ferdinand, heavily dependent on papal support, fought Protestantism in every possible way, while Szapolyai proved tolerant and gained many Protestant supporters. Until 1538, when the two rivals finally reached an agreement, the Hungarian capital Buda and much of the country's eastern portion was in Szapolyai's hand; Ferdinand ruled Transdanubia and a good part of the northern Uplands. In that year, under pressure from Ferdinand's brother Charles, who had become concerned that amid the bitter internal strife, defense against the Turks was being neglected, the two claimants agreed in the city of Várad that for the time being each would hold on to the regions he ruled, with the proviso that upon Szapolyai's death Ferdinand would inherit the throne alone. Szapolyai then married the Polish princess Isabella, and she in 1540 bore him a son. The father died shortly afterward and his retinue, ignoring the compact with Ferdinand, crowned the infant János Zsigmond king of Hungary. This proved to be the prelude to a century and a half of Turkish occupation of the middle of the country.

When Ferdinand laid siege to Buda to claim his inheritance, the leader of the Szapolyai party, Friar György Martinuzzi, prevailed on the widowed queen to ask for Turkish support. The support given was double-edged; Ferdinand's forces were driven back from Buda, but that city, together with the broad wedge south of it that eventually included one-third of the country, fell to the Turks. Suleiman exiled the queen mother and her infant son to Transylvania. There were now three Hungarian governments: Ferdinand retaining much of what he had had before, the Turks ruling the center of the country, and the Szapolyais holding on to Transylvania. The Turks eventually enlarged their area of occupation well past Buda, into the center of the Uplands, just north of the town of Fülek.

Martinuzzi, a political realist, saw clearly that in the last resort the struggle with the Habsburgs was secondary to the need to fend off the Turkish threat and sought agreement with Ferdinand, offering to unite the country under his rule once the Turks had been expelled. In 1541 Ferdinand did send a force against the Turks, but one which, according to contemporaries, was "too large for an embassy, too small for an army." Martinuzzi, disillusioned, turned to the Turks again; his secret negotiations were discovered and he was assassinated as a traitor. One after another Hungarian frontier post and fort fell to Ottoman power. Ferdinand, and even his successors, regarded their portion of Hungary more as a buffer against the Turkish menace than as a component part of their empire and allowed it to shrivel to near insignificance.

In 1570 Ferdinand's successor, Maximilian, reached another agreement with the Szapolyais at Speyer; János Zsigmond abdicated the crown of Hungary but was recognized as prince of Transylvania and of the counties east of the Tisza River, the so-called Partium. Upon the death of János Zsigmond, the noble estates elected a wealthy and cultured aristocrat, István Báthori, to succeed him. Báthori inspired a remarkable renaissance in his provinces; he beat back the forces Maximilian sent to extend his rule over Transylvania, and when in 1576 the much coveted throne of Poland fell vacant, he was elected to occupy it. Deeming the Polish crown of greater importance than the ever labile Transylvanian one, he ruled the latter province through his brother Kristóf. His ambition whetted, he hoped to gain the crowns of Bohemia and all of Hungary as well, then, as king of a multinational but united country, to expel the Turks from the Carpathian Basin. It was not to be. As king of Poland he became involved in an exhausting war with Russia and was never able to pursue his larger ambition. Transylvania, however, even under absentee rule, became a haven of tranquillity and peace compared to the southern and central portions of the country under Turkish occupation. In the latter, due to intermittent fighting, raids for slaves, sheer terror, and the wholesale flight of peasants, the countryside became virtually depopulated. Only some fearless herdsmen maintained a precarious existence. A few towns ruled directly by Turkish authorities offered some protection, and a number of these grew into cities, of significant size even today. Transylvania, in addition to its material prosperity, distinguished itself by religious toleration, remarkable at a time of wholesale persecution in many places. The Reformation begun by Luther spread with a rapidity and missionary zeal that caught the Roman Catholic Church off guard. The Vatican, refusing to believe at first that the organized protest against Catholic authority had staying power, sought to fight it with time-tested methods of excommunication and papal interdicts; but the movement, especially after Calvin's powerful voice was added to it, throve in face of persecution and threatened the unity of the "one true church." In the Holy Roman Empire, by and large identical with Germany, it took a number of fruitless attempts at compromise, then a prolonged armed struggle, to convince the two sides that neither threats nor the force of arms could decide the issue. In 1555, in Augsburg, Lutheranism and Catholicism reached an uneasy peace agreement, the result of mutual exhaustion rather than genuine reconciliation. In France it was only in 1598 that the farsighted Henry IV of the House of Bourbon issued his epoch-making Edict of Nantes, declaring full toleration (albeit not equality) for French Protestants. Transylvania's rulers went even further. A great part of the high and many of the lesser nobility had converted to Calvinism; as nobles they had the power to appoint clergymen to the communities under their lordship and they chose ones of the Calvinist faith, not always for spiritual reasons but because expenses

This illustration shows Hungarian women defending their town against the Turks, ca. 1551 *(Hulton Archive)*

were much smaller than with the decorous and elaborate Catholic worship. The Transylvanian estates then reached an agreement whereby Catholics, Lutherans, Calvinists, and Unitarians were all ranked as "established" churches, with equal freedoms and rights. The Eastern Orthodox faith to which most of the Romanians, numerous in the province, belonged, received only toleration.

In most of Europe the religious question was the primary one because nothing less than salvation or damnation after death was at stake; in Hungary, it was relegated to a secondary place by the unremitting warfare with the Turks. Vienna continued to be the chief target of Turkish expansion, but to reach Vienna the conquest of the as yet unoccupied parts of Hungary had to be accomplished. With no substantial aid coming from any quarter, Hungarians depended on the sturdiness of their chain of forts, built, then rebuilt, then fortified along the entire line of demarcation that separated Habsburg Hungary from the Turkish-occupied lands, and on the heroism of their often undermanned defenders. Some of the most legendary chapters of Hungarian military history date from this, the 16th, century. Temesvár, one of the southernmost of the forts, withstood a Turkish assault for five weeks with greatly inferior forces until the collapse of the water tower forced surrender; a promise of safe conduct by the Turkish pasha was violated and the defenders were massacred as they filed past their captors. At the fort of Drégely, commanded by a former serf, a force of 150 men fought a hopeless battle in which all were killed in the end. In Eger, which guarded the entry to the Uplands, the captain had some 2,000 defenders recruited from local peasants and artisans under his command. The siege lasted 58 days, during which women poured boiling tar and hot water on the Turks scaling the walls, until the latter abandoned the siege. At Szigetvár the aged Suleiman himself led the assault and the heroic Miklós Zrinyi defended the fort. There was no surrender; with the whole town burning, the defenders rushed out and fought with bare swords until the last of them fell. In this assault Suleiman, ill with fever, succumbed. There was no one else of his mettle and charisma in Constantinople. The fighting spirit of Hungarians had proved unconquerable and the Turks did not launch a major offensive again for a century.

With the long pause in the fighting, religious questions once again came to the fore. They were by no means limited to the theological sphere. It is a key question in the history of the Reformation how the struggle against Catholicism would have proceeded without the powerful forward jolt provided by the oppressed social classes. For millions of peasants Luther's message, in particular that each believer had the right and duty to read and interpret the scriptures for himself, led to a startled recognition of how far the church had strayed from the humble and forgiving spirit Jesus had preached. The "poor in spirit," who were to inherit the earth, in truth lived in the most degrading conditions of misery and serfdom, and the rich who were to be denied entrance into heaven ruled unchallenged. In the eyes of many peasants the Reformation was a call for the liquidation of the feudal system and even of a church that gave it its blessing. Neither Lutheranism nor Calvinism gave evidence, however, of condemning oppression by landlords, and both attempted to adjust themselves to feudal conditions. This was why many peasants turned to the more radical teachings of Anabaptism, which preached complete freedom for the individual, a return to the simplest, unpretentious ways of Christian worship, and an unencumbered choice among beliefs by postponing baptism until adulthood. Another denomination denied the dogmatic teaching of the Trinity. Unitarianism, also popular among the peasantry, gained, as we have seen, equality of place with the other three Christian religions in Transylvania, but in exchange its faithful had to pledge to discontinue their fight against feudalism.

After 1562, when the Council of Trent issued its definitive statement of Catholic dogma, and with the formation of the militant Society of Jesus (the Jesuits), a powerful counterattack against Protestantism, both in Hungary and elsewhere, began. Just as many of the Protestant clergy had come from Catholic ranks, most of the Jesuits and other "counterreformers" were converts from Protestant faiths. It was not merely a manner of speech when the Jesuits declared themselves soldiers of Christ; they were willing to fight for their faith with all the determination of self-appointed martyrs. This was why at times even rulers who invited them to their realms turned against them in time because religious fanaticism was not always compatible with the pursuit of political goals.

Given the intensity of these conflicts, it was astounding that the struggle between Hungary and the Turks almost entirely lacked a religious dimension. The sword of Islam seemed to lose its edge in the confrontation with Hungarians. The Habsburgs on their part lacked both the means and the inclination to make the defense of Hungary a phase in a crusade against Islam. It will be remembered that high Hungarian nobles had elected Ferdinand of Habsburg king in the hope that his military contribution would turn the tide against the invader. This hope was disappointed and Hungary was left to her own devices. The last time the country had a national force under unified command was in the Battle of Mohács—after that disaster the army disintegrated. Many great nobles still disposed of private armies, but they retained them for their own narrow, selfish purposes. Roaming in the fields could be found ragtag bands of *hajduk,* homeless or itinerant peasants and shepherds, ferocious in battle but lacking discipline and a sense of purpose. The Habsburgs were not opposed to the organization of a Hungarian "field army," but on condition that either the *hajduk* host was disbanded or that it was whipped and organized into a usable military force.

Either way, armies cost money, more money than the depleted Austrian treasury could produce. Noble cooperation was essential and many nobles used their Protestantism as an excuse for refusing contributions to the royal treasury. For its part, the Habsburg Crown used the expedient of filing lawsuits against nobles for inheritance or for treason to force them to pay up. Hand-in-hand with doing so, Vienna, under the general aegis of the Counter Reformation, launched a vigorous campaign to bring recalcitrant nobles under its authority on religious grounds. Churches and cathedrals confiscated by Protestants were forcibly brought back to the Catholic fold; attempts by nobles to bring the matter before their Diet were silenced by a royal decree that forbade the discussion of religious issues by lawmaking bodies.

The mood was revolutionary throughout the country. There was hardly a stratum of Hungarian society that did not nurse grievances; with the Turkish threat receding, the Habsburgs came to be looked on as the real enemy. The sounds of discontent reached the ears of a Transylvanian noble, István Bocskai, who had sought refuge in Turkey from Habsburg depradations. He now began to organize a force that, with Turkish help, would enable him to invade Hungary and become prince of Transylvania, the province the Habsburgs claimed as their own but which was kept beyond their reach by the Turkish-occupied center of the country. Vienna learned of Bocskai's preparations and, in 1604, sent an army under its foremost general Beglioso against him. The core of Beglioso's army was 5,000 former *hajduk,* enlisted in Habsburg armies and subjected to military discipline. However, upon learning that they were to be engaged against a Hungarian noble, they revolted and joined Bocskai's force. A surprise attack by this army against Beglioso's imperial forces resulted in the destruction of the latter. Bocskai then conquered a good part of northern Hungary, not the first or the last time that a rebellious noble wrested ill-defended regions from royal control, always to find in the end that conquest was easier than maintaining control. Bocskai, taking stock of the true power factors, concluded with the Habsburgs the peace of Vienna while he still wielded a powerful hand. The agreement made him prince of Transylvania, recognized the full power of the Hungarian Diet to make laws and, most important, guaranteed freedom of worship for Protestants. To guard these provisions, he settled scores of *hajduk* in major towns as citizens, freeing them of the obligation of military service.

At the end of December 1606 Bocskai died unexpectedly; the *hajduk* suspected his secretary of poisoning him, dragging him into the town square, and cutting him to pieces. They rightly felt that the willful and obstreperous Habsburg king and Holy Roman emperor, Rudolf II, would try to nullify many of the reforms Bocskai had wrested from him. When Rudolf indeed called a halt to settling the *hajduk* in cities, they revolted and demanded that Hungary have her own, Hungarian, king. Rudolf, an addle-brained mystic who spent most of his time in Prague engaged in black magic and other useless pursuits, was under attack in Austria and Bohemia as well for his inattention to his governing duties, and he was forced to abdicate. The court chose his brother Matthias (II) to take the throne, and, before being crowned king of Hungary, Matthias had to confirm the prerogatives of the Hungarian Diet and the privileges of the nobility.

Matthias ruled from 1608 until his death in 1619 and, during this time, religious peace reigned in the empire. He was succeeded by the zealot Ferdinand II, whom no political argument could convince of the wisdom of religious toleration. The Counter Reformation was in full swing and the Jesuits enjoyed, in Hungary and elsewhere, Ferdinand's unstinting support. Foremost among them was Péter Pázmány, born into a Calvinist family but converted in his youth to Catholicism. In time he became bishop and it was his great merit that he regarded cultural endeavors as the best instruments of conversion. In his many writings and rhetorical tracts he created a literary language that largely replaced the contemporary bastardized version of Hungarian with its many foreign adumbrations. Although a loyal Hungarian, he realized that to ensure Hungary's Catholic future, the continued rule of the Habsburgs was necessary and he became a leading supporter of such rule. However, in this—the belief that preservation of a Catholic state was the primary function of the ruling house—he had few supporters. In the eyes of the great majority of the population the Habsburgs remained unpopular and were often hated. They gave no evidence of being concerned with Hungary's welfare and future; even their occasional warfare against the Turks served only to defend the buffer in the west of Hungary rather than to liberate the country itself. This was why Transylvania, semi-independent and except for occasional incursions enjoying relative calm, was of such importance in the eyes of patriots. The Habsburgs claimed it but could not enforce their claim; the Turks left it generally unmolested as a counter-weight to German Austria. Even when a Turkish attack fell on this remote province, as it did in 1593, at the beginning of the so-called Fifteen-Year War, the thrust of the attack pointed westward, toward Vienna. If there was a defining feature in Hungarian history in the 16th and early 17th centuries, it was that the nation and its hard-pressed leaders had at every step to choose between two nearly equally undesirable alternatives: to hold off the Turk, Habsburg help was necessary; to avoid Habsburg domination, which was sure to ensue once victory had been won, some dependence on Turkey was called for. Meanwhile national life, politically, economically, and culturally, stagnated. Transylvania alone, and only for periods, stood as an exception.

CHAPTER THREE

At the opening of the 17th century, as we have noted, the appellation "Hungary" carried any validity only in the easternmost province, Transylvania; the rest of the country was under foreign occupation or in a state of devastation. By every legitimate measure the Habsburgs were kings of Hungary, but only the upper nobility, or that segment of it that regarded homage to the king as part of its Catholic duties, acknowledged that. By tradition, in Christian countries a noble's primary allegiance was to his monarch. The Catholic Church sanctioned the monarch's claim to the throne by divine right and the monarch in turn upheld the church's position and its laws by secular means. In Hungary the lesser nobility periodically asserted itself in defiance of this principle, but they never did so decisively. The majority had embraced Protestantism, mainly of the Calvinist variety, and they were in general more patriotic than the high aristocracy, yearning for a Hungary independent of foreign rule. Many of the lower nobility regarded the Habsburgs as a greater impediment to an independent Hungary than the Turks.

After Bocskai's death in 1606, following a two-year interregnum, Gábor Báthori, a young and gifted but unruly scion of the great Báthori family, was elected prince of Transylvania. He had vaulting ambitions, planning to unite his province with the Romanian principalities of Moldavia and Wallachia, and even with Poland, to create one empire. His dictatorial ways and lack of tact turned many of his friends into enemies and compelled one of his most devoted supporters, Gábor Bethlen, to emigrate to Turkey. The Porte, which kept a watchful eye on Transylvania, trying to prevent both its aggrandizement and its diminution, grew uneasy about Báthori's reckless enterprises and sent an army to unseat him. He fled and was killed by *hajduk* as he was on the run. The Transylvanian Diet thereupon elected the returned Gábor Bethlen as prince.

Bethlen's 16-year reign (1613–29), despite its many conflicts, is still remembered as the golden age of Transylvania, witnessing great economic and cultural improvements and the introduction of genuine religious toleration. The Turkish danger was in abeyance and Bethlen joined the anti-Habsburg faction, realizing that even Austria's occasional struggles against the Turks aimed at ensuring unimpeded Habsburg dominion over all of Hungary. When in 1618 religious strife broke out in the province of Bohemia (an uprising that in time grew into the climactic last act of the religious wars, the Thirty Years' War), Bethlen allied himself with the Bohemian estates whose defiance of the Habsburgs and election of a counter-king to the incumbent Ferdinand, a Protestant, had precipitated the conflict. Aided by Silesian and Moravian forces, Bethlen besieged Vienna, and, although he was compelled to lift the siege, in the process his armies succeeded in occupying most of Hungary; on August 25, 1620, a special session of the Diet elected him king of the country. Aware of the tenuousness of his hold, Bethlen refused to be crowned, awaiting developments in the widening religious conflict. As it happened, only three months after his election, Austrian forces crushed the Bohemian army in the Battle of White Mountain, and the prospect of humbling the Habsburgs instantly receded.

Bethlen did not waver. By sheer tenacity he forced King Ferdinand to conclude with him, in 1622, the Peace of Nikolsburg, granting Hungarian estates self-government in their respective provinces, and also, what for Ferdinand was the hardest concession to make, religious toleration. Given the intensity of the struggle between Catholics and Protestants, however, this could only have been an interim arrangement and its longevity depended on the outcome of the larger war. As that war dragged on, Bethlen joined forces with several Protestant powers against Austria and her Catholic allies. With the passage of years, the religious question became so intertwined with political and territorial issues and so many states were drawn into the conflict that a clear-cut victory by either side seemed impossible. Bethlen earned some partial victories, but all he had to show for them was the acquisition of seven eastern counties in the Uplands, which the Habsburgs agreed to cede to Transylvania under his rule.

An enlightened despot, Bethlen sought to ease the lot of the serfs and to protect them from excessive demands by their lords; he even forbade the latter to keep peasant boys who wished to be educated from attending school. His Protestantism did not blind him to the religious concerns of other denominations. He recalled the expelled Jesuits, authorized the founding of Catholic bishoprics, and exempted Jews from wearing the yellow star. He even invited an Anabaptist sect that found no protection anywhere else to settle in his province. His own princely court, and the palaces he constructed, became legendary for their magnificence; on the cultural scene he introduced the great novelty of the age, the Italian opera.

He died in 1629, and the Transylvanian Diet, rejecting the claims of his wife and his younger brother to the princely throne, in 1630, elected as prince György Rákóczi (I), the wealthiest landlord not only in the province but also in the Partium. Rákóczi lacked Bethlen's fighting spirit and diplomatic skill; he was ready to sacrifice both national and Transylvanian interests in order to live in peace with Habsburgs and Turks alike. The Thirty Years' War continued in spurts; in 1644 the French and the Swedes joined the anti-Habsburg coalition and Rákóczi decided to reenter the conflict. After raising an army of volunteers from the Uplands, he established contact with the Swedes and took the field. Despite some initial reverses in attempts to conquer the Habsburg-ruled western strip of Hungary, his armies turned the tide of battle and, in 1645, not only occupied most of the Uplands but even broke into the Habsburg hereditary province of Moravia. The Porte viewed these exploits with unease—if Rákóczi succeeded in expelling the Habsburgs from the Carpathian Basin he might turn against the Turks—and they ordered him to abandon the campaign. Rákóczi complied with surprising readiness—perhaps his heart was never in the struggle. He made peace with Ferdinand III of Austria (1637–57) and agreed to return the counties Bethlen had won in the Nikolsburg peace. His only gain was Habsburg consent to extending religious freedom to the serfs.

The Peace of Westphalia that ended the Thirty Years' War touched Habsburg interests only insofar as the Holy Roman Empire, of which they had been the titular heads for centuries, lost its political cohesion. Each unit became free not only to govern itself but also to make and break alliances. With their influence in Germany greatly diminished, the Habsburgs were all the more determined to assert their power within their own empire. They already had, in the spirit of royal absolutism that had gained a foothold in France and spread across much of the rest of Europe, reduced the legislative estates within their hereditary realms to practical impotence; now they attempted to do the same in Hungary. Entirely coincidentally, at this time, in the middle of the 17th century, the Turkish Empire, which had been in a state of steady decline since Suleiman's death, showed new signs of life. Viziers, mainly from the Köprülü family of Albanian descent, reorganized the army and revived its conquering spirit. In earlier times (in the 15th century) a large and well-governed Hungary had blocked the way to the center of German power; now a good part of Hungary lay prostrate, depopulated and militarily helpless. Transylvania alone survived relatively intact but was nowhere strong enough to withstand a major Turkish drive. The Habsburgs were generally content to let Ottoman power enjoy its piecemeal conquests at the expense of Hungary, reckoning that after its ultimate defeat they would repossess a country too exhausted to resist imperial claims.

At this point in time a Hungarian soldier of sterling qualities and with a family tradition of fighting the Turks stepped forward. Miklós Zrinyi was the great grandson of the Zrinyi who had fallen in the defense of the fort of Szigetvár. His family's estate in Croatia lay along the Turkish route of advance, and soldiering had become the obligatory career of every male in his family. The Zrinyis of earlier generations had belonged to those who believed that only Habsburg power could drive out the Turks, in the aftermath of which Hungary would be allowed to govern herself, with only a personal union tying her to Austria. Zrinyi at a young and ardent age (still in his 20s) had begun a literary career, seeking both to rouse with his poems the spirit of his people for a great crusade and to explicate the military imperatives for such a campaign. To be able to make the necessary preparations, however, he had to be chosen *nádor*, the highest position in Hungary below the king, in charge of military and financial affairs. The Diet of 1655 was about to bestow that dignity on him, but the court did not place his name in nomination, a fact that disqualified him. At this point Zrinyi broke with the pro-Habsburg family tradition and determined to wage a national struggle against the ruling house. Given military realities, the base of operations had to be Transylvania. Zrinyi used his influence to assure the election as prince of that province the only man who, as he saw it, could put himself at the head of the campaign, György Rákóczi II (1648–60), son of the Rákóczi who had fought the Habsburgs in the Thirty Years' War and then made peace with them. Zrinyi wanted to go so far as to have the young Rákóczi elected king of all of Hungary and thereby in effect dethrone the Habsburg Leopold I (who had just succeeded Ferdinand III). But at the Diet of 1655 the clergy, faithful to the Habsburgs, blocked the maneuver and Leopold was elected king. However, Rákóczi became prince of Transylvania. As it happened it was an unfortunate choice.

The young prince combined mediocre talent with reckless ambitions. Far from taking the lead in the great struggle to free Hungary, his ill-advised undertakings even devastated the province he ruled. He aspired to the throne of Poland and, without consulting the Porte of which he was formally a vassal, he led an army there, took Krakow and Warsaw, at which point the Porte moved against the obstreperous prince. It ordered its Tatar hosts in the Crimea to bear down on Rákóczi's force. The Tatars captured his whole army, marched it to the Crimea, then invaded defenseless Transylvania, which for half a century had enjoyed peace and prosperity, and visited on it the kind of destruction as had long been associated with the Tatar name. Rákóczi managed to escape with his life, but, arriving home, he found that the Porte had deprived him of his princedom.

Zrinyi foresaw the resultant sequence of events: the Turks, seeing the practical fall of the last Hungarian stronghold, would be encouraged to renew their offensive against Hungarians and Habsburgs alike. He foresaw also that the Vienna court, far from lamenting Rákóczi's tragic fate and the rape of Transylvania, rejoiced in the defeat of a Protestant prince and of a province where Protestantism held wide sway and where the Habsburgs were held in low esteem. They would seize the opportunity to make themselves masters of that province, a goal that had thus far eluded them. The Turks had their own designs. A large army was on the march and invested one Transylvanian fort after another. By the end of 1660 the key fort of Várad had fallen and Transylvania lay open to Turkish occupation.

There still remained regions, however, where maneuver was possible, specifically the western portions of the Upland, and Zrinyi decided to build a fort at a key point of passage, named for him, Zrinyi-Ujvár. The war council in Vienna, fearing that the plan would provoke the Turks into launching a new offensive against Vienna, vetoed the construction; Zrinyi proceeded anyhow. The court's fear was not groundless; in 1663 a new Turkish offensive was unleashed against northern Hungary. Zrinyi's tactical skills frustrated their project; he moved his forces south, took and burned the auxiliary bridge the Turks had built over the Drava River, and cut off their supplies.

Victory was within reach but Vienna wanted peace. It removed Zrinyi from command and appointed the Austrian general Montecuccoli in his stead. It was in this phase of the war that the Habsburgs showed their true intentions; they made no move to relieve the pressure on Hungary, allowed several forts to fall, and gave battle only when Vienna itself was in danger. By now French and German imperial troops bolstered the Austrian forces. In early August Montecuccoli joined battle at St. Gotthard and, thanks largely to the powerful artillery the French contributed, the Turkish army was destroyed or captured.

The weakened state of the Ottoman Empire was so evident that the time seemed ripe for the complete liberation of Hungary. Most of Europe did in fact take it for granted that Austrian armies would go on the offensive and, shoulder to shoulder with Hungarians, undertake this long overdue crusade. But, whether out of a genuine desire for peace (which was unlikely) or because their relations with France had taken a sharp turn for the worse and they feared a new war in the west, the Habsburgs made peace with the Turks, the Peace of Vasvár, which left most of the occupied portions of Hungary in Turkish hands.

This shameful peace produced a new alignment of forces. The great nobility of Hungary, for all its loyalty to the ruling house, had enough patriotic sentiment left to realize that the Habsburgs were always ready to sacrifice Hungarian interests to promote their own. A number of them, the majority of the Catholic faith, including the *nádor* and the bishop of the largest see in Hungary, approached French king Louis XIV with an offer of an alliance against the Habsburgs. They were even ready for a pact with the Turks, if the Porte recognized Hungarian independence. Zrinyi, however, who still had a commanding voice, clung to his romantic vision of Hungary gaining her complete freedom from both Habsburgs and Turks through her own national forces. Zrinyi was killed during a hunt in November by an enraged boar and another great presence passed from the scene.

The French king showed no interest in the offer of alliance, and in Hungary unhappiness with the Habsburgs simmered; the great nobles continued their idle conspiracies, though these lacked dimension and seriousness of purpose; internally they ignored the middle and lower nobility and showed no interest in relieving the lot of the oppressed peasantry. The conspirators still hoped that a call to arms against the Habsburgs would rouse the rank and file. They chose the exiled György Rákóczi to lead an uprising; he issued a call for the Upland counties to rise. The call produced no echoes, the conspiratorial plans were laid bare, and Habsburg reprisals were not long in coming. Nowhere did the imperial forces invading the country meet any resistance; most of the conspirators were rounded up, condemned by a tribunal composed largely of Germans, beheaded, their properties confiscated. Rákóczi alone was spared, thanks to the intercession of his wife, a fanatical Catholic.

A new nightmare of oppression descended on the country. The Habsburgs, blaming the entire nation for the conspiracy of a few, ended Hungary's special status within their empire, suspended her constitution, appointed an Austrian viceroy, dismissed without pay the soldiery defending the frontier fortresses, and replaced them with mercenaries in their own hire. Hungary, as the saying went, became the "garrison of Germans." Depradations by the military were appalling, tax burdens on the peasantry increased manifoldly. Hundreds of Protestant clergymen were accused of fraternizing with the Turks, tried, and, unless willing to convert to Catholicism, sentenced to death. In the end, however, most were marched to the Adriatic and sold as galley slaves.

Thousands, whether or not they had reason to fear persecution, chose to leave their homes and wander to remote frontiers, mainly in Transylvania. They came to be known as *bujdosók,* men in hiding or on the run, men without a country or a place to rest their heads, symbols of the sad fact that Hungarians were not free in their own country. In time these refugees from justice were joined by runaway serfs and began to organize in a military fashion. They took on the name *kuruc,* probably from the name used by György Dózsa's crusaders, the *cruciferi.*

The *kuruc* forces waged a guerrilla campaign of sorts against German occupiers, with little effect; matters changed only when they found a leader in a 19-year-old young man, Imre Thököly. Son of a large landowner from the Uplands, his father had been accused of conspiracy but died before justice could be meted out against him. The son took refuge in Transylvania, burning with desire to wreak revenge on the Habsburgs who had dragged the family name into disrepute. A born soldier, he had excellent leadership qualities. Under his command the *kuruc* forces went on the offensive and in short order drove Habsburg armies from the eastern Uplands. Thousands of volunteers, most of them lesser nobles, joined Thököly's forces. Within two years all of the Uplands were wrested from the Habsburgs. It was not easy going, however. There never was enough money to pay the soldiers and they often had to live off the land, causing much resentment and unrest. Only when Thököly married the widow of György Rákóczi and the huge wealth and estates of that family were his to use did his position become secure. The Porte grandiosely proclaimed him king of Hungary, but he satisfied himself with ruling the northern part of the country only. Although he maintained good relations with Constantinople, he spurned an alliance with the Turks and preferred to avail himself of the help of Louis XIV of France, who was by now only too happy to see the Habsburg enemy hard-pressed by its own subjects.

Leopold had to make concessions before the uprising in Hungary assumed more formidable proportions. He recalled his much-resented viceroy and reconvened the Diet after a 20-year absence. When it met, in 1681, Leopold reaffirmed noble privileges. The majority of the counties represented in the Diet were satisfied with these largely formal concessions, but Thököly did not trust Habsburg promises and continued the struggle.

Of Hungary's two perpetual enemies Turkey now seemed the more vulnerable. Since her armies had first advanced to the outskirts of Vienna in 1526, and established Ottoman power in the center of Europe, they had made many more attempts to conquer the city and all had failed. Now, with Thököly practically holding the Habsburgs at bay, they made one last thrust. Advancing from the east and the south, they set the suburbs on fire and were about to enter the city. Two relieving armies, one under Charles of Lorraine and another under Polish king John III Sobieski, arrived and scattered the Turkish host. Leopold, who had fled in panic as the Turks approached, returned and decided on a counter-attack. As a diplomatic prelude, he assured himself of the support of Pope Innocent XI; the alliance was joined by Poland and Venice to form the Holy League. At last a force capable of expelling the Turk from Habsburg lands was at hand.

The first victim of the offensive unleashed by the Holy League was Imre Thököly. Many of his *kuruc* fighters, attracted by the prospect of the Turk finally driven from their country, deserted him and joined the forces of the Holy

League. Thököly was deposed by the Vienna court but allowed to remain free. In July 1688 the Hungarian capital city of Buda, for over a century in Turkish hands, was besieged; it fell in September. The Christian forces turned south, maintained their momentum, and took Belgrade, key to the control of the Balkans. Thököly, now a refugee, chose the less than honorable course of making common cause with the Turks. He invaded Transylvania in 1690 and had himself elected prince, but, when the united Christian forces advanced against him, he fled the province.

For seven years the fortunes of the Holy League waxed and waned, but in September 1697, the great Austrian general Eugene of Savoy inflicted a decisive defeat on the Turks at the town of Zenta. That battle marked the end of nearly three centuries of Ottoman ascendancy.

In the Treaty of Karlowitz (concluded on January 26, 1699) all of Hungary, except the Bánát of Temesvár, was restored to the Habsburgs. Already in 1687 the Hungarian Diet, at the urging of the great Catholic nobles, had hereditary kingship vested in the Habsburgs.

Peace had at last come to the tormented land, but independence was still a distant prospect.

CHAPTER FOUR

With the Turks driven beyond the great rivers, the Danube and the Sava, which marked the southern boundaries of the country, Hungary was free of one enemy, but the Habsburgs exacted a high price for the liberation. They had their main claim satisfied as far back as 1687, the year after imperial troops reconquered Buda from the Turks; when the Diet formally relinquished its right to elect kings, it also renounced the closing article of the Golden Bull which empowered nobles to resist the monarch if key provisions of the Bull were violated. The Hungarian crown became hereditary in the House of Habsburg and no protest against the royal will was allowed to be raised.

The treasury, after a decade and a half of continuous fighting, was deep in debt and heavy new taxes had to be imposed to return it to solvency; as always, the serfs bore the brunt of the levies. Serf households were obligated to billet and feed imperial soldiery at a time when many barely had enough room and food for their own needs; the country was thrown open to exploitation. In general, the same extortionist legislation that two decades earlier had been inflicted on the populace as punishment for its rebellion were reintroduced as emergency measures in an attempt to shift the costs of the long war from Austria to Hungary. Now, as then, many peasants, rather than shouldering the burden, took to the hills and became refugees in their own country. The ruling house also compiled a long list of individuals who, by whatever definition, had cooperated with the Turks. The notorious general Caraffa set up a special tribunal in the town of Eperjes to try such cases; 24 well-to-do nobles and burghers were sentenced to death and loss of property while others suffered imprisonment, their confiscated estates given to Austrian generals. The heavy hand of absolutism extended to the religious sphere as well. As before, its chief instrument was the Society of Jesus. Hundreds of Jesuits were brought into the country and given a free hand in conducting their campaign against Protestants; in regions where the population had been decimated under Turkish rule thousands of Catholic Germans were settled. In the south, which had suffered most heavily, Serbian peasants were given land grants; even the Eastern Orthodox were favored over the Protestants, who were suppressed and their places of worship closed down. In the estimation of Vienna, Hungarians were by nature rebellious and contrary; to be governed effectively, their will had to be broken. Occasionally, as in 1697, peasants driven to despair would rise and occupy a fortified town or two, but for lack of outside support these uprisings collapsed.

The perennial search for a leader whom the nation could trust was perhaps never more evident. The Rákóczi family of Transylvania had twice in the past century produced such leaders, and although their work remained unfinished, they had written their names into the annals of Hungarian history. Another young Rákóczi arose in these black years of Habsburg oppression: Ferenc Rákóczi was the son of a father by the same name and of Ilona Zrinyi. Taken from his mother at an early age by the Habsburgs who hoped to expunge his Hungarian loyalties, educated by Jesuits, he went on to study at the University of Prague and then in Italy. Through his marriage in 1694 (to a princess of the German state of Hessen-Rheinfels), he became related to Louis XIV of France. Loyal to the Habsburgs, he several times turned down humble appeals that he place himself at the head of uprisings against them. How and why his outlook changed and whether his conversion to the cause of Hungarian independence was sudden or gradual is unrecorded in history. His closer acquaintance with conditions within Hungary, and the persuasions of great nobles he was in contact with no doubt opened his eyes to certain truths he had previously refused to face, but none of them could have come as a great surprise to him. He had been shocked by the bloody suppression that followed the failed uprising of serfs in the region of Hagyalja, and it had an undeniable impact on his conscience. Thus far he had seen the Habsburgs as paragons of royal virtue and as friends of his people. Now he witnessed an instance of their capability to engage in the most brutal conduct when their rule was in the least threatened. This discovery alone, however, was unlikely to turn him against the royal house. Possibly he had a personal grievance that research has failed to discover or that has been suppressed. In 1700, through a French intermediary, he contacted in secret Louis XIV of France, an enemy by tradition of the Habsburgs (though he was married to a Habsburg princess). The intermediary betrayed Rákóczi to the Vienna court, and he was arrested and locked up in the fort of Wiener Neustadt. With the help of his wife and her connections he escaped and fled to Poland, whose royal family was also closely linked to the French. It was while in Poland that he firmly committed himself to the cause of a Hungary free of Habsburg dominion. However, he remained out of touch with conditions in his country until a former serf of his, Tamás Esze, visited him with the news that a peasant army stood ready to strike against Austria; it only awaited a leader. Rákóczi sent his own envoys into Hungary to explore the situation; they reported to him in the same sense Esze did. In May 1703 Rákóczi crossed the border from Poland and called on "every titled and untitled Hungarian" to rally to his side.

Most of his volunteers came from untitled ranks, in fact most nobles watched the gathering uprising with unease and mistrust. Not without reason, because as Rákóczi descended from the Carpathians, his message to the peasants was unsettling to their masters: those who would fight for national liberation would be freed not only of the wanton plunder of German soldiery but also of feudal obligations. As the ranks of volunteers grew to a flood and major cities in eastern Hungary fell to Rákóczi's forces, a number of noblemen (usually such as were not threatened in their property) nevertheless joined Rákóczi's forces. Only the high priesthood stood apart and condemned the freedom fight.

The Habsburgs now faced another one of the seemingly perennial armed challenges to their rule. In 1700 they had been drawn into the War of the Spanish Succession and now the fight against France tied down the bulk of their forces. Rákóczi's free corps roamed almost unopposed in the Uplands and drew dangerously close to Vienna. Habsburg stubbornness and tenacity saved the day, though only temporarily. In 1704 Austrian forces defeated the French on the upper Danube and were able to transfer some of their troops to the eastern area of operations. What they faced by this time was open rebellion. The Hungarian Diet was so confident of the outcome that it met to plan the organization of the country free of any Habsburg connection. It elected Rákóczi prince and chose a senate of 25 men to make the major political decisions; an economic council was to deal with questions of taxation and feudal obligations. While they did not outright dethrone the Habsburgs, they demanded restoration of their right to elect kings and to disobey them if they breached their obligations under the Golden Bull. Rákóczi, who had been elected prince of Transylvania the year before, was satisfied to limit himself to that title; under the circumstances it was the only reliable foil to Habsburg absolutism.

Military fortunes, however, slowly turned against the insurrectionists. Although 40,000 Habsburg troops were tied down on the western front, a sufficient number of well-equipped and battle-trained forces remained in the east to oppose Rákóczi's poorly disciplined army. His appeals to Louis XIV brought no relief; the French were fighting a number of enemies besides the Austrians and needed their hard-pressed forces for their own defense. Rákóczi's proposal that French detachments link up with his *kuruc* forces in Croatia for a joint drive against Vienna did not even produce a reply. Overtures to Vienna for a cessation of the struggle on condition that Hungarian national and religious rights were guaranteed were turned down. Thereupon, in June 1707, a Diet meeting in the town of Onod declared the Habsburgs dethroned and vowed to continue the struggle.

The material conditions for that course were not present, however. What arms Rákóczi's forces acquired were purchased abroad and the tax burden on the impoverished population could not be further increased. Rákóczi tried to tax his fellow nobles, but they resisted. He promised liberation from feudal status to peasants who continued to fight, but that offer alienated the nobility who felt all too keenly the absence of its serfs. In August of 1708 a *kuruc* army suffered a great defeat at the hands of imperial forces, and the armed fight was in effect over. An outbreak of the plague decimated Rákóczi's remaining army, and he withdrew into the northeastern part of the country. More and more Habsburg troops released from the western front joined imperial forces fighting in Hungary. Rákóczi placed his last hope in enlisting Peter the Great of Russia against Austria. Peter responded favorably but could not, or would not, send military aid. Meanwhile Rákóczi had left for Poland, and his deputy at home, realizing the hopelessness of the situation, in April 1711 concluded with the Habsburgs the Peace of Szatmár. The new monarch in Vienna, Joseph I (1705–11), was magnanimous. He offered forgiveness to former rebels and pledged to respect the Hungarian constitution and freedom of religion.

Ferenc Rákóczi II
*(Hungarian Museum
of Photography)*

For Rákóczi that was not enough. Hungary was still a Habsburg province, not his homeland and he never returned to it. He stayed for a while in Poland, then transferred himself to Versailles, and from there, in the vain hope of resuming the struggle against the Habsburgs, he went to Turkey. In the town of Rodosto, he died in 1735.

In that year there sat in Vienna on the throne vacated by the untimely death of Joseph I his younger brother, Charles, Holy Roman Emperor as Charles VI and king of Hungary as Charles III. He had been slated to be king of Spain but the Habsburgs lost that throne in the War of the Spanish Succession. Charles did not follow in Hungary his uncle Leopold's high-handed absolutist methods. After the Peace of Szatmár he allowed Hungary at least the illusion of being a separate unit of his empire. But all administrative offices operated out of Vienna and the governing bodies, the State Council and the Secret Conference, had no Hungarian members. Still, after so many exhausting struggles, the small measure of conciliation the Habsburgs showed sufficed to disarm serious Hungarian resistance. In 1713, for complicated reasons and when he still could hope for a male heir, Charles issued the Pragmatic Sanction; as it happened its provision that in the absence of a male heir a female could inherit his far-flung possessions turned out to be its main feature. In 1722 the parliament in Buda solemnly accepted the document. It was not an entirely selfless action on part of the noble estates (the clergy voted for the document as a matter of course). Many titles, decorations, and a reaffirmation of noble privileges were awarded in gratitude for the vote.

The Pragmatic Sanction mandated not only internal unity (all parts of the empire had to follow the same law of succession, meaning that if one elected a monarch, whether man or woman, all the others had to follow) but also joint resistance to external aggression. In essence it meant that Hungarian noble estates, which for a generation had fought and bled in a struggle to dethrone the Habsburgs, now not only accepted Habsburg rule but vowed to defend it on the field of battle. A number of European monarchs also signified their acceptance of the terms of that unprecedented document, but given rising tensions, especially in the Holy Roman Empire, their pledges were of dubious value.

Charles III died on October 20, 1740, and the crisis he feared even as he dispensed prodigious amounts from the royal treasury to validate the Pragmatic

Sanction quickly engulfed the monarchy. His daughter, Maria Theresa, then 24 years old, succeeded him. She was married to Francis of Lorraine, a dynastic marriage but one of great personal warmth and mutual devotion. The Habsburgs had married in so many directions that the young heiress had hardly been crowned when claimants to her throne came forward. Some of these, rulers in the Holy Roman Empire, based their claim on having married Habsburg women, but the most dangerous foe was not an aspirant to the throne but the young king of the state of Prussia, Frederick II, equally eager to obtain the rich Habsburg province of Silesia and to put the large and well-trained army his father had left him to the test. Soon the Bavarians, the Spanish, and the Venetians took the field against the young queen and the Habsburg Empire seemed on the verge of partition. Desperate, bereft of resources, Maria Theresa, in June 1741 turned to the Hungarian estates for support. Nobles high and low repaired to Pressburg (Pozsony in Hungarian) to answer the call; on September 12, in a memorable demonstration of loyalty, they acclaimed in unison: *"Vitam et sanguinem pro rege nostro Maria Theresia!"* (Even now they pledged their life and blood to their *king*, Maria Theresa; to do so to a queen seemed incongruous.) Even though enemy forces were already inside the empire, the appearance of Hungarian forces on the battlefields did produce a change; the enemy was thrown back and when, in 1742, a truce was signed, only a part of Silesia was lost to the Habsburgs. The war continued, however, for the queen was loath to lose one of the most advanced and industrialized provinces in her empire. Still, this War of the Austrian Succession failed to dislodge Frederick II from Silesia.

Although the first woman ever on the Habsburg throne, Maria Theresa gave no sign of being insecure or irresolute. Her hand on the rudder was firm throughout her 40-year reign. Frederick II was quoted as saying, "The Habsburgs finally have a man on the throne, and even he is a woman." Hungarians liked to believe that their queen favored them over others in her empire, she gave so many evidences of it—she restored to Hungary the port of Fiume on the Adriatic and the Bánát of Temesvár, established a school in Vienna specifically for Hungarian nobles, organized a Hungarian bodyguard, and introduced a Hungarian royal decoration (the Order of St. Stephen)—but the truth was that she sought to forge her empire into a single political unit and could not have the largest component remain in a state of sullen opposition. All the same, Hungarians were beneficiaries of many of her reforms and showed their gratitude for it. The spirit of Enlightenment, abroad in Europe, informed many of her measures, at first under the influence of her chancellor, Prince Kaunitz, and later of her son Joseph, who in time would follow her on the throne. Only in religious matters was her enlightenment restrained: non-Catholics in the empire remained second-class subjects throughout her reign. Their freedom of worship was curtailed within the narrowest bounds and they could not be appointed to public office.

Characteristically, the nobility supported the queen only as long as she did not infringe on their privileges. When she called for noble taxation, they turned against her. It was just that, their freedom from taxation, that made the nobles a privileged class; for them to undertake the obligation of commoners would make them, in the eyes of the law, equal with them. Maria Theresa was undeterred and introduced noble taxation by executive decree. Another matter related to the landlords' freedom to impose monetary and labor obligations on their serfs. Already the ordinary peasant was greatly encumbered by the burdens deriving from the obligation to house and especially to feed and transport royal soldiery. When most military forces were withdrawn from Hungary, new hardships followed. Landlords began to enlarge the land on their estates that they retained for their own use, the manor as it was called. The rest, assigned to the peasants in small lots, were often in areas unsuitable for cultivation. In addition, as the land used by the landlord increased, more labor was required and that too fell on the peasants' shoulders. Rents payable in money were also increased. Repeated uprisings, pitiful and ill-organized affairs, drew the queen's attention to the problems on large landed estates. The royal treasury suffered because the less the peasant earned and the more his landlord demanded of him, the less was left over for state taxes and tithes.

The queen attempted to ease the serfs' burden by decreeing how much the noble could demand from them in labor and fees and by allowing them to bring their grievances through delegations before her "majestic presence." However, noble estates in parliament prevented royal authority from infringing on landlord-serf relations. Maria Theresa once again sought to settle the matter on her own. A royal edict of 1767 determined the minimum size of the land to be allotted to each serf, and also the rent to be paid for it. The size of the allotments varied from region to region, but on average, in addition to the one-*hold* (about 1.42 English acres) central lot that held the peasant's house and barns, he had to be allowed about 30 *hold* land for plowing and some 10 *hold* for forest and pasture. In addition to a small monetary rent, he also had to deliver to his landlord barnyard animals, milk, eggs, and butter; the *robot* was to be 52 days a year if rendered with a draft animal and double that if rendered by human labor. Maria Theresa showed her toughness in carrying through these measures despite vigorous noble objections.

The queen did not intend, however, that her domain remain a primarily agricultural economy. In western Europe manufacturing was for the day well advanced; in Habsburg lands only in Bohemia and in the tiny portion of Silesia left to them was there any industry at all. With the help of her son who was slated to succeed her, the queen introduced the mercantilist system in the empire. With so little and reluctant private enterprise, the Crown had to take a hand in modernizing the economy. Subventions and tax advantages were offered to those who established manufacturing plants, high tariffs protected their goods, and the Crown at times determined what was to be produced in what quality and quantity to make sure the goods would be competitive on the international market. Hungary at first had a modest place in this scheme: she was to provide much of the raw material for it and be paid for it with finished goods. It undoubtedly retarded the country's own industrial development, but it ensured a measure of prosperity Hungarians had not known before.

When Maria Theresa died on November 29, 1780, her oldest son (she had 16 children) Joseph was 39 years old. Since the death of his father, Francis of Lorraine, in 1765, he had been Holy Roman Emperor, a dignity he spurned. On succeeding his mother, he burned with impatience to carry her wavering enlightenment to the heights that he felt behooved an empire such as his.

In the history of Hungary, as well as the whole empire, a new era dawned.

Chapter Five

Enlightenment was the overriding vogue in many royal courts, large and small, during the 18th century. Some rulers treated it as a philosophical current and took vicarious pleasure in extolling its virtues while others, of deeper conviction and of a more practical mind, regarded it as a prescription for long overdue reform. These latter rebelled—against the intellectual tyranny of the Catholic Church, against a social order that kept the majority of the population in a state of bondage, against superstition and any belief not supported by reason. They held in contempt fellow monarchs who failed to understand the depth and magnitude of historic changes, who ensconced themselves in their palaces and lived for the day, trusting that the society they presided over would remain unchanged during their lifetime.

The most enlightened Austrian monarch, Joseph II, was intellectually utopian and temperamentally a despot, as most impatient reformers are. He seemed to sense that his time was short and reform was urgent. In Hungary he inherited a realm where the all-powerful social elite, the landowning magnates, set themselves against any social change that impinged on their prerogatives or sought to liberalize or liquidate feudalism. They had not been able to compel Joseph to take an oath to the constitution that guaranteed these prerogatives, as Joseph had declined the honor of being crowned and never took the obligatory oath that accompanied the coronation. He thus felt free to ignore not only the constitution but even the lawmaking body, the Diet, and during his 10-year reign he governed entirely by royal decree.

An account of Joseph II's reign is given in the section dealing with Austrian history pages 41–48 and in the current chapter we will confine ourselves mainly to how his many reforms affected Hungary. His religious decrees, although they diminished the dominant position of the Catholic Church in Austria, had no particular impact on Hungary, where Protestants enjoyed freedom of worship. Josephs's Edict of Toleration guaranteed them rights they already possessed, and its effect on Jews was minimal. What did cause consternation in Hungary was the series of edicts relating to feudalism, and it must be remembered that the feudal system was much more firmly entrenched in the Hungarian lands than in other provinces of the empire. Yet those edicts were by no means radical. Joseph's enlightenment did not go so far as to dismantle a system that for all its deplorable features had served as the bedrock of social stability for centuries. He put an end to manorial justice in which the landlord served as the sole judge of his serfs, and he forbade corporal punishment. He allowed serfs to leave their master's service and move freely, he allowed and even encouraged them to choose their occupation, and he forbade landlords to deprive serfs of their land allotments "without legal and sufficient reason." He even banned the use of the word "serf."

His language decree was another measure that caused deep resentment in Hungary (as well as in the Czech lands). Perhaps part of the resentment stemmed from the validity of his argument for the decree, namely, that the Hungarian language of the day lacked the sophistication and depth necessary for legal texts and elevated literary and philosophical tracts. For many technical terms it was dependent on Latin, a number of other influences had corrupted it, and it was essentially the vernacular of the lower classes. Laws and edicts were likely to be unclear, imprecise, or downright meaningless when written in Hungarian. Joseph had no patience with the use of the decorous but anachronistic Latin used in the church and in state administration: his language decree made German the uniform tongue in all official intercourse and all judicial proceedings. Hungarians (as other ethic groups) were confronted with the demand that they introduce German into state offices, and that in schools only German-speaking teachers be hired. The decree had a negative kind of success; while Hungarians generally rejected it, it increased their interest in their own language, which they sought to update to serve the needs of a modern society. A vigorous rehabilitation of the Hungarian language began.

As if intent upon further antagonizing Hungarians, Joseph ordered that the crown of St. Stephen, which had become a sacred symbol both of Hungarian royalty and of the country's special status, be transferred from Pressburg to Vienna and deposited in the royal treasury.

Hungary soon became the center of resistance to Joseph's sundry reforms. The country's administrative units, the counties, corresponded to the boundaries of ancient noble holdings and were still bastions of aristocratic power. Every royal decree had to find its way to the rank and file through a warren of bureaucratic centers on the county level; consequently, many of Joseph's edicts never reached the stratum for which they were intended. Joseph responded in a characteristically imperious way. He eliminated the counties as governmental units and divided Hungary into 10 districts, each headed by a royal official duty-bound to carry out the king's decrees. Even if Joseph had had time to impress his reforms on the Hungarian governmental system, it is doubtful that he would have succeeded. He was distant and the ruling lords were near. A telling example was the king's order that noble estates be surveyed and given addresses; the order, as well as one to hold a national census, foreshadowed an attempt to tax nobles and commoners alike. Neither measure passed beyond its very preliminary stages.

Some historians ascribe the failure of Joseph's far-reaching legislation to the outbreak of the war with Turkey in alliance with Catherine the Great of Russia, but most likely it was doomed by the haste with which it was introduced and by its deliberate flouting of tradition. Whereas that tradition might have been less than honorable, it was deeply embedded in the nation's life. The winds of change blowing out of France where a revolution was in progress had not yet reached Hungary or the empire; reform would come by slow measured steps, checkered with many setbacks. Before Joseph died in February 1780 of consumption, realizing that he had been trying to do too much in too little time, he withdrew all his reforms except for those affecting the serfs and the monasteries as well as his Edict of Toleration.

Judging from the reactions in Hungary to Joseph's passing, a heavy burden had been lifted and the nation seemed to breathe freely again. Within a month the crown of St. Stephen was returned to Buda amid general rejoicing, and people by the thousands donned native costumes in a backlash to the dead king's decree on Germanization. Officials in charge of carrying out his edicts were dismissed in droves. Data derived from the land surveys and the census were publicly burned. A number of nobles advanced the theory that Joseph's refusal to be crowned had ended the legitimacy of the Habsburg line in Hungary and the estates were once again free to choose their own king. Often even those who were supposed to benefit from the Josephine reforms turned against them. Serfs feared that by gaining their freedom they would be cast adrift and deprived of the security the system vouchsafed them; Jews looked on the measures speeding up their emancipation as a means to infringe on their religious practices and alienate them from their faith. The nation was in ferment and the fortunes of the Habsburgs were at a low ebb.

Joseph was followed on the throne by his brother Leopold II; the latter had been archduke of Tuscany and was in general sympathy with Joseph's reforms, though he was more modest in his expectations and more moderate in his methods. He quickly defused the two conflicts that kept his armies tied down and restricted his freedom of action; he terminated the war with the Turks at the cost of giving up certain conquered territories, including Belgrade, and came to an agreement with Prussia, which, in an effort to weaken the Habsburgs, had tacitly supported discontented Hungarian nobles in their opposition to Joseph's legislation. With his armies available for action, Leopold felt free to proceed against the ferment in Hungary.

Confident of prevailing over any opposition, he called the Hungarian Diet into session; he found the estates tamed and on the whole cooperative. They agreed to move their sessions to Pressburg, closer to Vienna and easier to control, and they duly elected Leopold king of Hungary. They even allowed the highest Hungarian authority after the king, the *nádor*, to be a Habsburg, namely, the king's youngest son, Alexander Leopold. The Diet also endorsed the ecclesiastical legislation and the feudal decrees of Maria Theresa and Joseph II. In exchange Leopold offered the largely meaningless assurance, incorporated as an article into the law code, that "Hungary is a free and independent country," a country that had to be governed by her own laws executed by her own officials.

At the same time Leopold took steps to ensure that Hungary would not be the only province with such special privileges in his empire. Bohemia, once the largest and most important component next to Hungary, had been reduced to a mere shadow of itself in the wake of its catastrophic defeat in 1620 and could not credibly serve as a privileged province; thus Leopold chose the South Slavs as a foil to Hungary's unremitting drive for a favored position. In the fall of

1790 an Illyrian congress met amid all the external trappings of a lawmaking body; its pretensions soon went far beyond what Vienna had been ready to grant. Slavs demanded a clearly defined national territory and government by their own officials. Croatian representatives present at the congress objected to Hungarian as the language of official contacts; not trusting the efficacy of Serbian for that purpose, they demanded the restoration of Latin. These assertions met with little success, as did others that sought to curtail the ultimate absolutism of the Vienna court; Hungary alone gained partial exemption from that absolutism.

What brought the House of Habsburg and the Hungarian aristocracy closer together in these years was what could broadly be called the Jacobin danger. The lofty ideals of the revolution in France had at first attracted many men of serious mind in Europe, and the attraction fairly cut across all social classes: the woebegone lower middle class in France, the sansculottes, embraced them as a means of social elevation, the propertied middle class hoped for equality before the law and the end to noble and ecclesiastical privilege, many guilt-stricken nobles sought to redeem the social sins of their class by making the slogan "Liberty, Equality, Fraternity" their own. But as blood began to flow in the streets and impassioned mob fury took the place of legal action, many were sobered. It was ironic that the first political club formed in the French National Assembly, the club that called itself the Society of the Friends of the Constitution, mainly educated young men hostile to the dogmas and assumptions of the church, gained their popular name from that of a religious association, the Jacobin order, when they rented its vacated premises in Paris. Ironic also that the club that in its practices observed upper-middle-class manners and habits, in time, under the relentless pressure of the Paris mob, drifted to the left and became the very epitome of social radicalism. It was the Jacobins who eventually used terror to maintain a flagging revolutionary spirit against all its enemies on the right and the left. When in July 1794 the sovereign legislative body, the National Convention, itself the object of Jacobin terror, arrested and executed the chief Jacobin, Maximilien Robespierre, the movement collapsed, its ideals discredited. In the year that followed, during the so-called Thermidorian Reaction, the revolution turned against itself, and the sansculottes, once its driving force, became its primary victims.

Because of its steadily shifting focus Jacobinism was not easy to define, but it came to be regarded as an enemy of royal power and especially of absolutism, of any kind of social privilege, any inequality before the law. It hoped to establish on the ruins of the old order what Robespierre termed a Republic of Virtue, a republic of equals freely obeying the law sanctioned by the Supreme Being, an ill-defined deity with no relation to the God of the Bible.

In Hungary, after the death of Joseph II, when an era of hesitant and failed reforms came to an end, Jacobin ideals exerted a certain attraction on intellectuals. These men did not fail to see how backward their country was compared to the west and how progress was being artificially retarded. One leading intellectual, observing this sorry state of affairs, wrote: "The flowering of science is far removed from our country; . . . ex-Jesuits spare no effort to prevent the translation of scientific books . . . ; they are afraid that the nation will achieve the enlightenment necessary for the introduction of a political constitution answering the demands of justice and the right."

Those who agreed with this assessment, by no means large in number, were recruited mainly from among writers, scientists, jurists, and the teaching profession; far removed from the ugliness of revolutionary extremism, they held these ideals practicable through social reform. They found a leader in a one-time religious brother and teacher of theology, Ignác Martinovics. He early rebelled against religious strictures, his interest resting in the natural sciences, and his philosophy teetered on the verge of atheism. He was also fiercely ambitious and hoped to rise to a high position in politics. He joined Leopold's secret police with the assignment of touring the country and reporting on public sentiment; he hoped in this way to gain the trust of the king and influence him in the direction of liberal reform. But Leopold died early (in March 1792) and was followed by his oldest son (Francis I in Austria, Francis II as Holy Roman Emperor). In contrast to his father, who retained what he deemed best and most useful of his mother's and his brother's reforms, Francis was a firm conservative whose announced program was to exorcise "the demon of the French Revolution." Martinovics and his reform plans went underground. In the spring of 1794 he organized two secret groups. The Society of Reformers, appealing to the lesser nobility, was tasked to carry out the first phase of the planned revolution by overthrowing the Habsburgs and depriving the high nobility and clergy of their special position. The second group, the Society of Freedom and Equality, would inherit a federal republic of associated nations and liquidate the last remnants of feudalism. The two societies were separate and neither was aware of the existence of the other.

Few elaborate conspiracies had a shorter life than Martinovics's. When would-be members expressed doubts about the future of his undertaking under an oppressive regime, he assured them of his connections with revolutionary elements in France and elsewhere; it was possibly his aggressive recruiting tactics that led to the discovery of his treason. In the summer of 1794 several members, including Martinovics, were arrested. During his interrogation he made such exaggerated claims about the size and appeal of his "societies" that by the fall some 300, practically the entire membership, were in custody. The trials were short and their verdicts predictable; in the end 18 death sentences were handed down and 16 defendants were sentenced to imprisonment in a fort. Of the death sentences seven were carried out on May 20, 1795, the others were commuted to life imprisonment. The trial quieted whatever revolutionary inclinations were still alive in the Habsburg monarchy.

By 1795 the revolution in France too passed from its sanguinary dictatorial to a more stable and less activist phase. The five men of the Directory who acted as the executive, facing nearly insuperable tasks in rehabilitating a bankrupt economy and a breakdown of public safety, exhausted much of their energies in trying to prevent both a royalist restoration and a return to the Jacobin system. Now the former, now the latter gained ascendancy in the two-house legislature and the directors had to employ extralegal means to prevent the deputies from taking their seats. But while the Revolution seemed to be at a practical end, victorious French armies carried its ideals abroad. France had been fighting a great coalition for years with fluctuating results; starting in 1796 she earned a series of brilliant victories under the command of a general from the lesser Corsican nobility, Napoleon Bonaparte. A new phase of the revolutionary adventure opened, as every country into which French armies entered was compelled to adopt the progressive and enlightened measures the Revolution had brought to France. The mainstay of traditional monarchy, the Catholic Church, suffered repeated humiliations and defeats.

Austria was from the start in the center of the successive coalitions ranged against revolutionary France. The high nobility who dominated the estates, fearing as much as the Habsburgs did the loss of their special position, dutifully voted the taxes and recruits necessary for the pursuit of the war. Only briefly, while Napoleon campaigned in the Middle East, did Austrian armies, in alliance with the British and the Russians, earn any victories at all. Once Napoleon returned and established himself as "first consul" and virtual dictator of France, French arms were again victorious and Austria suffered one defeat after another; in the shameful Peace of Pressburg she was compelled to accept such territorial losses that a good part of the empire was forfeited.

Napoleonic armies entered Hungary only twice for short periods of time, in 1805 and 1809; the first time a general, the second Napoleon himself, appealed to the Hungarian nobility to disown the Habsburgs and, as Napoleon put it: "Acquire once again your national existence!" There was no response to these appeals. The war in fact benefited the nobility, as it did landowners everywhere, because the needs of the armies raised the price of grain precipitously. This rise, to be sure, was often due more to inflation than to increased consumption, but it still created a robust faith in the future of the national economy. When, however, the government several times in succession devalued the currency, the true nature of the prosperity was revealed and the nobles became less enthusiastic about the continuation of the war. In 1812 the Hungarian Diet refused to sanction further debasement of the currency, and the alliance of royalty and nobility came to an end. Francis angrily dissolved the Diet and would not call it again until 1825.

Meanwhile Hungarian military units were repeatedly engaged in the wars against the French and made up roughly one-third of the Austrian army. In the final accounting Hungarian units suffered casualties amounting to over 120,000 and possibly as many as 150,000. One result of their long engagements so far away from home was that they became familiar with the social and technological conditions of more advanced western states. The effects of such contacts cannot be accurately measured, but later the very popular "westernizers" in Hungary drew from the wellsprings of a culture their fathers first came to know in the French revolutionary and Napoleonic periods.

Under the influence of nationalism to which the French revolutionary experiment gave such a powerful boost, in Hungary too there was a resurrection of the national spirit, though not of the superficial and ostentatious kind practiced after the death of Joseph II. It manifested itself mainly in the cultivation and modernization of the Hungarian language, which was purged of many foreign elements, and words of Hungarian roots were added.

In sum, both the ideals of the Enlightenment and the contact with Western cultures as well as the economic lessons learned from the long wars prepared the ground for a more progressive society, in Austria as well as in its dominions. At the same time, however, the very fact that these modern ideas had sprung from a series of events that were odious in the eyes of the monarchy and of the ruling elite rendered them suspect and in the end undesirable. Given the power monarchs and the high nobility still wielded, much depended on the flexibility and pragmatism of future rulers and future parliaments.

CHAPTER SIX

In the aftermath of the Napoleonic Wars the economic bust that often follows the boom cycle of war years hit Hungary, and especially the lesser nobility, particularly hard. While the fighting lasted, agrarian products were in high demand and fetched good prices; with Napoleon's final defeat, demand fell sharply. Grain of lesser quality due to inferior growing methods became hard to sell, as was wool shorn by primitive shepherds in a rough-and-ready fashion and put on the market unwashed and uncombed. Australian wool, despite the immense distances over which it had to be shipped, was cheaper and of better quality. As to grain, lack of scientific fertilization allowed it to be grown on only two-thirds of agricultural acreage; the rest of the land lay fallow in order to allow it to recover its fertility by natural means. A few enterprising landowners, mainly among the high nobility who possessed investible capital, managed to modernize their production methods. Smaller landowners, even if they had the inclination, which few did, could hope to do so only by acquiring loans from banks and financial institutions, and for the great majority of them such loans were unattainable.

The situation was aggravated by the rapid debasement of the currency. When the government in Vienna in 1822 demanded that taxes be paid in silver, an additional hardship was introduced, and, although it affected mainly the peasantry, it hurt the upper classes, too. Among nobles the gap between the ostentatious wealth of the great magnates and the economically strapped condition of the lesser nobility grew to obscene proportions. The former built palatial dwellings enriched with art works and artifacts of all kinds while many of the poorer nobles often had to work their land with their own hands and freedom from taxation was their only economic advantage. Placed between the two in economic terms, the gentry, with a few hundred or a thousand *hold*, although it could not afford pretentious luxuries, at least lived comfortably, without major financial worries.

However, all of them, whether high or low, suffered from the repressive Metternich system. Under the chancellor's dispositions, the Crown made another attempt to exclude the counties, in whose bureaucratic quagmire royal edicts were all too often diluted or sabotaged, from internal governance, and it sometimes used military force to install royal officials in place of the native ones. While theoretically the removal of small-minded bureaucrats made good sense, the result was growing confusion at the operational level, coupled with a decline in the maintenance of law and order. This was all the more unsettling to the Habsburgs as political troubles in Italy, where the movement of the Risorgimento was gathering strength, foreshadowed a nationalistic awakening. The royal house needed funds and military recruits, and tradition, at least in Hungary, demanded the convocation of the estates for that purpose. The latter had not been in session since the king prorogued it in 1812 for its refusal to approve his fiscal reforms, that is, the devaluation of the currency. The nobility had since ignored royal pleas for contributions; it thought of itself as *the* nation, and in the name of the nation demanded that the Diet be called. Vienna at first tried to placate the estates by other means: it restored to Hungarian sovereignty the port of Fiume that had been detached during the Napoleonic Wars and it reduced custom duties inimical to the interests of the landowning class. But passive resistance continued. And so, in 1825, the king recalled the Diet after an absence of 13 years.

A word about the organization of the Diet is in order. Meeting always at the king's summons, by custom every three years, its task was to vote taxes necessary to cover the state's expenses and to authorize the call-up of military recruits. It had an upper estate composed of Catholic bishops, archbishops, abbots, as well as secular lords—nobles by birth—princes, counts, and barons. The lower estate consisted of delegates, two from each of the 46 counties of Hungary, and also from the 40 to 45 royal cities; the latter, however, had only one vote collectively. In the early centuries, between 1000 and 1440, the estates had advisory functions; from 1440 on they acted as a legislature and all nobles were allowed to be present. Beginning in 1608 when, because of the Turkish occupation of the capital city of Buda, the Diet met in Pressburg, only the nobles mentioned above participated.

The Diet of 1825 at its opening session demanded the withdrawal of the illegal edicts issued in its absence; this Vienna refused to do but it did agree to restore the laws extant in 1791, specifically its obligation to call the Diet at least every three years and to levy military forces only with its consent. Once the noble estates had secured this much, they displayed little interest in social reform. When one speaker of their own class, otherwise popular for his eloquence, raised the issue of the wretched condition of the serfs before the meeting, the mood turned hostile to him. The estates even went so far as to vote that impoverished nobles who worked their own land should be made subject to taxation. (That measure was never enforced.)

The most notable event of the 1825 session occurred in November of that year; Count István Széchenyi, a high noble, offered a full year's income from his estates, 60,000 forints, toward the foundation of a Hungarian Academy of Sciences for the promotion of national culture. Other nobles soon pledged their own contributions, and in 1827 the project was voted into law.

Széchenyi was in his own lifetime called "the greatest Hungarian" for his selfless and high-minded promotion of Hungarian culture and all things genuinely Hungarian. Born to privilege, accustomed to a carefree, opulent life style, even as a young man he grew weary of the idle amusements of his caste. Intellectually he rejected the arrogant optimism of the great nobles who thought of Hungary in romantically exalted terms and parroted the slogan, *Extra Hun-*

gariam non est vita, si est vita, non est ita (Outside of Hungary there is no life, and if there is life, it is not of the same kind). Széchenyi by contrast regarded his country as a great wasteland. "Many," he wrote, "think of Hungary in terms of her past, I would rather think of her in terms of her future." When in 1830 his first great book, *Credit,* was published, it created a sensation. In it, he analyzed the reasons why the unavailability of loans secured by real estate stifled economic progress, on the land and in the cities. He was critical of his own social class, yet he realized that it alone possessed the education and sophistication to introduce meaningful reforms. For all his ardent patriotism, he did not think that Hungary, wedged between the powerful Germanic and Slavic peoples, was capable of independent nationhood. Much as he lambasted Habsburg policy, he saw Hungary's future secure only within the empire. He hoped that his reform plans would find understanding and support at the Vienna court.

There was no ready solution, however, for the problem that practically immobilized Hungarian society: the majority of the population were serfs, and while a narrow stratum of this bonded peasantry had managed to buy land with its own means and thereby to separate itself from the dirt-poor cottars who earned their living by hiring out for daily labor or working the tiny lots allotted to them from the landlord's estate, this very separation introduced class distinction even at the lowest social level. Grievances multiplied: the ever increasing taxes, the division of the once commonly used pastures into a separate landlord's and a separate serfs's portion, with the latter always of poorer quality, common resort to corporal punishment—all these fed the peasants' discontent.

In 1831 a cholera epidemic that had originated in India reached the borders of Hungary and soon claimed a quarter million lives, mainly among the poor. In places, authorities applied bizmuth powder to wells to kill the bacilli and the rumor spread that the drinking water was being poisoned to terrorize the peasants. In an Upland county an uprising broke out and soon spread to other counties. Most of the peasants were non-Hungarian—Slovaks, Germans, Ruthenians. In a state of rebellion, they refused the *robot,* attacked noble manors, and took terrible revenge for years of injustice inflicted on them. As all such jacqueries, this too was put down with brute military force.

The painfully evolving process of reorganizing the country's economic structure continued, and the lesser nobility took a leading part in it. A number of them came to the conclusion that their best chance for gaining a share of political control lay in an alliance with the peasantry, or rather with that portion of it that owned property and whose interests often coincided with theirs. Where the two classes differed was in their legal status: no restrictions encumbered the nobility, whereas the peasants, even when they had acquired land, were subject to sundry feudal regulations. There would be obvious benefits in allowing them to purchase their complete freedom: it would quiet the discontent that always simmered below the surface, and it would put badly needed money into the pockets of the nobles who let their peasants go.

When the Diet was called again in 1832, and sat for four long years, the middle nobility bent every effort to enact into law the many, often complex, measures necessary to accomplish the emancipation of the propertied peasantry. They, and society as a whole, may have been ready for them, but the Vienna court and the landed magnates whose huge holdings had value only with bonded labor in place were not. When King Francis opened the Diet, he warned against "the disease of innovation" and "the emulation of foreign lands." The warning did not deter the liberal segment of the Diet, labeled by the court and its allies "the opposition" from pursuing their goals. Its chief proposal was for a freely negotiated agreement between landlord and serf whereby the latter purchased his freedom and would no longer be subject to forced labor or delivery of part of his crop. Manorial justice would also end.

The bill actually obtained a majority of votes. However, the king vetoed it and it never became law. When the Diet finally disbanded, it had little concrete to show for its long session. Still, questions of pressing interest—and in addition to the one dealing with the position of the serfs, demands for Hungary's independence from Austria was the most conspicuous one—once raised, could no longer be silenced. Many outstanding spokesmen of the "opposition" in time became venerated heroes in Hungarian history. In this 1832–36 session of the Diet the foremost advocate of reform, the future architect of the compromise with Austria three decades later, Ferenc Deák, made his first appearance. Another young man, Lajos Kossuth, attracted attention of a different kind: he edited a sheet entitled *Parliamentary Reports,* and sent it out to selected readers in the country. To avoid the censor, he did not have it printed; the reports, often of a sarcastic tenor, were copied by young volunteers by hand.

King Francis died before the Diet ended. His mentally deficient son, Ferdinand, followed him but never exercised any real power; a five-member camarilla governed. With Metternich its leading light, it decided to scotch the "opposition" in Hungary. A number of liberal members of parliament, Kossuth included, were indicted on spurious charges and tried. Their trials elicited widespread protest. Kossuth was sentenced to three years, later raised to four years, in prison. He put the time to good use, he learned English and studied economics texts; he emerged, as he put it later, "rejuvenated" into the light of freedom. (Another young defendant was not so fortunate, he went mad in the damp underground prison in which he was sentenced to spend 10 years.)

The Vienna court once again came to the reluctant conclusion that strongarm methods did not work in dealing with Hungarians. Another Diet was summoned for 1839. Deák led the liberal opposition. When the court asked for an offer of military recruits—the primary reason why the Diet was called—Deák refused. The assembly later declared itself willing to offer 38,000 men, on condition that judicial procedures against political defendants would end; this request was granted. The assembly then proceeded to enact the bill that had failed in the previous session, allowing landlord and serf to come to terms for the permanent emancipation of the latter. Another measure raised Judaism to the same level of "acceptance" as other non-Catholic religions—with this measure Hungary became the first country in central Europe to begin the emancipation of Jews.

When Kossuth gained his freedom, the opposition, remembering his daring journalistic style, pressed him to edit a newspaper. The government gave its permission when a trusted publisher undertook to put out the paper, the *Pesti Hirlap;* it appeared twice weekly. Its colorful editorials made it immensely popular. Their tenor was unmistakably liberal. They dealt with conditions in prisons, with the squalor of subterranean apartments, with cruel and unusual punishments, with subjects that were of greatest interest to the emerging middle class. Yet to dwell on those while the class that made up over two-thirds of society continued to live in wretched squalor seemed to Kossuth abominable. He noted that though voluntary emancipation of serfs was now permitted by law, very few peasants could afford to pay for their freedom. He advocated making emancipation mandatory; when this proposal met an unfriendly reception in many quarters he ventured that the state should contribute to the price of the serf's freedom. He also wanted to end the nobility's exemption from taxation, as well as its monopoly on legislation. The nation, he argued, would be free only if its citizens were free.

Lagos Kossuth in old age *(Hungarian Museum of Photography)*

At this point in time, however, Kossuth did not yet make the most radical demand, for his country's separation from the Habsburg Empire.

Still, read in the proper vein, that was what many of his editorials suggested. And it was just this that provoked the anger and opposition of the other great public figure of the day, István Széchenyi. The latter accused Kossuth of advocating a catastrophic course; Hungary could never stand up to the awesome power of the Habsburgs. However, if the opposition worked hand-in-hand with the court, it could produce reforms which would lead the nation to freedom. In the ensuing debate most of the reformers ranged themselves behind Kossuth, or rather *against* Széchenyi. They either did not understand that Széchenyi aimed at forming a nonconfrontational political bloc that would by slow stages modernize the country and raise it to a level of development at which it could shape its own destiny, or they were too impatient for such a gradual approach.

Széchenyi's popularity began to decline; much against his better convictions he drew closer to the Vienna court.

What rendered the debate between Kossuth and Széchenyi almost irrelevant was that the rapid tempo of material improvement and the shift from an agrarian to an industrial economy had a far greater impact on national affairs than the most brilliant editorializing. As a result of this economic change effective political power began to slip from the grasp of the landowning nobility and into the hands of a sturdy, politically conscious middle class. With its material enrichment went its cultural elevation and a somewhat belated enlightenment. Whereas the status symbol of the nobility had been the possession of land and judicial authority over the peasantry, the status symbol of the bourgeoisie became education, more even than the acquisition of riches. Every generation thinks of itself as modern; to the generation of the early 19th century the word had no theological or other abstract connotation. It meant chiefly an enlightened understanding of how the application of science can improve the material condition of the masses and increase the standard of living to a degree undreamed of a generation earlier. Széchenyi had been the first to awaken the nation to this truth, but he did not go so far as to place himself in opposition to the existing political system that stunted initiative and looked on innovation with the greatest suspicion. Kossuth by contrast was an oppositionist, modern in both the political and economic sense. Yet in the end Széchenyi proved correct in his conceptions. The spirit of the times may have cried out for modernization, and the last thing the Habsburgs could be accused of after the traumatic experience of the French Revolution was being modern. Their power was deeply rooted in their past that the very notion of breaching tradition in the interest of economic improvement filled them with alarm. This should have made them, given realities, a doomed dynasty. But the Habsburgs—even such a pathetic ruler as Ferdinand V—had two assets that translated into power: a steadfastness that did not bow before any misfortune, and an army that in all critical situations proved *Hoftreu*, loyal to the court, led by dutiful generals, usually as mediocre as their masters, but firmly resolved to turn their forces against the citizenry when the situation so required.

※ ※ ※

Still another Diet met in Pressburg in November 1847. Despite the ferment that had been brewing in the country since its last meeting, there was no hint that it would be the last parliament meeting by estates, and that it would carry the nation into a prolonged and bloody revolution. The ideological divisions were as of old: the upper estate, consisting of the highest lay and ecclesiastical authorities, was determinedly conservative; the lower, composed almost entirely of the middle and lower nobility, was generally reform-minded. There were, however, a few enlightened men in the upper house, too. Kossuth sat in the lower, but no voice in the upper could equal his.

Months passed and there was little progress. The debate over feudalism, like a monotonous refrain, droned on, with no viable course of action in sight. So few peasants had been able to buy their freedom that the situation was not materially different from what it had been when the estates last met. The upper house opposed emancipation by royal fiat; it also opposed state subvention for freeing the peasant; the lower gentry found itself high-mindedly promoting the cause of a free peasantry while being economically unable to afford losing its labor force without major compensation. Peasant conditions could improve only if and when the national economy had so broadened its base by the introduction of industrial and associated enterprises that there would be a great increase in demand for agricultural goods, and such an upgrading of the economy could not be carried through by the conservative forces that ruled the country. At the same time the liberals could not hope to come to power until the still disenfranchised peasant strata gained emancipation—this was the vicious circle the parliament had to break.

For all the opposing and contrasting opinions the session would most likely have proceeded in an orderly fashion, as past sessions had, with some mild compromises emerging, sufficiently mild to ensure royal consent. But just how powerful were the passions beneath the surface became evident when news from abroad flashed before the legislators the possibility of achieving goals against the desires of the king and his political supporters. In the last days of February street disorders broke out in Paris over a trivial incident; within days the king, Louis Philippe of the House of Orleans, had to relinquish his throne and exile himself to England. In Paris liberal, middle-class elements came to the fore; whereas 18 years earlier, in a similar upheaval, these same elements recoiled from ending the monarchy and declaring a republic, this time they judged the time right for it. Suddenly it seemed as if Europe had awakened.

Within days there were disturbances in German states adjoining France as well. The granting of constitutions became the principal demand of the demonstrators then and later. On March 1 the news of the Paris events reached Pressburg as the Diet was in session. Kossuth, as if he had only waited for his cue, on March 3 demanded a constitution, not only for Hungary but for the entire Habsburg Empire, the liberation of serfs, and the recognition of basic rights for all. The court had no intention of granting any of these, though it refrained from openly saying so. It was still contemplating how to react to Kossuth's demands when, on that same day, a revolt flared up in Vienna. Students, workers, and a burgher's guard took to the streets, their principal demand being the dismissal of Metternich. The aged chancellor tried to demonstrate his firmness by refusing, but the frightened court ordered him to resign and leave the country.

The news galvanized the Hungarian people. Demands for reform spilled over from legislative chambers into the streets. A revolution began.

CHAPTER SEVEN

On March 15, 1848, the youth of Budapest spoke with the voice of the nation. Groups of university students and ardent spirits who joined them formulated a program of 12 points, incorporating demands that went far beyond narrow nationalistic goals; they expressed universal aspirations pronounced in the accents of revolution. They called for a free press and an end to censorship, yearly parliaments, equality before the law, the release of political prisoners, a national bank, and the unification of Hungary with Transylvania, which was still being governed as a separate province. They protested against Hungarian soldiery being sent abroad to fight for Habsburg interests. Other demands called for jury trials, a responsible ministry, and a national guard. The crowd proceeded to a printing press (the same that had published Kossuth's *Pesti Hirlap*) and had the Twelve Points, as well as an incendiary poem, *National Song* by the young poet Sándor Petofi, printed. Members of the crowd distributed them in the streets, ignoring existing laws against the dissemination of uncensored printed material.

Meanwhile the Diet in Pressburg voted for equal assumption of tax burdens by all, that is, for an end to noble privilege; it voted a further measure that had long been a bone of contention, namely, that the state compensate nobles for the loss of their serfs (the Twelve Points formulated by the students demanded an end to serfdom but made no mention of compensation). Once voted, these provisions were put in writing and a committee headed by Lajos Kossuth betook itself to Vienna to present them to the Crown. The committee returned to Pressburg two days later with the king's approval, and with his added promise to sanction whatever future measures the parliament would pass.

Nothing, it appeared, could stem the surge of revolution. On the 18th the Diet voted that serfs be immediately freed from all feudal obligations; it then frankly stated that compensation to the lords would take a while to be put into effect. In another measure church tithes were abolished; still another made the government, distinctly and independently Hungarian, responsible to what was now for all intents and purposes a parliament. Nobles and non-nobles had complete equality before the law, and provisions were made for the organization of a national guard. In line with the king's promise, these so-called April Laws received the court's sanction and, on April 7, Ferdinand appointed the first Hungarian cabinet under the nobleman Lajos Batthyány. Kossuth was of course a member of the cabinet but the premier, knowing Kossuth's radical views, assigned to him a politically neutral portfolio, that of finance. Széchenyi was appointed minister of transportation and public works in recognition of his many achievements in these fields. Ferenc Deák was named minister of justice. Parliament dissolved on April 11 and the new government began its work fully expecting that no obstacles would be put in its way as it carried out the April laws. That turned out to be a dangerously optimistic assumption.

Hungary was still a part of the Habsburg Empire, and the Pragmatic Sanction, which stated that royal authority applied in equal measure to all component parts, remained in effect. On April 14 the Hungarian government relocated from Pressburg to Budapest, where an immense enthusiastic crowd awaited it. Elation, however, was no substitute for the assets necessary, but missing, for the orderly conduct of affairs; the cabinet had no funds, no army, and, worst of all, no practical experience in running a country. If anything, enthusiasm in its ecstatic version was a drawback. It carried the conviction that everything was possible even against the greatest odds. The break with the Habsburgs was in most quarters taken for granted, though no practical alternative was being considered.

Batthyány was not unaware of the dangers of such heedless euphoria. He sought cooperation with Vienna and the reining in of revolutionary forces. Yet those forces were in the ascendant and in many places their actions got out of hand. Peasants began to encroach on noble property and in some places demanded radical land reform, miners and journeymen demonstrated against the system of guilds. Even more dangerous was the precipitously increasing separatism by nationalities. Lawmakers in Pressburg had assumed that Croats, Slovaks, Serbs, Ruthenes, all subjects of the Crown of Hungary, would be satisfied if the reforms granted by Vienna to Hungarians would be extended to them; they would then remain docile subjects within Greater Hungary. This was not the case—the minorities had caught the revolutionary fever. They demanded the right to govern themselves while remaining "children of the [Hungarian] fatherland"; they also demanded that in the conduct of official business they be allowed to use their own language. The Budapest government refused all such demands and was willing to concede only a measure of cultural autonomy. By the summer, Croatia, under the leadership of a lesser nobleman, Josip Jelačić, was in a state of revolt. Although Vienna, for the record, opposed such an act of defiance by a subject nationality, it perceived the opportunity to pit one rebellious nation against another and bring the Hungarians to heel. The Batthyány government on its part, pointing to the threat these separatist movements represented to the unity of Hungary, began to organize a national army.

When in early July the first parliament under the April laws met, it was a parliament chosen by an electorate that for the first time included commoners as well as nobles. The membership was still largely of noble rank. By now the position of the Austrian royal house had been substantially strengthened; it had overcome a major uprising in Lombardy, and also within Austria, and through the introduction of genuine parliamentarianism it had separated the bourgeoisie from the unruly masses, thus stymieing the forces of disorder. The royal court had, shortly after the outbreak of the revolution, left Vienna and moved for safety to Innsbruck, where it was received with pledges of unbending loyalty. In mid-August it felt confident enough to return to the capital.

Batthyány knew only too well that the concessions of the past spring had been wrested under duress and that a reaction would set in as soon as the court felt in control of affairs again. He hoped to anticipate forceful action by traveling to Vienna and offering to withdraw an earlier demand for separate Hungarian ministries of war and of finance; he was willing to agree that such ministries should be "joint," with equal Austrian and Hungarian representation. Vienna turned a deaf ear to the proposal and Batthyány returned to Budapest on September 10, sensing that an armed encounter was in the offing. Already Croatian troops under the command of Jelačić, whom the court had named governor of the province and asked "to act to the benefit of the entire monarchy," had broken into Hungary.

The situation appeared desperate. Small Hungarian forces in Transdanubia retreated before the Croatian army of 40,000. Croatian officers were so confident of a quick victory that they asked that their letters be mailed to Budapest. There the recently formed cabinet was in the process of dissolution. Batthyány resigned and Széchenyi, in a state of mental collapse, attempted suicide. Other cabinet members either retired from politics or went abroad. Vienna, seeking to assert its authority in what it regarded as an integral part of its empire, named a vice marshal, Franz Philipp Lamberg, commander in chief of *all* armed forces within Hungary. The parliament in Budapest declared the appointment unconstitutional, and when Lamberg arrived in the city, an angry mob lynched him. Parliament had earlier appointed a National Defense Committee under Kossuth's chairmanship to organize the nation for war. Kossuth addressed himself to the task with his usual energy. He called for volunteers and thousands responded. Hungarian soldiers serving in the Austrian imperial army tore off their insignia and replaced them with the red braids of the revolution. Kossuth traveled from town to town on a mission to raise an army. The response was overwhelming; it may have had something to do with the fact that the standing army which had thus far avoided open combat with the Croatian force and been in steady retreat, on September 29, at the town of Pákozd, made a stand. After an inconclusive artillery battle, the invading army withdrew.

The commanding general of the Hungarian force, János Móga did not, however, exploit this partial victory. Rather than giving chase, he allowed the Croatians to change direction and begin a march toward Vienna with the purpose of linking up with imperial forces. Meanwhile another Croatian division, moving toward Buda, was surrounded by units of the National Guard under the command of a young general, Arthur Görgey, and forced to surrender. The situation once again looked hopeful.

Vienna acted as if its authority in Hungary had been unaffected by these towering events. In Budapest the now all-powerful Hungarian Defense Committee, in order to meet the mounting expenses of full-fledged war, ordered the printing of banknotes and voted the recruitment of 40,000 soldiers. The king tried to veto the measures, but his veto was contemptuously ignored. The weak-minded king, or rather those around him, responded on October 2 by ordering the parliament to dissolve itself and placing Hungary under military rule, with Jelačić; in supreme command. The Croatian governor had by now arrived in Vienna, but he immediately ran into trouble. His assignment to bring Hungarian rebels to heel had become known, and Viennese radicals, sympathizing with the uprising in Hungary, created new boisterous disorders in the city. The frightened royal court once again fled, this time to the Bohemian town of Olmütz. When the defense minister, Latour, ordered the mobilization of troops to deal with the demonstrators in Vienna, he was seized and hanged from a lamppost. The radicals urged the Hungarian general Móga to march on Vienna; even the parliament in Budapest (which had defied the order for its dissolution) ordered him to do so, but Móga did not trust the strength of his forces and demurred. Thus the Vienna rebels remained defenseless. There had been an uprising in Prague too in response to somewhat extravagant demands made by a Slavic congress meeting there and that revolt was mercilessly put down by the Austrian marshal Alfred Windischgrätz, whose wife had been killed in the disorders. The marshal next led his forces to the walls of Vienna. The Hungarian army had in the meantime bestirred itself, crossing the Leitha River and moving toward Vienna. In the suburb of Schwechat, on September 30, it was defeated by imperial forces. The next day Windischgrätz bombed the Austrian capital into submission and an orgy of retribution followed.

The course of the uprising in Hungary shifted from the political to the military sphere. A beaten and disorderly army streamed home from under the walls of Vienna, but General Görgey was determined to shape it into an effective fighting force. Many officers, although their oath bound them to the king, refused service in the Austrian army ranged against Görgey; others had to be dismissed. By now Austrian troops had joined Croatian forces in a planned campaign against Hungary. In November Ferdinand named Felix Schwarzenberg (a brother-in-law of Windischgrätz) chancellor with authority over all Austrian lands. This resolute reactionary was determined to break the back of the uprising. But Hungarian armies fighting in the south, in Transylvania, and in the north, under competent and often brilliant leadership, proved too much for the imperial forces to overcome.

The camarilla in Vienna at last decided that Ferdinand, emperor of Austria, king of Hungary and Bohemia since 1835, was totally incapable of confronting the forces ranged against his dynasty and had to go. On December 2 he abdicated; his uncle Francis Charles, the first in the line of succession, at the prompting of his wife, the indomitable Sophie, who had raised her son one day to be emperor, stood aside, and the 18-year-old Francis Joseph was elevated to the imperial dignity.

Since late summer continuous incursions by Habsburg forces had kept Hungarian defenses off balance, but no major offensive had been launched. In mid-December Windischgrätz, having subdued two capitals within a month, engaged his armies against a third one, Budapest. Görgey, commanding a force of some 23,000 infantry against an imperial army of over 40,000, including 6,000 cavalrymen, opted for a gradual fighting withdrawal. Kossuth ordered one of Görgey's generals to give battle; after his army suffered defeat, the position of the capital became untenable. Parliament decided to transfer itself, and the cabinet, eastward, to the city of Debrecen. Attempts to negotiate a cease-fire met with Windischgrätz's stiff refusal. There could be no negotiations, the marshal said, only unconditional surrender. On January 5, 1849, his armies entered Budapest. Convinced that the back of Hungarian resistance had been broken, he announced a practical return to prerevolutionary political conditions and had Batthyány, who had remained in Budapest, arrested.

The two Hungarian armies in the field had, however, managed an orderly withdrawal, one under General Mór Perczel eastward, the other under Görgey to the north. It was at this point that Görgey, in a famous statement given in the town of Vác, assumed a position independent of, and in fact opposed to, that of his government. He refused to accept the authority of the Defense Committee and decided to follow only orders issued by the minister of war in Batthyány's now defunct cabinet.

In part because of this truculent manifesto and in part because of growing republican tendencies among the revolutionaries, which were unacceptable to the largely aristocratic officer corps, there were many desertions from Görgey's army. He persevered, however. In Transylvania the Polish general, Josef Bem, whom Kossuth had invited the year before to command a corps, was on the move and occupied several cities. Görgey moved northward and had similar successes in the Uplands. Windischgrätz's hope for a quick end to the campaign was dashed. In the first two months of 1849 imperial troops under General Puchner suffered repeated humiliating defeats in Transylvania. His troops were fortunate to escape from the province in relative safety.

Neither army however had victory in its grasp. Habsburg forces had the advantage of unity of command, a thoroughly trained and well-equipped army, and a loyal and professional officer corps. The Hungarians counted on revolutionary enthusiasm and inspired leadership in the field. In the spring Görgey's forces cleared the strategic region between the Danube and Tisza Rivers of enemy forces; the latter now had no option but to evacuate Budapest from where Windischgrätz a few months earlier had sent home word of complete victory. However, it was also obvious that the revolutionaries did not possess the reserves to make their victories permanent and decisive. Disillusionment gradually set in; many, especially among the lesser nobility, began to share Görgey's conviction that a compromise with the Habsburgs was the wisest course to follow. In April this conviction produced an ambivalent formula that bore some of the strengths and all the weaknesses of a compromise. Francis Joseph, early in March, had issued a manifesto speaking of an Austrian Empire in which Hungary and Croatia, while granted the trappings of independence, were designated as crown provinces; that is, they were in effect returned to the political position they held in prerevolutionary days. Thereupon, on Kossuth's initiative, the parliament in Debrecen declared the Habsburgs deposed and Hungary's complete national independence restored. But while parliament elected Kossuth president, it did not invest him with executive powers, which were entrusted to a ministry under one Bertalan Szemere who headed a cabinet disposed to compromise and cooperation with the Habsburgs.

The military situation continued uncertain. Görgey, not surprisingly, began to entertain political ambitions, believing that, with the disarray in Debrecen,

foreign influence from Italy. However, other than trying to enlist some states of the German Confederation on Austria's side, little was done in Vienna in the diplomatic field. Military preparations were just as lackadaisical. Incompetence culminated in a rash declaration of war on Piedmont without ascertaining whether the imperial armed forces in Italy were prepared to fight battles against a major foe. As a consequence, due to poor organization and faulty intelligence, three battles turned into bloodbaths, and Austria suffered grievous defeats and was forced to relinquish to Piedmont the province of Lombardy, while still retaining Venetia.

It was perhaps the first great lesson Francis Joseph learned about the necessity of cultivating the goodwill of the peoples he ruled. In the wake of the defeat he issued the Manifesto of Laxemburg, announcing his plan to reform lawmaking and administration. He next dismissed the widely hated minister of police, and, on August 22, Alexander Bach was given his walking papers. However, these were feeble promises and puny measures in the face of a deeply resentful mood in the empire. Voices hitherto silenced by tyranny began to be raised. The most powerful one was that of Count Széchenyi, whom the Hungarian nation still remembered as its greatest son. In 1848 he had slipped into such a state of mental confusion that he had to be committed to an institution, but during his slow recovery he observed all the iniquities of the Bach system. When in 1857 the interior minister authored an anonymously distributed pamphlet, hailing the success of Hungary's "pacification," Széchenyi replied in an open letter with scathing criticism. The Vienna police sprang to the alert. Keeping Széchenyi under surveillance but unable to silence him, in March 1860 they searched his apartment and threatened him with imprisonment. A month later he committed suicide. An extended period of mourning followed and the nation's mood turned sullen again.

The emperor's concern was heightened when, in the summer of 1860, an Italian revolutionary hero, Giuseppe Garibaldi, led a group of insurrectionists on a victorious campaign that resulted in the unification of Italy (except for Venetia, still held by Austria, and Rome, guarded by French troops, to ensure its possession by the Vatican). Slowly and reluctantly Francis Joseph realized the inefficacy of the terror that had become the sole mainstay of his empire. At the advice of some high nobles faithful to the crown he issued his October Diploma, which offered in place of the existing absolutist system one that, at least on the surface, was constitutional. There was to be an imperial council of 100 members in which the lands of the empire were to be represented, and which was to legislate in all matters except military and foreign affairs, which remained the exclusive realm of the emperor. In order to ensure compliance, he restored some of the governmental organs, notably county administrations, abolished after the defeat of the revolution, as well as parliaments for Hungary, Transylvania, and Croatia. All too obviously though, these concessions did not substantially alter the absolutist system. Discontent manifested itself in various ways; for instance, when votes were taken for county administrators, in many places exiled heroes of the revolution, such as Kossuth and Klapka, were elected. A parliamentary session, meeting in April 1861, was unanimous in demanding that the April Laws of 1848, which essentially assured Hungary's autonomous position within the empire, be restored. The more fundamental question of whether Francis Joseph should be recognized as Hungary's legal monarch produced a sharp division in that assembly. One faction, led by Ferenc Deák, deemed it wise to deal with the monarch and achieve reforms in cooperation with him; the other faction, led by a recently returned emigrant, László Teleki, declared the Habsburg king dethroned and wanted to address a proclamation to world opinion in support of Hungarian liberties. The debate was long and bitter and reached its climax in Teleki's puzzling suicide. Subsequently, by a narrow margin, parliament voted to adhere to Deák's formula. As stated, however, it was unacceptable to the emperor, because it assumed the right of a legislature to define the emperor's proper place in Hungarian government; the parliament was dismissed.

Realizing that the October Diploma satisfied practically no part of the empire, Francis Joseph had in the interim issued a new document, the February Patent, which addressed itself to some of the objections raised against the October Diploma. The Budapest parliament took no friendlier view of this document than it had of the previous one and in August 1861 it was again disbanded.

Hungary now constituted only one component of the Habsburg Empire, one which, even while its internal divisions continued, turned a uniformly hostile face to Vienna. Yet it was the component whose cooperation was crucial for the functioning of the whole structure. As Budapest saw it, it had never been part of the bargain with the Habsburgs that the nation relinquish its identity and submerge its culture in a polyglot empire ruled by a royal house by virtue of dynastic inheritance. Yet that had been the trend since the Turkish tide had retreated and the ruling house reclaimed its possession of the Carpathian Basin. When Hungarians at last revolted, they were put down by military means. They retaliated with passive resistance—but how long would it take for passivity to yield positive results? No help was forthcoming from abroad, and even internally things continued unsettled. The liquidation of the feudal system created many quarrels and much ill blood between landowning nobles and their serfs; Hungary's ethnic minorities were becoming increasingly restive. The question of whether claims put forth by one nationality could also be legitimately put forth by others was more than theoretical. Could Hungary hope for equal status with Austria while denying a separate status to her own minorities? This question lay at the very heart of the crisis of dualism, at this point still in the distant future.

The ostensible intent of the October Diploma and the February Patent had been to bring a measure of parliamentarianism to the empire, but the primary purpose of those documents was to conciliate the Hungarians; when that failed, they lost their rationale. There was no recourse but to return to absolutist government. Its instruments were in place and the methods had been tested—it had, however, also proved a failure. The result was a stalemate that cried out for a compromise. Still, that was just what both sides recoiled from. Men like Kossuth, now settled in Torino, indefatigably hatched plans for defying the Habsburgs; in 1862, he put forth a scheme for a Danubian Union, in which Hungary,

Romania, Serbia, and Croatia, separating themselves from Austria, would enter into a confederation with a joint parliament and joint ministries for defense, foreign affairs, and economics. He proclaimed his faith in the brotherhood of Hungarians and Slavs and saw in his plan "a smiling future for them all." Such utopian visions did little to engender a realistic solution—one that included, as it had to, Habsburg Austria. Only gradually did Hungarians, especially the propertied classes, realize that, even if the final settlement fell far below their expectations, it had to be accommodated within the larger empire of which their country was a part. They found their prolonged exclusion from politics degrading, but they also knew that a separate Hungary would mean a smaller market for their agrarian products and increased prices for imported manufactured goods. They were also aware of the dangers an independent Hungary would face on a continent dominated by competing great powers. To the north Prussia was energetically promoting the cause of German unity; to the east Russia posed as the champion of Pan-Slavism. A separate Hungary could find herself wedged between a Slavic and a Germanic power, with no effective means of resisting either.

Vienna, too, began to lean toward a softer stand. The empire's endemic internal problems caused its international situation to deteriorate. Prussia and Italy were hostile to it and relations with France suffered in the aftermath of the war of 1859. Internally, tax collection was erratic and finances were in continuous disarray. The current chancellor, Anton Schmerling, who practiced absolutism of a milder variety than his predecessors, was nevertheless a staunch champion of centralized government and as such an unsuitable instrument for smoothing the way toward a federal state structure. Francis Joseph dismissed him and, at the end of 1865, convened the Hungarian parliament again. Although the message was not explicit, the intention of making Hungary a cooperative partner in an orderly and politically stable empire was evident. Ferenc Deák, working mainly behind the scenes, became the moving force in semiofficial negotiations. By April 1865 he deemed the progress of talks promising enough to publish in a popular daily his so-called Easter Article in which the key sentence was this: "We will always be willing in a strictly legal way to harmonize our laws with the security demands of the empire." Although until now Deák and the majority of the legislators had insisted on the restoration of the April Laws of 1848, which provided for an independent Hungary tied to Austria only in a personal union, Deák now conceded the need for closer cooperation. Affairs relating to the international position of the empire and its military establishment would have to be administered jointly.

Although the final realization of the *Ausgleich,* the compromise between Austria and Hungary resulting in a dual monarchy, is often credited to the crushing defeat of Austrian armies at the hands of the Prussians in the Seven Weeks' War in the summer of 1866, the process had gathered such momentum by then that it would most likely have come about even if the defeat had not put the emperor and his government in a more conciliatory frame of mind. When concluded, it transformed the Habsburg Empire into a monarchy of two entities, separate in their internal affairs, jointly governed in matters of foreign policy and defense, as

Ferenc Deák
(Hungarian Museum
of Photography)

well as in financial administration relating to those two affairs. In February 1867, after the negotiations conducted on the Hungarian side by Ferenc Deák and Julius Andrássy (the latter a rebel from 1848 who had been sentenced to death and hanged in effigy), and on the Austrian side first by August Antal (in 1865) and later by foreign minister Ferdinand von Beust, the text of the agreement was presented to the Hungarian parliament for approval. That same month the emperor appointed Andrássy as the first premier of the newly autonomous country. Despite long and passionate debates, parliament at the end of May voted overwhelmingly in favor of the so-called *Ausgleich*. Kossuth from abroad urged rejection, perceiving in the compromise "the death of the nation," but by now his voice produced barely an echo. All strata of society welcomed the end to the long, bitter, and unproductive feud between Hungary and the Habsburgs. On June 8, amid the most elaborate pomp and circumstance, Francis Joseph was crowned king of Hungary. For Habsburg Austria, too, the source of its greatest and most embarrassing weakness had been removed.

CHAPTER NINE

The Great Compromise did not prove to be, especially in the first two decades of its operation, the potent formula for general pacification that its framers had hoped it would be. In an empire of so many nationalities a dualistic solution could not possibly be definitive. Even within Hungary there were many, united in the party of the extreme left (be it noted that the "left" in Hungary had no relation to the European left professing a Marxist program), who felt that only complete independence from Austria was compatible with the nation's dignity and historic mission. Because of the insistence of these patriots that the April Laws providing for such independence be reinstated, in time they came to be called the Party of 1848. Later still they were organized as the Independent Party and as such remained a political presence until the end of the Great War in 1918.

The largest and most influential party continued to be Deák's, and, despite its mixed political composition, it stood staunchly on the platform of the 1867 Compromise. To be sure, many opportunists, including large and medium land-holders and industrialists, who perceived the economic advantages that a large empire with ample natural resources and an open and free market offered, found common ground with political realists who understood the futility of efforts to break loose from the Habsburg realm, and also saw in the partnership with Austria a guarantee for Hungary as a force to be reckoned with in international politics. Between these two political groupings stood the so-called left-center party, under the leadership of Kálmán Tisza. It consisted mainly of large landowners with estates on the Great Plains east of the Tisza River. While not opposed in principle to the Great Compromise, this party chafed under its restrictions; it demanded a separate Hungarian army and greater economic independence. In the political struggles during the last third of the century the party distinguished itself by restraining the extreme left, and, by doing so, it was generally a force for stability.

The first challenge facing the Andrássy cabinet was to deal with discontented national minorities. When, in one of its earliest measures the government provided for the union of Transylvania with the Hungarian kingdom, Romanians and Saxons in that province protested against their formal subordination to the Hungarians who were in a numerical minority. Their separation, however, would have meant fragmentation of the province into minuscule entities; consequently, the unification of Hungary with Transylvania was duly enacted. The long festering question dating back to the Turkish occupation, namely, the constitutional status of Transylvania, was thus definitively settled.

The problem of Croatia was different because practically the entire population of the province was Slavic. A separate piece of legislation designated it as an "associated state." What this meant in practice was that in strictly internal matters it was autonomous, with a multiparty legislature and a cabinet under a governor, or *bán,* in Zagreb. To ensure participation in joint matters relating to foreign and military affairs, the Croatians sent 29 (later 40) delegates to the Hungarian parliament. In addition, a Croatian minister was included in the cabinet in Budapest. One outstanding question, the position of the port city of Fiume, was resolved when it was decided that it should constitute "a separate area joined to the crown of Hungary," to be administered by a governor appointed by the emperor-king. While the Croatian power elite accepted this general settlement, the public was inimical to it. Politicians and publicists alike demanded a status analogous to that of Hungary within the empire, and the question, especially under the impact of growing Pan-Slavist agitation, remained unsettled to the very end of the Dual Monarchy.

The other major Slavic nation, the Czech, was deeply disappointed with the terms of the *Ausgleich.* While Hungary had achieved parity of status with Austria, Bohemia remained subject to Austrian sovereignty and rule. In September 1870 the possibility of Francis Joseph being crowned king of Bohemia if the province was granted a proper position within the empire was discussed. The Czechs worked out a set of "basic articles" providing for a federal status based on parity with the other two major nationalities; it was brought before the Austrian Imperial Council (the parliament for the non-Hungarian parts) on October 20, 1871, by the chancellor of the day, Karl Hohenwart. At the meeting Julius Andrássy, Hungarian premier, countered the Czech claim with the argument that a federal scheme would render the very concept of a unitary foreign policy, so essential since the unification of Germany had changed the entire power balance in Europe, defunct. It would also sharpen conflict with Russia over Balkan problems. A few days after the meeting the emperor rejected the Czech initiative and Hohenwart resigned. Czech representatives withdrew from the Imperial Council. In the aftermath the emperor appointed Andrássy joint foreign minister.

The appointment was due largely to the fact that, unlike his predecessor, Beust, an avowed anti-Prussian, at the Ballplatz, Andrássy favored a German orientation as a counterweight to Slavic preponderance in areas that surrounded Hungary. Andrássy's first diplomatic move (which to be sure could be accomplished only with the active cooperation of German chancellor Otto von Bismarck) was the construction of a Dreikaiserbund, a Three Emperor's League, a loose alignment of Germany, Austria-Hungary, and Russia, which, while it provided for little more than an undertaking to consult with one another in case of warlike complications, defused to some extent the growing menace from the east. In Hungary, Andrássy was nevertheless assailed for making a compact with a nation, Russia, that had joined with Austria in crushing the Hungarian revolution in 1849. By this time, however, Bismarck's principle of Realpolitik was the guiding concept in European diplomacy—emotional factors were excluded from the making of foreign policy.

Andrássy's place as Hungarian premier was taken by the former minister of finance, Menyhért Lónyay, and with his appointment Deák's party lost much of its popularity. The reason was a controversial electoral reform bill aimed at extending the franchise so as to assure a broader base for the government party. Lónyay was an expert in financial matters and his tax legislation placed Hungarian finances on a solid basis, but he was personally unpopular, a fact responsible for the tangible weakening of the government party. Lónyay tried to recover some of his position by proposing the extension of the franchise; but, when he put his bill before parliament, the first filibuster in Hungarian history defeated it. Lónyay then employed less than honorable means, including bribery and intimidation, to achieve his goal. Although in the ensuing elections the government party lost votes, it still remained the largest in parliament and from this time on dishonest electoral practices became commonplace in Hungary.

Deák, aged and ailing, retired to his estate, and in his absence the government party lost much of its credibility and cohesion; it needed the infusion of fresh blood. By this time the left-center party headed by Kálmán Tisza had tired of its oppositionist role, a role that yielded it neither material nor political profit. Tisza, a fervent patriot, had originally opposed the Great Compromise. He had by now come to look on it as a mutable compact capable of evolving into an updated version assuring greater independence for Hungary, with a separate army and separate finances, and on that platform he chose closer cooperation with the government party. In 1875 the cooperation between the two became definitive. Tisza dismantled his political platform and simply joined together with Deák's government party under the name Liberal Party, creating in essence a coalition of great landowners. Its leaders would occupy the premier's chair for the next 30 years, during which, in the first 15 years, Kálmán Tisza headed the government. Despite his ingrained conservatism, the rapidly expanding economy and the growing class-consciousness of workers produced a cautiously progressive spirit in national politics, and, while the Liberal Party did little to promote it, it did not retard it. Indeed, it could in the end claim a small measure of credit for it.

Tisza was not a politician of sweeping conceptions, but rather a clever and indefatigable tactician. Much of the continued success of his Liberal Party depended on the support of the voters, and although the right to vote was tied to material wealth and literacy, he still judged the electorate, only about 6 to 7 percent of the population, but including many petit bourgeois, as too large. Unable to decrease the numbers legally, he hosted feasts, treating would-be voters to free food and drinks to promote a friendly spirit; but he also practiced gerrymandering until in most electoral districts his partisans had the majority. For the rest, the fact that voting was open and that casting a vote against the government party in full view of its agents, who might or might not be present as the tallies were taken, carried at least an assumed risk, and a majority could always be assured.

During Tisza's long tenure the nationality problem raised its head again, and he certainly did not possess the tact to soothe the ruffled feelings of non-

Hungarian minorities. In one instance he ordered the closure of a Slovak cultural center in the Uplands and subsequently banned any attempt at ethnic organization. He insisted that children of parents of any language group within the Hungarian kingdom receive their formal education in Hungarian. Nor did he have any patience with workers' organizations; he judged them to be potential centers of political agitation.

The hardest problem Tisza faced was that of the joint army, resented in Hungary since the conclusion of the Great Compromise. Entirely under Austrian command, the language of instruction and command was German, and its haughty officers had no respect for dualism; when stationed in Hungary, they acted if they were serving in a conquered country. It led to countless incidents, blown up out of all proportion by Hungarian hotheads. Tisza, by now a champion of dualism, sided with the emperor in efforts to make the army less divided and more efficacious. In 1889 he presented a new law concerning the defense forces. It provided for an enlargement of the imperial army, a limited right of control over it by the Hungarian parliament, and an obligation for Hungarian military officers to take examinations in the German language.

The bill produced an outrage of such proportions that it had to be whittled down to almost nothing. In March of 1889 Tisza was forced to resign.

✖ ✖ ✖

In the years since the *Ausgleich* Hungary experienced a great economic upswing. This was in part due to the improved availability of credit, as great amounts of foreign capital streamed into the country. Between 1867 and 1900 the number of investment companies increased in increments of 25 and investible capital of 10. Much of the money was earmarked for the expansion of railroads. In 1846 there had been one railroad in Hungary, between Budapest and Vác, about 50 kilometers in length. By 1848 there were 200 kilometers of track. By the time of the Great Compromise this had grown to 2,000 kilometers. From then on, in every year about another 500 kilometers of track were laid down and by the end of the century the network boasted rails of 17,000 kilometers in length.

In agriculture, the increased market after the removal of tariff barriers led to a corresponding increase in demand, which in turn necessitated bringing more and more acreage under cultivation. Marshes were drained, rivers, especially the Tisza, were improved, fallow land was put under the plow, the three-field system was abandoned. However, the social composition of the agrarian population changed very little. Too many of the emancipated serfs remained without or with too little land. At the turn of the century only 5.5 percent of agrarian land was in the hands of smallholders. At the same time over 31 percent of the land was in the hands of some 4,000 large landlords each owning a thousand *hold* or more. This disproportion was somewhat eased by the fact that most of the land—and the best at that—was in the hands of those who had the means and expertise to make it productive.

The Industrial Revolution came to Hungary in the closing years of the century and while its growth was most spectacular in branches related to agrarian products—mills, presses, distilleries—there was also a great increase in machine industries and in mining, especially of coal and iron. Still, the Hungarian economy remained fundamentally agricultural, in part because of tradition and in part because of the paucity of some essential raw materials for industrialization.

※ ※ ※

After the fall of the Tisza government, political stability seemed to be lost. In the last decade of the century four different premiers headed cabinets. Voices opposing the dualistic system once again multiplied. Nationalism of a not particularly constructive nature became the criterion of patriotism. When the exiled Kossuth died in 1894, his remains were brought home and the national mourning clearly showed how much the nation still cherished the memory of 1848. It boded ill for a continuing healthy partnership with Habsburg Austria.

Tisza's successor as premier was Count Gyula Szapáry, who had held several ministerial posts in past cabinets. Szapáry had neither Tisza's prestige nor his tactical skills. His proposed bills drowned in filibusters, a practice that had become distressingly common. In the end it was the ever-controversial religious question that led to Szapáry's fall. Already during Tisza's tenure bills promoting the legitimacy of civil marriage had been introduced and debated; they had passed in the lower house but failed in the upper. Under Szapáry the matter received attention from a different quarter. It was discovered that the Catholic clergy, ignoring the law that provided that sons born from mixed marriages should take on the religion of the father and daughters that of the mother, consistently registered such children as Catholics. The matter could be rectified if marriages were made civil and no declaration as to the religion of the children had to be made. Szapáry refused to support such a bill in its entirety and was forced to resign.

He was followed by Sándor Wekerle, a former minister of finance who had with great skill and tact succeeded in establishing a solid and reliable financial foundation for the entire monarchy by placing the joint currency, the krone, on the gold standard. (The fixed exchange rate against the dollar was 4.935 gold kronen.) He also steered through the legislative process, much to the chagrin of the emperor, a bill providing for civil marriages, and one which transferred the birth registry from ecclesiastical to civil jurisdiction. Another law guaranteed complete freedom of worship; the bill assuring the Jewish religion an equality of status with the other religions passed the lower house but failed in the upper; it was finally passed by both under the next administration.

Wekerle's ministry lasted only two years; deep currents of dissatisfaction flowed beneath the calm surface. Minorities kept up their agitation. The resentment of the agrarian proletariat, landless former serfs who lived an uncertain existence as day laborers and peasants who owned too little land to keep body and soul together, boiled over in the early 1890s, especially in the southeastern region of the Great Plains, soon fittingly dubbed the Storm Corner. Agitation, local uprisings, and repressions followed in quick succession. Demonstrations of this nature, however valid the grievances were, elicited little sympathy from other strata of society. One of the legacies of the French Revolution was an almost neurotic fear of the lower classes; every stirring by the poor raised the specter of socialism, and, with it, eruptions of mindless violence that the forces of law and order might not be able to control.

As the end of the century approached, these fears, and even the din of protests and the mood of uncertainty, were overshadowed by the extravagant celebrations of the nation's millennial anniversary in 1896. Preparations had been made for a decade. At midnight on New Year's Eve church bells struck all over the country reminding the people that their nation was celebrating its 1,000th birthday. In April parliament passed a resolution of gratitude to the founding father, Árpád, for the conquest of the fatherland, and to the Habsburg monarch for his magnanimity. The festivities, while they enhanced national pride, also served as a reminder that the nation was not entirely its own master; latent aspirations to rid it of the Austrian connection began to break onto the surface. The political parties had declared a truce for the millennial year, but in the September elections the truce broke down. The new premier, Dezsö Bánffy, a man committed to the policy of the iron fist, while striving to create a Hungary of Hungarians "by the most chauvinistic means," was also a champion of the *Ausgleich*. He found the new parliament of a different frame of mind. Aspirations for a separate nationhood were voiced in a variety of versions, and, whereas Bánffy could not silence them, he tried to smooth their political sting. A practical deadlock ensued, passionate debates and filibusters obstructed the legislative process, and no vote on the budget could be taken. By January 1, 1899, matters had reached a point whereby the government could no longer legally collect taxes or spend the money in the treasury. Bánffy was forced to resign. He was followed by Kálmán Széll, a liberal and a man from the world of high finance. He managed to quiet the turmoil by coming to terms with the National Party, the faction that had seceded from the Liberal Party during Tisza's tenure—it had called itself the Extreme Right Opposition before changing its name to the National Party. Its leader was a conservative, Albert Apponyi. Széll, in a gesture toward the Nationals, declared his support for the *Ausgleich*, but demanded that the system be purged of its polluting political features.

Such feeble concessions could not restore stability to a government torn by too many dissenting forces. Széll's cabinet fell on May 1, 1903, over the by now tired question of whether there should be one army or two. Owing to rising international tensions Vienna scheduled increased military call-ups; the nationalist opposition demanded that units from Hungary joining the colors use the Hungarian language and Hungarian insignia. When the recruitment bill came before parliament, the obstructionists resorted to filibuster and similar methods to prevent its passage, and a new parliamentary deadlock ensued. Széll's successor designate, István Tisza, son of Kálmán Tisza who had been premier a generation earlier, determined to put an end to such maneuvers by introducing new rules of debate that would make filibuster illegal. This move, and especially the methods by which he prevailed, led to such disorders, and even physical violence in the legislative chamber, that the session of parliament was suspended by royal order.

After such antecedents, the elections of January 1905 resulted in a great defeat of the government party that had run the country for the past 30 years. Tisza remained interim premier until the emperor named his successor, a former defense minister. Now the nationalist opposition was in the majority. It voted no confidence in the new government and campaigned for time-honored means of resistance, demanding that counties not collect taxes and recruits refuse to answer draft notices until a law providing for native Hungarian army units passed. Meanwhile the news of a burgeoning revolution in Russia in the wake of the lost war with Japan produced great excitement, especially among workingmen and their political party, the Social Democrats. Demonstrations and declarations of solidarity with oppressed Russian workers and peasants erupted in numerous parts of the country. Vienna responded by proposing to introduce universal suffrage and social reforms. With this it won over the Social Democratic Party, which had deserted the oppositionist coalition. (Universal suffrage was eventually introduced in the Austrian parts, but not in Hungary where the traditional power elite of the large landowning class was too strong in opposition.) Deadlock threatened the Hungarian political process. On October 5 the emperor actually considered bringing the country under military rule; provisional orders toward this end were sent to the commands of the major army corps of the joint army.

There was no need for military intervention after all. The opposition, deprived of the votes of the workers' party, was found to have no program beyond frustrating government initiatives; the discovery sapped its political strength and its appeal. Its leaders began to call for calm and for respect for the constitution—a program that gave the lie to their own actions over the past two years. They only asked that the righteousness of their demand for Magyarizing the military should be recognized "in principle"; the emperor replied by dissolving parliament by military force in February 1906. In April the opposition accepted an agreement practically imposed on it by the emperor; it undertook to form a government on the basis of the *Ausgleich* of 1867 and to abandon its nationalistic demands, which, if implemented, would have liquidated the Great Compromise and returned relations between Hungary and Austria to a state of chronic animosity.

A crisis was thus averted, but it had shown how feeble were the bonds that kept the Dual Monarchy together. The so-called nationalist opposition, seeking public support with its declamatory devotion to the Hungarian race and its traditions, was able to form transient coalitions with other parties, not on the basis of shared interests but by virtue of their hostility to Vienna. This was why a bare promise to consider extending the franchise to all adult males sufficed to separate the growing Social Democratic Party from the coalition, and why, apart from its nationalist posturing, the opposition was unable to erect a platform that attracted the masses of voters to its cause.

The future appeared dim indeed for the Dual Monarchy. The aged emperor labored mightily to keep his crumbling empire together, but more and more people, at home and abroad, began to believe that it was his person alone that held the structure together. Few dared to contemplate what would happen when he passed from the scene.

CHAPTER TEN

The prolonged crisis in the Hungarian government, pitting an ultranationalist opposition party against political realists who accepted the *Ausgleich* with Austria as the only viable framework for Hungarian-Habsburg cooperation, ended in 1905, with the victory of the opposition: an anticlimactic victory to be sure that brought neither stability nor purpose to national politics. The Independent Party, commanding a slim plurality that forced it into a coalition, had for so long stood on a platform of national independence that it could no longer disown it. Still, every political realist knew that it was an untenable position. It now launched a new initiative, one that turned out to be its only achievement during a short tenure: an educational statute that made Hungarian the sole language of instruction in schools for pupils of any ethnic group. Other items on the Independents' agenda—the introduction of Hungarian words of command in the military, a separate customs area, and universal franchise—remained unfulfilled.

Early in 1906 the emperor entrusted the government to Sándor Wekerle a second time; the latter succeeded in enacting measures that, although they benefited special interests, had a general usefulness: higher agrarian tariffs to protect the price level of Hungarian grain, state subventions for industry, and salary increases for civil servants. As to the franchise, it had become a burning issue that the government could not ignore at a time when almost every European state, even Russia, adopted the universal male right to vote. In 1908 the government introduced a complicated version of it that proposed extra votes for men of a certain age and education while illiterates, who made up 65 percent of Hungary's population, would receive one vote for every 12 of their numbers. The bill produced anger among the general public and was voted down in parliament.

The years around the turn of the century witnessed large-scale emigration, mainly among the small peasantry who were unable to make profitable the minuscule land allotments they received after their emancipation from serfdom. America was the destination of most emigrants; good farmland on that vast continent could be had almost for the asking, yet the majority of the new arrivals were absorbed in urban industries or in mining. The peasants who stayed at home grew restless, in places rebellious. The program of the Social Democratic Party, by now a movement to reckon with, with its advocacy of agricultural collectives, did not appeal to the small or landless peasants; they demanded land reform. After a Congress of Agrarians in 1897, an Independent

Socialist Party of agrarians was formed, and it openly advocated the breaking up of the large estates. In 1898 parliament had passed a law regulating the position of the agrarian proletariat; the purpose was to put an end to occasional but ever more frequent strikes on the land, especially at times of plowing and harvesting. It banned collective bargaining but at the same time prescribed strict penalties for landlords who dealt unfairly with hired labor.

In 1905, partly in response to the government crisis, a new wave of peasant unrest swept the countryside, especially in the Storm Corner in the southeast. The movement found a leader in a middle peasant, András Áchim, a passionate defender of peasant rights. He was a founder of the Independent Socialist Party and demanded the breakup, first of estates of over 10,000 *hold,* then of estates of over 1,000 *hold,* and their partition among the small peasantry. In 1905 he was elected to parliament and gained a position of influence seldom possessed by a man of his social class. In a weekly organ he edited, *Peasant News,* he kept agitating in a sanguinary prose for land reform. His passion for the cause was equaled by the anger of the large landowning class to whom the events in Russia during the revolutionary year of 1905 had demonstrated how life and property on the land could be threatened by an incited peasantry. Despite repressive measures against the movement, a peasant congress in 1908 attracted delegates from over 400 villages; they cheered as the statue of György Dózsa, the big-hearted nobleman who had led a peasant uprising in 1514 and died a terrible death at the hands of his fellow nobles, was unveiled. In 1911 two brothers of a large landowning family in the Trans-Tisza region assassinated Áchim, allegedly for insulting their family. The deed remained unpunished.

※ ※ ※

The government coalition of former oppositionist parties stood on shifting ground from the start, and in 1910 it fell from power. It was followed by partisans of the former Liberal Party who adopted the name National Labor Party. István Tisza stood as its leader and central figure. Although he had moderated his imperious manner in political dealings, his program still called for the preservation of the existing social order, dominated by the landowning aristocracy. This program seemed all the more necessary because of the spectacular rise of leftist movements, compared to which the opposition groups of past decades, for all their ill temper, appeared innocuous. When in May 1912 Tisza was elected president of parliament, an irate political left swung into action. On May 23 Budapest was the scene of a huge mass demonstration. In the face of police squads under orders to disperse the crowds, barricades were erected, streetcars were turned over, and in the end the military had to be called out to restore order. The occasion served as a pretext for Tisza to return to his strong-arm methods; he overrode parliamentary opposition and carried measures for increasing military preparedness, which, he claimed, not without reason, was essential, though he cited not internal disturbances but the threatening international situation.

Austria-Hungary's alliance with Germany had enabled the Dual Monarchy to take a firm stand in Balkan affairs, especially against Serbia, which, with uncertain Russian backing, was becoming ever more assertive. In the two Balkan wars, in 1912 and 1913, the Austro-Hungarian position, which crystallized in the determination to prevent Serbia from finding an outlet to the Adriatic Sea, prevailed even without major German support, as Russia was still too weak militarily to risk a major war in defense of the Serbs. This was the last time, however, that the Dual Monarchy could master an international crisis without outside help. Serbia had been kept from the sea, but the result was increased Pan-Slavic agitation directed toward already restive minorities within the monarchy. When a new crisis broke in late June 1914 with the assassination of Crown Prince Francis Ferdinand in Sarajevo by a Serbian youth, decades of accumulating tension and suspicion culminated in the Austrian resolve to bring Serbia down. Some leading politicians in Hungary, not familiar with or ignoring the perils of international complications, fanned the warlike mood. It was common knowledge that Francis Ferdinand had pronouncedly unfriendly feelings toward Hungary, feelings that were in many circles heartily reciprocated. Yet the larger question of whether Hungary would in the end be able to hold off the rising Slavic tide made many forget the sins of the dead heir to the throne. Albert Apponyi, one of the great orators of the day, at the funeral of the archduke called Francis Ferdinand "a royal scion of great gifts, of great will and great intentions"; another speaker asserted that the crown prince was "full of noble ambitions, and . . . he had been brought down by a murderous hand because he represented that very position of power that is in Hungary's vital interest."

It was at this point that Tisza assumed a critical role in the immediate events leading to the outbreak of the Great War. Constitutionally, as Hungarian premier, his consent was necessary for the Dual Monarchy to declare war; and his consent was not forthcoming. When he argued at a crown council in Vienna that a war against Serbia would not remain localized as the joint foreign minister Leopold Berchtold argued it would, Tisza had the interest of the whole country in mind. When, however, he expressed apprehension that Romania, an unreliable ally of both Germany and Austria-Hungary, would not honor her obligation to fight on their side but take the opportunity to break into Transylvania, he worried about Hungary's future in the Carpathian Basin. He also foresaw that the conquest of Serbia, which the Austrian military and foreign policy establishment confidently expected, would be followed by annexations, adding more millions to the Dual Monarchy's already heavy Slavic population.

Had Tisza only the Austrian government to contend with, he may well have prevailed in his opposition to war, especially as the fire-eating chief of the general staff Conrad von Hötzendorf admitted that the military was not prepared to deliver a quick strike against Serbia. But there was Germany, the most formidable power on the European continent, and German ruling circles feared for the survival of the Dual Monarchy if the Pan-Slavic menace was not energetically dealt with. In the end Tisza agreed that a nearly unacceptable ultimatum be delivered to Belgrade, and that, if it was rejected, war be declared. The consequences are tragically familiar. Far from remaining localized, the Austro-

Serbian confrontation quickly drew in Russia, Germany, France, and Britain in that order, with Japan joining on the Entente side soon after.

As it happened, the Russians were able to mount offensives much earlier than had been expected, both against East Prussia and against Austrian Galicia. The former attack, though defeated, drew two German army corps from the French front at a critical time, enabling the French to launch a counteroffensive against the exposed German flank and compel a stalemate that dashed the German hope of rolling up the western front in a matter of weeks. The Russian attack fell in the area of Lemberg between September 6 and 11 against the forces of the Dual Monarchy and was successful enough to enable the Russians to push into Hungary by way of a Carpathian pass. Only in December were Hungarian army units able to mount a counterattack, but six weeks later the Russians were again inside the Carpathians. After an extended winter lull, action flared up in May 1915; at that time, with German help, Austro-Hungarian troops achieved a major breakthrough at Gorlice and retook Galicia as well as large areas of White Russia. (In light of what the Germans did in these same areas in the Second World War, it is interesting to note that in 1915 retreating Russians murdered thousands of Jews whom they accused of collaborating with the Central Powers and it was the Germans who revealed these atrocities to the world.)

In the action against Serbia, Austria-Hungary did not as yet secure German help and, apart from a temporary occupation of Belgrade, Vienna was not able to achieve its goal of overrunning that small kingdom. The attack bogged down, in part because of the very difficult terrain and in part because of spirited Serbian resistance. In October 1915 German forces under General Mackensen poured into the Balkan kingdom and, sweeping the enemy before them, by early 1916 pushed into and occupied Montenegro and most of Albania. Bulgaria, long a competitor of Serbia, entered the war on the side of the Central Powers.

Italy, as a member of the Triple Alliance, was expected to honor the term of that alliance on the German-Austrian side upon the outbreak of war, but she failed to do so on the ground that she was not consulted during the diplomatic maneuvering that preceded the outbreak of the war. Her diplomats entered into secret negotiations with the Entente and in April 1915 secured promises of major territorial concessions after victory had been won. On May 4 they renounced their membership in the Triple Alliance and on the 23rd declared war against the Central Powers.

Romania did not immediately enter the war as Tisza had feared but kept a watchful eye on developments. When in June 1916 the Russians opened a massive offensive under the command of General Brusilov, which, if successful, could have taken Austria-Hungary out of the war, the Romanians decided the time had come for them to join the Entente. They did so, on August 17, in exchange for promises of territorial cessions that would double the area of their country: Bukovina, Transylvania, and a good part of the Trans-Tisza plains. Within a month, again with German help, Austro-Hungarian forces inflicted a crushing defeat on the Romanians; early in December they occupied Bucharest. The Romanian government, bereft of outside help, concluded peace with the Central Powers.

The hinterland of the Dual Monarchy was not entirely spared the stresses of war, but at first restrictions were not too onerous. Major firms were enlisted for war production and placed under military control. Shortages in certain staples occurred early and black markets flourished. Because of the absence of so many peasant boys from the farms, the harvests in wheat and other grains fell by one-third in volume in 1916, and they continued to slide. In the industrial sector, too, the places of trained and able-bodied men were all too often taken by women and even children, with the result that fewer goods of poorer quality were produced. The requisitioning of food and horses was soon introduced. Inflation was so rapid that in the course of the war the amount of printed money increased 15-fold and prices rose proportionately. Real wages fell by about one-half during the war.

On November 21, 1916, Emperor Francis Joseph died. National mourning was restrained and ceremonies were kept to a minimum. His successor, Charles IV (Charles I in Hungary) inherited a dismal situation. On the fronts the forces of the Dual Monarchy were either in retreat or bogged down in deadlocked trench warfare, as they were on the Italian front. Internally, shortages and the long and growing list of casualties produced a somber mood; workers' movements gained a new life and in 1917, for the first time in the war, May Day was celebrated with work stoppages and demonstrations for peace. Charles honestly intended to introduce reforms but with the best of will did not know where to begin, and most likely even a resolute and farsighted ruler would have been at a loss amid the welter of demands made, when the means of satisfying them were simply not available. On April 28, 1917, Charles, somewhat wishfully, directed the Hungarian government to make recommendations for improving national welfare and also to schedule a debate on the extension of the franchise. Instead of quieting the unrest, the news of these instructions increased it. Strikes and spotty mutinies multiplied. Tisza, still opposed to giving the right to vote to those who could not responsibly exercise it, resigned as premier on May 23. A young and rising politician, Moric Esterházy, formed a cabinet, but, unable to deal with rising public discontent, he too resigned three months later and the aged Wekerle stepped in his place. By now the only policy that had a chance to rally popular approval was one that could bring peace at almost any price, and none of Tisza's successors dared to take that course.

Actually, as early as the end of 1915, a liberal large landowner and member of parliament, Mihály Károlyi, had broached the subject of a separate peace and in the summer of 1916 he formed a new political party, the main plank in whose platform was peace without annexations and the reduction of the Austro-Hungarian bond to a personal union. At the time the military situation did not warrant such a radical solution to the Dual Monarchy's problems and the response was tepid. Even in 1917, after three years of stalemate at the fronts, there still were prospects of a victorious outcome for the Central Powers. The great French and British offensives of that year had been drowned in blood without achieving a breakthrough; several French divisions mutinied and in the French parliament there were cries of *"Il faut en finir!"* (Let's be done with it). On the Italian front the deadlock was abruptly broken when, on October 24, a powerful German-Austrian offensive breached the Isonzo front and advanced some 70 miles. Most important, the Russian front, long in a state of dissolution, practically collapsed after a futile July offensive.

Still, what the war-weary populace, in Hungary and elsewhere in the empire, could look forward to was either months or even years of more heavy fighting with a dubious outcome or a peace that meant certain defeat and the dissolution of the state that, for better or worse, it called its home.

CHAPTER ELEVEN

In the last year of the Great War Austria made several attempts to secure a separate peace with the Entente Powers, but all overtures met with rejection. In Hungary by contrast not even the nationalists, who had long sought divorce from Austria, tried to gain nationhood by means of their own separate peace. The armies of the Dual Monarchy remained a united force to the end and concluded an armistice as such. Signed in Italy, in the city of Padua, on November 3, 1918, the instrument of surrender contained no reference to territorial annexations, though it stipulated that the victorious powers had the right to occupy any such area as their military chiefs deemed to be of strategic importance. A French general, Franchet d'Esperey, who commanded a mixed French-Serbian force in the Balkans, lacking instructions as to the position he should take, claimed that the Padua armistice did not apply to the Balkans. He ordered his troops to move into Hungary and occupy parts of the southern and southeastern region. A special delegation of the Budapest government, headed by the new premier, Mihály Károlyi, betook itself to Belgrade to glean D'Esperey's intentions. The general drew a line on the map, separating Croatia, parts of the Bánát, as well as Transylvania from Hungary, and before the end of 1918 Serbian and Romanian troops, with French units operating in the area between them to prevent clashes, occupied these territories. A self-appointed Romanian National Committee in Transylvania had already declared the annexation of that province to Romania. The Budapest government in a last minute attempt to pacify disaffected minorities, promised to grant them autonomy. The declaration had no effect. In Belgrade, a Slavic National Assembly announced the annexation of Hungary's southern provinces to Serbia. By now, also, Czech military units had occupied most of the Uplands, in which the Slovak population was preponderant. Meanwhile, an Entente mission had ensconced itself in Budapest and made itself the final authority in all military and diplomatic matters involving Hungary. To Károlyi, a sincere friend of the Entente, these events, and the imperious conduct of French soldiery and of the Entente mission, was a bitter disappointment. His domestic support had never been strong and his inability to protect the country from rapacious neighbors further undermined his prestige. The problems he faced would have been overwhelming in any case. Inflation was nearly out of control and unemployment, due to the sudden cancellation of military contracts, was further increased by the hundreds of thousands of soldiers streaming home from the fronts. It was in these conditions that Károlyi decided to institute a program close to his heart, namely a

navy, Miklós Horthy, as minister of defense; Pál Teleki became foreign minister. Károlyi tried to bring some unity of purpose and a consensus of views to this ad hoc government, and when his attempts proved futile, on July 12 he resigned. Horthy, who did not deem the government's purely political organization sufficient to thwart the soviet regime, also distanced himself from it. He enlisted in Szeged the support of some men of finance and business for the organization of a counterrevolutionary military force. The first enlistees were almost all officers from the former Austro-Hungarian army. On August 4 a detachment began its march into Transdanubia. At this time a military mission from the peace conference, composed of high officers from the French, Italian, and American armies, arrived in Budapest to supervise the correct execution of the armistice conditions. The mission had little use or sympathy for Gyula Peidl's socialist government, which it regarded as the ideological successor to the soviet regime; on August 6, at the behest of some Hungarian officers of Horthy's camp, Peidl, having been premier for only three days, resigned. Already the nationalized businesses had been returned to their previous owners; on August 4 confiscated lands were likewise restored to private hands. The police and the gendarmerie, deactivated by the soviet regime, were also reinstated.

Peidl was succeeded as premier by one István Friedrich, a factory owner, whose popular support was nonexistent. During his two months in office various counterrevolutionary groupings jockeyed for position. Friedrich had the approval of the British and the Italians, whereas the French supported Horthy. His "army" was by now 25,000 strong. When a colonel in western Hungary placed a major force under his command at Horthy's disposal, its size reached 100,000. All that was needed now to legitimize the Horthy regime was the Entente's formal recognition.

When a British diplomat, Sir George Clerk, arrived in Budapest, he brokered an agreement among the various political factions. By its terms the Romanians were to evacuate Budapest, allowing a "national army" to occupy the capital. A formally democratic government representing various political groupings would then be formed. Romanian forces did leave Budapest on November 14; on the same day Horthy's army, led by the colonel who had placed his forces under Horthy's command, marched in. Two days later Horthy himself rode into the capital on his white horse. In front of the Gellért Hotel in Buda, replying to the mayor who greeted him, Horthy delivered an emotional homily. "This city has turned against its history of a thousand years, this city has dragged into the dust the Sacred Crown and the colors of the nation and has draped itself in red rags. It has thrown the best sons of the nation into prison, or had exiled them from their land. . . . Still, we will forgive this city steeped in sin if it returns to the service of the fatherland, if it will love with all the powers of its heart and soul the land in which the bones of our ancestors lie crumbling."

The long war, the two revolutions, the excesses of the soviet regime, the humiliations inflicted on the nation by the Romanian occupation and by the Entente Powers' imperious conduct, had produced a dangerous accumulation of collective anger. With a rightist government in power, the anger was directed mainly against those who served in the soviet regime, those who supported it, and those who were guilty by association. Among the last the Jews were the principal targets. Many leaders of the Communist government, including Béla Kun, had been Jews; rumors were on foot, some of them well founded, that Jewish manufacturers had sold the army military boots with soles made of cardboard, which had rotted off soldiers' feet in the Galician mud. In addition, there existed a sturdy residue of anti-Semitism from earlier times, a murky amalgam of superstition, resentment among peasants over usury, and the undeniable fact that many Jews, especially among the young, had been active in leftist politics and, embracing Marxist internationalism, were hostile to the national ideal.

Even before Horthy formally assumed power there had been instances of atrocities against Jews and they increased in violence in the early days of his regime. Many non-Jews also fell victim to the organized campaign of revenge.

Miklós Horthy
(Hulton/Archive)

Former Communists were arrested, tortured, and many survivors shot. On one day during these reprisals the chief of a terror action group wrote in his diary about the day's events: "In the courtyard of the inn we strung up five communists in the first half hour. The servant of the old count, who could have no complaints in his master's service, deserved the gallows above all—he escaped it only because the old count himself begged that he be spared. Thus he received only a hundred strokes of the stick; he nearly died of that too."

Altogether about 5,000 men and a few women fell victim to the White Terror, and over 70,000 were imprisoned or locked up in concentration camps. The terror had a predictably bad press abroad and the Entente Powers sent an observer to Hungary to investigate the reports of excesses. Interestingly the observer was an American Jew, Colonel Nathan Horowitz; after an investigation in Transdanubia he declared the rumors unfounded.

In the last week of January national elections were held. The previous November a decree had been issued providing for general, equal, and secret elections, in which every citizen 24 years old or more could participate; women were given the right to vote on condition that they proved literacy. The Social Democrats did not run. Over 80 percent of the electorate went to the polls, and when the returns were in and parliament met, the Christian Nationalists of the right and the Smallholders of the left were about equally represented. The assembly voted to maintain Hungary's position as a kingdom; until such time as a king could rightfully take the throne; a regent (a governor in Hungarian) would act as head of state. On March 1, 1920, Miklós Horthy was chosen to fill the latter dignity. The cabinet of the day, under one Károly Huszár, formed shortly after Horthy's assumption of de facto power, resigned and was followed by one under the equally colorless Sándor Semadam. A modicum of political peace returned to the reduced and tormented country.

Chapter Twelve

The treaties of peace between the Entente on the one hand and Germany and her wartime allies on the other had been concluded, new borders had been established, but the treaty with Hungary was still in a state of suspension. The short-lived soviet government had been promised an invitation to Paris to present its case for Hungary, but even had it met the conditions for the invitation, there never was a realistic prospect that the powers would deal with a revolutionary regime. (Even the Russian Soviet delegation had been conspicuous by its absence from the peace negotiations, ostensibly because of the civil war that ravaged the country, and when an invitation was finally issued, the proposed venue was a desolate island in the Sea of Marmora.) In Hungary's case, after the collapse of Béla Kun's soviet regime, the ensuing political flux contributed to the victors' reluctance to conclude peace; there simply was no government with sufficient authority to accept and enforce the peace terms. After Miklós Horthy finally succeeded in stabilizing the political scene, the invitation to send a delegation to Paris arrived on December 1, 1919. The three principal figures of the delegation included one old politician, Albert Apponyi, chosen for his linguistic skills and powerful oratory, and two younger men, Pál Teleki, a world-renowned geographer, who brought matchless expertise to the preparation of Hungary's plea that the economic and hydrographic unity of the Carpathian Basin be preserved, and István Bethlen, who had entered politics only in 1901 and represented the landowning elite.

While in Paris, the Hungarian delegation received sundry probing inquiries from French foreign ministry officials as to the country's willingness to participate in an anti-Soviet coalition—these approaches led nowhere. When the draft treaty containing the proposed new borders was finally presented, the delegation's worst fears were confirmed. Short of the total extinction of sovereignty, no harsher peace had ever been imposed on a European state. Formally the Hungarian side was invited to comment on, that is, to protest against, the treaty, but it was a foregone conclusion that such protests would be unavailing. By the provisions of the draft, all of the frontier regions of the former Hungary, some with extensive hinterlands, were stripped away. The sheer numbers convey the magnitude of the loss. The area ceded to Romania alone, 102,000 square kilometers, comprising Transylvania and parts of the Trans-Tisza region, was larger than the entire territory Hungary was allowed to retain (93,000 square kilometers). Austria received the Burgenland, a western strip of 4,000 square kilometers in extent, with 292,000 inhabitants; Czechoslovakia was awarded the Uplands, 63,000 square kilometers with 3.5 million inhabitants, of whom 1,072,000 were Hungarian. Of Transylvania's 3.5 million inhabitants 1,664,000 were Hungarian. The newly formed Serbo-Croat-Slovenian Kingdom received 21,000 square kilometers with 1.6 million people, one-fourth of whom were Hungarian. Altogether 3.2 million Hungarians found themselves under foreign rule. This flew in the face of Wilson's principle of national self-determination upon which the territorial dispositions were supposed to be based. When the Apponyi-led delegation requested plebiscites in the disputed regions, the neighbor states protested and the great powers rejected the plea. In the end the delegation had no alternative but to accept what was put before it and it signed the treaty, in the palace of Trianon, on June 4, 1920. At home, national mourning was declared, and for a full hour church bells all over the country tolled in a lugubrious chime.

The economic consequences of the treaty matched in severity the territorial losses. The unity and self-sufficiency of the Carpathian Basin was shattered; a series of small and intensely nationalistic states were established, each of which strove for an autarky that their limited resources made impossible to achieve. Hungary and Czechoslovakia, to cite one example, would have made ideal trading partners given the former's agrarian plenitude and the latter's industrial strength, but resentments over the treaty prevented them for a whole decade from reaching even a limited agreement for the exchange of goods.

It should be noted that at the time the final draft of the treaty was presented to the Hungarian delegation for signature, the president of the peace conference, French premier A. E. Millerand, in a letter that in its main section rejected Hungarian protests, held out the prospect of a later, peaceful, revision of the territorial terms. This promise became the basis for an active, unabating, agitation for such revision, which became the key endeavor of Hungarian foreign policy for the next two decades.

Internal consolidation was essential for the new independent Hungary to become a part of the European family of nations. The first parliamentary elections, as will be remembered, were held in January 1920, well before the peace treaty was even in its negotiating stage, and the outcome restored the political prominence of the old agrarian aristocracy. The premier (who, however, took office only after the signing of the peace treaty), Pál Teleki, although a staunch representative of that aristocracy, was a political moderate who put an end to the lawlessness of the extreme right and saw to it that some of those who had participated in the White Terror were brought to justice. A *numerus clausus*, instituted under his administration, was often looked on as an anti-Semitic measure, though actually its intent was to distribute university education among nationalities according to their percentage of the total population. Jews in general sought admission in much greater numbers than others, which was the reason why they were most adversely affected by the measure.

Even though Hungary was by parliamentary resolution a monarchy, the great powers, as well as Hungary's neighbors, insisted that the throne remain vacant. A return of the Habsburg monarch would imply the assumed legitimacy of his claims to all his lost possessions. In fact the chief reason why the parliament insisted on retaining the monarchy was to fortify its claim to Hungary's "crown lands." The monarchical question was, however, complicated by disagreements between, on the one hand, the legitimists, who wished for the restoration of the Habsburgs, and, on the other, those who preferred the installation of a Hungarian national king. The cleft between the two was never bridged.

Although the experience with the soviet republic had instilled a strong antileftist bias in the ruling classes, the Social Democratic Party was allowed to function on condition that it acted as a loyal opposition. A very limited land reform was also put in effect. Some half million families owning no more than two or three *hold* were given additional land as well as homesteads. Larger allotments were assigned to those with proven expertise in farm management. The lands so received carried a price tag that had to be paid over time in full. These modest reforms did not, to be sure, substantially alter the grossly unequal distribution of land ownership in the country (they affected only 7 percent of all arable land), and they stood in deplorable contrast to the much more liberal land reforms enacted in neighboring states. However, those states could afford to be generous, as so many landholdings had been abandoned by or been confiscated from former Austrian or Hungarian owners. A unique feature of the Hungarian land reform was that a special law had created a new order of *Vitézek* (Heroes) from among those who had earned military honors in the war; each of these, or, if they had died, their oldest son, was entitled to a land allotment.

On balance Teleki's government did much to normalize conditions in the country, considering that the radical territorial truncation and the passions engendered by the war and its aftermath made general normalization a very elusive prospect.

The sensitive question of royalty without a king was thrown into high relief when the deposed king, Charles, unexpectedly appeared in western Hungary and actually held discussions with Regent Horthy in the town of Szombathely. It developed that he expected French support, or at least tacit approval, for his return, but it turned out to be a misguided hope, as the Entente Powers protested in identical notes against any attempt at restoration. Charles departed for Switzerland; in October, he made a second appearance. The military garrison of the Hungarian town where he first stopped actually took the oath of loyalty to him; he went so far as to appoint a ministry and then proceeded in the direction of Budapest. Horthy ordered troops to block his passage. The king was exiled to the island of Madeira, where he died a few months later of inflammation of the lungs.

Parliament now took a step it had thus far refrained from taking: it declared the Habsburg dynasty dethroned and ineligible to wear the crown of Hungary. The crisis had shaken Teleki's cabinet. He resigned and István Bethlen formed a new government; it would with some changes in personnel remain in place for 10 years. Bethlen began his tenure with two small but significant foreign policy successes: the southern city of Pécs, which the peace conference had awarded to Hungary but which South Slav troops had kept occupied, was at last returned to Hungarian jurisdiction; another disputed town, Sopron, had originally been joined to Austria as part of the Burgenland, but vigorous protests led to the holding of a plebiscite, in which a great majority of the population opted to stay with Hungary. The city remained Hungarian. On the domestic front, Bethlen created a unified government party, in effect liquidating the second-largest party, the Smallholders, which had continued to agitate for a thorough land reform; he thus deprived the large Hungarian peasantry of formal parliamentary representation. In 1923 he forced the extremist Party of Race Protection out of the government coalition; from this time on until 1944 this rightist group functioned in an oppositionist role. The Social Democratic Party, on the other hand, was drawn more closely into the legislative process; the Communist Party was placed outside the law.

In a throwback to prewar days, and to ensure the kind of electoral outcome that best served his purposes, Bethlen once again restricted the franchise and, except in 12 cities, provided for open voting. This was in line with the ruling elite's mistrust of the political judgment of the masses. The predictable result was the government party's absolute majority in parliament and its submission to Bethlen's direction.

Foreign relations reflected the nearly helpless position of a defeated and impoverished state. Hungary was surrounded by hostile neighbors, each jealously guarding the territories it had gained from a once large and powerful Hungary. At Czechoslovak initiative three of the neighbors over the years joined in a series of bilateral treaties that came to be known, somewhat scornfully, as the Little Entente. Its avowed purpose was to prevent Habsburg restoration and to aid one another against any move by Hungary to effect a revision of the territorial status quo. For the rest, the Bethlen government was able to enlist the largely verbal support of certain British political circles for rectifying the mistakes of the Treaty of Trianon; overtures were also made to France, and it was mainly to promote this initiative that the government offered aid to the Poles (then enjoying French support) in their war against Soviet Russia. However, the French in the end opted to throw in their lot with the Little Entente instead of with Hungary, and from that time on the thrust of Little Entente policy was to isolate defeated Hungary from international connections.

Bethlen's government first breached this isolation by its rapprochement to Rome. Mussolini's Italy had designs in the Balkans, especially against the newly formed state of Serbs, Croats, and Slovenes, and she perceived in Hungary a useful partner. In April 1927 Bethlen traveled to Rome and signed an "eternal friendship" treaty between his country and Italy. Secret articles promised arms shipments to Hungary to promote revisionist aspirations. Another approach, to Weimar Germany, proved unsuccessful. So did cautious feelers toward official London and Paris. The postwar peace settlements had been achieved at the cost of so much wrangling and so many bitter compromises that none of the powers was inclined to open what could prove to be a Pandora's box. Only in Britain did the owner of the *Daily Mail,* Lord Rothermere, campaign for justice for Hungary; yet, responsible political circles never adopted his line.

In the matter of national welfare, adjustment to the greatly reduced economic base of the country proved a herculean task. In some spheres productive capacity outstripped the availability of raw materials, in others the opposite was the case. To cite but one example, the number of mills remaining in postwar Hungary had machinery able to grind 68 million quintal of grain—less than half of that was available. At the same time a good portion of the coal and iron that was mined had to go unused.

The monetary situation was chaotic. Hungary inherited part of the common currency of the Dual Monarchy, the krone; it validated it for the new conditions by superimposing a stamp of the Hungarian state on the banknotes. Attempts to overcome inflation had been started by Teleki's government when the latter curbed, then stopped, the issuance of new currency, reduced state expenses, and raised taxes. Even so, production of goods was so low that the money in circulation was many times larger than its purchasing value. By 1922 Hungary was unable to make its annual payment on reparations and was granted a year's deferral. The next year a major multinational loan, to which even two Little Entente states contributed, saved the country from bankruptcy. For two years an international commission supervised the nation's economy to ensure that the necessary measures for the repayment of the loan were effected. The results were so gratifying that by mid-1926 the supervision was lifted and the Hungarian currency was stabilized. In December of that year the krone was withdrawn from circulation and replaced by a new monetary unit, the pengő, one pengő was issued in exchange for 12,500 kronen.

With the country's political and economic position stabilized, Bethlen took additional steps toward conservative reform. These reflected the recognition that the straitened condition of certain social strata demanded state intervention; but, in no instance was that intervention supposed to promote the social uplift of the depressed or dispossessed classes. Bethlen restored the upper house of parliament against the possibility that a lower house with a majority of delegates who had radical leanings might be elected even under the restricted franchise. At the same time he had a social security system enacted that covered close to 1 million persons, that is, some 80 percent of the workforce. This mandatory old age and disability insurance program applied, however, only to industrial workers and left the large agrarian proletariat without protection. In 1928 the religious and racial prejudices of the *numerus clausus* law were eliminated. In the scientific field, the government established a number of institutions abroad to take advantage of the more advanced research methods and opportunities in the West.

Although officially Bethlen conducted his policy within the framework of the peace settlements, he could not, and most likely would not, lessen the intense resentment those settlements had left in Hungary. No government, no public person, could possibly declare himself reconciled to the Trianon peace and still hope to retain the nation's trust.

The stock market crash and the consequent economic crisis in the United States and much of western Europe affected Hungary at once, in part by the catastrophic plunge in the world market price of Hungary's chief export, grain, and in part because of the abrupt drying up of sources of credit. Within less than a year the price of industrial goods compared with that of agrarian prod-

small farms, thereby saving many farmers from bankruptcy; at the same time, however, he made no attempt to alter the grossly unequal pattern of landowning, which left many thousands of acres of the best land in the hands of great aristocrats and the Catholic Church. All the same, under his three-year tenure as premier the economic situation of the country definitely improved and the worst consequences of the Great Depression were avoided.

In foreign affairs too, despite his attraction to totalitarian systems, he was a pragmatist; given the extremely narrow limits within which he had to operate, he succeeded in extending Hungary's international connections. His diplomacy had to take into account the fact that for the past 400 years Hungary had not had an independent foreign policy and now had to build a diplomatic establishment from scratch. The task was made somewhat easier by the single clear and unchallenged (except perhaps by the Communists) foreign policy objective: the reconstitution of the borders that compressed the nation into an impossibly small area and left over 3 million Hungarians under foreign rule. Every diplomatic endeavor was informed by this imperative. Gömbös was perceptive in appointing as his foreign minister a man, Kálmán Kánya, who was not only a consummate diplomat but also fully dedicated to the policy of peaceful revision. Before the Nazi revolution in Germany, Italy alone among the great powers had been an active champion of overhauling the territorial provisions of the Paris peace settlements. It took some time for Hitler, who had risen to power on an anti-Versailles platform, to achieve the international stature Mussolini possessed, and Gömbös, although ready to find common ground with the Nazi dictator in a narrow sense, by no means endorsed his declamatory militancy and ideological extremism. He forbade the display in Hungary of the swastika, or of the symbol of the extreme rightist peasant party, the crossed scythes. He banned the Nazi-type militia that a rabid young aristocrat tried to organize, and when, in November 1933, anti-Semitic disturbances occurred in several universities, he had the institutions closed for a week. He opposed, as did Mussolini, Hitler's openly advertised plan of incorporating Austria into the German Reich. But such restraint had its natural limits. Hungary was surrounded by hostile neighbors; Austria alone, once the Burgenland problem had been settled, showed signs of friendship toward her former sister state. The Little Entente of Czechoslovakia, Romania, and Yugoslavia continued to be extremely defensive in face of Hungarian attempts at treaty revision, though Yugoslavia seemed far less concerned about such a development than the other two. The regions that had gone to the South Slav state were the least contested by Hungarian revisionists and Gömbös initiated a cautious rapprochement with Belgrade, mainly in the hope of weakening the Little Entente. The response was encouraging. Yugoslavia herself was in an increasingly precarious position. She had a defensive alignment with France dating back to 1924, but after the advent of Hitler the French were casting about for more potent allies against Germany, and they settled on Italy, as much opposed to German recrudescence as France was. Any approach to Italy had to take into account her increasingly tense relations with Yugoslavia, dating back to the territorial disputes following the peace settlements. In addition, Mussolini targeted Croatia, a restive province of Yugoslavia, as a sphere of Italian expansion. Until now the Yugoslavs could depend on French support against such pretensions but now they feared that France would sacrifice their security in pursuit of larger objectives. After laborious negotiations, they constructed the so-called Balkan Entente, aligning themselves with Romania, Greece, and Turkey; the express goal of the compact was the preservation of the Balkan status quo. Mussolini regarded this as a step hostile to Italy, for it aimed at excluding her from the Balkans, and in March 1934 he concluded with Austria and Hungary an agreement whereby the participants pledged to intensify their economic cooperation and to coordinate their foreign policies.

Gömbös's efforts to foster closer relations with Yugoslavia suffered a blow when on October 9, 1934, on a visit to France, the Yugoslav king Alexander II was assassinated by Croatian separatist terrorists. Investigations of the crime revealed that the assassins had lodged in Hungary before departing for France. In the League of Nations Yugoslavia accused Hungary of being accessory to the crime; the League left the discovery of who was responsible and to what extent to Hungarian authorities. The outcome was predictable, but relations with Yugoslavia suffered.

Increasingly in the 1930s German initiatives began to dominate the international scene. In January 1935 the French foreign ministry still labored to bring about a Danubian pact among Germany, Austria, Hungary, and Czechoslovakia, with the non-Danubian states of France and Poland, and with Romania, controlling the lower flow of the river, joining later. In March 1935 Hitler announced that Germany would no longer be bound by the military restrictions of the Treaty of Versailles and would build a strong army and an air force, both forbidden by the treaty. This brusque challenge to the military status quo drastically altered foreign policy concerns. France shifted her interest from Danubian cooperation to national security; on May 2 she concluded with the Soviet Union a formal military alliance directed against Germany. Two weeks later Czechoslovakia joined the pact and military compacts replaced economic ones.

The Italian orientation of Hungarian foreign policy continued, though it became increasingly doubtful whether Rome possessed the weight in international affairs to bring about territorial changes, even if those changes rectified manifest wrongs. Mussolini had, in the spring of 1934, proposed a four-power directory to impose peace on Europe *after* the peace settlements had been revised; the scheme, although no power rejected it outright, never came to realization. In December 1935 the Italians launched their first major imperial adventure when they attacked the African state of Ethiopia that bordered on Italian Somalia; the League of Nations voted economic sanctions against Italy, with only three states, Austria, Hungary, and Albania, abstaining. Although the sanctions had no effect on the conduct of the war and Italy's ultimate victory, her power position in the European constellation was substantially weakened. From 1936 on Germany became the dominant force in eastern European affairs.

Meanwhile, Gömbös made strenuous efforts to democratize his government. In his pursuit of a broad coalition he made overtures to smaller parties, first to the political right, then, moving progressively leftward, to the Smallholders'

Party. He briefly even courted the Social Democrats, only to meet a curt rejection. That workers' party opposed the premier's Italian and German orientation and advocated peaceful, economic cooperation with neighboring states, a position that rather cavalierly ignored the deep chasm that separated Hungary from its despoilers. Gömbös's efforts to build a mass party, the National Unity Party, were not futile, however. In the elections of April 1935 that party scored a landslide victory at the polls and gained 170 of the 245 parliamentary seats. There had been much intimidation and even falsification of returns, which cast a cloud over the results, but the victory of the party could not be ascribed to that.

Gömbös had reason to hope that Hungary, too, as Germany and Italy, could be turned into a one-party state. His labors in that direction made him many enemies, especially when he announced that he wished to replace labor unions and the Social Democratic Party with syndicates on the fascist model. A shrill concert of protest arose and Gömbös had to realize that, either because conditions in Hungary were not analogous to those in Italy and Germany or because he did not have the commanding position (or charisma) of a Mussolini or a Hitler, his endeavors would not succeed. Rightist forces opposed him because of his populist leanings and his concessions to the left; leftist forces because of his hostility to the labor movement in its every manifestation. Afflicted with a grave kidney disease, the premier lacked the energy to continue a struggle that was in any case hopeless. The regent, knowing he would not live long, allowed him to remain at his post. Gömbös went to Germany for medical treatment. He died in Munich on October 6, 1936.

His place was taken by his minister of agriculture, Kálmán Darányi, who had been heading the government in an acting capacity during Gömbös's illness. Unlike his predecessor, who had no social pedigree, Darányi was a member of the landowning elite with distinct conservative views. When he assured the nation that he would continue Gömbös's policies, he obviously did not have the latter's social experimentation or dictatorial pretentions in mind; he retained only the one item on which all Hungarians could agree, to undo at least some of the injustices of the Treaty of Trianon. Dependence on France had been abandoned when France had committed herself on the side of the Little Entente. The British orientation, which, as we have noted, had produced sympathetic editorializing but no concrete support, was also put on hold. Italy was progressively cast in the shadow of an emergent Germany. It was a foregone conclusion, if only from the programmatic portions of Hitler's book *Mein Kampf* that the chief thrust of Nazi Germany's foreign policy would be directed eastward and, with Italy in a gradual retreat from the Balkans and the Little Entente in an advanced state of decline, the field for German expansion was fairly open. Little Entente representatives met in the Slovakian capital of Bratislava at the end of 1936 and decided to abandon the practice, imposed by Czechoslovak foreign minister Edvard Beneš, of making foreign policy jointly, and to seek improvement in their relations with neighbor states, including presumably Hungary; it was obvious that each (with the exception of Czechoslovakia, which had the most to fear) wanted first of all a free hand in dealing with Germany. Hungary on its part announced her readiness to respond to overtures for improved relations, provided the Little Entente states recognized her equality in military matters and paid heed to the demands of the Hungarian minority within their borders.

No state overtly gave such an assurance, but Hungary's position was improved by the very fact that marching in step with Germany gave her at least an illusion of power. Ambivalence characterized the relations of each eastern European state with Germany. There was on the one hand the conviction that in order to promote one's position vis-à-vis rival states one needed German support, and on the other the fear that with each concession granted to her, Germany would become mightier and more threatening. Already her ascendancy had given a boost to rightist parties everywhere; and German minorities, the so-called *Volksdeutsche,* many of whom had so far been anxious to be assimilated into the native population, now discovered their German ethnicity. In Hungary some who had Magyarized their names readopted the former German ones; young *Wandervögel* from Germany came visiting as ambassadors speaking of the Nazi ethos and of a reborn Germany.

Darányi, although he had scant sympathy for Nazi goals and methods, found himself impelled to move in a rightist political direction; he even began putting out feelers to the domestic extreme political right. By now in Germany, including in what had been Austria before the *Anschluss* of March 1938, the position of Jews became a dominant domestic issue, the goal being to remove Jewish presence from the professions, the world of entertainment, and business. Nations in eastern Europe anxious to deal with Germany, or to have her support, found that the one reliable way to prove their bona fides was to come to grips with the Jewish question. In Hungary, Darányi left the task of framing a bill addressing that problem to his minister without portfolio, Béla Imrédy. On April 8, 1938, Imrédy introduced in the lower house of parliament a bill designed to restrict Jewish influence in the public sphere. Vocal protests accompanied the debate and it was not until May 29 that the measure became law. In no sense did it carry the severity of Hitler's Nuremberg laws: the definition of a Jew was based not on his racial identity but on his declaring himself a Jew; the law was lenient also in that, although Jews made up a little over 5 percent of the total population, it provided that "only" 20 percent of the membership of medical, legal, engineering, and commercial associations could be Jewish. Significantly though, it was precisely in these areas that Jewish presence was most numerous and influential. Opposition to the measure was most pronounced in conservative circles, which, though aloof from Jewish contacts socially and in their professional and business dealings, saw in the law a victory for those elements of society they most despised: the uncultured and ill-tempered lower classes flouting, in the absence of anything else to flout, their Gentile credentials and finding satisfaction in seeing those who lacked them victimized. Darányi, from all we know of him, shared the disapproval of his class and resigned two days after the passage of the law. He was followed by Imrédy, an economist by profession, a man of intelligence, as yet uncorrupted by the Nazi virus. The Jewish law, which he authored, as we have noted, was more noteworthy for its tolerance than for its punitive features. In his first major act as premier Imrédy took a hard stand against the Party of Awakening, home of Hungarian Nazis, and had its leader, Ferenc Szálasi, imprisoned. If by this he intended to serve notice that he would not follow the Nazi method of governing, his brave stance did not last long. The summer of 1938 was one of the most turbulent and emotionally charged of any period of peace in Europe. The rape of Austria in March had created sanguine expectations among the Sudeten German population in Czechoslovakia of being "liberated" from Czech rule, and Hitler took full advantage of the hysteria that followed. He correctly estimated that neither Britain nor France would risk a general war over a patchwork republic barely two decades old. He hoped to involve Czechoslovakia's enemies

Béla Imrédy
(Hungarian Museum of Photography)

in her planned destruction and, among those, Hungary had the most valid grievances. At the end of August Hitler invited the wife of Regent Horthy to christen a newly completed German battleship in Kiel. While in Germany, the regent, as well as foreign minister Kánya, and Imrédy, had some sharp words with Hitler and Foreign Minister Ribbentrop over Hungary's recent cozying up to the Little Entente instead of following the German lead in seeking to destroy it. In the end Hitler was grudgingly satisfied with receiving Hungary's territorial demands on Czechoslovakia as a means of trumping the almost desperate peace efforts of British prime minister Chamberlain. The ruse worked. Hitler was able to increase his own demands and by decision of the leaders of four great powers meeting at Munich on September 29 he was able to incorporate the entire Sudetenland into the Reich. It was, however, not at his but at Mussolini's insistence that the Munich protocol was accompanied by the pledge that if Czechoslovakia did not find means within three months to settle the claims of Poland and Hungary as well, the four powers would meet again to draw the new borders with those states. The Poles gained their demands quickly; the Hungarian side soon found itself involved in undignified haggling with the Slovaks over the size of the territory the latter should cede. In the end the Budapest government requested arbitration by the Munich powers; Britain and France, when invited, begged off. The Slovak area to be ceded to Hungary was determined, on November 2, by Ribbentrop and Italian foreign minister Galeazzo Ciano.

The first breach had been inflicted on the hated Treaty of Trianon. However, neither Hungarian diplomacy nor the Hungarian military could claim credit for it; the country received southern Slovakia as a gift. This was the case some five months later with another lost province, Ruthenia. Hitler decided, in mid-March 1939, to liquidate what had meanwhile become the hyphenated state of Czecho-Slovakia. He turned the Czech portions into a German protectorate, and ordered Slovakia to declare her independence, but he was somewhat at a loss as to what to do with the most distant and backward portion of the republic, Ruthenia. In the end he bestowed it on Hungary and gave the Budapest government barely two days' notice to carry out the annexation.

Within a short time Imrédy, of a generally moderate temperament, became mesmerized by Hitler's summary dispositions and by his peremptory ways of disposing of legal and constitutional encumberances. Already in 1938, at a meeting of the Hungarian cabinet on October 4, Imrédy announced his intention to govern by decree; three weeks later he so radically changed the procedural rules of parliament that that body was practically deprived of its legislative functions. In protest, about one-third of the delegates resigned, and Imrédy, far from being in a commanding position, had to resign as well. However, he did enjoy Hitler's confidence, a fact that became a major consideration at a time when no foreign policy gain could be made without German blessing, and the regent asked him to continue as premier. Imrédy then issued one decree after another, one aiming at strengthening relations with Germany, another at beefing up Hungary's military preparedness, still another at enabling the government to declare at its discretion a state of emergency. By now the leftist parties, never a substantial political force, had been reduced to practical impotence, and conservative elements, with István Bethlen in the lead, alone opposed Imrédy's high-handed "reforms" and his German orientation. In the end, what brought Imrédy down was not so much his radicalism as the discovery that one of his great-grandparents had been Jewish. On February 12, 1939, Horthy asked for his resignation. The next day the regent appointed Pál Teleki, who had been premier once before and had been a member of the Hungarian peace delegation at Trianon, to succeed Imrédy.

It was during Teleki's early tenure that Ruthenia was returned to Hungary but Teleki, unlike Imrédy, took little pride in receiving an old province from German hands. He too initiated quick action against extremist parties on the right, outlawing all those that fashioned their program on the Nazi German model. Imrédy, before his resignation, had been preparing a new anti-Jewish bill and now it fell to Teleki to navigate it through a reluctant parliament. Nazi influence was evident in the provision of the bill that defined Jewishness by race rather than religion. Regardless of one's identification with or practice of Judaism, anyone who had at least one Jewish parent, or two Jewish grandparents, was subject to its provisions. In place of the 20 percent quota in the professions, Jewish presence in them was reduced to 6 percent; the bill further stipulated that Jews could not be employed by the state or by public institutions, could not edit or publish newspapers, or own or manage theaters or cinemas. In every sense of the word Jews became third-class citizens. In certain circles the law was justified by the argument that it stole the thunder of the Hungarian Nazis, recently organized in a party by a new name, the Arrowcross Party. However, in reality the strategy did not work, because the votes cast for extreme rightist groups increased greatly during national elections held in May.

A year earlier the summer months had been heavy with foreboding over the Sudeten question, the summer of 1939 witnessed the dramatic deterioration of relations between Germany and Poland. Hitler, with his appeal to all Germans to return to the Reich, had liberated a ghost he could not control. A part of the Poland resurrected after the First World War had been carved out of the body of Germany. To ensure that he would not have to fight a two-front war (Britain had guaranteed Poland after the destruction of Czecho-Slovakia and France already had a defensive treaty with her) Hitler authorized secret talks to commence with the Soviet Union. When these bore fruit in a non-aggression pact signed on August 24, 1939, Hitler felt free to move against Poland when the latter would not concede his minimum demands.

Throughout the international crisis, Teleki followed a cautious middle-of-the-road course. As the war against Poland loomed, he wrote to Hitler: "Hungary will coordinate her own policy with that of the Axis [of Germany and Italy]. . . . There cannot be the slightest doubt, however, that such accommodation must not be allowed to infringe on our sovereignty and cannot raise obstacles to the realization of our national goals." He further anticipated German demands that Hungary join in the war against Poland by stating that Hungary was not, *out of moral considerations,* in a position to pursue such a policy.

Hitler was infuriated by being lectured like this; his mind was in any case made up. On September 1, 1939, German armed forces poured into Poland. The British and the French, although they were duty-bound to enter the conflict as soon as a German soldier entered Polish territory with hostile intent, waited three days before they declared war on Germany. But declare it they did, and only 20 years after the conclusion of peace at the end of the first European War, a second war cast its shadow over the continent.

CHAPTER FOURTEEN

It is possible to argue, as some historians do, that in the last resort it was the dogged revisionism of successive governments that dragged Hungary into the Second World War. This argument assumes, however, that had these governments not aligned themselves with the Axis in the hope of territorial gains, they could have kept the country out of the war—a farfetched assumption. In the early phases of the war, to be sure, Hitler requested no more than permission for German troops to move across Hungarian territory; when the request was denied, he did not press the matter. Judging from his occasional remarks, he understood well that it was self-interest and not ideological affinity that persuaded the Hungarians to side with Germany and take such symbolic steps as joining the Three Power Pact (of Germany, Italy, and Japan) and to declare, when it was convenient, their sympathy for Axis aspirations.

While things went well for Germany and the Wehrmacht marched from one stunning victory to another, there was no reason for Hitler and his military brass to be particularly concerned about Hungary's attitude. Premier Teleki's Anglophile sympathies were known to them; still, they did not call for his removal. It was, in fact, during Teleki's tenure that the richest prize yet, a good portion of Transylvania, returned to Hungary with Axis help. The antecedents were complex and unrelated to the merits of the Hungarian claim to the province. The central factor was Germany's vital need for oil, a good part of which came from the Ploesti wells in Romania. Hitler was anxious to assure the security of those wells by avoiding any development that might bring hostilities to the region. The preservation of the neutrality of Balkan states was one of the cardinal features of German foreign policy in the early stages of the war.

In August 1939, on entering into the nonaggression pact with the Soviet Union, in his haste to gain Soviet concurrence, Hitler had agreed to consign the Romanian province of Bessarabia into the Soviet sphere by recognizing the Soviets' "special interest" in the region. Stalin did not at once avail himself of the freedom of action that concession granted him; he was busy implementing other secret provisions of the nonaggression pact, specifically the military occupation of the Baltic states, and then, in punishment for the unexpected refusal of the Finnish government to cede a naval base to the Soviet Union, launching an attack on Finland, an enterprise that involved the Soviet armies in a series of humiliating defeats before their superior manpower finally prevailed. The position of Bessarabia continued in a contingent state; it was the rapid collapse of French resistance in face of the German attack in the spring of 1940 that made Stalin decide to fortify his western ramparts. A short-term ultimatum to Bucharest demanded the cession of Bessarabia. Romanian pleas to Germany to intervene went unheeded. Soviet troops occupied the province, bringing them into dangerous proximity to the Ploesti oil wells.

Still, as long as the rest of the Balkans remained quiescent, the Soviets were not likely to try to penetrate farther. But Hungarian policymakers smelled blood. Witnessing the helplessness of Romania, they judged the time ripe for advancing their claim to Transylvania, and to fight for it if the claim was rejected. They advised Berlin of this position. Hitler immediately perceived the danger of a war breaking out on the northern fringes of the Balkans. The Soviets, on the transparent pretext of restoring order, might send forces into Romania and penetrate as far as Ploesti. Hitler asked the Hungarians and Romanians to resolve their territorial dispute through negotiations. The two governments complied, though they knew full well that their respective positions were irreconcilable. When the talks did not lead to an agreement and Hungary threatened to go to war, Hitler arranged for another Axis arbitration. In the Second Vienna Award, on August 30, 1940, the northern part of Transylvania, plus the Székely enclave in the farthest eastern corner, were returned to Hungary.

The Germans did not wait long before asking for compensation. Hungarian citizens of German nationality had earlier been allowed to organize themselves into the Volksbund, which in some respects stood above the law; the privileges accorded to this organization were now increased. On a more practical plane, Berlin demanded extensive food deliveries. By degrees, Hungary, a nonbelligerent, was placed on a war footing. Defense legislation previously passed had already provided for stepped-up weapons production, though the country possessed neither the raw materials nor the infrastructure, nor for that matter the expertise, for such a radical retooling. As early as the fall of 1939 ration cards for certain food items were introduced and restaurants were ordered to hold two meatless days a week.

Now, after the Second Vienna Award, Hitler, in a talk with the Hungarian ambassador in Berlin, made it clear that Hungary could count on further German support only if she became firmly aligned with the Axis side. In view of continued German military successes, this indeed seemed the wise thing to do. All things being equal, at war's end Germany would dictate the terms, and, if Hungary's merits were meager, she not only would have to give up hope for further territorial enlargements but might even lose what, thanks to Axis generosity, she had received so far. The political right within the country began a concentrated campaign for entering the war on Germany's side. The most militant figure in this camp, Ferenc Szálasi, had recently been released from prison and gathered all the extreme rightist forces in the newly formed Arrowcross Party. It was largely in response to pressure from the Arrowcross that the government agreed, on September 30, 1940, to allow German military units to pass through Hungary, on their way to Romania, to assist in rebuilding that nation's military force.

In the months that followed, all considerations—territorial, military, and political—in the Axis camp were subordinated to the maturing German plan, which, once launched, would be the culmination of the war now nearly two years old: a German attack on the Soviet Union. The struggle against Bolshevism had always been the foremost item on Hitler's agenda of aggression. Tactical imperatives had caused it to be delayed, then put in an inactive status with the conclusion of the nonaggression pact. Now, with most other options exhausted, and the principal one, the invasion of Britain, having been indefinitely postponed, a war against the Soviet Union entered the realm of urgent possibilities. Hitler was receiving almost daily reports on the mighty efforts the Red Army was making to become battle ready; granting it another year or two to complete preparations might prove fatal to Germany. A last attempt to work out a joint plan of action between the Axis and the Soviets came to naught when Foreign Commissar Molotov, on a visit to Berlin in November 1940, proved intractable in pressing Soviet desiderata while treating German proposals for joint action against the British Empire with scorn. On December 18, 1940, Hitler issued his directive for Operation Barbarossa, a plan for a "swift campaign" against the Soviet Union.

The operational plans were from the beginning hampered by the fact that the anxiously guarded neutrality of the Balkan states had been upset. Mussolini, irked by the series of brilliant German victories, which his own ill-equipped forces were unable to match, in late October launched a poorly prepared and utterly senseless attack on Greece from recently conquered Albania. In the space of a week the Royal Air Force, taking advantage of the fact that Greece was no longer neutral, established itself there, bringing its bombers within striking distance of the Romanian oil wells. Worse, the Italian offensive bogged down almost as soon as it was started, and the Balkans became an active battleground. At one stroke the southern flank of the planned deployment against Russia became exposed. Hitler was forced to interpose an operation in the Balkans between the issuance of the Barbarossa directive and the actual start of hostilities against Russia. The objective of Operation Marita, to be launched in the spring of 1941, was to occupy Greece and clear British forces from the Balkans.

That Yugoslavia in time also became a target of German aggression was due to the bitter disapproval by the Serbian military of their government's agreement to allow German troops to cross the country on their way to Greece (an agreement given formal status by Belgrade's joining the Three Power Pact); a coup on March 27, 1941, removed the Yugoslav head of state and installed a new government. Hitler, almost on an impulse, decided to crush Yugoslavia as an independent state. He requested of Regent Miklós Horthy freedom of passage for German troops across Hungarian territory. Here was the opportunity for Horthy to make good a long-standing (though never actively pursued) territorial claim on still another neighbor state. Horthy promptly granted the German request and even offered Hungarian military cooperation. As it happened, in December 1940 the Hungarian government had concluded an "eternal friendship" agreement with Yugoslavia, an effective pledge that Hungary would not raise territorial demands similar to those put to Romania. Now Horthy reduced the eternal duration of the treaty to a few months.

He may not have been troubled by such a betrayal of trust, but Premier Teleki was. He secured a pledge from the Supreme Defense Council, which effectively acted as a cabinet, that Hungary would intervene in the war against Yugoslavia only to protect the Hungarian minority there, and then only if the country disintegrated. The day after the resolution Teleki had alarming intelligence from his ambassador in London: if a German attack against Yugoslavia was launched from Hungarian territory, Great Britain would sever diplomatic relations with Budapest. If Hungary joined in the war, she would have to be prepared for a declaration of war by His Majesty's government.

When Teleki realized that Horthy was, even in the face of that prospect, prepared to carry out his promise to Hitler, he wrote the regent a bitter letter of reproach, then, on the night of April 2 to 3, committed suicide. Possibly out of respect for a man of honor, or because cooler counsels prevailed in London, when Hungary did join the campaign against Yugoslavia, Great Britain refrained from declaring war.

Teleki's successor as premier was the foreign minister, László Bárdossy, formerly Hungarian minister in Bucharest, a man of decidedly pro-Allied sympathies. It became his dubious privilege to oversee another augmentation of Hungarian territory, the repossession of the Bačka from Yugoslavia, an action that, honorable or not, was greeted with general jubilation by the Hungarian populace.

It was obvious to all but the hopelessly gullible that conquests achieved in time of war lacked permanence and that if the country ended up on the losing side, the gains could prove more a liability than an asset. But, even if it was only for months, patriots relished the return of lands that for a millennium had been Hungarian and then were lost to a rapacious neighbor. The campaign against Yugoslavia was so brief, it entailed so few material sacrifices, that Hungary's participation in it did not even qualify for belligerency. In the larger context, however, the Balkan operation caused a postponement of the opening of the Russian campaign, though some delay would in any case have been necessary because unusually heavy rainfalls swelled the rivers the German army would have to cross on its way into Russia to flood levels.

Operation Barbarossa opened at dawn on June 22; two of Hungary's territorial rivals, Romania and Slovakia, declared war on the Soviet Union that same day. Hitler wrote Horthy a letter, delivered that same morning, informing him of his decision to destroy the Soviet Union, and assuring him that he was "acting in the spirit of the whole European civilization and culture in trying to repel and push back this un-European [Russian-Jewish] influence." The letter contained no invitation for Hungary to join, but its very tenor suggested that it was the duty of everyone imbued with the European spirit to do so.

The cabinet met on the morning of the 23rd. Premier Bárdossy still hoped that some gesture short of a declaration of war could preserve Germany's goodwill. He proposed to the cabinet that Hungary break diplomatic relations with the Soviet Union. After a heated debate the proposal was accepted. The German minister in Budapest, when informed of the decision, treated it with disdain. The chief of the Hungarian general staff, Henrik Werth, of German extraction, when urged by German liaison men in Budapest to put pressure on his government to abandon its half-hearted measures, sent an urgent memo to that effect to Bárdossy. The premier had before him another message as well, from his minister in Moscow, who had been summoned by Molotov with a plea for Hungary to abstain from hostilities and a broad promise of Soviet support for a thorough treaty revision if she complied. Bárdossy set the wire aside, and he did not report it to his cabinet or to Horthy either. (This omission became the chief count of indictment against him after the war.) In the hope that a rupture of relations would satisfy Hitler, he called in the German minister and explained to him in oblique terms that if Hungary went to war, she would have to fight side by side with Romania, her irreconcilable enemy. The minister listened to the argument without comment.

Matters were still in abeyance when, on the early afternoon of the 26th, with the Russian campaign four days old, some unidentified airplanes flew over the Hungarian town of Kassa, recently recovered from Slovakia, and dropped bombs. Thirty civilians were killed, many were wounded. A report to Budapest from a military eyewitness, stating that the planes, although unmarked, were recognizably German, was suppressed. The government, the media, in time the public, assumed that they were Russian. The cabinet met in extraordinary session and decided to communicate a declaration of war to Moscow. In point of fact, no formal declaration was made, either in Budapest or in Moscow. Bárdossy informed parliament of the state of war on the 27th.

A mobile corps with motorized units and two infantry divisions, altogether some 45,000 men, was dispatched to the Russian front. After the force reached the Dniester River, only the mobile corps continued the advance. The infantry was left behind for occupation duty. Because of heavy casualties incurred even in those secondary operations, at the end of the year the units were withdrawn. Not in time, however, to forestall a British declaration of war that reached Budapest on December 7.

※　※　※

Outstanding military experts in several countries had predicted after the launching of Operation Barbarossa that the Soviet armed forces would within weeks collapse under the impact of the German attack. The prophecies proved premature. Although the Red Army experienced several acute crises and was in almost constant retreat, it did not break. After the German failure to take Moscow, and after the Japanese attack on Pearl Harbor relieved the Soviets' Far Eastern Army for service elsewhere, the Red Army went on the counterattack. *Blitzkrieg* faltered and German victory in Russia became a rapidly receding prospect.

In Hungary, the military alliance with Nazi Germany once again gave heart to the extreme rightist groups whose ascendancy successive governments had vainly tried to curb. Before the year 1941 ended, parliament passed a third anti-Jewish law that forbade marriage, and even sexual relations, between a Jew and a non-Jew, characterizing such relations as racial pollution.

As the new year opened the German position in Russia was stalemated, though the military still maintained that only one final push was needed to bring the Red Army to its knees. To secure assistance to that end the head of the German high command, General Keitel, on a visit to Budapest in January 1942, spoke to Hungarian military and government officials. He demanded more extensive Hungarian participation in the war in the east. Reluctantly, and with a heavy heart—for the Russian front had become a monstrous meat grinder—the government agreed to commit one of its two armies, the Second, to that front. Military appropriations were greatly increased; but, due to the underdeveloped state of weapons production, only a fraction of those appropriations were actually expended. During the summer of 1942 the Hungarian Second Army followed the great German advance in the Don Basin; 300,000 strong, it was eventually deployed on the northern wing of German Army group B, in the area of Voronezh on the Don.

The year before, the German attack had been halted by the onset of winter, and the Red Army had been able to launch offensive operations; this time it did so before winter arrived. A two-pronged attack on the wings of the Stalingrad front resulted in the encirclement of the German Sixth Army and of the city itself. After the surrender of the Sixth Army at the end of January 1943, the Soviets began a general counterattack. The first blow fell on February 12 in the sector held by the Hungarian Second Army and it was devastating. The army was put to flight, often abandoning most of its weaponry, and by the end of the winter it had virtually ceased to exist as a fighting force. (It had in the process lost over half its manpower in dead, wounded, and captured.)

Although Regent Horthy had two years earlier waxed jubilant over the "crusade" against the Soviet Union, of which Hitler had informed him, he now held Premier Bárdossy responsible for leading the nation into a war with no end in sight, and on March 7, 1943, he asked for his resignation. Bárdossy's place was taken by a landowning aristocrat of old lineage, Miklós Kállay, whom the regent thoroughly trusted. Like so many of his predecessors, Kállay too preferred a western orientation. He had no faith in German victory and was fully aware of the fate that awaited his social class if the country fell to the Red Army. He planned to extricate what Hungarian forces were left on the Russian front and deploy them in the Carpathians facing eastward against a Soviet advance while seeking a separate peace with the United States and Great Britain. He was even willing to accept the "unconditional surrender" formula agreed upon by Roosevelt and Churchill at their meeting in Casablanca in January 1943, but only if that surrender was made to the Anglo-Saxons. An agent of his was able to make contact with an official British personage in Istanbul and offered surrender; when the Americans were advised of these approaches, they insisted that the offer be unconditional in every respect and advised the Hungarians to turn to the Soviets.

Hitler was informed of these contacts by an ally and had reason to believe that, as the Red Army breached the Carpathians, Horthy would surrender, opening a wide breach in the eastern front. On March 19, 1944, German military forces numbering about 300,000 men occupied Hungary. Kállay was forced to resign and after a brief hiatus the Hungarian minister in Berlin, Döme Sztójay, succeeded him. Of German roots, and a great admirer of Hitler and his system, he could be depended on, not only to keep Hungary in the war but also to carry out the action close to Hitler's heart, the mass deportation of Hungarian Jews to extermination camps. The expert in Jewish matters in the Third Reich, Adolf Eichmann, arrived in Hungary shortly after the occupation and with famed German thoroughness organized the concentration and transshipment of the Jewish population in the countryside to camps in Germany, especially to Auschwitz. Only when the gendarme units entrusted with the deportations reached the capital did Horthy use his authority to forbid further resettlements, ordering military units to disarm the gendarmes.

The action against the Jews had put a great strain on Hungarian rolling stock; only when it was halted were transportation facilities once again available for military use. Sztójay gave his consent to the country's other army, the First, to be deployed along the Pruth and the Dniester Rivers (A third army was in the process of being formed). Horthy was by now seriously considering surrender, even if it was to the Soviets. As a first step, he forced the resignation of Sztójay; the Germans tried to prevent it, but just then, near the end of August 1944, they suffered a great defeat in Romania and on the 23rd the government in Bucharest quit the war and a few days later declared war on Germany. These events deprived the Germans in Hungary of much of their political clout and Horthy was able to install a government under a military man of liberal leanings, General Géza Lakatos.

September 1944 was a crowded month and one in which Hungarian military forces, now fighting on their own territory, made a last attempt to salvage the gains they had made through Axis arbitration. Still in possession of northern Transylvania, they launched a series of attacks, against Romanian and later Soviet forces, for the recovery of the southern part of the province. After some early successes, by the end of the month the attacks petered out and elements of the Second Ukrainian Front, advancing from Transylvania, entered Trianon Hungary proper. Nothing could be gained from further resistance, and the hope of surrendering to Britain and the United States had been dashed when the Teheran Conference in November 1943 vetoed Churchill's plan of striking against the Germans from the Balkans. On September 28 Horthy dispatched a delegation to Moscow to ascertain conditions for an armistice. On October 11 a provisional agreement was signed in the Soviet capital. Nothing seemed to stand in the way of a separate peace with the Soviet Union, and subsequently with the United States and Great Britain.

Shortly after noon on October 15, a Sunday, Horthy caused a proclamation to be read on the radio, which in solemn accents renounced Hungary's alliance with Germany, a country that, as it was put, "instead of rendering military aid, seeks to deprive Hungary of its greatest treasure, its freedom and independence." He ordered all hostilities against the Red Army in Hungary to cease.

Horthy had underestimated the practical effect of the country's occupation by German forces. The Gestapo had, in anticipation of his announcement, arrested Horthy's son Miklós (his other son, István, designated to be his father's successor, had died in an airplane crash the year before), as well as other conspirators. Unable to find a respectable political figure to head a new governing Nazis. More than half of the cattle and hogs and other livestock had been slaughtered or shipped out of the country; 30 percent of agricultural machinery and some 50 percent of other types of machinery had similarly been plundered. The retreating Germans had blasted most of the railroad and other wheeled traffic bridges; they tore up railbeds to slow the Soviet advance. Many of the trains and engines they had used remained in occupied Germany. The currency, diluted by whimsically printed occupation banknotes, was rapidly losing all its worth.

On the political front the Communists, although they had fared poorly in the elections of November 1945, still commanded a measure of goodwill and many of the politically neutral elements in the population were willing to wait and see whether their program, the only dynamic and forceful one put forth, might solve the problem of regeneration. There was a fairly widespread recognition that past regimes had served narrow segments of society rather than the broad masses, and that the country's alliance with Nazi Germany, its servile readiness to deliver its Jewish population into the hands of murderers, had been sins for which the nation had to atone.

The Communists quickly capitalized on the general sense of outrage over Nazi crimes. Appointing themselves as the most authentic liquidators of the Hitlerite legacy, they quickly seized control of the political police. While the chief function of that police was to round up and deliver to justice Nazi criminals, many other persons unfriendly to communism were caught up in its net. The concept of the "enemy," repeatedly cited by Communist leaders and publicists as forces retarding progress, in a short time acquired the widest possible meaning; it was applied to the Catholic clergy, public officials of the past regime, former military officers, landowners, bourgeois nationalists (a term referring to people for whom the nation was a closer and dearer concept than international socialism), and owners of major business concerns. Remembering the stigma that had attached to the terms "communism" and "socialism" not long ago, party publicists used them sparingly; "democracy" was the operative phrase; in truth, it was a cover name for Stalinism. Although, as noted, Stalin as yet wielded a moderate hand, no major project could be undertaken without his knowledge and approval, and the judicial process, too, soon bore the unmistakable stamp of Stalinist methods.

The first major politicoeconomic undertaking occurred in the closing phase of the war, and, surprisingly, domestic Communists were not its initiators. It appeared that Marshal Voroshilov, the military commander of Soviet forces in Hungary, hoped to demoralize peasant boys in Szálasi's army still fighting on the Nazi side by announcing a major land reform. It was long overdue; too much good land resided in the hands of the Catholic Church and of large landowners; but its precipitousness and its means of enforcement worried not only members of the Smallholders' Party but also Western representatives in the country, who feared that it might prove the first step in a general confiscation of private property. It was nevertheless carried out; the haste in its execution produced many problems and petty quarrels, but on the whole it proved to be a felicitous measure.

As it had been after the First World War, the position of the Social Democratic Party was ill-defined. Its long practical experience in operating within a multiparty system (its leader, Árpád Szakasits, in fact spoke condescendingly to foreign journalists about the Communists who had acquired strange and immature habits in illegality) worked in its favor, and many voters of goodwill saw in it a civilized version of the militant Communist Party. The long-standing mistrust by Communists of Social Democrats, who were viewed as compromisers who could envision a thorough social transformation without the cleansing experience of a revolution worked against it. For the time being the pretense that the two parties were ideological cousins was preserved.

The Independent Smallholders' Party was a different proposition. In the elections it had garnered over 56 percent of the vote, and many former members of less moderate parties on the right had joined its ranks. Officially, the Communists cooperated with it as one, and in fact the major, party in the coalition, but their propaganda lambasted its "reactionary" political views, emotional attachment to the Catholic clergy, and demonstrative nationalism.

The Peasant Party, in character similar to the Smallholders, was more radical, and many viewed it as the agrarian arm of the Communist Party. There was also a Citizens' Democratic Party, made up largely of middle-class intellectuals and others who wished to participate in political life but found none of the major parties closely associated with specific programs to their taste.

The Communists also benefited from the growing economic crisis (in part caused by large-scale Soviet confiscations on top of reparations demands); they successfully insisted on the formation of a Supreme Economic Council (of whose three members one was a Communist and one a Social Democrat) with power to issue decrees, which later the parliament under Communist dictation raised to the status of laws. In this manner they became the effective directors of economic life. Then, on February 1, 1947, the royal tradition in Hungary was finally laid to rest when the first article of the law code for the year declared the nation a republic. Smallholders were placed in leading positions, Tildy became president of the republic and another Smallholder, Ferenc Nagy, was named premier. The decisive political voice, however, remained that of Mátyás Rákosi, who was proud to call himself Stalin's first Hungarian pupil, and who in fact had direct access to the Soviet dictator and knew only too well that all parties other than the Communist existed by tolerance and not by right.

When early in March 1946 a Left Bloc was forged from an informal cooperation between the Communist Party, the Social Democrats, and the Peasant Party, its slogan was, "Remove the people's enemies from the coalition!" Intimidated, the Smallholders excluded some 20 parliamentary representatives from their party—the liquidation of the political center had begun. At the same time strict penal laws were enacted against anyone who conspired or propagandized against the republic. The discovery and investigation of such activities was entrusted to the Communist-controlled political police.

Meanwhile, inflation, fueled by a catastrophic shortage of goods, mainly food and ordinary necessities, assumed such proportions that it is still cited as the worst recorded devaluation of currency in human history. Banknotes with a face value of millions of pengos were printed and lost half their purchasing power before they reached consumers' hands. For the issuance of a new, sta-

legally nonparty bodies, were invariably dominated by a secretary who was a member of the Communist Party.

The outbreak of the Korean War gave further impetus to the sharpening ideological struggle. Capitalist-imperialist forces, as decreed by Soviet propaganda, were trying to scotch the self-assertion of genuine democratic forces in the former colonial world. There were exhortations for greater productivity to serve as a fitting answer to the imperialist challenge, and workers were called upon to contribute to a Korea Fund to aid their brothers-in-arms in a distant land. In the end, what it all amounted to was that the already overstressed workers had to make still greater sacrifices for still smaller compensation. Meanwhile, Rákosi insisted that leading members of the Communist Party separate themselves from the common man by moving into villas; costly construction projects were undertaken toward this end.

With the merger of the two workers' parties in 1948 the distinction between a Communist Party and a Social Democratic Party had supposedly disappeared, but many old Communists felt uncomfortable, not to say insulted, in being lumped together with weak-willed compromisers. Rákosi put the matter bluntly in a speech to the Central Leadership of the newly formed Hungarian Workers' Party (MDP): "The Communist and Social Democratic parties had not yet fully merged. . . . A substantial portion of the party [assumedly the Social Democrats] is still on a low theoretical level and therefore we too face the danger of bourgeois nationalism, . . . of distancing ourselves from the Soviet Union, . . . of the opportunistic illusion that a peaceful maturation to socialism is possible."

Anyone familiar with Communist Party rhetoric knew that this was a declaration of war on the Social Democrats. Soon a number of them were arrested on a variety of charges; the first prominent victim of the purge was the former president of the Social Democratic Party whom Rákosi had recently persuaded to assume the presidency of the republic, Árpád Szakasits. He was accused of having betrayed to the police during the regime of Admiral Horthy a planned strike of construction workers, an act of treason that had already felled several victims. He was tried and sentenced to life in prison. Other convictions followed after a series of trials in which the case against the defendants was based entirely on putative charges. The minister of justice, taken in custody but not yet tried, died during the interrogatory process; another official, a recently appointed member of the all-powerful political committee, fearing arrest after a withering denunciation of his conduct during a meeting of the cabinet, apparently lost his reason, went home, killed his family, and committed suicide.

Stalinism in its most perverted form found a home in Hungary, directed by Rákosi's docile hand. Yet by now all that had been dynamic and creative in Stalin's work had been exhausted. The successive economic plans became parodies of themselves, the collectivization of agriculture had embittered the peasantry without succeeding in its chief function of providing the nation with an ample food supply, the claim that the working class had been liberated from capitalist exploitation sounded grotesque when workers labored long hours in unsanitary conditions without adequate safety provisions and with marginal health care. The nation's youth treated the political system with derision and alcoholism among the young assumed catastrophic proportions. Stalinist initiatives in foreign policy had proved humbling failures. The Berlin blockade of 1948–49, instead of squeezing the Western powers out of the former German capital, demonstrated both their resolution and their practical means of defeating the blockade. The campaign against Tito produced a gaping breach in the socialist camp without shaking the position of the Yugoslav dictator. The Korean War served definitive notice that the Western world, led by the United States, would resist every Soviet attempt, be it direct or by proxy, to extend communist rule elsewhere in the world. Terror remained the sole functioning feature of the Stalinist system.

Even practical and necessary measures were carried out in a manner that featured coercion in every aspect. In the years following the Second World War the population of Budapest had doubled. Most industrial enterprises were located in or around the capital; its cultural opportunities also attracted many. A decree that special permission was needed to move to Budapest was not observed and could not be enforced. The political committee, at Gerő's initiative decided to ease the apartment shortage by moving those among the populace who were judged unproductive or politically reactionary to the countryside. Considering that large comfortable apartments were often occupied by stalwarts of the former social order, retired professionals, or others whom Communists branded parasites, the measure did have some justification. But it was carried out by the political police in a fashion reminiscent of the Nazi deportations, and it produced disgust and outrage at home and abroad. Altogether nearly 13,000 persons were resettled to modest and often squalid peasant homesteads without substantially solving the shortage of living space in the capital. According to official reports the action had been directed against former government officials and military officers of the prewar Horthy regime, aristocrats, industrialists, and landowners; in reality, the deportations were often indiscriminate and included distinguished intellectuals and professionals as well as the physically disabled.

Among other Stalinist features, Rákosi eagerly adopted the cult of personality. He allowed several enterprises, including the largest industrial complex on Csepel Island in the Danube, to be named after him; portraits of his less than attractive visage, defined by his bald pate and fleshy features, were ubiquitous; and every aspect of the undeniably impressive accomplishments in the industrial field was ascribed to his prudence and foresight. When in March 1952 he celebrated his 60th birthday, it was the occasion for extravagant festivities. His biography was made compulsory reading in many academic curricula, and gifts in gross quantities were donated by workshops, collectives, industrial enterprises, and even by individuals who wished to express their profound gratitude for their liberation. In reality, whatever dubious popularity Rákosi had enjoyed in the early postwar years, due not so much to his political accomplishments as to his courageous endurance of long prison terms during the Horthy era, had long been expended by his dictatorial methods, by the open secret that the hated political police were his personal instrument, and, most of all, by the nagging suspicion that he had engineered and superintended the Rajk trial and, in so doing, had sacrificed an old and trusted comrade in the hunt for Titoists. To Rákosi's mind the whispering propaganda, of which he was well aware, was the work of "the enemy." He resented that his detractors groused over his occasional miscarriages of justice and did not give him credit for turning Hungary—true, at the price of great sacrifices by the working class—into a modern industrialized state. For now, however, the criticisms were muted and never publicly voiced; Rákosi possessed a far more potent asset than popular approval—Stalin's complete trust.

Stalin himself, deified by communist media the world over, had by now acquired a reputation for granite indestructibility, a leader not subject to the frailties of ordinary humans. During the XIXth Congress of the Communist Party of the Soviet Union (CPSU) in October 1952, however, he appeared frail and spoke for only five minutes. As if to quash rumors that he was in declining health, in successive months he plunged into a heavy schedule of activities. However, his paranoia, as evidenced among his final acts by the indictment of a number of physicians on charges of conspiring against the lives of high party officials, grew to pathological proportions. On March 3, 1953, the press announced that he had suffered a massive cerebral hemorrhage; on March 5 he died.

Mátyás Rákosi at the Rákosi Children's Home, Balatonaliga, 1952 *(Hungarian Museum of Photography)*

According to some party members in close contact with Mátyás Rákosi, he judged Stalin's departure from the scene as an opportunity for him to rise in stature among the leaders of international communism. He enjoyed seniority, a reputation for holding an exceptional grasp of Marxist (and Leninist) teachings, and he wore a halo of martyrdom for his long imprisonment as well. What Rákosi did not reckon with was that Stalin's death almost instantly discredited the infamous methods he had used throughout his long reign; the new Kremlin leaders, without ever mentioning Stalin's name, with one voice denounced the cult of personality as totally alien to Marxist principles. They also denounced the almost exclusive emphasis on heavy industry at the expense of consumer goods that Stalin had singlemindedly promoted. The abrupt release of the defendants in the doctors' plot was an implied condemnation of Stalinist judicial methods.

Hungarian public opinion viewed every criticism and denunciation of Stalinism as directed almost as much against Mátyás Rákosi. At the same time, terror, which Stalin alone could make authentic, lost much of its credibility; lips that were hitherto sealed began to open. The political police were denounced on radio and in the press for the liberties they had taken and the infamous chief official, Gábor Péter, had been removed even before Stalin's death. He was now put on trial for subversion of socialist justice and sentenced to a long prison term.

Rákosi's opportunity to advance his own position was further reduced when the new masters of the Kremlin summoned him and a few of his colleagues to Moscow and subjected them to a humiliating stream of criticism. They were roundly reproved for the forced tempo of industrialization when Hungary lacked the resources to see it through; for initiating an abnormal number of criminal cases against citizens, often on the flimsiest grounds; and for allowing the glorification of the name and person of one comrade, endowing him with almost superhuman qualities. Rákosi's defense that much of what he was criticized for he had done at Stalin's direction made no impression on his Soviet comrades; they were as interested in denouncing Stalin as they were in denouncing Rákosi. They ordered the delegation to separate the offices of party secretary and premier, both of which were at present held by Rákosi. He was to remain first secretary but a far more popular comrade, Imre Nagy, was to assume the post of premier.

Rákosi had long learned not to argue with his Soviet bosses. As he put it to the political committee at home, the Soviet comrades may err in minor matters but in the great defining questions of policy and power they were always right. He exercised unsparing self-criticism. Yes, he admitted, he had allowed his name and person to be extravagantly glorified, had interfered in judicial matters, had directed the political police as to whom to place under arrest and what methods of interrogation to use, and had often decided the nature of the penalty to be imposed. This time he offered no excuses or mitigating circumstances, though he characterized his misdeeds as errors in judgment rather than deliberate violations of Marxist ethical practices.

However, it quickly became evident that his self-criticism did not mean that he intended to relax his control over national affairs. He acted as though by owning up to his mistakes he had cleared the air and was free to resume governing, even if within somewhat narrower limits. The appointment of Imre Nagy as premier was an insult to him. Nagy's maiden speech in parliament, broadcast over the radio, amounted to an open challenge to Rákosi: not only did it speak critically of the very breaches of faith and legality Rákosi had in close party circles acknowledged but also it proposed an economic course diametrically opposed to that of his predecessor. It called for a thorough revision of investments in economic plans, a slowing down of industrialization, greater emphasis on the production of consumer goods, an easing of the burden of forced deliveries by individual landowners as well as collectives, and an effective end to the war on the kulaks, a term originally used to describe a well-to-do peasant but routinely applied to any peasant who refused to enter a collective or proved difficult in complying with delivery quotas.

After years of demoralizing material shortages and unremitting pressure on workers to give more and be satisfied with less, here was a human voice that addressed itself not to some remote future when the sacrifices of the present would bear fruit but to present and pressing needs. It was popularly referred to as the New Course. To Rákosi, it meant putting the brakes on an economic plan that had already produced impressive results, the virtual canceling of the new Five-Year Plan that was in an advanced state of preparation. Thus began a three-year tug-of-war between the two men, and, although the public heard only the disagreements that centered on issues of major national importance, it was a personal power struggle in the most traditional sense. Imre Nagy enjoyed popular support, especially the close and often passionate alliance of literary men, who, after years of unquestioning subservience, experienced a crisis of conscience, remembering how they had put their pens in the service of the lies the party had uttered and with the help of which it had victimized some of its finest sons, first and foremost László Rajk. For his part, Rákosi could count on the tactical skills he had honed during his exile in Russia and during years as head of the party—and there was something else. What had been unthinkable while Stalin was alive was now occurring—strikes and demonstrations broke out in East Germany, Czechoslovakia, and parts of Hungary.

The new Soviet leadership beat a hasty retreat. It invited a Hungarian government delegation to Moscow for a second time and the tables were turned. They criticized Imre Nagy for his political experimentation, his antiparty views, his wrong notions about the worker-peasant alliance (meaning he showed partiality toward the latter, a gross violation of Marxist concepts), and his playing with fire by proposing a Patriotic Front in which the Communist Party would be but one of many.

This criticism served as the basis of Rákosi's new, and this time concentrated, attack on his rival. He had so far abstained from criticizing the New Course, in fact admonished his comrades to act in its spirit; now, with Moscow once again in his corner, he turned against it. The struggle was waged ever more openly, in the Central Leadership which directed party affairs in the name of the party congress that met only at rare intervals, in the political committee, and even in the press. Nagy requested several postponements of the Central Leadership session, knowing Rákosi had assured for himself a majority on it; in January 1955 Nagy suffered what the press reported to be a "mild heart attack." Rákosi scoffed at the report, noted that Nagy's condition did not prevent him from maintaining lively contacts with literary figures, demanded that Nagy acknowledge, as he himself had two years earlier, his mistakes. When Nagy refused to submit a letter in this sense, Rákosi moved to deprive him of his party positions. The Kremlin sent a mediator to patch up the quarrel, but Rákosi had dug in his heels. Predictably, he prevailed. The Central Leadership, at his behest, condemned the rightist tendencies of Imre Nagy and by implication endorsed the policies Rákosi had pursued over the years. This session of the Central Leadership refrained from taking action against Imre Nagy, but a second one, in April, excluded Nagy from the Central Leadership and from the political committee, and appointed in his place a new premier, András Hegedűs. To all who cared to listen, Rákosi had won the battle in April 1955.

But his own days were numbered. He had always had a sovereign contempt for public opinion, yet public opinion had found a voice and would not be silenced. Several times when he spoke at public gatherings hostile questions were put to him and the demands for him to give a candid account of the Rajk affair became ever more insistent. A number of judicial cases based on obviously false or fabricated evidence were reviewed, and many convicted men, including Szakasits, were freed and rehabilitated. Rákosi would have made his peace with all that if only the Rajk case had been allowed to rest. However, it was not and, knowing he had to offer some explanation, he finally brought himself to admit that the case "had been based on provocation." He accused the political police of pulling the wool over his eyes, and such manifest mendacity enraged public opinion. Demands multiplied that Rajk's body be exhumed and reburied with honors. At a public meeting at which Rákosi was the main speaker the unthinkable happened: one listener, a respected historian, inquired why Rákosi did not draw the obvious conclusion and resign. All the first secretary could do was to charge that this was the voice of the enemy.

Moscow at last realized that in Hungary it had a satrap who had lost not only the trust of the people but also any substantial contact with them. It dispatched a Politburo member in July 1956 to prevail on the first secretary to resign, giving his failing health as the reason. Rákosi put up no resistance and agreed to move to the Soviet Union for medical treatment (in his farewell speech to the Central Leadership he could cite no graver condition to justify his resignation than hypertension).

Imre Nagy would have been the logical choice to step into Rákosi's place, but in the eyes of the Kremlin he was, despite his popularity at home, a played-out political figure. The choice fell on the party's gray eminence, Ernő Gerő, though his standing in public esteem was nearly as low as that of Rákosi.

The 11th hour was striking. No leading figure enjoyed public confidence any longer. Writers, even staff members of the party's daily organ, *Szabad Nép,* were in open revolt. The news of the successful resistance to the Kremlin by leaders of the Polish party electrified the public. The contents of the "secret" speech by the new general secretary of the CPSU, Nikita Khrushchev, at the XXth Party Congress in February, in which he had demolished the Stalin myth, were being bandied about. University students, gathering for the start of the new academic year, were in ferment. All the while Gerő complacently drew up plans for a new party congress and new elections.

On October 6 the remains of the martyr László Rajk were reburied amid general public mourning. Later that month Gerő, with a government delegation, traveled to Belgrade to clarify certain issues still unsettled after Tito and his party had been readmitted to the good graces of the Soviet and satellite parties. When the delegation returned to Budapest on the morning of October 23, revolutionary excitement was brewing. Students had framed a resolution stipulating a number of demands, the principal one being that Soviet troops leave Hungary and the nation be allowed to govern itself. The political committee immediately went into special session, but no resolution it could possibly make would stem the tide. In a very real sense, Hungary had become a revolution about to happen.

CHAPTER SEVENTEEN

In the orthodox Marxist view only one kind of spontaneous uprising deserves the designation of Revolution, namely, when the working class, conscious of its economic and consequently political strength and driven by a common will, takes possession of the means of production and replaces the existing governmental system that rules in the interest of a narrow propertied class with the dictatorship of the proletariat. Any other uprising, especially one that seeks to overthrow proletarian rule, is a counterrevolution, a political crime of the first magnitude, an attempt to retard and reverse history's natural progress, to deprive the working class, the only legitimate social stratum, of its hard-won freedom.

In this light the period of Hungarian history between 1945 and 1956 was a Revolution, attended to be sure by errors of judgment, "dogmatic" (i.e., inflexible) interpretations of Marxist theory, overly ambitious economic plans, but one that laid the groundwork for a vigorous workers' democracy in which former ruling social strata and anachronistic institutions such as Christian churches and castes based on birth had been relegated to historical memory. Anyone who judged this system by its errors rather than by its accomplishments was likewise an enemy of progress; anyone who took up arms against it was a counterrevolutionary.

In the eyes of those, however, to whom Hungary's assertion of her independence and restoration of her national dignity were duties imposed by history, the events of the end of October and early November 1956 were a glorious revolution and the enemies were those who in pursuit of personal power and fuzzy ideals accepted continued submission to a repressive great power, the Soviet Union.

The morning of the historic day of October 23 passed unremarkably. Streetcars and buses carried workers to their places of employment, workshops were humming and in the streets the customary weekday traffic flowed. Few were aware that the day before university youths, in Budapest and at other centers of learning, after announcing their demands calling for the withdrawal of Soviet troops from the country, for multiparty elections and the elevation of Imre Nagy to the post of premier, scheduled a demonstration for the 23rd in support of these demands. That demonstration, reluctantly approved by the Ministry of the Interior, drew alarmingly large numbers of people. Meeting at the statue of the hero of the March 15, 1848, revolution, Sándor Petőfi, the crowd emotionally recited his fiery poem with the refrain, "To the God of Hungarians we

A crowd of people surround the demolished head of the statue of Joseph Stalin, including Daniel Sego, the man who cut off the head, during the Hungarian Revolt, Budapest, Hungary. Sego is spitting on the statue. *(Hulton/Archive)*

swear, we will be prisoners no longer." The crowd then moved to another statue and finally into the large square before the parliament building; here cries hostile to and expressing hatred for the Soviet occupiers and their Hungarian lackeys went up. Symbols of communism were removed, red stars were cut out of the center of the Hungarian flag, leaving gaping, ragged holes.

At this point party first secretary Ernő Gerő, distraught and hapless, made the mistake, during a radio appeal calling for calm, of referring to the demonstrators as poisoners and counterrevolutionaries. Another large crowd began to congregate before the radio building, demanding that the students' demands be broadcast on the air. The building had been occupied by detachments of the political police and shots were fired, though it was not clear which side first pulled the trigger.

It was evening by now and so far only those who could afford spending daylight hours in protest and demonstration had participated in the outbreaks. But now a group of workers from the industrial plant named for Mátyás Rákosi, equipped with blowtorches and sledgehammers, betook itself to the giant bronze statue of Stalin that overlooked the avenue along which so many marches sponsored by the Communist Party had passed and, blasting away its foundation, to the cheering of tens of thousands, toppled it.

The premier, András Hegedüs, in one of his last official acts before resigning, called upon Soviet forces to assist in putting down the "disorders." At dawn on the 24th Soviet tanks appeared in the streets of Budapest; the demonstrators, far from being intimidated, attacked them with Molotov cocktails or with whatever crude weaponry they could lay their hands on. That day Imre Nagy was appointed premier by the party's frightened inner circle. He issued as his first order of business a call for the restoration of calm and order—but passions had become too raw and the taste of victory over the hated Soviet soldiery too enticing for his plea to be heeded. The uprising had by now spread to the provinces, strikes broke out in many factories and places of business, and revolutionary councils were formed in sympathy and cooperation with the demonstrators. The Soviet forces displayed ambivalent attitudes; many soldiers had been in the country for years, had developed friendships, and were reluctant to fire on their hosts. On the 25th, when another large crowd congregated in Parliament Square, some Soviet tanks had Hungarian flags affixed to their turrets. Only the local political police now stood in opposition to the revolutionaries; they fired a hail of bullets into the crowd, killing many. From this time on, insofar as the revolutionaries were concerned, it was open season on the ÁVH, the acronym for the hated political police. In one of the westernmost towns of the country, Mosonmagyaróvár, a confrontation between the ÁVH and a crowd of students resulted in over 100 dead, most of them students in their teens.

Nothing now could quell the fury of the revolution. Everywhere the most resolute fighters were the very young, the "Budapest kids" as they affectionately came to be called, youngsters who had grown up under communism and had served as the "blank minds" Lenin had demanded for the future success of the revolution. The minds, as it turned out, had the slogans of raw hatred of foreign occupiers and their Hungarian servants written on them. Soon these lawless adolescents and young adults ruled the streets. Some exercised arbitrary police powers, some dragged political policemen out of their apartments and hanged them from lampposts. Political and common criminals by the thousands were set free from camps and prisons, among them Cardinal Mindszenty, who was serving a life sentence, now under house arrest.

On October 25, Gerő, realizing that he had no credibility and no effective authority left, resigned as the party's first secretary and was replaced by János Kádár, a former minister of the interior and one who, like Rajk, had been caught up in the Byzantine maneuverings of the power elite and imprisoned on a variety of false charges, then released, though not rehabilitated, during the amnesty period following Stalin's death. The next day Imre Nagy, as premier, characterized the struggle then being waged as one for democracy and national independence (a dangerous program, as his definition of democracy was very different from that of the Kremlin and national independence translated into ending the association with the Soviet Union). Street battles continued, and Nagy was able to secure a Soviet pledge to pull their soldiery out of the capital;

the Soviet leaders agreed to this more because they no longer trusted the loyalty of their soldiers than to placate the new government. Nagy continued to tread on perilous terrain; in a radio address on the 28th he announced the evacuation of the capital by Soviet forces and added that soon the entire country would be free of foreign occupiers. The really dangerous step he took, however, was to announce, in a speech on October 31 from a balcony of parliament, that Hungary would initiate talks about withdrawal from the military alliance that tied satellite forces to the Soviet Union, the so-called Warsaw Pact. Given the dubious allegiance of member states to these imposed alliances, one defection could spell the end of the entire compact.

Already former political parties hitherto immobilized by the domination of the Communists were beginning to reorganize in preparation for renewed political life. On November 1 the leadership of the Communist Party (MDP) announced the liquidation of that party and the merging of socialist forces into a new party, the Hungarian Socialist Workers' Party (MSzMP). The same day Nagy made Hungary's withdrawal from the Warsaw Pact official and addressed an appeal to the UN secretary-general to place the "Hungarian Question" upon the agenda of the organization. On November 2 a coalition government was sworn in, including the parties that had formed such a coalition back in 1947.

Khrushchev's position as the Soviet leader, and his entire political future, were in jeopardy. He had none of the authority Stalin had wielded, was unable to make himself the sole political will in the Soviet Union, and the Stalinist faction in the Politburo blamed him for all the upheavals in the satellite realm, which, as they saw it, had been occasioned by his attack on the dead dictator at the XXth Party Congress. Even if Khrushchev had been inclined to let Hungary go her own way, the hard-line opposition in the Politburo would have removed him rather than let him have his way. Military leaders, too, embarrassed by what they viewed as a defeat of Soviet forces in Hungary, urged intervention. Surely a satellite could not be allowed to break loose from the Soviet bloc simply because its unruly youth took to the streets and denounced Soviet domination.

The Kremlin leadership, unable to control the situation by conventional means, all the while combined deception with rapid preparations for military intervention. Even as the Soviet ambassador, Yuri Andropov, assured Imre Nagy that all Soviet troops would be withdrawn and requested the appointment of a joint commission to discuss the details, Nagy had reports that fresh Soviet troops were pouring into the country. Khrushchev was feverishly lining up the support of sister parties for a military strike against the revolution, arguing that the defeat of socialism in Hungary would give heart to the darkest reactionary forces in socialist countries. The Chinese, now at odds with the Soviet party, whose liberalizing post-Stalin policies they distrusted, did not favor the intervention and Khrushchev reluctantly agreed to seek a peaceful solution. But after consulting hard-line comrades in Poland, Romania, Czechoslovakia, and Bulgaria, he found understanding for his plan to crush the Hungarian insurrection. The ultimate decision came from Marshal Tito. He had been, since Stalin's death, actively courted by the new Soviet leadership; Khrushchev had confided to a foreign communist that Stalin had not been in his right mind when he began his futile campaign against Tito, and that the damaged fences to the Yugoslav party had to be mended. A truce of sorts had been worked out, though relations between the two parties remained tense. Now Khrushchev had reason to fear that Tito would have nothing good to say about what amounted to a new military conquest of Hungary. To his surprise, the Yugoslav dictator, when he met with Khrushchev on the island of Brioni, was agreeable. The only sticking point was the choice of the comrade to head the new government of Hungary. Khrushchev favored Ferenc Münnich, a resolute hardliner who was reported (probably untruthfully) to have offered the lives of 50,000 captured revolutionaries as atonement for the upheaval; Tito argued for János Kádár, who would have a far better chance of gaining the confidence of the nation. Kádár, after October 23, had been a member of Nagy's cabinet, and on November 1 he in fact gave a radio speech praising the victorious revolution and announcing the rebuilding of the party in terms that suggested a more malleable organization. That day he disappeared; only much later was it disclosed that he had been taken to the Soviet embassy and from there to a town on the Soviet-Hungarian border, where he was given to understand that by heading a new government, grandiosely called the Revolutionary Workers' and Peasants' Government, he could ensure a peaceful and relatively friction-free return to the socialist system.

The decision to intervene having been taken, the Soviets gained time by continuing their entirely fraudulent negotiations with Hungarian political and military appointees over the specifics of a troop withdrawal that the Soviets had no intention of carrying out. On the afternoon of November 3, at Soviet initiative, the talks were transferred to the headquarters of their forces in the town of Tököl. This was an ominous move. The Hungarians had no protection against physical threats, but they accepted the change of venue in good faith. It was a mistake. Before the day was out the Hungarian delegation was placed under arrest in the first open breach of faith in what so far had been presented as friendly and constructive negotiations for an orderly transfer of power.

That evening, on November 3, the radio carried speeches from high religious personages, including Cardinal Mindszenty. While two other clergymen offered spiritual exhortations, Mindszenty's speech was blatantly political. The revolution in his words was the nation's fight for freedom. "The participants and inheritors of the failed system," he said, "will have to answer for their activities, their omissions, their procrastinations, their deplorable conduct." He demanded the immediate restoration of Christian institutions, free exercise of religion, and a free press. Perhaps he forgot that Imre Nagy, whom the great majority of the nation supported in his effort to break loose from Soviet domination, was himself an inheritor of the old system.

The few precious days of freedom were coming to an end. At dawn on November 4, as the capital lay in an exhausted sleep after 12 days of high excitement and street fighting, the iron ring of Soviet armor burst into the city and within hours took possession of it. Only isolated pockets of revolutionaries offered resistance. Imre Nagy had just time enough as a free man to deliver a last desperate radio address. "Our troops are battling [the invader]," he said. "The government is in its place. This is what I have to report to the nation and the world's public opinion."

The government, that is, Imre Nagy, was in his place for less than an hour after the speech. Realizing that he would be held responsible for his deeds and omissions, as Mindszenty had threatened the old rulers would, Nagy sought and received asylum at the Yugoslav embassy. Mindszenty watched the Soviet attack in the open street where he was accosted by a friendly Hungarian military officer and accompanied to the American embassy. He too became a fugitive from a retooled socialist justice system.

During the revolution hundreds of expatriates from the Horthy years had come back from West Germany to fight with the insurrectionists (who incidentally received these undisguised, fascist sympathizers with distrust at best and hostility at worst); they now hurried to the western border to return to exile. For days the border stood open and crowds of refugees, some to escape prosecution for their revolutionary activities, others to seek a new life, poured across it. In the free world the Soviet action was bitterly denounced and Soviet embassies in many cities were under virtual siege by demonstrators, but no great power offered a helping hand. The postwar arrangements continued to be observed: Hungary remained in the Soviet sphere of influence.

The revolution had not had the time to reach a level of maturity where it could show to the world that Hungary was capable of organizing a political system that, while salvaging the most constructive features of socialism (for at no point and from no quarter had there been a demand for the liquidation of socialism and a return to a system closer to Hungarian traditions), was nevertheless open to the free play of political forces and could serve as an example to follow for other satellite states. One reason why Khrushchev was in such a hurry to have done with the upheaval was precisely to prevent such a maturation. The revolution had produced instances of irresponsible, even criminal, behavior by its fighters, but far more blatantly it had produced acts of brutality by the political police and cowardice in crisis situations by much of the leadership. No leading Communist had bravely stood up and defended the party. Rákosi was in exile; Gerő and a few others soon followed him. Kádár was brought to the capital in an armored car two days after the Soviet invasion and ensconced himself in the parliament building under heavy guard. He had to tow a very narrow line: for him to defend Communist rule, of which he himself had been a stalwart, would have been suicidal because if one conviction united party members it was that Rákosi's system, a blind application of Stalinism to Hungarian conditions, was discredited, and that neither Rákosi nor any of his men could possibly be allowed ever to play a part in Hungarian government. On the other hand, discrediting the party in whatever version it assumed could not go so far as to implant the notion in people's minds that the fault for the country's sorry state lay with the failure of socialism. Socialism must continue to be the correct course; it had reached a crisis because many of its adherents had distorted Marxist principles and confused their own ascendancy with the victory of socialism.

As in 1944, when they first stepped on Hungarian soil, Soviet armed forces, or rather their political agents, now did all they could amid the violence that they brought to the land to pose as friends of "the working people," and convince Hungarians that their purpose was to preserve the gains and blessings of socialism. Huge shipments of food and clothing arrived from the Soviet Union as proof of this claim. Yet widespread strikes, some in the most vital branches of production, continued, and staple items were in dangerously low supply. Some 160,000 people had gone abroad, among them many professionals and highly skilled workers. The world outside condemned with almost a single voice the repression of the revolution. The Soviets on their part demanded that those Hungarians who had committed crimes, especially against the political police and Soviet soldiery, be found, arrested, brought to trial, and severely punished.

Again, as so often in the nation's history, the future looked dismal and national independence an unattainable goal.

CHAPTER EIGHTEEN

János Kádár, whose political activities had thus far been generally free of the deviousness so common in high party circles, found himself saddled with the almost impossible task of proving to his own people and to the outside world that the defeated uprising to which in its earlier phases he himself had subscribed and which had roused Hungarians to a passionate fight for freedom had been a betrayal of the best interests of the nation and a blatant attempt to divert Hungarians from the socialist path. The result of the betrayal, as the reactivated Communist propaganda had it, would have been a return to the rule of agrarian magnates, major capitalists, and the Roman Catholic Church bloated with wealth and insensitive to the needs of the working people.

When we say that Kádár addressed himself to the task with courage, we must add that it was courage born out of a lack of alternatives. If he had refused leadership, the original Soviet choice, Ferenc Münnich, would have taken his place and Münnich was an undeviating Stalinist at a time when Stalinism was bankrupt everywhere except perhaps in China, and he planned to punish the entire nation for its revolution. Kádár had a soft side, he had languished in Rákosi's prison, and he was probably the only Communist (other than Imre Nagy, a persona non grata in Soviet eyes) who could make credible a distancing from the Rákosi system, so essential for the restoration of trust. What he could not avoid, as Rákosi in his own time could not, was the public's perception of him as Moscow's docile puppet. And that was a distasteful feature even to many party men with deep socialist convictions. During the revolution in October 1956 workers' councils had been organized in many plants and factories, and, whereas this in itself was in line with Communist tradition, in the present situation it reflected a deep disillusionment with it. The councils were organized to defend workers' interests not against exploitative capitalists but against the very party that ruled in their name. Not only did the councils remain in place after the Soviet intervention, but on November 14 a Central Workers' Council of Greater Budapest was set up; in its first act it called for a general strike. When the call was heeded by many workshops and factories, the council extended its authority over the entire workforce of the nation. As a result, at a time when widespread damage and dislocations had already created critical scarcities, production almost completely stopped. Kádár had no option but to use force: by a decree of December 5 he ordered the workers' councils to disband. When response was spotty, on December 9 he proclaimed the civil equivalent of martial law. Enforcement of this drastic measure might have posed a problem, but the party still disposed of a cadre of loyalists to whom the counterrevolution posed a mortal threat. The old political police, the ÁVH, had officially been terminated at the height of the revolution, but its personnel still operated in the service of the state by a different name, and now, under close Soviet supervision, it began the prosecution of those defying the ban on strikes as well as of those who had actively, with arms, participated in the uprising.

Turning in such a wholesale fashion against the very workers who provided the Communist regime with legitimacy posed a serious ideological challenge and had to be explained in dogmatic Marxist terms. When the Provisional Central Committee of the reorganized Socialist Workers' Party met on December 3 to assess "the regrettable October events," it decided that those events bore all the criteria of a counterrevolution and were therefore criminal. A blanket denunciation of the uprising was nevertheless deemed to be unwise, and the Central Committee was moved to admit that there had been valid reasons for it: the Rákosi-Gerő clique had committed unpardonable errors in applying the Marxist system to Hungary. Imre Nagy, on his part, although he had been led by good intentions in opposing that clique, had in the process strayed onto counterrevolutionary ground and caused the nation to reject its Soviet connections. By doing this he enabled adherents of the old fascist system to use the upheavals for their own purposes and revive counterrevolutionary organizations. From abroad had come the voice and the agents of imperialist powers, abetting the uprising and making false promises. Gullible, misguided elements then plunged the nation into disaster.

Having explained the "regrettable events" in politically correct terms, the party was at pains to show that, despite the impression of a general uprising, in reality only a small portion of the nation had shown any interest in it and the great bulk of the working class had rejected it.

With the political side of the revolution thus receiving correct Marxist interpretation, the Central Committee turned its attention to economic questions. In this field it subscribed to the post-Stalin program of shifting emphasis from heavy industry to consumer-oriented products. The conferees decided to reinvigorate agriculture and deemphasize machine industry. They recognized that the attempt at economic autarky had failed. Hungary did not possess the raw materials or the infrastructure to pursue successive ambitious economic plans without outside help; she thus had to develop export items produced by light industry to pay for imports of goods she could not produce herself. Energy-intensive industries were to be downgraded, with the exception of electric railroad engines, and even the latter were to be complemented with diesel fuel engines. All this further necessitated the abandonment of economic planning on the old pattern, which had stultified initiative and was easily upset by any untoward development.

By now, however, economic planning had become second nature to orthodox communists. Although Kádár would have rejected any suggestion of orthodoxy, he agreed to the reintroduction of the multiyear plans after political tempers had cooled and public resistance became less likely.

That tempers did cool was in good measure due to the strenuous efforts of the new government to avoid the mistake of isolating itself from the people as the old regime had done; agents, trustworthy party officials, left their comfortable offices at party headquarters and literally went to the people, organizing party days, mass meetings, contacts with groups of shared interests, to explain as best they could that the October events, when observed from a sobering distance, were the work of immature or criminal elements lacking political purpose and interested only in tearing down all the secure pillars of the social order.

To provide concrete proof of this interpretation, the prosecution of law-breakers began in earnest. Estimates vary as to the number of people, most of them young and some very young, who paid with their lives in the aftermath of the revolution, but they ran into the hundreds. The majority of them, according to extant criminal law, were hanged; others, convicted mainly of concealment of arms, were shot. Some commentators later claimed that *all* the accused were innocent, at any rate of ordinary crimes; this is doubtful, and much depends on what in the extraordinary conditions qualify for ordinary crimes. When for instance at the height of the revolution it was announced that Soviet troops had left the capital, a crowd converged on the headquarters of the political police to settle accounts with those hated guardians of Communist rule. The terrified policemen in the building shot at the demonstrators. The crowd surged forward and broke down the gate. Most of the officers, ordering their men to keep firing, themselves fled. Demonstrators rushed up the stairs and threw several policemen out of the windows, led others into the square, where the captives pleaded that they had been recruited into the ÁVH and had not volunteered to serve in it; they were nevertheless shot. (Two survived severely incapacitated.) A number of the participants were subsequently put on trial for murder. What court without political prejudice could make a fair-minded decision as to the guilt or innocence of the accused? There were dozens of similar cases like this.

Most of the criminal investigations were conducted by officers of the Soviet political police, "assisting" their Hungarian colleagues. Beatings were commonplace; one of the accused, a young female graduate of a medical school, whose case to this day is wrapped in mystery, but who has been dubbed the Hungarian Joan of Arc, lost all feeling in the soles of her feet, assumedly from severe beatings. The purpose of the often lengthy and agonizing interrogations was to wangle confessions of guilt from the accused, which could then be paraded at public trials as proof that the revolution had been in the hands of depraved sociopaths who, far from fighting for national independence, indulged their basest instincts in the garb of high-minded patriotism.

The most celebrated case in the end was that of Imre Nagy, premier for just over a week during the revolution. It will be remembered that he had taken refuge in the Yugoslav embassy after the Soviet invasion. However, he left the embassy after being promised that he would be allowed to go home unmolested. The bus that carried him and several of his associates was held up by Soviet military police and its occupants were taken prisoner and subsequently deported to Romania, where they remained in Soviet captivity. Imre Nagy was a sore embarrassment to Kádár and his government. He was the legitimate premier of Hungary at the time Kádár returned under Soviet protection and assumed the leadership of the Revolutionary Workers' and Peasants' Government. The legitimacy of the new government could not be established until Nagy had resigned, recognized Kádár as his successor, and then retired from the political scene. Nagy, in a display of what he regarded as his moral duty (while others saw it as an exercise in futility), refused to do this. In practical terms his refusal failed to impede in the slightest Kádár's ability to govern; in fact, in time most foreign powers recognized his government. But this was a violent and unforgiving age and Nagy had become the ideological icon of the October events. Only by recognizing Kádár's government could he redeem himself in Soviet eyes. There was of course no assurance that even if he did he would be exonerated because by now he was a pawn in East-West relations, but it would at the least have saved his life.

More pressing problems had to be attended to, however, before judicial considerations took center stage. The neglect of agriculture had been the most sensitive shortcoming of the previous economic system. Kádár now pragmatically devoted himself to overcoming that problem. In the course of 1957 the obligatory delivery of agrarian products was ended. The pressure on individual peasants to join cooperative farms was eased. In this respect also, a total abandonment of Marxist practices would have been too bold a step for the government to take. By the end of 1958 it was obvious that collectives did not offer the advantages necessary for individually farming peasants to join them, as the government claimed they would, and the process of collectivization in effect came to a halt. Hard-liners perceived this to be an abandonment of socialist principles and advocated return to the system of coercion—but hard-liners no longer had support from any quarter. Although in those parts of the country suitable for agrarian pursuits, mainly the Great Plains, pressure on individual farmers continued, in other regions it almost completely stopped. Only indirect persuasion prevailed, not so much by plan as by the dynamics of the system; the peasant's passion for owning his own land was lessened by his desire to escape the burdens of ownership, the effects of bad weather, the fluctuations in the price of his produce. By 1961 three-fourths of agrarian land belonged to some form of collective; in addition, there were farms directly owned by the state. Individual farming had practically disappeared.

In industry the healthy practice of investing in productive branches at the expense of unproductive ones, continued and, while logic favored it, the public seemed to have its own view in the matter. For all too long people had been watching the output of capital machinery and military hardware and been asked to cheer on an empty stomach. This was, for good reason, the most often deplored feature of the Stalinist past, yet some investments in heavy industry proved beneficial to the nation's economic future. In the wake of the revolution the government continued to support mining, electric energy, and smelting, which would all have been for the best if it had not been at the expense of other investments. But in fact investment in health care, transportation, information services, and recreational opportunities received minimum attention. All the while the requirements of COMECON, the Soviet-sponsored economic union of socialist states, remained perforce a primary consideration. It provided for an interlocking system of economies in which each state produced what it was best suited to produce to avoid regional duplication; this way, at least on paper, an ideal balance was achieved. Khrushchev, fired by a determination to overtake capitalist countries in economic development, judged the chemical industry and the production of synthetic products as critical in this effort. The Hungarian chemical industry, qualitatively the most developed in Eastern Europe, had to build itself into a vast regional system, much to its disadvantage.

Internationally, except for its instant recognition by "friendly" (socialist) states, the Kádár government for a time existed in a diplomatic void. Relations with the United States were a case in point. In a strange coincidence, the resident U.S. envoy, C. N. Ravndal, had been recalled from his Budapest post days before the outbreak of the revolution, and his replacement, Edward Wailes, arrived in the midst of the political turmoil; he presented his credentials to Imre Nagy's foreign ministry practically hours before that government went out of existence. The foreign minister of the Kádár regime, Imre Horváth, made several appeals to Wailes to submit his letter of appointment. Wailes had no instructions to this effect and continued to carry out his official functions without being formally accredited. In the United Nations, at American insistence, the credentials of the Hungarian delegation were refused recognition.

It was not until April 1957 that the Kádár government presented to its people and the outside world a comprehensive case to prove that it had been established according to constitutional forms. A newspaper article accompanying the publication of this claim asserted: "The diplomatic representatives of certain western powers manifest a conspicuously impolite attitude toward the supreme state organs of the Hungarian People's Republic. . . . It is obvious that their [attitude] is designed to demonstrate that they contest the legality of the present Hungarian government." Such a position, the article contended, was unfounded. "The government was elected on November 4, 1956, by the competent state organ, the presidential council of the People's Republic. The presidential council is the organ embodying the will of the people." It went on to state: "There is no single government in the world that has a better . . . claim to validity and a constitutional legal status than the Kádár government."

Predictably, this announcement persuaded only those who did not need to be persuaded, and relations with Western governments, especially the United States, remained in an uncomfortable limbo. When Wailes continued business as usual while refusing to present his credentials, Washington was asked to recall him. His successor continued the practice and in time he too was recalled.

The case of Imre Nagy, whom the United States and other Western powers had recognized, and continued to recognize, as the legitimate head of the Hungarian government, became an appendage to the diplomatic imbroglio in several directions. Nagy's illegal arrest had already thrown Yugoslav-Soviet, and consequently Yugoslav-Hungarian, relations back to a frosty status quo ante. When Khrushchev arrived in Hungary on April 2, 1958, for an eight-day visit, he delivered a speech that contained a blistering indictment of Yugoslavia as a state that was trying to follow an independent line from that of other socialist states.

That the Western powers joined in condemning the treatment accorded to Imre Nagy was, however, a much more serious matter. Khrushchev, on the transparent pretext that the Hungarian events were a domestic matter that did not have to affect relations among other states, was pressing for a summit meeting with Western leaders. As he judged matters, he was leading from strength: the Soviet Union had just launched a spacecraft into outer space, an achievement that placed western space technology at an apparent disadvantage. A summit attended by all major powers would restore the image of the Soviet Union as a peace-loving nation. Khrushchev realized that in the tense postrevolutionary days the fate of Imre Nagy, more than anything else, would indicate whether the new Hungarian government, under Soviet guidance, intended to follow a hard Stalinist line or whether it would act in a reformist spirit to appease the West. In this matter, however, the Kádár government had gone too far to retrace its steps. Validating Nagy's views, in whatever modest fashion, would also validate his government, and invalidate Kádár's. The propagandistic version that emerged was that Nagy, a counterfeit Marxist, had capitalized on the mistakes of the Rákosi regime and sought to carry reform so far that it was stripped of all genuine and necessary Marxist features.

When Imre Nagy, who had been returned to Hungary from Romanian captivity, persisted in his claim that he was the country's legitimate premier, there was no alternative to putting him on trial for assorted political misdeeds. The trial, and that of his associates, opened on February 5, 1958; it was almost immediately halted. The media reported that its suspension was in deference to the "comradely opinion" of the Soviet party, as "the sentencing of the chief perpetrators of the counterrevolution must be subordinated to the cause of peace." The Soviet comrades feared, so this version had it, that Nagy's trial "would serve as a pretext for 'leading imperialist circles' to squirm out of Soviet-sponsored peace talks."

However, nothing came of the peace talks (the Geneva summit meeting of 1955 had shown that there was no basis for agreement on substantial issues), and Imre Nagy's fate was sealed. The trial was resumed in a hurry and on June 15 three of the defendants, including Imre Nagy, were sentenced to death. The sentences were carried out the next day. Western governments expressed their shock, but the Hungarian public, still numb after the tragic "October events," manifested no emotion.

CHAPTER NINETEEN

It was a measure of János Kádár's political moderation and strength of purpose that, although since 1958 he shared power with hard-liner Ferenc Münnich, who served as premier, he never allowed the latter to wield any major influence. Once his own position was solidified and he earned the respect of the Soviet leaders, in November 1961 he summarily dismissed Münnich and assumed the top government position himself. He subsequently purged high party and government positions of other hard-liners, mainly of those who refused to learn the bitter lessons offered by the October events and stubbornly sought to return to prerevolutionary days. Khrushchev and his colleagues, far from showing displeasure with Kádár's high-handed actions, demonstrated their confidence in him by withdrawing Soviet advisers attached to key ministries, allowing Hungarians greater control over their own affairs.

Achieving public trust was a different and more sensitive matter. For years after the revolution the majority of Hungarians looked on Kádár as a traitor who had placed himself at the disposal of a foreign power against his own people. Gradually, however, they began to realize his finer qualities, his sober realism, and few could mistake his pronouncement that "he who is not against us is with us" as a deliberate challenge to the Communist position that one had to be an active Marxist to escape the charge of being an enemy of historic progress. In 1961 Kádár ended the practice of demanding party membership of anyone aspiring to a position that required specialization. In general his every act gave evidence of a highly pragmatic party man who was ready to sacrifice orthodoxy if it was necessary to achieve useful and tangible results.

The Eighth Congress of the Socialist Workers' Party in November 1962 was probably the high point of Kádár's long and checkered career. By now he had achieved mastery over his political opponents and he used the congress for a wholesale removal of hard-liners, whom he then replaced with his own candidates and supporters. Resolutions of the congress also reflected his desiderata: they set high standards for party membership, they called for an end of what in present-day America we would call "affirmative action," whereby young people from worker and peasant backgrounds were granted marked preference in admission to institutions of higher learning, and while they did not negate the importance of party membership as a criterion for obtaining a leading position, they did not make that a sine qua non.

However, the state of the economy was again a cause for concern. As we have noted, the liberalization inspired by the revolution had produced good initial results. As pressure on independent farmers eased, food became more plentiful and the productivity of industrial workers increased. In the eyes of many Marxist purists, however, these results were achieved at the cost of sacrificing socialist principles. Conceivably these critics could have been silenced had supply continued to meet and at times even outstrip demand—but that was not the case. The nation's natural resources and technical know-how were simply not equal to the demands of multilayered and sophisticated production, in industry or in agriculture. Enlightened economic experts, Marxist by conviction but realistic in practical application, were brought to the realization that "market forces and the law of value exist in a socialist economy too, and if we want to develop, we will have to put them to use." The most outspoken advocate of this view was a secretary of the party's' Central Committee, Rezsö Nyers, and he proposed to go beyond piecemeal adjustments aimed at meeting immediate needs and wanted to reform the entire socialist economic system. This raised the most sensitive question of all and one that would confound the political leadership for the remainder of Communist rule in Hungary: could the economy play by its own rules while the political structure remained centrally directed and dictatorial, or was the economy doomed to stagnation unless the political structure thoroughly reformed itself? A whole generation had grown up since the Second World War that knew no other system than that of Marxism and whose indoctrination had stressed the exclusive legitimacy of that one system. No propagandistic sleight of hand, no exercise in doublethink could reverse this line of argument. Yet how was the argument to be maintained in the long run if it had no solution for the worsening economic crisis?

One fact was indisputable: Hungary depended, as it had since 1919, on foreign trade for its economic well-being. To continue to compete on the world market she had to drastically upgrade her technology and production methods, and socialist practices were not conducive to this. To preserve a modicum of prosperity, Hungary had to import consumer items she could not produce herself, and, to pay for them, she had to produce export items of at least equal value. Yet such was not the case. Capital investments had all too often been made in nonproductive enterprises for reasons that were political and had little to do with market forces. Quality had in many cases been substandard, leading to an accumulation of unsalable goods.

By 1966 these problems were obvious and cumulative enough to demand serious attention. In May of that year the Central Committee decided on a major departure from the established economic system and dubbed it the New Economic Mechanism (NEM). The very phrasing filled devoted reformists with dismay because it spoke not of a new economy but merely of a new mechanism (no doubt not to alarm the hard-liners unduly), implying that, although certain innovations in production and distribution would be introduced, the strict socialist character of the economy would remain in place. Had Khrushchev, who himself had constantly been experimenting with new formulas, still headed the Kremlin leadership, he would no doubt have given his blessing to the scheme. However, Khrushchev, whose often scandalous behavior (not to mention his political miscalculations) had brought disgrace on Soviet leadership, had been removed in October 1964, and the new leadership under Leonid Brezhnev was far less enthusiastic about departures from the Marxist model. Kádár, firmly bent on reform, was not discouraged and pronounced that the "political attitude" of his government would not change "one iota." What that political attitude amounted to in practice was that if Hungary wanted to achieve a healthy trade balance, it had to develop its own production priorities, and the means of achieving them, regardless of COMECON requirements. This to be sure was hardly pleasing to the Moscow leadership; on the other hand, it was equally reluctant to allow its troublesome satellite to slip back into economic stagnation that might breed further unrest. Yet stagnation, and worse, was clearly indicated by the economic indexes: vital agricultural production had fallen 5.5 percent, industrial output was also on the decline, and the government was forced to increase production quotas and raise prices to prevent supply and demand from going out of kilter.

The two key features of the NEM were, in the first place, that the achievement of profit and not the fulfillment of planned production figures was the key criterion of the success of an enterprise, and in the other, that central planning applied only to overall figures of production. On the operational level individual firms did their own planning and set their own wages, prices, and means of marketing. Although these changes were decided on in May 1966, it was only on January 1, 1968, when the new, free, price system went into effect, that it was formally inaugurated. On paper the plan contained many welcome innovations in addition to its broad scheme of decentralization. Once again emphasis was placed on light instead of heavy industry, a recurring shift that, however, seemed to lack staying power. In foreign trade, decisions over capital investment and allocation of resources were left largely to individual enterprises; these, however, were expected to make a profit and pay a tax on it. In the spirit of a freer economy, state subsidies to firms were eliminated, except where the acquisition of basic raw materials was concerned.

One may say with fair confidence that had the new economic mechanism been carried out in a constructive spirit and without political second-guessing, it would have been at least a limited success. But the time had not yet come when a system embracing the essentials of free enterprise could find a home in Hungary. Even the most devoted advocates of the new mechanism had to consider socialist strictures and build brakes into the system. This was the chief weakness of the NEM, namely, that every economic decisionmaker had to look over his shoulder to ascertain a measure of political correctness.

The most pressing problem was "concealed unemployment." It was the proudest claim of orthodox Marxists that in a true socialist economy there could be no unemployment, and the state was able to guarantee everybody able to work a useful job. That in practice this was not the case was a sad truth that had to be concealed at any price. Full employment was a myth; it merely meant that the person was assigned a place of work where he was expected to report and was given a, usually minimal, salary. If the NEM was carried to its logical conclusion and each firm, bent on making a profit, decided on its own employment practices and wage scales, obviously some superfluous employees would have to be dismissed. While this was sound economics, politically it was unacceptable. Here then was one of the brakes inserted into the cumbersome system of the new mechanism: make your own employment policies but do not feel free to remove employees who cannot be usefully employed.

The most significant achievement of the NEM was one the planners had not bargained for: the emergence of a "second economy." However comprehensive the state-directed economy strove to be, it could not satisfy the myriad individual demands for goods and services unavailable in state-owned enterprises. The birth place of the second economy were the private plots that members of collective farms were allowed to keep while the bulk of their holdings had been absorbed by the collectives. It was on these holdings that the spirit of enterprise was most alive and most innovative. Not only did the owners grow readily marketable farm products on their plots but a whole cottage industry sprang into being. Soon the principle became common in the industrial field. The state found itself impelled to license small enterprises; these were often run by workers whose main job was in a state-owned enterprise but who, after their regular hours, worked several more hours in a second job, thus substantially increasing their income.

The New Economic Mechanism as a whole did not live up to expectations. It amounted to a mixed economy for which there was no instructive precedent and no guiding principles. After their experience with the Czechoslovak reform movement in 1968, the Soviet leaders soured to economic experimentation, which always seemed to bring in its wake undesirable political consequences; and the "leftists" within Hungary, supported by some large enterprises that suffered from competition with newer and more freely managed companies, and even some workers who feared for their jobs, turned hostile to the NEM. At the same time Moscow tightened the rules of COMECON, proclaiming that there were no "independent roads"; every socialist country had to follow the Soviet example. Kádár, aware that he by now enjoyed the trust of the general population, offered to resign rather than see his program emasculated; in the early part of 1972 the hard-liners were not yet confident enough to take him up on his word. By the end of the year, however, they gathered enough strength to rein in the program. The signal was given by the Communist Party organ *Népszabadsàg,* which in October branded as anticommunist all those who, by propagating different economic models for different parties, fostered nationalism and created dissension among Communist Parties. In November 50 large enterprises, which produced one-half of the country's industrial output, were deprived of their autonomy and placed under ministerial supervision. A number of small firms that had competed with the behemoths were restricted in their activities. Anticipating workers' protests, wages were increased. However, prices were not allowed to find their own levels but were centrally controlled and some were subsidized by the government. Several party leaders, among them the premier, Jenö Fock, who had been partisans of reform, were forced to resign. The "strong man" of the new system was Béla Biszku, an old Stalinist and former interior minister who in face of every evidence that controlled economy was a prescription for weakness, placed political imperatives before pragmatic economic considerations.

János Kádár
*(Hungarian Museum
of Photography)*

Further deterioration caused by the oil crisis of 1973 and later years para-doxically strengthened the hand of the hard-liners because they were able to argue that the crisis was caused by capitalistic manipulation and that the Hungarian working class had to be protected from such practices. But protection proved possible only by keeping consumer prices artificially low while production costs, due mainly to higher energy prices, increased, causing an ever growing deficit. The government chose to cover it by accepting loans from foreign,

almost exclusively Western, banks; the practice that soon grew to critical proportions, of ensuring a measure of prosperity at the cost of progressive indebt-
edness ominously began.

Meanwhile the return to a centrally controlled economy brought with it a
restriction of the private sector, a move that could be taken only at considerable risk. To support it, Communist propaganda began a hysterical campaign
against those who made their living not from labor but from enterprise. When
the 1975 congress of the Socialist Worker's Party solemnly proclaimed that "the
state is the chief instrument of socialist reconstruction," a return to the old
Marxist economic system became the order of the day.

The leadership, of which Kádár was a progressively less influential member,
did not find the means though to remain faithful to its political convictions and
still provide the material means to keep the great consuming public content.
How long, after all, can any government claim that its political line is unfailingly
correct while unable to feed and clothe the people and provide even the essentials of health care? What rescued the regime, if only temporarily, was an accumulation of surplus capital in the West somewhat frantically searching for
investment. When the choice came between loaning to private enterprises with
questionable collaterals and governments, the decision usually went in favor of
the latter. In the next five years, between 1975 and 1980, the Hungarian government took loans to the tune of $8 billion, and, although the domestic econ-
omy was in the doldrums, the standard of living modestly improved.

Another consequence of such unbalanced economy was that consumer
prices in Hungary were substantially lower than on the world market, creating
an awkward situation, especially in exports. Starting in 1978 another wave of
reforms aimed at correcting these deviations was introduced; the price system
was revamped to make exports profitable. Internally, whereas only a few years
earlier large enterprises enjoyed government subsidies and protection, the new
tendency was to break them up into smaller more manageable firms. Starting
in 1982 the government legalized private enterprise on a small scale, adding a
new dimension to the second economy. Economic concessions were accompanied by modest political liberalization; parliamentary delegates who until now
had served as passive rubber stamps in voting for legislative proposals put
before them by the party were encouraged to take a long critical look at these
bills and vote on them as their conscience dictated. In 1983 the practice of a
parliamentary seat being contested by a single party nominee was ended and
a minimum of two candidates were mandated for each seat, allowing the voters at least an illusion of a choice. Although these changes were symbolic, they
signified an acknowledgment, observable in the entire Soviet bloc, that a measure of political freedom was a precondition for social progress and economic
development.

However, as long as Hungary was politically restricted by and economically
dependent on the Soviet Union, genuine progress was not possible, and by the
mid-1980s all sober and practical minds realized this. Being tied to the Soviet
economy—as was the case by COMECON dispositions—was a virtual guarantee of obsolescence and technological backwardness. At the same time Hun-

gary depended on the West for the loans that enabled her to ensure at least a modicum of economic prosperity. Soon new loans had to be negotiated for the repayment of old ones, and within seven years the national debt doubled to nearly $20 billion. Inescapably, a spiral of inflation followed.

It was left to a new reformist premier, a former printer and parliamentary deputy, appointed in June 1987, Károly Grösz, to take the burgeoning economic crisis seriously. An income tax, a taboo until now (if it was a workers' state, to whom did the worker pay taxes?) was introduced to curb consumption. Another painful truth was faced when unemployment was accepted as a feature of the new economic order and the prices of many consumer items and utilities were sharply increased. Ideologically the never clearly articulated concept arose that the innovations and reforms were incompatible with Marxist philosophy and practices and that further insistence that socialism was an answer to accumulating social and economic woes had to be abandoned. Perhaps less than fairly, János Kádár was singled out as the person responsible for decades of misman agement. When a party conference met in May 1988, Grösz replaced Kádár as secretary general of the party, and reformers such as Rezsö Nyers, Imre Pozsgay, and others were appointed to the Central Committee. At a congress in October, leadership of the party, now renamed the Hungarian Socialist Party, was entrusted to a group of four men, all dedicated reformers. The disintegration of the socialist order, long in the making, entered its final phase.

There was no open talk yet about a multiparty system but the democratic impulses of politicians and ordinary people asserted themselves. In September 1987 a debating society calling itself the National Opposition convened for an open discussion. Its announced modest purpose was to wangle acknowledg ment from the government of the legitimacy of oppositionist groups and oppositionist pronouncements. The popular reformer Imre Pozsgay launched the debate by having a highly controversial pronouncement from the September debate printed in a middle-of-the-road newspaper, and in it he demanded the establishment of a Hungarian Democratic Forum to serve as "the scene for a continuous and public dialogue." Soon a number of "clubs" and associations, as yet with rudimentary agendas, sprang up while parties that had been emasculated or put out of existence by the Communists, such as the Smallholders' Party, the Union of Free Democrats, and the Social Democratic Party, emerged and gained new life. An irresistible political ferment engulfed the nation.

Just as back in 1956 the reburial of a group of victims of a gross miscarriage of justice signaled the coming of a revolution and the overthrow, if only for a short period, of communism in Hungary, in June 1989 the solemn exhumation and reinterment of the bodies of Imre Nagy and his associates marked the beginning of the final collapse of a system that, for all its extravagant claims of historical necessity, had been unable to organize a viable economy or to gain the confidence of the people, least of all perhaps of the people in whose name it ruled, the working class. It was sadly ironic that in each instance the victims were Communists, and what the assembled multitudes memorialized was not their political achievement but their martyrdom in a cause they themselves had helped to bring to the nation.

That September a seemingly minor incident opened the floodgates when the Hungarian government allowed a group of East German tourists to cross the border into free Austria, thereby violating an extant agreement among socialist states not to allow citizens of the member states to leave their territories for a nonsocialist state. There could be no further talk after that of a closed communist bloc, for the borders had opened and the Iron Curtain had ceased to be.

Between March 25 and April 8, 1990, parliamentary elections were held. Predictably, no single party obtained a majority, and so the Free Democratic Forum, the Smallholders, and the Christian Democrats combined to form a government. The Hungarian Socialist Party, an heir to the defunct Communist Party, which for the past 40 years had advertised itself as the only legitimate and historically valid political force, garnered less than 10 percent of the vote. With the introduction of multiple political parties and free elections, the government began to issue reforms, including freedom of press and assembly, as well as the right to own a private business. The newly elected premier, József Antall, pushed Hungary toward a free-market economy as the nation's enterprises became privatized.

The presence of Soviet troops on Hungarian territory could no longer be justified, and the government of Mikhail Gorbachev in Moscow was not inclined to use force to impose its rule in foreign nations. In June 1991 the withdrawal of Soviet troops from Hungary began and was completed by the end of the year, upon which the nearly half-century-long forced association with the Soviet Union ended.

Antall died in 1993 and was succeeded by Péter Boross. The Socialists reclaimed power in the 1994 elections, with Gyula Horn as prime minister, and established a coalition with the liberal Free Democrats. Despite its former ideologies, this government welcomed a free-market economy and encouraged capitalism and foreign investment.

Árpád Göncz was elected president in 1990 and reelected in 1995 while Viktor Orbán became prime minister in 1998. Hungary joined the North Atlantic Treaty Organization (NATO) in 1999 and elected Ferenc Mádl as president the following year. Péter Medgyessy was chosen prime minister in 2002. Hungary's continuing economic growth and strengthening ties to Europe make the nation a viable candidate for membership in the European Union in the near future.

CZECHOSLOVAKIA

CHAPTER ONE

Created in the closing days of World War I from provinces of the disintegrating Austro-Hungarian Dual Monarchy, Czechoslovakia proved to be, mainly because of its ethnic conflicts, one of the most troubled and impermanent political entities in 20th-century Europe. There was no historic precedence for the unity of the Czech (Bohemian-Moravian) and the Slovak and Ruthenian peoples. The former had enjoyed, until 1526, an independent existence whereas Slovakia and Ruthenia had, since the 10th century, been parts of the kingdom of Hungary. Ethnic affinity did provide a bond, but in times of stress or crisis that bond proved to be of a weak fiber.

It was due to accidents of dynastic inheritance that in 1526 both the Bohemian-Moravian and the Hungarian crowns fell to the Habsburgs of Austria; in this way a loose and arbitrary connection among Czechs, Slovaks, and Ruthenes was established but it never acquired an organic character. Three centuries later, during the revolutionary events of 1848, there was a tentative awakening of a Slavic identity in the Czech lands, but it left the Slovaks and Ruthenes largely unaffected. From that time on, and especially after the conclusion of the Great Compromise in 1867 that established the Austro-Hungarian Dual Monarchy, there was increasing agitation among the Czechs to secure, not separation from the Dual Monarchy, but equal status with the German and Hungarian nationalities. As late as the decade preceding the outbreak of the Great War, only some small and radically inclined groups, especially the so-called Young Czechs, thought in terms of a separate Czech nation. Neither of the two men who in time would be responsible for establishing a Czechoslovak state, Tomáš Masaryk and Edvard Beneš, advocated separation from Habsburg lands; the Dual Monarchy had acquired an aspect of permanence and economic coherence that few statesmen of serious mind and purpose were inclined to disturb.

The outbreak of war had an almost instant radicalizing effect on national movements in Europe. When hostilities did not end in a matter of months as optimistic forecasts had predicted, the vulnerability of the Dual Monarchy was gradually exposed. The Hungarians, or rather the extreme nationalistic elements within the nation, had for some time been clamoring for complete independence from Austria, although they themselves were unwilling to concede any measure of autonomy, let alone independence, to their own subject nationalities. The war mobilization brought many Czech and Slovak units into the joint army. At first they fought dutifully under the banner of the Habsburg monarchy on the Russian front, but by 1915 their loyalty to Austria-Hungary began to waver. Soldiers in droves left the front; many among them, and even ordinary prisoners of war, volunteered to fight on the Russian side against forces of the Dual Monarchy. Slavic political aspirations took a sharp turn toward separatism under the influence of these events.

In the early phases of the war, Czech politicians were unable to formulate a coherent plan for a unitary Slavic state. Masaryk, a member of the Austrian parliament when war broke out, saw little prospect for a consensus among the feuding factions, and in December 1914 he left the country. He went to Switzerland, where he was joined by a former student of his, Edvard Beneš, and the two men began to lay plans for a postwar Czecho-Slovak republic, to be pieced together from fragments of the Austro-Hungarian Monarchy. Masaryk was the leading spirit in these preparations but even his plans remained tentative; only gradually was he brought around to the idea of a united Czech, Slovak, and Ruthene state. On the Slovak side a young astronomer, Milan Rastislav Štefanik, offered his cooperation.

From Switzerland Masaryk moved to Britain, and he began seeking contact with influential Czechs there and abroad, with a view of gaining foreign support for his maturing plan. In the spring of 1917 he attended a Slavic congress in St. Petersburg in Russia and was instrumental in founding a Czecho-Slovak National Council; this council became the authoritative voice of Czechs and Slovaks within the monarchy as well as abroad. Another step in this direction was taken later in 1917 when Masaryk assisted in forming in Russia a separate fighting unit of Czech and Slovak deserters and prisoners of war, the so-called Czech Legion; the new state had an army before it had established borders and a government, or before it had been recognized by any of the powers.

The problem of Slovakia's proper place in the emerging state had still not been resolved. From Russia Masaryk took a long journey via the Pacific to the United States; there a Bohemian National Council had been formed and its interest in a Czecho-Slovak state was keen. President Wilson's Fourteen Points, promulgated in January 1918 and promising free opportunity for the "autonomous development" of member states in the Dual Monarchy, had brought the prospect of realization nearer. Masaryk, in a declaration at Pittsburgh, Pennsylvania, assured the Slovaks that they would have their own Diet and administration and law courts in a Czechoslovak state. By now the Czech Legion (which, by resisting attempts by communist forces in Siberia to disarm it, had precipitated the Russian Civil War) was on its way to France. The Allied powers, on June 3, 1918, recognized the Czechoslovak state that at the time was still barely more than an idea, as a member of their alliance. However, its legal existence did not begin until October 14 of that year, when the Allied powers extended formal recognition to the Czecho-Slovak National Council, then sitting in Paris, as the provisional government of the future state. Another government was already in existence in Prague, under Karel Kramař, a former leader of the Young Czechs; the two governments merged when Masaryk and Beneš arrived home. Union with the Slovaks remained in abeyance. The first proclamation of independence, in Prague, on October 28, referred only to the

"Historic Lands" of Bohemia and Moravia. The next day Slovak national leaders met in the town of Turčansky Swaty Martin and proclaimed that Slovakia
would be an integral part of the new Czechoslovak nation. On November 14,
Tomáš Masaryk was elected by a National Assembly meeting in Prague to be
first president of the First Czechoslovak Republic.

Dr. Tomáš Masaryk
with his youngest
grandson *(Hulton/
Archive)*

Members of the assembly had not been elected by popular vote but were
chosen by committees of the leading political parties. Karel Kramař was
appointed premier; he had in 1915 been under a death sentence for sedition but
later reprieved. Beneš served as foreign minister, a post he would hold until his
elevation to the presidency in 1935. The position of the government, and of
the new state itself, was somewhat shaken in the first half of 1919 when troops
of the soviet government of Hungary, responding to a hostile invasion by the
Czechs, penetrated deep into Slovakia. After those troops were ordered by the
Entente to withdraw, the independent life of Czechoslovakia began.

The peace conference, meeting in Paris early in 1919, treated the newborn
nation generously, and in the process violated Wilson's principle of national self-
determination. In order to give the republic natural defensible borders, which
in the south of Slovakia were provided by the Danube River, some 1 million

Hungarians found themselves citizens of Czechoslovakia; in the west the mountainous Sudeten regions, inhabited by nearly 3 million Germans, were included in the new state; a territorial dispute with Poland over the coal-rich province of Teschen was resolved by a partition of the region, which left both sides dissatisfied.

In February 1920 the republic adopted its first constitution. It bore some resemblance to the American constitution, except that at the executive level there were to be a president and a premier as well. The legislature consisted of a Senate and a Chamber. Guarantees of individual freedom and human rights were broad-based. The great multitude of parties vying for political prominence also marked a major difference from the American political system. In elections between 1920 and 1935 over 30 parties participated. However, leading figures in government remained the same for long periods of time, and the Bohemian civil service, trained and brought to maturity within the Dual Monarchy, proved efficient and honest. Masaryk was reelected to the presidency in 1920, 1927, and again in 1934. In that office he displayed none of the adventurousness and polemical bent that he had in his academic career; rather, he was instrumental in reconciling differences among Czechs, Slovaks, Ruthenes, Germans, and Hungarians.

For all the potential divisive forces within the republic, political stability characterized its first decade. This stability was reinforced by economic strength, at least until the coming of the Great Depression. The currency in circulation when the republic was born was the old Austrian krone, greatly depreciated; the new finance minister Alois Rašin was expeditious in introducing the Czechoslovak koruna, providing the state with a firm financial base. The economy achieved a healthy balance between the industrial strength of Bohemia and the agricultural and timber resources of Slovakia and Ruthenia. The agrarian sector remained productive and prosperous despite the Reform Law of 1919, which decreed the division and distribution of large landed estates. The reform was quite thorough on paper, but in practice it left many estates, especially in Slovakia, intact or only slightly diminished.

In the 1919 municipal elections Kramař's National Democratic Party suffered substantial losses, and the Social Democrats emerged as the winners; their leader, Vladimir Tusar, formed a new government. The political strength of the party was confirmed in parliamentary elections early in 1920. But the traditional split in workers' ranks became evident here too when, shortly after the 1920 elections, a faction seceded from the Social Democrats to form the Czechoslovak Communist Party. This was a blow to the more moderate party; its position was further shaken when it called a general strike, which ended in complete failure. The premier, Vladimir Tusar, resigned and was replaced by a nonparty government dubbed "Cabinet of Bureaucrats."

Of the many political parties populating the scene only a few were of any significance. The National Democrats, generally a party of the affluent middle class, professed strong and less than noble principles: they harbored an ill-concealed hostility to national minorities, especially Germans, as well as to socialism in its every variety. They were distrustful of the Catholic Church, which they suspected of continued loyalty to Habsburg Austria and hostility to the new state.

Another political force was the National Socialist Party, a name that in time, in a different environment, acquired a sinister reputation; the only feature Czechoslovak National Socialists shared with the German was their militant nationalism. The party had been formed in Habsburg days to occupy a middle ground between the Young Czechs, who sought social reform on a national basis, and the Social Democrats, whose professed outlook was international. It was and remained a strong advocate of the underprivileged. Its support came from a wide spectrum and counted Edvard Beneš among its members.

The strength of the Social Democrats had at first been concentrated almost exclusively in the Czech lands, among the working class, but in time it made significant inroads in Slovakia as well. Besides the Czech party there were also distinct Hungarian and German Social Democratic Parties; there was, however, scant collaboration among the three until the late 1930s, in response to the growing Nazi threat. The Czechoslovak party, as mentioned, was weakened by the desertion of its communist faction, and it never overcame the loss in membership and influence it suffered as a result. The Communists had the advantage of appealing not only to industrial workers, who provided the main strength for the Social Democrats, but also to poor peasants and other economically disadvantaged groups in Slovakia and Ruthenia. Their membership included many Germans and Hungarians.

In a number of ways the strongest party was the Agrarian. It too dated back to Habsburg times and, despite its assumed appeal to the workers of the land only, it attracted votes from many quarters. The Czech-based party merged with the Slovak Agrarians to form the Czechoslovak Republican Party, but it continued to be referred to as the Agrarian Party. It did not have the peasant character of agrarians in other states. Most of its members were well-to-do and well educated, some belonging to prosperous cooperatives practicing advanced production and marketing methods.

The most onerous task of the Prague government from the start was establishing the parity of power and influence between the Czech and the Slovak regions that the founders had envisioned and promised. The historic experience of the two nations was widely different. Slovakia had never known independence and in "historic" Hungary the great bulk of the Slovaks had been serfs; their emancipation in 1848 barely affected that status. Their educational opportunities had been almost nonexistent. In the closing decades of the Dual Monarchy many had been Magyarized, had changed their names to stress their absorption into the Hungarian stock, or, conversely, a number of Slovak names became so familiar in Hungary that their origin was ignored or forgotten. The Czechs, by contrast, looked back on periods of glorious independence; before their grievous defeat in the Battle of White Mountain in 1620, they had enjoyed equal status with the Germans of Bohemia, and even in successive centuries had many opportunities to advance themselves. By contrast, Slovak nationalism among the masses was an almost unknown phenomenon; an organic connection with the Czechs was a novelty that few Slovaks embraced with any conviction. They were glad to be free of their former Hungarian masters, but in the minds of many the Czechs took the place formerly held by Hungarians.

The republic, to run efficiently, needed a large and well-trained officialdom and the Slovaks made only a paltry contribution to that. Many administrative positions even in Slovakia were occupied by Czechs. The typical Czech civil servant was liberal in his outlook and manners, far too liberal to please the narrowly Catholic Slovaks. The virtual monopoly of Czechs on government positions was presented as a temporary state of affairs, assumedly until the Slovaks developed an educated officialdom themselves, but the government in Prague appeared in no hurry to accomplish that and kept stressing the concept of a single "Czechoslovak nation." Still, educational opportunities for Slovaks *were* steadily increasing, as did their employment in the administration, albeit only in minor positions.

Mistrust between the two nationalities was increased by the religious question. Czechs, even the many good Catholics among them, were traditionally anticlerical; in Habsburg days this sentiment had been encouraged by the disproportionately large number of German bishops in Czech lands. It was with a certain satisfaction that the Czechs applied the Land Reform Act of 1919 to church lands; a year later a "National" Czech church was founded and it seceded from the Roman Catholic Church. In one of its first acts it took steps to secularize education. An open breach with the Rome church took place in 1924 when members of the government participated in the anniversary memorial of the martyrdom of Jan Hus, the Czech Protestant reformer who had been burned at the stake for his refusal to bow to the demands of the Catholic Church. In response, the Vatican severed diplomatic relations with Czechoslovakia. Only in 1928 were relations resumed.

In that same year Czech-Slovak tension rose to a new high when a leader of the Slovak People's Party, Professor Voytech Tuka, published an article asserting that Slovak adherence to the Czech state in the proclamation of Turčansky Swaty Martin contained a secret article, according to which the union was made for only a period of 10 years, during which the conditions of Slovak autonomy would be tested. The promised autonomy, he claimed, had not been granted, giving the Slovaks legal right to secede from the republic. Tuka was put on trial, in the course of which he was found to have had treasonous negotiations with Hungarians, seeking Slovak association with that country; he was sentenced to a prison term of 14 years. Following this, the People's Party moderated its stand, but the Slovaks, or the most politically conscious among them, were never fully reconciled to the unequal union with the Czechs.

One reason for continuing tension was that the economic position of Slovakia was distinctly inferior to that of the Czech lands. As part of Hungary, the Slovaks had had a ready market for their iron and timber; also Slovak peasants in the mountain regions often found employment in the great Hungarian plains, where in seasons of plowing, planting, and harvesting labor was often in short supply. The intense economic nationalism following the peace treaties now cut off these opportunities. Slovak iron works could not compete with the far more advanced methods of Bohemian operations and the border was tightly sealed for workers seeking employment on the other side. The sale of Slovak products in Bohemia was further impeded by the long distances across which they had to travel, adding unacceptable costs of transportation to the basic price.

If muted hostility characterized Slovak adherence to a unitary Czechoslovakia, indifference marked the attitude of the Ruthenians in the eastern reaches of the republic. While in the last years of the Dual Monarchy there had been vigorous movements of self-assertion in Bohemia-Moravia, generally for trialism within the Dual Monarchy but in some instances for total separation, there had been little of that in Slovakia, and almost none in Ruthenia. A primitive mountain people, Ruthenians accepted Hungarian rule without disadvantage or protest; the small intelligent stratum consisted almost solely of Jews and Hungarians, and they had had little quarrel with the monarchy. Separatist sentiment was almost wholly confined to the Ruthenians living in the United States, and it was they who had undertaken negotiations with Masaryk in 1918 in the matter of their homeland joining a Czechoslovak state. In the so-called Philadelphia Agreement Masaryk had promised Ruthenia autonomy similar to that granted to Slovaks, and full Czechoslovak citizenship to Ruthenians; the agreement even assigned to them certain territories that belonged to Slovakia.

In this remote part of the republic too the promises were only partially kept, not because of bad faith but because there was so little potential for self-government. In 1920 an American Ruthene, Zatković, who had returned to effectuate the agreed-on union, was appointed governor of the province, but realizing the slowness of the central government in granting autonomy, he resigned in 1921. Here, as in Slovakia, the Prague government found that in the absence of a trained and educated civil service, it had to assume responsibility for governing the province. Centralization rather than autonomy became the operative system.

Economically Ruthenia's separation from Hungary created problems where there had been none before. Timber was the main product; large quantities had been floated down the Tisza River to the treeless Great Plains; this market too was now closed. The cutting of timber continued nonetheless, at times so indiscriminately that, with the tree barrier holding back the great accumulation of snow at high altitudes removed, downpourings of melted snow swelled the Tisza, often producing devastating floods downriver. In addition, although it would have made little difference to the economy, the promised Slovakian districts were never transferred.

Ruthenians suffered from a confusion of identity that in all reality could never be completely unraveled: ethnically they were closest to the Ukrainians, but they had for so long been separated from that body of Slavdom that there was no sense of commonness between the two: Those with a measure of sophistication identified with the Hungarians, who had ruled them for some thousand years without any attempt at integrating them into their nation. Nationalism of a purely Ruthenian brand was nonexistent. As educational opportunities increased in the republic, the unitary Czechoslovak trend gained force, though there probably was no great difference in the condescension of the Czech element from that of the Hungarians.

In the last reckoning it was the peculiarity, and also the great weakness, of the republic that practically everybody in it belonged to a minority. Of the 13.6 million; people, Czechs, or those who called themselves Czechs, numbered 6.6 million, Slovaks 2.2 million, Germans about 3 million, Hungarians about 900,000, Ruthenes 460,000, Jews, the majority of them Hungarian-speaking, 180,000. The ideal of the Republic of Czechoslovakia provided a feeble bond. For all that, it enjoyed relative inner peace, perhaps—though that would be hard to document—because it practiced exemplary toleration and scrupulously observed democratic principles. Its great test of strength, as would be the case in other European states, came with the Great Depression. Its economic impact was bad enough, but it also brought nationalistic tensions into sharp relief.

CHAPTER TWO

Owing in part to her multinational character, and in part to foreign minister Edvard Beneš's enterprising, and at times meddling, diplomacy, a significant portion of the history of the First Czechoslovak Republic was played out in the field of foreign affairs. One may argue that given the republic's sensitive ethnic and geographic composition, and her territorial disputes in at least two directions—toward Poland and Hungary—an astute and alert diplomacy was necessary. However, it is also true that Beneš took his position far too seriously and was inexhaustible in proposing new schemes for enhancing, by his own lights, the security of the republic. He spent altogether too much political capital on plans that either came to naught or, when realized, proved ineffectual. Two items of his diplomacy stand out: efforts to strengthen the League of Nations by affirming Czechoslovakia's devotion to its principles, and forestalling any attempt to restore even a semblance of the old Habsburg Empire.

Beneš was aware that the Trianon peace, just as the Versailles peace, was an imposed treaty and not one of reconciliation, that upholding it necessitated unwavering great power support. In the immediate aftermath of the war there were a number of influential men, in France and Britain, who felt that the breakup of the Dual Monarchy had been a veritable tragedy, economically as well as politically. They feared a Balkanization of the region and a chronic instability from which in time the flanking powers, Germany and Russia, would benefit. No one of course seriously contemplated the restoration of the Habsburg realm, but plans for a confederation of the successor states were repeatedly put forth. Of such a confederation, by virtue of her central position, Hungary would be the pivot, and her price for taking a constructive part in the scheme would no doubt be a revision of the Trianon frontiers. This was what worried Beneš on the political side; at the same time he was aware that the economy of Czechoslovakia, and of the entire region would enormously benefit from a combination of states that included Hungary. How to reconcile the two positions?

After the collapse of the Hungarian soviet republic in August 1919, and the subsequent installation of Miklós Horthy as head of state the French sought to prevail on Horthy to support Poland's war against Soviet Russia, a plea that other successor states also received and rejected. During preliminary talks with the Hungarian peace delegation in Paris there were lively contacts between members of the delegation and certain French government officials regarding Hungarian participation in an anti-Soviet war, and the Hungarian side hinted that the key condition was the restoration of parts of Slovakia to Hungary. These were very unsettling developments so far as Beneš was concerned.

To him the realization that his country, as well as other successor states, was a mere pawn in the high politics of the great powers was distasteful; Beneš strove to be a statesman of commanding influence in his own right. His importunities in Paris and London during 1920 and 1921 were numerous and often not a little annoying. At the same time he made several overtures toward Romania and Yugoslavia for a common front against any Hungarian striving for territorial revision. On February 6, 1920, at his initiative, the three states issued a joint memorandum stating their opposition to Hungary's revisionist maneuvers. A Budapest daily paper sardonically referred to this combination as the "Tiny Entente"; that supercilious sobriquet was later modified to the more polite Little Entente.

Beneš aimed at more than an ad hoc joint pronouncement. He wrote to the Romanian premier: "With a view of the situation in Hungary, and of the fact that Hungary's intentions toward Romania and Czechoslovakia are completely identical, the time has come for the two states to take common steps against the Hungarian danger." He sent a similar note to Belgrade. Of the two capitals Belgrade was the more receptive and in August 1920 Czechoslovakia and Yugoslavia signed a two-year agreement essentially obligating themselves to affirm and maintain the Trianon peace treaty. In a secret appendix the two states undertook to lend each other military aid, in case of either a defensive or an offensive war with Hungary. Toward this end military conversations were to be held.

Whatever dubious advantage accrued to Czechoslovakia from this agreement (for a war with disarmed Hungary was a totally unlikely prospect), it was counteracted by the negative reaction from Paris. The French accurately foresaw that Hungary, as well as Austria, would now seek closer ties with Germany, and possibly Italy, and those two states would be drawn into the affairs of east central Europe in which France hoped to be the only power of influence. The French foreign minister warned Beneš that he had chosen a dangerous path. French disapproval also ended whatever inclination Romania might have had to join the Czech-Yugoslav compact. An additional factor was that Romania wanted a regional agreement directed not only against Hungary but the Soviet Union as well, in order to protect her recent acquisition of Bessarabia. She also resented the joining of southern Máramaros, to which she had laid claim at the peace conference, to Czechoslovakia, as well as the division of the Bánát province between Romania and Yugoslavia; all this boded ill for Romanian adherence to the Czechoslovak-Yugoslav combination.

Italy was the first power to take advantage of the fluid conditions in the Middle Zone (the designation applied to the broad strip of land between Germany and Russia). She saw the opportunity to inject her influence into the region. In a reversal of her conflict with Yugoslavia over the possession of Dalmatia and Fiume (both of which had been promised to Italy when she entered the war in 1915, but were later, at Wilson's insistence, awarded to Yugoslavia), Italy and Yugoslavia concluded the Rapallo agreement, obligating the two powers to the maintenance of the peace treaties and to joint resistance to any attempt to restore the Habsburgs in Austria or Hungary. Two months later Beneš announced adherence of his own country to the Rapallo agreement, assuring Italy that the republic was a party to the provision rejecting a Habsburg restoration.

Italian involvement put an end to the incipient French attempts to make Hungary a center of her own aspirations in the region; after the Polish victory in the war against Russia the danger of Soviet expansion into the center of Europe abated and France had to choose her allies with a view to the new realities. The secretary general of the foreign ministry, Maurice Paléologue, who had championed the Hungarian connection, was forced to resign; he was replaced by Philippe Barthelot, committed to the maintenance of the general territorial status quo. Indirectly this meant an endorsement of an anti-Hungarian combination among successor states.

A new element was introduced into the political picture by the unexpected arrival in Hungary, on March 26, 1921, of the Habsburg pretender Charles, to occupy his throne, if not in Austria, then in Hungary. It was a foredoomed enterprise, because political developments had by now far outdistanced the possibility of a defunct and discredited monarchy reestablishing itself in the center of Europe. But Beneš regarded Charles's return with the utmost seriousness and declared it to be a casus belli. Only Yugoslavia adhered to this extreme position, but, as it turned out, protests from Britain and France more than sufficed to make Hungarian regent Horthy politely persuade the hapless monarch to leave the country.

During the affair Romania had again taken a less drastic stance than her Little Entente partners (in part because of rumors, albeit false, that it was France who had sponsored the return of the dethroned king), but in its aftermath, decided to make common cause with the Prague-Belgrade combination against future such attempts. In April 1921 she concluded a pact with Czechoslovakia, and in June with Yugoslavia; the latter instrument differed from the former only in that it applied to Bulgarian revisionist attempts as well (both Romania and Yugoslavia had gained territory from Bulgaria). With this the Little Entente was complete.

None too soon because on October 20 Charles of Habsburg made a second attempt to return to Hungary and the March scenario was, at a much higher decibel level, reenacted. The chorus of protest came from western Europe as well as from the Little Entente and at Beneš's behest the attempt was again declared a casus belli. Serious military preparations were made. Czechoslovakia mobilized an army of half a million. However, Charles was expelled by the Hungarians in very short order. In retrospect all the to-do and diplomatic posturing appeared absurd and hysterical. Czechoslovakia, however, kept the mobilized troops under arms for another two weeks, as if the Czech leadership had expected either a repetition of the affair or some bellicose move on the part of Hungary.

By now the grave economic consequences of the breakup of the Dual Monarchy were evident, not only to the successor states but also to France and

Britain. Businessmen of the latter had been accustomed to dealing with a single well-coordinated economic unit operating with a single currency under a single customs system; now they had to adjust to doing business with several individual parts, calculating prices in five different currencies and dealing with five different customs regulations. Plan after plan emerged in London and Paris for some manner of economic combination in the Danubian region, from a customs union to a federative system. Beneš made it clear early on that his government would not hear of any scheme that bore even a distant resemblance to the old monarchy. A system that included both Austria and Hungary was unacceptable to him, though he was not opposed to bilateral economic agreements with them that he could control and in which Czechoslovakia would have the upper hand.

The Little Entente was not able, however, to transfer its politico-military cooperation into the economic field. It suffered from the weakness of any alliance based on a single item of common interest. In their political philosophies the three countries were sharply divided. Czechoslovakia was a democracy with a generally enlightened and liberal outlook; Romania and Yugoslavia were monarchies governing in a dictatorial fashion. The three did have one common concern apart from resistance to Hungarian revisionism: a fear of the spread of bolshevism. Since the revolution in Russia that fear afflicted whole societies, yet there was no agreement among them as to how to deal with communist Russia: whether to employ outright ostracism or cautious accomodation. In Czechoslovakia Kramář's National Democrats favored exclusion of the Soviet Union from Europe; the Masaryk-Beneš duo would settle for an economic boycott. Both prescriptions were thwarted when, in April 1922, in the course of an international economic conference in Genoa, Italy, the two pariahs of postwar Europe, Germany and the Soviet Russia, made common cause, resumed diplomatic relations, canceled mutual financial claims, and agreed on broad commercial exchanges. Beneš saw his earlier prediction that "Russia will have to take her place in Europe" vindicated and from then on, in the officious manner that characterized much of his diplomacy, he made repeated representations in western capitals against any policy that sought to isolate the Soviet Union. In 1924 he worked out a plan for the recognition of the Moscow government and the normalization of relations with it; he met with such protests within his own country and from the other states in the Little Entente that he shelved the idea. Economic as well as political motives had influenced Beneš in promoting the plan; Czechoslovak industrial products found a ready market in the Soviet Union, whereas there was little that the agrarian economies of Romania and Yugoslavia could offer.

Another interesting, though not fully verifiable, diplomatic initiative of Beneš, dating back to pre–Little Entente days, was to offer, in properly veiled fashion, certain territorial cessions of Slovakian territory to Hungary in exchange for Hungary granting minority rights to its sizable Slovak population in the Great Plains. Assuming that the plan (which according to sources originated with Masaryk) was serious, the quid pro quo character of the offer was obviously for the sake of form, because Slovaks in Hungary suffered no discrimination or indignities. Beneš's intent might have been to stabilize the republic's contested borders in one direction, in order better to ensure its defense in another, which could only have meant, with Poland. It might also have been a first step toward a much needed economic agreement with Hungary. Czech nationalists, first and foremost Kramář, opposed the plan, and even Beneš argued for it only halfheartedly. According to his memoirs, talks toward this end, in Brno, were interrupted by Charles's first attempt to return to Hungary, and they ended altogether after his second attempt, but it is hard to believe that, if the offer was indeed seriously meant, an imbroglio lasting less than a few days on each occasion, and totally without consequences, would have put a definitive end to it. Furthermore, had there been any realistic basis for a deal with Hungary, Beneš would not have pursued the Little Entente combination with such zeal.

Nevertheless in the following years several probings of this nature reached Budapest from Prague. The government of István Bethlen treated them with disdain, judging them to be tactical attempts to realize a Hungarian-Czechoslovak economic agreement from which the latter party would reap most of the advantages. He made it known that the expectably small territorial cessions Prague had in mind would not persuade the Hungarian side to renounce its claims to other lost territories.

Beneš had a rather naive faith in the potential of the League of Nations to safeguard peace and ensure the integrity of its member states and was one of the most engaged statesmen in that organization. It did not prevent him, as we have seen, from pursuing bilateral agreements, and when France began actively to seek allies in eastern and central Europe, Beneš responded. A 1922 military defense agreement between France and Poland was supposed to form the core of a cordon sanitaire to isolate the Soviet Union from the rest of Europe, but in practical terms it was directed more against Germany. In case of a French-German war, however, Poland was a paltry prospect for a second front and the French foreign ministry undertook to support the Little Entente largely with a view of obtaining additional allies in eastern Europe. In January 1924 an alliance was signed between France and Czechoslovakia, though on somewhat less definitive terms than those contained in the Polish-French alliance; the contracting parties pledged to coordinate their foreign policies in case either found itself the object of an attack. The following year this alliance was placed within a broader framework when, largely at German initiative, the powers signed the so-called Locarno Agreements, intended to allay French fears of a resurgent Germany. Although in this connection the Franco-Czechoslovak treaty was reaffirmed, and Czechoslovakia also concluded with Germany an arbitration agreement, on balance the Locarno Agreements posed unrecognized dangers to France's eastern allies because, whereas Germany pledged to respect her western borders (with France and Belgium) and accept them in perpetuity, no such pledge was made in regard to her borders with Czechoslovakia and Poland. The claim of the German government was that it would be brought down by public outrage if it recognized the much-resented eastern frontiers, though it promised not to try to alter them by force. Thus the Locarno Agreements specified, without alluding to them, two kinds of borders, the inviolate and the problematic ones, and the border with Czechoslovakia belonged to the latter category. At the time this seemed to be of only semantic significance, but there was no telling what interpretations unscrupulous politicians might give it in the future. For now, the "Spirit of Locarno" was so brimming with optimism that this weakness of the agreements was not recognized.

Optimism was increased when, in 1928, at the initiative of French foreign minister Aristide Briand, first France and then the United States, and subsequently over 20 other states, signed an agreement—the so-called Kellogg-Briand Pact—that, although without teeth or guarantees, foreswore war as an instrument of national policy.

It would be a mistake to characterize Czechoslovak foreign policy in the 1920s as a failure, because the republic's subsequent problems and ultimate tragedy had very different roots, but it must be said that Beneš's foreign policy was overproductive. He involved his state in agreements and obligations that were oversized for its capabilities and in the process antagonized several other states. The Little Entente is probably the most typical example of this because the only bond among its members was preparation for an entirely hypothetical situation and it engendered the hostility not only of Hungary but of Austria and Germany as well. The French alliance was similarly of little value; at the time it was made Germany had no claims on Czechoslovakia but had a tense relationship with France (owing to the recent Ruhr invasion), and there was a question of whether, in case of a conflict between France and Germany, it would be in Czechoslovakia's national interest to participate. Negotiations with Hungary were based on nonexistent premises. There was no prospect of the republic, if only because of internal opposition, yielding any territory to Hungary; the Hungarians understood that better than Beneš and assumed a negative stance from the start.

Still, all these considerations are ultimately irrelevant because in the long view much of the futility of the international agreements in the 1920s sprang from the meteoric rise in Germany of Adolf Hitler, who had not the slightest respect for pacts made before his own assumption of the chancellorship and within three years tore all of them, including the Treaty of Versailles, to shreds. His rise in turn was a direct result of the Great Depression whose onset, at least in Europe, was hastened, if not caused, by the breakup of the Austro-Hungarian Monarchy. And so the chain of causation continues.

CHAPTER THREE

When President Woodrow Wilson proclaimed that the Great War was being fought "to make the world safe for democracy," he seemed to have seriously expected that the impending victory of the great democracies would serve as proof to totalitarian or semi-totalitarian regimes that only by adopting democratic standards could they avoid future devastating conflicts. In the immediate postwar period, after the collapse of four empires, there were promising signs in that direction. Germany became a republic, so did Austria, and where monarchy survived it was combined with a parliamentary system. The League of Nations itself reflected a measure of democracy and was designed to ensure the very conditions that democracies cherished.

Then something went wrong with Wilson's calculations. In countries where democracy had deep roots, it survived, albeit leadership was distressingly mediocre and the national purpose ill-defined. In Europe east of the Rhine, popular sovereignty was gradually subverted to autocratic forms. Even where it was preserved in form, the drift toward one-man rule, or the rule of a small elite, proved irresistible. To this general pattern Czechoslovakia alone was an exception. Notwithstanding her chronic inner conflicts, government proceeded in an almost flawlessly democratic fashion and even the perpetually disgruntled elements exhibited respect for it. The dominant Czech nation made sincere efforts to have other ethnic groups share in government; in 1926 the cabinet included two Germans; some time later three Slovaks, members of the Slovak People's Party, were added to it. Programs to increase the educational level of the Slovak and Ruthene population were seriously taken in hand as part of an effort to reduce and eventually eliminate cultural disparities. Had the economic situation remained stable, had unemployment, especially in industry, continued low, there was every reason to believe that democracy would be strengthened and the uneasy multinational character of the early years replaced by a fairly well integrated system.

Czechoslovakia was, however, among the states most immediately affected by the Great Depression. The health of her economy had from the very beginning depended on the export of industrial finished goods, and it was in that area that the effects of the downturn were most seriously felt. Within months of the stock market crash in New York demand for the products of Czech industry declined precipitously. In the following four years the value of its exports fell by 70 percent, and unemployment increased from 42,000 jobless in 1929 to 738,000 in 1933. Nearly one-fourth of the families in the republic had no breadwinner. The slump most noticeably affected Slovakia, where no economic mechanism had yet developed to deal with a downturn; also badly hit was the German-inhabited Sudetenland where manufacture was largely of nonessential goods. In that province resentment was increased by the fact that the great system of fortifications to protect the republic in a future war was being built in the Czech lands and Germans did not benefit from the employment opportunities it offered.

Perhaps never before in European history had economy been so politicized. Every scheme put forth to deal with the Great Depression had a political side that obscured the merits of the proposal. In May 1930 French foreign minister Aristide Briand floated his Pan-Europe plan, aiming at an economic union of European capitalist states (not unlike the present European Union), with the thinly disguised political purpose of lessening British and especially American influence on the Continent. According to the plan, within Europe, excluding the Soviet Union, tariff barriers would be phased out to make possible free trade with all its benefits to national economies. It was a bold and constructive plan, but in the end it was its political underside that doomed it. Nevertheless, Beneš perceived its possibilities and prevailed on the other two Little Entente states to approve it—another one of his spectacular but futile interventions.

Barely had the French initiative been taken off the table when the news that Germany and Austria planned to enter into a customs union to mitigate the economic crunch in their countries, a version of Briand's plan on a much smaller scale, hit Europe with unexpected impact. In purely economic terms the plan made perfect sense, not only for Germany and Austria but also for the other Danubian states, because the union would have absorbed products that individually neither Germany nor Austria could or would buy. However, the French saw in it a first step toward an *Anschluss,* a political union that they had been determined since the end of the war to prevent.

They were not alone. Beneš too saw the plan as a threat, both in the economic sense, because the union would exclude Czech exports (31 percent of which went to these two countries), and in the political sense because it would lead to a great material strengthening of Czechoslovakia's western neighbors and have an unhealthy appeal to the 3 million Germans in the republic. He saw to it that his Little Entente partners, both of whom were inclined to favor the union (a good prospective market for their agrarian exports), awaken to the dangers of it. He had his way and, at the League of Nations meeting in May 1931, all three states voted against the Austro-German customs union. The project was eventually referred to the international court at the Hague and that forum ruled that it was at variance with the terms of the Treaty of Versailles.

Conceivably, had the union become a reality, the German government of the day, headed by the conservative Heinrich Brüning, who had already gained some popular support by his tough stand on the question of disarmament, would have proved more durable and given pause to Hitler's surging National Socialists. As it was, the failure of a perfectly sound economic plan due to political pressures was a new humiliation to Germans (in Austria and the Sudetenland as well as in Germany) still smarting from their recent military defeat, and inclined them to pay closer attention to Hitler's intensely nationalistic rantings.

Within Czechoslovakia, the Sudeten Germans soon accused the Prague government of deliberately prolonging their economic misery by withholding direct aid and preventing the implementation of indirect measures to assist their recovery. Even before Hitler's actual appointment as chancellor, extremists in the Sudetenland, grouped in the National Socialist Workers' Party, hostile to the republic since its very birth, fashioned themselves on the Nazi model and endowed their Turnverein, a sports organization, with a strong nationalistic character. They invited Nazi speakers from Germany to address their rallies. Rising national sentiment made the position of the German members of the cabinet and of German delegates in parliament increasingly problematic. The government responded to Sudeten German provocations by banning quasi-military uniforms and forbidding visits by Nazi officials. In 1932 it closed down the youth organizations of the National Socialist Party and arrested some of its leaders.

Hitler's appointment infused new strength into the movement. It also intensified efforts by the Prague government to suppress it. The National Socialists, anticipating a total ban, dissolved themselves but transferred their numbers and adherence to a new organization, the so-called Heimatfront, under a genial young bank clerk and gymnastics teacher, Konrad Henlein. In 1935, the same year when the ailing Masaryk resigned as president (creating an imperceptible weakening of the republic), and was replaced by Beneš, the Heimatfront was renamed Sudetendeutsche Partei (SdP); in the ensuing elections it won 44 seats in parliament, making it the second-largest party after the Agrarians. By now the organization was receiving regular funding from German foreign ministry coffers to the tune of 180,000 marks annually. It is not clear whether Henlein himself was from the start of his political career an enemy of the republic; in his early pronouncements he professed loyalty to it and its institutions, but after 1935 he was for all practical purposes an agent of Hitler and a fifth columnist. During the Olympic Games in Berlin in 1936, he met the führer and from then on the Sudetenland was viewed in Germany as a Gau, an administrative district of the German Nazi Party.

Gradually many Sudeten Germans (excluding the Social Democrats among them), until then hesitant, realized the possibility of attaching the German-inhabited portions of Czechoslovakia to what Hitler projected to be a Greater Germany. Henlein intensified his activities. Defying the ban on militias, he copied German Nazi methods in organizing a paramilitary unit on the model of the German SS, the Freiwilliger Selbstschutz (Volunteer Self-Defense). By now however his self-effacing personality was overshadowed by the impact Hitler was making on Germans (and even on non-Germans) at home and abroad. The führer's speeches, broadcast on the radio, acquired a large mesmerized audience within Czechoslovakia. Anticipation of a German move on behalf of the Sudeten Germans became almost palpable.

Beneš, who, as foreign minister in the 1920s and early 1930s, had reason to think of himself as a statesman of international stature (and indeed his ideals, if not his practical proposals, enjoyed great respect in many quarters) at first seemed to think that the Nazi danger could be mastered by conventional means. He was tireless in devising new measures for strengthening his country's position and that of the Little Entente. Each of these attempts, however, only showed how feckless traditional methods were in an age of totalitarian diplomacy. He sought to strengthen the Little Entente by setting up an executive organ, the Permanent Council, as well as a secretariat, and he undertook to work out the details. He believed that there was a growing need for fortifying the alliance for the purposes it was supposed to serve. In January 1933 Austrian railway workers discovered that several freight cars en route from Italy to Hungary carried illegal weapons. Even if it had been a major shipment, which it was not, it would have constituted an insignificant violation of Hungary's disarmament as mandated by the peace treaty. Beneš transformed it into an instance of war preparation, and he began an accusatory campaign that predictably led nowhere. He also initiated a tripartite agreement among the Little Entente states to replace the three bilateral treaties; it was hard to see what difference that made, but its satisfied Beneš's love of order.

After Hitler's coming to power, Beneš proposed a revamped plan for a Danubian federation of Austria, Hungary, and Czechoslovakia. It was actually Masaryk who first put the idea to the Austrian envoy, Ferdinand Marek: "In the given position we cannot remain with the status quo. For our states and for all of Central Europe it would be the best, and possibly only, solution that the three of us once again unite. In short, we would have to bring about a new Austria-Hungary. Unfortunately there is little possibility that the Hungarians will come to their senses."

Neither Masaryk nor Beneš offered particulars of what they projected would be a Dual or Triple Republic, but it was an example of the nervous probing toward solutions for problems they themselves never properly defined. Not that the nervousness was entirely baseless. The position and security of the republic became progressively weaker, and the Little Entente guarantees proved slender reeds in the face of threats from abroad. Hungary's claim to at least the Magyar-inhabited southern regions of Slovakia was in itself not a serious threat, but, when combined with the aspirations of other powers, it could be a potent factor. Poland had never reconciled herself to the loss of a part of the Teschen region and Polish statesmen, in plotting its return, integrated efforts to secure it in some more grandiose plans. According to these, Teschen would in its entirety be joined to Poland, Bohemia-Moravia would become a separate entity that, in close cooperation with Poland, would block German expansion eastward, and Slovakia and Ruthenia would be detached, either to be returned to Hungary or to be attached to Poland. The plan did not seriously consider whether Slovakia-Ruthenia could be a viable independent state.

All these plans and ambitions suffered a shocking blow when, on March 12, 1938, Hitler marched into Austria and, within days, annexed it to the Third Reich. Bohemia-Moravia was now surrounded on three sides by German power and its already restive Sudeten population, with an ever rising voice, demanded "self-determination." The majority, it appeared, took the view that,

tance government buildings and other key installations in Bratislava. The Slovak premier, Monsignor Tiso, was unceremoniously removed, and a new, pliant, government under one Karel Sidor was installed.

Prague had taken a step that under existing conditions in the Middle Zone amounted to a brazen defiance of the commanding position Germany had assumed, and no one seriously believed that it would pass without challenge. There is no certainty as to when Hitler decided that the rump republic must be destroyed to bring the process that began at Munich to a definitive close, but it was fairly evident that the events in Bratislava of March 9–10 came as an unpleasant surprise to him. If he allowed the status quo to stand (and this seemed to be the desire of the people in both provinces), his one valid pretext for intervening would vanish. In the next few days there was another series of frenetic moves aimed at destroying the newfound relationship between Czechs and Slovaks. The German Volksgruppe in Slovakia, an ethnic minority that had been granted special privileges to please Berlin, rose in revolt against Czech presumptions and occupied the main government building in Bratislava. For Czech forces to retake it would now amount to an armed provocation, not of a local militia but of Germany herself.

It was most likely on this day, March 11, that the final decision to liquidate the remnant of the republic was taken in Berlin. What Hitler still had not decided though was how to partition the doomed state. Bohemia and Moravia would be taken under German "protection" and Slovakia, formally declaring her independence, would become a German satellite. But what about Ruthenia? She might be left as part of Slovakia, a solution that, however, would inescapably lead to the same kind of conflict as currently existed between Czechs and Slovaks.

The final decision to join Ruthenia to Hungary was almost certainly taken not so much to please Hungary as to please Poland. Hitler assumed that a Hungarian Ruthenia was what the Poles wanted and his diplomacy at this stage sought accomodation with Poland as an ally in future action against the Soviet Union. In the end Hungary was given two days to prepare a takeover of Ruthenia.

What Hitler had scarcely anticipated (though a correct reading of the signs would have made it fairly clear) was that the Slovaks had no great enthusiasm, or even interest, in independence. Their new government, instead of being at loggerheads with the Czech inhabitants, fully cooperated with them, and, apart from demonstrations by the German minority, the public mood was quiet, as if for the first time since the founding of the republic its two chief components, after the fractious minorities of Germans and Hungarians had been removed, had recognized their interdependence.

It was time for a new exhibition of totalitarian diplomacy. At dawn on March 13 Monsignor Tiso (no longer premier) was gotten out of bed and handed an invitation to go to Berlin for an interview with Hitler. He informed the Slovak cabinet of his impending trip, and the latter, though it thought it ominous that the invitation had gone to Tiso and not to the present premier, Sidor, agreed, on condition that Tiso would make no commitments.

In Berlin Hitler bitterly reproached Tiso for Slovak hesitations. Had he known, he said, that Slovaks had so little interest in their independence, he would not have disappointed "his friend" Hungary, which had designs on the province. He wanted a firm answer as to Slovak intentions. He was ready to support and guarantee Slovakian independence. If Bratislava refused that course, "he would leave the fate of Slovakia to events for which he was no longer responsible."

Tiso took with him to Bratislava the text of a declaration of independence prepared for him in Berlin. He first showed it to Sidor, who, upon reading it and realizing its significance, resigned. Tiso then read out the declaration to the cabinet and it was adopted without a debate. At noon on the 14th the independence of Slovakia was promulgated. That same afternoon the Hungarian government sent Prague a 12-hour ultimatum, demanding, among other things, the evacuation of Ruthenia by "Czech-Moravian troops." The next day Hungarian military units began their march into Ruthenia.

As to the Czech lands, Hitler sought to endow their military takeover with a veneer of legality, probably in deference to Anglo-Saxon sensibilities. The for-

A parade of German light tanks in Wenceslas Square, Prague, Czechoslovakia, 1942 *(Hulton/Archive)*

mula he devised was that Bohemia-Moravia, after the separation of Slovakia, found its own independent survival problematic and appealed to the German Reich for protection. President Hácha would accordingly beg to be invited to Berlin to put his case personally to Hitler.

When the special train that carried the president and foreign minister Chvalkovsky, and Hácha's daughter, arrived in Berlin at 10:30 P.M. on the 14th, unknown to Hácha, the fate of what was left of the republic had been decided. The ailing president, after an initial polite reception, was subjected to brutal pressure lasting for hours to prevail on him to sign a document assigning his now pathetically shrunken state to Germany's good graces. When, on the brink of physical collapse, he finally surrendered, German troops had already crossed the border into Bohemia and were on their way to Prague. Hitler betook himself there the next day and spent the night in the Hradčany Castle. Hungary had taken possession of Ruthenia, and Czechoslovakia, the nation that Hitler in one of his diatribes had labeled "the monster child of Versailles," had ceased to exist.

CHAPTER FIVE

The First Czechoslovak Republic had been known and admired for its tolerance both toward its non-Slavic citizens and toward political dissent, and it was a tragedy that this very virtue proved in the end the cause of its downfall. It is no exaggeration to say that during the war years former president Beneš *was* in effect Czechoslovakia, dramatizing the fact that the republic had never had the distinct identity that, in an age of national self-determination, justified its existence. He had transferred himself from the United States to London, to be in closer touch with European statesmen who, he assumed, would determine the postwar settlements. There, first as a simple political exile and later as head of a shadow government, he sought to pave the way for a rebirth of the defunct republic. Although that involved many maneuvers and negotiations, the ex-president's central concern, as he himself wrote in his memoirs, was to find a solution for the Sudeten problem. He could not deny that there had been a large bloc of Sudeten Germans, mainly Social Democrats, who had been loyal to the republic and who, after the German occupation, suffered as badly as other undesirables did, but whom the very designation Sudeten German made in many eyes enemies of Czechoslovakia. Beneš knew that widespread sentiment at home favored the expulsion of these Germans from a reconstituted Czechoslovakia and it became for him a *cas de conscience* to decide whether he should support this view or to resolutely take the humanitarian line, punishing the traitors, but allowing loyal Germans to remain in the republic as citizens with equal rights. Months, then years of sporadic negotiations with a Sudeten exile group of Social Democrats, the so-called Treuegemeinschaft, headed by one Wenzel Jaksch, produced tentative agreements, drafts, and often venomous disagreements, but the problem was as controversial when the war ended as it had been at its beginning. However, what fatally prejudiced the more liberal line toward the Sudeten Germans were the unspeakable atrocities inflicted on Czechs (and many Slovaks) by the German occupiers during the war. The Second Czech Republic, its leadership drawn largely from Communist ranks, began its existence with a hardened and uncompromising bias against at least two of its former minorities, the Germans and the Hungarians.

The new government, formed while some two-thirds of the country was still under German occupation, was determined not to repeat the mistakes of the first, and it began its equally troubled career by announcing the expulsion of its disloyal citizenry. In the case of the Sudeten Germans, where international opinion was concerned, the expulsion did not present a major problem: not only did Stalin, during a visit to Moscow by Beneš in March 1945, give his sanction, but subsequently the Potsdam Conference of the victorious powers, convening in July 1945, in effect mandated the expulsions. Desire for revenge was the dominant motive, but it could also be argued that no nation was obliged to accommodate minorities who, despite all the opportunities for self-expression offered to them, proved themselves irreconcilable.

The process was to be nonpolitical in the sense that it was supported by a broad consensus, but in the end it redounded to the advantage of the Communist Party of Czechoslovakia. As in other countries with multiparty governments, in Czechoslovakia too the Communists chose to join a coalition of center and left-center parties in order to avoid a defeat at the polls; given their tight discipline and organizational skills, they invariably came to dominate the coalition. Even if it garnered only a plurality of votes, the Communists hailed it as a rousing victory for "progressive" forces; their own militant progressivism was naturally beyond question.

Prague was "liberated" by the Red Army, whose first units drove into the city on May 9, 1945, two days after Germany had surrendered. The country as a whole was fortunate in that it had escaped the physical devastation that its neighbors to the north and south had suffered. In addition, unlike Hungary and Austria, Czechoslovakia was not saddled with reparations obligations— that too promised a quick recovery.

A program proclaimed in April 1945 in the first major liberated town, Košice in Slovakia, provided the framework for political organization: it justified the formation of the National Front with the argument that it would minimize differences of opinion during the electoral contest. The National Front did not achieve official status until after the war when a hastily elected Provisional Assembly under the presidency of Edvard Beneš sanctioned it. The leadership pledged to call a constituent assembly to draw up a new constitution. Meanwhile retribution for wartime crimes, mostly for cooperation with the Nazis, began in all seriousness. Former president Emil Hácha, who had, under duress, signed away the independence of Bohemia-Moravia, was arrested and died in prison. The former Slovak premier, Monsignor Tiso, was put on trial for high treason, condemned, and shot. The last German Reich protector, Karl Herrmann Frank, was extradited to the republic by American forces, tried, and hanged.

Elections for the constituent assembly took place in May 1946. The largest number of votes within the National Front, 38 percent, went to the Communists; the rest to other parties. Beneš was elected president of the republic. He appointed Klement Gottwald, head of the Communist Party, as premier; eight other members of the 12-member cabinet were also Communists. The post of foreign minister, not of great political importance at the moment, went to the former president Tomáš Masaryk's son Jan, but the all-important post of interior minister was entrusted to a Muscovite communist, Václav Nosek. The new government launched a two-year economic plan on the Soviet model and concluded a commercial agreement with the Soviet Union.

The country enjoyed two additional advantages that, under a stronger hand than that of Beneš, could have helped it to escape a one-party dictatorship. It had a reservoir of goodwill in the west, where many still remembered with shame the betrayal at Munich, and as a victor state it was not under Soviet military occupation. In countries where such occupying forces were present in large numbers, communists acted with much greater vigor and boldness knowing that, if challenged, they could count on the support of the Red Army; public officials of whatever description acted with the greatest circumspection so as not to anger the Communists. Czechoslovakia was an exception only in that her steady drift toward communism was a homebred phenomenon in which the Soviets played a marginal role until conditions for a putsch were already ripe.

In addition, President Beneš, whose past experience with Moscow dated from an era when the Soviet Union, an ostracized and diplomatically vulnerable country, tended to honor her international obligations, trusted that the same correctness would guide Moscow's foreign policy in the postwar era. Even the fact that Stalin, whose territorial greed knew no bounds, demanded the cession of Ruthenia to the Soviet Union did not free Beneš of this illusion; Ruthenia had never fitted comfortably into the Czechoslovak republic and its population was ethnically Ukrainian. The cession was carried out while the war was still in progress. With the fighting at an end, Stalin's greed became political in that he sought to bring the greatest possible number of governments in Europe, certainly in the eastern portion, under Soviet control. In the case of Czechoslovakia, unlike in Poland, Romania, and Bulgaria, there was no need to apply strong-arm methods. The indigenous party worked with great skill and persistence to sovietize the republic.

In Czechoslovakia the Communists, capitalizing on the passionately negative feelings toward the political right, forbade the formation of any party outside the National Front. On the argument that swift and decisive action was called for to reconstruct the nation, they conceded only a negligible legislative power to parliament. They quickly introduced the key feature of the communist system, the nationalization of industry. The decree to this effect, issued on October 28, 1945, at first applied only to firms with over 500 employees. At the same time however abandoned businesses in the Sudetenland, where the forcible expulsion of Germans had begun, were also subject to nationalization unless they were of a small size and found a purchaser.

In the political arena the Communists earned a significant victory by persuading their coalition partners to outlaw the largest party of prewar days, the Agrarians. The stated reason was that some members, especially in the leadership, had professed pro-fascist views and during the war had cooperated with the enemy. This, to the extent that it was true, was a slender argument for deactivating a party that had broad public support, but the Communists felt so confident of their power position that they did not go to great lengths to justify even the most arbitrary act.

In addition to the usual "enemies"—capitalists, large landowners, the church, and fascist military officers—there existed the massive body of Germandom whose enemy status had been confirmed from all quarters. Although when the deportation of the Sudeten population began, officially a distinction was supposed to be made between "good" and "bad" Germans, the process was too summary and emotions were still too raw for such differentiation to be effective. Expulsions were on the whole indiscriminate and often carried out in such an inhumane manner that for a long time after the Sudetenland had been practically emptied of Germans, the particulars of the process were kept from outside investigation. The argument over whether the murderous methods employed by the Nazis during the war justified adopting similar, if on the whole milder, measures against Germans has continued and will probably never be resolved.

As we have noted, in the opportunistic manner Communists employed, they were able to turn the punishment of Sudeten Germans to their advantage. They harped on the theme that they alone were truly dedicated to extirpating the last remnants of fascism and they posed as the executors of the national will to bring the republic's former enemies to justice. Justice in the Sudetenland had no judicial features, unless occasional recognition that some Germans had fought and suffered in defense of the republic counted as such. Through their control of the Ministry of the Interior and also the Ministry of Agriculture, Communists carried out most of the actual expulsions. They were also in charge of the subsequent distribution of abandoned goods. Not only did these agents of the party see to it that Communists and fellow-travelers gained most of the booty, but also anyone receiving goods formerly owned by Germans became beholden to the system, since rule by the Communists alone could ensure their continued possession of the assets gained.

Communist propaganda also played upon the Pan-Slavist theme; it stressed the Slavic character of the nation, which owed allegiance to the Soviet Union not only because the latter's armies had liberated it from Nazi rule but also because the liberators were fellow Slavs. The concept and theme of the "enemy," so routinely used by Communists to justify extralegal acts, surfaced in Czechoslovakia with particular virulence. Premier Gottwald put it baldly: "The Red Army freed our nation from the Germans, [but] we have to free ourselves of the enemy within our own ranks." He reserved for his party the right to determine who the internal enemy was, and by a logical extension of the principle, the enemy was whoever questioned or opposed communist policies.

In line with the democratic traditions of the country the Communists hoped to attain untrammeled power by electoral means. Their following, however, did not appreciably grow after their May 1946 victory and other means had to be employed to make the republic a communist state. Here the organizational skills of the party came to the fore with striking results. It had long been a feature of communist mentality, initiated by Lenin, that national opinion was properly that of the working class, and a further elaboration of this thesis was that only the "politically conscious" part of the working class, that is the Communists, had the wisdom and vision to be allowed to express that opinion. Gottwald and his colleagues worked hard on what they labeled "the mobilization of the masses," seeking to show that the great bulk of the population, though politically still immature, knew what its interests were and was eager to voice them when given an opportunity. They organized mass demonstrations, dispersing their own agents in the crowd, so that when they spoke up they gave the impression of the same views being voiced from all quarters;

these agents were instructed to demand enactments and decrees that had been hatched in close party circles. At the same time the party was careful not to abandon the trappings of democracy. Gradually but inexorably a coup by the Communist Party was being prepared; other parties, as well as President Beneš, either did not see the handwriting on the wall or were helpless in halting the onrushing events.

In retrospect there was no reason why the Second Czechoslovak Republic could not have become a democratic haven even among the totalitarian states in the Soviet sphere. The president had the authority to dismiss the incumbent premier and appoint a new one, and the Soviet Union did not have direct means of coercion as it had in states where its military was present in large numbers. But the Czechoslovak government had granted the Soviet Union the right to move troops across its territory from one satellite state to another. Consequently there were always Red Army troops in the country, if only in transit. The psychological factor proved a powerful one.

When, in June 1947, U.S. secretary of state George Marshall announced his plan for European economic reconstruction and invited states in need of aid to first explore possibilities for their own solutions before making requests to meet their needs to Washington, Prague at first signaled its readiness to participate. Stalin was at this point undecided as to what to make of the mammoth offer of a virtual giveaway. Characteristically, it was in the end he who decided that the Marshall Plan was a shrewd scheme to make Europe, devastated by war, dependent on American largesse in the expectation that the dependence would continue and produce a permanent market for American goods. During a visit to Moscow of Klement Gottwald and some members of his cabinet, Stalin shared his misgivings with the Czech premier and strongly hinted that he would take a dim view of Czechoslovak acceptance of Marshall aid. It must have been a painful decision for even a diehard Communist like Gottwald to forgo an offer with no visible strings attached, but by now Stalin's authority brooked no opposition. The American offer was politely rejected.

Churchill's prophecy of a year earlier, namely, that an Iron Curtain was descending across Europe, was coming true. So was the "Two Camps" concept promulgated by Stalin's ideological chief, Andrey Zhdanov, which warned nations that there was no middle ground between the communist and the capitalist camps; they had to choose one or the other and live with the consequences, which, in the case of capitalist countries, was the exploitation of the working class, and in the case of communist countries its liberation. Gottwald and his colleagues had taken their cue. The kind of mixed system that Czechoslovakia represented had become an anomaly. A declaration of adherence to one camp or another was imperative.

The showdown in Prague had a prehistory of concrete events, but there is no doubt that it would have come in any case given the definite shift in favor of the Communists. The minister of interior, Václav Nosek, had for a time used his authority in a high-handed manner to remove politically "unreliable" police officials and replace them with communist ones. On February 12, 1948, in an abrupt move, he ousted 12 chiefs of police stations in Prague. The noncommunist members of the cabinet met and decided to demand that the order be rescinded. When Nosek refused, on the 20th the ministers resigned in a body. They naively expected that this would occasion a government crisis and Gottwald would have to resign. A crisis did indeed follow, but it was that of the existing system. Gottwald quickly filled the vacated posts with his own men. As it happened, the Soviet deputy foreign minister Valerian Zorin was in Prague on a trade mission and, with his expertise in political manipulation, superintended the transfer of power. He reportedly brought Gottwald a personal message from Stalin, offering military help to consolidate the communist hold on power if it proved necessary. It did not prove necessary but Zorin's offer amounted to an unspecific promise for the future; a communist Czechoslovakia would be one of those states in which the Soviet Union would protect the survival of socialism, by force of arms if necessary.

In one of his last political acts, President Beneš on February 25, approved the new, essentially communist, government. The only member of the cabinet still from the old school was Jan Masaryk, who wielded too much authority and prestige to be removed as unreliable. In the morning of March 10 his dead body was found below an open window of the foreign ministry building, an apparent suicide.

Nothing now stood in the way of Czechoslovakia becoming a soviet state, in fact if not in name. Gottwald called a new constituent assembly and it obeisantly adopted still another constitution. Beneš, rather than endorse it, resigned on June 7. Gottwald became president, and another communist, Antonin Zápotocký, a trade union leader, became premier. In May new elections were held. Communists still did not trust their own electoral strength sufficiently to run on a separate ballot, but the National Front, which they headed, garnered a great majority, a majority that might, however, have disappeared had the one and a half million blank or invalid ballots been counted.

More important for the new regime than the number of ballots cast in national elections was the numerical size of the Communist Party. If enough new members, especially young ones, could be enrolled and properly indoctrinated, they would contribute to a political transformation that would either make elections obsolete or, if held, would yield the desired results in overwhelming numbers. An energetic drive to increase the membership began and met with great success. In a six-month period the number of card-carrying Communists nearly doubled (from 1,409,000 to 2,675,000). In the process, in July 1948, the two workers' parties, the Communist and the Social Democratic, merged. It was part of a concentrated effort, not so much to swell workers' party numbers as to undermine whatever residual strength other parties had.

The sovietization of the country was now seriously taken in hand. The Moscow-trained Czech cadre was competent enough to carry it out, but the Gottwald government bowed to Soviet insistence that operatives appointed by Moscow "assist" the Czech comrades in the reorganization of the political and economic system. Numerous Soviet experts were placed in key positions, mainly in the army and the political police but also in large industrial enterprises, assumably to prevent errors of judgment in technical and political matters.

In January 1949, after the successful completion of the Two-Year Plan, a Five-Year Plan was inaugurated and during its course the economy was wholly nationalized. The emphasis, following Stalin's wishes, was on heavy industry, since in the COMECON scheme Czechoslovakia was to be a chief source of machine production, to counterbalance other, more agriculturally oriented nations. The consequence was the gradual emasculation of light industries, such as porcelain and lace, which had a long tradition and of which the country was justly proud. Another consequence was a growing dependence on the Soviet Union for raw materials because Bohemia, the main base of heavy industry, did not possess the necessary amount of minerals to carry out the onerous demands of the new plan. There was the accompanying destruction of spiritual and cultural values as well. Although after the war the state and the church had worked out a compromise that very nearly amounted to a separation of the two, by 1949 the tolerance had ended. Roman Catholic bishops were imprisoned or sent to concentration camps. Religious orders were abolished. Monks and nuns by the thousands suffered imprisonment or exile. Churchgoing was regarded as unpatriotic; if a party member was discovered attending services, he was ousted from the party and most likely from his job.

Equally hard hit was national culture. By Communist Party standards there was only one legitimate theme that should inform creative work: the struggle of the laboring man to find recognition and achieve his dignity. All other subjects were deemed frivolous or, worse, reactionary. Hundreds of books, many by venerated Czech writers, were banned. In some schools Communists and teachers intimidated by them called on their students to cull their parents' collection of books and, if they found any that were not politically correct, to bring them to school so they could be consigned to the ash heap.

Political terror was moderate until the eruption of the Tito affair in the summer of 1948; after that, as in all satellite countries, a veritable witch-hunt of Titoists, including persons who by some association could be suspected of that political crime, began. Until then, most of the victims of the political police had been stalwarts of the old order, "reactionaries," as they were called, enemies of communism by definition. After Tito's alleged treason most suspects were Communist Party members, many with years of faithful service and with impeccable ideological credentials. These proceedings were at times tainted with anti-Semitism, particularly repugnant only a few years after the Holocaust had decimated Europe's Jewish population. Stalin, who had been the first to recognize the newly born state of Israel, soon perceived it as a mainstay of Jewish nationalism and upon investigation was appalled to find how many Jews were in leading position in the Communist parties of satellite states. In Czechoslovakia the first and most prominent victim of this bias was the second in command in the Communist Party, Rudolf Slánský. Not an attractive person by any means, he was heard to say, after the trial and execution of László Rajk in Hungary, that what Czechoslovakia needed was her own László Rajk. Little did he suspect that in the course of time he would fill that prescription. When Gottwald received Stalin's personal envoy, Anastas Mikoyan, who brought orders for the arrest and trial of Slánský, he complied without a word of protest, although Slánský had been his friend and comrade for many years. Slánský, with 10 other defendants, was tried and hanged. In Czechoslovakia, as in Hungary, many more Communists were tried and victimized by a communist regime than had been by previous "reactionary" regimes; the revolution was devouring its own children.

Only Stalin's death in March 1953 caused a slowdown, then a nearly complete cessation of the terror, but ineradicable scars had been inflicted on the national consciousness; the revulsion against the terror could be controlled only with more terror. And a regime based on terror, as historic evidence shows, has a short life span.

CHAPTER SIX

Klement Gottwald caught a chill while attending Stalin's funeral and died a few days later of pneumonia. His body was embalmed and displayed in a mausoleum in Prague; this very emulation of the practices of the Stalinist past served as a sign that the new Czechoslovak leadership did not contemplate any deviation from its present policies. Antonin Novotný, a hard-core Stalinist, replaced Gottwald as secretary general of the Communist Party; Antonin Zápotocký was chosen president and Viliám Siroký premier. The latter two were not disinclined to ease political repression, and they may have been able to do so, but when on May 30 the government introduced the long planned "financial reform," a euphemism for the devaluation of the currency that deprived many, including the middle peasantry, which by now constituted the backbone of society, of much of its savings, reaction was shockingly hostile. The official explanation, namely, that the "reform" was necessary to put an end to the differential in prices between the controlled and the free segments of the economy, convinced no one. There were violent protests, especially in the Lenin Works in Pilsen, where enraged workers tore down symbols of communist rule and trampled pictures of Stalin and Gottwald underfoot. The leadership had a taste of what awaited it if it relaxed controls. Even some of the police fraternized with the demonstrators, and army units had to be called out to restore order. Subsequently, official propaganda blamed the disorders on "bourgeois and Social Democratic provocations" and mobilized the party apparatus, as well as the labor unions, to condemn the demonstrations. Novotný's iron fist philosophy seemed to be justified. He also enjoyed the support of the new Soviet party leadership, specifically that of the general secretary, Nikita Khrushchev, who laid great stress on personal relations among comrades and had taken an instant liking to the new head of the Czechoslovak party.

Thus, whereas in the Soviet Union and countries such as Poland and Hungary controls were relaxed, concentration camps nearly emptied, and persecutions of political crimes practically ceased, in Czechoslovakia, if anything, repression became greater. An old Communist, the Slovak Gustav Husák, in preliminary custody since 1951 for "Slovak bourgeois nationalist" pronouncements, was sentenced to life in prison, and so were many others. The Kremlin raised no objection to the Czechoslovak party marching to a different drummer from all the others in its orbit including the Soviet Union itself, for in truth it did not fully trust its own dismantling of a system of tight control. The fragility of a government depending on terror was quickly revealed when, after Stalin's death, disgruntled voices began to issue from sundry quarters, most unsettlingly from literary men, and sporadic strikes by workers occurred in various places. Czechoslovakia became a test case of how long protest can be held in check by methods that, although discredited, still held potency. Hungary in particular provided an example of the dangers of liberalization. The noisily advertised "New Course" of Imre Nagy, a popular challenger of Stalinism, found such enthusiastic reception that soon the monopoly of power by the Communist Party itself seemed in danger. In the end, Nagy was removed as premier on Moscow's order. In Czechoslovakia, no such crisis occurred. Liberalization was never attempted, thus its consequences were never tested.

In February 1956 the celebrated XXth Congress of the CPSU, or, rather, its aftermath, foreshadowed another break with hard-line policies. There is no certainty to this day as to why Khrushchev, who already had reason to regret that he and his colleagues had plunged into the liquidation of the Stalin legacy in such unthinking hurry, went one big step further in that direction when, in a six-hour speech at the congress, he denounced Stalin and his methods in intemperate terms; the most likely yet least satisfying explanation lies in his impetuous nature, which often led him to act before he considered in any depth the likely consequences. On the other hand, only by separating himself from Stalinism in the most definitive manner could he make himself authentic and credible as a more humane leader—there was much to commend this argument on moral grounds, but in the practical sense it implied a renunciation of political coercion at a time when it was most needed.

Hard-liners in the satellite states, especially Novotný and his colleagues in Czechoslovakia, immediately perceived the dangers of repudiating Stalin's system of consent by terror, and their fears were soon justified: at a congress of writers in Prague a number of speakers denounced the tyranny of the Stalin era, charged that it was being perpetuated in their own country, and demanded more freedom. The government bristled but did not at first make an issue of the matter. It could call itself fortunate that the revolution that broke out in Hungary later that year, also initiated by writers and journalists and then taken up by university youth and finally by workers themselves, so alarmed the Soviet leadership that it put down the uprising with overwhelming military force. In the aftermath, repression once again received sanction from the highest quarters. The Czechoslovak government belatedly proceeded against liberal-minded authors; many were expelled from the leadership of the Writers' Union, denounced as agents of the "enemy," and replaced with faithful Stalinists.

From this time on it became official party policy to regard writers and intellectuals as ideological enemies of the regime, bent on undermining the socialist system. The ire and venom of the controlled media were unleashed against them. A century earlier, in Russia, the term "intelligentsia" had referred to a group of people who not merely earned their living by intellectual work but directed their intellect toward subversive ends and, under false moral assumptions, set themselves against the official order. A very similar view was adopted by the Czech leadership in the late 1950s and the 1960s. The targets were professionals, especially in literature and the social sciences. *"Ty inteligente"* (you intellectual) became a common term of abuse. In addition to suggesting that the *inteligente* were politically unreliable, there was also the implied charge that they lived a parasitic existence made possible by the labor of the honest, politically loyal, working class. Simultaneously, efforts were undertaken to elevate members of that class to professional ranks; preference in schooling was given to children from peasant and worker families. However, the program never had enough time to be tested. It would have taken two or three generations for youngsters from economically underprivileged families, which provided little intellectual inspiration, to rise to the achievement level of children from the middle class, who, even if not motivated, had imbibed culture by osmosis.

Some intellectuals in Czechoslovakia and elsewhere remained unrepentant and, if engaged in creative work, continued to produce literature that the party denounced as bourgeois and decadent. However, the majority, out of fear or conviction, adjusted to the demands of proletarian culture, both in the choice of their subject and in their mode of expression. Even in their dress habits, and in their vernacular, they stooped to vulgarity.

Although from what the public saw, the party leadership was united in its political outlook and in its choice of methods to achieve it, disagreements, not fundamental but serious, continued. Zápotocký as president never carried Novotný's authority, and although of a milder temperament, he had to yield to the general secretary's rigid hard line. As in most communist states, agricultural policy was the true test of a leader's conviction. Marx had had little to say about the peasantry and Lenin had treated it, or a portion of it, as petit bourgeois. Stalin's most prolonged and brutal struggle was against a hardheaded peasantry that refused to sacrifice its private holdings to fulfill the Marxist vision of all means of production, including the land, being commonly owned. In that struggle even the usually unbending Stalin had had to yield to the extent of allowing peasants in a collective to have their private plots, thereby creating what some mordant wits called a gray desert dotted with green patches, the underworked collectives interspersed with blooming private plots. The agrarian question was never resolved: both the opinion that the peasant must be forced into economically viable collectives and the counter-opinion that the willing cooperation of the peasant could be gained only by allowing him to own his own land had their advocates.

The conflict between Zápotocký's lenient and Novotný's hard line had been out in the open well before Khrushchev's anti-Stalin diatribe in February 1956. Zápotocký, in a speech on August 1, 1954, criticized forced collectivization and, like Imre Nagy in Hungary, wanted to give peasants already in collectives the right to return to individual farming. Novotný could not allow such a challenge to go unanswered. Later that fall, in the Moravian city of Brno, although he did go so far as to admit that collective farms operated at a deficit and that some were on the verge of bankruptcy, he denied that that was reason enough to break them up. However, since this is precisely what was happening—peasants in collectives were withdrawing their former holdings—Novotný resolved on energetic measures to halt the process. In the political committee (the ruling body of the party) he branded Zápotocký's position petit bourgeois deviation, insisted that problems of collective farming had to be solved not by liquidation but by better organization and, when he could not get a majority, referred the matter to the Kremlin. Khrushchev himself had been in favor of easing the agrarian tyranny of the party and, as an agricultural expert, he saw the merits of Zápotocký's argument, but, for political reasons, he sided with Novotný. This settled the matter, for the time being anyhow. When the Czechoslovak party held its Xth Congress that year, Novotný drew the political conclusions from his policy having been sanctioned over and above Zápotocký's. He weightily announced: "The leading force is the party; it cannot be placed on an equal rank with the state apparatus." End of debate.

It appeared that the 1956 events—the Khrushchev speech and upheavals in Poland, Hungary, and the German Democratic Republic—left Novotný unimpressed and his hard-line policy on course. The intellectuals were driven into silence. The agricultural collectives continued to plod along. Ideological vigilance, repeatedly called for, was ensured by a censorship that extended over all means of expression. The XIth Party Congress of 1958 pledged itself to complete socialist reconstruction, remove the remnants of the exploiting classes, and liquidate the kulaks (independently farming peasants) "as a class in the countryside."

These were no empty threats. In the next two years the number of private farms was reduced by one-half (from 542,000 to 256,000), placing 90 percent of agrarian holdings in collectives or into state-owned farms. Private businesses, however small in size, practically disappeared. Those that remained belonged to small tradesmen, cobblers, tailors, blacksmiths, and the like. Culturally, the search for "bourgeois vestiges" continued with grim persistence. Anyone who had served the former regime, who had been branded a "class enemy" (landowner, businessman, clergyman), was dismissed from his (her) job or relegated to the lowest level on the pay scale. It was Novotný's dream to be able to make the announcement, before any other Soviet bloc state did, that Czechoslovakia had come to full maturity as a socialist state. He authored a new constitution, adopted in 1960, by which the country was renamed the Czechoslovak Socialist Republic. The key role of the party was once again stressed when Novotný declared:

> The leading force in society and the state is the vanguard of the working
> class, the Communist Party of Czechoslovakia, a voluntary combative union
> of the most active and conscious citizens from the ranks of the workers,
> peasants, and the intelligentsia.

The constitution also formalized the "comradely cooperation" of Czechoslovakia with the Soviet Union and the other states in the Soviet bloc.

❉ ❉ ❉

The history of the eight-year period after 1960 could properly be titled "The Decline and Fall of Antonin Novotný." It had all the features of a political disaster caused not by any specific mistake (though Novotný did commit at least one in his needless provocation of Slovak leaders) but by unreasoning insistence on principles and policies that the passage of time had shown to be outdated. Rigidity had served Novotný well when he defied Soviet leaders by clinging to the Stalinist system of governing; his country escaped the upheavals that shook other satellites. Not to anger his chief mentor, Nikita Khrushchev, he periodically paid lip service to trendy themes like the denunciation of the cult of personality and of perversions of socialist justice, but he never took a single step toward correcting these mistakes. In 1956, after the Khrushchev speech, a committee had been set up to review the Czechoslovak show trials held between 1949 and 1952; in a few instances the convicted were set free but they were never rehabilitated, giving the whole process a character of commutation rather than admission of miscarriage of justice. No one was charged with engineering these trials and steering them through their predictable courses. The policy of immobility did not, however, prevent problems from multiplying and increasing in bulk. Agriculture continued to stagnate and industrial performance was so lackluster that the third Five-Year Plan had to be canceled in the summer of 1962. Growth in production of goods slowed, from 11.7 percent in 1960 to 8.9 percent in 1961 to 6.2 percent in 1962; in the following year it stopped altogether. Undeterred, the government began to draft the blueprint for a Seven-Year Plan. However, planners had to consider a factor previous plans had been free to ignore: the growing shortages in food production traceable directly to the policy of forced collectivization, aggravated by bad weather and partial crop failures. The Czech regions of the republic had always served as the model for industrial development in eastern central Europe; now, under Communist Party management, they stumbled from one failure to another. Disappointment, widespread at the grassroots, gradually penetrated to the leadership cadres. The interior minister, Rudolf Barak, an ambitious and decisive person, reputedly a confidant of Khrushchev, placed himself in opposition to Novotný's ineffective one-man rule. When, at the XXIInd Congress of the Soviet party Khrushchev renewed his anti-Stalin line, erasing lingering suspicions that at heart the Soviet leadership still clung to Stalinism, Novotný's position was seriously shaken. However, he did not succumb without a fight. Speaking before the Central Committee of his party, he presented himself as a devoted supporter of the Soviet general secretary; to give proof of this in a manner that could do him no harm, he announced that the giant statue of Stalin in the center of Prague would be dismantled. He also referred to the legal monstrosities of the 1950s but blamed them (perhaps with some justification), on Klement Gottwald, who could no longer defend himself. He said Gottwald at that time had grown old and was surrounded by bad advisers. He himself, continued Novotný, had no influence on the direction of those political trials. Whether because of these maneuvers or because of his long entrenched position, he still had enough clout to cause, in June 1962, the arrest and conviction of the interior minister, Rudolf Barak, on charges of sabotage and exploitation of public resources.

This new trial, which Khrushchev did nothing to prevent or delay, assured Novotný that he still had Moscow's support and, in his hard-pressed position, that was the ultimate assurance he needed. He might have paused to ask himself whether, if by chance, *he* found himself at the rough end of a political confrontation the Soviet statesman would speak up on *his* behalf. Such a confrontation was not a farfetched possibility. A group of reformers in the Central Committee, a body that in the 1960s was called more often than it had been in the past and consequently assumed greater authority, placed itself in undisguised opposition to Novotný. A respected professor of economics, Ota Šik, was the most prestigious and most outspoken among the critics. He recognized the ossifying effect of central planning and supervision on which Novotný insisted, and he advocated greater freedom and decision-making power for managers heading the state enterprises. A 1966 meeting decided to do just that, the first phase to be introduced in 1967, the second in 1968. Another decision taken, much to Novotný's dismay, was to encourage tourism in order to attract Western currencies. However, when discussion in the Central Committee turned to the truly serious subject of applying for foreign credit to finance new investments, the first secretary had his way and the motion was denied.

If Novotný had been satisfied with frustrating economic reformers in small ways, not because he really believed that they were wrong but because they placed themselves in opposition to him, he might have clung to power considerably longer than he did. But then came his undignified quarrel with Slovak comrades. Its roots dated far back because the Slovaks, as we have noted, were a perennially discontented nationality in the republic. The 1960 constitution had formalized Slovakia's subordinate role; it was also a rather conspicuous fact that many of the Slovak defendants convicted of political crimes had been charged, among other things, with unpatriotic conduct, implying that they had a more suspect devotion to Czechoslovak unity than the Czechs. Certainly Slovaks, especially the intellectuals, were sterner foes of Stalinism than many of the Czechs, though these intellectuals found some solid supporters among their Czech colleagues. As early as 1962 Slovak men of letters began a determined campaign against Prague's hegemony, demanding that the republic be turned into a federation of two coequal parts: Czechs and Slovaks. The most vocal advocate of this formula was Gustav Husák, the Slovak Communist recently released from prison and rehabilitated.

In 1963 the party in Slovakia secured a new leader, Alexander Dubček. That same year Novotný, by now increasingly on the defensive, parted with his hardline premier, Široký, and replaced him with a Slovak, Josef Lenart, an advocate of "controlled liberalization." Already an important, though largely symbolic, step toward liberalization had been taken when the committee charged with reviewing the political trials of the 1950s had declared as not guilty some 70 victims; as far as the Slovak defendants were concerned, the Central Committee ruled that the charge of "bourgeois nationalism," which had been the chief count of indictment against most of them, was without foundation.

In October 1964, in Moscow, the politburo of the CPSU ousted Khrushchev from his post as general secretary for unbecoming conduct; Novotný alone among satellite leaders expressed disapproval to the Kremlin leadership. With Khrushchev, he lost his chief supporter in Moscow, and this at a time when his quarrel with the Slovaks and their non-Slovak partners was entering a critical stage.

It is a matter for speculation how genuinely the Czech reformers empathized with the Slovak cause, but it certainly was a convenient instrumentality for embarrassing and eventually removing the hated first secretary. To the chorus of captious voices from writers and intellectuals there were now added the voices of university students, unhappy with their poor living conditions and their regimented curricula (the study of marxism was obligatory regardless of one's discipline).

At a Central Committee meeting in October 1967 Novotný, in a clash with Slovak members, once again and for the last time, resorted to the hoary charge of "bourgeois nationalism," party jargon for placing national interests above the cause of the international working class as defined by Moscow. The charge frightened nobody and Novotný, in a last desperate attempt to save his political skin, appealed to Khrushchev's successor, Leonid Brezhnev, to visit Prague and back him up against the unruly members on the Central Committee. Brezhnev arrived on December 8 but showed no interest in giving any support to the man who had opposed his, Brezhnev's, ouster of Khrushchev. Novotný, assailed from all sides and defended by no one, offered his resignation as first secretary of the Communist Party. The January 5, 1968, meeting of the Central Committee accepted it but allowed Novotný to remain president, an empty dignity he had held since 1957. It also allowed him to choose his own successor as first secretary. His choice fell on Alexander Dubček, by now the leading figure among Slovak Communists. An era had truly come to a close.

※　※　※

Dubček was 46 years old when he assumed the most responsible position in the republic. Between the wars he had lived in the Soviet Union and had received his primary and secondary education there. He had returned to Prague after the end of the war, but in 1955 he was once again in the Soviet Union, and for three years studied political science at Moscow University. Back in Slovakia again, he embarked on an utterly ordinary career in the party and showed no particular distinction in any endeavor. Certainly no one expected great things from him when he assumed the leadership of the Czechoslovak party. This impression was confirmed when shortly after his appointment he went to Moscow, as was the duty of every newly appointed high functionary, to receive proper instructions. Reporting to the public after his return he resorted to the usual verbiage, promising "socialist democracy," without being specific about it. Conceivably at this point he did not intend any thoroughgoing change, nothing that would place him in disfavor with the Moscow leadership. Reformers around him pushed him to make good on his promises. Party rallies and informal meetings held all over the country multiplied in number, and demands for a new course were so pressing that it was obvious that the rank and file would not be satisfied with half measures or counterfeit reforms. Pressure began for Novotný to give up even the presidency, and on March 22, 1968, he complied.

Most of his supporters followed suit, resigning either under pressure or because they knew that their careers were at an end. Novotný's place as president was taken by a general, Ludwik Svoboda. Svoboda had played a major part in the 1948 putsch in assuring a triumph for communism, but precisely because of the debt of gratitude the Soviets owed him, he seemed an assurance that they would respect Czechoslovakia's independence.

An exultant mood swept over the country. With Soviet control, which for two decades had lain like a physical weight on the nation, removed, everything seemed possible. Newspapers, radio, and television began to broadcast uncensored news and commentaries; demands were voiced for an investigation of the assumed suicide of Jan Masaryk, with obvious suggestions that he had been murdered. On April 5 the Central Committee adopted an Action Program, sanctioning the connection between political and economic reform. It also accepted an autonomous status for Slovakia. It promised a revised constitution that would guarantee complete human freedom and civil rights. It provided for the separation of the Communist Party from government power; government would henceforth be conducted by a National Assembly as a legislature and an executive branch named by the assembly, and there was to be no political interference in the judicial process. In elections, Communist candidates would have to contend with candidates from other parties—in short the monopoly of the Communist Party over political life, the bedrock of Soviet-style governments everywhere, would be ended. Dubček claimed it would still be socialism, but "with a human face."

Stalin had been dead for 15 years and the Soviet government in Moscow had done much to eradicate even the vestiges of Stalinism. It did so with some confidence because it could control the process in its every phase, ease restrictions when it could safely do so and tighten them again when expectations soared too high. This was not the case in the satellites. Depriving the Communist Party of its legislative and executive power could be only the first step toward creation of a multiparty democracy, with the next step being a complete break with the Soviet Union. Cautionary voices issued from Moscow in April; in May Dubček made another visit to Moscow, trying to assure Brezhnev and company that he still followed the socialist path and that his reforms presented no threat to Soviet security. The Kremlin bosses were not satisfied. They alerted leaders in satellite states to the dangers the daringly independent course chosen by Dubček represented. Late in July Brezhnev, with the entire Politburo of the CPSU. traveled to Slovakia and met with Dubček in a small town to discuss their differences in a frank spirit. Already Soviet and satellite military forces were gathering and maneuvers were being held in southern Poland. The talks revealed that there was no basis for agreement. Left alone, the Dubček regime would go too far in "reforming" communism in Czechoslovakia, and once the process came to full term, it could no longer be reversed. On August 20 a mixed army of Soviet, East German, Polish, Hungarian, and Bulgarian forces invaded Czechoslovakia. There was no opposition to speak of. But military occupation could not be translated into political victory. Dubček and several of his "reformist" colleagues were seized and taken to Moscow; returning

Soviet tanks in the center of Prague, Czechoslovakia, during Soviet occupation, 1968 (Hulton/Archive)

them proved a problem, however: if they eschewed the reforms they had previously endorsed, everybody would know that they had been brainwashed and none of their pronouncements would be credible. In the end the Kremlin leaders brought two more malleable comrades to Moscow: Swoboda and Husák. They were not outright liabilities as Novotný had been, and they could be trusted to curb Dubček's reforms according to Soviet wishes. They agreed to Soviet troops being permanently stationed on Czechoslovak soil on the transparent pretext that they would help to defend socialism were it again threatened by reformers who did not know where to draw the line to reform.

Husák did not return to the mindless and stubborn oppression of Novotný, and even made a bid for popular support by backing economic improvements, but he could not live down the stigma of being chosen by a foreign power and kept in office by a foreign military force. Many arrests were made at Soviet request, more for deterrence than for punishment, but extreme sentences were avoided. Dubček himself escaped arrest—a far cry from Stalinism—and was appointed first as ambassador to Ankara, and later to an insignificant job in the forestry service.

By the 1970s, it was clear that Soviet leaders were dedicating themselves not to the preservation of socialism but to their own political survival. One superannuated party chief followed another, young blood was shunned; men like Dubček had given the leadership a taste of what the new generation of Marxists could be like.

As it happened, with the eventual passing of the Old Guard, the ideology and the system passed away as well.

CHAPTER SEVEN

Events in Czechoslovakia following the demise of the Prague Spring were symptomatic of the growing crisis of Soviet leadership within the satellite empire, and indeed even within the Soviet Union itself. Khrushchev had lacked Stalin's political base held together by intimidation, and he had had to form transient political alliances to keep himself in power. During the Hungarian revolution of 1956, he found that only Stalinist terror bolstered by military force could maintain Soviet dominance in the region. At the same time he continued his de-Stalinization campaign, and his liberal initiatives mixed poorly with the heavy-handed methods of implementation. In general, he proved inept in matters of high politics, and his fanciful foreign ventures drove him to a confrontation with the United States. The fallout from the Cuban missile crisis proved fatal to his political future.

His successor, Leonid Brezhnev, whatever his true political instincts were, by and large abandoned political and economic reform and satisfied himself with the preservation of the status quo. The pursuit of socialist progress yielded to the necessity of keeping the ruling elite in power; socialism became a mere label under which that power was exercised. The Politburo continued to be manned by the superannuated personnel brought to political maturity under Stalin and dedicated to the maintenance of control by means introduced and perfected by the late dictator.

The Czechoslovak scene faithfully reflected these principles. Had Dubček's proposed reforms been given the benefit of open discussion, their usefulness, in both the political and the economic sphere, would no doubt have been recognized. This very fact was their most dangerous feature because open discussion would have revealed that the Soviets opposed reform not because of its shortcomings but because it loosened their control over a vital satellite. Control was no longer automatic as it had been in Stalin's time; it had to be exercised over specific pieces of legislation as well as over expressions of loyalty and admiration for the Soviet Union. Small incidents acquired overblown significance. In March 1969, the last month of Dubček's tenure as party chief, the Czechoslovak ice hockey team defeated the Soviet team for the world championship, and this occasioned passionate anti-Soviet demonstrations throughout the republic. The Soviets used these as proof that Dubček was losing control, and three weeks later he was forced to go. Whatever interest the Kremlin bosses had had in helping Czechoslovakia to achieve her full economic potential was subordinated to making her an obedient satellite. Their policy, duly communicated to the new Czechoslovak leadership under Gustáv Husák, was to condemn reform for jeopardizing socialist unity. The course of action they chose instead they euphemistically dubbed "normalization," and it consisted in the reversion to old and largely discredited policies pursued by governments under Gottwald and Novotný. In practice it meant purging the political leadership of all reformist elements and staffing responsible party and government positions with men of leftist or left-centrist persuasion, to whom reform was as distasteful as it was to the Kremlin bosses.

In a subsequent purge of the Central Committee of the Czechoslovak Communist Party, 54 of the incumbent 115 members were removed. The same principle was applied to lower levels of leadership, and even to the rank and file, with the result that party membership in short order shrank from about 1.7 million to 1.2 million. Means of mass communication—publishing houses, theaters, motion picture companies—often had their entire leadership replaced in order to ensure adherence to new censorship laws applying to the printed word and branches of entertainment. Simultaneously even in the forever sensitive religious sphere in which the government had in the past been able to produce some accommodation, all tolerance was ended and a campaign of militant atheism was introduced.

To formalize Czechoslovakia's close adherence to the Soviet bloc, the Husák regime signed, in May 1970, a Treaty of Friendship, Cooperation, and Mutual Assistance with the Soviet Union; the use of the treaty for Moscow lay not in its obligatory expressions of goodwill but in that it authorized the stationing of Soviet troops on Czechoslovak territory and placed the military forces of the republic under Warsaw Pact (i.e., Soviet) command. It further accepted Soviet advisement (i.e., control) in the Ministry of Interior and the security police.

Hundreds of thousands of citizens, unable freely to vote at the ballot box, voted with their feet; by 1971, 170,000 had fled the country, many of them highly trained technicians and professionals. The Husák regime was willing to accept such a brain drain if it meant the removal of hostile or obstreperous elements. When in May 1971 the XVIIth Congress of the Czechoslovak Communist Party convened, Husák felt justified in announcing that normalization had been completed and that the party's chief task now was to consolidate its gains. Gains were manifested not in higher productivity or more broad-based education but in a more ready submission to political dictation. In the November elections, in which only the party's own selected candidates were allowed to run, with reportedly 95 percent of voters casting ballots, these candidates received 99 percent of the vote.

Deep disaffection with the regime in the next few years was somehow mitigated by the fact that the performance of the economy proved equal to the growing needs of the nation, and this despite rigid central planning and a rather lenient attitude toward work discipline, which tended to be lax. However, this stemmed from reaping the benefits of a strong industrial base inherited from earlier times rather than from a continuous upgrading of the means of production. By the mid-1970s obsolescence began to take its toll. Stagnation, then recession, set in. The government tried to mitigate its effects by encouraging consumerism and by closing its eyes to a growing black market, but such tolerance could go only so far. The oil crisis following the Arab-Israeli war of 1973, which led to a precipitate increase in the world price of petroleum, caused a further decline in productivity. Gradually all the easily attainable measures for increasing production proved inadequate substitutes for thoroughly modernizing the infrastructure; for such modernizing the necessary capital and international goodwill were lacking.

In 1975 a popular but politically suspect playwright, Václav Havel, made the first wave on the tranquil waters when on April 8 he published an "Open Letter to Gustav Husák," pointing out the many deleterious effects of "normalization." Husák chose to ignore the letter, but a breach had been inflicted in the party's solid ideological front. Three weeks later, as if in defiance of any challenge to his authority, Husák added the largely ceremonial post of president of the republic to his title of party chief.

Even in a system of political and intellectual intolerance the fiction that Czechoslovakia respected the fundamentals of human and civil rights had to be maintained. In August the government added its signature to the so-called Helsinki Final Act, passed by a Conference on Security and Cooperation in Europe. The human rights covenant of the Final Act consequently became incorporated in the law system of the republic, and while the government may have taken a cynical attitude toward it, it became vulnerable to future demands for accounting once political oppression eased.

Such a demand was in effect voiced when, early in January 1977, several West German newspapers published a manifesto composed by Czechoslovak intellectuals under the title *Charter 77*. Its original version had reportedly been signed by 243 persons, most of them prominent in the arts, literature, and the political sphere. The collective authorship referred to itself as "a loose, informal, and open community of people," devoted to the protection of human rights. It saw its task as calling attention to individual violations of such rights and suggesting remedies. More signatures, by prominent as well as unknown citizens, were added, and although the number remained relatively low (about 800 by the end of the year), in the general atmosphere of repression every signature amounted to a courageous defiance of the regime. (Many of the signatories were subsequently interrogated, punished, or deprived of their jobs.)

The wisest course of action for the government to take would have been to ignore the charter and consign it to oblivion. But it is the principal weakness of a totalitarian system that it cannot afford to close its eyes to any initiative not originating with it. Far from ignoring it, the Husák government gave it the widest possible exposure by furiously denouncing it, releasing "anti-Charters" and collecting signatures to them, and instructing the press to denounce or hold up to ridicule a document that demanded nothing more than what the government had formally committed itself to undertake.

Fifteen months after issuing *Charter 77*, some of its authors formed a group devoted to a more concrete task. The Committee for the Defense of the Unjustly Persecuted set itself the goal of examining some individual criminal cases (almost always of a political character) that resulted in miscarriages of justice and seeking to advise current defendants against whom the government's case rested on false or insufficient evidence.

By now the Prague government had been deprived of the palliative effect of a humming productive economy; shortages occurred ever more frequently and foreign competition posed a challenge to the backward state of the Czech economy. In 1980 the government was for the first time forced to acknowledge negative growth in the gross national product, blaming it largely on the low technological level of industries. The day was rapidly approaching when the government would have nothing left on the credit side to justify its blind oppression of freedom of conscience, economic liberty, and cultural expression. Police power would then be the only means to keep a discredited regime in power.

The coming of that day was hastened when, in 1985, after the death in Moscow of the last Stalinist secretary-general of the CPSU, Konstantine Chernenko, a relatively young party man brought to maturity in a different political climate, Mikhail Gorbachev, assumed that position. Perhaps naively, Gorbachev believed that communism as an economic and social system had enough staying power to sustain itself without consistently deceptive propaganda and without police oppression. He advocated *perestroika*, an economic restructuring which proposed to ignore many narrow socialist prescriptions, and *glasnost*, or openness, about the problems that kept socialist countries in a permanent state of instability and economic stagnation.

In Czechoslovakia these proposals had the same effect as had Khrushchev's denunciations of Stalinist methods and the cult of personality; the leaders looked at themselves and saw their own mistakes being pilloried. Nevertheless when the XVIIth Congress of the Czechoslovak Communist Party met between March 24 and 28 in 1986, it dutifully adopted *perestroika* as an operating principle, and it pledged reform in the social and economic fields, without, however, providing specifics as to its nature. That reforms were necessary was beyond question, but the problem was not only how they were to be achieved but how to explain to a discontented public that a fundamentally strong economy had been allowed to go downhill for so long just so that certain hard-core principles dating from a bygone era would be upheld. The Husák regime had no effective means of dealing with this dual task; it was by now adept only at repression.

Hopes of reformers were cautiously raised when Gorbachev visited Prague in April 1989, but his boldest pronouncement turned out to be the admission that the Communist Party had "no monopoly on the truth," a fact that was by now clear to everybody though it had not previously been pronounced from official lips.

Three months later the Soviet leader took a great step forward, when in a speech delivered in Strasbourg on July 6 he declared in defiance of the Brezhnev Doctrine that all nations had the right to change their social system free of outside interference. The statement, in essence, gave a green light to oppositionist forces in the Soviet orbit.

The process of disintegration that threatens every system lacking the means to reform itself accelerated. During 1988, in Czechoslovakia, a religious revival, as political as it was spiritual in content, occurred in several parts of the republic.

After some 600,000 signatures had been appended to a petition demanding religious freedom, pro-Catholic demonstrations were held in Prague and Bratislava, and in September some 60,000 participated in a religious pilgrimage to a holy site in western Slovakia. The 20th anniversary of the Warsaw Pact invasion in August had drawn some 6,000 demonstrators to St. Wenceslas Square in Prague.

On October 15 a loose conglomeration of civil rights clubs and movements came together in founding the Movement for Civil Liberties. Its unifying feature was the rejection of the leading role of the Communist Party in public and political affairs, and its slogan was "Democracy for All."

Like wildfires in a desiccated landscape, protest demonstrations sprang up almost daily, and the recurrent theme was a demand for the release of political prisoners and for freedom of expression, association, and the press.

The opening act of what came to be called the Velvet Revolution was played out on November 17, 1989. A peaceful demonstration by thousands of students commemorating the closing of Czech universities by the Nazis in 1939 was brutally broken up by riot police when it acquired more immediate political overtones, and a number of students were seriously wounded. Out of the disorders emerged a fusion of the *Charter 77* movement and a variety of pro-democracy groups in an umbrella organization that called itself the Civic

Václav Havel, six months before he became president of Czechoslovakia (Hulton/Archive)

Forum. Its leader was the same playwright who had been one of the original signers of *Charter 77,* Václav Havel. Refusing to call itself a party to avoid the odium that had come to be attached to that designation in the past decades, and lacking any formal organization, the Civic Forum soon gained the loyalty of millions of Czechs; a Slovak counterpart called Public against Violence, under one Vladimir Meciar, also attracted large numbers.

The Communist Party of Czechoslovakia was by now a mere shadow of itself. It had failed both in inspiring confidence in its political agenda and in finding answers to the country's multiplying ills. In December President Husák and party chief Jakeš resigned simultaneously; on the 29th Václav Havel was elected president of Czechoslovakia. In the new cabinet Communists were now a small minority.

The first free elections since 1946 were held in June 1990 without controversy or disruption. More than 95 percent of those entitled to vote cast ballots and the Civic Forum in the Czech lands and the Public against Violence in Slovakia swept to landslide victories. The electoral triumph, however, was due not to a comprehensive and viable program that these parties presented to the electorate; it was a protest vote amounting to a wholesale rejection of communism in political life. Much of the latter half of 1990 passed in a spirit of sober recognition of the fact that the overthrow of Communist Party rule did not in itself assure effective government. In parliament political "clubs" began to emerge, each with its own agenda. The one that attracted most of the political forces was the Civic Democratic Party headed by a former prime minister, Václav Klaus.

Given the increasingly sluggish performance of the Czechoslovak economy in the past decade, working to achieve an increase in the living standard should have been the first priority of the new coalition government, but the most urgent issue that waited to be addressed was Slovak separatism. In the first republic the bond that held the disparate parts of the state together was assumedly Slavic solidarity, with non-Slavic minorities pacified by receiving broad democratic freedoms. In the second republic marxism with its supranationalist platform was the presumptive bond. The latter failed as thoroughly as had the first one. No ready explanation can be given for Czechs and Slovaks finding it so problematic to form one nation and to acknowledge their economic interdependence by political unity. The backward status of the Slovaks had been a vitiating factor in the first republic and Czech monopoly of leading state positions had bred much resentment. The disparity had largely disappeared during the second republic. The Communists certainly made more earnest efforts to groom the Slovaks for equal status than the Masaryk-Beneš regime had in the 1920s and 1930s. Although Slovak nationalist aspirations had at times been condemned as manifestations of bourgeois nationalism, such persecutions constituted part of a much broader pattern of political intolerance that searched for and found enemies in every corner. The most popular groundbreaking politician in the second republic, Alexander Dubček, was a Slovak, and so was his successor as party chief, and later as president of the republic, Gustáv Husák. Czechs and Slovaks had found common ground in the struggle against Communist monopoly of power, especially in the 1980s, but once the totalitarian government collapsed and the new coalition government began to turn its attention to the practical problems confronting the nation, the cleavage between the two nationalities opened up again. During 1991 and 1992 the effective functioning of a central federal government was increasingly complicated by Slovak insistence, at every level, on dealing separately with the problems at hand. The split became more evident in the June 1992 elections, in which Václav Klaus's Civil Democratic Party campaigned on a platform of economic reform and Meciar's Movement for Democratic Slovakia, which garnered most of the votes in the province, on a platform of Slovak autonomy. President Václav Havel, and others devoted to federalism, tried their level best to heal the fissure, but the movement for Slovak separatism had gone too far. Realizing the futility of his efforts, Havel resigned as president in July, though Klaus, also a federalist, continued as premier. During the rest of 1992 Klaus worked hand in hand with Meciar in hammering out an agreement for a formula by which the Czech lands and Slovakia would become different political entities. The separation had to be enacted by the federal parliament and that body had by now effectively divided into a Czech and a Slovak faction; the one question on which the two could agree was the need to break up the republic. A law to this effect was passed on December 27, 1992. Effective January 1, 1993, Czechoslovakia was divided into its western portion, now called the Czech Republic, and its eastern portion named Slovakia. A three-quarters century long experiment in Slavic solidarity in the center of Europe had come to an end.

Despite the fall of communism in 1989, the Communist Party fared well in the Czech Republic's most recent parliamentary elections, held in June 2002. The Social Democratic Party won 30 percent of the vote, however, and Vladimír Spidla was appointed prime minister. Václav Havel served as president from 1993 to 2003. He was succeeded by Václav Klaus. The Czech Republic has been a member of NATO since 1999, with membership in the European Union on the nation's agenda.

YUGOSLAVIA

CHAPTER ONE

Nation-making is one of the most arduous and historically significant tasks that any leader or group of people can undertake. Each component of the would-be nation has its own ends in sight, its own values to protect, its own traditions to preserve, its own fears of being submerged in a larger unfamiliar entity to overcome. For decades after the unification, or longer, differences and apprehensions continue, and, unless the common bond is strong and comprehensive, they may never be resolved.

The formation of Yugoslavia in 1918 was an instructive example. Tradition, the most powerful force, did not support the ideal of South Slav unity. Although the several nationalities in the Balkans had for centuries lived under Ottoman rule, each had maintained its distinct character, determined by language, religion, and, in part, by geography. The South Slav, or Yugo-Slav movement, an offshoot of the Pan-Slavic idea championed by Russia, did not make its appearance until the 1860s, and even then it was more the invention of a fervent idealist, the Croatian bishop (of German background) Strossmaier, than an authentic grassroots movement. The bishop's exhortations produced echoes in Serbia, especially among the gradually emerging middle class, and in Dalmatia, a Slavic province that had been assigned to Austria by the Congress of Vienna. As the unification process gathered strength, the leading role fell to the Serbs, mainly because they had been the first to secure for themselves a measure of autonomy under Turkish suzerainty (as the result of the 1804–13 uprising led by George Petrović, popularly called Kara George, and in 1815 as a result of another revolt under Miloš Obrenović). Over half a century passed, however, before Serbia, pursuant to the dispositions of the Congress of Berlin in 1878, achieved complete independence. In 1882, under the Obrenović dynasty, thanks to Austrian magnanimity, the rank of the ruler was elevated from prince to king. However, a majority of the Serbs continued to live under foreign rule, some in the Habsburg, others in the Ottoman Empire.

The first concrete step toward South Slav unity was taken in 1905 by two Dalmatian Croats, Franjo Supilo and Ante Trumbić. At a congress of Serbs and Croats in Fiume, these two men initiated a loose Serbo-Croatian coalition, which, at that point, was little more than a gathering of like-minded individuals with no hint that they envisioned an eventual independent Yugoslav state. The political goal of the coalition was "trialism," the transformation of the Austro-Hungarian Dual Monarchy into a state in which the Slavs enjoyed equal rights with Germans and Hungarians. In subsequent years Hungarian opposition rendered the prospect less and less promising, and Serbo-Croat militancy increased. Even so, the aspiration for separate statehood was confined to the Serbs; in Croatia, as far as it gained a focus at all, it aimed for autonomous status within the Dual Monarchy. Croats spoke the same language as the Serbs, but they were Catholic, (whereas the Serbs were Greek Orthodox) and the native Catholic establishment, the Vatican, as well as a good part of the intelligentsia, opposed a political union with the Serbs, whom they regarded as backward and culturally inferior.

This arrogant perception was by no means general; the great majority of Croats were peasants, and the cleavage between them and the educated and religiously devout Croatian middle class, which the peasants thought of as the *gospoda,* the ruling class, was wide and deep. It was the peasant class that, in the early years of the 20th century, produced two able rulers, the brothers Ante and Stjepan Radić; the former, while unassuming, possessed a sound political sense, whereas Stjepan's forceful personality was put in the service of a somewhat muddled political program of vaguely socialist ideas combined with an incongruous insistence on the sanctity of private landownership. The latter's political goal was the formation of a Croatian republic in which the peasantry would hold the dominant position and which would carry out a thorough land reform. Hence Croat commitment to the larger South Slav ideal was hedged with many qualifications. Croats did refer to Serbs as brothers and they spoke with pride of their own Slavic ethnicity, but union with the Serbs was not an item on their political agenda.

The Great War proved a catalyst. The final collapse of the Ottoman Empire quickened the momentum for the creation of a Slavic state that, by dint of its size and population, would be a power factor in the Balkans. During the war the active agent of the drive was the so-called Yugoslav Council sitting abroad, composed mainly of politicians who after the outbreak of the war had emigrated from the Dual Monarchy. Besides its comprehensive project, the council had a narrower concern as well. The London Treaty of April 1915, by the terms of which Italy entered the war on the Entente side, promised her extensive territorial rewards, including the entire Dalmatian coast; thus, even before its formation, the Yugoslav state faced the prospect of competition with Italy over lands populated by Slavs. When after the end of the war the peace conference assembled in Paris, Italy was a member of the Big Four charged with working out the particulars of the peace treaties.

There was also the fact that the Yugoslav Council, the majority of which was made up of Croatians, did not speak unequivocally for all South Slavs. A number of emerging statesmen retained, if only for sentimental reasons, loyalty to the Habsburg Empire; even as that empire crumbled, they leaned toward a trialistic solution. As late as May 1917 the South Slav deputies in the Austrian parliament declared themselves in favor of an autonomous position for South Slavs *within* the Dual Monarchy. By the middle of the next year, however, any formula that reckoned with the survival of the monarchy had been overtaken by events. In October 1918 even the Slovenes of Austria joined the budding plan for creating a separate state in the south. A formal agreement to that effect

Provisional National Assembly was composed of members drawn from the assemblies of those states. All governmental units dating back to the Dual Monarchy were dissolved as were military formations of mixed ethnic composition; the only army of the new state was the Serbian, and at this stage officers from former units of the Dual Monarchy were not allowed employment in it. As to territorial integrity, there was no assurance that the arrangements made unilaterally by the government would be allowed to stand without challenge; they did not as yet have international recognition. Furthermore, for the state to have a legal foundation, a special assembly had to be called to draw up a constitution.

International recognition proceeded fairly smoothly; on February 10, 1919, Washington, on June 1 London, and on June 6 Paris accorded full diplomatic status to the new state. These governments were not as generous however in honoring the far-reaching territorial claims as the Serbs had hoped they would be. By virtue of Serbia's belligerent status on the Entente side, Yugoslavia was now counted among the victors. However, so were Romania and Italy, and both had their own claims that the great powers could not ignore. The drawing of the final borders involved a great deal of acrimony and delay, and not until the conclusion of the peace treaties with Bulgaria and Hungary, the latter as late as June 1920, did the Kingdom of the Serbs, Croats, and Slovenes acquire its definitive territorial shape. The central core remained unchanged, but in the west, after all the bargains and dispositions had been made, Italy had acquired Trieste, the Istrian Peninsula, the Kvarner Islands, and Zara, as well as the southwestern strip of Slovenia. The port city of Fiume had been a bone of bitter contention during the Paris peace conference. At Wilson's insistence it was given to the new kingdom, but in September 1919 units of an Italian free corps seized it. In the final settlement it was made a free city. (In 1924 it was annexed to Italy.) In the east, both the Yugoslav state and Romania wanted all of the Bánát; in the end Romania received the larger, eastern, part of it. In the north, Yugoslav troops had waged irregular warfare for the possession of northern Carinthia, claiming that its German majority was the result of the forced Germanization of the population under Austrian rule. In the end a plebiscite, ordered by the Entente, produced a great pro-Austrian majority. As to the northern Croatian border, it was finalized in the Treaty of Trianon with Hungary: the Yugoslav state was awarded the broad strip between the Drava and Sava Rivers, and additional territories along the Mura River. Territories in southern Hungary, however, including cities such as Baja, Pécs, and Baranya that South Slav troops held under military occupation, had to be evacuated. By terms of the Treaty of Neuilly with Bulgaria, the Yugoslav state once again received the part of Macedonia that Serbia had gained in the Second Balkan War in 1913, and in addition a strip of land of Bulgarian habitation to secure the Niš-Saloniki railroad. The greatest disappointment for the new government was the denial of the right to occupy northern Albania, which would have provided an outlet to the Adriatic. In its final extension, the United Kingdom of Serbs, Croats, and Slovenes occupied a territory of 247,000 square kilometers and had a very mixed population of 12 million inhabitants, roughly fivefold larger in size and fourfold in population than the Serbia of 1912.

Parliamentary government required political parties, and it was with the formation of these that the highly complex, not to say makeshift, character of the new state was revealed. There were three general groupings: the Greater Serb parties professing a centralist platform, of which the Radical Party and the Democratic Party were the most important; the second was the bloc forming around the Croatian Agrarian Party, with a federalist program, definitely opposed to a government with strong central powers; the third and least robust grouping, although also federalist, eschewed an oppositionist program and sought accommodation with the Greater Serb parties. It was made up of the Slovenian National Party and the Yugoslav Muslim Organization.

The largest and strongest party, officially called National Radical Party, now headed by Nikola Pašić, the man who, as premier in 1914, had led Serbia into war, had originally been a peasant party; by now it had become the party of choice of the middle class (while it continued to attract the bulk of the peasant vote) and adopted a strong nationalistic character. A dissident group with milder Greater Serbian convictions had split off from it and, together with Serbs living in Croatia, had formed the Democratic Party, the second-largest party in Serbia. This party too, like the Radicals, favored a central government to which the various provinces were subject, though it showed greater tolerance for the autonomous endeavors of other nationalities. Somewhat surprisingly, the third largest party represented in the National Assembly was the Communist. There had been a Socialist Party in Serbia before the war, but both because of the absence of an industrial proletariat in whose ranks it could prosper and because in the minds of many it had a German character, it never commanded a large following. Its leaders, as almost everywhere, were restless intellectuals; however, in Serbia, unlike elsewhere, the great majority of the membership was made up of peasants. The revolution engendered by the Bolsheviks in Russia had made a deep impact, though more because it was Russian than because it was socialist. All over Europe a split occurred in the labor movement, creating a moderate Social Democratic and a radical Communistic faction; the Serbian party chose the latter course. Deplorable economic conditions fed the discontent, which in turn tended to radicalize the labor movement. In the 1921 elections the Communist Party won 54 seats in the National Assembly. Strongest in Serbia, it also garnered a substantial number of votes in Bosnia and the Vojvodina. But in the summer of 1921 a young Communist assassinated the minister of the interior, and this gave the government the pretext to suppress the party. Communist delegates in the assembly were deprived of their mandates, the party newspaper was banned, and sympathizers became subject to political and judicial persecution. There still remained the small Social Democratic Party, from which the Communists had split off, but it never achieved political importance.

The elections of 1921 also produced a surprisingly large vote for the Croatian Peasant Party under Stjepan Radić. In the Dual Monarchy, where the franchise had been restricted, the peasant masses of Croatia had never been given a chance to make an impact on the political scene. Now theirs was by far the largest party. Its significance was increased by the influence on the membership exerted by its leader, Stjepan Radić. When back in November 1918 the Yugoslav National Council announced the union of Serbia and Croatia, Radić had cast the only negative vote. It had scarcely mattered then, but now he was in effect the political head of Croatia. A peasant himself, men of the soil were the only ones he really trusted, and he seemed to have in mind a peasant brotherhood of the type Marx had envisioned for industrial workers. His political ideal was a republic dominated by agrarians, and he had little faith in or hope for the ruling monarchy. With a clearer purpose and a less antagonistic political style he may have become a serious threat to the kingdom, or at least to its unity. But oppositionism was his hallmark as a reformer and, even had he listened to the calmer counsel of his brother Ante, he could not control his temperament. One of his key decisions after the elections was to withdraw his party from parliamentary participation on the premise that its absence would make a stronger political statement than would active opposition or even practicing obstructionism.

In any case, the conflict between centralism, as represented most forcefully by Nikola Pašić, and federalism, promoted by Radić, transcended personalities. In the end Pašić and his supporters from a wide political spectrum carried the day. The so-called Vidovdan constitution of 1921 (so named because it was proclaimed on St. Vitus' Day, a Serbian national holiday, which happened also to be the day of the year on which Francis Ferdinand was assassinated) provided for a centralized government. The king was given almost exclusive powers over the army, with a restriction that the army must be kept out of politics. He was to name the premier from the largest party in parliament. The parliament was unicameral, to be elected every four years by direct, secret, and general vote of the adult male population. There was also a provision for complete religious freedom.

The weakness of the constitution, as it turned out, was not that in many of its articles it lacked specificity or that the congeries of nations it sought to unite was too diverse (of the nearly 12 million citizens 9 million were identified as Serbo-Croatian, a highly dubious identification), but that there was no moral consensus for making it work. The excitements of the war had generated passions for South Slav unity, but, with the war over, passions had cooled and differences began to reveal themselves in discouraging proportions.

CHAPTER TWO

The first parliamentary elections after the promulgation of the constitution, held in March 1923, did not produce major surprises; in Serbia the Radical Party gained an overwhelming victory while in Croatia Radić's Peasant Party emerged as the great winner. The former had 108 seats of a total of somewhat over 300 in parliament and the latter 70, but Radić continued his boycott of legislative sessions for another year. In July 1924 Pašić resigned as premier and his place was taken by a Democrat, Ljuba Davidović, a former schoolmaster; he won the trust of the Croatian Peasant Party, which now decided to take its seats in parliament. However, Davidović's cabinet lasted only a short time, and in October Pašić once again assumed the premiership. He immediately proceeded against the Agrarians. Davidović had amnestied Radić, who had been banned from political participation for his boycott. However, the Peasant Party leader had made the mistake of visiting several foreign capitals seeking support, among them Moscow and, on the basis of the anticommunist law of 1921, Pašić accused Radić of association with the Comintern and declared his party illegal.

Repression did not bring civil peace, however. The centralist program of the government could silence opposition in the lawmaking chambers but not in the streets. Pašić hoped to hasten the collapse of the Croatian Peasant opposition by holding new elections ahead of schedule, in February 1925. The Peasant Party, being outside the law, could not seat its delegates in parliament, but it was still allowed to participate in the elections, probably in order that its electoral strength could be assessed. The results were sobering: the majority of the ruling Radical Party in parliament shrank to a low of 163 against 152 opposing delegates. The Peasant Party received 67 mandates; of those Pašić on dubious grounds invalidated 58, thus precipitating a new round of protests. At this point the king intervened. He hoped to achieve a measure of political consensus by appeasing Radić, and toward this end prevailed on Pašić to form a partnership with the party he had thus far persecuted. Radić, who for his part hoped that working within the system would enable him to transform it in his own party's image, and also that many representatives in parliament who stemmed from peasant roots would in time be attracted to the Agrarians, agreed publicly to renounce his republican aspirations. On March 27, 1925, he formally accepted the Vidovdan constitution. The second-largest party in the kingdom thus passed from illegality to respectability and was given four portfolios in the cabinet. Peace seemed at hand and when, in August, the king visited Zagreb to help celebrate the 1,000th anniversary of the founding of Croatia, he was enthusiastically received.

As is the case with coalitions that rest on nothing but expediency, the Radical-Peasant alliance did not last long. As a member of the ruling coalition, Radić could scarcely work to undermine it, but he and Pašić never had the personal relationship that would have made their cooperation free of friction. In April 1926 Radić quit the government; within two weeks, Pašić resigned when he learned that his son was a major figure in a corruption scandal. He died shortly afterward. The short-lived coalition between the Serbian-based Radicals and the Croatian-based Peasant Party came to an end. The new alignments, between the Radicals, who had a permanent majority of varying size in parliament and were the government party, and other parties and splinter groups represented in the legislature are too complex and confusing to recount here. The departure of Pašić left a vacuum that no other politician could fill. It was in any case doubtful that even if another man of his stature and prestige had emerged he would have been able to find the middle ground necessary for compromises. More and more political forces tended to the extremes.

In the elections of September 1927 the government coalition garnered 218 parliamentary mandates out of a total of 315, but by now parliamentary majorities counted for little amid the farrago of political, ethnic, and religious affiliations. An outrage committed in June 1928 by a Montenegrin delegate, a member of the Radical Party in parliament, further compromised the political situation and indirectly led to the liquidation of democracy. On the 20th, during a meeting of parliament, he rose from his seat and shot five members of the Peasant Party, including Radić, who had insulted him the day before. Two of the five died on the spot; Radić was seriously wounded, and then seemed on the way to recovery when, on August 8, he too succumbed. The Peasant Party suspected a Radical plot behind the assassinations and turned against the government. Throughout the rest of the year there was a series of disorders and demonstrations in Zagreb and elsewhere among Croatians; repeatedly the military had to be called out, but peace was restored only temporarily.

During these months the question that had been critical even before the formation of the Yugoslav state,—whether it should be a voluntary conglomeration of South Slavs of diverse traditions and religions, with only an overarching ideology uniting it, or a Greater Serbia in which the smaller components accepted the cultural and political leadership of the Serbs (as the many individual ethnic groups in the Russian Empire had accepted the leading role of the Russians)—again surfaced. The South Slav ideal, such as it was, had had a certain attraction under the Habsburg Monarchy when Slavic soldiers and subjects had to obey commands in German or Hungarian, and when Pan-Slavist agitators preached to the Greek Orthodox that their western masters were forfeiting salvation with their materialism and arid rationalism. However, once the South Slavs had a state of their own, the divisive rather than the unifying features became conspicuous. The conflict between Serbians and Croatians in particular is usually ascribed to the religious differences (Serbian Greek Orthodox and Croatian Catholic), to a cultural divide (the Croatians having benefited from their continuous ties with the papacy and the West while the Serbians had been largely isolated from the cultural mainstream of Europe) but it should be noted that the Balkans, and in fact the whole region up to the Baltic Sea, had always been one of chronic instability, which only the weight of Russian, Austrian, and Turkish power had kept in check. The breakup of those empires had left a vacuum that the so-called successor states, hastily patched together after the Great War, by their very fragmentation made more gaping. This in part explains the Serbian insistence on a unitary state under a dynasty of some prestige and tradition, which alone could serve as a bond. That unity had to be abandoned in favor of the Serbo-Croat-Slovene coalition, which, in turn, had produced not stability but an almost permanent political rift. Radić's place as head of the Croatian Peasant Party was taken by one Vlasko Maček, who engineered an ephemeral coalition with Pribičević's splinter party of Independent Democrats; together they revived the idea of a federal Yugoslav state in which only foreign, defense, and financial affairs would be centrally administered, each federal province would have its own military, and the king would serve merely as a symbolic head of state. It would be in his person that South Slav unity, the ideological bond of the state, would be embodied. This formula, as in 1918, was unacceptable to Alexander. He briefly considered shedding Croatia as a constituent unit of his kingdom, allowing it to be independent on territory of purely Croat habitation, expectably of minuscule proportions. The plan never entered its realization phase. Left to its own devices, Croatia would have been easy prey for Italy, still unhappy over her exclusion from the Balkans in the peace settlement. But Alexander also realized that the pressure from Croatia was not compelling and that the province could conveniently be integrated into a Greater Serbia, which he had by now decided to create. In full command of the military, on January 6, 1929, the king suspended the constitution, dissolved the National Assembly, introduced censorship, placed political parties outside the law, and announced a royal dictatorship. His choice to head the government was General Petar Živković, and it was the latter who proclaimed the new fundamental law, by which the king was the sole source of power in the land. Legislatures not only on the national but on the provincial and even local levels were declared defunct and mayors were replaced by persons named by and responsible to the military.

After a decade of continuous political turmoil, the change was greeted with relief rather than distress. The name of the state was changed from the United Kingdom of Serbs, Croats, and Slovenes to the Kingdom of Yugoslavia. The traditional borders among the several provinces were erased and the kingdom was divided into nine districts (with Belgrade forming a separate administrative unit); the lines of demarcation were so drawn as to pay minimum attention to the ethnic character of the units. The hope no doubt was that with local and provincial loyalties dissolving, a Yugoslav sense of nationality would at last develop. Everywhere the principle of Serbian domination prevailed. In six of the nine districts Serbs formed the majority; in Belgrade their majority was absolute. The civil service was also heavily Serbian, although Alexander made sincere efforts at involving minorities in government. To the extent that he succeeded, it did little to appease the disappointment of the minorities with their unconcealed subordination.

In September 1931 Alexander issued a new constitution, one that did not even pretend to stem from the will of anyone but its author. Parliament would henceforth have two houses; one half of the membership of the upper would be appointed by the king, the other half to be chosen by administrative bodies of the newly constituted districts. The lower house was elected directly by the voters but voting was done in the open. In the prior system the cabinet was responsible to the legislature; under the new constitution, it answered solely to the king. None of the enactments of parliament were valid unless the king approved them. Political parties were tolerated but only if they did not have an ethnic or religious character. Whichever party secured a plurality of the votes received two-thirds of the seats in parliament. This provision guaranteed the practical rule of the government party, the Serbian Radical (it was soon renamed the Yugoslav National Party). In the elections held in November 1931, boycotted by a number of parties and registering a very low turnout, this government party won all the 306 seats in parliament.

Serbians were now masters of the kingdom, but even their own civil and political rights were severely restricted. As Alexander had not, until this time, displayed a tyrannical temperament, he would most likely have on his own eased the strictures of his constitution had the economic downturn not threatened further unrest. The Great Depression arrived late in Yugoslavia, but it arrived, and by 1933 the gross national product was one-half of what it had been in 1927. Political dissent increased, most vocally, according to expectations, from the Croatian Peasant Party. In November 1932 its leaders drew up the so-called Zagreb Articles, sternly criticizing the royal dictatorship; the Slovenians joined in the protest in December, demanding autonomy for their province. The unrest soon spread to Serbia itself and several groups demanded the restoration of constitutional forms. The government responded with repression, arrests, and trials for treason. A number of oppositionist politicians were forced to emigrate. Soon the very men who had played a leading role in making a separate Yugoslav state a reality found themselves in prison or in exile.

The foreign policy of the state moved in two complementary directions. In the narrower sphere Yugoslavia became a member of that awkward and on the whole ineffective alliance called the Little Entente; she had bilateral agreements with Czechoslovakia and with Romania, for the dual purpose of resisting Hungarian territorial revision and to prevent the restoration of the House of Habsburg. The Little Entente, mainly at the initiative of Czechoslovak foreign minister Edvard Beneš, developed an elaborate consultation system and secretariat, but in time fell victim to Hitler's territorial reordering and passed out of existence. In the broader sphere Yugoslavia became a part of the French security system in eastern Europe. In November 1927 the two countries concluded an agreement providing for consultation in case a third power threatened their external security or sought to alter the status quo by force. In any such case the two states would immediately consult about joint steps to take "within the framework of the Covenant of the League of Nations."

With the rise of Hitler in Germany the French alliance became of special importance to Yugoslavia. It was partly due to this, as well as to growing apprehension about Italian designs, especially on Croatia, that Alexander undertook a state visit to France in October 1934. By this time, with Italian backing, a Croatian Revolutionary Union (popularly known as the Ustaša) had been organized, and it periodically cooperated with another revolutionary group based in Macedonia, the VMRO. Upon arriving in Marseilles Alexander, together with French foreign minister Louis Barthou, was shot and killed by VMRO assassins acting on behalf of the Ustaša. The latter, as far as the motives of political terrorists can be ascertained, aimed at the disintegration of the Yugoslav state and the emergence of an independent Croatia and possibly also of Macedonia.

However, the impetus for such independence lacked wide popular backing. The transition at the top in Belgrade was smooth enough; the dead king was succeeded by his 11-year-old son Peter, though of course actual governing was in the hands of a regency, headed by Alexander's cousin, Prince Paul. Paul raised himself above the political passions of the day and soberly faced the task of governing the troubled kingdom, on the one hand refraining from major constitutional changes and on the other mitigating those features of the present system that had given rise to so much unrest. To demonstrate goodwill, a number of political prisoners were amnestied and police powers were curtailed. However, elections were still manipulated and political freedom was kept within narrow limits. In the May 1935 elections the United Opposition representing no coherent bloc but running against the government party with a hodgepodge program,

The assassination of King Alexander I of Yugoslavia and the French Foreign Minister Jean-Louis Barthou in Marseilles. The assassin Petrus Kaleman, a Croat separatist, is being apprehended by Colonel Poillet, an outrider in horseback, and by the chauffeur of the royal car. He was later lynched by the furious crowd. *(Hulton/Archive)*

received nearly 40 percent of the vote, but still took only 67 of the 301 seats in parliament, with the Yugoslav National Party taking the rest.

In June a Radical politician, and one who had had serious reservations about the introduction of royal dictatorship, Milan Stojadinović, was named head of the government. In part because of his moderate views, but more likely because of a general weariness with political conflicts, his three-and-a-half-year-long tenure was relatively free of friction. It was not free, however, of political manipulation. The democratic ideal, which President Wilson had hoped would prevail over adversarial strivings, never gained ground in this part of Europe. On the contrary, the conviction was growing that stability and peace on the political and the labor fronts could be achieved only by authoritarian methods. Mussolini's fascist government, which for over a decade had stood the test of time, served as a model for leaders who were unable to establish domestic peace through compromise. In Austria Engelbert Dollfuss, in Hungary Gyula Gömbös, and most persuasively in Germany Adolf Hitler imposed a disciplined social order by eliminating all opposition and silencing labor unrest. Stojadinović also chose this path. He replaced the Yugoslav National Party with the Yugoslav National Community, essentially the old Radical Party, fortified with the Bosnian Muslim Party and the Slovenian National Party. Attempts to draw the Croatian Peasant Party too into the coalition failed because of the continued separatist ambition of the Croatians. The ultimate goal of Stojadinović was of course to become the Yugoslav Duce, to make himself the single political figure of consequence in the state, but his efforts in this direction never got far. Apart from other reasons (e.g., the resolute opposition of the regency council) Yugoslavia lacked the ethnic homogeneity that made the introduction of a dictatorship, as in Italy, Germany, Austria, and elsewhere, possible. An example was the conclusion, in July 1935, of a concordat with the Vatican aimed at defining the legal status of Catholics in Yugoslavia. By its terms Catholics and their church were to enjoy equal status with the Greek Orthodox to which the great majority of Serbians belonged. The agreement produced immediate opposition among the Orthodox—they realized that the Vatican would ensure for the Catholics an international sanction and protection that the Orthodox did not enjoy—in due time the concordat was declared invalid in the eastern half of the state. In unity is strength and in disunity weakness; given the growing tensions in Europe, many of them centering on efforts to revise the peace treaties, Yugoslavia sorely needed a political consensus to reflect a commanding strength. The *Anschluss* of 1938 made the country a neighbor of Nazi Germany; Mussolini's Italy was registering her own claims in the Balkans. The Croatian Ustaša, still seeking separation from Yugoslavia, had strong support from Italy and many of its emigrant politicians lobbied for a separate Croatian state. A national consensus, far from solidifying, was growing more tenuous every day. The Serbian-Croatian conflict entered a new phase and it became increasingly evident that on its resolution depended the future of Yugoslavia.

CHAPTER THREE

With each passing year Yugoslavia became more divided against itself, and as the war crisis deepened the question arose whether its stresses would divide it further or bring the hostile component parts closer together. The Croats demanded autonomy, but what they really wanted was independence, though every thinking person, including the new head of the Peasant Party, Vlasko Maček, realized the precariousness of such a claim in a world where even states with a long tradition of independence, which Croatia certainly could not claim, trembled for their very survival. As for the larger Yugoslav state, it was viable only if Croatia was appeased and pacified. Prince Regent Paul valiantly struggled with the dilemma. Elections in December 1938 did produce a majority for the government party, but a greatly reduced one, and although by the electoral law in effect the party maintained its two-thirds majority in parliament, the election result amounted to a defeat, and in February Stojadinović resigned as premier. His place was taken by a member of his cabinet, Dragiša Cvetković, and Cvetković made the resolution of the impasse with Croatia the principal item on his agenda. Talks began in April, a month after the *Anschluss*, which had served as a warning to Germany's neighbors to put their political houses in order. Four months of tenacious negotiations produced a compromise a mere 10 days before the Second World War broke out. It provided for a thorough territorial reorganization of the state. Croatia would henceforth embrace Slovenia and the larger part of Bosnia-Hercegovina, and as such would form a separate autonomous *banate;* as constituted, of its 4.4 million inhabitants three-fourths were Croatians, the rest Serbs and Muslims. Its legislature, the Sabor, was revived and was given the right to appoint an executive, but the formal appointment was made by the king and all legislative decisions were subject to his approval. There were the traditional "joint" matters, foreign affairs, foreign trade, the military, finances, customs and duties, but Croatia still enjoyed a measure of autonomy, which, in a charitable interpretation, amounted to virtual independence. One problematic feature was the inclusion of the Croatian Peasant Party in the central government; it was positive in that it accorded respectful recognition to a party that had been the chief source of discord since the formation of the kingdom, but also negative in that it made the effective separation of Croatia from the rest of the kingdom illusory. It demanded loyalty to a Serbian-dominated federal government, a loyalty that was hard to reconcile with the assertion that Croatia was genuinely autonomous. Another negative result of the compromise was that other minorities, Slovenes, Muslims,

Albanians, and Macedonians, began to put forth their own demands for autonomy. The situation resembled conditions in the Dual Monarchy after the Great Compromise, when minorities bitterly resented the undisguisedly privileged position of the Germans and Hungarians.

However, such problems appeared progressively more trivial in face of the crisis that engulfed the entire European state structure with the onset of war. For its external security, Yugoslavia had for too long depended, on the one hand, on her French alliance and, on the other, on the Little Entente, both of which with the passage of time proved unreliable supports. The Munich Agreement had removed Czechoslovakia from the Little Entente and rendered that never very sturdy alliance worthless; it also resulted in London and Paris conceding predominance in eastern Europe to the Axis. We have seen that when it came time to implement the addendum to the Munich Agreement, which called for the arbitration of Hungary's claim on what was now Czecho-Slovakia, Britain and France begged off, leaving the decision to Germany and Italy. The pillars of Yugoslav security, never reliable, were thus wholly removed.

The logical foreign policy line to follow would have been accommodation with the Axis—but from that, Belgrade shrank. It was by now, 1940, obvious that an Axis orientation meant almost total submission to Italy or Germany, and that was more dangerous than standing aloof. As a tentative alternative, Belgrade decided on a rapprochement with the Soviet Union, with whom her relations had until now been unsettled to the point of hostility. On June 25, 1940, the two states resumed diplomatic relations. The date was significant: only three days after the surrender of France, an event that made the prospect of Germany turning east real and very dangerous. Warming up to the Soviet Union had the potential of severing the last ties Yugoslavia had to the West (Moscow was, by virtue of the nonaggression pact the year before, aligned with Nazi Germany), and that was another step the Yugoslav government was loath to take. Only Romania in the East European sphere (other than hapless Slovakia) declared herself to be unequivocally in the Axis, or more precisely the German, camp. Yugoslavia, while ostensibly courting Germany, tried to preserve a modicum of good relations with Great Britain, and even with the United States. To demonstrate to those states their standing apart from the Axis, the Yugoslavs on December 12, 1940, concluded an "eternal friendship" and nonaggression pact with Hungary. In Belgrade's calculation, apart from making a good impression on the West, the pact amounted to a friendly gesture toward Germany, which had just helped Hungary acquire the northern slice of Transylvania from Romania and had included Hungary in the Tripartite Pact of Germany, Italy, and Japan. To that latter pact the little states of East Europe hastened to append their signature in the hope of earning merits in Germany's eyes for a postwar territorial reordering.

It is by now a well-worn commonplace that Yugoslavia's involvement in World War II was due not to Hitler's territorial greed but to Mussolini's ill-advised decision to launch an utterly pointless and militarily disastrous attack from recently acquired Albania against Greece. Il Duce had watched for years as his Axis partner gobbled up countries and led his armies to spectacular victories while Italy's only crumb of satisfaction had been the conquest of tiny Albania. He was impatient to prove his own military mettle. Had he advised Hitler of the planned invasion, the latter would surely have dissuaded him. Germany's most essential raw materials, especially oil and nonferrous metals, came from the Balkans and Hitler wanted to keep that peninsula politically neutral and stable; this became even more important after he took the decision to attack the Soviet Union. Any disarray on his southern flank could jeopardize the success of that campaign. The Italian attack on October 28, 1940, came as a complete and most unsettling surprise to Hitler, more unsettling still when the Italian divisions became stymied by the rugged terrain and bad weather. The British took instant advantage of Greece's belligerent status by sending troops and an air squadron, placing them within striking distance of the Romanian oil wells. Within days after their landing, Hitler issued an order for a campaign against Greece to precede the launching of the attack on the Soviet Union. The land approaches to Greece were vital: Bulgaria and Yugoslavia had to be prevailed upon to allow passage of German troops when the attack became timely. Bulgaria agreed without protest; she joined the Tripartite Treaty and became a firm partner of the Axis. Hitler next approached Belgrade, asking for no more than benevolent neutrality. Regent Paul, an Anglophile, and a man not dazzled by the series of German victories, was discomfited by the request; he was firm in his conviction that Germany would in the end lose the war. German pressure mounted, and the Yugoslavs procrastinated. Opposed to joining the Axis, they also realized the dangers of defying it. At last, on March 25, 1941, on condition that no military obligation attached to it, they put their signature to the Three Power Pact.

Their adherence to that infamous compact lasted less than two days. On March 27 the government that had bowed to the German demand was overthrown by a military coup. The motives of the overthrow are still not clear, but the sequence of events is well established. The cabal under the air general Dušan Simović, which now seized power, removed Prince Paul from his regency, declared King Peter of age, and formed a new government. To make the significance of the change more weighty, on April 5 the new government concluded a friendship treaty with the Soviet Union, and at the same time began military conversations with the British.

It did not, however, abrogate the pledge of the previous government to join the Tripartite Pact; in fact, it assured Berlin of its readiness to cooperate. But Hitler knew that the mood in the country, and especially in the military, was violently anti-German; in any case, he brooked no delay in the timetable of Operation Barbarossa. He ordered the inclusion of Yugoslavia in the anti-German front that had to be conquered and occupied. The campaign was prepared with unbelievable swiftness; on April 6, the German attack was unleashed, with dive bombers swooping down on Belgrade and the as yet invincible Wehrmacht invading Yugoslavia from all directions.

Hitler had almost at the last minute found another military ally. The Hungarians, although they had only four months earlier concluded an "eternal friendship" treaty with Belgrade, recalled how in 1918 the newly formed

Yugoslav forces, together with the French, despoiled Hungary's southern provinces; here was the opportunity to recover whatever could be gained with German help. The Hungarian attack did not begin until April 11, the day after Croatia declared its independence; its stated rationale was not the reconquest of lost provinces but that Yugoslavia had ceased to exist and that Hungarians in the Bačka had to be protected.

Yugoslav resistance in face of the concentrated attack lasted only days. Their military units were deployed along the border in clusters, with large gaps between them, and they were untrained in and unprepared for mechanized warfare, which gave the German attack a commanding advantage. Croatian and Slovenian soldiers deserted the Yugoslav army in droves. On April 10, an Ustaša leader, Slavko Kvaternik, in Zagreb, proclaimed an independent Croatia. Two days later Belgrade fell. On the 15th King Peter and the Simović government fled to Greece (from where they eventually found their way to London, a city that, as a century earlier, had become a haven for deposed royalty and displaced politicians).

Defeated Yugoslavia was a country that practically begged to be partitioned. German and Italian conferees met in Vienna between April 20 and 22 to make the dispositions. Eastern Macedonia was awarded to Bulgaria, Hungary got the Bačka and the small triangle at the confluence of the Danube and the Drava Rivers as well as other smaller enclaves. The Yugoslav portion of the Banat, to which both the Hungarians and the Romanians registered a claim, remained under German military governance. Kosovo, enlarged, was joined to Italian Albania; only its northern strip, rich in minerals, remained with Serbia, by now a mere figment of a state under complete German control. Roughly two-thirds of Slovenia was absorbed in the Reich, the rest went to Italy. One-half of Dalmatia became Italian, the rest remained with Croatia. Thus three putatively independent states emerged from the former Yugoslavia: Serbia, its territory corresponding to the pre-1914 Serbian kingdom, Montenegro under Italian auspices, and Croatia, over which Germany and Italy shared supervision.

When Germany launched her war against the Soviet Union, a war that required the commitment of nearly all her battle-worthy divisions, the pacification of the former Yugoslavia became imperative. To facilitate the task, Hitler posed as a benefactor of the Serbians by installing in Belgrade a "government of national renewal," headed by the former minister of defense, Milan Nedić. Like most military men, Nedić was essentially nonpolitical; if he had any ideology, it was that of Greater Serbian nationalism. He hoped to preserve for the duration of the war the diminished Serbia left after the recent defeat, to be augmented by the addition of the stripped away territories in a postwar settlement. His cooperation with Germany was most notable in his efforts to make Serbia *Judenrein,* free of Jews. Both in that country and in Croatia the war against the Jews was waged with such abysmal thoroughness that by the time of the Axis collapse there remained only tiny enclaves of Jews in the area that was once Yugoslavia.

If for Serbia the Second World War was a period of lying low until her interwar greatness could be reestablished, for Croatia it was the fruition of an age-old ambition. It took a bold leap of faith to regard the state that on April 10 emerged from her uneasy partnership with Serbia as truly independent, but it was undeniably closer to independence than it ever had been in its long history. Adopting the name Independent Croatian State (NDH), it had a population of 6.3 million, of which only 3.3 million were Croatians; there were nearly 2 million Serbs and some 800,000 Muslims. Germany's satellites, as well as Spain, Japan, Burma, and Manchuria, granted it recognition and it adhered to the Tripartite Pact. While the Germans controlled the larger and more important northern sphere of the country, Mussolini was allowed to select the head of the national government and he chose Ante Pavelić. Formally, because Mussolini and Pavelić opted for a monarchy, an Italian prince was designated to be the monarch. He took the name Tomislav II, but showed no interest in his kingdom and did not visit it once. Thus Ante Pavelić was in effect head of state.

As a younger man, in the 1920s, he was still a parliamentarian (in 1927 he had been elected to the central legislature), but in 1929 he emigrated and offered his services to Mussolini in the expectation that in time he could return to his homeland as a leader under Italian protection. It proved a 12-year wait, but in 1941, by Mussolini's disposition, he became *poglavnik,* chief administrator, and gained full scope for both his dictatorial impulses and his brutal governmental methods. A dictatorship appeared imperative when, in May 1941, Pavelić was compelled to relinquish a good part of Dalmatia to Italy, a cession that proved so unpopular that he could no longer depend on broad national support. The Peasant Party leader, Maček, in the interest of national unity, several times exhorted the public to loyalty to the regime, as did the Catholic church too, but loyalty to the government that Pavelić instituted was beyond the emotional capacity of most of his fellow-citizens. Within days of the state's formation, laws were issued for racial protection directed against Serbs, Jews, and Gypsies. Pavelić liked to contend that Serbs were really Croatians who had abandoned Catholicism for Eastern Orthodoxy and reconversion was one of the methods for them to return to their national roots—as it turned out, for many Serbians that proved to be the only means of saving their lives. Those who remained true to Orthodoxy often had to find ways to go abroad to escape death. Atrocities on the part of one side often provoked atrocities from the other, and Croatia became the most blood-soaked country in Europe among those not at war; between 250,000 and 350,000 Serbian civilians lost their lives between 1941 and 1945. The Jewish and Gypsy population of Croatia was virtually annihilated.

The rising partisan movement further aggravated the unstable conditions in the former Yugoslavia. In the spring of 1941 Hitler had been so concerned that the campaign against Yugoslavia and Greece might unduly upset his timetable for Operation Barbarossa that he mistook military victory for pacification. German units were often withdrawn from the Balkan theater while a battle was still in progress, many Serbian soldiers escaped capture, and caches of arms remained hidden from the Germans. The result was an early rise of guerrilla activity, which the Germans were never able to control or subdue. Within a month of the surrender of the Yugoslav army a detachment consisting largely of Serbian officers had established itself in the forests of Ravna Gora under the command of a royal colonel Draža Mihailović. By January 1942 the Yugoslav government in exile in London promoted Mihailović to minister of war, and the troops under his command were referred to as the Četnik Detachments of the Yugoslav Army. The colonel's contacts with the exiled government, and even with the British government, continued throughout the war. However, his battlefield effectiveness was questionable. His "army," made up almost exclusively of Serbs, was never forged into a unitary fighting force, and his control over it was loose and at times nonexistent. More damagingly, realizing that he had to contend with another, communist-directed, partisan army, in the later phases of the war he became more involved in the fight against Communists than in the fight against Germans. At times, though this was never conclusively proven, he cooperated with Nedić's government in Belgrade, and even with the Germans, to stem the rise of Tito's communist partisan movement. Politically he was a Greater Serb; he saw no future for the mosaic of peoples that had been helter-skelter pieced together after the First World War; if they were to be reunited, he believed it would have to be under Serbian rule.

Opposed to Mihailović's četniks, politically and militarily, were the "partisans" under the command of Josip Broz Tito, an old Communist appointed by the January 1939 decision of the Comintern to head the Yugoslav Communist Party (an illegal organization, it will be remembered, since August 1921). In its early years that party, beset by many problems of organization and compelled to operate underground, paid scant attention to the question of whether a centralized or a federative system best answered the needs of the Yugoslav state. Gradually though, and in part because the membership came from practically every ethnic group in the kingdom, a federal solution emerged as the party's political platform. The practical result during the wartime fragmentation of the state was that the Communists were the only party who could establish themselves and operate in every part of the former Yugoslavia. When the fight against the German occupiers began, it was accordingly waged on a broad front and, during the first three months of the German campaign against Russia, an area of about 20,000 square kilometers in southwest Yugoslavia was wrested from the occupiers. The Germans steadily had to drain soldiery from the already strapped Russian front to deal with the partisans in Yugoslavia. Unable to wage set-piece battles, they resorted to unspeakable atrocities, decreeing that for every German killed 100 Yugoslavs were to be put to death. The četnik response to the terror was greater caution verging on timidity; Mihailović, firmly confident of eventual allied victory, saw no sense in sacrificing hundreds of Serbian lives in a cause that would be victorious even without the sacrifice. While there was humanitarian logic behind this strategy, it did little for morale. Often his units were inactive for months and many simply dispersed.

For nearly two years Tito's partisans also fought an uphill battle. The Germans, after their Balkan victory in April 1941, had left only four divisions in the former Yugoslavia; these were augmented by two Italian armies, Hungarian and Bulgarian units, and Croatian contributions of various size; later the Germans brought in SS volunteers from non-German countries, notably the Netherlands. In addition to reprisals against civilians, these formations inflicted many defeats and great casualties on Tito's partisans, but in time they learned that winning battles did not add up to winning the war. Their repeated encirclements failed to capture Tito and his staff; partisan activity shifted from province to province and with the passage of time drew many recruits. By March 1943 the standoff was so complete that the two sides agreed on a truce combined with exchange of prisoners; the break favored the partisans, who needed time and manpower to fight not only the occupiers but also Mihailović's četniks.

It was in the course of 1943 that Tito's forces clearly showed their superiority in battle tactics and morale over the četniks. When the heads of government of the Grand Alliance met in Teheran in November of that year, they decided to give their support to Tito. Churchill had favored the četniks from the start, as much for political as for sentimental reasons. After the Teheran decisions London and Washington made several attempts to reconcile the two resistance movements, but, given the fact that Yugoslavia would most likely fall into the Soviet sphere, Tito saw no profit in cooperating with his monarchist rival, whose striking power had in any case greatly diminished.

By the summer of 1944 the Germans were on the defensive everywhere in the Balkans; their manpower needs on the Russian front had become critical and they were forced to withdraw more and more men from the Yugoslav region. In September the first Soviet units reached the Yugoslav border; shortly afterward Tito flew to Moscow. In his talks with Stalin he coordinated the military actions of his partisans with those of Red Army units and also extracted a promise that once the war ended Soviet forces would leave Yugoslavia. After Soviet and partisan forces took Belgrade on October 20, most of the rest of Yugoslavia was liberated by native forces. Fighting continued even after Berlin had fallen and the Germans unconditionally surrendered to the Americans. However, Tito carried on the struggle against the četniks, not only against their armed units but also against any such member or collaborationist whom his forces managed to capture. He wanted to make amply sure that a communist-dominated Yugoslavia would emerge from the cataclysm of the Second World War, and in that, with Soviet help, he succeeded.

CHAPTER FOUR

Thanks to the leading part it played in Yugoslavia's liberation, the Yugoslav Communist Party was in an exceptionally strong position when the war ended. Unlike in other East European countries, where the party faced political forces generally hostile to communism, in Yugoslavia there were no powerful left-overs from the prewar system, and those still in existence were thoroughly intimidated. During the partisan struggle against the Axis forces there had come about, in November 1942, an organization called Yugoslav Anti-Fascist Liberation Council (AVNOJ), and although for tactical reasons its first head was not a Communist but a Croatian parliamentarian of prewar Yugoslavia, the actual direction was in the hands of Josip Broz Tito. In subsequent months members of the AVNOJ, with Communists always in the forefront, labored mightily to make that organization the sole political force in liberated areas. The emphasis from early on was on creating a security apparatus, including a political police and other organizations, whose announced task was the maintenance of internal order, but whose actual purpose was ensuring Communist Party control.

The state that emerged from the ravages of war, one that included the entire territory of the interwar Yugoslavia, bore the name Democratic Federative Yugoslavia. Its first provisional national assembly, organized in the closing phase of the war, had to take cognizance of the fact that constitutionally Yugoslavia was still a monarchy, with the king, now of age, in exile. As King Peter showed no interest in returning to his homeland controlled by forces hostile to the very idea of monarchy, the assembly set up, against the protest of the absent king, a regency council. This council, as early as January 1945, empowered Tito to form a government. It was formally installed on March 7, 1945, and gained the recognition of all the major powers. Tito was premier and minister of war, and most portfolios went to members of the AVNOJ. Temporary legislative power was vested in an assembly drawn from "trustworthy" members of the last Yugoslav parliament, elected in 1938, with the addition of persons the assembly coopted. The first task of the assembly was the preparation of national elections.

True to Communist practice in states where the party was not confident of its popular support, in Yugoslavia too the Communists decided to enter the electoral battle within the framework of a National Front. At two congresses, held in August and in November 1945, the front laid down as its fundamental principle a guarantee of individual freedom and property rights. The Communists, probably so as not to show their hands too early, agreed to it; they also agreed that the AVNOJ be made more democratic by adding to it several noncommunist members. In general, the government at this point went to great lengths to ensure that, in an official sense, every party had equal rights and an equal opportunity to participate in the electoral contest; in reality, the conduct of the Communist-controlled security police gave the lie to these pretenses. Communists, steeled in partisan battles against foreign occupiers, and having spearheaded the nation's liberation, regarded it as less than fair that they should have to compete with bourgeois and peasant parties on equal terms. A number of smaller political groups, either won over by this argument or powerless to contradict it, joined the National Front in the full knowledge that it was an instrument of the Communist Party, and that the other parties within the front would have to play by its rules. Not so the Croatian Peasant Party, a thorn in the side of every government since the formation of Yugoslavia, or the Serbian Democratic Party, which had never embraced the Greater Serbia policy of the ruling Radicals; these two refused to join the National Front. (A leftist faction of the Peasant Party, calling itself the Croatian Republican Peasant Party, in the last minute did enroll in the National Front). The boycott of these two parties was circumvented by presenting to the electorate not separate parties but a single list, with the option of voting for or against it.

Nationwide elections were held on November 11, 1945; they were direct and secret, and for the first time in Serbian or Yugoslav history women were allowed to vote. Rumors were current that although voting was secret, the government had means to determine who cast a "yes" and who a "nay" vote. In the end, 88.7 percent of registered voters went to the polls and 90.8 percent of those voted for the National Front. Whereas the front was officially a conglomeration of a number of parties, and although pressures of all kinds had undoubtedly swelled the number of "aye" votes, a sober analysis of the outcome left little doubt of the popularity of the Communist Party. Even in entirely unencumbered elections that party, had it run separately, would have defeated any other party or combination of parties, though perhaps not with an absolute majority. In effect, before the year of 1945 was out, Yugoslavia had a one-party political system.

A constitutional assembly was convened after the elections, and on November 29 it voted to abolish the monarchy and to proclaim the Yugoslav Federal People's Republic; it further validated the provisional decrees issued by the AVNOJ until then. In January 1946 it adopted a new constitution on the Soviet model. The media continued to refer to the National Front as the defining political authority, but there could no longer be any doubt as to the meaning of that assurance.

The state's international position was ambiguous. When the peace conference convened in Paris on February 10, 1947, to hammer out treaties with former German satellite states, the wartime Grand Alliance was in tatters and the cold war had begun. Yugoslavia in Western eyes was a Soviet client state; at the same time, the fact that she had fought a brave and sustained battle against the Axis had to be acknowledged and her claims had to be given a sympathetic hearing. These claims, to the Istrian Peninsula, as well as to Fiume and Zara, formerly all Italian, were honored, but not the one to the harbor city of Trieste with its heavily Italian population. The Soviet delegate energetically supported the Yugoslav position, while Britain and the United States opposed it. An impasse occurred; in the end, the fate of the city was kept in abeyance by creating a Free Trieste Zone, with one part of it placed under British, another under Yugoslav administration.

When the constituent assembly of the Yugoslav People's Republic had voted to sanction the AVNOJ measures previously decreed, it referred primarily to the nationalization of major industries. By the time the constitution was enacted, private enterprise had in large measure been liquidated, except in the agrarian sector and in small industry, and in time even those were brought under state control. A gradual land reform had begun as early as August 1945 with the confiscation of church estates, at the same time private landholdings of over 45 hectares were also made state property. One portion of these lands was later distributed among small farmers, the other was converted into either state farms or collectives. In the process even the most objectionable feature of Communist agrarian policy, the obligatory delivery of farm products, also became official state policy. All indicators pointed to a program of forced collectivization as practiced in the Soviet Union—then the sharpening tension between Belgrade and Moscow, and the actual break in June 1948, reversed the process.

Economic planning at first concentrated on physical reconstruction, later on rapid industrialization and the electrification of the countryside. The country had suffered terrible material damage in the war: more than 1 million people had lost their lives, two-fifths of the industrial plant and one-quarter of the living quarters had been destroyed, and the transportation network was in shambles. An UNRRA grant of $400 million, as well as reparation payments from Italy, helped somewhat. A Five-Year Plan was implemented to achieve full reconstruction by increasing industrial production fivefold over the 1939 level and agricultural production by one and a half. As was the case with successive economic plans in the Soviet Union, these projections were unrealistic, but they served the purpose of energizing much of the productive capacity of the labor force.

Alone among East European satellites, Yugoslavia was organized as a federal state. The leadership, harking back to the endemic conflicts among the constituent parts between the wars, sought to allay regional misgivings. The country was divided into six people's republics, each of which had the right, on paper, to secede. The six were Serbia, Bosnia-Hercegovina, Montenegro (Crna Gora), Macedonia, Croatia, and Slovenia. With small exceptions, the borders were drawn along historically established lines. Outwardly the system was eminently fair and none of the republics had rights denied to others, yet there was a centralization more complete than there had ever been under the monarchy. In each republic the Communist Party was in effective control and it received its instructions from the center in Belgrade (the official name of the national party was the Yugoslav Communist Union). More important than the party's monopoly of political power was Tito's commanding personality; and, as time was to show, it became the defining feature and force of Yugoslav unity.

The rupture between the Soviet Union and the Yugoslav Communist Party in the summer of 1948 was one of the most startling events in European history after the Second World War. Until then communist media indefatigably advertised the solidarity of the international working class under the leadership of "the Great Stalin," and the unbreakable strength of the "socialist-democratic camp," in opposition to the "capitalist-imperialist camp" directed from Washington. Yugoslavia was a pillar of the former camp, and even before the war ended, as we have seen, she had concluded with the Soviet Union a treaty of friendship, cooperation, and mutual aid. In the three years following the war the Yugoslavs faithfully toed the Soviet line in foreign affairs. When in September 1947 the representatives of the Communist parties of Eastern Europe and of France, and Italy were summoned to a Polish resort in Silesia to coordinate their ideological endeavors and facilitate the transmission of information, the Yugoslavs were given the task of upbraiding the French and Italian comrades for their lackadaisical conduct in opposing the pro-American policies of their governments. The meeting established a Communist Information Bureau to serve as a center of communication among parties, and at Moscow's behest Belgrade was chosen as its location. In the West Britain in particular looked with unease at Belgrade's unambiguous Soviet orientation. During the war, when Stalin and Churchill worked out an informal division of interest spheres in the Balkans, Stalin put an approving check mark on Churchill's scheme, which stipulated a fifty-fifty division of influence for the two powers in Yugoslavia. By the end of 1947 there was no division at all; Yugoslavia was totally under Soviet influence. That same agreement had assigned Greece to the British sphere, but now a civil war between royalist and communist forces raged in that country and Tito lent generous support to the latter. Also, the Yugoslavs, although they had been more than fairly treated at the peace conference, continued their territorial probings, seeking to round out their border republics with additional annexations. Certainly no country appeared to be more firmly built into the Soviet camp than Tito's Yugoslavia.

Seldom were appearances more misleading. Although solid political reasons underlay the rapidly increasing tension between the Yugoslav and Soviet governments (Stalin, for instance, resented Tito's high-handed initiative in forming a Balkan League with Bulgaria and Albania, neglecting to ask for Soviet guidance), in the end it was the clash between two strong-willed individuals that accounted for the ultimate rift. Stalin was stunned to realize that there was a satellite leader in his sphere who dared to defy him and set himself against the Kremlin's wishes. There were in Belgrade, as in other satellite capitals, a number of Soviet "experts," whose advice was supposed to have the force of law. Tito treated these with growing disrespect, ignoring their guidance, especially when they urged a more strenuous tempo in agricultural collectivization. At the same time the Soviets failed to deliver a good part of the aid promised for Yugoslav reconstruction. On March 1, 1948, Tito called a meeting of his party's leadership and presented to it his complaints, among them that the Soviet-Yugoslav "joint" companies established after the war benefited almost exclusively the Soviet side, and that Moscow demanded a political union between Yugoslavia and Bulgaria that would imperil Yugoslav independence. With his comrades' approval, Tito set his complaints down on paper and forwarded them to Stalin.

The only reply he received was a note saying that Moscow was withdrawing its advisers from Belgrade, as they were "surrounded by hostility." The correspondence, conducted from the Soviet side by Foreign Minister Molotov, became ever more heated and personal. Molotov charged that accusations circulated within the Yugoslav party, for instance that the Communist Party of the Soviet Union (CPSU) was "degenerate," that, "the USSR is trying to dominate Yugoslavia economically," and, perhaps the most insulting one, that "socialism in the USSR had ceased to be revolutionary," were "dishonorable, underhanded and hypocritical."

The exchanges and recriminations continued until the breach could no longer be healed. A hastily called meeting of the Cominform at the end of June 1948, acting at Stalin's express wishes, excluded the Yugoslav party from the organization. The resolution stated that "showing their poor understanding of the international situation and their intimidation by the blackmailing forces of the imperialists, the Yugoslav leaders think that by making concessions, they can curry the favors of the imperialist states." The denunciation was unprecedented. A deep chasm within the communist camp was laid bare for the world to see.

From this point on the demonstration of Tito's treachery, not only within the narrower context of his quarrel with Stalin but also in an inclusive manner that embraced his entire political career, became a major industry in the Soviet Union and in the satellites. The most undignified charges ("chained dog of imperialism") were hurled at the Yugoslav dictator, and data were provided to show that even his partisan struggle in the war had been a sham, that he had fought not for the victory of socialism but in the service of capitalist-imperialist interests, and that his strategy had been to preserve Axis forces while apparently at war with them so they could fight another day.

Nor was it enough to rail against Tito alone. It had to be shown that the Yugoslav dictator had enlisted in his conspiracy a number of other leaders who posed as Communists while seeking to undermine socialism in countries where it had at last been established. The result was a series of political trials in satellite states (it could never be admitted that the Titoist plague had infiltrated the Soviet Union); old and until then trusted Communist Party leaders were put on trial on patently false charges, convicted, and executed. Yet amid this orgy of denunciation and falsehood, Tito remained firmly in control as head of the Yugoslav Communist Union, defying Stalin's worst invectives, as well as a boycott by socialist states.

Not that he failed to take the threat seriously. Stalin's authority was such that few Communists opposed it with impunity. As one of Tito's comrades, Edward Kardelj, wrote in his memoirs: "A life-and-death struggle began. We mobilized not only the army but a good part of the nation as well. In our border regions with neighboring Eastern European states we dug ditches and erected fortresses. . . . Daily one or another party member, officers, officials, diplomats, deserted us. The number of these refugees was never large, but [the result was that] we still had to live in an atmosphere of constant uncertainty."

Josip Broz,
Marshal Tito
(Hulton/Archive)

Abandoned by other socialist states, Yugoslavia had to take steps to make herself independent in essential spheres. The method the party chose was to allow both the federal republics and the productive enterprises the greatest possible degree of self-government. It was a bold experiment at a time when there was so much need for a centrally controlled system that mobilized all the forces of the state to withstand the Soviet challenge. In order to give the laboring man, especially in industry, a greater sense of responsibility and pride, workers' councils were formed and entrusted with effective governance of the enterprise. When the experiment yielded gratifying results, the parliament in June 1950 passed a "fundamental law" providing self-government for all state-owned businesses as well as economic cooperatives. While almost revolutionary in the history of communist states, such decentralization was in line with the Marxist premise that as the means of production passed into collective hands and workers looked after their own affairs in the workplace as well as in their social environment, the government would progressively wither away.

Once started, the process continued by its own momentum, and it unavoidably began to display symptoms of the capitalist free enterprise system. Not that any productive property was placed in or returned to private hands, but the principles of market economy received ever more attention as stultifying central controls were gradually abandoned. To be sure, the changes never stepped across the line where the state's final authority over production, labor relations, or remuneration was relinquished. When in November 1952 the party's Sixth Congress met, it announced a "new type" of leadership role for the party: it would be limited to ideological and political guidance, with minimum interference in the economic sphere, or even in politics at the lower level.

Stalin died on March 5, 1953, and one of the first steps taken by the new Kremlin leadership was to mend the ruinously damaged fences with Yugoslavia. Within two months of the great leader's death diplomatic relations were restored and the Soviet leadership (much to the chagrin of its hard-liners) in effect admitted that it had been wrong in victimizing the Yugoslav leader and his party.

Still, the resumption of inter*state* relations left the proper relations between the two *parties* unsettled. That was an all the more thorny problem because so many good and loyal Communists had ended up on the gallows for the supreme sin of Titoism. Interparty relations could be restored only if Tito was vindicated; in that case, however, "Titoism" would become an empty charge and it would have to be admitted that stalwart Communists had been victimized for no good reason at all. Hard as the matter was, Stalin's successor as head of the CPSU, Nikita Khrushchev, finally swallowed his pride. Accompanied by Soviet premier Bulganin, he made an official visit to Belgrade in June 1955. He admitted the false and misguided nature of the campaign against Tito and placed the blame for it on the by now purged head of the Soviet security police, Lavrenty Beria. To Tito such shifting of responsibility was an insult, and the Soviet delegation was accorded a frosty reception. Moscow never withdrew—most likely because of an oversight—the gravest charge, namely that Yugoslavia was not a socialist but a capitalist state. To correct this omission, the XXth Congress of the CPSU in February 1956 (the one that listened to Khrushchev's epoch-making denunciation of Stalin) in its closing resolution, inserted the following sentence: "Important achievements in the construction of socialism have also been made in Yugoslavia."

However, how long the improved relations between the two socialist countries would last, and to what extent Yugoslavia would remain a socialist state, was still a wide open question.

CHAPTER FIVE

Among party faithful in Yugoslavia the break with Moscow produced much agonized soul-searching and incomprehension. How could the unthinkable, an open clash between the high priest of world communism, Joseph Stalin, and the Yugoslav party of Josip Broz Tito have occurred? Edward Kardelj, in reflecting on the crisis, wrote: "The hardest task was to come to terms with our own consciences. I have been in the communist movement since I was 16 years old, I had unconditional faith in Stalin, and in the Soviet Union. When in 1934, as an emigrant, I first laid foot on Soviet land, my joy brought tears to my eyes. . . . Now I had to overcome a deep inner crisis. It was not that I had doubts when I had to take sides in the quarrel; . . . what Stalin did to us was so obviously based on lies and innuendo that I would have demeaned myself if I had given credit to these fabrications and [absurd] charges. My inner crisis had its roots in these questions: How could all this have happened, what are the causes of this terrible metamorphosis of socialism, what are the perspectives of the future development of socialism, what do we have to do to avoid ourselves these crass historic mistakes and false directions?"

Tito did not appear to be subject to such bouts of conscience. He did seek to mitigate Stalin's ire by voting with the Soviet bloc on international questions—when for instance a conference on Danubian navigation was held in August 1948, a conference in which nonriparian states like the United States, Britain, and France also participated as voting members, the Yugoslav delegation sided with the Soviet in demanding that only states served by the Danube should sit on the navigation commission—but within Yugoslavia Tito undertook a thorough purge of Stalinists. Between 1948 and 1952 some 60,000 members of the Yugoslav party were expelled on charges of siding with the Comintern, and their hope of obtaining any kind of employment was dim indeed. At the end of 1948 two concentration camps were set up on desolate islands in the Adriatic and in following years over 16,000 erring party members were sent there. Meanwhile the Soviet embassy in Belgrade as well as embassies of satellite states that sided with Moscow were under virtual siege and snubbed diplomatically.

It had been one of the sources of Stalin's unhappiness with the Yugoslav brand of socialism that it did not pursue agricultural collectivization with sufficient vigor. Yet Stalin of all people should have understood how the bitter Soviet experience with that program in the 1930s, and the enormous price paid in human lives and human suffering, discouraged the Yugoslavs from introducing it in their own land. Tito did try to placate Stalin when, in early 1949, he increased pressure on individual farmers to consolidate their holdings; by 1951, one quarter of the cultivated land belonged to collectives. Peasant resistance was too strong, however, and Tito could not ignore the fact that if his quarrel with Moscow led to war—not a far-fetched possibility—his army would be made up primarily of peasants, whose loyalty therefore had to be fostered. A couple of bad harvests due to drought also gave the process pause. As early as December 1949, by decision of a party assembly, pressure on individually farming peasants was eased, then halted altogether.

In March 1953 a decree inaugurated a new direction in agrarian policy. As a first step, a peasant already in a collective was allowed to leave, taking a maximum allotment of 10 hectares with him. Existing collective farms were transformed into self-governing agrarian enterprises. After the program had time to evolve to its concluding phase, the great bulk of the agricultural land remained in private hands, but under a mixed system of cultivation, by which basic aspects of farming were performed individually while others (especially those that entailed the use of machinery) were undertaken jointly with state or collective farms, and the harvest was divided according to the respective contribution to its production.

The break with the Soviet party allowed Yugoslav Communists a certain latitude in political and economic experimentation; without admitting the unorthodoxy, they no longer felt bound by rigid Marxist concepts. During the 1950s, as we have seen, they made earnest efforts to shift both decision making and responsibility to the productive units in the economic sphere, and to the federal republics and their constituent units in the political sphere. All this had a liberating effect on cultural and religious life; local or regional tradition gradually took pride of place over Marxist prescriptions. There were a few taboos to be sure that could not be breached: the one-party system, the fraternal unity of the Yugoslav people, and Tito's commanding place in party and society.

More by necessity than by choice, the foreign policy of the country was, in the immediate aftermath of the party's exclusion from the Cominform, entirely reoriented. Apart from the campaign of vituperation waged against it by other socialist states, a practical economic boycott ostracized Yugoslavia from trade with COMECOM nations; that trade had accounted for fully one-half of her exports and imports. Tito was compelled to act against his political convictions and turn to Western states, notably to Britain and the United States, for economic cooperation. His overtures were at first received with reserve; the Soviet-Yugoslav break had been so unexpected and so baffling that there was speculation it might have been staged to encourage the West to channel some of its surplus into the communist orbit. As these suspicions proved groundless, however, a limited but still useful exchange between Yugoslavia and the West developed. In addition, Yugoslavia received direct aid to the tune of $400 million from the United States in the next five years.

Normalizing relations with the Cominform after the death of Stalin was an uncertain and halting affair. Many of the satellites, especially Hungary, dragged their feet in resuming relations; the leaders, deeply involved in the show trials of the years 1949–52, saw no practical way of rehabilitating Tito without admitting their own miscarriages of justice. The Soviet leaders on their part could scarcely justify their past outbursts against Tito and the Yugoslav party if they admitted, as they now would have to, that they knew that the charges had no basis in fact. Thus they composed a resolution that in essence cleared the Yugoslavs of any wrongdoing but at the same time defended the Cominform decision to expel their party as a praiseworthy exercise in interparty solidarity. It was hardly a resolution the Yugoslav party could embrace.

The lingering tension flared into open hostility in 1956. The Hungarian revolution in October of that year, clearly directed against heavy Soviet presence in Hungary, once again necessitated a consensus among socialist states on the need to deal with the uprising. Khrushchev consulted Tito several times and even agreed to install Tito's choice as head of the reorganized Communist Party in Hungary, János Kádár. During the discussions between the two men the fate of the current Hungarian premier, Imre Nagy, who in the heady days of the uprising proposed to break away from the Soviet camp and its military alliance, the Warsaw Pact, was left undecided. The day when Soviet forces reentered Budapest to subdue the revolution, November 4, 1956, Nagy asked for and received political asylum at the Yugoslav embassy. With that, Belgrade assumed responsibility for his and his ministers' personal safety. Nagy eventually left the embassy under a safe conduct promise given by the Soviets to the Yugoslav government; he was arrested before he reached home and was never a free man again. A year and a half later he was tried for his "crimes" during the revolution, condemned, and hanged. All this elicited dismay and protest in Belgrade.

Tito did not to intend for the affair to result in a complete break with the Soviet camp. He proposed to Khrushchev a resumption of their dialogue. They were to meet in Bucharest in August 1957. Khrushchev first went to Prague to reassure Novotný's hard-line government there that, notwithstanding recent cataclysmic events, there would be no deviation from Marxist dogma; in a speech given to Czechoslovak Communists he sharply criticized the Yugoslav party for advertising its self-governing workers' cooperatives as examples to follow in all socialist states. "We acknowledge that there are many roads," Khrushchev said, "but the most important one is the common road."

When Tito met his Soviet counterpart in August, he tried to be accommodating. As a special concession, he promised to give full recognition to the East German government, a recognition he had thus far withheld. He also promised personally to attend the November celebration in Moscow of the 40th anniversary of the Great October Revolution, an event to which the leaders of all Communist parties were invited. As the proceedings of the celebrations opened however, Tito discovered to his disappointment that the principal foreign speaker was Mao Tse-tung of China, who delivered an undeviatingly orthodox Marxist address, condemning by implication the revisionist initiatives Tito and his party had taken, and confirming his, Mao's, faith in strict centralism, a practice the Yugoslav party had by now foresworn. Khrushchev had not intended to go that far, in fact at the by now legendary XXth Party Congress he himself had spoken against such obviously Stalinist principles; at the present meeting he kept a diplomatic silence, neither endorsing nor opposing Mao's line.

However, it was scarcely a subject on which any Communist Party leader could remain noncommittal. Tito had assumed that his presence at the conference at Soviet invitation suggested at least a partial approval of his polycentric practice of running party and government—now he felt betrayed. A congress of the Yugoslav party was scheduled to open in April 1958; Tito wanted it to serve as an unambiguous endorsement of the "Yugoslav way." On March 13, a month before the opening of the congress, the party made its agenda public. It warned of the dangers of bureaucratic centralism, confirmed the legitimacy of different roads to socialism, and expressed faith in the effectiveness and true socialist nature of self-governing workers' cooperatives. Most provocatively, it insisted on the equality and independence of all Communist parties and demanded a pledge of noninterference in one another's internal affairs. It condemned Stalinism and "monolithism"; taken together, his speech was a powerful rejoinder to Mao's address at the Moscow conference. Khrushchev, deeply chagrined, announced that he would not send a Soviet delegation to the Yugoslav congress.

When the congress opened in Ljubljana and its program was announced, Beijing reacted sharply; it confirmed that the deviations for which the Yugoslav party had been expelled from the Cominform in 1948 were still in evidence. Soon a storm of criticism from capitals such as Sofia, Tirana, Prague (seats of hard-line Communist regimes) rained down on Tito and the Yugoslav party. Khrushchev, still dwelling in the shadow of his de-Stalinization campaign, lost his way in the present confusion. He did not join the condemnation, but later, under Chinese pressure, canceled the $285 million credit he had promised the Yugoslav economy in 1956. In June he was more outspoken when, during a visit to Sofia, he made a speech referring to Yugoslav revisionism as the wooden horse that sought to undermine communism from within. He even accused Tito of being bribed by the economic aid he received from America. (It is interesting to note that a few weeks earlier Khrushchev had sent word to President Eisenhower saying that his country would gladly accept long-term credit for economic improvements.)

The execution in Budapest on June 16 of that year of Imre Nagy and three of his codefendants, although officially an internal matter, further envenomed Soviet-Yugoslav relations. The impulsive Khrushchev, whose zigzag course often led him onto totally unexpected terrain, began to realize that Mao Tsetung's often intemperate outbursts against Tito were really directed against him, hinting that it was he who had opened the floodgates that led to a wholesale discrediting of Stalinism, the very policy that the Chinese party uncritically embraced and practiced. In his heart Khrushchev would probably have preferred to side with Tito in the current quarrel but he had gone too far in condemning the latter's "revisionism" to retrace his steps. He confined himself to discreetly begging satellite party leaders not to censure Tito too harshly, lest the unity of the socialist camp be rent beyond repair.

The spats—for in retrospect they amounted to little more than that— between Tito and leaders of sister parties had their milder counterpart *within* Yugoslavia. The argument that the transfer of decision-making power from the central government to local workers' councils marked a beginning of the government's withering away had a measure of Marxist validity, but purists could also argue that the withering would have to await the final, communist, stage, when the abolition of private ownership had eliminated social classes. Reformers, as always, paid less attention to dogma and more attention to pragmatic principles. Such a group formed around Edward Kardelj and it urged that decentralization be continued and economic policy be geared to market forces. The conservatives, champions of centralization, gathered around Alexandar Ranković, the founder and the feared head of the UDBA, the security police. Their objections to reform were only in part based on dogma; they also feared that in a freer atmosphere, amid economic competition, the underdeveloped regions of Yugoslavia would fall behind even more, or, to use a Marxist prophecy, that the rich would get richer and the poor poorer. Their position was strengthened when a new wave of reforms in 1961 failed to improve the economic picture. The intent had been to extend the autonomy of the workers' councils, allow prices to find their own levels, and shift the authority for granting credit from the government to banks. The currency, the dinar, was drastically devalued to make Yugoslav exports more competitive. The government, to bolster its reform measures, took a $100 million loan from the United States and a $75 million loan from the World Bank. Additional loans were later secured from the World Bank and the United Nations.

The new program of reforms failed to produce the expected results, in good part because Tito simply could not decide whether he favored it (in which case he would have had to commit himself totally to it) or whether he feared a gradual weakening of the party's authority if the business sector was granted too much discretionary power. He felt more comfortable with reforms in the political sphere, which could be more easily controlled. In April 1963 the federal parliament accepted a new constitution. Yugoslavia was no longer a people's republic but a federal republic. (People's Republic had a pronouncedly communist connotation.) Its productive forces were state-owned, but they operated on the principles of market economy. The constitution stipulated a four-year limit on the mandate of anyone who held a leading position (Tito naturally being an exception); it established a special court to deal with constitutional questions and broadened individual freedoms. In addition to the federal and the republican parliaments, it set in place elected councils in charge of economic, cultural, welfare, health, and political-administrative matters. The consistent feature in the administrative provisions was the dispersal of authority and responsibility; thus, after years of seesaw battles between conservatives and reformists, the latter finally gained the upper hand.

Yet, Tito was unable to embrace the reformist platform whole. Concern for the position of the party, which ultimately meant himself, was always uppermost in his mind. In a speech in Split in July 1962 he warned liberals and intellectuals not to draw the wrong conclusions from political and economic changes and not to go too far in their bid for cultural freedom. When in December of that year he visited Moscow, he took with him, not Kardelj, whom the Soviets distrusted, but Ranković, whose program was still undeviatingly con-

Yugoslavia the disintegration proceeded in a somewhat more formal fashion than in the other states where the system simply went out of existence. In January 1990 the Yugoslav Communist Union held what turned out to be its last congress and the principal item was once again the decision as to whether the Communist Union should be a centralized structure in which the will of the highest decision-making body became law for the subordinate organs or whether it should be the free union of national parties, each of which had the right to direct its own affairs. Milošević and his Serbian group favored greater centralization, but they no longer had the means to enforce their will. When no unity of views was achieved, the Slovene delegation walked out. The Croats caucused as to the course to take, then they too left the congress. With this the Yugoslav Communist Union, the last unifying bond in the South Slav state, ceased to exist. Serbians, to whom the breakup meant an end to their hitherto unassailable position in a larger Yugoslav party, reacted bitterly. Almost overnight the ethnic hatred thus far directed against Albanians turned against the Slovenes, who were held chiefly responsible for the disintegration of the party and by extension of the state. Serbian media unearthed, or invented, a series of charges to "prove" that the Slovenes had always been a disruptive element in Yugoslavia, and had been the cause of most of the economic woes. The hate campaign reached such proportions that many Slovenes felt compelled to hide their ethnicity and even to conceal their speech pattern not to become objects of discrimination and possibly violence.

No one now had a formula for what kind of Yugoslav state should replace the old one bequeathed to the nation by Tito. Elections were supposed to provide an answer, and these were held in December 1990, in the individual republics only, not in Yugoslavia as a whole. Milošević placed himself at the head of the Communist Union of Serbia and hoped to clean up its tarnished reputation by renaming it the Serbian Socialist Party. Most likely the party would have gained a substantial majority in any case, but Milošević took no chances and rigged the elections in old time-tested ways. In the end the party won 194 seats in the 250-seat parliament. To enhance its popularity, Milošević also arranged for a major loan from a Serbian bank to bolster the Serbian economy, obviously a short-term measure but it helped avoid an immediate economic crisis.

However, his position was by no means unassailable. He still did not possess a solid political base; the Serbian Socialist Party was a makeshift creation, with no political conviction behind it. In the minds of many Serbians, deeply disillusioned with communism in its every variety, the new party, by whatever name it went, was a liability; others were turned away by Milošević's Greater Serbian pretensions, which they feared would lead to further internal conflicts. Most politically sober Serbs realized that Slobodan Milošević's cause was not a high-minded solution for Serbia's, or Yugoslavia's, multiplying problems, but the political future of Slobodan Milošević. Many resented the way in which, once he became the top political figure in Serbia, he ruthlessly ousted his former mentor and benefactor Ivan Stambolić, who had been severely critical of his militant nationalism. That nationalism most forcefully manifested itself not in Serbia itself, where it had no convenient targets, but in the autonomous provinces of Kosovo and Vojvodina, where, he asserted, the Serbian population (10 percent of the total in Kosovo and 57 percent in Vojvodina, a former Hungarian province), had to be protected. In truth, while the position of Serbs in Kosovo might have given some cause for concern, certainly there was no threat to them in Vojvodina; yet, Milošević, claiming the opposite, proceeded to strip that province of its autonomy as early as 1988. Kosovo followed a year later. He then cast his eyes on Montenegro, Bosnia-Hercegovina, and Croatia, though only in the last of these could any case be made for a need to protect Serbian ethnic interests. It didn't matter. Milošević needed a forceful and fighting stance to keep himself in the political picture. Communism had lost its appeal, as did the Yugoslav ideal; Serbian nationalism alone possessed the potential for attracting a large following. The rest of his drive to power could then be accomplished by political manipulation.

Yugoslavia's presidency was, since Tito's death, vested in a collective body of eight men; one from each of the six republics and one each from Kosovo and Vojvodina. Each member of the council served as its president for one year, then yielded the office to the next in the rotation. For Milošević to acquire full power he only needed to take the short step of gaining the vote of the majority of the eight. In May 1991 the presidency was to devolve to the Croat member, Stipe Mesić. The current president was a Milošević partisan, Borisav Jović, and Milošević had in addition four other votes. These votes prevented, in an illegal maneuver, the presidency from passing to its next lawful candidate. The normal process of government was thus aborted, and Milošević, the single Serbian member on the presidential council, was poised to seize power for himself. Such a development foreshadowed a much-feared Serbian domination in a future, "third" Yugoslavia. Neither Croatia nor Slovenia was willing to remain a constituent unit in such a state and both made clear their intention to secede. Various last-minute proposals were put forth from inside and outside of Yugoslavia for the preservation of the state; even the U.S. secretary of state of the day, James Baker, offered a formula. Bosnia-Hercegovina proposed a scheme whereby the two secessionist republics would be reintegrated, not in a federal but

Slobodan Milošević
*(Michel Porro/
Getty Images)*

in a confederal status. The federal premier, Ante Marković, personally pleaded with the Croat and Slovene parliaments to stay within Yugoslavia. All in vain. On June 25, l991, both northern republics announced their independence. A day later Marković ordered the Yugoslav National Army to move into and take possession of Slovenia.

In the resulting Ten-Day War the Slovene armed forces, including the national guard, proved more than an equal to the by now disorganized Yugoslav force. A truce was brokered by the European Community on July 7 for a period of three months; after it elapsed, on October 8, Yugoslav forces evacuated the republic and Slovenia was granted its independence. (Milošević's rather dubious position throughout was that he had no interest in keeping Slovenia within Yugoslavia.)

What made the situation in Croatia different from that in Slovenia was the large Serbian ethnic minority there. The deep-seated antagonism between the Catholic Croats and the Eastern Orthodox Serbs dated back centuries, and memories from the Second World War, when Croatians, under Nazi protection and with Nazi help, had waged a war of extermination against the Serbs, were especially fresh and painful. Hence the Serbians within Croatia vigorously opposed the secession of the republic, and they had the outside support of the Yugoslav National Army, 70 percent of whose officers were Serbian. During the fall of 1991 irregular warfare raged within Croatia, which practically cut the republic into two, separating the prosperous Adriatic region from the hinterland, and providing instances of brutality and violations of human rights all too familiar in the region. Little distinction was made between military and civilian targets. The Yugoslav army, when it attacked Croatian strongholds, such as in the city of Vukovar, destroyed as much Serbian as Croatian property in its indiscriminate shelling. A Yugoslav attack on the landmark medieval town of Dubrovnik, which over the years had drawn millions of tourists to Croatia, had no military significance and was clearly aimed only at depriving Croatians of one of their chief sources of revenue.

When the fighting finally abated under United Nations auspices in November 1991, about one-third of Croatia was in Serbian hands and appalling casualties had been inflicted on both sides. The United Nations (UN) took responsibility for keeping the two antagonists apart, and it was a position not unpleasing to Milošević and the Serbians because an international force essentially protected the Serbian gains.

However, it proved impossible for the UN and the European Community (EC) to recognize the independence of two former constituent units of Yugoslavia while ignoring the others. Either there was a Yugoslavia or there was not, and if there was not, provisions had to be made for the successor states. When the EC foreign ministers met on December 16, they decided to consider applications for independence by individual republics (though not for Kosovo, which was formally still a province of Serbia). There was no difficulty in granting the applications of Croatia, Slovenia, and Macedonia, each of which spoke essentially with one voice, but Muslim Bosnia-Hercegovina was a different matter. Too complex ethnically to be assigned to any one nationality (and it should be noted that Muslim in this context was regarded not as a religious but as an ethnic designation), an EC commission decided on a referendum in the republic to gain some guideline as to the orientation of the population. In the last census, held only a few months earlier, nearly 44 percent of the population had identified itself as Muslim, 31 percent as Serb, 17 percent as Croat, and a tiny minority as Yugoslav. Nor did these ethnic groups form recognizable blocs that could provide convenient lines of separation; the mixture was bewildering. As far as the options before the republic were concerned, it could remain part of a reduced Yugoslavia (which was the choice of its Serbian population) or become independent (a course the Muslim and Croat portions of the population favored). As it happened, neither would be a felicitous choice. Within Yugoslavia Bosnia would be a small underprivileged republic, another Kosovo; a choice of independence on the other hand would surely result in determined Serb, and possibly Croat, countermeasures. Both Serbs and Croats, driven by the territorial greed that the impending breakup of the state had produced, had their eyes on hapless Bosnia, and Croatian president Tudjman, and Serbian president Milošević had in September 1991 secretly agreed on a formula for its division. The Bosnian president, Alija Izetbegović, unaware of secret plans, in the spring of 1992 tried to keep his republic out of the more violent phase of the Yugoslav breakup, but the most he could achieve was to have the EC produce a formula

A United Nations armored personnel carrier escorting humanitarian aid from Zenica to Tusla through "bomb alley," an area regularly targeted for shelling by Serbian troops *(Hulton/Archive)*

for a separate Bosnia, of three component parts. Serbia countered the proposal on March 27 by announcing, in a declaration, that Bosnia-Hercegovina was a constituent part of the Serbian republic. The EC, on its part, responded by recognizing an independent Bosnia, which brought in its wake a Serbian attack against that republic on April 6, 1992.

The announced purpose of the invasion was the protection of the Serbian minority, but it was a transparent pretext because the nationalities in Bosnia had long lived in relative harmony with one another; it was more likely that Milošević, apart from his territorial ambitions, sought to divert attention from the catastrophic state of the Yugoslav economy, with its 500 percent annual inflation rate and its 750,000 unemployed. Expected to be of short duration, the Bosnian conflict lasted three and a half years and exposed the worst features of Serbian intolerance and brutality and the basest instincts of the man, Slobodan Milošević. The latter had made himself Serbia's leader with only the scantest popular support and went on to use Serbian nationalism as an instrument for personal advancement, an enterprise that eventually led to his dishonor. War casualties in the end accounted for a smaller loss of life than did the accompanying genocidal actions by Serbians termed "ethnic cleansing." Not a new phenomenon in the region, it had been practiced, mainly against Muslim populations, after the First and the Second Balkan Wars, in 1912 and 1913, and their aftermath; the conquest from Turkey of Macedonia; and in the wars of the 1990s. The first atrocities in this new round of "cleansing" occurred in eastern Croatia, against ethnic Croats, when the Serbs invaded that province to punish it for its declaration of independence in the fall of 1991. It sank to abysmal depths during the war against Bosnia, when most of its victims were Muslims and the process was so thorough that at one point one-third of the population of the province fled for its life and accepted the most dismal conditions rather than be exposed to Serbian ire.

Soon the news of these atrocities reached the West and the UN found itself obliged to act, as the UN Charter demanded it should when human beings were victimized en masse. Not surprisingly, its action was not only ineffectual but exposed the victims to greater danger because, by imposing an arms embargo in the region, it in effect preserved Serbian military superiority. The U.S.–brokered Dayton peace accord, which essentially divided Bosnia into a Muslim and a Serbian-dominated half, proved to be a paper treaty, although after it was signed in 1995, trade sanctions were lifted, and a year later, the UN Security Council ended its weapons embargo.

In July 1997, Milošević became president of the Federal Republic of Yugoslavia. The following year, the Yugoslav army and Serbian police force began attacks on the province of Kosovo, focusing primarily on ethnic Albanians (Muslims) who made up the vast majority of Kosovo's population, as an extension of Milošević's effort to unite all of Serbia politically and ethnically. Because Kosovo was an official province of Yugoslavia, NATO hesitated to intervene as it had done during the conflict with Bosnia in 1992, but evidence of civilian massacres provoked a response, led by the United States, which threatened a military air strike. After negotiations proved unsuccessful, NATO began air strikes in 1999 but failed to prevent Milošević from deporting and murdering Kosovo's civilians. Hundreds of thousands of refugees escaped to Albania and Macedonia.

NATO did not commit ground troops in the conflict, but Serbia eventually accepted a peace agreement and withdrew its forces. The UN indicted Milošević for his crimes against ethnic Albanians, but he remained president until September 2000, when Vojislav Kostunica won the federal elections. Milošević's refusal to accept the results led to countrywide public demonstrations that eventually forced him to withdraw. He was arrested in April 2001 by Yugoslavian authorities and put on trial in June by the UN International Criminal Tribunal for crimes against humanity. Upon his arrest, the United States contributed $50 million to Yugoslavia, and the government was recognized by the international community.

In March 2002, the nation of Yugoslavia became a federation comprised of Serbia and Montenegro, that will facilitate a possible move to independence by Montenegro in the near future.

In conclusion, if the breakup of the old Yugoslavia and its reduction to the provinces of Serbia, Montenegro, Vojvodina, and the still contested Kosovo, together with the simultaneous establishment of Slovenia, Croatia, Macedonia, and Bosnia as independent states can be termed a successful solution of the Yugoslav problem (as in the same time frame the breakup of the Soviet Union into its constituent republics can be called a solution of the Greater Russian problem) then we may say allegorically that the deep political fault line that crisscrosses the Balkans had lapsed into quiescence. Few observers familiar with the dynamics of Balkan politics would, however, take such an optimistic view. As our survey in the previous chapters has shown, the hope that the communality of South Slavs would prove a powerful enough bond to overcome whatever religious or political differences existed had often run high, and it was invariably disappointed.

HISTORICAL DICTIONARY
A–Z

A

Adler, Victor (1882–1918)

Austrian socialist and one of the founders of the Social Democratic Party in Austria

Son of a wealthy Jewish family in Prague, upon completing his medical training, he opened an affluent office in his father's villa in VIENNA. His early political orientation was that of a liberal German nationalist; he was one of the authors of the so-called LINZ PROGRAM of 1882, which proposed to reconstruct the Dual Monarchy on the basis of the supremacy of the German element. Later, realizing the downtrodden, destitute condition of the working class, his political interests turned to this problem. He became known as the "physician of the poor" and forewent the brilliant prospects of a wealthy and socially well-placed professional. Convinced that the problem of poverty demanded a thorough social transformation, he became one of the founders of the Social Democratic Party, organized at a congress in Hainfeld in December–January 1888–89. He believed that much of the energy of the labor movement was drained away in narrow doctrinal debates, and he was instrumental in resolving opposing viewpoints and dedicating the party to a practical political agenda. It was his further belief that capitalism was destined to collapse, and he advocated a policy of patience and moderation. The new party soon attracted some of the finest political minds in Vienna and campaigned for universal franchise and a democratization of the state. Although its growth was slow, after the 1907 elections it emerged as one of the strongest parties in parliament. By 1917, under the stresses of war, a strong leftist faction emerged, with OTTO BAUER as its outstanding member. The Adler family acquired a grim notoriety when, in 1916, Victor's son Friedrich, himself an ardent revolutionary, shot and killed the Austrian chancellor Count Karl Stürgkh.

After the retirement from political affairs of Emperor Charles on October 16, 1918, a provisional government was formed under the Social Democrat Karl Renner in which Victor Adler became the foreign minister. He died shortly after his appointment, on November 11.

Ady, Endre (1877–1919)

revolutionary rejuvenator of Hungarian poetry, one of the greatest Hungarian poets

Son of an impoverished family of the lesser nobility, his father, Lőrinc, started as a smallholder, and never owned more than 100 *hold*. His mother, Maria Pásztor, came from a Calvinist clerical family. From autumn of 1888 Ady studied in a Piarist school, where he concluded his secondary education. In March 1896 his first poem appeared in print; it was titled *March 20* and he signed it A.E. That same year he entered law school in Debrecen. Beginning in January 1897 his poems appeared regularly under his own name. In 1898 he discontinued his studies in law and joined the editorial board of the *Debrecen Hirlap*. His poems appeared quite regularly from this time on, in that paper and in several others. The first volume of his poetry, simply titled *Poems,* was published in June 1899. Those pieces, as well as his articles condemning the clergy and the remnants of the feudal order, early testified to his revolutionary outlook. From May 1901 on, he was assistant editor of a radical newspaper. On September 27,

1902, his theatrical play, *In the Workshop,* was performed. At the end of January 1904 he traveled to Paris, and from there he sent articles home to newspapers and magazines. His year in Paris proved to be significant for his poetic and political development. It was there that he became acquainted with French symbolic lyric poetry. In January 1905 he returned to BUDA-PEST; in February 1906 he published his volume, *New Poems,* which had a dramatic impact on Hungarian poetry. His symbolic language, which hinted at decadence, and the obvious debt he owed to a foreign culture, incurred the wrath of the Hungarian feudal ruling class. In June 1906 he went back to Paris for another year. He interrupted his stay to travel with his lover, Lada, to the Mediterranean, staying in Venice and Nice. In the years before the outbreak of the Great War he made several more journeys to Paris, and in the summer of 1911 to Rome. His book entitled *Blood and Gold,* published in 1907, occasioned even more virulent attacks from his critics. By now, however, the camp of his followers had also grown. In 1909 he received the only official recognition for his poetry when he won the 2,000 korona FRANCIS JOSEPH prize. From 1909 he was in close contact with university youth, who, like he, were seeking a revolutionary road to poetic expression. His health began to fail and from 1909 he spent much time in sanatoria in Hungary and abroad. In 1912 he broke off with Lada and at the same time became a member of the Free Masons' chapter. In these years his poetry began to reflect a disillusionment with his earlier faith that the peasant and the middle classes would produce a social revolution and a democratic renewal. He found them inert and bereft of idealism; more and more he turned to the urban proletariat as the prospective vanguard of the revolution. When a mass demonstration by workmen broke out in Budapest in 1912, he sided with them and published the poems, "Let the Earth Quake" and "The Rush to Revolution." That year he married the daughter of a Transylvanian landowner and moved with her to his castle in Boncza. When war broke out he condemned the slaughter in several eloquent poems.

In 1917, as his health deteriorated, he moved to Budapest. In August 1918, in a volume entitled *Head of the Dying,* he compiled most of the poems he had written during the war. In parliament in November 1918 he participated in the festivities proclaiming the republic and was elected president of a literary academy.

Ady represented a sharp and widely resented departure from the native character of Hungarian poetry and was often attacked by literary, political, and cultural figures for depriving Hungarian poetry of its native roots. His poems were in many ways prophetic of the changes that the Great War would bring about and it was symbolic that he died when the war ended.

Aerenthal, Aloys, Baron Lexa (from 1909, Count) (1854–1912)

Austrian diplomat, ambassador to St. Petersburg, foreign minister of the Dual Monarchy from 1906 to 1912

The man who owed his place in history largely to a single diplomatic event, though one of far-ranging consequences, the BOSNIAN CRISIS, had a dubious social pedigree. According to a never fully confirmed or discredited account by German chancellor Bernhard von Bülow, one of Aerenthal's grandfathers was a Jewish grain merchant in Prague, with the last name of Lexa, who, upon being ennobled as baron, took on the name Aerenthal, meaning "Valley of Grain." This suspicion of a Jewish strain in Aloys's ancestry made him, according to some, insecure and anxious to prove his worth both as an Austrian and as a diplomat, a striving that would account for his not infrequently brusque manner and scheming diplomatic maneuvers. His many years as ambassador in Russia, from 1896 until his elevation to foreign minister in October 1906, made him a champion of Austrian-Russian cooperation and, although previous experiences of that nature (in the so-called Dreikaiserbunds of 1873 to 1879 and 1881 to 1886) had been less than successful, as ambassador he labored for a new alignment. His moves in this direction did not, however, elicit a positive response, from Berlin or from Vienna. After his appointment as foreign minister, Aerenthal continued his cautious inquiries, both in VIENNA and in Berlin, as to the feasibility of a new Dreikaiserbund, but again with no success. Undaunted, he endeavored to conduct a foreign policy in cooperation with Russia, or at least one that would not be objectionable to St. Petersburg. Ironically, his first major diplomatic sally brought his country into direct confrontation with Russia.

An activist by temperament, he had been impatient with the quietist, timid foreign policy of his predecessor, the Polish count Agenor Goluchowski, a policy that did not reflect the great power status of the Dual Monarchy. At the time of Aerenthal's appointment, Russia too obtained a new foreign minister, Alexander Izvolsky, and he on his part felt that Russia's power position needed to be restored after her defeat by Japan in 1904–05. As it happened, a quid pro quo that could accomplish both goals just then presented itself. While a great deal was subsequently read into the bargain these two men, Aerenthal and Izvolsky, struck in September 1908, providing for Austria's acquiescence to the opening of the Turkish Straits to Russian warships and Russia's consent to Austria's annexation of the Balkan provinces of Bosnia and Hercegovina, the most likely reason for the imbroglio that followed was not deliberate deception on Aerenthal's part but a casualness bordering on negligence with which the two diplomats concluded their agreement. Although Aerenthal announced Austria's annexation of the provinces (on October 6) before Izvolsky gained his point with the powers regarding the Straits, and thus there was really no quid pro quo, nothing changed in the European, and Balkan, power constellation. Austria merely altered the *legal* status of BOSNIA-HERCEGOVINA, which she had occupied and controlled for 30 years; he even softened the blow by giving up control of the adjoining Sanjak of Novibazar, also under Austrian occupation since 1878. The move nevertheless came at a time when both Serbia and the newly reorganized Turkish gov-

ernment had an acquisitive eye on the provinces and thus the ramifications were considerable.

There was no prospect that Austria, once she had carried out the annexations, which in a sense were long overdue, would reverse herself; and what followed was not so much power politics as a series of diplomatic skirmishes of which Aerenthal proved an adept practitioner. He quickly assured Berlin that he had no plan "of territorial gain or of embarking on a policy of prestige," adding that a war with Serbia at this time was out of the question as it would entail far greater risks than the promised benefits justified. He was able by his assurances to allay German resentment over his failure to give advance notice of the annexations. Still, his often provocative attitude toward Russia, and personally toward Izvolsky (whom, in a letter of March 8, 1909, he threatened with publishing embarrassing documents and correspondence) led to the escalation of what originally was no more than a misunderstanding to the level of a major diplomatic crisis. In the end Aerenthal gained his point and in the process strengthened the German alliance so vital to Austria. He retained his emperor's trust and remained at the Ballplatz until January 1912; he died on February 17 of that year. His reputation among historians is generally unfavorable, with suggestions that the sharp worsening of relations between Austria and Russia, as well as between Germany and Russia, following the Bosnian crisis opened the door to developments that led to the outbreak of the Great War.

Aix-la-Chapelle, Congress of See CON-CERT OF EUROPE.

Alexander I (1888–1934)
regent of Serbia, from June 1914, king of the United Kingdom of Serbs, Croats, and Slovenes, later renamed Yugoslavia, from September 1921 to October 1934

He was a member of the House of Karageorgević, one of the two Serbian dynasties (the

King Alexander of Serbia *(Hulton/Archive)*

never fully trusted him. In the 10-year period before 1929 when Alexander opted for an authoritarian regime, there were 23 governments, with seven premiers, of whom only one was a non-Serbian, and Serbs held most of the portfolios and the commanding positions in the army.

Much of Alexander's political energies were drained away by mediating between the two leading political figures in the Yugoslav parliament, Nikola Pašić, head of the Serbian Radical Party, favoring a Greater Serbia, and STJEPAN RADIĆ, head of the Croatian Peasant Party, of republican persuasion, who strove for a federal structure in the Yugoslav state. At Radić's persuasion, until 1924 the Peasant Party boycotted parliament and sabotaged Alexander's efforts toward Yugoslav unity. When on June 20, 1928, a Montenegrin deputy shot Radić and two of his followers during a session of parliament, Alexander perceived a chance. But Radić's successor, Dr. Vlasko Maček, proved just as obstreperous as his predecessor had been, and on January 9, 1929, Alexander suspended the constitutional form of government. He prorogued parliament, banned political parties, except for the Radical Democratic Peasant Party, constituted to be unquestioningly loyal to the government. He appointed the commander of his bodyguard, Peter Živković, premier. All agencies of government at all levels were invalidated and replaced by royal appointees. Labor unions and cultural institutions were also suspended. On October 3 of that year the name of the country was changed from the United Kingdom of the Serbs, Croats, and Slovenes to the Kingdom of Yugoslavia.

On September 3, 1931, Alexander issued a new constitution, which, although it provided for a two-house legislature, was designed to assure the king's dictatorial powers. Until then, opposition to royal dictatorship had been muted, but in the early 1930s, in part because of the economic crisis growing out of the Great Depression, resistance rose precipitously. Arrests and deportations multiplied.

other one being the Obrenović). When his aged and ailing father Peter proved unable to bear the burdens of ruling, Alexander assumed the regency of Serbia on June 24, 1914, only a few days before the assassination of Archduke FRANCIS FERDINAND of AUSTRIA-HUNGARY. He had been educated in Russia at the court of czar Nicholas II, where he developed strong Pan-Slavist sentiments. He served in the Serbian army in the two Balkan Wars of 1912 and 1913, and subsequently in the Great War. Temperamentally neither a soldier nor a politician, his interests were intellectual, with a contemplative bent.

After the war and the proclamation of the United Kingdom of Serbs, Croats, and Slovenes on November 24, 1918, of which his father was the king, with himself serving as regent, he assiduously labored at creating a unitary Yugoslav state, although sentimentally he favored a Greater Serbia. The other component parts of the kingdom, especially the Croats and Slovenes,

Alexander deemed it necessary to ensure support for his policies from the other two members of the LITTLE ENTENTE in which Yugoslavia was a partner, as well as from France with which she had a military alliance. It was with the intention to shore up French support that Alexander sailed to France early in October 1934. Arriving in Marseilles on the 9th, he was shot to death, together with French foreign minister Louis Barthou, by Croatian terrorists. The latter hoped that the king's death would result in the dissolution of Yugoslavia. But in an orderly succession, Alexander was followed on the throne by his 11-year-old son Peter, with Alexander's cousin serving as chairman of the regency council.

Algeciras Conference (January 16– April 7, 1906)

an international conference convoked at Algeciras, Spain, ostensibly to settle the Moroccan question

The Moroccan controversy arose from the agreement among Great Britain, Spain, and Italy to support France's protectorate over that country, in violation of the Treaty of Madrid of 1880 whereby all matters relating to Morocco were subject to the assent of the 13 powers party to that treaty. What was really at stake, however, was the success or failure of the German attempt to disrupt the recently concluded Entente Cordiale between Great Britain and France, by discouraging Britain from backing up France for fear that the crisis could issue into war. For Austria, which also attended, it was an opportunity to express solidarity with her principal partner in the Triple Alliance, Germany. As it happened, partly because Germany was represented by an arrogant and unbending negotiator (Count Tattenbach) and partly because Germany's ulterior motive of driving a wedge between France and Britain was all too obvious, Austria alone sided with her when the participants voted on crucial questions. The only point Germany gained was to secure agreement that the Moroccan police force charged with maintaining order in that troubled country was placed under international supervision. This provision was accompanied by a perfunctory declaration upholding the integrity and independence of Morocco as well as its "economic liberty without inequality." In the aftermath, the Entente Cordiale emerged strengthened and crucial military conversations between France and Britain soon followed.

Andrássy, Count Julius, the Elder (1823–1890)

Hungarian revolutionary, politician, and statesman, who served most of his political career in the House of Habsburg, as prime minister and defense minister of Hungary and later as joint foreign minister

During the revolution of 1848–49 he was a member of KOSSUTH's radical reform party. He was elected to the Hungarian Diet in 1847. As a batallion commander, he participated in the armed struggle against the Habsburgs in the War of Independence of 1849. After the defeat of the uprising, he fled abroad, was sentenced to death in absentia, and was in fact hung in effigy in VIENNA's marketplace. During his exile he visited several west European countries and thoroughly familiarized himself with the intricacies of European politics and diplomacy. Amnestied in 1857, he returned to Hungary. Working hand-in-hand with FERENC DEÁK, he was instrumental in drafting the Hungarian terms of the compromise with the Habsburgs that by painful degrees emerged after Austria's defeat at the hands of Prussia in the summer of 1866. He was later, together with Deák, one of the participants in Vienna in the discussions that led to the conclusion of the AUSGLEICH in February 1867. From that time on he was continually active in political life, in the service first of Hungary and then of the Dual Monarchy. After the Great Compromise he was named, at the recommendation of Deák, prime minister of Hungary. It was he who placed the crown of St. Stephen on the emperor's head when the latter was crowned king of Hungary on

June 8, 1867. As prime minister he relaxed the stringent censorship of the press that since the revolution had hampered free expression; he also mitigated the repressive legislation against the Jews.

Having been born in northern Hungary (in Kassa, in the largely Slovak-populated Uplands), he feared somewhat extravagantly that the Hungarian nation would become submerged in the Slavic sea; for that reason he strongly favored dualism—that is, close links to Austria—as well as alliance or alignment with Germany as a means of keeping Russia, protector of Slavs in the empire and in the Balkans, in check. When plans were developed in Vienna for giving Bohemia with its Czech population equal status with Hungary in the monarchy, he strenuously opposed such a measure.

In 1871, when Emperor Francis Joseph abandoned his plans for revanche against Germany and sought rapprochement, he dismissed the anti-German FRIEDRICH BEUST as joint foreign minister and, on November 14, 1871, appointed Andrássy in his stead. The brunt of Andrássy's foreign policy was resistance to Russian expansion in the Balkans and curbing Serbian ambitions to become the center of a South Slav federation. When revolt broke out in BOSNIA-HERCEGOVINA against Ottoman rule in 1875, he strongly advocated the absorption of those provinces into the Dual Monarchy, as well as that of the sanjak of Novibazar, which separated Serbia from Montenegro and which in Austrian hands could serve as an *Ausfalltor* (springboard) for the monarchy into the Balkans toward Saloniki. He achieved these goals at the CONGRESS OF BERLIN in the summer of 1878, following a war between Russia and Turkey.

Pleading ill health, but most likely because he was discomfited by criticisms of his Balkan policy, he resigned as foreign minister on October 8, 1879. First, however, he put his signature to an Austro-Hungarian alliance with Germany, directed chiefly against Russia. He remained a member of the Hungarian upper house to the end of his life.

Andrássy, Julius, the Younger (1860–1929)

son of the great JULIUS ANDRÁSSY THE ELDER, he was active in Hungarian politics as a Liberal

In 1894–95, he was named state minister for service with the king; on October 24, 1918, in the closing days of the Great War he succeeded Count Stephen Burián as foreign minister with the express purpose of terminating the alliance with Germany, which his father had concluded in 1879.

After the war he was a member of the legitimist movement and in fact served on its general staff. He died at the end of 1929.

Anschluss movement

A program aiming at the political union of the German and the Austrian state. Its most active phase fell between the two world wars, but it had its theoretical beginning in the 1880s, specifically as an agenda item in the LINZ PROGRAM. Austria, together with Bohemia, had been a member of the German-Roman, or Holy Roman Empire, and, as such, of the German commonwealth. Even after the demise of the Holy Roman Empire in 1806, and its reconstitution as the German Confederation, Austria retained its dominant position. That position was gradually eroded by the rising power of another German state, Prussia, and after a war between the two powers in 1866, Austria was effectively ousted from German affairs. Not only military defeat but the fact that the great bulk of the Austrian Empire was non-German contributed to this exclusion. In 1882, in the Linz Program referred to above, earnest Austrian intellectuals voiced concern over the German element being overwhelmed by Slavs and Hungarians, and they urged closer relations with the German Reich, although not yet a political merger with it.

No empire after the Great War experienced such extensive territorial fragmentation as the Austrian. French premier Clemenceau, in reviewing the European political landscape, slightingly declared, *"L'Autriche c'est le reste,"*

Austria is a leftover. From this time on a union with Germany became to the minds of many, in Austria as well as Germany, the only viable course. During the war the former German chancellor Bernhard von Bülow had declared: "Even if we lost this war, with the annexation of Austria we can be winners in the end." The victorious powers, quite cognizant of this truth, included in both the German and the Austrian peace treaty a clause forbidding a political, or an economic, union between the two countries.

As Austria's initial grave economic problems, which twice necessitated intervention by the League of Nations, gradually diminished, particularly as industry showed remarkable recuperative powers, the idea of an *Anschluss* lost much of its attractiveness. This state of affairs changed drastically when the Great Depression hit both Austria and Germany in 1930. Austrian chancellor Schober visited Berlin in February of that year and worked out a plan for the preparation of a customs union. When the plan was put to the test of international opinion, it met vehement objections, especially from France, supported, with somewhat less resolution, by Great Britain. In the end the International Court of Arbitration at the Hague, on September 6, 1931, by a single vote ruled that a customs union between Germany and Austria was at variance with the international obligations undertaken by both. France gained a political victory that would come back to haunt her later. With the project of the customs union frustrated, the economic position of both Germany and Austria went from bad to worse, and it was largely the resultant political crisis in Germany that facilitated ADOLF HITLER's rise to the chancellorship in January 1933.

Hitler had made it clear in the first sentence of his book *Mein Kampf* that it was his lifelong dream to bring about a union between his country of birth (Austria) and the German Empire. Obsessively consistent with the goals he had expressed early in his political career, union with Austria remained a cardinal feature of his foreign policy. Although at first he was content to pro-

mote the fortunes of the National Socialist Party in Austria, when that attempt suffered repeated reverses, at a conference with Austrian chancellor KURT VON SCHUSCHNIGG in February 1938 at Berchtesgaden, he made wide-ranging demands that would place Austria's internal and military policies in the hands of Nazi officials. When Schuschnigg tried to frustrate this attempt by scheduling a referendum in which Austrians were asked to vote on the question: "Are you for a free and German, independent and social, Christian and united Austria?" Hitler, to prevent the vote whose outcome was a foregone conclusion, sent his troops into Austria on March 12, 1938. He did not intend an immediate *Anschluss,* but when protests from the League of Nations and from Britain and France were feeble and irresolute, he incorporated Austria into the German Reich.

anti-Semitism in the successor states

The degree of anti-Jewish sentiment in Austria, Hungary, Czechoslovakia, and Yugoslavia, respectively, after the First World War seemed to depend on the mood the peace treaties had left in their wake in each. In general, where the terms had been favorable, the attitude was one of tolerance and even acceptance; where they were harsh, the resultant bitterness was often directed against the Jews. In Hungary the resentment over the drastic territorial truncation was increased by the radical actions taken by the native soviet government that seized power in March 1919 and held it until August of that year; many of its members were young Jews who placed the cause of international socialism above that of the fatherland. The overthrow of that regime was followed by localized outbreaks of "white terror," to which several thousand Jews fell victim. The new head of state, Regent HORTHY, at first tolerated these outrages as a means of appeasing the fury of nationalist elements, then forbade further illegal violence. During the 10-year premiership of ISTVÁN BETHLEN anti-Semitism took the muted form of *numerus clausus,* a limiting of Jewish students in institutions of higher learning, to 5 percent. Even that measure was eased in 1928 and Jews became quite numerous and prominent in the professions, and also in publishing, entertainment, and business. In 1928 Jewish rabbis of high station were given a place in the august Upper House, side by side with those of other religions.

In Hungary, as in other states in eastern and central Europe, the position of the Jewish population was profoundly affected by the rise to political power of ADOLF HITLER in Germany. Official anti-Semitism of the past had targeted religious affiliation; Hitler regarded Jewishness as a matter of racial identity, which neither conversion nor nonaffiliation or nonobservance could alter. His infamous Nuremberg Laws of 1935 introduced into public consciousness the image of the Jew as the eternal enemy, not of Christianity but of an orderly moral society. As ADOLF HITLER's domestic and foreign successes multiplied, his obsessive anti-Semitism gained ever wider currency. In Hungary, 1938 witnessed the passage of the first anti-Jewish law, "zsidótörvény," which placed a limit of 20 percent on Jewish participation in the professions and in commercial and industrial enterprises. A second such law, in 1939, in effect accepted the racial definition of Jewishness and drew some 100,000 persons who had converted or had not been classified as Jews before, under its provisions; it further reduced the ratio of Jewish presence in the professional and commercial fields to 5 percent.

The proportion of Jews in the general population, which ebbed and flowed as the national territory shrank, then increased by piecemeal revisions of the peace treaty, remained fairly stable at about 6 percent. The 1930 census listed 444,567 Jews in a population of slightly over 8 million; by 1941, after portions of Slovakia, Transylvania, and the Bácska had been added to the national territory, of a total population of 14,683,000, 725,000 Jews were counted, about one-quarter of whom lived in the capital. In that year under a third zsidótörvény, over 58,000 more persons were made subject to the restrictive

measures previously enacted; the law also forbade intermarriage between Jew and Christian.

Although the Holocaust did not come to Hungary until the spring of 1944, small-scale deportations, especially from areas recently joined to Hungary, were periodically carried out, and there was an organized massacre of some 1,000 Jews in the Bácska, mainly in the city of Ujvidék, in 1942. Confiscatory legislation as well as further measures aimed at excluding Jews from the country's economic life followed, but their execution was half-hearted and in the early 1940s Hungary was something of a haven for refugees from neighboring countries suffering from summary persecutions.

In the early part of 1944 the Germans, suspecting that Hungary, which had seen her entire Second Army destroyed in the depths of Russia, was maneuvering to leave the war, occupied the country on March 19. They installed a pro-Nazi government, and with its cooperation in the following three months they deported the entire Jewish population from the provinces, the great bulk of it to the extermination camp at Auschwitz. Only men of military age serving in labor battalions both inside Hungary and on the Russian front escaped ghettoization and deportation. The casualty rate among the latter, although substantial in Russia, was generally smaller than among the civilian population. By the time the German occupiers and their Hungarian allies were ready to undertake the deportation of BUDAPEST Jews, foreign pressure and a hesitant change of heart by the head of state, Regent Horthy, had set itself against further such action. Horthy, aware that the war was as good as lost, in October of that year made a forlorn effort to seek peace with Hungary's enemies. The gamble failed. With active German support a Hungarian Nazi regime under FERENC SZÁLASI came to power and aborted the attempt at a separate peace. The persecution and deportation of Budapest Jews was begun, but the hour was late. Over 100,000 were crammed into ghettoes and about half of them were marched under atrocious conditions to the German border. Many died on the way, but railroads and other facilities for wholesale systematic deportations were no longer available. Deaths, both on the road and in the ghettoes, occurred mainly from starvation, exposure, and individual murder.

It is impossible to estimate with any accuracy how many perished in the conflagration whose scale surpassed anything Hungarian Jews had experienced in their tumultuous history. The most approximate count lists about 565,000 (of an estimated total of 825,000) dead, and about 260,000 survivors. After the war there were instances of resentment among the Gentile population at the number of returning Jews who reclaimed assets that had been taken from them during their deportation, but that is not a quantifiable phenomenon. The question of whether and how much anti-Semitism there still is in Hungary time and again surfaces; certainly, the institutional kind is long gone. After the collapse of communism political parties with a platform hostile to "minorities" had made a paltry showing in national elections. On the emotional level the question remains part of the much larger problem of the acceptance or nonacceptance of Jews as equal members of a national community.

In Czechoslovakia, after its founding in 1918, traditional patterns of anti-Semitism were muted by the liberal outlook of the republic's new leaders, TOMÁŠ MASARYK and EDVARD BENEŠ, as well as of a number of prominent cultural figures. In general, until the mid-1930s the lenient national minority policies of the government fully applied to Jewish citizens as well, although small extremist groups and parties, especially in Slovakia, such as the National Union and the Czech Fascist Community, kept the flames of intolerance alive. Slovaks were wont to accuse Jews of cosmopolitanism, which in this case meant adherence to the greater Czech rather than to Slovak nationality. Jews living in the Sudetenland were on their part often suspected by Czechs of pro-German sympathies and of German rather than Czech cultural affiliations. At times, in all regions, they were accused of favoring communism. In general, however, Jews were not subject to any official discrimination. They were present in large numbers in the pro-

fessions, as well as in business enterprises. What first began to erode the edges of the generally benign attitude was the growing number of refugees, first from Romania, where in 1938 an emphatically anti-Semitic government came to power, then from Austria after the ANSCHLUSS. Although most of the refugees were well educated, well-to-do, or well trained in the arts and crafts, they were often regarded as a parasitic presence in difficult economic times. Also ADOLF HITLER's increasingly vehement anti-Semitic outbursts had an incendiary effect on many, especially in the Sudetenland. It had become a political imperative for any government seeking Germany's favors to introduce some manner of anti-Jewish legislation, which in Hitler's eyes was the chief criterion of being a legitimate member of his planned "New European Order."

At the Munich Conference on September 29, 1938, the premiers of France and Britain, anxious to avoid war, granted Hitler the right to annex the Sudetenland. Shortly after the conference, Slovakia achieved partial separation from the Czech parts and the name of the republic was hyphenated to Czecho-Slovakia. In the latter province the Jews made up roughly 4.5 percent of the population (in Bohemia-Moravia the percentage was about 1.1, whereas in Ruthenia it was over 14 percent). The six months after Munich were a twilight period in which some anti-Jewish measures were enacted but a comprehensive exclusion of Jews from public, professional, and commercial life was not yet official policy. In mid-March 1939 Hitler destroyed the remnant of Czecho-Slovakia by incorporating Bohemia-Moravia into the Reich as a "Protectorate," allowing Hungary to take Carpatho-Ruthenia, and proclaiming Slovakia an independent state, though, under a separate "treaty of protection," essentially a German satellite. In internal matters the Slovaks were still allowed a measure of autonomy and their form of government continued to be republican, with civil rights guaranteed to all, including Jews. This state of affairs ended in the summer of 1940, after the German victory over France. A joint resolution by German and Slovak leaders in

Salzburg on July 28 established a Slovak government on the National Socialist model. The solution of the Jewish question was seriously taken in hand. Two German experts on Jewish affairs, Adolf Eichmann and Dieter Wisliceny, were dispatched to Bratislava to "advise" Slovak leaders on the consecutive steps to take for the total removal of Jews from national life. Within a year all Jewish enterprises of any size were either liquidated or "aryanized" (transferred to Gentile ownership); Jews thus rendered unemployed were assigned to labor centers, which in time became forced labor camps.

In the winter of 1941–42 the battle in Russia was stalemated, with no prospect of an early end, and the labor shortage within Germany became acute. In February the German government requested that 20,000 able-bodied young Jews be sent to the Reich to work in war industries. This measure, which Slovak authorities mitigated somewhat by insisting that families should not be separated in the process, marked the beginning of the mass deportation of Jews from Slovakia, first to labor and then to extermination camps. In the spring and summer of 1942 some 60,000 were transported into German-occupied Poland, the bulk to Auschwitz where most of them perished. It was from among these that two inmates managed to escape and make their way back to Slovakia, bringing with them news of the operation of extermination camps. It was the time when mass deportations from Hungary were getting underway, but the news, which quickly spread even beyond the confines of German-dominated Europe, produced no effective intercession. The governments in Washington and London rejected appeals from Jewish persons and organizations that the approaches to Auschwitz be bombed on the plea that they were not a military target.

When in the fall of 1944 a Slovak national rising erupted against German domination, a rising put down only with difficulty, thousands of Jews fell victim to the reprisals that followed the failed revolt. Practically all the Jews remaining in Slovakia, excluding those who lived with false papers or were in hiding, were now deported to Auschwitz. When the war and the terror finally ended, over 100,000 Slovakian Jews had perished and less than 5,000 had survived.

In BOHEMIA and Moravia, under German occupation throughout the war, persecution generally ran on a parallel course with that in Slovakia, although here the Jewish communities, more organized than in the sister province, made concerted efforts to save as many of their coreligionists as they could by assisting in legal and illegal emigration and by instituting educational programs that promoted both Jewish consciousness and confidence. The German concentration camp in the Protectorate, at Theresienstadt, was first intended to be a model camp that might even pass international inspection, but in time most of its inmates were transferred to extermination camps and the Theresianstadt camp itself deteriorated to nearly the level of those. The final count of the victims in Bohemia-Moravia was as grim as in Slovakia; of a total of over 80,000 Jews deported some 70,000 had died in camps and over 5,000 had met their deaths through other violent means. By the end of the war only some 2,800 Jews remained alive in Bohemia-Moravia.

In the postwar period institutional anti-Semitism ceased to exist, but here as elsewhere undercurrents of hostilities toward Jews continued. An unexpected added development was the anti-Semitism within the Communist Party in the late 1940s and early 1950s, a result of Stalin's preoccupation, first, with the inordinate number of Jews in high party positions, and second, with the attraction of Jews to the newly formed State of Israel (which, incidentally, his government was the first to recognize among the major powers), as a force for Jewish nationalism, in defiance of the Marxist principle of internationalism.

Very few urban centers in postwar Czechoslovakia, and later in Slovakia and the Czech republic, respectively, have organized Jewish communities at present; emigration, mainly to Israel and the United States, had been unusually heavy.

It is difficult to present a comprehensive essay on Jewish life and its virtual extinction during the Second World War in Yugoslavia because its regions had different historic, cultural, and religious traditions, which greatly influenced the Jewish experience in each. In Hungary and Czechoslovakia, anti-Semitism had deep roots and was easily rekindled by an untoward event or an accusation of some religious perversity, such as a blood libel. This was not the case in Balkan areas that for centuries had been under Turkish domination in conditions of a thorough ethnic and religious mix; the dominant faith, Islam, was generally tolerant toward minorities. When after the First World War a unitary Christian state, first called the United Kingdom of Serbs, Croats, and Slovenes, emerged, there was

no organized Jewish life on a national scale. In their religious practices Jews were sharply divided between the Sephardim, of Spanish provenance, and the Ashkenazi, who had lived in central Europe for centuries. There was a further division between the Orthodox and the *neolog*, or conservative, Jews. The latter did form, as far back as 1919, a "Federation of Jewish Communities," which however, even though it received government sanction, the Orthodox refused to join. Nevertheless the king appointed a spiritual head for the entire Jewish population, whose rank was on par with the Greek Orthodox patriarch, the Catholic archbishop, and the Muslim religious leader.

Nazi soldiers and party members watching Jews being forced to scrub the pavements of Vienna *(Hulton/Archive)*

There was, in the interwar period, no institutional anti-Semitism or restriction of any kind on Jews. Before the outbreak of the Second World War Jews in Yugoslavia numbered somewhat over 70,000. When, in April 1941, the country was designated by Hitler as one of the states whose independence was to be extinguished as part of the hastily devised plan to make the Balkans safe against possible British landings, the fate of Yugoslavia's small Jewish population was sealed. Unlike in other states under Nazi occupation, from where the intended victims were as a rule deported to extermination camps, the great majority of Yugoslav Jews were murdered where they had been caught or where small groups were concentrated, usually by being shot. At first, it is true, they had been put to work to repair war damage, but after the invasion of the Soviet Union in June 1941 by the German Wehrmacht, summary extermination of Jews and Gypsies became the rule. In August 1942, a report from German military authorities in Yugoslavia stated matter-of-factly that the "problem of Jews and Gypsies has been solved; Serbia is the only country in which this problem no longer exists."

In other parts of Yugoslavia, notably CROATIA, under the terroristic rule of ustaša, an extreme nationalistic grouping, similar fate awaited the Jews, although there the process, at first in the hands of local authorities, was more gradual than in Serbia. The general pattern, as most everywhere else, was that at first the population and the authorities of a region felt bound by the constraints of their legal code; once the Germans moved in and became in effect the source of all legality they authorized mass deportations and executions, mainly on racial grounds. Elements of the local population, feeling released from the strictures of their own national laws, often willingly joined the Germans in their destructive work; so hypnotic was the effect of the unceasing series of German triumphs that the possibility of an ultimate collapse and retribution never seemed to occur to these murderous collaborators. In all of Yugoslavia only the regions occupied by Italians proved to be a haven for Jews; Italian officers, honor-bound, refused to sanction the persecution, let alone murder, of civilians. Under German pressure, and to control the flood of refugees into these Italian-occupied regions, most of the Jews were in time interned, but the internees were generally humanely treated.

At the end of the war only a pitiful minority of about 15,000 Jews remained in the territory of Yugoslavia. After the establishment of the State of Israel 8,000 of these were allowed to emigrate there. Most of those who remained were very old or very young. In Yugoslavia, as in other countries in eastern and central Europe, the future of Jewish life and survival appears precarious.

Austrian anti-Semitism after the Great War cannot be regarded as an autonomous phenomenon because already in the 1920s it was deeply influenced by the tide of anti-Jewish sentiment in Germany, and subsequently by the Nazi Weltanschauung. However, two circumstances did influence Austrian national attitude toward Jews: one was the rapid rise of Zionism, which in its very fundamentals denied the possibility of Jewish assimilation; the other was the conspicuously large Jewish presence in Austria's economic and cultural life. There was also the fact that in the almost exclusively Catholic provinces only a tiny fraction of the population was Jewish and they were viewed as unwelcome outsiders. Adding to a seldom clearly articulated hostility to Jews was the disproportionate participation of Jews in the Social Democratic movement whose professed internationalism many Austrians passionately rejected.

The government after the Great War at first made serious efforts to avoid the stigma of anti-Semitism. Although it took some restrictive measures—it segregated Jewish students at universities and denied voting right to Jews who had settled in Austria after the outbreak of the war—it did not interfere with Jewish domination of such varied enterprises as scrap iron, banking, furniture and shoe trades, textiles, the theater and cinemas, oil, and the professions. When in

1934 political parties were replaced by the single Vaterändische Front (Fatherland Front), Jews were allowed to join it. Jewish writers, scientists, and musicians, such as Stefan Zweig, Franz Werfel, SIGMUND FREUD, and Bruno Walter attained international recognition and fame.

The ANSCHLUSS in March 1938 put an end to whatever tolerance there was in Austria toward Jews. The infamous Nuremberg Laws, providing a racial definition of Jewishness, introduced in Germany in 1935, were applied in Austria, too. The emigration of Jews was seriously taken in hand, but at the same time many in public life, or those who refused to relinquish property rights to their enterprises, were arrested and taken to concentration camps, especially to Dachau near Munich. Several spontaneous anti-Jewish riots occurred in provincial locations. Persecution was at first tentative and exceptions were made in special cases; by the outbreak of the Second World War nearly 110,000 Jews had succeeded in emigrating. From 1939 on persecution became systematic and in November 1939 Adolf Eichmann, in charge of Jewish affairs, told leaders of the Jewish community that all Jews who did not emigrate within a year would be deported to recently conquered Poland. Indeed from 1940 on, deportation to camps in the east became the common means of dealing with the Jewish problem. By the summer of 1943 only Jews in hiding were still left in VIENNA, and none in the countryside. By the end of the war Austrian Jewry, except for those who had emigrated or had been in hiding, had effectively been destroyed. Most Jews present in Austria were of foreign nationality, largely Hungarian, who survived deportation there in the closing months of the war. The majority of these subsequently emigrated overseas, or to the newly founded Jewish state. In conclusion it can be said that while Hitler by and large succeeded in making Europe *Judenrein* (free of Jews) he also occasioned a new definition of Jewish identity for the survivors and contributed to the establishment of the State of Israel, which drew its lifeblood from survivors of the Nazi Holocaust.

Apafi, Mihály (1676–1713)

the last prince of independent TRANSYLVANIA, ruling between 1690 and 1695

After the defeat of the Turks in the long war ending in the Peace of Karlowitz (1699), and their evacuation of the central part of Hungary that separated Transylvania from the western part of the country ruled by the Habsburgs, Leopold I named a governor responsible to him alone to manage the affairs of the province. With this, an independent Transylvania came to an end. Before the Turkish conquest of central Hungary, it had been an integral part of the country, but now, by disposition of the VIENNA court, it was governed as a separate province. Apafi and his wife were transported to Vienna under orders from the Habsburgs never to return to Transylvania.

Apponyi, Albert (1846–1920)

Hungarian conservative politician, vigorous defender of Hungarian constitutional rights under the Great Compromise

He was one of the leaders in parliament of the United Opposition, a loose grouping of moderate conservatives and moderate liberals devoted to the Hungarian national ideal. United Opposition later became the National Party and Apponyi ended up as a member of the Independent Party. He was president of the lower house of parliament in 1901–03. As minister of education, in 1907, he was the chief author of the Education Act, whose principal object was the Magyarization of nationalities under Hungarian rule.

When, after the fall of the soviet government in Hungary, the conclusion of a peace treaty to end Hungary's belligerence in the Great War became possible, the Entente Powers on December 1, 1919, invited a Hungarian delegation to come to Paris. Apponyi, who was an outstanding orator and spoke several languages, was chosen to head the delegation. His mighty efforts to gain a revision of the harsh terms put to the delegation (see TRIANON, PEACE OF) proved unavailing, and he signed the peace treaty on June 4, 1920.

Arad, martyrs of

The revolutions of 1848 and 1849, especially in Hungary, imperiled the very existence of Habsburg rule and, after their defeat, the reprisals were correspondingly severe. Somewhat puzzlingly, on August 16, 1849, after the surrender of the insurrectionist Hungarian armies, the imperial council of ministers passed a resolution calling for lenient treatment for those who had participated in the uprising. Former imperial officers were to be allowed to reenter the army or apply for retirement. Political leaders could freely go abroad. But four days later, at the behest of Prime Minister FELIX SCHWARZENBERG, who, to a plea of a foreign statesmen that the government show indulgence toward the insurrectionists, had cynically replied, "Yes, we will, but first we'll do some hangings," instructed Hungary's military dictator, Julius Haynau, to take all political leaders as well as military officers who had participated in the uprising into custody and conscript ordinary soldiery into the imperial army. Summary trials and convictions followed. On October 6, in the town of Arad, 13 former generals (Lajos Aulich, János Damjanich, Arisztid Dessewfy, Ernö Kiss, Károly Knézich, József Nagy-Sándor, György Lahner, Vilmos Lázár, Károly Leiningen-Westerburg, Ernö Pöltenberg, József Schweidel, Ignác Török, and Károly Vécsey) were hanged; in BUDAPEST the premier of the short-lived revolutionary government, LAJOS BATTHYÁNY, was shot. Only the commander of the revolutionary army, ARTUR GÖRGEY, was, at the intervention of Russian czar Nicholas, spared and exiled to Carinthia. Less than a year later Haynau, who in his role as military dictator had acted with uncalled-for brutality, was retired.

armistice of November 3, 1918

The official act that ended Austro-Hungarian participation in the First World War. A month earlier, on October 3, 1918, the German, Austrian, and Turkish governments had sent simultaneous notes to Washington, asking for an armistice. The reply was slow in coming and meanwhile component parts of Austria-Hungary—Bohemia, Slovakia, Galicia, later Ruthenia, Croatia, and Slovenia—separated themselves from the Dual Monarchy through resolutions passed by hastily constituted national committees. By the end of October only the Italian front was still active; on November 1 the Italian high command in Padua handed emissaries of the Austrian army the conditions for ending the fighting, conditions decided upon by the Supreme War Council in Paris. By its terms Austria was to evacuate the areas that the London Treaty of April 1915 had assigned to Italy. The Entente reserved to itself the right to occupy such "strategic points" within the Dual Monarchy as its military chiefs deemed necessary. After Emperor Charles of Austria signified acceptance of the terms, the Austrian army on the Italian front ceased fighting at 3 A.M. on November 3. The Italians, wishing to capture as many prisoners and as many supplies as they could, did not abide by the armistice until 3 P.M. on November 4. All hostilities had still not ended, however. French general Franchet d'Espérey, commanding a mixed French-Serbian force in the Balkans, claiming that the Padua armistice applied to the Italian front only, occupied Belgrade. When he was at last willing to deal with the Hungarian delegation, his terms designated large areas of southern and southeastern Hungary for occupation by French and Serbian forces. These areas in time were joined to the United Kingdom of Serbs, Croats, and Slovenes.

The fighting was at last over but the peace that would demolish what had once been the Austro-Hungarian Dual Monarchy still waited to be made.

Árpád

Tradition knows him as the founding father of the Hungarian nation, though most likely he was but one of three leaders of the tribes that entered the Carpathian Basin in A.D. 896, and possibly earlier. His father was the chieftain Álmos. About 889–890, Hungarian tribes settled in the area between the Dnieper and Dniester Rivers, which they came to refer to as the

Etelköz. Here, disorderly conditions prevailed, owing largely to the fact that the seven tribes, one of them Khabar, did not recognize a single leader—they cooperated as voluntary allies. Battles with the ferocious Petchenegs, pressing westward from the Volga and the Don, pointed up the need for unified command, and the choice fell on Árpád, who stood out by dint of his courage and intellect. According to national chronicles, the chieftains lifted Árpád on a shield and introduced him to the people held high. At the same time they defined their relationship with him. The seven chieftains cut their arms and let the blood flow into the sacred pot used for soothsaying and concluded the so-called Contract of Blood. Their oath provided that: (1) as long as Árpád descendants lived, the prince of the Hungarian people would come from his line; (2) whatever they conquered by united strength they would divide justly; (3) as the chieftains elected Árpád of their own free will, none of their descendants would be excluded from the royal council; (4) if anyone among their descendants turned against the prince, their blood would flow as the blood of those that took the oath did; (5) anyone in future who violated this oath would be excluded from the tribe. These became the founding principles of the Hungarian constitution. It is not at all certain that the undertakings were as precisely defined at the time, but they were kept and honored in the sense the chronicles state.

Barely had the tribes settled in the Etelköz than Byzantine emperor Leo VI sent an embassy to ask Árpád to join him in a war against the Bulgarians on the lower Danube. Árpád obliged and in 894 sent his son, Levente, with a force to the Danube. Levente returned with a large booty and with the ransom paid for the prisoners he had taken. But now the beaten Bulgarians allied with the Petchenegs, and while Árpád campaigned in the north, they laid waste to the region inhabited by the Hungarian tribes. Because of the Petcheneg threat the Hungarians no longer felt safe in the Etelköz, and they began another westward move. There are different versions of the route they took, depending on the chronicle one reads.

According to the most likely one, Árpád's host besieged Kiev, and although the Slavs defending the city were allied with the Cumans, he defeated them. Subsequently the racially related Cumans, and even some of the Slavs, joined the Hungarian host. Árpád led it to the Carpathians. It scaled the mountains at Verecke Pass and entered the basin in the neighborhood of present-day Ungvár in the county of Bereg. Inside the ring of mountains, the area west of the Tisza River was under the rule of Bulgarian king Zalan (Salaman?). Árpád sent an embassy, claiming that the land belonged to him as a scion of Attila, though he demanded only part of it. In time he sent tribal chiefs to other parts of the Carpathian Basin with similar demands. In the third year after he scaled the Carpathians, he reached the left bank of the Danube. The region situated beyond the Ipoly River was ruled by the Moravian king Svatopluk. In time Árpád's host conquered that land too. And now Zalan, seeking to preserve his kingdom, ordered Árpád to evacuate the Carpathian Basin. Árpád refused and the two armies met on the plains of Alpár. Árpád won a great victory and Hungary was his.

Auersperg, Prince Wilhelm (1814–1890) (Carlos)

Austrian prime minister from January to September 1868

Son of a Bohemian family of the old aristocracy, Auersperg professed views extraordinarily liberal for his time. The Great Compromise with Hungary of the year before he assumed his high office left many constitutional questions in abeyance and it was the task of Auersperg's brief ministry to address them. Because of the number of bourgeois ministers in his cabinet, it was referred to as Bürgerministerium, ministry of burghers. The laws it pushed through had an almost militantly liberal character, including separation of the judiciary from the executive; abolition of the ministry of police, which had acquired an evil reputation during the BACH Era; and granting peasant landowners the right freely to dispose of their property. The most conspicuous and controversial measures, however, concerned church-state relations, thus far governed by the restrictive clauses of the CONCORDAT OF 1855, which had made the Roman Catholic Church virtually a state within the state. Civil marriages were now declared legal and public schools were freed from ecclesiastical control. All religions were given equal status before the law. In case of mixed marriages, upon the death of a parent boys inherited their father's religion, girls their mother's. Free-thinkers were no longer subject to imprisonment for expressing their views. These measures, although popular enough to elicit general jubilation and the illumination of the capital, were opposed vigorously by the Austrian clergy and the Vatican itself, but in the end in vain. What Auersperg's ministry could not resolve was the Slavic clamor for rights similar to those granted to the Hungarians in the AUSGLEICH; in September 1868 Emperor FRANCIS JOSEPH dismissed Auersperg from office.

Auersperg, Prince Adolf
(1821–1885)

Austrian politician, younger brother of Prince WILHELM *(Carlos)* AUERSPERG, *who was appointed prime minister in 1871*

After the failure of the experiment of his predecessor, Count Charles Hohenwart, aiming to transform the Dual Monarchy into a genuine federalist state, Auersperg's cabinet was composed mainly of Austrian Germans who called themselves Liberal in the narrow sense of the word at the time, anticlericals and centralists, intolerant of assertive national minorities. Regarding, with good reason, the Bohemian Czechs as the most determined foes of the dualism of Austrians and Hungarians, Auersperg moved swiftly to silence all voices of protest in that province. In order to strengthen German influence in political life, Auersperg proposed to the imperial council that governed the Austrian parts of the Dual Monarchy a new electoral law whereby deputies would be selected not by provincial assemblies but by electoral districts so drawn that they assured a German majority. The

bill passed largely due to the boycott by Czech deputies in the Reichsrat (Imperial Council) session when the vote was taken. The elections of 1873 proved the success of Auersperg's experiment when a heavy Austro-German majority was elected to the Reichsrat.

Auersperg had to resign in 1878, following the CONGRESS OF BERLIN, when he opposed the occupation and administration by Austria of BOSNIA-HERCEGOVINA, though not for the obvious reason that it was likely to lead to a collision course with Russia, but because he argued that it would bring too many Slavs into the empire and further undermine the predominance of the German element. As it happened, there was no felicitous choice between preserving the German character of the empire and at the same time pursuing imperialist goals (in the Balkans) that Austria's great power status demanded.

Augsburg, Peace of (1555)

The first conciliation, after years of warfare, between the Catholic and the Lutheran faiths in the Holy Roman Empire. The Protestant estates, supported by France, which, although Catholic, pursued the political goal of opposition to the Habsburgs, formed the Schmalkaldic League, to defend their interests against Catholic princes, the Holy Roman Emperor, as well as the Vatican, who fought vigorously against religious pluralism in the empire. When armed hostilities failed to settle the matter, the two sides finally agreed to a negotiated peace. The Diet of the empire, called to draft the terms of the settlement, met in February 1555 and sat until September in the city of Augsburg. Neither Holy Roman Emperor Charles V nor any papal representative was present. Two popes had died in quick succession in March and April before a third one, Paul IV, agreed to a formula regarding religious affairs in Germany.

After lengthy negotiations, in September of that year FERDINAND I of Habsburg, to whom his brother Charles V had yielded the imperial dignity, published the so-called Augsburg Recess containing the provisions of the agreement. It had four principal articles: (1) Lutheran princes, knights, and free cities enjoyed the same security and protection as Catholic estates did; (2) each state was free to choose between Catholicism and Lutheranism (the phrase enshrining this principle, *cuius regio, eius religio,* although widely used, was not part of the written agreement), but only the prince could make that decision and the population had to adhere to it; (3) all lands seized by Protestant estates and granted to them by a previous agreement (the Peace of Passau of 1552) could be retained by them; and (4) by the so-called ecclesiastical reservation, if a Catholic bishop, archbishop, or abbot chose to convert to Lutheranism, he could do so but would forfeit his title, land, and privileges. It was understood, though not officially stated, that only Catholicism and Lutheranism would be recognized in the empire, thus leaving the position of Calvinist estates in doubt.

As later events were to show, the Augsburg settlement was a peace of exhaustion rather than of genuine reconciliation; each religion sought to advance its position and the ecclesiastical reservation was repeatedly violated. The final showdown between the two camps came in the first half of the next century, in the so-called THIRTY YEARS' WAR.

Ausgleich (1867)

A series of agreements concluded between the imperial court in Vienna on the one hand and Hungarian statesmen on the other regarding the position of Hungary within the Austrian Empire. On the part of the Austrian government the agreement reflected a realization, enhanced by two recent military defeats (at the hands of France in 1859 and Prussia in 1866), that Hungarian cooperation was essential for the effective functioning of the imperial structure. The finalization of the agreement was preceded by prolonged negotiations and the submission of a number of proposals and counterproposals; it might well have failed had it not been for the wise initiatives and moderating influence of the Hungarian statesman FERENC DEÁK. In essence

the *Ausgleich* recognized two distinct entities within the empire, Hungary and Austria, each with their possessions. The links between the two were the Habsburg monarchy, which, as long as a Catholic male line existed, would have sovereign rights in both parts and joint ministries for military, foreign affairs, and finances necessitated by the first two. The ruler had a dual title, emperor of Austria and king of Hungary. In terms of sovereignty the two titles were inseparable; the ruler could not abdicate his crown in one country without also abdicating it in the other. To possess his imperial and royal dignities he would have to be separately crowned in Austria and in Hungary, and take the oath to respect and protect the laws and liberties extant in each country. He would appoint both the common ministers and the ministers of the Austrian and the Hungarian cabinet. For the rest, the two countries were in effect independent from one another, and the formal name of the state was changed from Austrian Empire to the Austro-Hungarian Dual Monarchy. There was no common citizenship; a person was either an Austrian or a Hungarian citizen and if he chose to change his citizenship, he had to be naturalized in the country of his choice.

As for the "joint" ministries, the ministry of defense would be charged with the organization and management of the Dual Monarchy's fighting forces but would have no jurisdiction over the national levies in each realm, the Landwehr in Austria and the Honvédség in Hungary. These latter would be controlled by a separate defense ministry in each country. In the joint army the language of instruction and command was German, except where allowance was made for the native tongue of non-German recruits. For the determination of the length of service and the size of the annual conscription levies, the consent of both parliaments had to be obtained.

The foreign minister was entrusted with the conduct of the Dual Monarchy's foreign relations and the appointment of ambassadors and consular officials. For the conclusion of international trade treaties he had to consult the minister of commerce in each realm and gain the consent of the parliament of each.

The joint finance minister supervised common revenues derived from contributions by both entities as well as customs receipts. It was his responsibility to prepare annual budgets for such finances as were necessary for the conduct of foreign and military affairs. Every 10 years the two countries jointly set tariff rates and decided the share each would shoulder for joint expenditures. If any international undertaking involved financial obligations, these would have to be voted on in a parallel fashion by the two separate parliaments. Finally no person could be a common minister and at the same time a minister in the cabinet of his country.

To give weight to the principle of separation as the Hungarians saw it, and to avoid providing a core for an eventual central parliament, the delegation system was instituted at the initiative of Count JULIUS ANDRÁSSY THE ELDER of Hungary. Every year each of the two parliaments elected from its membership a delegation of 60 members, 20 from the upper house, 40 from the lower. The delegations met alternately in VIENNA and BUDAPEST. They deliberated and voted on issues of common interest separately. If disagreements arose between the two delegations, they met in common session and voted on the contentious issue without prior discussion. In case of a tie, the emperor cast the deciding vote.

The system, despite its potentialities of controversy and fundamental disagreements, worked fairly smoothly for the remaining decades of the Dual Monarchy, although toward the end growing Hungarian aspirations for separating the two units cast a cloud over the conduct of "joint" affairs. No other entity in the Dual Monarchy ever received equal status with the two principal ones.

Austerlitz, Battle of

Napoleon Bonaparte's most celebrated victory on December 2, 1805, his lucky day as he called it (he had been crowned emperor of the French on that day the year before). In the prolonged warfare against the Third Coalition, Napoleon entertained the notion of breaking British sea power and invading the island kingdom, somewhat fancifully claiming that he could accomplish the landing if he could rule the English Channel for six hours. He chose a somewhat irresolute admiral, Pierre de Villeneuve, to accomplish the task by a series of complex maneuvers that involved luring the main British fleet to America to gain his six hours' freedom in the Channel. The plan failed, and Villeneuve's fleet was eventually destroyed by Nelson's squadron at Trafalgar.

But on land Napoleon's forces proved invincible. Intent on preventing the two main armies of the Third Coalition, the Austrian and the Russian, from combining, he sent one of his armies, the Grande Armée, which had been gathered around Boulogne in preparation of the invasion, to the Rhine and then to the Danube. At Ulm Napoleon hemmed in Austrian general Mack's army of 50,000, cut it off from all provisions, and forced it to surrender. He subsequently marched his forces practically unopposed to Vienna, which he entered on November 12. However, two Russian armies, under General Kutuzov and Czar Alexander I were bearing down from the north and were joined by one of the two Austrian armies in the field (the other under Archduke Charles campaigned in northern Italy). For days Napoleon had been riding on horseback over the rolling terrain near the Moravian town of Austerlitz surveying the opportunities it offered. The highest of the hills, Mount Pratzen, once taken, offered a vantage point for artillery from which the entire field below could be strafed. Napoleon drew up his army, its right and left wings six miles apart; the elite corps under Marshal Soult had the task of scaling and occupying Mount Pratzen, from which they would command the entire battlefield. He promised his soldiers that "The victory will put an end to the campaign, and we shall then be able to turn to our winter quarters, where we shall then be joined by the new armies which are forming in France; and then the peace which I shall make will be worthy of my people, of you and of myself."

The night of December 1, as word spread in the ranks that the emperor was coming (he had been touring the prospective battlefield all day), in a burst of enthusiasm they made torches from the bundles of straw they had been given to sleep on and formed a spectacular corridor of fire, hailing their commander.

When the sun rose in a clear sky the Austro-Russian armies, sensing that the weight of French forces was on the left wing, drew troops from their center to outflank it. The marshals around Napoleon impatiently begged him to order the attack, but he restrained them, saying, "When the enemy is making a false move, we have to be careful not to interrupt him." He gave the signal shortly after 8 o'clock and the marshals rode to their respective corps at full gallop. The battle was on.

Soult's forces battled their way up onto Mount Pratzen, and by noon the French standard waved at the summit. Soult then sent his troops down the other side of the hill into the valley, where he joined the Imperial Guard in combat. Some 7,000 of the enemy fell in the confused battle and were trodden underfoot. Others tried to retreat across a frozen lake. With some 2,000 men on the ice, Soult ordered his artillery to pounce on them. The ice yielded, and the men drowned in the icy water. Panic completed what the weapons had left undone. The allied armies retreated with a loss of 20,000 lives. That evening Napoleon addressed his triumphant troops. "Soldiers," he said, "I am satisfied with you. In the Battle of Austerlitz you have justified all my expectations of bravery; you have adorned your eagles with immortal glory, and it will be enough for one of you to say, 'I was in the Battle of Austerlitz' to draw the reply, 'Here is a brave man.'"

Czar Alexander fled in tears and Francis sued for peace. In the ensuing Peace of Pressburg, Austria suffered extensive territorial losses.

Austria-Hungary

Created by the *AUSGLEICH* of 1867 it was formally known as the Austro-Hungarian Dual Monar-chy. Of its two constituent parts only Hungary was defined as a national state; the other part was referred to as "the lands and countries represented in the Imperial Council." Such unity as there was between the two parts was provided by the person of the ruler (*Kaiser*, emperor, in the Austrian parts, *király*, king, in Hungary), and by three "joint" ministries—for foreign affairs, defense, and such finances as the first two necessitated. The term "personal union," embodied by the sovereign, had different meanings in the two parts: in Austria, the emperor was the source of all authority; in Hungary, authority was vested in the houses of parliament, which then transferred it to the king, but only after he had been crowned with the crown of St. Stephen, Hungary's first Christian king, and taken the oath to the Hungarian constitution. All these and related governmental issues were spelled out in the *Ausgleich* of 1867.

Territorially Austria-Hungary constituted much the greater part of eastern and central Europe and was the largest state on the continent after Russia. In 1914 it comprised 676,615 square kilometers (by comparison the German Empire in Europe had a territory of 547,888 square kilometers, France totalled 536,464, and Britain comprised 317,915). The westernmost point of the Dual Monarchy was Bangs in the Vorarlberg, the easternmost, Chiliseni in Bukovina. The distance between the two was 1,247 kilometers. The northernmost location was Hilgersdorf in Bohemia, the southernmost Spizza in Dalmatia. The distance between these two was 1,046 kilometers. The total population of the Dual Monarchy including Bosnia-Hercegovina according to the 1910 census was 51,390,223. (Germany at the same time had a population of 64,925,993, Britain 46,533,896, France 39,602,258, Italy 34,671,377.) In the monarchy the density of population was 76 persons per square kilometer. (In Germany it was 118.5, in France 74, in Britain, 149, in Italy 121.) The Austrian part of the Dual Monarchy was more densely populated than the Hungarian, with 95 inhabitants per square kilometer over Hungary's 64.2.

In Austria for every 1,000 men there were 1,030 women, in Hungary l,019 women. The birth rate in Austria for every 10,000 people was 315, in Hungary 363. The death rate for each thousand persons was 220 and 233, respectively. Of the monarchy's citizens 25 percent were German, 17 percent Hungarian, 13 percent Czech, 11 percent Serb and Croatian, 9 percent Polish, 8 percent Little Russian (Ruthenian), 7 percent Romanian, 4 percent Slovak, 3 percent Slovene, 2 percent Italian, and 1 percent mixed.

After its annexation in 1908 BOSNIA-HERCE-GOVINA comprised an integral part of the Dual Monarchy; the promulgation announcing its integration stated that its precise legal status was to be defined—it never was. In the meantime it was jointly governed by Austria and Hungary. Bosnia's capital was Sarajevo, Hercegovina's Mostar. The provinces were under the administration of the joint finance minister of the Dual Monarchy.

Each nation in the state had its own colors; the Habsburg escutcheon with the two-headed black eagle merely symbolized the rule of one royal family over the farflung dominions included in the monarchy. The Austrian colors of black and yellow dated back to the Holy Roman Empire, from whose banner they were taken. The Hungarian flag of red-white-green was also of ancient origin; the Habsburgs abolished it, then restored it after the revolution of 1848. The naval colors of both countries were red-white-red, dating back to Babenberg times. (As legend had it, when Prince Leopold of Babenberg, after a battle, removed the belt from his blood-stained shirt, it left a white band in the middle, with red on either side.)

The Austro-Hungarian Dual Monarchy was an anomaly in an age of rising nationalism, and indeed ethnic tensions proved to be the most disruptive force throughout its life of 41 years, and yet its historic function was precisely, as it had been of the Austrian Empire before it, to prevent the many nationalisms within its borders from turning against each other and set the sprawling region ruled by the Habsburgs on fire. This recognition was the source of the remark so often quoted as an historical verity that if the Habsburg Empire had not existed it would have had to be invented.

Austrian Netherlands

When MAXIMILIAN I of the House of Habsburg, as a very young man, married Mary of Burgundy, only child of the Burgundian prince Charles the Bold in 1477, he inherited not only his bride's home country but the Netherlands as well. Burgundy slipped from his grasp when, in the Peace of Arras of 1482, ancient French claims to it were recognized, but the Netherlands remained in Habsburg hands. A loose confederation of 17 provinces, Dutch-speaking in the northern seven provinces and French-Flemish speaking in the southern 10 Belgian provinces, it lived in internal peace under Habsburg rule until the Reformation shattered traditional loyalties and internal peace. The grandson of Maximilian I, CHARLES V, began the persecution of Protestants in the Netherlands, but it was under his son, Philip II, ruling from Spain, that the persecution caused a deep political split and wholesale internal disruption. Repeated attempts by the absentee Philip to overcome resistance to his religious policies, especially in the northern Dutch, Calvinist provinces, proved unavailing, and in 1579, as the 10 provinces in the south united in the League of Arras, reaffirming their loyalty to the House of Habsburg, the northern provinces declared their separation in the Union of Utrecht, declaring their virtual independence from the ruling house and from their southern sister provinces. The separation did not receive international sanction until 1713 when, in the Peace of Utrecht, ending the War of the Spanish Succession, the 10 southern provinces were temporarily assigned to the Republic of Holland, with the proviso that they would, after the resolution of some border disputes, be turned over to Austria; after that time they were known as the Austrian Netherlands. These provinces were, however, conquered by the French during the Revolutionary Wars of 1792 to 1814 and remained parts of the French Empire until the Congress of Vienna, when they were attached to Holland as part of the United Netherlands. A revolution in Belgium in 1830 eventually resulted in its separation from Holland; in 1839 the powers recognized the independence and permanent neutrality of Belgium.

Austrian Succession, War of the

The PRAGMATIC SANCTION, a document issued by CHARLES VI of Austria, seeking to preserve the unity of Habsburg lands and ensure orderly succession even in the absence of a male heir, gained the signatures of a number of European monarchs, though some of them doubted its legitimacy. Among the doubters was Frederick II of Prussia whose father, a signatory, had died the same year Charles VI did. Frederick, concerned about the small size and population of his Prussian kingdom and fiercely dedicated to making it into a great power, repudiated his father's adherence and, on December 16, 1740, invaded Silesia, a province of Bohemia and a Habsburg possession. He assured European powers that the purpose of the annexation was to free Protestants in Silesia from Habsburg oppression. He treated the newly conquered province with extreme solicitude. But within weeks of the invasion Austrian troops poured into Silesia in order to retake it. Sensing Austrian vulnerability, the European states swung into action. France hoped to take the AUSTRIAN NETHERLANDS and was joined by Spain. Britain, at war with France over parts of America, entered on Austria's side. Charles of Bavaria, a descendant of the daughter of Leopold I of Austria, laid claim to Upper Austria and Bohemia. The king of Saxony aspired to Moravia. Soon the original issue of Silesia was lost from sight.

In 1742 the hard-pressed Maria Theresa made peace with Prussia alone, temporarily ceding Silesia. But the war continued in the west. The French earned a great victory in Belgium and seated their candidate, Charles of Bavaria, on the throne of the Holy Roman Empire. But overseas, in America, the fortunes of war turned against the French and Paris, in fear of losing its American offshore colonies, offered peace.

The treaty of Aix-la-Chapelle of 1748 restored the status quo ante in Europe, and Frederick II was left in possession of Silesia.

Austro-French War of 1859

One of the significant wars of the 19th century fought over an issue extraneous to the relations between the two nations: Italian unification. The Congress of Vienna had compensated Austria for the loss of the AUSTRIAN NETHERLANDS with the two Italian provinces of Lombardy and Venetia; these were incorporated into the Austrian Empire. Even in the other Italian principalities (the Kingdom of the Two Sicilies in the south, the Papal States in the center, the grand duchies of Tuscany, Modena, and Parma north of Rome), though not in Piedmont-Sardinia in the northwest, Austrian influence was paramount, if only because internal unrest and external threats could be opposed only with the help of Austrian military might. Thus, when Piedmont achieved national maturity after the revolutions of 1848, its king, Victor Emmanuel (who succeeded his father Charles Albert after the revolutionary upheaval), and his chief minister Count Camilo di Cavour, perceived Austria to be the main obstacle to Italian unification. Cavour was also only too well aware that unification would mean the extinction of the independent Papal States and he sought to reduce the role of the church in secular affairs as a preliminary to the inevitable clash with the Vatican. In foreign policy he recognized the need to enlist allies, for Piedmont could not stand up to Austrian power alone. An opportunity offered itself with the outbreak, in 1854, of the Crimean War, in which both Britain and France fought Russia in the Black Sea. Cavour overrode parliamentary opposition by committing Piedmont to a struggle in which she had no direct interest. The first Piedmontese troops landed in the Crimea in April 1855. One foot soldier was heard to remark: "Out of this mud, Italy will be built."

After Russia surrendered in January 1856, a peace conference was called in Paris and Cavour participated as an equal. It was here that he first called attention to the plight of "the unhappy peninsula" dominated by Austria. Although he made a deep impression, more than international sympathy was needed to secure military help in a war with Austria. Napoleon III of France was a champion of the nascent movement of nationalism, had fought in a revolution in Italy in 1830 on the side of the romantic revolutionary group called the carbonari and had seen his older brother killed. Since then he had several times expressed himself in favor of Italian unification. But it took two attempts on Napoleon's life by Italian patriots to frighten him into the realization that his life and that of his family was not safe as long as he failed to commit himself to the cause of a united Italy. As a first step he proposed a marriage between his nephew (son of Napoleon I's brother Jerome) and the 15-year-old daughter of the Piedmontese king, Clotilde. After a series of exchanges between Napoleon and Cavour, on this question and others, the two men met in the French spa town Plombières, near the Piedmontese border, in July 1858. They at first envisioned four Italian states to emerge from a conflict with Austria: the Kingdom of the Two Sicilies, a central Italian kingdom, the Papal States, and a northern Italian kingdom under Piedmont. The four would be joined in a loose confederation under the pope's presidency. But later Cavour advanced more ambitious plans and Napoleon tentatively agreed that once Austria was defeated, northern and central Italy, including the provinces of Lombardy and Venetia, would be joined to Piedmont under the House of Savoy. France was to be compensated for her military and diplomatic aid with the provinces of Nice and Savoy.

As the year 1859 opened, both Napoleon and Victor Emmanuel made statements hinting at a coming conflict. The wedding between Prince Napoleon and Clotilde of the House of Savoy in January foreshadowed a close alliance between Piedmont and France. Indeed in that month a secret agreement was concluded, in which Napoleon pledged an army of 50,000 on Piedmont's side in case of war with Austria, on condition that Austria would be the aggressor. Czar Alexander II of Russia proposed a congress to deal with the Italian question and, as a preliminary to it, Britain and France proposed that both Austria and Piedmont disarm. Austria, opposed to the congress, especially as Napoleon called for the participation of all Italian states in it, now demanded Piedmont's unilateral disarmament. When an April 23 ultimatum to this effect was rejected, Austria declared war.

Even before actual fighting started, there were revolts in Tuscany, Parma, and Modena, and the populace, by calling for Piedmontese protection, in effect opted for union with that state. After the French-Piedmontese army defeated the Austrians at Magenta, three other states, Romagna, the Marches, and Umbria, also asked to be placed under Piedmont's protection. On June 24 came the costly battle at Solferino, whose savagery so shocked Napoleon that he offered Austria separate peace. This violated Article 6 of his secret treaty with Piedmont, which pledged joint struggle to the end. In the Peace of Villafranca Austria ceded Lombardy to France, on the understanding that France would confer it on Piedmont. Venetia remained with Austria. Decision as to the future of Parma was left to Napoleon. He, together with Austria, would strive to return the thrones of Modena and Tuscany to their former rulers, but no force would be used toward this end. To make the agreement more palatable to Cavour, Napoleon abandoned his claims to Nice and Savoy. But Cavour was not to be appeased and resigned as premier. He wrote to a friend: "I feel such exhaustion that it warns me that [all this] is too much for me—old age has begun, premature old age, caused by moral pain of unparalleled bitterness."

In less than a year, however, Cavour came to realize how much Piedmont had gained and

the premier Nicola Pašić, Austrian-Serbian relations deteriorated sharply. Pašić's pan-Slavic aspirations threatened Austria's already precarious position in the Balkans; at the same time, Serbia's waxing power acted like a magnet on the Dual Monarchy's large Slavic population. Austria had earned a Pyrrhic victory in the BOSNIAN CRISIS OF 1908–09, when she incorporated the provinces of BOSNIA-HERCEGOVINA, which, until then, she had only administered, into her empire, thus frustrating Serbian designs there, while Austria's ally, Germany, warned the Russians off intervention. The result was increased Russian pan-Slavic agitation in the Balkans. In VIENNA it became a dogmatic conviction that every Serbian gain redounded to Austria's disadvantage. A new crisis could well bring matters to a head.

When, in September 1911, Italy, having been given a free hand by France to claim the North African Ottoman province of Tripolitania (present-day Libya), declared war on Turkey and, in a series of quick actions, expelled her military forces, the nearly terminal weakness of the Ottoman Empire was revealed. The time seemed ripe to drive the Muslim Turks from Europe altogether. It was against this background that the First Balkan War erupted. No single state on the peninsula was strong enough to challenge the Ottoman Empire alone; thus an entirely opportunistic alliance, the Balkan League, was quickly formed. The Russian envoy in Belgrade, Hartwig, was feverishly active, often without authorization from St. Petersburg, in promoting this compact. The first treaty of alliance, between Serbia and Bulgaria, was concluded on March 13, 1912. It provided for the distribution of territorial gains in case of a Turkish defeat. On May 29, Bulgaria and Greece entered into a similar alliance. French president Poincaré, during a visit to St. Petersburg in August, was shown the text of the Serbo-Bulgarian alliance and at once realized its potential for war but, although such a war might involve Russia and, in consequence of her alliance with France, that country too, he did not object, only urging an increase in Russian military strength in Poland.

The first shots, on October 8, were fired not by any of the contracting parties but by tiny Montenegro; 10 days later Serbia, Bulgaria, and Greece declared war on Turkey. The armies of these allied states earned a series of quick victories. Bulgaria in particular, following battles at Kirk Kilissé, then at Lulé Burgas in Thrace, drove to the very gates of Constantinople. The Serbians at the same time earned a great victory in the three-day battle of Kumanovo.

Although Austria was not directly involved, the reaction in Vienna was alarm. A greatly enlarged Serbia, especially if it gained access to the Adriatic Sea, would undermine Austria's entire position in the Balkans. Serbian forces, on November 10, reached the Adriatic, prompting the Austrians to announce their firm opposition to such a territorial gain. Italy, with her own ambitions in the Balkans, supported Austria while Russia supported Serbia.

On December 17, after an armistice had been reached by Turkey, on the one hand, and Serbia and Bulgaria (not Greece), on the other, an ambassadorial conference met in London in an attempt to reconcile the many conflicting interests. But the conflicts proved too deep and, when the Turks refused to surrender some key points demanded by the Balkan allies, the conference adjourned and war resumed on February 3. After a new series of defeats Turkey agreed to the key allied demand, the cession of Adrianople; the conference in London reopened and drew new borders, greatly to Bulgaria's advantage and to Serbia's disadvantage (for she was not allowed to retain her Albanian conquests). Disgruntled with their meager gains, Serbia and Greece, on June 1, 1913, concluded a new alliance, this time against Bulgaria, a preliminary to the Second Balkan War (June 29–July 30). Turkey and Romania, each hoping for territorial gain, entered the anti-Bulgarian coalition and, within a month, Bulgaria suffered resounding defeat. By the Treaty of Bucharest of August 10, she lost most of the territories she had gained in the first war to the coalition ranged against her. It was, however, not this treaty, but the aftermath, that

A Bulgarian field gun being positioned for the siege of Adrianople, occupied by the Turks, during the Second Balkan War *(Hulton/Archive)*

alarmed Austria and led to a new worsening of Austro-Serbian relations. The Serbians, still unreconciled to their exclusion from the Adriatic, invaded Albania and for weeks skirmished with Albanian forces. Possibly, in different circumstances, Austria might have opted for military action while the position in the Balkans was still fluid, especially as she had 60,000 fighting men, largely reservists to be sure, in Bosnia-Hercegovina. But, both a misreading of the military odds (the high command had expected Bulgaria to hold her own against her Balkan enemies), and an embarrassing scandal in the military (the so-called Redl affair) had a demor-

alizing effect on Austrian military initiatives. There were also vocal criticisms of Austria's Balkan policy in both the imperial and the Hungarian parliaments. Archduke FRANCIS FERDINAND, the weightiest voice in military matters, was on vacation in Holland in July. Thus any Austrian military intervention was mired in uncertainties and hobbled by personal disagreements. There was no disagreement, however, where the necessity of forcing Serbia to evacuate territory belonging to the newly formed Albanian state was concerned. A visit to Vienna early in October by Serbian premier Pašić produced no reconciliation of views in this respect. When the

Serbians continued to drag their feet in leaving Albanian territory, on October 18, 1913, VIENNA addressed an ultimatum to Belgrade, demanding evacuation within eight days. Serbia, abandoned even by Russia, yielded. But the wounds inflicted on Austrian sensitivity and Serb national pride never healed.

Bárdossy, László (1890–1946)
Hungarian diplomat, politician, premier

His father, Jenö, was a jurist, also active in politics. Bárdossy took his doctorate in political and juridical studies at Budapest University. He subsequently studied in Berlin and Paris as well. His early positions were in the educational field; from 1913 he was a superintendent of schools and also served in the ministry of religion and public education. Between 1922 and 1924 he was deputy head of the foreign ministry's press office; in 1924 he was appointed its head. In 1930 he was named counselor at the London legation; from October 1934 he was the envoy and first minister at the Bucharest legation. After the sudden death of Count ISTVÁN CSÁKY in February 1941 he was appointed foreign minister. Two months later, when the premier, Count TELEKI committed suicide in protest against Hungary's involvement in the war against Yugoslavia, Regent HORTHY chose Bárdossy to be premier while letting him continue as foreign minister. When Germany attacked Yugoslavia in early April of that year, Bárdossy authorized the occupation of areas that had before the First World War belonged to Hungary, but allowed the employment of troops only after Yugoslavia had in effect ceased to exist.

The fateful turn in his life and career occurred when Germany launched her campaign against the Soviet Union. Although Hungary's neighbors, Slovakia and Romania, joined the campaign that same day (June 22, 1941), Bárdossy hesitated, especially when, on June 23, Soviet foreign commissar Molotov assured him of Soviet goodwill toward Hungary and promised Soviet support for Hungary's territorial claims.

Bárdossy never shared this message with either regent Horthy or his cabinet; it took a mysterious air attack on the Hungarian town of Kassa for him to prevail on the regent to declare war on the Soviet Union; he announced this decision to parliament on June 26. Although he did not say so, his expectation, strongly supported by chief of the general staff Henrik Werth was that, after the swift German victory most everybody expected, Hungary would be rewarded with great territorial cessions. From here on, he had no option but to fall in with all Axis initiatives. After ADOLF HITLER's declaration of war on the United States in December 1941, Bárdossy followed suit, announcing a state of war between Hungary and not only the United States but Great Britain as well.

Early German victory on the eastern front did not materialize and Hitler faced the unthinkable: a winter war in the depths of Russia. In January 1942 he demanded of Hungary fuller participation in the war and Bárdossy authorized the deployment of one of the two Hungarian armies on the Russian front. In his internal policies he sought to continue the work of GYULA GÖMBÖS, who had died in 1938: he pursued a rightist radical course with an accent on racial protection. He initiated the third Jewish law that banned intermarriage between Jews and Gentiles, terming such a union racial pollution. However, he either did not realize or ignored the strength of conservative political forces in Hungary to whom both the anti-Jewish law and the state of war with Britain and the United States were disagreeable; they demanded his dismissal as head of government. Horthy did request, and obtained, his resignation on March 7, 1942. Thereafter Bárdossy occupied himself with creating a common front of extreme rightist politicians and in 1943 became president of the United National Christian League with just such a program. But if nothing else, the rapid advance of the Red Army made it obvious that the day of such racist elitist organizations had passed. Knowing what fate awaited him in a Hungary dominated by the Soviets, in late 1944 Bárdossy retired to his native town, Szombathely. In early 1945 he received permission to settle in Bavaria. There he secured an immigration visa to Switzerland, but once there he was placed in a concentration camp. On May 4, 1945, he was expelled to Germany, where American authorities arrested him and, together with other Hungarian war criminals, sent him back to his native land. He was put on trial on October 29, 1945, and although he offered an expert and intellectually superior defense, on November 3 he was sentenced to die by the rope. An act of clemency changed that sentence to death by firing squad. He was shot on January 10, 1946.

Bartók, Béla (1881–1945)

Hungarian musician, composer, pianist, teacher of music

Son of a school principal who died at age 33, and of a mother of German stock, he had one sibling, a sister. He married twice, had a son, Béla Jr., from his first marriage, and another son, Peter, from his second. His parents early discovered his musical gifts and began giving him piano lessons when he was five. Soon he composed minor pieces. His father died when Bartók was seven and his mother, an elementary school teacher, returned to her earlier occupation as a piano teacher. In 1891–92 Bartók enrolled in the Gymnasium at Nagyvárad, but by now music had become his dominant, indeed sole, interest. He gave his first piano concert at age 11 and performed, among other numbers, his own composition, *The Flow of the Danube*. The family moved several times, and finally settled in Pressburg, where Bartók began his musical training in earnest. He earned a diploma from the Pressburg Gymnasium in 1899. By now he had composed his first mature pieces, chamber music in the style of the German romantic masters. Pressburg being only a short distance from VIENNA, it would have been natural for Bartók to take his further training in that city immersed in music, but he came under the influence of Hungarian composer Ernö Dohnányi, only four years his senior, and he decided to place himself under Dohnányi's tute-

Béla Bartók *(Hungarian Museum of Photography)*

lage in BUDAPEST. When he gave his first Budapest concert on October 21, 1901 (Franz Liszt's H-moll Sonata), he was already an accomplished pianist, but his output as a composer lagged behind. He gained new inspiration when, in February 1902, he heard Richard Strauss's *Thus Spake Zarathustra*. Another motif that entered Bartók's musical imagination was the swelling tide of Hungarian nationalism, and it manifested itself in his demeanor as well: he began wearing a native attire and in other respects too stressed Hungarian themes. His "symphonic poem," *Kossuth,* performed on January 14, 1904, caused a great stir. In the fall of 1903 he joined Dohnányi in Gmunden, Germany, to upgrade his piano technique. During 1904–05 he gave several concerts in Vienna, Berlin, Pressburg, and Budapest. Taking a long vacation in a Hungarian peasant village in 1904 he first fell under the spell of folk music.

He decided to collect a large trove of such songs and orchestrate them. He met a Hungarian fellow-composer, Zoltán Kodály, who was engaged in a similar endeavor. In 1906 the two published a collection of 20 pieces, 10 by each of them, under the unassuming title *Hungarian Folk Music.* However, the reception was not friendly; the snobbish music establishment took a less than kindly view of melodies plucked from the peasant environment. Still, the two composers were undaunted. In 1911 they formed the New Hungarian Music Association in order to gain for their work a larger and friendlier audience, but that did not prove a successful venture either. Bartók retired from performing in public. His more serious compositions, *The Prince Carved from Wood* (1914–16) and his opera, *Castle of Bluebeard* (1917–18) had a better reception. In the decade after the First World War he gave several concerts abroad; in 1919 his last operatic work, *The Wondrous Mandarin,* was performed. In 1928 he gave concerts in both the United States and the Soviet Union. Gradually he achieved world fame. But his political views engendered hostility in Hungary; he had an unwelcome sympathy for his country's neighbors who had, in the wake of the Great War, detached large chunks of the "historic kingdom." It was a measure of his character that he remained a faithful Hungarian without translating this loyalty into chauvinistic antagonisms. Between 1920 and 1930 he orchestrated a vast collection of folklore. In 1923 he married Pásztory Ditta and they settled in the United States. He suffered from repeated ailments during these years. He was hard at work on a composition when he died in 1945. His significance as a composer did not diminish with the passage of time; he had discovered in the folk music of eastern Europe, especially of Hungary, the noble wellspring for a new, rich, musical culture.

Báthori, István (1533–1586)
prince of Transylvania, later king of Poland
Son of István, former prince of TRANSYLVANIA, and Kata Telegdi. His life and reign fell into a period of Hungarian history when the rivalry between the Ottoman Turks, occupying the central third of historic Hungary, and the Habsburgs, reigning over the western strip while laying claim to the entire country, was at its height. Transylvania benefited from the stalemate by clinging to a semi-independent status, but it was obliged to pay annual tribute to the Porte. It elected its own Diet, which in turn elected the prince of the province. As a young man, Báthori studied at the university of Padua, then served as a page at the court of Habsburg king FERDINAND I in VIENNA. But when Ferdinand's rival for the Hungarian throne, János Szapolyai, became prince of Transylvania with Turkish support, Báthori transferred his loyalty to him; then, after Szapolyai's untimely death, to his infant son János Zsigmond. When the latter also died young and the Vienna court appointed one Gáspár Bekes prince, a defiant Transylvanian Diet elected István Báthori, then 36 years old, in his place. Bekes led an army into Transylvania but he met a series of defeats at Báthori's hands. Habsburg attempts to extend authority over Transylvania were once again foiled.

Meanwhile, in 1572, the throne of the House of Jagiello in Poland fell vacant. Several houses, the Habsburg included, aspired to it. The Polish Diet first elected the younger brother of French king Charles IX, Henri, to the throne, but when the latter returned to France after his brother's death, the Diet chose Báthori as prince. He was crowned in Krakow on May 1, 1576. He subsequently married Anna, the sister of the last Jagiello king. Being absent from Transylvania, he entrusted its governance to his younger brother Kristóf. After Kristóf's death in 1581, István Báthori appointed a governing council to handle routine matters in the province, but he had items of importance referred to himself. During the closing years of his reign he promoted a scheme for an alliance of Poland, Hungary, and Transylvania as a bulwark against both Habsburg and Turkish power, but he was not able to bring the plan to fruition. He died in Grodno, Poland, on December 22, 1586. The Poles still remember him as one of their greatest kings.

Batthyány, Count Lajos (1807–1849)

president of the "first responsible Hungarian ministry" during the revolution of 1848

His father was Count Sándor Batthyány, his mother was Borbála Skerlecz. He had no sisters or brothers. In 1834 he married Countess Antonia Zichy, from whom he had one son and two daughters. He studied at the Vienna Klinkowstrom College and received his higher education from a private instructor. In 1826 he joined the army. At first he served in the infantry; a year later he transferred to the cavalry. Owing to his spendthrift habits he accumulated many debts, as did his mother with her expensive lifestyle. After the elder Batthyány died, Lajos became involved in a long legal battle with his mother over his father's legacy. Finally, at the behest of the Hungarian chancellor in Vienna, they compromised. When Lajos came of age in 1831 he left the army and took over his paternal inheritance. His estates had been neglected, their restoration proved arduous and costly, but it forced him to adopt modern methods of agriculture. He became active in the political life of Vas County where his estates were located. His debut in national politics came during the 1839–40 session of parliament; he joined the opposition grouping of young noblemen in the upper house. In the early 1840s he fell under the influence of the rising politician LAJOS KOSSUTH and his political views became more radical. Radicalism at the time meant the dual endeavor of achieving for Hungary a measure of independence from Habsburg rule and an enlightened approach to the mitigation or abolition of feudalism. By 1843 Batthyány was one of the commanding influences in circles opposing Habsburg rule. Together with Kossuth he was aware of Habsburg machinations to scotch all opposition. A telling object lesson was the way the royal house countered an attempt by Polish nobles in Galicia to resist Habsburg dominion by encouraging a peasant rebellion that put those very nobles on the defensive. Batthyány and Kossuth urged the speedy liquidation of feudal conditions to prevent a similar outbreak in Hungary. In 1847 it was under Batthyány's presidency that the lower house of parliament produced the Oppositionist Pronouncement in preparation for founding a new party of the opposition. But it was only under the impact of the revolution in Paris in February 1848 that the political climate became receptive to the reforms advocated by the oppositionists. In the beginning parliament, especially the upper house, resisted precipitate changes, but after the success of the revolt in VIENNA and the resignation of Metternich on March 13, it became more responsive. On March 15 it dispatched to Vienna a delegation, of which Batthyány was a member. A reluctant court agreed on March 17 that he become the head of a Hungarian government. He occupied his position on March 31 and organized his cabinet on April 7. Between April 19 and May 23 he provisionally also headed the ministry of defense. By now what had been demands for reform had escalated to the Hungarian desire for a separate state. At Batthyány's initiative the government set up the Military Council of the National Guard, over which he alone had supervision. It was one of his tasks to oversee the recruitment of the Honvédség, a separate Hungarian military organization in May 1848; he was also made responsible for negotiating with the Croatians who were attempting to do vis-à-vis Hungary what Hungary was doing vis-à-vis Austria, declare their independence, and were mounting an armed attack. Meanwhile the attitude of Vienna stiffened under the influence of military successes in northern Italy against Italian rebels and the king did not receive the Hungarian delegation. After his return to Budapest on September 11, Batthyány resigned and agreed that the National Assembly endow Kossuth with executive power. But when news came of a Croatian attack against Hungary, on September 12 he again agreed to form a government. His choice of cabinet was not accepted by parliament; he governed as acting premier with the help of state secretaries. On September 13, determined to resist the Croatian invasion, he called for a national uprising; he could not, however, find a competent leader. On September 27 the king dismissed him. The Vienna court then appointed a royal commissioner, F. Lamberg, to govern Hungary, but on the very day of Lamberg's arrival the people of BUDAPEST lynched him. Batthyány betook himself to Vienna in order to find a solution for the disagreements, but as the court did not deal with him as an equal, on October 2 he tendered his final resignation. He even abdicated his parliamentary mandate and returned to his estate in Vas County. However, he continued to support the cause of the revolution and fought as a national guardsman. On October 11, 1848, in a battle, he fell from his horse and broke his arm. After his recovery he was once again chosen parliamentary deputy and participated in the work of the October 1848 parliament, which the king had declared illegal. When proposals were made to transfer parliament to Debrecen for safety in the face of an advancing imperial army, he opposed it. It was at his initiative that on December 31, 1848, parliament agreed to send a peace delegation to the commander of the Austrian army, Marshal WINDISCHGRÄTZ. Batthyány himself was a member of the delegation; Windischgrätz demanded unconditional surrender and, instead of negotiating with Batthyány, on January 8, 1849, arrested him. He was at first locked up in the barracks in Buda, later transferred to Pressburg, then to Laibach. In August 1849 a court martial sentenced him to prison; later under pressure from the Vienna court, he was sentenced to death but recommended for clemency. He did not acknowledge his guilt or the competence of the court. Subsequently, he was brought to Hungary and, when Julius HAYNAU became military commander with full powers, he approved Batthyány's death sentence by the rope. On the day before his execution, with a dagger smuggled in by his wife, he inflicted a serious wound on his neck. The next day he was executed by firing squad.

Bauer, Otto (1882–1938)

Austrian jurist, socialist theoretician, one of the most influential members, together with VICTOR *ADLER, of the Austrian Social Democratic Party*

Present at the party's 1899 congress in Brünn (Brno) in BOHEMIA, he represented the viewpoint that the nearly crippling nationality problems of the Dual Monarchy were manifestations of the class struggle; in his 1907 book *Die Nationalitätenfrage und die Sozialdemokratie* he subjected the thesis to a profound analysis, concluding that nationalism was in the last resort a part of the ideology of the exploiting classes; at a time of rampant nationalism he held fast to the conviction that no class-conscious working man could identify himself with the national ideal. In this formative period of international socialism such a dogmatic conception was not uncommon, even though it ignored the many changes brought about by the Industrial Revolution as well as the jealous possession by nations of their countries' natural wealth. From 1907 he was a parliamentary deputy. During the Great War, and especially during its closing phases when the collapse of the Dual Monarchy seemed imminent, he advocated union with Germany, but, unlike other more moderate socialists, he favored such a union only if Germany chose the socialistic, or at least a genuinely democratic, path. As for his native country in its final death throes, he subscribed to the unconditional right of each component unit to shape its national destiny, including the right of secession.

With the empire dissolved even before the end of the war, on October 21, 1918, a provisional national assembly of "the independent state of German [as distinct from a multinational] Austria" met in VIENNA. This assembly, on October 30, formed a provisional government, of which the principal figures were Social Democrats, with Karl Renner as premier. Victor Adler was named foreign minister, but when he died on November 11, Otto Bauer succeeded him. The next day the assembly declared Austria a republic.

As foreign minister Bauer diligently promoted an ANSCHLUSS with Germany; in fact at the beginning of March 1919 he traveled to Berlin and, with German foreign minister Brockdorf-Rantzau, enunciated the conditions under which such a unification of the two German-speaking nations could be achieved. These were essentially that Austria would become a federal state within Germany while reserving to herself the right to conduct her relations with the Vatican and the successor states of the Dual Monarchy individually. But soon after the conclusion of this agreement conditions changed drastically in both Austria and Germany, and Bauer deemed his own policy mistaken. "The question of where a state belongs," he stated, "is a problem of centuries, which cannot be decided by the demands of the moment." He continued to hope, however, that if "progressive" forces triumphed in German political life, a unification of the two states would still be viable.

French statesmen, firmly opposed to any common basis between Germany and Austria, treated with mistrust a government in Vienna whose foreign minister was a determined champion of an *Anschluss*. When on June 2, 1919, the Austrian government received from the Allies the peace terms, many attributed their harshness to Bauer's maneuvers. On July 13, Bauer resigned as foreign minister. He had other reasons as well: Italy would make no concessions in the matter of the South Tyrol, an Austrian province that she demanded for herself, and the impending collapse of the soviet government in Hungary dashed all hopes of the strengthening of socialist forces in the Danubian region.

Out of office, Bauer felt freer to fight for his socialist convictions. The Austrian economy and its fiscal position were so hard-pressed that repeated deficits forced the government to turn to the League of Nations for financial aid. The granting of a loan was tied to strict conditions. Principal among these was Austria's pledge that for the next 20 years she would preserve her national independence (i.e., forswear the very idea of union with Germany) and, in the interest of a balanced budget, that she would radically decrease the number of state employees; this meant the dismissal of about 200,000 working people. Otto Bauer, and the Social Democratic Party in general, were opposed to such a restriction on the government's freedom to con-

duct its own internal and external policy. Bauer in particular argued that with greater financial sacrifices, Austria could achieve stability by her own efforts and not depend on the League of Nations for financial rescue. He was overruled and the loan was accepted with all the conditions attached to it.

Those same conditions did not bind Germany, however, and in that country the financial consolidation produced by the Dawes Plan, which moderated German reparations payments and provided for large international loans, led to vigorous expansion and heavy investments in Austrian business concerns, especially in smelting and electric energy production. All this revived the *Anschluss* idea in a new form, namely as a solid foundation for international business interests. Bauer was not slow in perceiving how an idea he had held dear since his early political days was subverted from one conceived in the spirit of Marxist internationalism to one serving rapacious capitalist interests. This recognition however, as well as his previous declarations in support of a union with Germany, remained, on the theoretical level. Bauer's merit in Austrian history is not that he was able to bring his socialist convictions to practical fruition but that he always acted as a moderating force on their potential militancy. It was due largely to his moderation that segments of the middle class at times looked on the Social Democrats (in contrast to the tiny Communist Party) with less hostility and even at times with indulgence.

Bauer remained active in Austrian politics, though with less and less effectiveness, until the *Anschluss* in March 1938. Fearing almost certain arrest and detention, he fled to Czechoslovakia, and there, in Brno, during the few months left to him, he edited *Der Sozialistischer Kampf,* in which he returned to his earlier idea of an all-German socialistic revolution within the framework of an *Anschluss*. But *Anschluss* of a very different nature had already taken place. Bauer died on July 4, 1938. The editorial offices of his paper were, after his death, moved to Paris.

Dr. Edvard Beneš *(Hulton/Archive)*

direction of his country. Although France lent diplomatic support, it was the last time she showed any fighting spirit on behalf of her eastern ally. When Hitler pressed his claims to the German-inhabited Sudetenland in Czechoslovakia, and threatened war in case of refusal, the British government headed by Neville Chamberlain discouraged France from backing the Czech position. At the infamous Munich Conference on September 29, 1938, the dismemberment of Czechoslovakia (which Hitler contemptuously referred to as "the monster child of Versailles") began. At Hitler's insistence Beneš resigned as president on October 5 and left his native land soon after. He first went to Britain, then to the United States, where he became visiting professor at the University of Chicago. When in March 1939 Hitler destroyed the remainder of Czechoslovakia, Beneš moved to Britain, where he became head of the Czechoslovak National Council and president of the Czechoslovak government in exile.

Beneš was one of those among political exiles who early realized that the future of eastern and central Europe would in good part be determined by the Soviet Union. He was also among those who hoped that this would not necessarily mean Soviet interference in the domestic affairs of those countries, especially the ones that emerged from the war as victorious states or that were victims of Nazism. In March 1945 he led a delegation of Czech and Slovak politicians to Moscow; he was assured by Stalin and Molotov that his government would be allowed to exercise full control within the pre-Munich borders of Czechoslovakia, though this promise was subsequently qualified by a Soviet claim to the easternmost province of the republic, Ruthenia.

Beneš consented; in fact, U.S. ambassador to Moscow Averell Harriman reported home that Beneš "did not seem particularly exercised over the possibility of losing Ruthenia."

On April 3, 1945, Beneš reestablished his government in the Slovakian city of Košice, and on May 16 he reentered Prague to resume his presidential office and duties. In ill health—he suffered two strokes in the course of 1947—he was unable to resist growing Communist Party influence in the government. In February 1948, when the Communist premier Klement Gottwald demanded that Beneš install a cabinet consisting largely of Communists, he surrendered. He refused, however, to sign the new constitution, resigned on June 7, 1948, and died on September 3, having once again failed to preserve his country's independence.

Berchtold, Leopold von (1863–1942)
(Leopold Anton Johann Sigismund Joseph Korsinus Ferdinand, Count von Berchtold)
Austro-Hungarian diplomat, ambassador in St. Petersburg from 1906 to 1912, when he succeeded ALOYS AERENTHAL *as foreign minister of the Dual Monarchy*

Descended from an Austrian baronial family, he acquired large landed estates in Hungary as well as in Bohemia, married a wealthy Hungarian woman, and became, emotionally and in habit, a Hungarian. Given to the pleasures of the high aristocracy (he owned a racing stable and attended horse races regularly), he did not take easily to the often rigorous demands of the diplomatic service and accepted his elevation to the post of foreign minister with sincere reluctance. One historian's description of him as "wavering in his decisions and of unfathomable ignorance, he treated his office as a secondary occupation, of less importance to him than clothes or the Turf," is probably too harsh, but all those who knew him seem to agree that whereas his predecessor, Aerenthal, had kept a firm hand over his ministry, Berchtold was unsure of himself and easily influenced. It is in any case one of his-

tory's cruel ironies that a man of his caliber was at the helm of the foreign office at the time when the Dual Monarchy entered its most serious international crisis.

That Berchtold had, by his own admission, little understanding of the South Slav problem was evident during the First BALKAN WAR, in which an alliance of Serbs, Montenegrins, Bulgarians, and Greeks fought for no other purpose than to divide the Balkan portion of the Ottoman Empire among themselves. Berchtold insisted that the territorial status quo be preserved, in the naive hope that this would prevent Serbia, which had become the greatest threat to Austria's survival as a multinational empire, from acquiring land and influence. That policy proved unsuccessful, but when in the second Balkan War Serbian forces reached the Adriatic Sea in Albania, Berchtold did succeed in preventing such aggrandizement by organizing the London conference of ambassadors, which in the end opted for an independent Albania rather than allowing any portion of it to pass to Serbia.

What assured Berchtold an indelible place in history was his role in the dispatch of the Austrian ultimatum to Serbia, on July 23, 1914, an act that proved the opening salvo in the diplomatic crisis that rapidly led to the outbreak of the First World War. Berchtold was under the influence of the saber-rattling chief of the Austro-Hungarian general staff, FRANZ CONRAD VON HÖTZENDORF, who had been urging war against Serbia for years. Both Aerenthal and Berchtold had resisted Conrad's urgings, but the assassination of the heir to the throne, the Archduke FRANCIS FERDINAND, on June 28, 1914, created a new situation because of the live suspicion that high-ranking Serbian officials and even statesmen had abetted the deed. Assured by Conrad that the army was ready, Berchtold, once he had the German kaiser's blank check to take any action against Serbia his government deemed fit (he told Conrad on July 7 that "Germany advises us to strike at once . . . [She] will support us unreservedly even if our march into Serbia lets loose a great war"), was determined to put demands to Serbia that were impossible to fulfill and thus provide a pretext for an attack on her. The only objection to this plan came not from abroad but from within the monarchy, where Hungarian premier Count ISTVÁN TISZA, convinced that a war between Serbia and the Dual Monarchy could not be localized, advocated a diplomatic solution to the crisis.

Meanwhile Berchtold had sent the legal adviser of his ministry, Dr. Wiesner, to Belgrade to investigate culpability for the murder. Wiesner reported on July 13, "There is nothing to show the complicity of Serbian government in the assassination or its preparation." But he left the possibility open that other officials were involved; on the basis of this report Berchtold, on July 14, prevailed on Tisza to drop his opposition to the ultimatum. (Tisza later claimed that he yielded because of the intemperate tenor of the Serbian press.)

Berchtold instructed his minister in Belgrade, Giesl, to deliver the ultimatum at 6 P.M. on July 23 with the demand that it be accepted in toto within 48 hours; failing that, Giesl was to break off relations and return to Vienna. The Serbian reply, delivered an hour before the deadline, was not satisfactory and the situation was further compromised by the fact that at 3 P.M. on July 25 the Serbian government ordered general mobilization. That evening Berchtold gave his approval to the mobilization of seven Austrian army corps to be deployed against Serbia. German military men (the kaiser was on an extended cruise) watched the development of events and, together with Chancellor Bethmann-Hollweg, wanted Austria to act quickly before a coalition hostile to her, and by extension to Germany, could crystallize. But now Berchtold had a rude awakening. When on the evening of July 26 he told Conrad that the government wanted to declare war as soon as it could "in order that various influences may cease," Conrad replied that the military would not be ready before August 12. Crestfallen, Berchtold replied, "The diplomatic situation will not hold that long."

Indeed, it did not. The next day British foreign secretary Grey decided to initiate mediation between Austria and Serbia, and possibly between Austria and Russia. Such mediation, if successful, would prevent Austria from settling scores with Serbia, and the potent threat in the south of the empire would continue and get worse. What Grey actually proposed was that Britain, France, Germany, and Italy mediate between Austria and *Russia*. For this purpose he envisioned a conference in London, of the kind that had settled the Balkan crisis of 1912–13. But now Germany's spine stiffened and Bethmann-Hollweg advised Grey that "we cannot drag Austria in her conflict with Serbia before an international tribunal." He then called Vienna and urged a fait accompli. Berchtold called in Conrad and demanded that he agree to an immediate declaration of war against Serbia. Conrad gave his reluctant consent, "provided diplomatic considerations make it seem necessary." Thus, at 11 A.M. on July 28 Berchtold wired the Austrian declaration of war on Serbia to Niš, whither the Serbian government had retreated. The next day Austrian cannon bombarded Belgrade. Two days after that, Europe was aflame.

In the final reckoning the outbreak of war amounted to a failure of Berchtold's policy. In January 1915 the court requested his resignation and he tendered it on the 13th. He was then assigned a high office at court. After the war and the collapse of the Habsburg monarchy he retreated into anonymity.

Bethlen, Gábor (1580–1629)

son of a Transylvanian family of lesser nobles that over the centuries gave numbers of outstanding politicians and statesmen to Hungary

His father was Farkas Bethlen, his mother a Croatian, Družina Lázár. Gábor was prince of TRANSYLVANIA between 1613 and 1629. The entire 17th-century history of Hungary was marked, and scarred, by a two-pronged struggle against the Turks in the south and the Austrian Habsburgs in the west, as well as by religious conflict. Bethlen, fighting for Hungarian (or alternately Transylvanian) independence, at times had to seek the support of one enemy power against the other. Throughout his life he was in the center of these shifting alliances and changing political fortunes.

He grew up at the court of Transylvanian prince Zsigmond Báthori and began his military career at an early age, participating in some bloody battles, particularly against the Habsburg general Georg Basta, whose attempts to extend Habsburg authority over Transylvania brought a period of unprecedented terror to the province. Bethlen sought Turkish help against Habsburg tyranny. Having fled to Ottoman territory, he established contact with another Transylvanian noble, ISTVÁN BOCSKAI inside Hungary, urging him to lead an uprising against the Habsburgs. For this purpose he secured the Porte's support for Bocskai's assumption of the princely dignity in Transylvania in 1604. Bocskai, however, died two years later. Bethlen, unwavering in his opposition to Habsburg rule, in 1611 was again forced to take refuge in Turkey; in 1613 the Transylvanian Diet nevertheless elected him prince. His 16-year rule marked the high noon of Transylvanian prosperity. Peace at last reigned in the province, trade and commerce flourished, and government coffers bulged with unprecedented surpluses. In his political philosophy Bethlen was beholden to the English king James I of the House of Stuart, embracing his idea of royal absolutism and rule by divine right. But, unlike James, he exhibited exemplary religious tolerance and chose his advisers on the basis of merit, regardless of their religious affiliations. Rejected by the Habsburgs, he continued to lean on the Porte, but he managed throughout his reign to avoid subservience.

The most active phase of his foreign policy was bound up with the THIRTY YEARS' WAR which broke out in 1618 and during whose early, Bohemian, phase a strong Protestant movement developed in Hungary; Bethlen was its outstanding political and military leader. He led a major force into northern Hungary, then under Habsburg rule, occupied several towns and cities, and eventually brought all of Habsburg Hungary under Protestant rule. In 1619 he besieged VIENNA. However, learning that a Hungarian general allied with the Habsburgs had invaded Hungary in his rear, he retreated. A Diet elected him king of Hungary; by then, however, the Habsburgs had fought the victorious Battle of White Mountain, decisively defeating the Bohemian Protestant forces, and Bethlen was forced to conclude the Peace of Nikolsburg, relinquishing his royal title. He did receive, however, in compensation seven counties in northeastern Hungary as well as the princedoms of Oppeln and Ratibor in the Holy Roman Empire. In 1824 he launched a second attack against Habsburg Hungary, with even less success, and had to conclude the Peace of Vienna, that confirmed the Nickolsburg peace but forced him to give up the German provinces he had gained in the latter. He now sought to make common cause with the Habsburgs and asked for the hand of the princess Cecilia Renata in marriage. After being politely rejected, he married a Protestant princess, Catherine of Brandenburg, who, however, under the influence of Catholic nobles, converted to Catholicism and became a supporter of the reunification of Transylvania with the rest of Hungary under Habsburg rule. Bethlen joined a Protestant grouping of states organized by Cardinal Richelieu of France, including Denmark, England, and the Netherlands. This alliance induced the formidable Catholic general Wallenstein to bring an army to Hungary in the summer of 1625; Bethlen prepared to meet him in battle. Each side maneuvered well late into the season and the battle was never fought. Bethlen then abandoned military hostilities, and no enemy entered Transylvania during the rest of his reign. He died on November 15, 1629, at age 59.

Bethlen, Count István (1874–1946)
Hungarian landowner, politician, statesman, premier

Scion of one of the old Transylvanian noble families, he represented the pride, values, and political interests of the large landowning class. After earning a degree in law from the University of Budapest, he spent a year of study in Britain; upon his return home he served a year in the military. A member of the Hungarian parliament from 1901, he repeatedly changed his party affiliations, always championing a conservative, nationalistic political line. He served throughout the First World War on a number of fronts. When at the end of the war a progressive nobleman, serving as premier, MIHÁLY KÁROLYI, embarked on a broad program of land reform, Bethlen placed himself in strong opposition. During the short-lived soviet regime in Hungary he stayed in VIENNA and headed the anti-Bolshevik Committee. When time came for Hungary to make formal peace with the Allied Powers, he was appointed to the peace delegation led by Count ALBERT APPONYI. He was first elected to the postwar parliament in 1920 and continued to serve until 1939. Amid the political turmoil of the early 1920s, although he remained a stalwart of the old social order dominated by the landed aristocracy, he accommodated financial and commercial interests, at the time largely in the hands of Germans and Jews.

During his 10 years as premier he also held, in 1921, the finance portfolio; in 1929, the justice portfolio; and in 1924, the justice, foreign, and the agricultural portfolio. Although a royalist by sentiment, he was instrumental in preventing, in 1921, the return of the last Habsburg king, Charles IV, and in fact in December of that year he had parliament pass a measure depriving the Habsburgs of their right to the throne. In line with his elitist convictions, Bethlen was mainly responsible for limiting the franchise, thus further ensuring majority for his Christian Smallholders' Agrarian and Bourgeois (Unity) Party, and for reintroducing open voting in BUDAPEST and several other municipalities. At the same time he rid the party of its extremist, racist, faction.

In foreign policy, after the staggering losses Hungary suffered in the peace treaty, he was an ardent supporter of territorial revision and perceived opportunities to break the unity of the LITTLE ENTENTE, formed to oppose such revision,

Count István Bethlen *(Hungarian Museum of Photography)*

specifically by separating Yugoslavia (which feared Italian imperialism and the threat that Hungary might act in concert with Italy) from that bloc. He prevailed on Mussolini to assist in the rearmament of the Hungarian army by shipping weapons captured by Italy in the war to Hungary. A large shipment was indeed discovered by the Austrians, and occasioned a vigorous protest by the Little Entente to the League of Nations; however, the incident was smoothed over with British help. In April 1927 he concluded with Italy a friendship and arbitration agreement. Being a realist in economic matters, he overrode his undisguised hostility toward another Little Entente state, and in 1927 he concluded with Czechoslovakia a three-year economic agreement in order to find a market for Hungary's surplus agrarian products and receive badly needed finished products in exchange. This agreement was not renewed upon its expiration.

The Great Depression had created new conditions, and in 1931 Bethlen concluded trade treaties with Germany, Austria, and Italy; he also secured a large state loan from France to support the Hungarian currency, the pengő.

In August 1931, under increasing pressure for his unpopular economic measures at home, he resigned the premiership although he remained a close adviser of Regent HORTHY and continued to serve in parliament. In 1939 he was made a life member of the Upper House. Although he remained an active advocate of restoring to Hungary some of her lost provinces, he opposed the nearly exclusive pro-German orientation that the rightist governments following his own pursued. He deeply disapproved of Hungary's entry into the Second World War and remained one of those who advocated retention of contacts with Britain and the United States. After the Germans occupied Hungary in March 1944, he retreated into hiding. He was arrested by invading Soviet forces in December of that year and taken to the Soviet Union. He died in Moscow on October 6, 1946. His remains were returned to Hungary only in 1994.

Beust, Count Friedrich Ferdinand
(1809–1886)

Saxon politician and diplomat, Austrian foreign minister and premier

During the 1848 revolutionary period he was Saxon ambassador in Berlin; from 1849 until 1866 he was Saxon minister of culture and of foreign affairs; from October 1866 he served as Austrian foreign minister, from February 1867 as premier; from June 1867 to November 1871 as the first joint foreign minister of the Austro-Hungarian Dual Monarchy. Emperor FRANCIS JOSEPH chose to appoint this Lutheran Saxon diplomat to head his foreign establishment largely because Beust had strong anti-Prussian sentiments and the emperor smarted under the humiliating defeat suffered in the AUSTRO-PRUSSIAN WAR of 1866 and was bent on revanche. He saw in Beust a possible counterweight to Prussian chancellor Bismarck and glossed over the

fact that Beust had only the most cursory familiarity with the *internal* affairs of the Austrian Empire. However, Beust did recognize and appreciate the fact that a compromise with Hungary was the only way to restore the empire to a power position in which it might challenge Prussian power and he actively promoted that compromise. He also realized the need for allies and saw in France the best prospect, as France and Prussia were at odds over territories along the Rhine. From his appointment as foreign minister to the outbreak of the Franco-Prussian War in June 1870, Beust conducted intermittent negotiations with French foreign minister the Duc de Gramont with a view to an alliance. Of the two statesmen, surprisingly, Beust was the less forthcoming. Personally he might have favored an alliance with France, but he accurately calculated that, being clearly directed against Prussia, such an alliance would antagonize the generally pro-Prussian Hungarian estates (it was after all Prussia's victory over Austria that had brought the emperor around to the idea of a compromise with Hungary) and a large part of the Austro-German nobility as well.

In August 1867, when Napoleon III and his wife paid a visit to Salzburg, ostensibly to express their condolences to the emperor for the recent violent death of his brother Maximilian in Mexico, the French first broached to Beust the proposal of an anti-Prussian alliance: it might result in Austria gaining the allegiance of the south German states, at present unaligned, and France helping herself to areas along the Rhine. Beust declined, for the above-mentioned reasons, and proposed instead an alignment against Russia (Austria's rival in the Balkans), or possibly against a Russian-Prussian combination. For the rest of his tenure Beust's chief diplomatic activities were exhausted in these largely futile negotiations with the French (with whom he at one point mooted the possibility of a triple alliance of Austria, France, and Italy), while the commanding hand on the rudder of European diplomacy remained that of Bismarck, who was already steering toward a Prussian-French confrontation. After the Prussian victory in 1870,

would have postponed the annexation indefinitely; what made up his mind, all other things remaining equal, was the revolt in Turkey by a group of army officers, popularly known as the Young Turks, who compelled the sultan, Abdul Hamid, to reissue a constitution he had proclaimed under great-power pressure in 1876, then canceled as soon as the powers lost interest in it. This measure was followed by appointing competent and responsible men to government positions, thus replacing the sultan's moribund administration with a modern system of governing. Legally Bosnia and Hercegovina were still under Turkish suzerainty, and Austria had only temporary rights to govern them; now a progressive regime far more responsible to the subject people's needs than the previous corrupt one had been installed, and it was fully expected that the new government would seek to resume its sovereign rights in the provinces. Aerenthal felt that this had to be prevented by quick action, before the powers took an unwelcome interest. The time had come to put the agreement over the annexation of Bosnia-Hercegovina, on the one hand, and the granting of passage for Russian warship through the Straits, on the other, into concrete form.

The Austrian ambassador in St. Petersburg, LEOPOLD VON BERCHTOLD, placed his country estate in Buchlau, Bohemia, at the disposal of the two foreign ministers. They met for two days, on September 15–16, 1908. No staffs were present and no minutes were kept. The agreement made was oral. It should be noted that the bargain Izvolsky proposed was on unequal terms and he knew it: Austria needed only Russian agreement to her annexation of Bosnia-Hercegovina, whereas Russia needed the consent of all great powers for the satisfaction of her request. Even if the agreement had been put in writing, there was no getting around this fact. To make Austria responsible for the objections of other powers to the Russian scheme was unrealistic. In any case, while the memos on the discussion subsequently prepared by both ministers stated that Austria agreed to raise no objection to the Straits being

opened to Russian warships and Russia would not object to Austria's annexation of the sister provinces (with the proviso that the latter's troops would be withdrawn from the Sanjak), by Aerenthal's version the execution of one action did not hang on the other, in Izvolsky's account the two were to be put in effect simultaneously, or, at the very least, Aerenthal would give ample advance notice of the annexation.

Izvolsky resumed his tour of European capitals, encountered no difficulties in Rome and Berlin, but found both France and Britain opposed to his request. Amid these talks came the news, on October 6, that by an imperial rescript Austria had annexed Bosnia and Hercegovina. In a transparent attempt to cushion the blow, the rescript promised that Bosnians would receive "a voice when decisions are taken concerning their native land, which, as hitherto, will have a separate administration."

The announcement produced fury in Turkey, Serbia, and Montenegro, and Izvolsky felt betrayed. Even Austria's only dependable ally, Germany, was angry, because she had not been consulted beforehand. German relations with Turkey, in a sensitive phase because Germany was pressing for a concession to build the Baghdad railway, might now be put in danger. However, Germany had no alternative to supporting her ally. Still, what Bismarck had always feared, that Austrian adventurism in the Balkans would drag Germany into a war that could bring her no gain seemed to be happening.

Austrian chief of staff Conrad, fearing possible Russian intervention, inquired of the German chief of staff Moltke what Germany would do in such a case. Moltke was authorized by the kaiser to say that "the moment Russia mobilizes, Germany will also mobilize." The position seemed serious enough for Moltke to disclose to Conrad the essentials of the German plan for a two-front war authored by Alfred von Schlieffen.

It was by now clear to Izvolsky that he had made an unfortunate bargain, due to his own negligence in failing to nail down the agreement in writing and, with saving face his only remaining recourse, he demanded that the matter of the annexations be placed before an international congress on the argument that the status quo Austria had violated had also been determined by such a congress and could not be altered unilaterally. Austria was willing to agree to this demand only if the annexation was sanctioned in advance. German chancellor Bernhard von Bülow supported this position, out of loyalty to Austria, but also because he hoped to weaken the Triple Entente of Russia, France, and Britain by humiliating one of its members.

It is uncertain how far Izvolsky was ready to go in saving his own and his country's prestige, but what little support he had melted away. The Young Turk government in Istanbul, initially indignant about the annexation, abandoned its claim to the provinces in exchange for a cash payment. France informed Russia that she saw no casus belli in the situation. Bülow, in early March 1909, proposed to Izvolsky that Russia and Germany together lay the matter of the annexations before the powers with the proposal that it be considered settled. Izvolsky turned down the offer and, despite Russia's military weakness, war appeared to be a distinct possibility. Bülow, as well as the German chief of staff Moltke, saw the moment auspicious for an Austrian war on Serbia, an action that, if successful, would have pulled the poison tooth of the Balkan conundrum. Expecting to lay bare Russia's impotence, Bülow, on March 22, 1909, sent Izvolsky an ultimatum, demanding that his government recognize the annexations and prevail on Serbia to do likewise. Weighty voices in Vienna were not satisfied with such a solution. Conrad urged a cabinet meeting on March 27 to order mobilization, for Serbia would not be eliminated as a power factor by diplomatic means. But the decision for war or peace was being made elsewhere.

Izvolsky, even though his conference proposal found no backing from any quarter, might still have held out by making an alternative offer or asking for clarifications, but Bülow's note contained an unmistakable threat. "An evasive, involved, or vague answer would have to be regarded by us as a refusal." No room was left for procrastination. Izvolsky accepted Bülow's proposal.

Serbia, with no friend left, abandoned its claim, not only to the provinces but even to compensation, and promised to live on good terms with Austria. The crisis ended but the bitter feelings it engendered would linger.

Brezhnev Doctrine

A semi-official declaration by the general secretary of the Communist Party of the Soviet Union following Soviet armed intervention in Czechoslovakia in August 1968, ending the so-called PRAGUE SPRING, an introduction of reforms in a number of fields that the Soviet leaders deemed excessive and dangerous. Once this rebellion, spearheaded by the former general secretary of the Slovakian party, Alexander Dubček, had been put down by military means and a new hard-line Communist leadership under Gustav Husak was installed, Brezhnev publicly asserted the right of the Soviet party to intervene in any socialist country where the foundations of Marxism-Leninism were threatened. It was in the West that this declaration was dubbed the Brezhnev Doctrine.

Budapest

Capital of Hungary, second-largest city and, youngest metropolis in the Dual Monarchy. Until 1872 Buda and Pest were separate royal cities. In that year they were united, with the addition of the farm community of Óbuda and the island of Margitsziget, into one municipality. Buda is the ancient coronation city but its growth was restricted by the hilly terrain, whereas during the 19th century Pest developed by leaps and bounds. After the Compromise of 1867 architects in Budapest sought to rival the preeminence of Vienna and its scenic attractiveness. They had the advantage of the majestic Danube River flowing through the center of the

Owing to the felicitous marriages of his grandfather Maximilian and of his father, he became heir to large European territories and subsequently to the New World, minus Brazil, which, by papal verdict, fell to Portugal. Born at Ghent in the southern Netherlands, he grew up in a court cherishing anachronistic medieval traditions of chivalry and of the sanctity and inviolability of the Roman Catholic Church. His mother tongue was French but, having a quick and receptive mind, he in time learned Flemish, Spanish, Latin, and German as well. A taciturn man who held that silence was one-half of good diplomacy, of him it was said that he could be diplomatically silent in five languages.

In 1515 he became ruler of the Netherlands, which he regarded as his homeland to the end of his life; in 1516, upon the death of his grandfather Ferdinand, he inherited the crowns of Castile, Aragon, and Naples-Sicily. He sailed from Antwerp to Spain to occupy his newly won throne; his ship went astray, landed on a desolate rocky shore, and it took days of trekking for Charles and his party to reach the port where a delegation of high Spanish nobles awaited the arrival of their new ruler.

On Spanish soil he met for the first time his younger brother FERDINAND, whom to the end of his life he treated with a condescension bordering on disdain. It was in that year, 1517, that Martin Luther offered his challenge to the Catholic Church, a movement that for a while threatened to engulf Europe north of the Alps, and Charles from this time on to the end of his life waged a faithful Catholic's battle against the "heresy."

When his grandfather, Maximilian I, king of the Austrian hereditary lands and Holy Roman Emperor, died, Charles at once announced his candidacy for the vacant imperial throne. He had to vie with such older and more established rulers as Francis I of France and Henry VIII of England, but a bribe to the electors of 850,000 gold marks, 500,000 of which he had borrowed from the Fuggers, ensured his election. He journeyed from Spain to Germany and, once there,

realizing the gravity of the Lutheran challenge, he summoned a Diet of German kings, princes, and ecclesiastical dignitaries to the town of Worms, where he first laid eyes on the Augustinian monk whose questioning, first of church practices and then of church doctrines, had placed Catholicism in an unprecedented defensive position. Luther's refusal at the Diet to renounce his doctrines threatened the severance of the German confederation of states from Rome and the Catholic Church.

The burdens of ruling his own far-flung empire as well as a divided Holy Roman Empire began to weigh on the young king-emperor. By the Treaty of Brussels, a year after the Diet of Worms, Charles allowed his brother Ferdinand to succeed to the thrones of the Austrian lands; it marked the effective division of the Habsburg realm into western (Spain, Naples-Sicily, Netherlands, Americas) and eastern (the Austrian lands, soon to be adumbrated by Hungary, BOHEMIA, Moravia, and Silesia) sections.

To Charles's religious-political challenges were soon added a war with France and a conflict, looming ever larger, with the Ottoman Empire, which, since its conquest of Constantinople in 1453, had brought most of the Balkans into its sphere, defeated the Hungarians in the BATTLE OF MOHÁCS, and, three years later, pushed to the very gates of VIENNA. There were only brief periods of respite in these sustained states of belligerence. The Netherlands, which had become a distant province of the empire, had to be held and strengthened because of the war with France. There were disputes over Flanders, Alsace, Burgundy, Savoy, Milan, Naples-Sicily, territories to which the Habsburg claim rested on dubious foundations. There was also an ideological clash between Charles and French king Francis I. Charles was a champion of the universal ideal represented by the Catholic Church, and to his mind the Holy Roman Empire would in time encompass all of Christianity. Francis ruled over a *nation* and devoted his energies to enlarging and strengthening it; although a good

Catholic, in politics he spurned universality. If fortunes in war were an indication of divine favor, God favored Charles's vision, his armies earned several victories over Francis's forces, though never a truly decisive one.

In 1524 Charles, with his eyes on another territorial gain, married the Portuguese king's daughter Isabella. In 1527 their son, Philip, was born. Charles's unending troubles left him little time to rejoice over the birth of an heir. At one point he had to make temporary peace with the Protestant princes of Germany to obtain their military help against the Turks; when the help turned out to be unnecessary because of Turkish weariness with the long siege of VIENNA, Charles resumed his struggle against Lutheranism. In 1536 the war with France, in abeyance for 10 years, broke out again and did not end until 1538, with papal mediation. Then there was trouble in the Netherlands, a Protestant uprising in his native town of Ghent threatened to spread. In the Holy Roman Empire open warfare raged over the religious question, complicated by the fact that many princes, and even some bishops, chose Lutheranism more to wrest land from Catholic estates than from religious conviction. As proved to be the case in all religious conflicts, neither side could achieve final victory. Discouraged and disillusioned, Charles in 1555, gave his reluctant approval to the PEACE OF AUGSBURG, which ended, though not conclusively, the Catholic-Lutheran contest in Germany. In October of that year, in a solemn ceremony that brought tears to many eyes, he abdicated his title to the Netherlands. Returning to Spain, which he had not visited in years, he laid down his Spanish and Neapolitan crowns as well. His son Philip inherited these western lands; Charles's brother Ferdinand became Holy Roman Emperor. Charles retired to a little castle he had built next to a monastery near Yuste, and there lived quietly, reading, hunting, receiving visitors, and occasionally giving political advice. He died on September 21, 1558.

Charles VI of the House of Habsburg (1685–1740)

younger son of Leopold I, Charles was the last male member of the Austrian Habsburg line, archduke of Austria

King of Spain as Charles III by his own proclamation from 1706 to 1714, from 1711 to 1740 Charles was Holy Roman Emperor as Charles VI, Hungarian king as Charles III, and Czech king as Charles II. His reign fell into that critical period of Habsburg history when both the Spanish and the Austrian male line became extinct and, in the case of the Spanish succession, the French Bourbons advanced a forceful claim to the throne. In the resulting WAR OF THE SPANISH SUCCESSION the maritime powers of Britain and Holland also participated, both arrayed on Austria's side against France. So far as the Habsburg family was concerned, the succession to both thrones was governed by the secret family contract drawn up in 1703, the *pactum mutuae successionis,* whereby the scepters of the Spanish and the Austrian lines would remain separate except in the event that the male line on either side became extinct; in that case the legitimate heir of the other line would inherit it. The *pactum* also provided for female succession should the male line to either throne end.

Pursuant to the *pactum,* Charles of Austria proclaimed himself king of Spain after the male line there ended in 1701 (his older brother Joseph would succeed to the Austrian throne), but his assertion was purely theoretical as the War of the Spanish Succession was already in progress and French king Louis XIV claimed the throne for his grandson Philip. In Austria, Charles's father Leopold I still ruled, and, because of the separation of the two crowns, neither he nor his son Joseph could claim the Spanish throne; thus Charles was the legitimate Habsburg successor to that throne. Leopold I died in 1705 and Joseph inherited the Austrian, Hungarian, and Czech crowns as well as the Holy Roman emperorship; the disposition of the Spanish crown was still being contested. Joseph died in 1711, leaving his crowns in the Austrian realm to Charles, who also became Holy Roman Emperor as Charles VI. That fact laid his claim to the Spanish crown to rest.

The *pactum mutuae successiones* was made public in 1713, under the heading of Pragmatica Sanctio. At that time the matter of female succession was not of any urgency as Charles was a young and virile man; in fact, three years later a son was born to him. However, the infant Leopold died that same year, in 1716. The next child, born a year later, was a daughter, MARIA THERESA. By now the War of the Spanish Succession had ended, and although militarily it had been a draw, the Spanish throne had passed to Philip of Bourbon. The *pactum mutuae* thus no longer had any mutuality; the Spanish throne was lost to the Habsburgs. From this time on Charles's foreign policy abandoned the traditional Habsburg goal of extending influence and gaining new territory and, as no more sons were born to him, narrowed to having the all-German Diet endorse the Pragmatic Sanction, thus assuring that even in the absence of a male heir Habsburg lands would not be divided or pass to a foreign ruling house. The Prussian king Frederick William I was the first to promise agreement, and in fact pledged that, as one of the electors in the Holy Roman Empire, he would vote for Maria Theresa's future husband to be Holy Roman Emperor. In this light it was of the greatest importance that Maria Theresa make a fitting marriage. There was talk that the Prussian crown prince Frederick, then that the Bavarian elector, marry the princess, but neither prospect came to fruition. In 1736 she married Francis Stephen Leopold of Lorraine, who became her consort. By now Britain had subscribed to the Pragmatic Sanction, and after Prussia and Saxony did the same, the imperial Diet gave its sanction. One by one the others, within and without the Habsburg Empire, fell in line.

Charles had, for the time being anyhow, achieved the continuity of the Habsburg line, albeit on the female side only; his last years were, however, troubled. When in 1732 the Polish king died, the Saxon king, Frederick Augus-

tus, demanded in exchange for his continuous support of the Pragmatic Sanction that Charles on his part support his candidacy to the Polish crown. Charles was agreeable, as was the Russian czarina, Anna, but the majority of Polish nobles supported Stanislas Lesczinski, whose daughter had married Louis XV of France, and Louis sided with his father-in-law. In the resulting War of the Polish Succession, Austrian forces fared poorly and lost most of their Italian possessions, Naples, Sicily, and Milan; Lorraine, hitherto part of the Holy Roman Empire, although formally still belonging to it, was awarded to France. Austria's only consolation was that Frederick Augustus was confirmed as king of Poland; Lesczinski was made duke of Lorraine, a purely symbolic title as it belonged to the lawful heir, Francis Stephen, and on him it was conferred after Leszcinski's death.

Charles VI died on October 20, 1740; Maria Theresa followed him as archduchess of Austria, queen of Hungary and of the Czech lands, and Francis Stephen of Lorraine followed Charles as Holy Roman Emperor. The House of Habsburg from this time on became the House of Habsburg-Lorraine.

church and state in the Dual Monarchy

This was how Count Joseph Roth Chojnicky in his book *The Radetzky March* (1886) expressed the relationship between church and state in the Austrian realm: "The Monarch, our Monarchy, is founded on piety and on the belief that God has chosen the Habsburgs to rule over so many Christian people. Our emperor is a secular brother of the Pope, royal-imperial apostolic majesty. No ruler is as apostolic as he, but no ruler so much depends on the grace of God and the people's faith in God. The German emperor rules even if God abandons him, possibly by the grace of his people. But the emperor of the Austro-Hungarian Monarchy can never be forsaken by God."

Indeed in the Dual Monarchy church and state, specifically the Roman Catholic Church and the Habsburg lands, were so organically intertwined that many believed that the church, the mass, the clergy, even God, were institutions of the monarchy. Given this widespread and emotionally held belief, other religions, even when they were granted legal status, were essentially tolerated minorities. According to the census of 1910, 78 percent of the total population of the Dual Monarchy were Catholics, although not all Roman Catholics. There were, in relatively small numbers to be sure, also the *Greek Catholics*. Their history dated back to the schism of 1054, when the western church excommunicated the eastern and the latter refused to acknowledge the authority of the pope. The emperor in Constantinople continued to have the final word in religious as well as secular matters. But after the Turks conquered Constantinople in 1453, many eastern Christians returned to papal jurisdiction, and these were known as the Greek Catholics. In terms of Christian dogma there was no difference between the Roman and Greek denominations, but there were several differences in ritual and eastern priests were allowed to marry. In the Dual Monarchy, almost all Greek Catholics were Ukrainians, or Ruthenians. Their religious status had been established in 1596, when Ukrainians under Russian rule signed the Union of Brest, returning the eastern (Kiev) church to the authority of Rome. After the partitions of Poland, Russian czars and czarinas applied enough pressure to force many of these adherents of Rome back into the Russian church. Only in the provinces of Galicia and Bukovina did Greek Catholics remain. They had a religious center under a metropolitan in Lemberg.

There were in addition the *Greek Orthodox*. They differed from Greek Catholics in that they did *not* recognize the pope's authority; their liturgy was, however, the same. In the Dual Monarchy west of the Leitha River, the emperor named Greek Orthodox bishops and metropolitans; in the rest of the Monarchy elected synods made the selections; the emperor merely confirmed them.

Protestants, although not large in numbers, had since the days of the Reformation been the most contentious elements in the Christian commonwealth. In the Austrian (German) parts there were only the Lutheran and the Calvinist denominations. They were organized in 10 church districts, each with a superintendent at its head, a position just beneath the bishop. Neither church had permanent headquarters or an administrative center; the center happened to be the residence of the superintendent chosen for that year.

In Hungary Protestants made up a substantially larger proportion of the population than in Austria, and there were, in addition to Lutherans and Calvinists, the Unitarians. Unitarians denied the doctrine of the Trinity as well as Jesus' divinity, although they embraced his teachings. They, like the other two Protestant faiths, enjoyed state protection and their freedom of worship was constitutionally guaranteed, as were their political and civil rights. Calvinists in Hungary were organized into five church "counties," each made up of a number of congregations. Several counties made up a church district under a religious head (bishop) and a secular head (supervisor). The members of this church were practically all Hungarians, with their religious center in Debrecen, often referred to as the Calvinist Rome. The Lutheran faith was more diversified, ethnically and religiously. There were among them, apart from Hungarians, many Germans and Slovaks, the Germans mainly among the Saxons in TRANSYLVANIA; these did not follow the Augustinian confession of the Hungarians but their own Saxon ritual.

There were in very small numbers also the *Old Catholics*, who had broken away from the head church after the proclamation of papal infallibility in 1870. Disputing such powers, they no longer accepted the supremacy of the pope. Subsequently they discontinued confession and fasting, did not accept the indissolubility of marriage or the obligation of priestly celibacy, and discontinued Latin as the language of the church.

for that purpose that the congress convened in Berlin. Although many of the disputed points, especially between Russia and Britain, as well as Russia and Turkey, were settled *before* the opening, the congress still proved a protracted and often acrimonious affair. The Russians, though they gained some valuable territory (they were allowed to reannex from Romania Bessarabia, the province they had lost after the Crimean War, and to take from Turkey a strip of land between the Black and the Caspian Seas), were bitterly disappointed that their military exertions, whose outcome often hung in the balance, were so poorly rewarded while powers that had not shed blood gained so much. Austria was allowed to occupy and administer (though not for now to annex) Bosnia-Hercegovina, to garrison and, if the need arose, to occupy also the strip of land south of it, the Sanjak of Novibazar, that separated Serbia from Montenegro. British desiderata were satisfied in two ways. The large Bulgaria outlined in the Treaty of San Stefano was trisected, with only the northern third above the Balkan Mountains independent, though still tributary to Turkey; the middle third, called on English insistence Eastern Rumelia, autonomous under a Christian prince but under Turkish suzerainty; the southern third, Macedonia, containing the Aegean littoral, was returned to Turkey. The congress also recognized a bargain struck earlier between Britain and Turkey, whereby the latter would cede the island of Cyprus in exchange for a British commitment to defend Turkey's Asiatic possessions. Nothing was said about concessions to France, but by a tacit undertaking on the part of the great powers (except Italy), her right to turn the Ottoman province of Tunis into a French protectorate was recognized. The Italian foreign minister, Corti, alone returned home "with clean hands." Germany made no direct gains either—it was precisely her disinterestedness that enabled Bismarck to act as the "honest broker"—but her international prestige was greatly enhanced.

As at the CONGRESS OF VIENNA over half a century earlier, the Berlin Congress too ignored minority rights (with this exception that Bismarck insisted that Romania grant her Jewish subjects citizenship) and nationalist aspirations. Sovereignties were shifted and territories reassigned with total disregard of the desires of the peoples who inhabited them. This held particularly true for Austria. Her foreign minister, COUNT JULIUS ANDRÁSSY, actually opposed the inclusion of more Slavs into the Dual Monarchy, but he could not allow the ever troublesome provinces of Bosnia-Hercegovina to remain under Turkey and be a bait for waxing Serbian power.

Congress of Vienna

A year-long congress in the Austrian capital (November 1, 1814–June 8, 1815), it met to accomplish the reconstruction of Europe after the disorders and dislocations caused by the French Revolutionary and Napoleonic Wars. Properly speaking it was not a congress, for it had no formal organization, agenda, duly elected or appointed officers, and, except for ceremonial purposes, it did not hold plenary sessions. The Austrian chancellor, KLEMENS VON METTERNICH, was the unofficial chairman, and his influence, conservative though not reactionary, dominated the procedures. He utilized Austria's position as the power that had longest fought against revolutionary France to the best advantage, glossing over the fact that in the last years of the war Austria had in fact been an ally of Napoleon, a compact sealed by the marriage of the Austrian emperor's daughter to Napoleon. None of those present showed any interest in the nationalistic aspirations that had been awakened by the French Revolution, but Metternich, himself of an international background and serving a multinational empire, was the most determined opponent of any concessions to submerged nationalities. He was also the first to oppose the plan presented by Russian czar Alexander I, calling for the reconstruction of Poland (which had been partitioned by its neighbors in the previous century) as an independent nation with Alexander as king. The Prussian chancellor Hardenberg was willing to consider giving up the part of Poland Prussia held, in exchange for the much richer kingdom of Saxony, but Metternich was supported in his opposition to the Russian plan by the British foreign secretary Castlereagh; in the end Russia's claim to all of Poland was thwarted, and Alexander became king of a rump Polish state referred to as Congress Poland.

The congress strove to apply the principle of legitimacy, but only in order to have some guideline determining the lawful occupant of a throne; in territorial arrangements the principle was generally overlooked. Where the latter arrangements were concerned, outside of Europe Britain gained most, though some of the territories conceded to her were already firmly in her possession: Heligoland island in the North Sea, Malta and the Ionian Islands in the Mediterranean, the Cape in South Africa, Ceylon in Asia, and several islands in the Atlantic. In Europe, Austria gained most. Metternich was quite willing to consent to the loss of the AUSTRIAN NETHERLANDS that were difficult to govern and to defend from afar, when Austria received in compensation the provinces of Lombardy and Venetia in northern Italy, additional territory in the Tyrol, as well as Dalmatia, a long strip of seacoast along the Adriatic Sea. Even though the lost Netherlands were among the most densely populated areas of Europe, after the congress the Austrian Empire had nearly 5 million more inhabitants than it had before the wars.

Metternich also brought to the congress the principle of the balance of power, an arrangement by which any power bent on aggression would find itself opposed by a coalition it could not hope to overcome. The fact that, except for short local wars, Europe was at peace for the next 100 years is often credited to the wisdom and diplomatic skill of the Austrian chancellor. However, it must also be remembered that the cavalier way in which the congress treated nationalist claims led to recurrent revolutions and that nationalism proved a potent force and was one of the factors that brought on the Great War. It must also be considered that the many economic and social changes that came to Europe

in the 19th century so absorbed the powers (including even the most stubbornly conservative Russia) that they discouraged foreign adventures, except, in a limited way, in the Balkans in the latter part of the century, and there it was largely thanks to Bismarck's diplomatic gifts that the balance was upheld.

At its end, the congress produced two alliances, both with the essential intent of preventing any recurrence of the upheavals that that had rent Europe for a quarter of a century, the QUADRUPLE ALLIANCE and the HOLY ALLIANCE.

Conrad von Hötzendorf, Franz (1852–1925)

chief of staff of the Austro-Hungarian military forces from 1906 to 1911, and again from December 1912 to March 1917; from November 1916 marshal

Count Conrad von Hötzendorf was one of the most controversial figures in the history of the Dual Monarchy and of the prehistory of First World War. The only child of a veteran of the Napoleonic Wars, he served briefly in Bosnia as an infantry officer in 1878–79, lectured on military tactics at the war college, and commanded Austrian troops posted along the Italian border. One observer, the British military attaché in Vienna, described him as a "delightful little man, dapper, erect, alert, with grey hair . . . over a keenly intellectual and rather ascetic face . . . [a man] of great moral courage, frank and straightforward, but essentially a one-sided man . . . certainly the bright star in a rather dull constellation, and all the foreign attachés had great regard and affection for him." Unlike most military men, Conrad had a profound interest in, and a fair understanding of, international affairs and judged the Dual Monarchy's position as particularly threatened in the south, by Italy, an ally he did not trust, and by the South Slavs in the Balkans. He perhaps best understood how the prolonged internal conflicts in the Dual Monarchy had affected the morale of the army and he used his influence with FRANCIS JOSEPH to urge reforms to improve the striking power of the joint armed forces. Believing that the military was the staunchest expression of national will, he argued that the internal weakness of the Dual Monarchy could be compensated for by an aggressive and assertive foreign policy. He espoused the cult of the offensive, had no use for military display such as parades and marches, and held that only field exercises prepared the soldiers for combat. Many of the officers on his staff came from among the students he taught at the war college, and he presided over a general staff that through his political as well as military advocacy achieved a status greater than that of the war ministry. Yet, his political judgments were oversized and adventurous. He insistently kept urging preventive war against both Italy and Serbia. The latter project, while rash, at least had some strategic rationale behind it; the former revealed his bellicosity rather than his sagacity. It brought him into sharp conflict with foreign minister AERENTHAL, who finally insisted that Conrad be dismissed. The emperor reluctantly complied and in November 1911 removed Conrad as chief of staff. Conrad was replaced by General Blasius Schemua, but the heir to the throne, the Archduke FRANCIS FERDINAND, an ardent supporter of Conrad, successfully argued with Francis Joseph that Schemua lacked the experience and the strategic grasp of his predecessor and, in December 1912, Conrad was reinstated. He continued in his position until March 1917. It has been discreetly suggested that behind his constant urging of military action lay his passionate love for a married woman, many years his junior, the mother of six, who would not yield to his entreaties and whom he hoped to impress by waging, and winning, a great battle. That hoped-for victory never came but he did win his woman when after her divorce in 1915 the aged emperor gave permission for him to marry her.

Even while urging action against Italy and Serbia, Conrad's eyes were on Russia and most of his strategic plans envisioned a great battle in the east. Yet these plans did not achieve the maturity with which a great military thinker might have endowed them. While there was some precision in his offensive plans against Italy (Plan I) and against Serbia (Plan B), his dispositions against Russia (Plan R) remained vague and contingent, for they were plagued by uncertainty over whether, in case of war, the bulk of Austrian forces should be deployed in the south or in the north, primarily against Serbia or primarily against Russia. As to the latter, he believed that Austria's German alliance would deter the Russians from making war on the Dual Monarchy; if such were not the case, Austria would have to wage a defensive war in Galicia while dealing with Serbia in an offensive confrontation. In a war with Russia, Germany would have to bear the brunt of the fighting. This at any rate was Conrad's scenario until 1909, when he learned from his German counterpart, Helmuth von Moltke, the broad outlines of the Schlieffen Plan, which in case of a two-front war called for an initial massive German attack against France. Until this campaign was concluded, Austria would have to hold off the Russians in the east. From this time on Conrad's plan against Italy was placed in inactive status while the choice between Plan B and Plan R was made dependent on how the war crisis developed.

That crisis came on by stages, with several dress rehearsals, and while these might have served to clarify the odds, they in fact confused them. In the First Balkan War of 1912 Serbia and her allies, Bulgaria and Greece, made discomfiting gains at the expense of Turkey, and the specter loomed of a hostile Serbia with greatly increased territory and population. Conrad was out of office and Schemua carried little weight in high councils. Francis Ferdinand urged immediate war on Serbia. After Conrad's reinstatement in 1912, and especially after the Second Balkan War, when only joint great-power pressure restrained Serbia from acquiring Albania and thus gaining access to the Adriatic Sea, he pressed more firmly than ever for preventive war against the Dual Monarchy's southern neighbor. He held it incompatible with the great-power status of AUSTRIA-HUNGARY that a small Balkan state with a negligible military force should keep it in permanent tension and tie down a part of its army, one that in case of a general war would be badly needed on the front against Russia. But while before the BALKAN WARS Russia, in consequence of her defeat by Japan in 1905, could hardly contemplate war against a major power, by 1912 she had sufficiently recovered to be a player in an international crisis. Thus, while Serbia remained the immediate enemy to the unity of the Dual Monarchy, Russia posed by far the greater military threat. Conrad, nevertheless returned to his conclusion that in a general war Serbia would have to be dealt with first. By his scheme, after the completion of Plan B, the larger part of Serbia would be absorbed into the monarchy, the rest assigned to Bulgaria, and the Serbian problem would be laid to rest.

This theoretical scenario was put to an abrupt test with the assassination, on June 28, 1914, of the heir to the Austrian throne Francis Ferdinand and his wife in the Bosnian capital of Sarajevo. The assassin was a Serbian youth and preliminary investigation suggested that high-ranking Serbian personages were, at least in an ancillary sense, parties to the deed. Among the impassioned voices in Vienna calling for quick military action against Serbia, Conrad's was the loudest and strongest. As foreign minister LEOPOLD BERCHTOLD reported later, Conrad's constant advice was "War, war, war!" He at first assured the emperor that the Austrian military was ready, but as time passed, his sanguine resolution began to waver. At a ministerial council on July 7, he revealed his long-standing dilemma of whether to concentrate his main military forces against Serbia or against Russia. The danger was that if he opted for the former, his forces in Galicia could not face a major Russian attack. In that case territory would have to be conceded on the Russian front. But even in such a case, he held it was better to fight a war now rather than later.

In Conrad's calculation the decision between Plan B or Plan R could be made as late as on the fifth day of Austrian mobilization. When the emperor ordered partial mobilization on July 25, Conrad was still committed to Plan B. One reason was that he did not wish to provoke Russia

needlessly; another was that mobilization did not proceed with the speed necessary for an unencumbered choice between one plan or the other. In fact Conrad, who four weeks earlier demanded immediate hostilities, now wanted to postpone the declaration of war against Serbia until the (partial) mobilization was completed. Such caution seemed justified when intelligence reached him of mobilization by Russia in the military districts facing the Dual Monarchy. Yet, determined to fight Serbia, Conrad kept moving troops from Galicia southward even before the deadline was reached that he himself set for being certain whether or not Russia would enter the war. At the height of the crisis, as the German military urged an immediate attack on Serbia to create a fait accompli, when the foreign minister's inquired as to when Austria should actually declare war on Serbia Conrad was forced to answer that that the earliest date was August 12. He drew the melancholy reply that "the diplomatic situation will not hold that long." Austria actually declared war on Serbia on July 28. Full mobilization, however, was not ordered until August 4, and, by then, with Russia in the war, Conrad had to opt for Plan R, and the troops in transit to the Balkan front were redirected northward. The net result was that Conrad had insufficient forces on both fronts and could not succeed on either. The Serbian front was not conquered until the end of 1915, and then only with German help. On the Russian front, too, initial Austrian moves failed. Conrad then drew up a plan of battle for a joint German-Austrian offensive in Galicia in 1915; a breakthrough was achieved, but from then on the Austrian general staff was in effect subordinated to the German. In 1916 Conrad launched an offensive on the Italian front; on the verge of success, at a critical time he had to divert forces to the threatened Russian front and again could not gain victory on either.

When Charles IV became emperor in 1916 he dismissed Conrad as chief of the general staff. Conrad then commanded an army group in Italy. He retired from active service after the war and wrote his memoirs in six volumes: *Mein Anfang,*

minorities they had ruled since their conquest of the CARPATHIAN BASIN.

Hlinka was arrested, charged with sedition, suspended from his priestly duties, and imprisoned. His parishioners rallied to his cause and obtained ecclesiastical permission to build a new church. The bishopric dominated by Hungarians assigned a new priest to the church, who was ordered to proceed to Csernova and dedicate it. On the way there he and his party were confronted by a hostile mob, which threatened the priest's life if he did not turn back. His party, and the accompanying gendarmes, were pelted with stones, whereupon the latter opened fire and killed 16 of the crowd and wounded many more. The gendarmes subsequently arrested a number of the participants; these, including Hlinka's sister, were put on trial and sentenced to prison.

In the aftermath of the affair both sides voiced their predictable arguments; the Slovaks, generally supported by the foreign press, charged Hungarians with depriving the population of the Uplands (northern Hungary) of their national and cultural rights; the Hungarian side pointed to the incendiary effect of the activities of men like Hlinka, which roused a generally peaceful population to frenzied outbursts. It should be noted, as later developments were to show, that incidents like the Csernova affair were the exception rather than the rule for Slovak behavior. In general Slovak peasants, who made up the great majority of the nation, did not understand, or particularly resist, the subtler means and motives of their Magyarization, and many, in areas where Hungarians were in the majority, quite readily adopted the Magyar language. It took the upheavals of the Great War and the enticements of the Czechs to awaken in them a collective feeling, which translated into Slovak nationalism.

Czech Legion

A military force composed of Slavic soldiers who had served in the Austro-Hungarian army in the First World War and had either been taken prisoner or, unwilling to serve a power that had held them in subjugation, surrendered of their own volition. By 1917 there were some 200,000 such Slavic prisoners in Russian captivity. The Czech government in exile proposed that those who volunteered to fight against their former masters be enlisted in a Czech Legion that would be deployed on the Russian front. In time the Legion numbered between 40,000 and 50,000 soldiers, armed and serving under their own officers. In early July 1917 parts of it participated in the Kerensky offensive against the Central Powers; even though that offensive ended in a general rout, the legion maintained its cohesion. But when, in March 1918, the Bolshevik government signed the peace treaty of Brest Litovsk, the presence of the Czech Legion in Russia became superfluous. The allies, largely at French initiative, decided to transport it to the western front in France. Westward passage being impossible, as every possible route lay through enemy territory, it was decided, in agreement with the Bolshevik government, that the Czechs be sent, via the Trans-Siberian Railway, to Vladivostok, and thence by sea to France. It proved a slow and frustrating journey aboard crowded freight cars and the soldiers became restive. On May 14, 1918, a row broke out in one train between some members of the Czech Legion and Hungarian prisoners of war. The local soviet at Chelyabinsk arrested several Czech soldiers. Thereupon other members of the legion attacked the Red Guard units in town, disarmed them, and released the prisoners. Emboldened, Czech detachments strung out along the railway began to take over town after town in western Siberia and the Ural region. Leon Trotsky, as commissar for war, ordered them disarmed, but the Czech Legion had become a law onto itself. By June 8 it had occupied the capital of the central Volga, Samara, and the Bolshevik position in the entire Ural region was imperiled. Already before the Czech rising Bolshevik governments in Siberia—in Biinsk, Omsk, and Krasnoyarsk—had been overthrown; it now became doubtful that Lenin's regime would be able to maintain itself in and beyond the Urals at all. Until now resistance in Russia to the Bolsheviks had been limited to local peasant risings and had been easily dealt with by semi-regular Red Guard units. Now the entire region along the Trans-Siberian Railway was threatened.

During the foreign intervention in the Russian Civil War in the summer of 1918, the Czech Legion was placed under allied command and it fought against the Red forces continually until November of that year. With the Great War at an end, its activities, as well as those of the Allied forces, became pointless, and the Czech Legion sought a way out of Russia. Some members managed to get to Vladivostok and sail away, others were taken prisoner by the advancing Bolshevik forces.

D

Darányi, Kálmán (1886–1939)
premier of Hungary

Son of Béla Darányi and Antonia Nagy, he had one brother, Gyula, a medical scientist. In 1909 he earned a doctorate from Budapest University in political science. In 1913 he married Margit Magyary. He served in several local and county positions. In the Great War, between 1914 and 1917, he served on the Russian front as a reserve cavalry lieutenant, and later as a first lieutenant. In 1917 and 1918 he was lord lieutenant of Zólyom County. After the war and during the period of upheavals he retired to his estate in Veszprém County. He emerged in 1920 and held a series of positions at the county level. In 1927 he was elected to parliament where he served until 1939. Between 1935 and 1938 he was minister of agriculture in the Gömbös cabinet and, during the latter's sickness, he twice (from May to August and from September to October 1936) acted as premier. From October 10, 1936, to May 14, 1938, he was premier in his own right and head of the Party of National Unity. As premier he discontinued GÖMBÖS's policies, especially his dictatorial ambitions; in April 1937 he banned Ferenc SZÁLASI's extreme rightist

Kálmán Darányi (seated, third from left) and his cabinet members, 1936 *(Hungarian Museum of Photography)*

Party of National Will. He was a champion of the secret ballot but sought to mitigate its effects by literacy tests and by raising the age for voting. He also retreated from Gömbös's pronounced pro-German orientation and championed a Polish-Hungarian-Yugoslav axis to counteract German influence in the region. After his November 1937 visit to Germany, however, his foreign policy underwent substantial change. He began to work for closer relations with the Reich; domestically he even warmed up to Szálasi's party. He also worked hard to make the army an effective fighting force. On April 8, 1938, he introduced in parliament the first anti-Jewish law, restricting Jewish participation in the professions. When it was revealed that he had personal connections with Szálasi and several of his collaborators, he lost the confidence of the conservatives and Regent HORTHY asked for his resignation. From December 1938 to his death he was president of the lower house.

Deák, Ferenc (1803–1876)

Hungarian politician and jurist, affectionately known as the Sage of the Fatherland, he was the chief architect of the AUSGLEICH of 1867

He was born into a wealthy noble family in the county of Zala. His mother died giving him birth, his father never recovered from the loss and died five years later. Ferenc was reared by his brother and sister, both many years older than he. Already in his lower schooling he gave evidence of great intellectual gifts and a prodigious memory. He went to law school and became a jurist. A voracious reader, not only in his native Hungarian but also in Latin (then the language of the judicial process) and German, he acquainted himself with the works of the Enlightenment, mainly in German translations from the original French. Deeply impressed by Montesquieu's *Spirit of the Laws,* he found it applicable to his native land. He was particularly attracted to the model of a constitutional monarchy in which the branches of government were separated; it became the leitmotif of his plans for mitigating the absolutism of the Habsburgs that ruled the

Austrian Empire, especially after the revolutions of 1848–49. As assistant prosecutor in his native county between 1824 and 1832, he had consistently fought against the manifest inequalities before the law as well as against the fundamental inhumanity of the feudal type of jurisdiction.

A bachelor to the end of his life, Deák devoted his energies unstintingly to his public duties. In 1833, at age 30, he was elected representative from Zala County to the Hungarian Diet meeting at Pressburg. His passionate interests as a legislator included the causes of the reform of feudalism (in particular the easing of the lot of the serfs) and of freedom of expression.

Although a devout Roman Catholic, Deák opposed church decrees he judged high-handed and imperious, especially those that banned intermarriages except when the non-Catholic party pledged to bring up the children in the Catholic faith. "The Church," he declared, "can only absolve sins, not create them."

He played a rather modest role during the revolutionary upheavals of 1848–49, although he was named minister of justice in Kossuth's government. Legal questions interested him more than the momentous political ones that grew out of Hungary's defiance of Habsburg rule. When the Hungarian parliament, transplanted from Pressburg to Buda, made a further move to Debrecen to separate itself from the part of the country ruled by imperial forces, he did not follow it there but retired to his estate in Kehida. From there he encouraged LÁJOS KOSSUTH to continue his struggle, though he could not agree with his more radical aspirations, especially the proposed total break with the Habsburgs. Thanks to his absence from Debrecen he was not indicted for insurrection in the period of reprisals; but when he was invited to VIENNA to give his advice about means of reconciliation, he refused to go. He became the very symbol of the passive resistance that in the end broke the will of the Vienna court and brought it around to a compromise with Hungary. The court tried by means of the OCTOBER DIPLOMA and the FEBRUARY PATENT to purchase Hungarian consent to a very limited autonomy, but Deák, who, by virtue of his moderation and unbending purposefulness, became the most weighty voice on Hungarian affairs in dealings with Vienna, insisted that the laws passed by the Hungarian parliament in 1848 serve as a basis for negotiations with Vienna. It took his infinite and wisely measured patience to progress toward a compromise, unbending on fundamentals but ready to concede what could not be gained without resort to violence. When, for instance, the Hungarian parliament was convened in the spring of 1861, Deák supported its majority position that both the October Diploma and the February Patent be rejected. In a celebrated letter to the emperor of May 13, he reiterated the demand that the 1848 laws be recognized as valid, but he added that those laws may be revised to conform to the provisions of the Pragmatic Sanction. FRANCIS JOSEPH rejected the appeal, not for its substance but because it did not specifically affirm the emperor's right to Hungary's throne.

Years passed and the question of Hungary's special position within the empire hung fire. But passive resistance by Hungarians began to wear down Austrian firmness. Deák, both in his writings and in his informal negotiations with the Vienna court, advanced the conditions that in time became the basis for dualism, namely, Austria and Hungary equal partners within the empire. When parliament met again in December 1865, it adopted Deák's plan for a compromise with Vienna. Shunning publicity and the limelight, Deák left the practical conduct of negotiations to JULIUS ANDRÁSSY while he remained its ideological guide. Reading the final draft, he admitted that it was not perfect, "but we are not able to prepare one that better serves our purpose and is at the same time capable of execution."

After the conclusion of the Great Compromise Deák gradually withdrew from political life. The parliamentary party he had forged, once its central endeavor had been accomplished, began to disintegrate. Although Deák continued to fight for liberal and nationalistic causes, both in parliament and in print, they did not attract the consensus his constitutional efforts had. Plagued by failing health (he had long been suffering from a heart condition), he officially ended his political career in November 1873, when he left parliament for the last time. He died on January 28, 1876, in his 73rd year.

de-Stalinization

This was the term used for the general easing of controls and mitigation of terror in the Soviet Union and its satellites following Stalin's death on March 5, 1953. Symbolically it began with the rehabilitation of the physicians who, in the last weeks of Stalin's life, had been indicted on charges of conspiring to murder high party officials. The frame-up was exposed and those among the doctors who had not died during interrogation were released. Other measures quickly followed. The secret police was deprived of its separate status and placed under party authority, forbidden to make administrative arrests or hand down sentences. A great number of inmates in concentration camps were released. In the initial phases of liquidating Stalin's legacy, the new premier, Georgy Malenkov, laid stress on ending the nearly exclusive reliance on heavy industry as the backbone of the socialist economy that Stalin had introduced and pursued to the very end. Countries lacking the material foundations for such a demanding economic program, notably Hungary, inaugurated a "NEW COURSE," which emphasized the production of consumer goods and began to phase out the forced delivery of foodstuffs by the peasantry and by collectives. Such wholesale deemphasis of heavy industry, mainly of a military nature, found vigorous opponents among the hard-liners, the Soviet equivalent of the industrial-military complex, whose economic and political well-being depended on continuing production of military materiel. After Khrushchev replaced Malenkov as head of the Soviet government, the downscaling of heavy industry was declared to be in conflict with socialist principles of production, especially at a time when the capitalist-imperialist camp posed such a danger to the socialist-democratic camp. But there never was a complete return to the Stalinist model of creating states of iron and steel.

One feature of the de-Stalinization period was that the name of Stalin virtually vanished from public mention. Whereas before his death there was hardly a newspaper editorial, a public speech, or an encomium that did not praise Stalin in extravagant terms, now his very name seemed to recede into anonymity. His portraits disappeared from public places. Whereas before 1956 he was not subjected to direct criticism, the rapid denunciation of many of the principles he promoted and defended in itself amounted to that. The change was most noticeable among the communist literati. While Stalin was alive, they mindlessly put their not insignificant talents in the service of socialist realism, deeming only one theme worthy of literary (and artistic) treatment: the struggle of the working class to free itself from wage slavery and achieve its dignity. In the process they not only "schematized" literature, they deprived it of freedom of expression and put it in the service of a political cause. Now many writers revolted against their own submission to a dictatorship. As one conscience-stricken poet wrote:

> I dwelt in elevated regions
> And saw nothing but the bright
>   and fine;
> My good fortune drew a curtain
> which concealed from my eyes the
>   dismal truth;
> I lived exultantly amid wondrous
>   numbers
> and great results that did not show how
> my people carried and dragged on their
>   shoulders
> the heavy exhausting burden of their
>   fate.

De-Stalinization reached its definitive stage at the XXth Congress of the Communist Party of the Soviet Union when party chief Nikita Khrushchev, in a "secret" speech to chosen delegates, tore down beyond repair the myth of Stalin's infallibility. He also recited a long cata-

logue of Stalin's many miscarriages of justice and his victimization of comrades who had fought long and hard for the victory of the revolution.

Djilas, Milovan (1911–1995)

Yugoslav Communist Party dignitary and statesman, one of the many once ardent revolutionaries who became disillusioned with communism

Born on June 12, 1911, in Podbisce in Montenegro, a talented and dynamic young man in a repressive society, at age 18 he was admitted to the University of Belgrade. His early interest centered on literature, and his poetry and short stories gained quick recognition. It wasn't long before his restless mind and temperament turned to the revolutionary doctrines rife among university students of the day; in 1932 he joined the illegal Communist Party of Yugoslavia. He graduated in 1933 and soon shared the fate of many of his activist comrades. He was arrested by the Yugoslav Royal Police for opposition to the absolutist monarchy of his country. After being tortured, he was imprisoned for three years. The hardness of spirit so common in young revolutionaries in those years sustained him and, no sooner free, he again plunged into revolutionary activities. At age 27 he was elected to the Central Committee of the party, and in 1940 he became a member of the ruling Politburo.

After the Germans occupied Yugoslavia in April 1941, Djilas joined the partisan movement and fought heroically to the end of the war. By 1944 he was a partisan general and as such joined a military mission to Moscow. His position was paradoxical because officially Yugoslavia was still a monarchy and the ambassador in Moscow, with whom he had frequent contact, was a monarchist, whereas Djilas was a professed Communist. After the end of the war he became a minister in Tito's government, one of Tito's most trusted confidants. He was a member of a second, this time political, mission to Moscow; he met and held talks with Stalin, Molotov, and other Soviet leaders. In 1947 he represented Yugoslavia at the founding of the COMINFORM. A year later, in April 1948, as Soviet-Yugoslav relations were headed for a breakdown, he visited Moscow a third time, together with Tito and other officials in order to forestall a break. The attempt was unsuccessful, even though Stalin was still amiable and called Tito a comrade. Two months later the break was final, the Yugoslav party was expelled from the Cominform, and a virulent campaign against Tito began.

Djilas served his superior loyally; early in 1953 he became one of four vice presidents of Yugoslavia and in December president of the People's Assembly. But, even though Stalin was by now dead and the new Soviet leadership made obsequious approaches to Tito, the latter remained rigid and defensive, not only toward the Soviets but also among his own compatriots. When Djilas pressed for liberalization, Tito relieved him of his official posts. In April 1954, Djilas resigned from the party of which he had been a member for 32 years. He was given an 18-month suspended sentence. He violated his parole when at the end of 1956 he wrote an article in an American magazine in support of the failed Hungarian revolution of that year and was imprisoned. Captivity did not bend Djilas's independent spirit; he published his books in the West, drawing additional prison sentences each time he did so. In *The New Class* he argued that communism in practice was not much different from capitalistic societies. He was released from prison in 1961, but arrested again a year later for publishing *Conversations with Stalin* in the West. He was amnestied in 1966, and, living in Belgrade, he published five more volumes, *Memoirs of a Revolutionary* in 1973, *Wartime* in 1977, *Tito: The Story from Inside* in 1980, an autobiographical collection of essays, *Rise and Fall* in 1985, and *Of Prisons and Ideas* in 1986.

Dobi, István (1898–1968)

Hungarian Smallholders politician, minister of agriculture, premier, and president of the republic

Son of a poor peasant family, he only completed six years of elementary education. In 1916 he became active in the construction workers' movement. Under the Hungarian soviet regime in 1919 he served in the Red Guards, and he was later captured by HORTHY's "White" forces and interned. In 1921 he returned to his native village but was placed under police surveillance. He showed some interest in joining the Social Democratic Party, but the strictures placed on it discouraged him and in 1936 he joined the Independent Smallholders' Party, in which he held several responsible positions. During the Second World War, as national secretary for the Peasant Alliance and president of its construction division, he was part of the left wing of political life that was spearheaded by the still illegal Communist Party. In 1944 he joined the resistance movement but was called to the colors; he was captured by the Red Army and returned home in the summer of 1945. He was, subsequently, minister of state until November 30, minister of agriculture, then, until September 24, 1947, minister of state again. He was vice president and then, from June 3, 1947, president of the Independent Smallholders and was largely responsible for the leftward shift of that party. In purging its ranks of "reactionary" elements he did the bidding of the Communists who were intent on breaking the political power of the Smallholders. From December 10, 1948, to September 5, 1949, he was premier; from September 6, 1949, until his retirement on April 14, 1967, he was president of the presidential council, in effect president of the republic. During the revolution of 1956 he sided with the "old order," that is, with socialist reconstruction and the forces that remained loyal to the Soviet Union. In the fall of 1959 he applied for membership in the Hungarian Socialist Workers' Party, and, when accepted, he became a member of the Central Committee. After his retirement in 1967 he became a parliamentary deputy and was active in the socialist organization of agriculture. He earned several awards, among them that of Hero of Socialist Labor in 1967.

Dollfuss, Engelbert (1892–1934)

Austrian Christian Socialist politician, president of the Austrian railroads 1930–31, minister of agriculture 1931–32, chancellor 1932–34

Son of an old Austro-German family from the town of Texing in hereditary Austrian lands, he studied law in VIENNA and economics in Berlin and became an expert in agrarian matters. He was appointed chancellor at the height of the Great Depression, and he managed to alleviate the acute economic crisis by securing a major loan through the League of Nations. He was soon buffeted by rival political forces, which even the most resourceful diplomacy was unable to reconcile. Devoted to the Greater German ideal, he favored *Anschluss* with Germany, but ADOLF HITLER's rise to power and the anti-Catholic bias of National Socialism sobered him of this preference. Of the two options for counteracting Nazi influence within Austria, an alliance with leftist-democratic forces on the one hand or with the conservative religious right on the other, he chose the latter and established close relations with the HEIMWEHR, the militia of conservative, nationalist forces. In foreign relations his resistance to pressure from Nazi Germany required the active patronage of another great power, and Italy willingly offered it. At a meeting with Mussolini on August 19, 1933, at Riccione in Italy, Dollfuss agreed to several onerous demands put to him: the Austrian constitution would be amended to become more authoritarian, political parties would be abolished and replaced with a single government-sponsored front, and a sweeping attack would be launched against the strongest Austrian party, the Social Democratic. In return Italy would resist, by force of arms if necessary, any Nazi move, either from inside Austria or from Germany, to seize power.

Shortly after this meeting, on September 11, 1933, Dollfuss in a speech forecast the impending dissolution of political parties. "Liberal mentality," he declared, "Marxist-Leninist deception of the people," the rule of parties, are things of the past." Against this program the Social Democrats alone registered protest. However, aware that an authoritarian party committed to Austrian independence was the only viable alternative to a union with Germany, the Social Democrats were willing to grant Dollfuss's government five years of dictatorial power, on condition that the freedom of trade unions was preserved.

Dollfuss was not inclined, however, to shape his domestic policy at the sufferance of the political left. In September 1933, in a bold move, he proclaimed the Vaterländische Front (Fatherland Front) as the sole party in the nation, abolished parliament, and proclaimed a corporative state on the Italian fascist model. He then made an attempt at accommodation with Germany, but he found the German conditions for harmonious relations, namely, the appointment of Nazi officials to major positions, unacceptable.

As the Social Democratic Party refused being absorbed into a single front, especially in one dominated by the right-wing Heimwehr, and maintained its agitation against Dollfuss's maneuvers, and as Mussolini persisted in his demand that the workers' party be liquidated, Dollfuss, not without misgivings, decided to strike against the Social Democrats. Between Februay 11 and 13, 1934, Austrian military and police units supported by the Heimwehr, assaulted the workers' quarters in Vienna, bombarded a number of buildings, and in effect destroyed Social Democratic strength. The action may have satisfied the conservative, Catholic Heimwehr, but it did not satisfy the Austrian Nazis. In the last reckoning the action against Social Democrats was part of Dollfuss's design to prevent union with and domination by Germany. A group of Austrian Nazis, acting on their own but not against Hitler's wishes, on July 25, 1934, invaded the chancellery in Vienna and shot Dollfuss, allowing him, while they barricaded themselves, to bleed to death. Any possible help from Germany to the conspirators was forestalled by Mussolini, who rushed troops to the Austro-Italian border (as did the Yugoslavs), serving notice that he would not tolerate the absorption of Austria into the German Reich.

When he chose to marry Sophie Chotek, countess from a family of unequal rank to the Habsburgs, FRANCIS JOSEPH and court officials made strenuous efforts to dissuade him from his choice. The emperor in the end gave his blessing, but only after Francis Ferdinand renounced the succession to the throne of the children born from the marriage. Sophie was made a princess. The marriage was happy and three children were born: Sophie in 1901, Max von Hohenberg in 1902, and Ernst von Hohenberg in 1904.

Francis Ferdinand engaged in politics from 1906 on and was especially active in frustrating Hungarian aspirations for complete independence from the Habsburg monarchy. His military bureau in the Belvedere Palace became a kind of second court. Here plans were laid for the time when Francis Ferdinand would become king. He planned restrictions on Hungarian rights under the AUSGLEICH, and in this he counted on Slovak, Romanian, and Croatian support. In opposing Hungarian aspirations he was even ready to employ military force. In general a conservative and a clerical opposed to democracy, still, he wanted to expand the rights of minorities, most likely as a means to weaken Hungarian power.

He strove to avoid international complications and opposed AERENTHAL's ambitious Balkan policies. He maintained close personal ties with William II of Germany and sought rapprochement with Russia. He strove to revive the moribund Dreikaiserbund. His plans for trialism, granting to Slavs equal status with Hungarians in the Dual Monarchy, are not convincingly documented, but he was an ardent foe of Serbia, a fact that lends credence to the theory that he wanted to neutralize Serbian appeal to the Slavs in the monarchy by making the latter the third component nationality.

In August 1913 he became inspector general of the combined armed forces and as such attended military maneuvers in Bosnia in June 1914. After their completion he proceeded to an official reception in Sarajevo, and there he was assassinated together with his wife on June 28.

Hard-working, intelligent, and conscientious, his private passions were less attractive; he was an avid hunter, boasting that he had shot over 200,000 wild animals, including hundreds of tigers. Addicted to blood sports, he was not popular with the general public.

Francis Joseph (1830–1916)
Austrian emperor, king of Hungary and Bohemia-Moravia

Oldest son of Archduke Francis Charles, son of FRANCIS I, and of Bavarian princess Sophie, he was christened Francis (Franz). Born in Vienna, on August 18, 1830, Francis Joseph died in Vienna on November 21, 1916. He had three younger brothers; one, Maximilian, the ill-starred "emperor" of Mexico, met his end before a firing squad in 1867. The emperor's slogan was: *Viribus unitis* (with united strength). His mother energetically prepared him and his character for ruling, made him aware of his royal dignity which he was taught owed no accounting to anyone but God. When the feeble-minded Ferdinand V, uncle of Francis Joseph, was forced to abdicate among the pressures of the revolutions of 1848, queen mother Sophie was instrumental in prevailing on her husband to step aside in favor of the succession of his 18-year-old son. With his coronation as emperor on December 2, 1848, in the Czech city of Olmütz, whence the royal family had retreated from the revolutionary violence in VIENNA, Sophie's dominant ambition was fulfilled. Upon the advice of the premier of the day, FELIX VON SCHWARZENBERG he added to his given name the name Joseph, for the still lovingly remembered reforming king JOSEPH II. Although by no means subservient, Francis Joseph followed his mother's direction, in full agreement with her principles. He regarded the military and the Roman Catholic Church as the dual foundation of the society he ruled; the arts and the sciences, literature, philosophy, theories of statecraft did not interest him and were absent from his education. His inculcated sense of mission early isolated him from his people, even from his younger brothers. At the time of his coronation as emperor, Hungary and Bohemia denied him recognition as sovereign. In one of his first acts, he invited Russian intervention against Hungarian revolutionary forces. After the defeat of the revolution he lent his imperial authority to the severe reprisals and executions that followed and this action poisoned relations between VIENNA and BUDAPEST for some two decades.

With the 1851 New Year's Eve Patent, issued at the prompting of Schwarzenberg and of the returned Metternich, the young emperor reverted to the practice of absolutism. He canceled the constitutions for Austria and Bohemia issued under duress in 1849, which bore his signature. He disbanded the Kremsier Assembly elected in Bohemia under that constitution. Leading democrats were imprisoned. All this made him, and his mother who had the greatest influence over him, very unpopular. In 1853 a Hungarian "patriot" János Libényi, tried to kill him by assaulting him with a knife.

After Schwarzenberg's death in 1852, Francis Joseph took over the direction of internal and foreign affairs, with bad results; his first fiasco was Austria's isolation in the Crimean War. His CONCORDAT OF 1855 granted the Catholic Church wide powers in education and marital matters, which represented a sharp attack on freethinkers. The empire became a police state. In 1854 he married his first cousin, 16-year-old Bavarian princess ELISABETH. In love with his Sisa, he found her eccentric and willful, a fact that caused no end of problems, especially as the young bride refused to adhere to the rigid protocol of court life insisted upon by the queen mother. The marriage produced four children: Sophie, in 1855, Gisela, in 1856, Rudolf, born in 1858, and Maria Valeria, in 1859.

The 1859 declaration of war on Piedmont, the Italian state that strove to unite northern Italy under the House of Savoy, was in part due to the emperor's boundless self-confidence; it resulted in Austria's defeat by Piedmont's French ally and the loss of the Italian state of Lombardy. The defeat had a sobering effect on the emperor and led to some mitigation of absolutism. The OCTOBER DIPLOMA of 1860 and the FEBRUARY PATENT of 1861 were hesitant first steps toward recognizing the legislative powers of parts of the empire.

Francis Joseph had inherited from his predecessors a dominant position in all-German affairs. The Austrian delegate under his instructions in the Diet of the 39 states that made up the German Confederation, the successor to the Holy Roman Empire, was at all times president of that assembly. But that position was progressively eroded by the ascendancy of Prussia, especially after Otto von Bismarck became minister president of that state. Francis Joseph, attempting to be his own foreign minister, was no match for Bismarck's manipulations and allowed himself, in 1866, to be dragged into a war in which Austria faced Prussia in the north and Italy in the south. Although Austrian forces prevailed against Italy, they suffered a major defeat in the Battle of Königgrätz against Prussia. It put an end to Austria's preponderance in German affairs. It further made it necessary to reorganize the Austrian state structure. Pro-Hungarian Elisabeth used her influence in the interest of an AUSGLEICH with Hungary. Dualism was born and Francis Joseph now ruled over two entities, an empire (Austria) and a kingdom (Hungary). On June 8, 1876, the royal pair was crowned in Buda as king and queen of Hungary. The promised Czech coronation never materialized.

During the 12 years of liberal government (1867–79) that followed the Great Compromise, the Concordat of 1855 was cancelled, and educational and press policies were liberalized. The Czech problem continued to rankle. There was also a great deal of controversy over Austria's acquisitive Balkan policies, which liberals in both parts of the Dual Monarchy opposed. The cabinet of the younger Auersperg brother fell in 1879, and it was followed by one under Francis Joseph's childhood friend Count TAAFFE (1879–93). Taaffe governed conservatively, but he also passed laws for the protection of workers. The 1882 electoral reform gave the right to vote to many peasants and petit bourgeois. The years that followed witnessed the growth of the Christian Socialist Party and Social Democratic Party, both laboring, though in very different ways, for the improvement of the lot of the working class.

The last 20 years before the Great War were marked by increasing ethnic tensions and the emperor became more and more a symbolic link among mutually hostile elements. He suffered many personal tragedies. In 1867 his brother Maximilian was executed in Mexico; his only son Rudolf committed suicide in 1889; in 1898 his wife Elisabeth was assassinated in Geneva by an enraged radical. In his late years Francis Joseph strove mightily to preserve the Dual Monarchy's great power status while his heir apparent FRANCIS FERDINAND vainly tried to persuade him to make the political structure more equitable for all ethnic components. However, Francis Joseph feared that the tenuous unity of the empire would fall apart if major changes were made.

In 1914, although he liked to be called "emperor of peace," it was he who signed the unacceptable ultimatum to Serbia on July 23, and on June 28 the declaration of war. In the next two years he witnessed the repeated reverses of his forces on the Russian, Serbian, and subsquently Italian fronts; only German interventions rescued them from complete defeat. He was growing physically feeble but labored at paperwork to the very end of his life. He worked at his desk on the morning of November 21, 1916, retired to rest in the afternoon, and asked for "a little water." These were the last words he spoke. Unable to swallow it when it was offered he died minutes later. In a very true sense his death marked the end of an era.

Freud, Sigmund (1856–1939)

Austrian physician, founder of the school of psychoanalysis, arguably the most influential figure in the study of the human psyche, its passions and means of expression

He was born in Freiberg, Moravia (then part of the Austrian Empire, today in the Czech Republic) to a Jewish wool merchant, Jakob, who had been twice married and widowed, and who married his third wife, the 19-year-old Amalie Nathanson, when he was 39. His two sons from his previous marriage were of approximately the same age as his new wife. One of Freud's nephews, Johann, to whom he was closest, was a year older than he. When Freud was four years old, his family moved to VIENNA, a cosmopolitan city far more tolerant of religious differences than the narrowly Catholic environment in Moravia. Although Freud never was a practicing Jew, he had a strong emotional bond to Judaism and maintained lasting ties with Jewish organizations. There are indications though that he felt less than comfortable about the field of psychoanalysis being closely associated with the Jewish analytic intellect.

At the Gymnasium in Vienna that Freud attended between 1866 and 1873, he studied the classics, mathematics, the natural sciences, and history. He was an outstanding student and entered the university at age 17. He had considered the study of law but apparently a lecture on Goethe about nature inclined him to devote himself to medicine. In part because he vacillated between clinical medicine and theory and research and in part because of the compulsive thoroughness of his inquiries, he took seven rather than the usual five years to complete his doctorate in medicine.

He married a young Hamburg woman, Martha Bernays after a five-year long-distance courtship in 1886, and in time they had six children. (The youngest, Anna, became an eminent psychoanalyst in her own right and a preserver and perpetuator of her father's legacy.)

Freud earned his medical degree in clinical neurology but his theoretical interests persisted. During a stay in Paris in 1885 he made the acquaintance of the French neurologist J. M. Charcot and under his influence came to recognize hysteria as a distinct neurological disorder. Returning to Vienna, he found that an older colleague, Josef Breuer, pursued studies similar to his. Breuer had discovered that when he queried a patient, almost always a woman, about the earliest manifestations of her hysteria, in conse-

Sigmund Freud *(Library of Congress)*

quence of speaking about it the symptoms disappeared. It was the beginning of talk therapy. Breuer did not aver, and neither did Freud, that hysteria was merely an exalted form of behavior without neurological roots, but both maintained that it could be influenced by discovering its origins and changing the ideas that brought on the symptoms.

Where Breuer and Freud parted company was that in Freud's view neuroses had sexual origins, dating from early childhood, producing inner conflicts that had never been resolved. Key among these, in Freud's view, was what he called the Oedipus complex, the repressed desire of the male child to take his father's place in his mother's affection, a desire so strong that it involved the wish to remove the father from the relationship altogether in order to possess the mother freely. Unresolved conflicts such as this

were in time buried in the unconscious, and their repression was the source of all neuroses.

Freud published in 1901 his study *The Interpretation of Dreams*, based primarily on the consideration of the mood and content of his own dreams. In this work he argued for the first time that a person's dreams, as the examination of his neurotic symptoms, serve as a "royal road" to understanding the unconscious. Ultimately the unconscious determined a person's behavior. Following the practice of Charcot, Freud had at first experimented with hypnosis as a means of laying bare the contents of the unconscious; he later turned to the subtler method he had worked out with Breuer, called "free association." By this method Freud encouraged the patient to express random thoughts in response to often unrelated subjects. The patient could thereby circumvent the obstacles that conscious thought and the dictates of convention placed in the way of expressing deeply unconscious motifs. The encountering of such obstacles in the course of therapy at times produced prolonged silences, defective speech, visible unease; these Freud termed resistance. Overcoming them was essential to penetrating the unresolved conflicts lying deep in the unconscious. However, the process must not be allowed to be purely intellectual; it has to be *experienced*. Given the painfulness of recovering the memory, the reason why it is repressed, at first produces regression rather than recovery. This is why therapy, to be successful, must be of such long duration.

Following up on the theme developed in his essay on dreams, Freud wrote a number of other essays, exploring unconscious mental and emotional processes, often exploring such seemingly trivial subjects as slips of the tongue and gaps in memory. These events he discussed in his book *The Psychopathology of Everyday Life* (1901); the peculiar roots of humor in *Jokes and Their Relation to the Unconscious* (1905), the roots of creativity in *Leonardo da Vinci and a Memory of His Childhood* (1910), and the influence of cultural institutions on the psyche in *Totem and Taboo*

(1912). Probably his most insightful and most controversial work was his *Three Essays on the Theory of Sexuality* (1905), in which he explored the stages and conflicts of infantile sexuality.

Beginning in 1902 Freud held weekly sessions with friends and colleagues to read and discuss papers on psychoanalysis. It marked the beginning of the psychoanalytic movement. In Switzerland a similar circle was formed around Carl Jung, and in 1908 the first psychoanalytic congress was held in Salzburg. In 1909, upon the invitation of Clark University in Worcester, Massachusetts, Freud gave five lectures, and the occasion marked the beginning of his international recognition.

Yet his subsequent theories, like his earlier, were never conflict-free. In the beginning phases of his career, in treating hysterical women, Freud often came to the conclusion that as young girls these women had been seduced, usually by older male relative and repressed the trauma, which continued to live in their unconscious. His later empirical studies, however, led him to believe that the women's confessions were often the products of sexual fantasies rather than actual cases of seduction. Instead of abandoning his theories on infantile sexuality altogether, he allowed wider scope to the influence and effect of sexual fantasies, which in some ways could leave as deep a mark on the unconscious as an actual sexual experience. Nevertheless, his partial retreat from a previously firmly held theory, however creative, led to several of his associates breaking with him and establishing schools of their own. Alfred Adler, Otto Rank and Wilhelm Reich were the most prominent.

Freud was a chain smoker of cigars and in 1923 he developed cancer of the mouth. He had 33 operations which he bore with courage, and it took his cancer 16 years to take his life. His last years were nevertheless every bit as productive as the earlier ones had been. It was now that he fully developed his theories on the divisions of the psyche into the ego, the superego, and the id, probably the most influential of all his writings.

When Austria was occupied by Nazi Germany in March 1938, Freud and his family, as Jews, were placed under house arrest. Through the intervention of several illustrious and highly influential persons, among them a Greek princess, an eminent British psychoanalyst, and the American ambassador in Paris, the Freuds were allowed to leave Austria in June 1938. They went to London, where Freud had one more operation for his cancer. He died on September 23, 1939, his reputation as a pathblazer in the study of the human psyche and the unconscious firmly established.

G

Gerő, Ernő (1898–1980)
leading figure in the Hungarian communist movement

Between the two world wars Gerő was active in the Communist International and resident agent in Spain of Soviet military intelligence during the Spanish Civil War. After the Second World War he became one of the top Communist Party functionaries in Hungary, heading at different times a variety of ministries utilizing his economic expertise. His family name was Singer, and he was one of 10 children of a Jewish retail merchant. Gerő completed his secondary education in the BUDAPEST suburb of Ujpest. In 1916 he enrolled in medical school but did not finish his studies. He became involved in the communist youth movement and soon was an outstanding member of the fledgling party in Hungary. During the Hungarian soviet regime of 1919 he volunteered for the Red Army but did not see military service. After the fall of the soviet regime he fled to VIENNA and actively participated in organizational work in a number of foreign locations. After his return to Hungary he defied recent legislation that authorized the death penalty against Communist agitators; with several comrades he edited and published the illegal newspaper *Commune*. He was arrested and in May 1923 and sentenced to 16 years in a penitentiary, but a year and a half later he was deported to the Soviet Union. The party soon sent him to France where, between 1925 and 1928 he was in charge of the Hungarian subsection of the party. After his return to Moscow several other foreign assignments—in Belgium, Sweden, Finland, Yugoslavia, and finally Spain—awaited him. During the Spanish civil war he

directed the campaign against "Trotskyites" in the International Brigade and earned the epithet of "Butcher of Barcelona." The outbreak of the Second World War found him in Moscow again, and there he remained for the duration of the war. After the dissolution of the Communist International in 1943 he was in charge of propaganda directed at enemy forces and prisoners of war. He was widely regarded as the prospective head of the Hungarian party once that party could, under the protection of Soviet military forces, reemerge as a legitimate political force. But Stalin's choice fell upon a Hungarian Communist with a much more checkered career, MÁTYÁS RÁKOSI. Gerő was nevertheless among the very first communist functionaries to return to Hungary in early November 1944. Later that month he flew back to Moscow to participate in the discussions concerning the terms under which Hungary would surrender to the Soviet Union. Back in Hungary in December of that year he was one of the chief organizers of the provisional assembly that was empowered to conclude an armistice with the victorious powers. After the liberation of Budapest he moved his activities there and, until the arrival of Rákosi on February 22, headed the party apparatus in the war-scarred capital. From then on, he served as a member of the all-powerful political committee of the party and also held the commercial and transportation portfolios in the government. He was instrumental in bringing about the fusion of the Communist and the Social Democratic parties in 1948. Known as the gray eminence, he in many instances had more authority than Rákosi. His interminable memos laid down the law within the party and his drafts for various

Ernő Gerő (middle)   *(Hungarian Museum of Photography)*

pronouncements or agendas for congresses were often adopted verbatim. After serving a year as finance minister, from 1948 to 1949, he became head of the Planning Bureau and was responsible for the wholesale nationalization of private firms and for the successive Three- and Five-Year Plans that demanded ever heavier sacrifices from the workers in whose name the party ruled.

While Stalin was alive the allocation of party responsibilities and the broad outlines of the economic plans remained unchanged, except that in 1952, at Stalin's request, Rákosi became, in addition to general secretary of the party, premier as well. (It was in line with Stalin's inten-

tion to transfer the substance of political power from the party to the government.) After Stalin's death in March 1953, the new leadership in the Kremlin became aware of the exaggerated proportions of industrialization in the satellites, especially in Hungary. Twice Gerő was a member of a government delegation summoned to Moscow to explain and justify the unrealistic expectations of the economic plans. Together with Rákosi he obediently accepted the criticism, and also the appointment of a liberal reformist, IMRE NAGY, instead of Rákosi as premier. Gerő now had the unenviable task of soft-pedaling the measures he himself had declared as imperative, measures aimed at transforming Hungary into a "land of iron and steel." Although he was even more of a taskmaster than Rákosi was, in the public eye he did not suffer from the odium of gross miscarriages of justice, and he never practiced, as Rákosi did, the cult of personality. Thus, when the pending bankruptcy of communism in Hungary sufficiently alarmed Soviet leaders that they realized the necessity of a major change, in the summer of 1956 they demanded Rákosi's resignation as party chief and placed Gerő in his place. Always dutiful and an assiduous worker, Gerő began to draw up plans for a new party congress and for new national elections. In October 1956 he headed a delegation to Belgrade to settle some pending matters with the Yugoslav government and, in his absence, the political situation at home reached a breaking point. Returning to Hungary on October 23, he found a revolution in progress. His appeals for calm and for support of the party went unheeded. At a meeting of the party's central leadership that evening he blamed the press, which had taken inexcusable liberties lately, for the turmoil in the streets, and he also charged that fascism had much deeper roots in Hungary than anyone had suspected. He was relieved of his post as first secretary on October 25 and flew to the Soviet Union for safety. He returned to Hungary only in 1960, but the new, chastened, party leadership held him responsible for sundry miscarriages of justice and in 1962 expelled him from the party. He was granted a modest pension and to supplement it he did translations, mainly from Hungarian into Russian. A man who had in every sense of the word devoted his entire life to a political cause found himself victimized, not so much by the cause as by its terminal weakness and ultimate failure.

Golden Bull of 1222

Royal document issued by Hungarian king András II in response to a widespread demand by both the high and the middle nobility, who greatly resented the king's practice of giving away whole counties, as well as crown estates and fortress estates, in an attempt to gain followers and increase royal income. Resentment further increased when, early in 1222, under papal pressure, András exempted the clergy from taxation and from civil jurisdiction. Eleven years earlier he had already incurred the ire of many by inviting into eastern Hungary the Teutonic Knights to deal with the heathen Cumans in TRANSYLVANIA. The knights also enjoyed freedom from taxation and a number of other privileges not granted to the local nobility. On St. George's Day in 1222 a large crowd gathering in the town of Fehérvár demanded the issuance of a bull guaranteeing cessation of the resented practices. In the Golden Bull, so-called from the golden seal dangling from a ribbon fastened to it, Andrew pledged not to grant entire counties, or high dignities, as permanent possessions, and further that he would in future not deprive anyone of an honestly earned estate. The document limited the number of foreigners who could be given high office or granted landed estates and banned the employment of Jews as land-stewards or customs officials. To prevent the devaluation of money it provided that currency must be kept valid and in circulation for at least one year. It called for the removal of bailiffs who treated serving nobility unfairly and it assured the serving nobility of the right to choose the heir to their estates as well as the right to refuse to fight outside the borders of the country. It forbade the harboring of legally convicted individuals. It forbade the accumulation of multiple dignities. It granted a special right to the high nobility in Article 31, which stated that if a king violated provisions of the document, the high nobles had a right to disobey his orders.

Goluchowski, Count Agenor, the Younger (1849–1921)

Polish-born aristocrat appointed foreign minister of the Dual Monarchy

Scion of an old Polish aristocratic family, his appointment as joint foreign minister in May

1895 caused considerable surprise. The appointment was possibly due to the fact that his predecessor, Count Gustav Kálnoky, recommended him as his replacement, and FRANCIS JOSEPH was favorably impressed by the fact that the Goluchowskis had long been among the Polish aristocrats most loyal to the House of Habsburg. His father had been Austrian viceroy of Poland and, between 1859 and 1860, minister of interior for the empire. The younger had served in the Austrian diplomatic service for years, without, however, distinguishing himself in any way; his most responsible assignment had been minister in Bucharest. Personally he was well liked for his cheerful and casual ways. His sentiments, if not his active politics, were pronouncedly anti-Russian. He favored British adherence to the Triple Alliance of Germany, Austria, and Italy, an arrangement by which Austria, together with Britain, and supported by the German alliance, could frustrate Russian schemes in the Balkans. By this time Britain had herself made probings in the direction of an alliance with Germany (in 1899 and later), and Goluchowski's plan lost much of its timeliness. Prompted largely by fears of broader involvement that the Greco-Turkish war of 1896 had inspired, Goluchowksi and his emperor, in 1897, paid a visit to St. Petersburg and reached a "gentlemen's agreement" that essentially confirmed the status quo in the Balkans. This agreement, strengthened by Russia's revived interest in the Far East, neutralized the Balkan problem for a decade.

Also in 1897 Goluchowski concluded an oral agreement with Italy, confirmed in writing in 1901, acknowledging equality of rights between Austria and Italy in Albania. The Italians were exerting intensive diplomatic, as well as cultural, efforts in the Balkans, with Albania and Montenegro their chief targets. In line with his easygoing disposition Goluchowski saw no danger in this, certainly not as long as the Austro-Russian détente in the Balkans held. Upon signing the agreement with Italy in 1901, he rather complacently assured his government that the agreement would prevent any changes in the Balkans

"prejudicial to [Austria's] vital interests or involving danger for her position in the future."

Austria's position suffered another setback in June 1903, when the pro-Austrian king of Serbia, Alexander Obrenović, was murdered and replaced by Peter of the anti-Austrian House of Karageorgević. Austria responded by placing an embargo on Serbian livestock, a step that resulted in cancellation of Serbian orders for heavy machinery from the Bohemian Škoda Works. It is not clear what part Goluchowski played in the implementation of these measures; always seeking to avoid conflict, he most likely passively acquiesced in them. Whether because of the failure of the anti-Serbian action or for reasons of his own, he resigned in October 1906, to be replaced by the far more activist ALOIS AERENTHAL. His departure coincided with the end to the relative calm in the Balkans and also with the détente with Russia.

Gömbös, Gyula (1886–1936)
rightist Hungarian politician and premier of a racist persuasion

Gömbös's father was a high school teacher, his mother a housewife. As a professional military officer, he served in the First World War on the Russian front. He was wounded in June 1916; following his recovery he did duty in the ministry of defense, then in VIENNA at the Central Supply Office. After the war he served briefly as military attaché at the Zagreb legation. From the end of 1918 he headed the Balkan section of the operational division in the Ministry of Defense. He started his political career in 1919 when he was elected to head the newly organized Hungarian Self-Defense Society (MOVE). He was active in organizing a committee in Vienna against the soviet regime in Hungary and in the summer of 1919 he represented in that city HORTHY's provisional government then being formed in Szeged. In 1920 he was elected to parliament. In October of the following year he played a major part in foiling the attempt by King Charles IV to return to Hungary and claim his throne. In

January 1922 he joined the National Unity Front of Premier ISTVÁN BETHLEN but in the summer of 1923 he left it and organized the Hungarian National Independence Party with a racist program. Failing to attract a large following, in 1928 he returned to Bethlen's party and became state secretary for defense. On September 19, 1932, after the resignation of Bethlen, he became premier. His irrepressible ego (he was in the habit of saying, referring to himself, that it was enough if there was one clever man in a country) induced him to put forth a program for the reorganization of Hungarian society by rightist dictatorial means, on the model of Italian fascism. His "Ninety-Five Points," issued after his appointment to the premiership, contained promises for every stratum of society and envisioned a corporative state in which employers and employees formed corporations with government mediation.

In June 1933 he was the first head of government to pay ADOLF HITLER a visit. In addition to premier, he also retained his post as defense minister, and in the first two months of 1933 was also foreign minister. Although his ideas had a certain appeal to the lower and the middle classes, they had no support from realistic political groups. He concluded a commercial treaty with Germany and supplemented it with additional provisions in 1933 and 1934. These did have some mitigating effect on the country's economic crisis. In 1934, by the Rome Protocols, he established a tripartite commercial and foreign policy connection among Hungary, Italy, and Austria. Thus fortified in the diplomatic field, he made the peaceful revision of the TREATY OF TRIANON his principal goal, and he saw in Hitler's Germany the best guarantee for achieving his end. In 1934 he launched a new domestic program in which he sought to end the unhealthy practice of open voting. He also supported a large-scale resettlement of indigent farmers. His plans met opposition from the left and the right alike. In March 1935 he prevailed on Horthy to dismiss parliament and hold new elections. In the same month he became the sole head of the

government party, which already in 1931 had been renamed the Party of National Unity, but his attempts to create a totalitarian state on the German and Italian model failed. By 1936 he lost even Horthy's support; the regent refrained from dismissing him only so as not to aggravate his ever-worsening kidney disease. From May 14, 1936, Gömbös was on sick leave in Germany. He died on October 16, 1936, in Munich.

Görgey, Artur (1818–1916)

Hungarian military officer, commanding general of the Hungarian Honvéd army during the revolution of 1848–49

Son of an impoverished noble, he began his military studies in the sapper school at age 14; at age 21 he was promoted to lieutenant in the bodyguard; in 1842 he became first lieutenant in the cavalry. After his discharge in 1845 he studied chemistry at Prague University. When revolutionary events in March 1848 took a sudden turn toward Hungarian independence from Habsburg rule, he offered his services to the new government. On June 13 he was promoted to captain, and a month later to major. In November the National Defense Committee of the Hungarian parliament, at the recommendation of LÁJOS KOSSUTH, promoted him to general. That winter he made his mark by employing quick maneuvers against the invading Habsburg army and with his skill he succeeded in demolishing the enemy line with concentrated artillery fire. Politically, however, he promoted compromise with the Habsburgs, a course that favored the interests of the middle nobility to which he belonged against the high aristocracy that owned immense estates and wielded dominant political influence. He defied Kossuth's order to engage the enemy in open battle and, in a pronouncement at Vác in January 1849, announced his readiness for compromise. By doing so he isolated himself from the National Defense Committee and that winter he acted independently. By spring military realities compelled him to join up with an army on the Upper Tisza, which acted in concert with the

Defense Committee. After spectacular military successes that spring, he made common cause with the peace party and placed himself in open opposition to Kossuth and the radicals who strove for a complete break with the Habsburgs. His position gained enough support for him to be named minister of defense from May 7 to July 14. He entered the field again after the Russian army, which the new emperor FRANCIS JOSEPH had invited to help put down the Hungarian rising, invaded the country. Realizing the overwhelming odds against his forces, on August 13, at the town of Világos, he unconditionally surrendered to the Russian army. During the heavy reprisals that followed, he was a prime candidate for being tried for treason but, at the intercession of Czar Nicholas I, he was spared and exiled to Klagenfurt in Austria.

Gottwald, Klement (1896–1953)

Czech Communist politician, premier, then president of Czechoslovakia

Illegitimate son of a small farmer, he had only an elementary education. At age 12 he was sent to VIENNA to apprentice in the carpenter trade. He became a socialist at age 16. After the outbreak of the Great War he served in the Austro-Hungarian army on the Russian front, but deserted and became a prisoner of war. He drew new inspiration for his socialist convictions from the revolution in Russia. He returned home in 1918 and joined the left wing of the Social Democratic Party, which later seceded to become the Communist Party. In the Slovak capital of Bratislava he edited the party newspaper. In 1925 he became a member of the party's Central Committee and then of its Political Committee. As the leader of the party's left wing, he shaped the Czechoslovak party according to the wishes of Stalin. In 1929 he was elected to parliament and

served until the truncation of Czechoslovakia following the MUNICH AGREEMENT. In November 1938 he emigrated to Moscow, where he organized the Czechoslovak National Front under communist direction. He returned to his homeland with the advancing Red Army in April 1945; it is with his name that the so-called Košice Program, which proposed the collective deprivation of Hungarians and Germans of their political rights, is associated. He became deputy premier in the first postwar government appointed by President EDVARD BENEŠ. Between July 1946 and June 1948 he was premier and he headed the coalition government that negotiated the Czechoslovakian-Hungarian population exchange. He gradually brought the Czechoslovak army, then the national militia, the labor unions, and the youth organizations under the direction of his party. It was thus that he prepared the ground for the Communist seizure of power in February 1948. When President Beneš resigned in July of that year, Gottwald became president of the Czechoslovak People's Republic. He foisted a Stalinist constitution and governmental system on the country. He liquidated freedom of the press and of expression. He was responsible for the abnormal acceleration of heavy industry development, which by degrees ruined the once flowering Czech economy. He settled scores not only with the enemies of the system but with his own personal rivals as well. During the conceptual lawsuits of 1949–51, 230 men were sentenced to death. Among them was RUDOLF SLÁNSKÝ, previously general secretary of the party; tens of thousands were imprisoned or sent to labor camps. During Stalin's funeral on March 9, 1953, he caught a cold and died two weeks later of pneumonia.

Great Compromise See *AUSGLEICH*.

H

Habsburgs

According to a story concerning the foundation of a cloister in Mur in Aargau canton in Switzerland, written in the 12th century, the founding father of the House of Habsburg was one Guntram the Rich who lived in the second half of the 10th century. The name Habsburg was a contraction of the name of the family castle—Habichtsburg (Hawks' Castle). Guntram may or may not have been the same person as a count by that name who in 952 was shorn of his estates by Otto I (the Great) for treason. According to this version Guntram's son was Lanzelin, who acquired Mur. Lanzelin's own son, Ratbod, founded a cloister in a municipality that in time became the burying place of many Habsburgs.

Ratbod shared the family estate with his younger brother, Rudolf. He himself kept the Aargau and Klettjan estates; Rudolf obtained Upper Alsace and Rauben. As Rudolf had no children, after his death Ratbod secured all the possessions, and these he left to his three sons.

The political rise of the Habsburgs began with Rudolf I of a much later generation who was elected Holy Roman Emperor in 1273. In 1278 he defeated the Czech king Ottokar II, and he conquered Lower and Upper Austria as well as Styria, all held by the latter. Rudolf did lose, in 1315, his Swiss provinces; after that the Austrian possessions became the central holdings of the Habsburgs, together with Carinthia and Carniola. The family later acquired Tyrol and the Vorarlberg, in 1369 and 1375, respectively. After the death in 1473 of Sigismund of Luxembourg, who was emperor of Austria and king of Hungary, his son-in-law, Albert II of Habsburg (1437–39) inherited the Hungarian and Czech crowns, as well as the Holy Roman emperorship; the latter remained in the House of Habsburg until 1806 (though from 1741, when MARIA THERESA's husband Francis of Lorraine was elected emperor, it rested properly in the House of Habsburg-Lorraine).

In the 15th century the true rise of Habsburg power began. Through Maximilian I's marriage in 1477 to Mary of Burgundy, Burgundy and the Netherlands became Habsburg provinces; when Maximilian's son Philip the Handsome married the oldest daughter of Ferdinand of Aragon and Isabella of Castile, Juana la Loca, these lands, minus Burgundy, which passed to the French crown, eventually devolved upon their son Charles. In 1526 Hungary, Bohemia-Moravia, and Silesia also accrued to the Habsburgs. The emperor CHARLES V, before his abdication in 1556, separated the empire into a western and an eastern part; the western eventually passed to the Bourbons in the WAR OF THE SPANISH SUCCESSION while the eastern empire remained under the House of Habsburg until the end of the First World War.

Havel, Václav (1936–)

Czech dramatist, essayist, politician, last president of Czechoslovakia, first president of the Czech Republic

Havel's literary reputation rests mainly on his work as a playwright, but his role in history was initiated and deepened by his trenchant political essays in which he exposed the soulless bureaucracy under a Communist Party system, a system that stunted free expression and genuine

ernor and regent for the absent Habsburg king Charles IV. Fourth son among five born to the Protestant nobleman Stephen de Horthy and his Catholic wife Paulette de Halasy, he and his brothers attended a Protestant church in their native town of Kenderes while their only sister worshipped in the Catholic church with her mother.

Until age 14 Horthy attended a Reformist Gymnasium in Debrecen, then he enrolled in the Imperial Naval Academy at Fiume. In 1886 he became an ensign in the imperial navy; in 1900 he was promoted to lieutenant. The sea his passion, he was on board ship on many voyages and once sailed on a frigate to the South Seas escorting a scientific expedition. In 1901 he married a commoner, Magda Purgly; she bore him two sons and a daughter. In 1909 he was named aide-de-camp to Emperor FRANCIS JOSEPH. His promotion to captain came just before the outbreak of the First World War. He first commanded the battleship *Habsburg,* then the cruiser *Novara.* In 1917, after the Allies set up a blockade on the Adriatic, Horthy made himself a name by breaking through it at the Otranto Straits. Wounded in the leg, he managed to return his ship to port safely. The next year he was made vice admiral. After the military collapse in 1918, in line with agreements his government had worked out with the Serbs and the French, he delivered the Austro-Hungarian navy to Serbian authorities.

His political career began when he allied himself with forces hostile to the soviet government in Hungary that had established itself in March 1919. In the city of Szeged in southern Hungary he joined a hastily formed reactionary government. (The government printing office, charged with publishing his "secret papers" in 1962, summarized these events as follows: "The bloody suppression in February 1918 of the revolt of seamen in Cattaro gave [Horthy's] name notoriety. On the basis of his counterrevolutionary merits thus attained, he became minister of war in the counterrevolutionary government in Szeged, and later commander in chief of the so-called national army. After drowning the soviet republic in

blood, he transferred his headquarters to Siófok [on Lake Balaton] and directed his terrorist gangs from there. When the occupying Romanian army evacuated Budapest, on November 16, 1919, he entered the terrified capital. With the help of his [terrorist] detachments, on March 1, 1920, he had himself elected governor. He managed to use his position as head of state to augment his personal power and promote his dynastic ambitions. It was in pursuit of these goals that he repeatedly foiled [Habsburg king] Charles IV's attempt to return and forced the extension of his own governmental powers.")

In its essentials the account is accurate; what it omits to say is that the soviet government Horthy's forces crushed was immensely unpopular because of its exactions and confiscations and for its predominantly Jewish leadership, whereas Horthy, once installed, commanded the loyalty of the vast majority of the people. His official residence was in the vast royal palace in Buda, where he had a small and none too tidy office, but he and his wife spent as much time as they could in Horthy's ancestral home in Kenderes.

In his first 10 years as head of state Horthy left most of the business of governing in the hands of his premiers, especially ISTVÁN BETHLEN, who was able to lift Hungary from an economically devastated to a fairly prosperous state and earned the truncated country a measure of respect in international councils. In the 1930s, largely under the impact of the Great Depression, which had hit Hungary hard, and of political events in Germany, Horthy took an increasingly active interest in governmental affairs. Personally he had no respect for Adolf Hitler, but he gradually realized that the TREATY OF TRIANON, which deprived Hungary of two-thirds of her prewar territory and population, could be revised in Hungary's favor only through Hitler's intercessions. He also supported Hitler's militant anticommunism. He was able to keep his country out of the Second World War for two years, but after Hitler launched his campaign against the Soviet Union, he could not resist the pressure by the military and by extremist political elements to join the "crusade." After initial advances, the Second Hungarian Army he had agreed to contribute to the German war effort was destroyed on the Don in January 1942 in the last phase of the epic battle for Stalingrad. Hungary, as so often before, found herself in a losing war. Horthy and some of his ministers made several attempts to arrange a surrender to United States and Britain rather than to the Soviet Union. When these efforts failed and the Red Army stood at the Carpathians, Horthy attempted to pull his embattled nation out of the war. However, a Hungarian Nazi coup supported by the Germans frustrated the attempt, and Horthy was arrested and taken to Germany. After the war he fell into American hands; he was imprisoned for a few months, then released without a trial and allowed to move to Portugal. He died in Estoril on February 9, 1957. He lived long enough to witness the crushing of the heroic uprising of his people against Soviet rule, and a campaign of vendetta launched against the "counterrevolutionaries," a term that had carried an heroic ring when Horthy came to power but had become a mortal crime under Communist rule.

I

Imrédy, Béla (1891–1946)
Hungarian rightist politician, premier

Son of Kálmán Imrédy and Karolin Vajkay, Imrédy had two brothers and a sister. In 1912 he earned a diploma in judicial studies from Budapest University. In 1913 he spent a year studying economics in western Europe. In 1917 he married Irén Nelky; no children were born. He served on various fronts during the First World War as a cavalry lieutenant. From 1919 he worked in the ministry of finance in various capacities. In 1921 he left government service and held several high positions in banks and financial institutions. Between 1928 and 1932 he represented his country at a number of international economic conferences as an expert adviser. In 1932 Premier GYULA GÖMBÖS asked him to work out the economic aspects of the government program he called his National Work Plan. In October 1932 Imrédy became minister of finance. In his first trip abroad as minister he visited Germany and conducted intensive negotiations with Hitler's minister of finance, Hjalmar Schacht. In January 1935 Regent HORTHY appointed him president of the National Bank. He had been a member of the lower house of parliament since 1933, and in 1935 he was appointed to the upper house. Whether under the influence of Hitler's successes or through his own convictions, he adopted an uncritically pro-German attitude and strove to bring a rightist dictatorship to Hungary as well. His conduct in parliament became ever more contentious. In November 1938 he authorized unfettered campaigning by the German Volksbund within Hungary. The first VIENNA AWARD, which returned to Hungary a part of the northern uplands that she lost in the TREATY OF TRIANON, further strengthened his pro-German sentiments. To bolster his dictatorial ambitions, in January 1939 he announced the formation of the Fascistic Party of Hungarian Life. Conservative elements in parliament, who were resolved to uphold the constitution, thereupon demanded his dismissal. They were able to produce documents to show that Imrédy, who pursued an undisguisedly racist policy, had a Jewish forefather. He resigned in February 1939, but he was not chastened. Abandoning the government party, in October 1940 he founded the ultrarightist Party of Hungarian Renewal and became its parliamentary representative. He established close relations with the German National Socialist Party as well as with FERENC SZÁLASI'S Arrowcross Party. After the outbreak of the Second World War he became a champion of German war aims as he had been a champion of the German Nazi political system. When the Germans occupied Hungary in March 1944, they intended him to head a government, but Regent Horthy refused to appoint him and he became minister without portfolio in the government of DÖME SZTÓJAY. Deeply disillusioned when he realized how consistently and ruthlessly the Germans sought to exploit Hungary's economic resources, he nevertheless supported the Arrowcross seizure of power in October 1944. After the lost war he departed for Germany, where the Americans arrested him on October 3, 1945, and returned him to Hungary. On November 23, 1945, he was sentenced to be hanged as a war criminal; the method of execution was later changed to death by firing squad. He was executed on February 28, 1946, another gullible victim of the Nazi dream of a "New Order" in Europe.

J

Jelačić, Count Josip (1801–1859)

vice marshal in the Austrian army, governor of Croatia, Dalmatia, and Slavonia

Son of an impoverished Croatian family, Jelačić had two younger brothers. In 1850 he married Countess Sophie Stockau, lady-in-waiting at the Vienna court. They had no children. He received his military education in the Theresianium Military Academy in VIENNA and, at age 19, became a lieutenant. By 1837 he was a major in an infantry regiment and aide-de-camp to the governor of Dalmatia. The unexpected outbreak of revolution in the Austrian Empire in 1848 gave him his chance to become the spokesman, then the appointed leader, of the Croatian nation in opposition to its Hungarian overlords. On March 23, 1848, Emperor Ferdinand V named him governor and commander in chief of the armed forces of CROATIA. He began his assignment on April 18 in the capital city of Zagreb. His first open defiance of Hungary occurred on April 25 when he proclaimed the liberation of the serfs in his homeland and forbade Croatian administrative organs to have any contact with Hungarian authorities. The BUDAPEST government, early in May, appealed to the emperor to instruct Jelačić to obey Hungarian laws. Ferdinand V at first obliged, but Jelačić, who by now had formed his own government, in a proclamation to his people defied the order on the plea that the Hungarian government acted against the interests of the Croatian nation and threatened the unity of the empire. On June 10 Ferdinand V suspended him as governor for overstepping his authority, but on the 21st the Croatian parliament declared the royal suspension invalid. By now Vienna became alive to the possibility of using a defiant

Croatia as a counterweight to Hungary's own secessionist ambitions, and on June 24 it granted her a large amount of money to cover military needs. On June 29 the Croatian government endowed Jelačić with dictatorial authority. He traveled to Vienna and at the end of July made an agreement with Hungarian premier COUNT LAJOS BATTHYÁNY, each pledging to withdraw his national forces from the Drava River that formed the border between Hungary and Croatia. On September 7 the emperor officially restored Jelačić to the office of governor, and the latter, emboldened by Vienna's trust and by the rapidly deteriorating relations between Austria and Hungary, on September 11 crossed the Drava with a main army (about 40,000 men) and began a drive toward the center of Hungary. On September 13 Premier Batthyány ordered a national uprising in the Transdanubian counties threatened by the invasion. On September 18 the Hungarian national army destroyed Jelačić's rear guard, but on September 26 his main forces occupied Székesfehérvár, only 50 kilometers from Budapest. On September 29, 1848, the Hungarian army defeated him in the Battle of Pákozd. Its victorious general, János Moga, wasted much time in leisurely pursuit and Jelačić withdrew his forces toward Vienna. At this juncture Emperor Ferdinand V absurdly named him commander of the Hungarian armed forces, a nomination that the newly formed Hungarian National Assembly declared illegal. On October 8, fleeing toward Vienna from a pursuing Hungarian army, he avoided battle and placed himself under the command of the imperial marshal PRINCE ALFRED WINDISCHGRÄTZ. He took part in Austria's struggle against the Hungarian revolution. On December 30, 1848, an army corps under his command gained a significant victory. In 1849 he at first fought successfully against the Hungarian army but in July suffered defeat and was expelled from the imperial army. These events marked the end of both his military and political career.

Jews in the Dual Monarchy

Jews had probably lived in lands that subsequently were ruled by the Habsburgs as early as Roman times. Their numbers remained small and were further reduced by periodic forced expulsions, from Styria in 1496, from Carinthia and Carniola in 1513, from the Tyrol in 1518, and from Upper Austria in 1596. The cycles of persecution and tolerance were not different from those experienced by Jews in most western European states. In Austria, by the Age of Enlightenment, only the families of "court Jews," tolerated by royal dispensation, were allowed to live in VIENNA; their number was estimated to be less than 500. The number of Jews was far greater in the non-German areas. Bohemia-Moravia counted about 40,000, mainly in and around Prague. In Hungary, the small number who remained when the Turkish occupation ended increased significantly, chiefly through immigration, and by 1776 amounted to about 80,000. The partition of Poland, which brought Galicia with its large concentration of Jews into the empire, nearly doubled the total number. They lived in ghettoes, were forced to wear special distinguishing garments, and were subject, over and above regular taxation, to the so-called Judensteuer, a tax on Jews. Nevertheless many individual Jewish families attained high position and became dominant in Austrian economic life.

During the reign of JOSEPH II (1780–90), the emperor's enlightened principles overrode his personal dislike of Jews, but his PATENT OF TOLERATION aimed more at Germanizing Austrian Jews than at allowing them unhampered economic and cultural development. He encour-

aged Jews to engage in agriculture and urged the use of the German language in their commercial and official activities. To hasten their assimilation he abolished the obligation that they wear distinguishing clothing and badges. Judicial autonomy, allowing legal rulings to be issued by rabbis, was discontinued. Jews were inducted into the army and in time became quite numerous in the lower commissioned ranks.

Emperor FRANCIS I (1792–1835), although far less enlightened than Joseph II, made his own efforts to integrate Jews into the German community of Austria. Rabbis were required to study German philosophy and to use German in public services and Jewish children were required to attend Christian schools. At the same time many Jews of great wealth and influence were instrumental in developing Austrian railroads and industry.

The revolutions of 1848–49 had a general liberalizing impact, and although in the so-called BACH Era that followed the defeat of the revolutions, the Vienna court did all it could to dampen that spirit, after the Great Compromise of 1867 it was revived. The constitution of that year formally recognized Jews as a religious community. Article XVII of the law code in effect provided for their emancipation. Starting in 1895, Judaism was a legitimate religion in the Dual Monarchy. Rabbis acted not only as clergymen but also as advisers and judges in cases involving Jews.

The percentage of Jews was highest in Galicia and Bukovina, most of them refugees from Russian pogroms; among Bosnian Jews many had come from Spain. The Jews of Bukovina belonged to two religious branches, orthodox Talmudists (who regarded the Torah as a literal divine revelation), and the neologs, or Reform Jews.

The center of the Hasidim (pious ones) was in Sagadir in Bukovina, home of many *wunderrabbiner*, rabbis endowed with special gifts of prophecy and legal wisdom. This particularly eastern movement arose about 1750 in the Carpathians and stressed emotional over rational acceptance, in which blind faith in the laws was replaced by natural revelation (association between God and man must be maintained by ecstatic prayer). In general, until the end of the Dual Monarchy in 1918, Jews enjoyed equal rights and encountered very few obstacles to personal advancement.

Joseph II (1741–1790)

archduke of Austria, king of Hungary, Holy Roman Emperor; leading figure of the Enlightenment

One of the most attractive and intriguing figures in the Habsburg dynasty, like so many in his family, Joseph was early made conscious of his royal dignity, its prerogatives and responsibilities. When he was six, the Prussian ambassador to VIENNA wrote of him: "He already has a high conception of his station." Joseph early displayed impatience with the otherworldly concepts his Jesuit tutors sought to instill in him. He was enlightened already as a child.

Contemptuous of noble presumptions and pretenses, as a young man he dressed in worn clothing and rode on horseback. He visited the provinces of the empire to gain firsthand knowledge of the conditions endured by the common folk. At age 19 he married Isabella of Parma, granddaughter of French king Louis XV, 18 years old and beautiful, but melancholy and possessed by the desire to die young. She was by her own admission deeply enamored of her sister-in-law, Marie Christine, and wrote to her that she could never be happy at the side of her husband. She died three years after the marriage of smallpox; it was a blow from which Joseph never fully recovered. He married, in 1765, Josepha of Bavaria, a woman whom he found repulsive and kept at arm's length to the end of his life.

In March 1764, when his father, Francis Stephen of Lorraine, was still alive, Joseph was elected Holy Roman Emperor, and he was formally crowned after his father's death a year later. At home, he shared the governance of the empire with his mother, MARIA THERESA, who, distrusting his liberal impulses, limited his sphere of authority largely to military affairs.

King Joseph II of the Romans, and the Holy Roman Emperor *(Hulton/Archive)*

She died in November 1780. Joseph refused to let himself be crowned, unwilling to take the coronation oath that would bind him to honor aristocratic privileges, an act that earned him the moniker, "king in a hat."

His early decree, aimed at restricting the extensive and often unwarranted participation of the Roman Catholic Church in public affairs, were elaborations of the earlier decrees issued (largely at his behest) by his mother. But the PATENT OF TOLERATION, in which he granted equal civil rights to Protestants and Greek Orthodox, went far beyond what his mother would have condoned. Although he had little sympathy for JEWS, he sought to assimilate them into the citizenry by ordering the removal of the stigmatizing badges they were forced to wear, stipulating that Jews conduct their official and commercial affairs in German instead of Hebrew, encouraging them to engage in agriculture, and enlisting their young men in the armed forces.

His pronounced bias against the Catholic Church prompted Pope Pius VI to make a month-long visit to Vienna in an attempt to mitigate the antichurch measures. These efforts were unsuccessful and the visit was subsequently dubbed "reverse Canossa," a fitting description, except that unlike the visit of King Henry IV to Pope Gregory VII in 1076, which produced the desired result, Pius VI's visit did not. All the same, it cannot be said of Joseph that he was anti-Catholic; he merely placed the interests of the state forcefully above those of the church. Regarding himself, as Frederick the Great did, the first servant of the state, and adopting the latter's slogan, "Everything for the people, nothing by the people," Joseph labored mightily to replace the political fragmentation of his polyglot empire with a firm centralized government. Latin, the language of official business and government, was no longer suited for contemporary terminology; he replaced it with German. In fact, his Language Decree made German the only language of official intercourse (in schools, in courts, in government agencies), and he allowed three years for non-German subjects to learn the language. The measure met with stubborn resistance, as did another, aimed at increasing state revenue, one that ordered a general census and the surveying of all landholdings. The nobles feared with good reason that it was preliminary to ending their age-old privilege of exemption from taxation.

Joseph's long-standing determination to free the peasantry from bondage received a powerful boost when rumors in TRANSYLVANIA that serfs would be enlisted in the border guards as a means to their emancipation led to a full-scale uprising by the largely Romanian peasantry, which refused obedience to their masters. The revolt was put down, but it served as a rationale for making the serfs free citizens. In 1784 they were allowed to leave their masters' service, enter the trades, and freely dispose of their property.

A commission of jurists reformed the law code, lightened draconian penalties, and abolished capital punishment. Another commission eased censorship of books and articles, except those that contained "immoral utterances and unclean obscenities," especially directed against the Catholic Church.

Joseph's program of reforms suffered a setback when war erupted with Turkey, a war in which Russia was Austria's ally. Owing to poor leadership and a lack of cooperation by nobles who refused to deliver needed supplies and horses, the war went badly at first; later General Loudon, the newly appointed commander, reversed the series of defeats, but the war brought no gain to either belligerent.

Joseph did not live to see the coming of peace. Exhausted by his taxing labors, and afflicted with consumption, he died early in 1780. Realizing as he lay dying that his reforms, well intentioned though they were, had been issued before their time and engendered resistance rather than compliance, he withdrew them, leaving only the emancipation of the serfs, the Patent of Toleration and the decrees affecting religious orders in force.

K

Kádár, János (1912–1989)
postwar leader of Hungary

Hungarian politician, minister of the interior, Budapest County party secretary, general secretary of the Communist Party, premier, Kádár's family name was Csermanek before 1945. He was raised by foster parents in the village of Kapoly. From there, in September 1918, he moved to BUDAPEST, where he completed a trade school course. He married Maria Tamáska; they had no children. In 1929 he became a journeyman typewriter technician. In the same year he joined the youth division of the Iron Workers' Union and, in September 1930, the Communist Working Youth. In November 1930 he was arrested for his political activities but set free for lack of evidence and placed under police supervision. In the summer of 1933 he was again arrested and in October was sentenced to two years in prison. He completed the second half of his sentence in the infamous Csillag Prison in Szeged, where many political prisoners languished in often atrocious conditions. There he made the acquaintance of the imprisoned Communist, MÁTYÁS RÁKOSI. After his release, he was appointed to several positions in the illegal Communist Party. His primary job was to reorganize and guide local cells and committees of the party. In December 1942 he was a member of the Central Committee's secretariat, a key assignment, for it was here that most personnel decisions were made. In February 1943 he became its secretary. When the Comintern, an association of all Communist parties to coordinate policies, was disbanded in May 1943, he filled the consequent void in Hungary by organizing the so-called Peace Party. Following the German occupation of

the country in March 1944 he initiated the formation of the Hungarian Front, a political grouping of liberal elements hostile to Germany and ready to work with the Soviet Union, and he played a leading part in the selection of the three-member military committee. In April 1944, at the instruction of the party, he left for Yugoslavia to seek contact with Tito's partisans. He was arrested at the border but was sentenced only to two years in prison for attempting to leave the country. After his return to Budapest he became the leading secretary of the Central Committee but was again arrested. In November 1944, as he and others were being evacuated to Germany, he managed to escape and make his way back to Budapest. After the liberation of the capital, he was named deputy police chief by the provisional government. During 1945 he held several party and government positions. Until August 1948 he headed the Budapest party committee, then he was appointed minister of the interior. In 1949 he played a still not entirely clarified part in preparing the trial of László Rajk, an old party faithful, falsely accused of "Titoism." In June 1950, at his own request, he was released from his office as minister of the interior, but remained a member of the leading organs of the party. At the end of April 1951, he was arrested in the intensifying hunt for unreliable party members and, in May, was excluded from all party positions. On December 26, 1952, the highest court sentenced him to life in prison. He was amnestied in June 1954 and appointed to several party organs. In March 1956, at a session of the Central Leadership (the Hungarian version of the Soviet Central Committee) he raised a question about the legality of the ousting from his party offices of IMRE NAGY, a violation of party discipline that once again placed him at odds with the hard-line leadership. Furthermore, as a critic of the miscarriages of justice of which he himself had been a victim, he became a defining personality in the oppositionist wing of the party. In an atmosphere of growing liberalization, which had been gathering strength since Stalin's death, his position began to represent the mainstream. In July 1956 he was once again included in the ruling Politburo, and he became secretary of the Central Leadership. When revolution broke out in Hungary at the end of October 1956 and Imre Nagy formed a government, Kádár became minister of state. On the surface he associated himself with the revolution; his radio speech on October 30 bore witness to that fact. When, on that day, the Hungarian Workers' Party (Communists) was formally dissolved, he was instrumental in forming the Hungarian Socialist Workers' Party (MSzMP), which differed from the old party only in name in that it excluded former leaders who by their oppressive policies had lost the trust and support of the people. On November 1, 1956, he went to the Soviet embassy in Budapest, supposedly to negotiate the withdrawal of Soviet troop from Hungary. He was taken to Moscow, where on November 2 and 3 he discussed with leaders of several socialist countries the Hungarian situation. On November 3 Soviet leader Khrushchev received the assent of Yugoslav president Tito to an armed Soviet intervention in Hungary to deal with the revolution, and he, on his part, accepted Tito's proposal that Kádár should head the newly organized party in Hungary. On November 4 Kádár met with Khrushchev in Ungvár, near the Soviet-Hungarian border, where he was given his new mandate. That afternoon he went to Szolnok in central Hungary and formed the "Revolutionary Workers' and Peasants' Government." He arrived in Budapest with a Soviet military convoy on November 7, 1956.

There now began the liquidation of all the residual traces of the recent revolution and the hunting down of those who participated in it.

Kádár's government at this point had no public support; strikes continued for weeks, and sullen resistance characterized the mood of the populace. The government responded by organizing a new workers' militia and authorizing mass arrests. At the same time it made an effort to win over certain portions of society one by one. It offered raises in pay and improved living standards, some of it with Soviet material help. It tried to separate the peasantry from the striking workers by ending the system of forced deliveries of farm products. In December 1956 the trials of arrested revolutionaries began and hundreds of death sentences were handed down. At the same time certain mitigating measures were introduced. The tax for being childless was abolished, Easter Monday, as well as both days of Christmas, were declared holidays, members of collective farms were given pension rights. In November 1956, Kádár was named president of the executive committee of the MSzMP. His position became firm only in March 1957, when, in exchange for his agreement to start proceedings against Imre Nagy for the part he played in the 1956 revolution and his subsequent refusal to relinquish the premiership, Moscow agreed to exclude Mátyás Rákosi, Kádár's chief rival, from the Hungarian government and party. On January 28, 1958, Kádár resigned the largely meaningless post of minister president and became state minister in a new government formed by Ferenc Münnich, the most resolute hard-liner, while he remained head of the party and the sole effective political will in the country. However, his position remained ambiguous because, although he sought to separate himself in every way from Rákosi's legacy, he had to apply the very methods he had condemned Rákosi for in dealing with continuing resistance to Communist rule. He remained a strict Marxist but, in reality, pursued a program that deviated from marxism in many respects. He tried to conceal these contradictions by proclaiming a struggle on two fronts, against the Stalinist holdouts on the one hand, and against those who sought to abandon

Marx's prescription for a socialist society on the other. In 1958, yielding to Soviet pressure, he agreed to hold a trial of Nagy and he did not intervene when Nagy was condemned and executed. The *justizmord* produced international outrage and made even Kádár's person unacceptable abroad. In order to improve his reputation, in the beginning of the 1960s he gradually abandoned open terror in consolidating his rule and began to apply subtler forms of oppression. He regarded it as one of his chief tasks to end Hungary's international isolation. He pursued this goal during secret U.S.–Hungarian negotiations in October 1962. One beneficial result of the discussions was that the "Hungarian Question," occasioned by the illegal liquidation of the 1956 revolution, was taken off the agenda of the United Nations. In March 1963 he issued a general amnesty and, with the exception of a few hundred men, the political prisoners were set free. His government tried to settle the strained relationship with the Vatican as well; the latter, in a 1964 agreement, recognized the Kádár government and acknowledged its right to fill church positions. As a result of successful foreign policy actions, by 1965 Hungary's diplomatic relations with several great powers, France and Great Britain included, were once again raised to the ambassadorial level.

During his second premiership, the country's international isolation was further reduced. Kádár's position as head of the party was firm, although there were several attempts to arrange his fall. From the beginning of the 1970s the economic situation in Hungary showed great improvement, and Kádár's relatively liberal politics made his name ever more acceptable in the West. Even the fact that he loyally followed Moscow's political line did not change that. In the 1980s, however, serious economic problems arose, owing largely to the fact that foreign credit, which had made improvements thus far possible, had become exhausted. Kádár vainly tried to salvage an ever-deteriorating balance sheet and his position within the Hungarian party was undermined. A party conference in May 1988 "promoted" him to the party's presidency, a hollow title, thus depriving him of the substance of power. His fall was quickened by the fact that in the Soviet Union Mikhail Gorbachev came to power and Kádár tried to isolate himself from the political and economic reforms he introduced in the Soviet Union. Already gravely ill, Kádár died on July 6, 1989, the same day when the chief victim of his political retributions, Imre Nagy, was officially rehabilitated.

Kállay, Miklós (1887–1967)

Hungarian large landowner and a leading politician in the HORTHY administration, premier
Youngest child among seven of Lord Lieutenant András Kállay and Vilma Csuka. He married in 1914 and had three sons. He received his higher education in law and political science at Budapest University and also studied briefly at institutions in Dresden, Geneva, and Paris. He held several public positions on the county level. In 1918, amid the political upheavals that followed the war, he retired to his estates in Kállosemjén. He returned to a political career in 1922. As Lord Lieutenant of Szabolcs County he endeavored to give public education wider scope, but his chief interest was in developing the country's commerce and industry. In 1929 and 1930 he was secretary of state for commerce. In 1931 he was elected to parliament as a deputy of the government party. From October 1932 to January 1935 he also served as minister of agriculture in the Gömbös government. Between 1936 and 1942 he was president of the national irrigation office. On March 9, 1942, Regent Horthy named him premier in place of LÁSZLÓ BÁRDOSSY. The appointment meant victory for those elements in government who judged Bárdossy's exclusive pro-German orientation dangerous for Hungary's future and did not want to break off all contacts with Britain and France. Accordingly, although he continued the war against the Soviet Union even after the catastrophic defeat of the Hungarian Second Army ar Voronezh in January 1943, Kállay also sought a connection with the British in order to negotiate an armistice with them rather than

with the Soviet Union. In this period he persecuted Communists and other leftist forces and
disarmed the fledgling National Front, which on
its part prepared for a peace arrangement with
the Soviet Union. His two-faced policy did not
succeed. The western Allies insisted on the formula of unconditional surrender and his secret
and unofficial negotiations with the British
became known to the Germans, who in that critical period of the Second World War wanted
complete control over Hungary's economic and
military resources. On March 19, 1944, the Germans occupied the country; on that same day
Kállay, fearing for his freedom, asked for asylum
in the Turkish embassy in BUDAPEST. When he
voluntarily left it some time later, the Germans
arrested him and sent him to a concentration
camp. Liberated in April 1945, he settled in Italy
and, in 1951, moved to the United States. His
book, *Hungarian Premier,* a personal account of
his nation's struggle in the Second World War,
was published in New York in 1954.

Karageorgević dynasty

The progenies of Karageorge (George Petrović),
leader of the first Serbian national uprising
against Turkey between 1804 and 1813, who in
the 19th century, alternately with the Obrenović
dynasty, and from 1903 continuously, sat on the
Serbian and subsequently the Yugoslav throne.
After a quarter century rule by the Obrenović
dynasty, Alexander Karageorgević was prince of
Serbia from 1842 to 1858. Starting in the latter
year, the Obrenovićs sat on the throne of Serbia
until 1903. During their tenure their title was
elevated from prince to king. In 1903 a bloody
coup enthroned Peter I (1844–1921), grandson
of Karageorge, who was king of Serbia from
1903 to 1921 and of the Kingdom of Serbs,
Croats, and Slovenes from 1919 to 1921. From
1914 his son, ALEXANDER I (1888–1934) acted as
regent for his ailing elderly father until the latter's death in 1921. Starting in that year Alexander was king of what, from 1929 on, was no
longer the Kingdom of Serbs, Croats, and
Slovenes but rather the Kingdom of Yugoslavia.

Unable to devise a viable federal system in
which the Serbs comprised the dominant
nationality, he ruled as a dictator. On October 9,
1934, he was assassinated in Marseilles by a
Croatian terrorist organization, the Ustaše. Peter
II (1923–70) was king of Yugoslavia between
1934 and 1945, although from March 27, 1941,
when a military coup removed him from actual
ruling for his friendship treaty with the Axis, his
son Paul carried out the royal duties. From April
15, 1941, the end of the "first Yugoslavia," Paul
lived in exile.

Károlyi, Count Mihály (1875–1955)

*liberal, democratic politician, provisional pres-
ident of the first Hungarian Republic after the
abdication of the Habsburgs*

Scion of the great Károlyi family, which owned
immense landed estates, Mihály was a member
of the Liberal Party from 1901, but when he
entered parliament in 1905 he represented the
Independent Party, and although such party des-
ignations meant little amid the plethora of political groupings, his orientation was consistently
liberal. Opposed to the outdated principles of the
Hungarian ruling classes, especially to the
aggressive policies of Premier ISTVÁN TISZA, he
demanded among other reforms the introduction of the universal franchise. Before and during the First World War he also disapproved of
the military policies of the Dual Monarchy and
its alliance with Germany. At a time when war
enthusiasm was still running high, in 1916, he
advocated a search for peace, and in the last year
of the war conducted pronounced antiwar agitation, coupled with demands for domestic
democratic reforms. As a member of the left-
wing Independence Party, he gradually gained
popularity among the war-weary masses. At the
time of the democratic revolution in October
1918 he was the leading political figure and
president of the National Council that took over
for the defunct official government. On October 31, 1918, King Charles I, (Charles IV as Austrian emperor), under popular pressure, named
Károlyi premier in one of his last official acts. On

January 11, 1919, Károly became president of the republic. He launched a bourgeois democratic reform program and a moderate land reform. He parceled out his own estate at Kalkápolna. But his popularity suffered when he could not secure favorable peace conditions for the country, and invading Czech-Slovak, Romanian, and Serb troops occupied ever greater areas of Hungary with the approval of the peacemakers in Paris. On March 21, 1919, he resigned as president, and it marked the beginning of the seizure of power by a soviet regime or, as communist histories put it, by the working class. Disillusioned, at the beginning of July 1919, Károlyi emigrated to western Europe. He found no political friends there, however. Neither could he return home because he disapproved in equal measure of the revolutionary soviet regime and of HORTHY's "counter-revolution." In countless articles and speeches from abroad he lashed out against the White Terror that raged in Hungary in early 1920 and against the undemocratic methods of the new government. Later he went on a lecture tour in the United States. He also visited the Soviet Union. He was uncompromisingly hostile to every manifestation and policy of fascism. During the Second World War he lived in England. He returned to Hungary in May 1946 and in the following year was appointed ambassador to Paris. In 1949, in protest against the growingly totalitarian methods of the government at home, he resigned his post. He retired from politics and spent the last years of his life in France. His remains were returned to Hungary in March 1962 and placed in a mausoleum.

Kaunitz, Count Wenzel Anton Eusebius Rietberg (1711–1794)

Austrian diplomat and foreign minister in the reign of MARIA THERESA

Between 1750 and 1753 Kaunitz served as Austrian ambassador to France and from 1753 to his death as court and state chancellor in Vienna. He was one of the two Austrian foreign ministers with extremely long tenure in the tumultuous

century between 1749 and 1848, the other one being KLEMENS VON METTERNICH. Kaunitz attained fame by producing the so-called Diplomatic Revolution, reversing the traditional system of alliances that had obtained during the WAR OF THE AUSTRIAN SUCCESSION; Metternich by constructing a power balance in Europe that lasted a century. In 1749, when Kaunitz first caught the eye of Maria Theresa, an Austrian diplomat of any rank could only have one cause to which to devote his talents and energies: to undo the shattering damage to Austrian prestige and interests inflicted by the loss of the province of Silesia to Frederick II of Prussia, and the failure to reconquer it in the war between 1740 and 1748. In that war Austria faced a number of enemies, France being the most powerful, with only Britain, far more interested in colonial matters than in Silesia, fighting at her side. The War of the Austrian Succession had ended in the Peace of Aachen (Aix-la-Chapelle) at which Kaunitz, then an official in the foreign ministry, represented Austria. When in 1749 Maria Theresa called a state conference at the highest level to discuss matters of foreign policy, Kaunitz, to general surprise and spotty dismay, argued that Austria's best chance for a successful revanche against Prussia was to enlist France as a future ally. By this time, although Austria had been fighting against Turkey for over two centuries, Kaunitz judged not that power but Prussia to be Austria's most dangerous enemy. Austria ruled over much greater territory and a substantially larger population than Prussia, but in an age when no power could field a force greater than 100,000 the advantage would be with the nation that had more allies and thus could engage the enemy on several fronts. If France was won over, Kaunitz argued, Spain, now under Bourbon rule, would follow, as would Saxony and the Palatinate, and Prussia would be isolated. The notion was indeed revolutionary because for the past two and a half centuries Austria and France had almost uninterruptedly been at war with each other. But Maria Theresa, even though her husband Francis of Lorraine remained determinedly anti-

French, was willing to give Kaunitz's scheme a chance. In May 1750 she appointed him as her ambassador to the Versailles court. During his three-year tenure in France his feelers met little response, but in 1753 he was nevertheless elevated to foreign minister and his place in France was taken by Prince Starhemberg. The latter managed, over the heads of French ministers opposed to any overtures to Austria, to enlist the support of Madame Pompadour and, through her, to reach the ear of King Louis XV and convince him that Prussia was no longer a reliable ally for France because she was making common cause with England, whose interests in America clashed with those of France. Indeed in a conference at Westminster in January 1756 Prussia won British favor by pledging not to attack Hannover (the native land of British royalty) in case of war while Britain undertook to restrain Russia from attacking Prussia. Although the agreement was secret, Starhemberg got wind of it, intimated it to the French king, and the groundwork was laid for Kaunitz's grand design. At the insistence of his ministers, Louis XV only demanded that after victory in war Austria relinquish to France the Belgian provinces. On May 1, 1756, an alliance on these terms was concluded at Versailles. Kaunitz did not wish to rush into war. Rather he preferred to wait until the planned internal reforms, especially the greatly improved taxation system, had taken effect in Austria. But Frederick of Prussia, concerned about the shift in alliances, precipitated matters when in August 1756 he sent his armies into Saxony, and in September into BOHEMIA, and a new war ensued. Kaunitz's patient diplomacy seemed to pay off. The French sent two armies against Prussia, and early in 1757 Russia and Sweden joined the war on the Austrian side. The Russians took the key Prussian city of Königsberg and the Swedes occupied Pomerania. The preponderance of manpower Kaunitz had aimed at was now ranged against Prussia and the resources of Frederick II were strained to the limit. That the war, known as the SEVEN YEARS' WAR, did not end with Austrian victory, and that in the end Prussia retained Silesia, was due less

to any weakness in the alliance system Kaunitz had built than to the Prussian king's military genius and unbroken tenacity, and even more to the fact that in January 1762 Czarina Elizabeth died and her successor Czar Peter III, a German prince, long an admirer of Frederick, withdrew Russia from the war with Prussia and even considered reentering it on Frederick's side when a coup masterminded by Peter's wife, Catherine, removed him from the throne. The new czarina's eyes were on Turkey and she was not inclined to resume the war with Prussia. In the Peace of Hubertsburg on February 15, 1763, Maria Theresa with a heavy heart accepted the loss of Silesia and the war with Prussia ended. From then on Kaunitz's diplomatic talents were absorbed in routine matters, more concerned with the maintenance of peace than with constructing new alliances. In the late years of his chancellorship the burdens of conducting the foreign office fell largely on the shoulders of his deputy Baron Johann Thugut.

Kossuth, Lajos (1802–1894)

Hungarian politician, statesman, reformer, finance minister the head of government during Hungarian uprising against the Habsburgs in 1848–49

His father, László, of Slovakian stock, was Lutheran, a lawyer by profession, representing landowners in his county of Zemplén. His mother, Karolina Weber, was German. An older sister died in childhood. Lajos had four younger sisters. In 1841 he married Terezia Meszlényi who bore him three sons and a daughter. He attended the Protestant academy Sárospatak and also studied law there, but it was only in 1824 that he obtained his law degree from University of Budapest. Unable to find a government position, he began to work for one of his father's clients, Etelka Andrássy, with whom he was reported to have had a close relationship. He first attracted public attention with a major speech he made in the summer of 1831 on behalf of the Poles, who were then fighting a heroic battle against the Russians for their independent nationhood. In 1832 Mme. Andrássy arranged for him to serve as a deputy delegate in the national Diet at Pozsony, an assignment that somewhat relieved his narrow, confining existence. In Pozsony he established contact with various reform-minded politicians. Noting that no minutes were kept of the proceedings of the Diet, he began to write informal reports, in colorful, arresting prose. Some of his colleagues copied his reports and distributed them. His political philosophy had no clear focus, but he was oppositionist in temperament and found much to oppose in the Habsburg Empire, whose policies were still directed by the heavy-handed and stubbornly conservative KLEMENS VON METTERNICH. Kossuth's term of service in Pozsony ended in 1836; by then his reports had attracted so much attention that the Pest County Assembly invited him to cover its proceedings as well. He published these accounts under the title *Törvényhatósági Tudositások* (Municipal board reports), but whereas in Pozsony he had been protected by his parliamentary immunity, in Pest he was a freelancer, responsible for what he wrote, and in 1837, after a long investigative detainment, he was sentenced to four years in prison. His "crime" was to attack feudal privilege and to speak in favor of Hungary's constitutional independence and in defense of civil liberties. For all his liberal posturing, he was an elitist, firmly believing that his contemplated reforms could be accomplished only under the leadership of the nobility.

Amnestied in 1840, he already had a wide following. But his views also provoked criticism from conservatives and he became involved in a sharp exchange with them in articles and pamphlets. The owner of a biweekly publication *Pesti Hirlap* (Budapest courier) hired him as an editor. He remained a controversial figure. Apart from antagonizing the landed magnates whose prosperity depended on serf labor, he also angered Croats and other subject nationalities by advertising and defending the superiority of the Hungarian nation over them. His most notable debate was with another reformer of much more conservative bent, ISTVÁN SZÉCHENYI, who

attacked Kossuth in a book, *Kelet Népe* (People of the East) and in articles, accusing him of carrying his people to the grave with his immoderate demands, especially for a complete break with the Habsburgs, who were too powerful to be challenged in their imperial rights. Although, as publicists and historians noted, Széchenyi spoke to the mind and Kossuth to the heart, it was the latter who commanded wider support. But as his language became more fiery, he was dismissed from the *Pesti Hirlap* for inciting too much controversy. He had an offer from VIENNA to put his journalistic gifts in the service of the government but that offer he refused. He became briefly fascinated with the possibilities of industrial development and sought to promote them in Hungary, with little success.

It was the revolution of 1848 that catapulted him to national, and eventually international, recognition. Elected to the national Diet in 1847, he was a leading figure in the so-called national opposition that sponsored a number of reforms, all with the ultimate goal of securing Hungary's independence from the Habsburg Empire. The program, seemingly stillborn when it was first introduced, gained impetus when the news of the revolution in Paris reached BUDAPEST early in March 1848. Kossuth then demanded that his reform program be enacted without delay. Not only did he succeed, but he was chosen as a member of the delegation that carried the set of demands passed by the Diet to Vienna, where a terrified court fearing for its very survival accepted them. When LAJOS BATTHYÁNY formed a cabinet in April 1848 with the reformist program, he made Kossuth his finance minister. Used to controversy and glorying in it, Kossuth soon antagonized many of his fellow ministers who were not inclined to go as far as he and wanted to avoid a complete break with Vienna. However, such a break could no longer be avoided. The imperial government, facing an armed uprising in its Italian provinces, readied a force to defeat it and proposed to include Hungarians in it as well. Kossuth countenanced such inclusion only on condition that promises were made for the recognition of a measure of Hungarian independence. When the royal court refused to make such a promise, he prevailed on the Diet to reject the request for troops and at the same time to raise a national Hungarian force, on the argument, not without foundation, that the subject nationality of Croats were making ready to invade Hungary. He had a measure passed to call up 200,000 recruits and to provide for a defense fund of 2 million forints. In September 1848 he ordered the issue of Hungarian bank notes (*Kossuth bankók*). He also called for a national defense commission to organize the country's defense. In that same month, during a highly successful recruitment campaign, he called the people of the Great Plains to arms to protect the achievements of the revolution. After the resignation of the Batthyány government following a Croat invasion, Kossuth was named head of the national defense commission and became the virtual dictator of the country. From this time on he devoted all his energies to the solution of the complicated political, economic, and social problems that beset his nation. Firmly opposed to the "peace party" that sought conciliation with the Habsburgs, he succeeded in rendering them ineffectual. Imperial armies were invading Hungary and the government moved to the east-central city of Debrecen. There Kossuth's volcanic energies and his unbridled temperament determined the course taken by his government. When on December 2, 1848, the emperor "Benevolent Ferdinand" (so called because he was weak-minded and could be cited only for his good intentions) was removed and replaced by his nephew FRANCIS JOSEPH, Kossuth prevailed on the Diet to reject both the removal and the replacement. When Vienna defied him, the Diet, now called National Assembly, on April 14, 1849, announced the removal of the Hungarian crown from the House of Hapsburg. At the same time Kossuth was nominated governor president of Hungary. However, the rapid deterioration of the military situation, Russian intervention on behalf of the beleaguered Habsburgs, and conflicts within his own leadership, forced Kossuth on August 11 to resign. He transferred his powers to the military commander, Artur

Görgey. Knowing that defeat was unavoidable and that the Vienna court would be unforgiving of his treason, Kossuth fled to Turkey. Both the Austrians and the Russians asked for his extradition, but the sultan, under western pressure, refused. Kossuth first lived in Vidin and Sumen, in European Turkey, but he was later exiled to Asia Minor. The American government invited him to visit and he responded, in 1851, stopping on the way in Britain. He was accorded an enthusiastic reception in both countries. From 1852 on he lived in London. He judged the conflicts among the great powers as the best way to restore Hungary's independence. In emigration he worked out several plans toward that end. In 1859, as war between France and Austria loomed, French Emperor Napoleon III approached him with the commission to organize a Hungarian national uprising against the Habsburgs. This commission Kossuth accepted, but the plan failed when Napoleon III made a premature peace with Austria and lost interest in the Hungarian cause. From 1861 Kossuth lived in Italy and in his so-called Cassandra letter he sharply criticized the AUSGLEICH of 1867. He lived out his remaining years in Torino, Italy, in poverty, abandoned by friends and onetime supporters. When he died in 1894, at age 92, his body was returned to Hungary and interred amid national mourning.

Kreisky, Bruno (1911–1990)

Austrian Social Democratic politician, foreign minister, chancellor

His chancellorship between 1970 and 1983 was the longest in Austrian history. Although of Jewish birth and upbringing, he enjoyed great personal popularity in a country that a quarter century earlier had been the scene of a wave of Nazi-sponsored anti-Semitic measures and in the course of the Second World War saw its once thriving Jewish population reduced to a few thousand survivors. Born to Max Kreisky, managing director of textile works, and Irene Felix (on January 22, 1911), Bruno's primary education began in 1916, and his secondary education

Bruno Kreisky *(Hulton/Archive)*

in 1921. He early displayed an activist spirit; at age 15 he joined the Socialist Youth movement, and he participated in several protest demonstrations. When in 1929, upon completion of his secondary studies, the leader of the Austrian Social Democratic Party, Otto Bauer, told him about the dearth of good lawyers in the party, Kreisky changed his original plan of becoming a physician to study law.

He did not cease his political activities, though, even after the Socialist Party (SPÖ) was outlawed in 1934. For his activism he was arrested in 1935 and sentenced to 18 months in prison. (His speech in court in his own defense had wide coverage in the international press.) After being released, he resumed his previously interrupted studies in law at the University of Vienna. The Nazi takeover of Austria in March

1938 found him preparing for his final examinations. He was arrested by the invading Germans and held in several prisons for five months. In August 1938 he was released on condition that he leave the country. At the invitation of a leading Swedish Socialist he emigrated to that country.

He spent the war years in Sweden, working for a consumer cooperative and also contributing articles to Swedish and foreign journals. Returning to Austria at war's end, he entered the foreign service and for four years worked at the Austrian embassy in Stockholm. After returning home, he was appointed state secretary for foreign affairs at the critical time when Austria was involved in intense negotiations with the occupying powers to regain her full sovereignty. Kreisky played a significant role in the process.

In 1956 he was elected to the federal parliament, and in July 1959 he became foreign minister in the government of Julius Raab. Careful, perhaps excessively so, not to allow his Jewish identity to influence the direction of Austrian foreign policy, he at times drew criticism, as foreign minister and later as chancellor, for his refusal to ostracize such pronouncedly anti-Israel figures as Yassir Arafat and Muammar Qaddafi. Despite controversial stances in domestic and foreign policy, his down-to-earth style and his accessibility (his home phone number was listed in the general directory even after he became chancellor), made him greatly popular with a majority of Austrians and his evenhanded policies were much respected abroad.

Kreisky's political career remained closely associated with the SPÖ. In June 1966 he was elected chair of the party in Lower Austria; in February 1967 he became chair of the national party. When in April 1970 the SPÖ garnered a plurality of votes in the federal parliament, Kreisky, as chancellor, formed his first government. In October 1971 the plurality was transformed into a fractional majority and, in November, Kreisky formed his second government. Because of his durability he was soon referred to as "Kaiser Bruno," in reference to the ruler of imperial times who was always assured of his position as head of state and government. Kreisky's popularity was furthered by the long period of economic prosperity and almost full employment under his tenure. His foreign policy motto reflected his sober political pragmatism: "The task of Austria is to earn maximum trust in the West, while engendering only a minimum of mistrust in the East." Given her history and Catholic tradition, Austria was naturally an integral part of the West; at the same time, the task of ensuring her permanent neutrality and a stability in the center of Europe demanded avoidance of any conflict with the Soviet Union.

Throughout the electoral struggles of the 1960s and 1970s the SPÖ ran a very close race with the other major party, the Austrian People's Party (ÖVP). Kreisky, realizing that the balance might shift any time, vowed not to head a coalition government. In the elections of 1983 the shift occurred in favor of the ÖVP, and Kreisky resigned as chancellor. He carried with him into retirement a great deal of goodwill and was able to devote his remaining years to humanitarian activities.

His wife died in 1989, a year before Kreisky died on July 30, 1990. He was survived by a son, Peter, and a daughter, Suzanne.

Kun, Béla (1886–1939)

Hungarian communist politician, founder of the Party of Hungarian Communists, foreign minister, minister of defense, for 133 days effectively dictator of his native land

Born Áron Kohn on February 20, 1886, in the village of Lele, Szabolcs Country, where his father was a notary, Kun worked in his early years as a reporter on a newspaper in Nagyvárad. Upon the outbreak of the First World War he was called up as a noncommissioned officer and sent to the Russian front. Taken prisoner in 1916, Kun's political interests and ambition were galvanized by the victory of the Bolshevik Revolution in Russia. He joined the Bolshevik Party and, in November 1918, with fellow-communists in Moscow, decided to form a Hungarian branch of the Communist Party. He was sent back to Hungary to do propaganda work. A fearless and unscrupulous agitator, he belonged to that small circle of young Hungarian communists who fanatically believed in the victory of the oppressed proletariat over the moribund bourgeois system. It was thanks to his labors that Hungary became the only country in Europe outside Russia to have a full-fledged soviet government, albeit for only a little more than four months. Taking advantage of the vacillations and internationally hard-pressed position of the first postwar government of MIHÁLY KÁROLYI, Kun engineered a fusion with the more moderate Social Democratic Party and seized power on March 21, 1919. The official head of the new government was a colorless party operative, Sándor Garbai, but it was Kun, enjoying the trust and support of the Bolshevik regime in Russia, who wielded actual, dictatorial power as foreign commissar, and then, after April 4, also as commissar for defense and commander in chief of the freshly raised Red Army.

As if sensing the brevity of time history had vouchsafed him, Kun, as well as his collaborators, most infamously Tibor Szamuely, his deputy as commissar for defense, acted swiftly and unscrupulously in their attempt to introduce a proletarian dictatorship into Hungary. They put a quick, if temporary, end to ordinary jurisdiction and the law courts that administered it and introduced revolutionary tribunals with power to issue sentences of life or death, allowing the defendants, accused more often than not of political rather than ordinary crimes, no effective legal protection. Wholesale expropriation of landed and industrial private property began, and banks were placed under government ownership. As head of the Red Army, it fell to Kun to defend Hungary against invading troops of Romania and recently formed Czechoslovakia. His army was signally successful in expelling the Czechoslovak invaders but made little headway against the Romanians, who drove past the Tisza River and eventually occupied Budapest.

The most potent enemies of Kun's soviet regime, however, were the governments of the

Western Powers convened in Paris to work out the peace settlements after more than four years of devastating war. It was they who ordered the Hungarian Red Army to retreat from Slovakia, who refused to curb the marauding Romanian forces that had French military support, and who in the end effectively demanded the resignation of the incumbent Communist government.

In the end the attempt to sovietize Hungary failed disastrously. On his last day in power, July 31, 1919, Kun issued a forlorn appeal to the workers of the world to rise to the support of soviet Hungary. There was no response. On August 1, l919, Kun and his cabinet, lacking all internal support, and recognized only by the new Russian government and a few neutrals, was forced to resign. Austria offered its members asylum. Szamuely was nevertheless arrested by Austrian gendarmes at the border and committed suicide.

For a while Kun made himself at home in Austria. In 1920, of his own accord or at the request of the Austrian government, he transferred himself to Bolshevik Russia. There he worked for the Communist International; after the outbreak of the Spanish Civil War he was sent to that country but failed in his assignment. There is no concrete information on how he met his end, but, as best can be determined, he fell victim to Stalin's countless purges.

L

Lajos II (1506–1526)
the last Hungarian (and Bohemian-Moravian) king of the Jagiellonian line

Lajos's untimely death bequeathed the Hungarian and Bohemian-Moravian crowns to the Habsburgs, with whom they remained until the fall of the house and its empire in 1918. Lajos was the son of Ladislaus II of the House of Jagiello and of French princess Anne of Candale. His sister Anna married Ferdinand I of Habsburg, a connection that formed the basis of the claim by the Habsburgs to the thrones of Hungary and Bohemia-Moravia. Lajos's mother died giving him birth and his father, enfeebled by a cerebral hemorrhage, sought to ensure his infant son's claim to the throne by arranging that he marry one of the granddaughters of Holy Roman Emperor Maximilian I. Lajos was barely one year old when he was engaged to Princess Maria of Habsburg, whom he married in 1515. His father, still alive, had him crowned king on June 8, 1514; upon the death of his father he was declared of age and on March 13, 1516, at age 10, he occupied the throne. A regency council of 28 nobles ruled in his stead. His education was put in charge of two humanists of the age, Jerome Balbi and James Piso. His father, before his death, had appointed the bishop of Esztergom to be his foster parent. The influences acting upon the young king at court were, however, frivolous and irresponsible, and he grew up to be just such a man. Actual government was in the hands of ambitious, unscrupulous noble families who placed personal interest above the welfare of the nation.

Riotous spending emptied the treasury and at a time when the Turkish menace loomed ever more threateningly, no money was found to outfit an armed force. When a Turkish host stood at the very borders of the country, the king was so deep in debt that he had to pawn court valuables. In 1521 Sultan Suleiman II took two of the key border fortresses and opened the road to the interior of the country. A hastily assembled royal army converged on the town of Mohács but an epidemic so decimated it that it had to be disbanded. In 1525 Suleiman asked permission of Lajos for free passage through the country so he could besiege VIENNA. Lajos refused the request. Thereupon, in April 1526, the Turkish host began its northward march from Constantinople, and on July 2 crossed the southern frontier line of Hungary, the Sava River. Panic at last struck the disorganized royal court; appeals for foreign aid produced promises but little else. In July Lajos called for a national uprising to oppose the approaching Turk; the response was disheartening. The final BATTLE OF MOHÁCS took place on August 29, 1526, on a plain some seven kilometers from the town. It lasted barely two hours and the Hungarian army was disastrously defeated. Many of the high nobility and clergy remained dead on the battlefield. The king escaped but as he crossed a brook his horse tripped and threw him; he drowned in the swollen water. His body was recovered some time later and buried in October 1526. By then the competition for the crowns of Hungary and Bohemia-Moravia had begun.

Linz Program

A political agenda drawn up in September 1882 by five Austrian intellectuals, the physician VICTOR ADLER, the lawyer Robert Pattai, the historian Heinrich Friedjung, the radical deputy GEORG SCHÖNERER, and the writer Engelbert Pernerstrofer. These five, at one on certain racial principles at the time, would in subsequent years move in widely divergent political directions. The program, more declamatory than businesslike, was motivated by the fear that the German element in the Dual Monarchy was being submerged by the increasing Slavic population and influence. The framers were quite willing to relinquish much of what the Habsburgs had acquired over the centuries in order that Austria become an all-German state. They proposed that Galicia, Bukovina, and Dalmatia be separated from Austria and either be attached to Hungary or be made autonomous. Hungary itself should be joined to Austria only by a personal union. The remainder of the monarchy was to be organized as a German state, with German as the sole official language and ties to the German Reich strengthened by a customs union, provided for in the constitution. Their manifesto well reflected the emotional content of the program: "We protest against all attempts to convert Austria into a Slavic state. We shall continue to agitate for the maintenance of German as the official language and to oppose the extension of federalism." Furthermore: "[W]e are steadfast supporters of the alliance with Germany and the foreign policy now being followed by the Empire."

Given the strong nationalist prejudices of the framers, the universalism of the Roman Catholic Church was of course unacceptable to them and they became passionate partisans of the *Los von Rom!* (Away from Rome!) movement, which gathered strength after the 1870 proclamation of papal infallibility. It was ironic and telling that two of the framers, Adler and Friedjung, were Jewish; that apparently did not disqualify them from being regarded as racially German. The Linz Program never found broad support in any quarter and in time, to different degrees, its framers dissociated themselves from it.

Little Entente

A series of bilateral military alliances (ultimately made trilateral) uniting Czechoslovakia, Romania, and Yugoslavia in common resolution to resist Hungarian revisionist aspirations as well as attempts at Habsburg restoration in the Danubian region. The earliest origins of the Little Entente can be traced to a French plan, conceived and promoted by the secretary general of the French Foreign Office, Maurice Paléologue, supported by President Alexandre Millerand, early in 1920, before the peace treaty with Hungary was concluded in June of that year. Paléologue, alarmed by the victory of the Red Army over the White armies in Russia, and later over Poland, intended to construct a cordon sanitaire of which, in its incipient version, Hungary would have been the centerpiece. He kept in close touch with the Hungarian peace delegation in Paris and, through it, initiated secret conversations with the HORTHY government. Hungary, in exchange for revisions in her favor of the borders already established, would contribute 200,000 troops to Polish forces battling Soviet armies in Poland, and contract with French firms, especially the Creusot works, for large-scale construction projects in Hungary. The Horthy government demanded the restoration of large areas of the new Czechoslovakia in return.

Intelligence reports about these contacts reached the ear of Czechoslovak foreign minister EDVARD BENEŠ, which deeply alarmed him. French support of Hungarian revisionism, not to mention the fact that any troop transport to Poland would have to move through Czechoslovakia, would jeopardize the entire system of little states that had emerged from the debris of the Austro-Hungarian Dual Monarchy. The first joint action among the "successor states" occurred on February 20, 1920, when the peace treaty with Hungary was still in its earliest phases. The three states bordering Hungary handed a joint memorandum to the peace conference, stating their existing demands on Hungary. One Budapest newspaper sardonically referred to this compact as the "Tiny Entente"; the name, in its somewhat mellower version, stuck.

The ever busy Beneš, while peace negotiations between Hungary and the Entente Powers were still in progress, wrote to the Romanian premier: "In view of the Hungarian situation, as well as of the fact that Hungary's intentions vis-à-vis Czechoslovakia and Romania are entirely the same, the time has come for the two countries to take steps in the face of the Hungarian danger." A similar note was sent to Belgrade as well. Although neither country was at first in favor of such an alignment (possibly because they did not perceive a particular danger from truncated and disarmed Hungary), France's continued flirting with the idea of a solid East European bloc of which Hungary too would be a member, and the deliberate delay of the Horthy government in ratifying the TREATY OF TRIANON, signed on June 4, 1920, sufficiently concerned at least the Yugoslavs to heed Beneš's appeals. On August 14, 1920, Czechoslovakia and Yugoslavia signed a two-year political and military compact, whose stated goal was the maintenance of the status quo as determined in the Trianon peace treaty. The key paragraph read: "In case one of the High Contracting Parties is the object on the part of Hungary of an unprovoked aggression, the other party undertakes to come to the aid of the state so attacked in a manner defined by Article 2 of this treaty." A strictly secret military convention, which formed part of the treaty, spoke emphatically of a *defensive* intention, but it also envisioned a possible offensive situation. "In case one of the contracting parties attacks Hungary alone, without previously notifying the other party, the latter obligates itself to remain neutral toward its ally, and to keep on its border with Hungary not fewer than two mobilized divisions."

When Beneš proposed to Romania a similar compact, he met with a hesitation that bordered on refusal. The main reason was that the French reaction to Beneš's initiatives was downright hostile. The French Foreign Office felt that such a treaty, directed not only against Hungary but against Austria as well, would drive those two countries into the German sphere. The Czechoslovak ambassador in Paris, noting these objections, was of the opinion that it would have been better to wait with the Yugoslav treaty until the Romanians became more forthcoming. Apart from French objections, Romania was disinclined to join a Little Entente because it wished to direct any military compact against Soviet Russia as well as Hungary and aimed at Poland's inclusion in it. Romania had unsettled border questions with both Yugoslavia and Czechoslovakia as well.

The subsequent change in Romania's attitude was due largely to a change of policy in Paris. Afraid that its support of Hungary would result in a loss of influence in eastern Europe, as well as the distancing of Great Britain, the French Foreign Office replaced the pro-Hungarian Paléologue with the pro-Czech, anti-Hungarian Berthelot. But the truly decisive reason for Romania's change of policy turned out to be the attempted return to Hungary, on March 26, 1921, of the deposed Habsburg king Charles IV. This caused near panic in the successor states. Czechoslovakia and Yugoslavia, in their notes to the western powers, termed the event a casus belli. Romania was more moderate, but she too was disquieted—sufficiently so, now that her plans for a larger eastern European bloc had lost all reality, to communicate to Prague, on April 14, 1921, her readiness to join the Little Entente. On April 23, the Czechoslovak-Romanian pact was duly signed. It was followed, on June 17, by a Romanian-Yugoslav treaty. This last one differed from the previous two only in that it was also directed against any territorial revision in favor of Bulgaria. The final version of the Little Entente was complete.

Lueger, Karl (1844–1910)

Austrian attorney, politician, parliamentary deputy from 1890, mayor of Vienna from 1897; a founder of the Christian Socialist party

Two very different endeavors make Lueger's name memorable in Austrian history. One was his political militancy, his demagogic outbursts against capitalists and Jews, his general extremism, which twice prevented him from becoming mayor even though he won at the polls. The second was his prominent role in the Viennese *Grunderzeit,* the dramatic enlargement and renewal of the city of Vienna in the closing years of the 19th and the early years of the 20th century. Himself of humble roots, he spoke the little man's language and he spoke it to great dramatic effect. In 1875 he was elected to Vienna's City Council, and it was in that office that he began his verbal attacks on the corruption of vested interests and always managed to identify the worst elements with Jewish business and public figures. In 1885 he was elected to the Reichsrat, the Austrian parliament. It was now that the "Christian Social Union," which was to develop into the Christian Socialist Party, attracted, through KARL VOGELSANG, his attention. The party first ran in the elections of 1891 and won 14 seats. Although in its program it continued to harp on the Jewish question, it made it clear that, unlike GEORG SCHÖNERER, who first made anti-Semitism a political weapon, it regarded the Jewish problem as a social, not a racial or religious, issue.

In Lueger's oratory, however, such a distinction was by no means apparent; his hostility was generic so to speak. (It was remarked nevertheless that he had a number of Jewish friends and, in any case, with the passage of years his enmity seemed to mellow.) His demagoguery, far from turning the electorate off, gained him many adherents. Half in jest he was referred to as "the uncrowned king of Vienna." Perhaps another part of his popularity stemmed from his similarly outspoken hostility to the Magyars, those forever unreconciled partners in the Dual Monarchy. When, in 1903 Czar Nicholas II stopped off in Vienna and the Social Democratic Party protested his visit, Lueger reminded them that it was Russian help that had defeated Hungary's armed struggle against the Habsburgs in 1849.

By 1895 Lueger's popularity helped him secure the position of deputy mayor; that same year he was thrice elected mayor, but for such an election to become valid, the emperor had to approve it and FRANCIS JOSEPH withheld his approval because of Lueger's undisguised hostility to Jews and Hungarians. But in 1897, when the incumbent mayor, Strobach, resigned his office, Lueger was finally permitted to occupy it.

From this time on he expended his constructive energies in rebuilding and embellishing the capital city. It was said later with some justification that it was Lueger who turned Vienna into a true metropolis. His first step was to free the business of building the infrastructure from entrenched monopolies. Many public companies were made properties of the municipality. In the early 1900s he superintended the electrification of Vienna's public transportation system, soon to be followed by electric street lights. It was under his tenure that three new bridges were built to span the Danube, the large market halls were erected, and the aqueduct, built many years earlier, that brought fresh alpine water into the city, was enlarged and a second one built.

As one history of Vienna states: "It was also to Lueger's credit that despite the enormous expansion of the past decades, Vienna did not become a desert of stone. He remained true to his pronouncement, 'It is my will that where there is space in Vienna for a tree, one should be planted.'" A number of large parks were laid out, and by 1909 the city had 198 public parks encompassing nearly 10 million square meters.

Lueger died on March 10, 1910. As one paper reported, "The emperor walked behind the coffin of the son of a school servant, when his earthly remains were taken to the Stephanskirche." Four years after his death, Vienna counted as the fifth-largest city in the world.

M

Maria Theresa (1717–1780)

Maria Theresa was the oldest daughter of Austrian emperor Charles VI and Princess Elisabeth Christina of Braunschweig. (Her slogan was *Justicia et clementia:* Justice and clemency.) Four years before her birth, in 1713, Charles VI had issued the Pragmatic Sanction confirming the indivisibility of Habsburg lands and the principle that in the absence of a male heir a female could inherit the throne. Her early education conformed to that accorded to princesses—she learned music and dance, she was introduced to the works of classical authors, she learned Latin from her Jesuit tutors, also Italian and Spanish, as well as French, which since the momentous reign of Louis XIV had become widely used in aristocratic circles. Studying the history of the Habsburgs and their far-flung possessions served as a valuable lesson in geography and dynastic principles. (Frederick II of Prussia thought that she had had a bad education, but her brilliance overcame that handicap.) Her father, even though he knew early enough that she would inherit his throne, did not make her privy to political and governmental affairs.

Before she was 19 years old, in 1736, she was married to Francis Stephen of Lorraine who in time, after a short-lived challenge by the king of Bavaria, became Holy Roman Emperor. Theirs was a happy and fulfilling marriage and Maria Theresa became the mother of 16 children. It was Francis Stephen, from 1732 on viceroy of Hungary, who acquainted her with the techniques and intricacies of governing a multinational empire.

Her reign was not yet two months old when several European rulers presented claims to her throne and Frederick II of Prussia offered his support against these claims in exchange for the cession of the rich province of Silesia. Thus the 24-year-old queen, mother of a daughter and an infant son, began her reign amid an acute crisis that threatened to dismantle her empire. In her despair she turned to the Hungarian estates, and their chivalrous nobles enthusiastically voted her support. Soon the empire was involved in war in several directions, known as the WAR OF THE AUSTRIAN SUCCESSION. Initial successes against the Bavarians and the French were negated by Prussia's occupation of Silesia. The fact that despite lengthy and exhausting wars, between 1740 and 1748, and then between 1756 and 1763 in the SEVEN YEARS' WAR, she was unable to regain Silesia embittered the queen to the end of her reign. Her grief was somewhat eased by the gain of Galicia in 1772, in consequence of the first partition of Poland, carried out with Russia and Prussia, both of the latter also gaining extensive territories. Another territorial adventure, in 1778–79, to which she consented at the insistence of her son and coruler, Joseph, the incorporation of Bavaria into Austria, was less successful; gaining only a small region along the Inn River.

Devoted to the principle of enlightened absolutism, she tried, with the help of her husband Francis Stephen (who died in 1765), and then of her son Joseph, to tighten royal control over her extensive possessions. A well-trained and loyal bureaucracy that proved the most efficient instrument of Habsburg rule into the 20th century was largely her creation. While nobles occupied most leading positions, in the lower and middle ranks could be found increasing numbers of bourgeois.

Although a devout Catholic, she allowed herself to be persuaded to lessen the influence of the church in many state and private affairs. She was alarmed by the great increase in church property, often due to churchmen offering indulgences in exchange for sinners' property being bequeathed to the church. Very young women, unaware of the lifelong obligation they were undertaking, were induced to take vows by the urging of priests or nuns. Maria Theresa forbade the participation of church officials in the drawing up of last wills, taxed church property and did not allow taking the veil before a woman was 21 or older. Many Jesuit teachers were replaced by laymen and curricula were broadened with the inclusion of history and the sciences. Papal encyclicals could be published only with the queen's permission; she forbade the heads of religious orders who lived abroad to visit Austrian monasteries and confined ecclesiastical jurisdiction to religious issues only.

She sought to ease the serfs' lot by concretizing the demands their masters could make on them, thus preventing wanton exploitation. Toward the end of her reign she extended the frontiers of her empire southward. In 1776 she acquired Fiume and its environs on the Adriatic, thus for the first time giving Hungary an outlet to the sea. In 1778 she restored the Bánát of Temesvár, which had been pledged as security by a previous king, to the empire.

Her impeccable private life stood in stark contrast to the scandalous behavior of many kings and nobles in Europe's ruling houses. Despite the constraints she placed on the Catholic Church, her private beliefs continued to conform strictly to Catholic teachings. Her close contact with *illuminati,* including her son JOSEPH II, convinced her that human beings were fundamentally good and she repeatedly did penance to expiate her sins.

A good and devoted mother to her many children, she raised them prudently and with discipline. She chose her daughters' husbands carefully. Maria Carolina (born 1740) was married to the younger son of the king of Spain and king of Naples, Ferdinand; Amalia to Ferdinand,

prince of Parma. The last and most celebrated marriage was that of her youngest daughter Marie Antoinette to the French dauphin, the future Louis XVI. Maria Theresa did not live to witness the tragic fate of her youngest daughter in the turmoil of the French Revolution. She died on November 29, 1780.

Martinuzzi, György (1482–1551)
cardinal, bishop of Várad, one of the most politically active churchmen in Hungarian history

Born in CROATIA into an impoverished noble family, his father's name was Utjesenič, his mother's Martinuzzi; he used both names alternately. Hungarians generally know him as Friar George, for he joined at an early age the Paulian order and remained an active member of it throughout his life. His career is associated with one of the most tumultuous periods in Hungarian history, when two kings, the Habsburg FERDINAND I, the choice of the conservative nobles, and a rival, János Szapolyai, ruled respective realms. During the resulting hostilities Szapolyai had to take refuge in Poland. A member of his small retinue was Martinuzzi, possessing great gifts of diplomacy and intrigue, and he became Szapolyai's most trusted friend and adviser. In recognition of his services, his master appointed him bishop of the see of Várad and royal treasurer. It was largely at Martinuzzi's behest that Szapolyai, in 1538, concluded with Ferdinand the peace of Várad, whereby each of the two kings would rule over the land they then controlled, but with the proviso that after Szapolyai's death, even if he had a son, his territories would pass to the Habsburgs.

Szapolyai subsequently married the daughter of Polish king Sigismund I, and in 1540 a son was born to the couple. Being the father of a son persuaded Szapolyai to violate the crucial provision of the Peace of Várad. Gravely ill, he left his throne to his infant son, naming a relative and Martinuzzi as regents, and bidding them to enlist the aid of the Turkish sultan to keep his son, John Sigismund, on the throne. It is hard to know whether Martinuzzi accepted the assign-

tion for the German princes who had been dispossessed by the French of their territories west of the Rhine. After appointments to the Saxon and Prussian courts, he was named, in 1806, Austrian envoy to Paris, where he met Napoleon, and gained useful insight into his character and ambitions. In 1809 he returned to Vienna. By then Austrian emperor FRANCIS I had been forced, owing largely to Napoleon's summary dispositions, to abdicate his title of Holy Roman Emperor, and Austria, with two-thirds of its population non-German, lost its organic connection to German lands. With nationalism on the rise, attempts were made, especially by Francis's younger brother Archduke John, to rouse German patriotic feeling as a cohesive force, but to the minds of both Francis and Metternich such patriotism smacked of revolution. Yet when in 1809 Britain was able to enlist Francis in the Fourth Coalition, an upsurge of national feeling did sweep Austria; it quickly subsided when, in July of that year, Austrian arms suffered another great defeat in the Battle of Wagram. On October 8 Francis appointed Metternich foreign minister. In one of his first acts Metternich put his hand to a humiliating treaty with France, the Peace of Schönbrunn, in which another precious Austrian province, the Tyrol, was lost. Francis, although ruling an exhausted, financially bankrupt country, was determined to continue the fight against Napoleon, whom he saw as an enemy of tradition and of monarchy, but Metternich deemed Russia, not France, to be the true menace to the European equilibrium. Appreciating the need to appease France for the present, he persuaded Francis to give the hand of his 18-year-old daughter, Marie Louise, in marriage to Napoleon, then 40 years old, to seal an alliance. The marriage took place in April 1810.

When Napoleon prepared his campaign against Russia, Metternich's position was that Austria must not exempt herself from participating, because in case of French victory she would be left out of the spoils, but, on the other hand she must contribute only a small force so as to keep her hands free for the postwar fallout. As it happened, this freedom proved crucial

after Napoleon's Grand Army was virtually annihilated in the depths of Russia. Czar Alexander pressed Austria to join a war of liberation against France, but Metternich hesitated; neither of the options before him was attractive. France, which for two decades had kept Europe off balance, was losing the war and Russia, whom Metternich regarded as Austria's potential nemesis, was on the ascendancy. He at first kept Austria neutral and sought to mediate between Napoleon and the new coalition forming against him. But, as the fortunes of war changed from one battle to the next, either one side or the other proved unbending. Metternich was required to exercise a supreme sense of timing in order not to join the coalition too early and thereby strengthen Russia's position, but not too late either so that Austria would not be among the victors. In the summer of 1813, as Austrian troops foregathered in Bohemia in anticipation of an impending declaration of war on France, Napoleon invited Metternich to Dresden for what turned out to be their last meeting, trying to persuade him to keep Austria neutral. Metternich on his part tried to prevail on his vis-à-vis to make concessions. When Napoleon proved obdurate, Metternich declared, at a meeting in Reichenbach, Austria's accession to the coalition. The allies stipulated May 10 as the date by which Napoleon would have to accept the conditions put to him, conditions that were on the whole mild, allowing France to keep many of her early conquests. When the date passed without a French answer, Austria declared war. After a series of armed encounters, the French and the allied forces fought, between October 16 and October 19 of 1813, the historic Battle of the Nations, in which the French forces were defeated. By the end of March 1814, Paris fell; two weeks later Napoleon abdicated, and the revolutionary nightmare was over.

Given that Austria had fought longer against France than any other power, and that Metternich had been instrumental in coordinating policies since his accession, the congress called to put Europe on its feet again met in Austria. The

CONGRESS OF VIENNA represented the high–water mark of Metternich's career. In British foreign secretary Castlereagh he found a man who completely shared his ideas about a European balance of power. The prominent role Metternich played at the congress enormously increased his sense of self-importance and he began to think of himself as infallible and indispensable. He displayed all the pompousness and self-veneration of an abnormally inflated ego. "I say to myself 20 times a day," he once pronounced, "how right I am and how wrong the others are. And yet it is so easy to be right." He did have unquestionable gifts, but they were almost exclusively in the field of foreign policy. He had only the most cursory understanding of the domestic problems of the Austrian Empire, of the financial ruin the long wars had brought on, and he treated the desire of the rising middle classes for constitutional protection with cynical contempt. The dynamic force of industrialization either remained beyond his comprehension or he feared the effect of a great concentration of workers in factory centers as breeding grounds for revolutionary unrest. He favored cottage industries or small workshops, with marginal returns for the workers. He wrote to Czar Alexander: "The labours to which this class—the real people—are obliged to devote themselves are too continuous and too positive to allow them to throw themselves into vague abstractions and ambitions."

Although he deemed nationalism the most potent legacy of the French Revolution, poisonous and lacking legitimacy, within the empire he promoted certain national aspirations, especially of the Germans and Hungarians, later of the Czechs as well, in the same spirit of balance that he advocated for Europe as a whole. Catholicism served as still another balancing force. He instituted church monopoly in education; even university students were obliged to attend lectures on Catholic theology.

By professing principles most European monarchs agreed with, viewing them as insurance against a revival of revolutionary activism, and by sponsoring congresses of the CONCERT OF EUROPE to coordinate policies on European affairs, Metternich played a dominant role in the international community as well as in all-German affairs; in fact historians refer to the entire period between 1815 and 1848 as the Age of Metternich. Yet in retrospect the very principles he so assiduously upheld were responsible for his political demise.

Metternich was married three times; his first wife died in 1825; two years later he married the Baroness Antoinette Leykam; when she died in 1829, another two years passed before he married the Countess Melanie Zichy-Ferraris. She died in 1851. His son by the Baroness Leykam, Richard, proved an outstanding diplomat as Austrian ambassador in Paris.

The revolutionary events of 1848 demonstrated the failure of the policies Metternich had advocated and pursued during his long tenure as foreign minister and, from 1821, as imperial chancellor. Discontent over his refusal to yield to popular desires, long suppressed by police methods, burst into the open when the news of the revolution in France reached the Austrian capital. On March 13, 1848, a small student demonstration opened the floodgates to armed clashes with the police and to large-scale workers' demonstrations. Among the demands put to the hapless emperor Ferdinand, the dismissal of Metternich figured most prominently and, before the day was out, the imperial chancellor was forced to resign. He took the long road of exile to Britain.

He returned to Austria after the revolutionary events and his advice was occasionally sought, but his political career was at a definitive end.

Milošević, Slobodan (1941–)

Serbian politician and statesman, chief of the Serbian and later of the Yugoslav Communist Union, president of the Republic of Serbia (1989–97), and subsequently of Yugoslavia (1997–2000)

He was born in the industrial city of Pozerovac in central Serbia in 1941. Both his parents were school teachers, apparently in a troubled relationship. His father left the family and, in 1962, committed suicide. Slobodan's mother, a devoted

Communist, imposed strict discipline on her children; she herself died a suicide in 1973. As a student, Slobodan was hard-working and conscientious but withdrawn. He forewent extracurricular pursuits and had few friends. He did fall in love, however, with a classmate, Mirjana Marković, also from a family of dedicated Communists. He eventually married her and she remained a strong influence in his life.

Slobodan joined the Communist Party in 1959, at age 18, and for several years acted as an economic adviser to the mayor of Belgrade. During the same time he studied law at the University of Belgrade. His stay at the university proved to be significant, not so much for its academic content as for the personal connection he established with Ivan Stambolić, a Communist functionary five years his senior, who would in time become his mentor and the most important promoter of his political future. Slobodan's early positions were in the business sector, first as a director of a factory, later as president of Beobanca, a major national bank. He proved himself a hard worker and a superior organizer.

Although he lacked the oratorical skills and the commanding writing style so important in public life, Milošević was early drawn to a career in politics. In this pursuit Stambolić's generous support proved indispensable. As his own career progressed, Stambolić took care that his protegé almost routinely occupied the positions vacated by himself. In 1984 Stambolić advanced from chief of the Belgrade party organization to become head of the Serbian Communist Union, and Milošević stepped into the Belgrade party position. Two years later Stambolić was elected president of Serbia and Milošević inherited his position as head of the Serbian Communist Union.

At this stage his political activities were still limited to maneuvering in close party circles. This rather unexpectedly changed when he began championing the Serbian cause in the non-Serbian republics of Yugoslavia, especially in the province of Kosovo, an integral part of Serbia but plagued by growing antagonism between Serbians and the indigenous Albanians. The 1974 constitution of Yugoslavia had granted Kosovo autonomous status, recognizing the Albanians' right to self-government. Serbians, however, had an abiding emotional affinity with the province: it was on the plain of Kosovo Polje that, in 1389, in a historic battle they lost their independence to the advancing Ottoman Turks. Here were the makings of a deeply divisive ethnic conflict, rendered more serious by the fact that in the course of time the Albanian population steadily increased, while the Serbian became a diminishing minority. During Tito's lifetime the conflict had been held in check by his refusal to favor either ethnic group over the other, but after his death in 1980 the simmering resentments broke onto the surface. Milošević, recognizing a potent political opportunity (but also seriously committed to the Serbian cause), made the Kosovo imbroglio a launching pad for his political ambitions. In April 1987 he traveled to Kosovo and, with a passionate call for Serbians to defend themselves in a province so dear to them, he roused his audience to a fury against the Albanian majority. In November of the next year, in another much-advertised political appearance in Belgrade, he persuaded tens of thousands of striking workers to return to work. At the 600th anniversary of the battle of Kosovo Polje in 1989, he made another impassioned speech in Kosovo, and his reputation as a political figure of influence was established.

It was the year when socialist rule in the European satellites collapsed with almost frightening rapidity. Milošević was instrumental in making the breakdown of the Yugoslav Communist Party a slower and more orderly process. Although his attempt to make the Serbian party under his leadership the center of the entire Yugoslav Communist Union failed when delegates from various republics walked out in succession rather than be subject to a central party under Serbian domination, he remained the single most authoritative political figure in both Serbia and Yugoslavia. However, his authority did not suffice to prevent the gradual disintegration of the Yugoslav federation as separatist tendencies prevailed over an encompassing Slavic unity. While he did accept, reluctantly, the secession of Slovenia, CROATIA,

Macedonia, and Bosnia, he drew the line at Kosovo's bid for independence and even for autonomy. Barred from serving a third term as Serbia's president in 1997, he was elected president of a greatly reduced Yugoslavia (composed of Serbia, Montenegro, and the Vojvodina). His refusal to make concessions in Kosovo, and escalating Serbian atrocities billed as "ethnic cleansing" against Albanians in the province, this in Bosnia in time led to NATO military intervention, largely from the air. Serbians responded by deporting hundreds of thousands of Albanians from Kosovo. In the end however they were forced to withdraw from that province and Milošević was charged with and put on trial before the International Criminal Tribunal at the Hague for crimes against humanity. As recently as September 2002 he vehemently denied any responsibility for atrocities, including the Srebrenica massacre of Muslims in Bosnia in 1995, in which he charged that it was the Muslims of Bosnia, abetted and aided by the French, who had orchestrated that massacre.

Mindszenty, József (1892–1974)

Hungarian Catholic clergyman, archbishop of Esztergom, cardinal, political prisoner

His family name was Pehm. Born in the village of Csehmindszent, he derived his ecclesiastical name from the place of his birth. His parents were farmers. He began his secondary grade studies at the Gymnasium in Szombathely at age 11; eight years later he entered the town's Catholic seminary. He was ordained on June 12, 1915. In 1919 he was assigned as priest to the Zalaegerszeg parish. In 1921 he was promoted to archdeacon; in 1937 to papal prelate.

A strong-willed conservative, a confirmed legitimist, he repeatedly placed himself in opposition to both the political and the ecclesiastical establishment. As a determined enemy of the National Socialist movement that flourished in Hungary in the 1940s, he used the pulpit to denounce its partisans, and although he himself was of Swabian German stock, he criticized members of the Volksbund, who flaunted their German ethnicity over the Hungarian. On March 4, 1944, he was named bishop for the Veszprém diocese, though his appointment was opposed by the regent, MIKLÓS HORTHY, because of Mindszenty's continued devotion to the House of Habsburg, and also by the archbishop of Esztergom, Jusztinian Serédy, the highest church authority within Hungary, who judged Mindszenty to be insufficiently prepared and temperamentally too impatient and intolerant to be effective as bishop. What more likely defined Mindszenty's character was his sense of personal mission and his disposition to martyrdom; after the extreme right Arrowcross Party seized power in Hungary in October 1944 and declared its intention to honor Hungary's alliance with Nazi Germany, Mindszenty addressed a letter to the new national leader, FERENC SZÁLASI, pointing out the senselessness of continuing the war. He was arrested and sent to a concentration camp in western Hungary. Soviet troops liberated him on April 1, 1945. On August 16 Pope Pius XII named him archbishop of Esztergom in place of the deceased Serédy.

With a government under strong Communist Party influence and supported by Soviet troops whose behavior was often outrageous, Mindszenty's impatience and crusading zeal found ample scope for combat. When in October 1945 national elections were scheduled for the next month, he issued a pastoral letter, read from all Catholic pulpits, in which he deemed the euphemistic "people's democracy" unworthy of the voters' support and instead advocated a democracy based on Christian virtues. Whether under his influence or because of political and practical reasons, the Communists did suffer a major defeat at the polls. Mindszenty continued to denounce the scandalous behavior of Soviet soldiery and the political maneuvers of the feared political police, the ÁVO. In April 1948 the government announced the "nationalization" (meaning the secularization) of church schools. Mindszenty so vigorously opposed the measure that the Communist Party chief MÁTYÁS

Cardinal József Mindszenty *(Hungarian Museum of Photography)*

RÁKOSI denounced him as a fascist. Although few others went that far in their criticism, Mindszenty's appeal was by no means broad-based. The Hungarian envoy in Washington, Rusztem Vámbéry, called him a reactionary whose main gripe was the land reform carried out in the spring of 1945 that deprived the church of large holdings; the Esztergom bishopric alone lost 87,000 acres. Mindszenty was also suspected, with some reason, of desiring a new world war, because only that could produce the upheaval that would restore deposed monarchs, especially his beloved Habsburgs, to their thrones. Even Western democracies had little patience with a churchman who consistently meddled in politics. When Mindszenty urged the American gov-

ernment to intervene in defense of church schools in Hungary, the U.S. envoy in BUDAPEST gently reminded him of the reluctance of Americans to breach the principle of separation of church and state.

By the end of 1948 church-state relations in Hungary had reached a state of crisis. Rákosi, addressing the central executive committee of the Communist Party, said, "The people now fault us for showing such weakness in the face of Mindszenty's fascist religious services." He went on, "[Since] agreement is not possible, we will defend democracy—as the people demand that we should—and will strike not only against the lower clergy but against the responsible higher clergy as well."

On December 23, 1948, Mindszenty, with 13 suspected co-conspirators, was arrested on charges of treason, espionage, and illegal currency trading. During his detention he was, according to his own account, beaten, abused, humiliated, and given "truth drugs." As he later wrote in his memoirs, "During my torture I had to remember the immense suffering that was inflicted on our nation [under communism]: among them the Hungarian girls raped by the thousands, the state of mind of nuns and mothers; they too must have suffered an inner collapse."

The trial was held in a small and cramped courtroom between February 3 and 5 and it created a worldwide sensation. There were demonstrations in many Western capitals against placing a prelate of the Catholic Church on trial on manifestly false charges. Mindszenty and the other accused were found guilty and Mindszenty was sentenced to life in prison. There are reasons to believe that he expected a national uproar, or such firm interventions from abroad on his behalf as the Hungarian government would be unable to fend off, and he was bitterly disappointed when none of that happened. Although never an entirely forgotten man, his case disappeared from the political and judicial agenda. Even the Vatican did not exert itself to secure his release. By 1954 he was sufficiently humbled to submit to the Hungarian government a "Pro Memoria," reminding it that he had been in prison for five years, that his state of health was unsatisfactory, that he suffered from lack of air and a proper diet and did not have the opportunity to carry out his religious duties. His memo did not elicit immediate reply but in the summer of 1955 Mindszenty was transferred to an old summer palace of bishops, and in January 1956 to a "nationalized castle." He regained his freedom, albeit only briefly, during the revolution in Hungary in 1956. When Soviet arms crushed that revolution in November, he was escorted by some loyalists to the U.S. embassy where he was given asylum. He remained there for 15 years, refusing papal entreaties to come to the Vatican. He finally did heed the appeal and left the embassy in Budapest on September 28,

1971. At the Vatican Pope Paul VI greeted him, took the cross from his own neck, and put it around Mindszenty's. But the honors bestowed on him did not mean that the church fully endorsed his past deeds and was not apprehensive about his future behavior. A month after his arrival in Rome he traveled to VIENNA. According to his memoirs, after a joint mass at the Vatican, the pope remained alone with him and said in Latin, "You are and remain the Bishop of Esztergom. Continue your labors and if you meet difficulties, turn to us always with trust."

Yet Mindszenty's continued militancy and his intemperate attacks on the Communist regime in Hungary did not suit the Vatican's current policy, which sought accommodation with East European governments. On February 5, 1974, a papal nuncio handed him a letter in effect announcing his retirement; Mindszenty refused to accept it. At odds both with his church and his state, he died on May 6, 1974.

Mohács, Battle of (August 29, 1526)

Arguably the most catastrophic military defeat Hungary ever suffered in her long history. It opened the way for nearly two centuries of Turkish occupation, which literally divided the country and depopulated large portions of it. It also enthroned the Habsburg family, against whose rule Hungarians would fight many prolonged and futile battles, terminated only by the AUSGLEICH of 1867. The Ottoman Turks had been steadily pushing northward since they had gained a foothold in the Byzantine Empire in the 14th century. They extinguished Serbian independence in the Battle of Kosovo in 1389; in the next century their advance was temporarily halted by successful Hungarian resistance. But under Suleiman II they resumed their drive aimed at the center of Europe. The Hungarian estates were divided between the high nobles and the squirearchy, at odds over issues of religion and land tenure and not until the Turkish host reached the Sava River that marked the southern border of Hungary did defensive preparations begin. A small army, collected

The Battle of Mohács, where the Hungarian army of King Ludwig II met the Turkish army under Suleiman the Magnificent and were decisively defeated *(Hulton/Archive)*

under the command of Bishop Pál Tomori, tried but failed to prevent the Turkish crossing of the river. The young king LAJOS II at last collected an army of his own, but it was pitifully small as the landed gentry refused to rally to the country's defense. Lajos and the high nobles tried to hire mercenaries with monies realized from the sale of holy objects. As the king's army slowly, with repeated delays in the hope that its ranks would swell with volunteers, made its way toward the town of Mohács, Tomori, to its south, was unsuccessful in foiling a Turkish crossing of the Drava River as well. There were debates in the Hungarian army over who should have overall command; the person most suited, János Szapolyai, with another small force, was at too great a distance from the expected scene of battle and the choice fell on Bishop Tomori. He was eager

to confront the Turkish host, though other members of the war council preferred to wait until reinforcements arrived. When the king's and Tomori's armies merged, their manpower amounted to 25,000. Facing them was a Turkish army of 60,000 regulars and a large host of support troops.

On the morning of August 29 the Hungarian army deployed in two attack formations, the front one of heavy infantry and cavalry, the rear of the retinues of high nobles and high priests. The king and his bodyguard took up position in the latter. In the opening phase of the battle the Hungarian frontline broke through the Turkish battle array and fought itself into a trap. Janissaries counterattacked and Turkish cannon strafed the Hungarian lines. The battle raged on, the Hungarian formations, front and rear, reached the Turkish artillery deployment but were unable to dislodge it. Meanwhile Anatolian cavalry engulfed the left wing of the Hungarian battle array and destroyed it. In the furious final battle seven bishops (including Tomori), 28 high nobles, and the bulk of the cavalry perished. The king fled, was swept off his horse in a swollen creek, and drowned. The Turkish host proceeded to the Hungarian capital, Buda, took it and burned it to the ground.

Mozart, Wolfgang Amadeus
(1756–1791)

Austrian composer, one of the authentic musical geniuses, in an era brimming with extraordinary talent, perhaps of all time

His father, Leopold Mozart, himself an accomplished composer and concertmaster, subjected his son, as well as his daughter Anna (Nannerl) to such intensive musical training that Wolfgang started playing the keyboard at age three and by age five was composing minuets. His father, ambitious both for artistic recognition and financial rewards, in 1762 arranged for his son to perform at the imperial court in VIENNA, then, for a three-year period between 1763 and 1766, took him and his sister on an extended musical tour with stops in all major musical centers, Munich, Augsburg, Mannheim, Frankfurt, Brussels, and Paris, and finally to London where they stayed for 15 months. The response, then and in later years on tours, was always the same: great admiration and accolades for the scintillating talent of the child prodigy but very meager material benefits. In London Mozart met the youngest son of Johann Sebastian Bach, Johann Christian Bach, himself a celebrated musician, and he composed his first symphonies, of which only three survive, under his influence. After his return to Salzburg, he wrote instrumental works; in 1768 he wrote his first *Singspiel,* musical drama with spoken dialogues, *Bastien und Bastienne,* and subsequently his first full scale opera, *La finta semplice.*

Between 1769 and 1773 Mozart visited Italy three times; it was said, though never verified, that after hearing the opera *Allegri's Misere,* he

Wolfgang Amadeus Mozart *(Library of Congress)*

tried to obtain the score, and when he could not get it, wrote it down from memory. In Italy he received much recognition. In Rome he was inducted into an honorary knightly order by the pope, in Bologna into the *Academia Filarmonica,* despite being underage for the honor. During these years he produced his operas *Mitridate* (1770), *Ascanio in Alba* (1771), and *Lucio Silla* (1772). He also wrote string quartets.

Returning to Salzburg in 1773 he at last received an appointment as concert master of the local archbishop's court musicians. He wrote several religious pieces. His ambition was to be promoted to chapel master, but the newly appointed archbishop of the city looked unkindly on the perennial wanderings of the Mozarts and the promotion was not forthcoming. Frustrated, Mozart took up temporary residence in Munich. Here he wrote and produced an opera buffa, *La finta giardiniera,* to great critical success, but once again with meager financial gains. He returned to Salzburg and, as he complained, with some zest to be sure, he was totally surrounded by and absorbed in music. He wrote nine symphonies, a number of divertimenti, and concertos for violin and other instruments.

In 1777 he set off on another extended tour with his mother, hoping to find a post at a princely court. He stayed at Munich, Augsburg, Mannheim (where he fell in love), and finally in Paris. This last stay was overshadowed by his mother's sudden death in July 1778. The next year Mozart returned to Salzburg as court organist, conductor, and violinist for the archbishop. At last in 1780 his chief ambition was fulfilled when he was commissioned from Munich to write an opera. *Idomeneo*, although seldom performed nowadays, was in its own time on the cusp of the dynastic opera series.

In the last 10 years of his life Mozart lived in Vienna. In 1781, due to growing tension between himself and the archbishop, he resigned his post as concert master, much to the chagrin, not only of his employer, but of his father as well. In Vienna, in 1782, he married Constanze Weber at St. Stephen's Cathedral. In the same year his opera *Die Entführung aus dem Serail* (Abduction from the seraglio), the first product of his infatuation with the Italian opera, was performed. He supported his young wife by teaching music and composing. His own music became more involved and complicated in these years and even his most ardent fans found it difficult to follow it; many jealous rivals disparaged him and Mozart, bitter and disillusioned, paid them back in their own coin. But his last operas were successes: in 1786 *La nozze de Figaro* (The Marriage of Figaro), in 1787, the year his father died, *Don Giovanni* premiered in Prague National Theatre, in 1790 *Cosi fan tutte* was performed at the Burg Theatre in Vienna. In that year Mozart was offered the opportunity to compose in London, but he declined the offer.

In his last opera, *Die Zauberflöte* (The Magic Flute), performed in 1791, Mozart returned to the themes and expressions of German opera. It was the last year of his life. He composed dance music for the Vienna court and was appointed chapel master for St. Stephen's Cathedral, with no pay. His last project was the mass, *Requiem*, commissioned by an anonymous benefactor. Mozart, already gravely ill, labored under the premonition that he was writing the piece in preparation for his own death. He completed only the first two movements and died in the first hour of December 5, 1791, apparently of rheumatic fever.

Munich Agreement (September 29, 1938)

Four-power accord marking the first stage of the liquidation of the First Czechoslovak Republic. Ever since the ANSCHLUSS the great majority of the German population in the Sudetenland, then an organic part of Czechoslovakia, kept up a steady and mounting agitation for "self-determination," which, as Czechoslovak president EDVARD BENEŠ could not help being aware, was a euphemism for breaking away from Czechoslovakia and securing annexation by Germany. This was eminently in line with ADOLF HITLER's vision of Grossdeutschland, or Greater Germany, in which all *Volksdeutsche*, namely, German minorities in foreign countries, would be brought home to the mother country. The rabidly nationalistic Sudetendeutsche Partei under the leadership of KONRAD HENLEIN was instrumental in creating chaotic conditions in the Sudetenland to demonstrate the urgency of solving the Sudeten problem. Hitler at first urged patience. He did not want to precipitate a foreign adventure so soon after the *Anschluss,* but, after the MAY CRISIS of 1938, he determined to destroy Czechoslovakia by military means. In pursuit of this goal he had to consider Czechoslovakia's military alliances with France and the Soviet Union, and a possible British intervention on France's side as well. But British prime minister Neville Chamberlain was determined not to allow his country and its dominions to be drawn into a general war over a local ethnic dispute in the center of Europe. This determination lay at the heart of "appeasement." As conditions in the Sudetenland steadily deteriorated during the summer, with daily clashes and atrocities on both sides, the western powers feared that Hitler would use the occasion of the annual Nazi Party rally in early September to declare war on Czechoslovakia. Chamberlain returned early from his summer vacation in Scotland and conceived Plan Z, whereby he would pay Hitler a surprise visit, in an effort to find a solution for the Sudeten problem. Although the surprise element was avoided, he actually made not one but three visits. During the first, at Hitler's retreat in Berchtesgaden, he was treated to an angry diatribe, together with the demand for "self-determination" for the Sudeten Germans, a demand he subsequently presented to his cabinet, the French, and finally the Czechoslovaks, with the peremptory recommendation that it be accepted. On September 22 he met Hitler a second time, in the German city of Godesberg, to advise him of the acceptance of his terms. But Hitler at once put additional demands, which the prime minister reluctantly agreed to transmit to the forums, where acceptance or rejection lay. This time the concurrence he sought was not forthcoming, not from his cabinet, not from the French, not from the Czechoslovaks. By September 26 Europe was on the verge of war. Chamberlain sent two letters to Hitler, through his friend, Foreign Office official Horace Wilson, the first urging bilateral negotiations between Berlin and Prague, the second stating that if France in pursuit of her treaty obligation came to the aid of Czechoslovakia if attacked by Germany, Britain would be bound to support France. The threat left the dictator unimpressed. He was resolved to carry out the promise of the previous May, to destroy Czechoslovakia by military means. However, the French on their part were resolved to fight for Czechoslovakia. Chamberlain, in a speech to the House of Commons on September 28, in effect admitted the failure of his efforts to save the peace. He had by now dispatched a letter to Italian dictator Mussolini asking him to intercede with Hitler. The latter complied and at his instance Hitler agreed to a four-power conference to be held the next day in Munich. Chamberlain was speaking in the

House of Commons when a message to this effect was thrust into his hand. He triumphantly announced to the House the news, adding that French premier Daladier had accepted the invitation and he did not need to say what his own reply would be. On the afternoon of the next day Hitler, Mussolini, Chamberlain, and Daladier, with their aides, congregated at the Nazi Party House in Munich. A Czech delegation was present but was not admitted to the negotiations. The Soviets, although they had a defense treaty with Czechoslovakia, were not invited. As all the principles upon which an agreement would be based had in essence been settled, the long hours of the conference in Munich were taken up with largely meaningless details, as for instance Chamberlain's feeble inquiry as to whether Czech farmers leaving the areas assigned to Germany could take their cattle with them. It was at 2:15 A.M. on September 30 that the Czech representatives waiting in an anteroom were handed the text of the agreement. By it, German occupation of the Sudetenland would begin the following day and proceed in stages, to be completed by October 10. The timetable for the first four stages, delimiting the areas to be evacuated by the Czechs and occupied by the Germans, were drawn up at the conference; the parameters of the fifth would be determined by an international commission on which, in addition to the Munich powers, Czechoslovakia too would be represented. This commission would determine the regions subject to plebiscites and lay down the conditions of evacuation. At the insistence of Daladier, two of the powers present, Britain and France, "proposed" to guarantee what was left of Czechoslovakia after the cessions. Germany and Italy undertook a guarantee only after the territorial claims of Poland and Hungary had been settled.

For Chamberlain, who had set the whole process of appeasement of which the Munich Agreement was the crowning event into motion, the real value of the settlement lay in the informal agreement he concluded with Hitler on the forenoon of September 30, in which the two declared that they would regard the agreement as symbolic of their determination to solve all future outstanding issues peacefully and never to go to war against each other again. The prime minister waved that paper upon his arrival back to London, affirming his belief that it meant "peace for our time."

"Our time" in this instance would mean 11 months. The international commission convoked soon after the conference did Hitler's bid-ding, no plebiscites were held, and even areas beyond the German-speaking enclaves, such as those that contained crucial Czech fortifications, were assigned to the Reich. Five months later, on March 15, 1939, Hitler sent his armies into the rump portion of Bohemia-Moravia. Of the other two parts of the republic, Slovakia declared itself independent and Ruthenia was awarded to Hungary. From then on the plunge toward a general war was unstoppable.

N

Nagy, Imre (1896–1958)

Hungarian Communist politician, minister of agriculture, minister of the interior, premier

Son of József Nagy, a telegram delivery man, later coachman, and Borbála Szabó, Nagy had three younger sisters. In 1925 he married Mária Égető; they had one daughter, Erzsébet. Between 1907 and 1912 he attended the Gymnasium in Kaposvár, then left his studies and became a laborer. In 1915 he was called up for military duty and sent to the Russian front. In July 1916 he was taken prisoner. Freed in June 1918, he participated in the Russian Civil War on the side of the Reds. He became a member of the Communist Party and returned to Hungary in 1921 with instructions to organize party cells. He joined the illegal Hungarian party and initiated a peasant movement demanding land reform. In 1925 he was a founding member of the Hungarian Socialist Workers' Party, a front organization for the Communists. In 1928 he emigrated to Austria but twice returned to his homeland for illegal organizational activities. In 1930 the party sent him to Moscow as a delegate to the Second Comintern Congress, where because of his ardent support of the peasantry (assumedly at the expense of the urban proletariat) he was accused of rightist deviation and expelled. He remained in Moscow, worked for the agrarian section of the Comintern, then, until 1944, he was editor of the Hungarian-language broadcasts of Moscow radio. In l944 he prepared a comprehensive plan for land reform in Hungary. In November of that year he returned to his native land and became a member of the Central Leadership, consisting of four party leaders. In December he served as a member of the delegation that negotiated the armistice terms in the Soviet Union. Returning to Hungary, he became a delegate to the Provisional National Assembly, then minister of agriculture in the provisional government. In the spring of 1945 he saw his plans for land reform put in effect. In this formative period of the legalized Communist Party he first came into conflict with other leaders, MÁTYÁS RÁKOSI, ERNŐ GERŐ, and Mihály Farkas, hardened Stalinists who accused him of passivity and who, in March 1946, forced him to resign as minister of the interior. He was given several, largely decorative, government and party positions. But fundamental personal and policy differences separated him from the top party leadership. He lacked the ruthlessness and uncompromising hardness that in the latter's opinion the socialist reconstruction of the country demanded. Politically he continued to be a spokesman for the peasantry, including the "kulaks" whom the party deemed exploitative and destined for eventual extinction. When, in the fall of 1949, he was excluded from the party's ruling body, the Politburo, for a short time he became a university lecturer. In December 1950 he was appointed minister of foodstuffs; in 1951 he returned to the Politburo. His partial rehabilitation may have been due to the fact that he was the one "Hungarian" (Gentile) in a leadership composed mainly of Jews and just then Stalin demanded that the imbalance be rectified. After Stalin's death in March 1953 the new Soviet leadership insisted that party leader Rákosi yield his other key title, chairman of the Council of Ministers, to Nagy. Thus began a prolonged political, as well as personal, power struggle

Imre Nagy *(Hulton/Archive)*

between the two men. Nagy, upon his appointment as premier, promulgated a program he referred to as the "New Course," a general softening of the exacting demands the old leadership had made on worker and peasant alike involving a shift from a disproportionate emphasis on heavy industry to the production of consumer goods, a moratorium on forced collectivization of farms, and an increase in wages and a corresponding lowering of the prices of consumer goods. He disbanded concentration camps and put an end to summary and administrative jurisdiction. He also initiated the so-called Patriotic Front intended to end the Communist Party's monopoly of government by legitimizing other parties, though their intended role in government was never clarified. All these reforms

coincided with growing unrest in other satellites, especially in East Germany and Czechoslovakia, and the Soviet leadership had a change of heart about the wisdom of the kind of changes Nagy was introducing. Rákosi and his partisans capitalized on the Kremlin's growing distrust of Nagy and conducted a concentrated attack on him and his policies. His position was further weakened when his one solid supporter in Moscow, Georgy Malenkov, lost much of his power base to Nikita Khrushchev, secretary general of the Soviet party. In January 1955 Nagy suffered a minor heart attack and Rákosi used medical arguments to limit his political activities and isolate him. An April meeting of the Central Leadership stripped Nagy of all his positions and excluded him from the party. Even the Hungarian Scientific Academy was forced to remove him from its membership. But while officially a nonperson, Nagy became a hero among the restless and rebellious literary and journalistic elite. At the same time, especially after Khrushchev's "DE-STALINIZATION" speech at the XXth Party Congress of the Communist Party of the Soviet Union, the position of Rákosi, the quintessential Stalinist, was shaken and calls for his resignation multiplied. In June 1956 Soviet Politburo member Anastas Mikoyan arrived in Budapest and demanded in no uncertain terms Rákosi's resignation. Rákosi was replaced with Gerő and the latter continued the campaign of exclusion against Nagy. The entire political structure as it existed until then came crashing down on October 23, 1956, when a spontaneous uprising in Budapest, quickly spreading to the provinces, toppled Gerő and placed the dominant position of the Soviet Union in Hungary in question. On October 24, by wide popular demand, Nagy was named chairman of the Council of Ministers. He negotiated with Soviet ambassador J. V. Andropov a truce between the insurrectionists and the Soviet military. On October 29 he announced on radio the withdrawal of Soviet troops from Hungary. Distrusting Moscow's true intentions, on November 1 he announced Hungary's withdrawal from the Warsaw Pact and her neutrality. By now Moscow had decided to crush the uprising in Hungary and, at dawn on November 4, sent fresh troops into the country to reestablish its position. Nagy, after an appeal on the radio, took refuge in the Yugoslav embassy. A new government headed by JÁNOS KÁDÁR took over, but Nagy, despite the hopelessness of his situation, refused to resign as premier. On November 22, having been granted safe conduct, with several members of his government he left the Yugoslav embassy. Notwithstanding the guarantee for his safety, he was taken into custody by Soviet agents aided by Hungarian authorities. Transferred to the Romanian town of Snagov, he was held in preliminary custody. The intention was not so much to punish him as to induce him to resign expressly in favor of

János Kádár. Repeated attempts in that direction failed. He was formally arrested and imprisoned. An elaborate legal case was constructed against him with the help of Soviet police authorities. When put on trial, he rejected the charges against him and refused to offer a defense. On June 15, 1958, a people's court found him guilty of attempting to overthrow the people's democracy and high treason, and sentenced him to death. He refused to ask for clemency and was hanged the following day. After a hasty burial his body was removed to a cemetery where many other executed revolutionaries were buried. In the spring of 1989, with a number of martyrs of the revolution, he was rehabilitated and reburied with full honors.

Neue Freie Presse

Viennese newspaper started in 1864 and having significant circulation, as well as influence, until the very end of the First World War. The paper's predecessor, named simply *Presse,* had been launched by one August Zang, a man of many interests and a restless temperament who had grown rich in Paris running a bakery of Viennese products and, galvanized by events in his native land in 1848, returned to Vienna and founded a newspaper, the *Presse.* The watchful censorship in the BACH era often found fault with the paper's critical editorials, but it was precisely its bold voice that made it widely read and increasingly popular. In 1864, at a time when censorship had been significantly relaxed, some of the journalists on the *Presse* defected and launched a daily of their own, which, as its title indicates, was new and free. Its independent journalistic voice was a novelty, not only in Austria but in many other countries as well, and the *Neue Freie Presse* became a kind of guidepost for freedom of expression in the press. By no means radical, it was uncompromising in demanding freedom from oppression of any kind. It advocated adherence to the constitution and championed the unity of the Dual Monarchy, it was also sharply critical of the Slavophil tendencies of the 1880s. In general its editorial line was that of the German Liberals who voiced distress over the growing Slavic population and feared for the future of German culture and dominance within the Dual Monarchy. In time its reputation became sufficiently established for government organs to use it at times to reflect official policy and opinion. This did not prevent the editors from raising frequent critical voices, especially on issues of foreign policy. Although the *Neue Freie Presse* catered to the general reading public, it maintained to the end a high literary and stylistic quality. Meanwhile the parent organ, the *Presse,* possibly as a result of competition from its own offspring, succumbed in 1894.

New Course

The name informally given by IMRE NAGY, recently appointed premier of Hungary, to the economic program he laid before parliament on July 4, 1953, in which he proposed to ease the exactions that had been placed on society, and especially the working class, under successive economic plans, to improve living standards, and discontinue coercive measures against the peasantry. These reforms were not only authorized but mandated by the Moscow leadership, which was alarmed by the unrest in several satellite countries following Stalin's death. In mid-June 1953 an eight-member Hungarian delegation composed mostly of members of the Communist Party were summoned to Moscow to "discuss" the increasingly critical economic situation in Hungary. The visitors were subjected to severe browbeating for doing the very things the deceased Soviet dictator had ordered them to do: forced industrialization in the face of insufficient resources, neglect of the production of consumer goods, imposed collectivization of individual farms and, ancillary to all this, gross abuses in the justice system. MÁTYÁS RÁKOSI, both premier and party head, had to bear the brunt of criticism for concentrating too much power in his hands, paying no regard to the close relationship between the Communist Party and the laboring masses, and practicing

the same cult of personality that Stalin had been guilty of in the last years of his rule. The Hungarian delegation returned from Moscow chastened and, at a meeting of the party's Central Leadership, on June 27 and 28, Rákosi exercised contrite self-criticism. Following the demands of the Soviet leadership, he also relinquished his post as premier to the reformist Imre Nagy. Nagy then announced, both at the party and the government level, the policy he proposed to pursue as premier, and referred to it as *"uj szakasz,"* New Course. Although he abstained from pointedly criticizing his predecessor's policies, he made it clear that the blueprint for economic development would henceforth serve not some grand plan to make Hungary a country of iron and steel but to improve the general living standard and allow the peasant the freedom to choose between cultivating his farm individually or in a collective manner. The production quotas between heavy and light industry were to be drastically revised in favor of the latter, and much of the investment thus far earmarked for the production of capital machinery would be diverted to agriculture. A collective farm in which the majority of the membership voted to recover its holdings would be disbanded. Arrears in obligatory deliveries to the state would be reassessed and, when unreasonable, cancelled. In general, the New Course aimed at humanizing a system that had a well-deserved reputation for regarding human beings as mere productive instruments with only such rights as the Communist government was willing to grant them while still preserving the primacy of the party in political and economic life. Unhappily the success and permanence of the New Course depended on Imre Nagy's political skill and clout, and he lacked both. The Soviet leadership soon became worried that the reforms would lead to extravagant expectations that, if unfulfilled, would cause further unrest; less than a year after installing Nagy as premier they lost faith in him and reined in his New Course, with disastrous consequences as it turned out.

O

October Diploma

An imperial rescript of October 20, 1860, issued by Emperor FRANCIS JOSEPH, it was a tacit acknowledgment that the centralized absolutist system introduced after the failed revolutions of 1848–49 had produced neither internal peace nor efficient government. The document's chief purpose was to pacify the Hungarians, whose passive resistance and occasional participation in anti-Austrian foreign adventures (a Hungarian contingent, for instance, fought with the Piedmontese forces against Austria in the war of Italian unification in 1859) had been the greatest obstacle to making an absolutist empire a going concern. The October Diploma was issued as a "permanent and unalterable basic law," and it introduced, instead of the existing centralized system, a limited constitutional government, with only foreign and military affairs remaining the exclusive province of the emperor. All other laws, including taxation, had to be submitted to an enlarged Imperial Council sitting in Vienna, and subsequently channeled through the parliaments of the separate provinces of the empire. The council was competent in matters concerning the empire, such as weights and measures, customs duties, commerce, transportation, and military needs; all else fell to the purview of the provincial parliaments. In Hungary the earlier, purely administrative, districts were abolished, and the historic counties were restored, as were the Hungarian, Transylvanian, and Croatian parliaments. The central interior and cultural ministries were also abolished; matters handled by them were assigned to the jurisdiction of provincial agencies. The Imperial Council was to have 100 members, with each province represented on it in proportion to the size of its population. In the case of Hungary, Francis Joseph offered additional concessions to ensure the cooperation of at least the high nobility, although the April 1848 laws, providing for the taxation of nobles, admissibility to public office without regard to rank, and emancipation of the serfs, although unpopular with that nobility, were confirmed.

The Hungarian people were not satisfied and insisted on the implementation of Hungary's 1848 April constitution, whereby Hungary would have a separate government responsible both to the emperor and to its own parliament, with only "joint matters" to be handled centrally. A mass protest in Budapest took place on October 23, 1860. In many places the two-headed eagle, symbol of the Habsburgs, was destroyed, and certain elements in touch with emigrant circles prepared for an armed uprising. It did not take the emperor long to realize that the October Diploma failed in its chief purpose and had either to be withdrawn in favor of a new absolutist system or updated to meet Hungarian demands at least halfway. The result was the FEBRUARY PATENT of 1861.

P

Patent of Toleration (1781)

One of the most significant edicts issued by JOSEPH II in the first year of his reign, it reflected his dedication to Enlightenment ideas as well as to some of the ingrained Habsburg prejudices he had by no means shed. The intent of the decree was to end the crippling religious restrictions on personal liberty and freedom of enterprise. Since the start of the Reformation, Lutherans, Calvinists, and Greek Orthodox had been prevented by law from freely participating in national life and in the economy; the JEWS were subject to additional humiliating disabilities. The Patent of Toleration still pronounced Catholicism to be the dominant religion in the empire, but it allowed Lutherans, Calvinists, and Orthodox, in places where they were present in substantial numbers, to build their own churches and schools, own land, pass beyond the journeyman status to become masters in the craft guilds, hold positions in the civil service and the educational system, and join the armed forces. They were further relieved of the imposition of taking oaths that violated their religious beliefs. Jews were freed of the obligation to wear distinguishing garments or badges, they could attend Christian schools if they so wished, could enter academia and the professions, and practice crafts and trades, although they could still not become masters in their chosen crafts nor could they become burghers of towns.

Significantly, Joseph, who before his death canceled most of the reforms he enacted in his lifetime, refused to repeal the Patent of Toleration; even his successor, Leopold II, clung to that position.

Pázmány, Péter (1570–1637)

Jesuit priest, later bishop, outstanding figure of the Counter Reformation in Hungary

After the Council of Trent (1546–62) which in effect launched the Counter Reformation, the Roman Catholic Church, largely through the services of the Jesuit order, undertook to "prove" the heretical errors of the Protestant churches and led Protestant converts back into the "one true church." In Hungary the Counter Reformation was officially launched at the Council of Nagyszombat, in 1611. Often the most effective churchmen in its service were themselves converts from a Protestant denomination.

Pázmány was the son of high-born Calvinist parents and was brought up in the spirit of that religion. While attending a Calvinist Gymnasium in the city of Nagyvárad, he made the acquaintance of several Jesuits, one of whom so deeply affected him that in his 13th year he converted to Catholicism. He transferred to the Jesuit Gymnasium in Kolozsvár and upon graduating journeyed to Rome to continue his studies in the Jesuit college there. After receiving his degree, he himself joined the order. In 1601 he was sent to the town of Kassa in Hungary, where the principal church was in the hands of the Calvinists. He conducted his services in the small chapel of the mayor. In rebuttal of statements in the book of a Lutheran preacher, which blamed Hungary's misfortunes under Turkish occupation on the intolerance of the Catholic Church, an intolerance that so angered God that He fastened the yoke of heathen conquerors around Hungarians' necks, Pázmány replied that he dated the decline of Hungary's fortunes from the time when Protestantism began to make inroads in the country. He was soon transferred to Graz where, in 1613, he published his major work, *Guide to God's Truth,* in which, in over 1,000 pages, he sought to discredit every Protestant challenge to Catholic teachings. He carried on his reforming activities with such eloquence and zeal that in 1616, when the bishop of Esztergom died, he was appointed to replace him. Under the impact of his writings and sermons, so tradition has it, he returned 30 high noble families, who had converted to Lutheranism or Calvinism to the Catholic fold. Because it was the nobles who appointed the clergymen to serve on their estates, the common folk attending the services once again heard the Catholic gospel.

To ensure the continuity of Jesuit teachings Pázmány founded several monasteries in the country and other educational institutions in VIENNA. In 1635, two years before his death, he founded a university of sciences at Nagyszombat. It was later moved to BUDAPEST, where it bore his name until the Communist Party government after 1945 "secularized" it.

Sándor Petőfi *(Hungarian Museum of Photography)*

Petőfi, Sándor (1823–1849)

Hungarian lyric poet, generally regarded as the most authentic voice in native poetry and the foremost representative of the Romantic school in Hungarian literature

Of Slovak origin, his family name was Petrovich and his father, István, was a butcher and innkeeper. Petőfi called Kiskunfélegyháza his native town but his actual place of birth is still being debated. He attended schools in various locations, seldom staying longer in any one of them than a few months. It was while attending school in the town of Aszód that he began to write poetry; it was there too that he became interested in acting, an interest he never abandoned. While at still another school, he grew tired of his studies, at which point his father ceased to support him. He found temporary refuge at a distant relative's home in a village, but when he began to write love letters to the daughter of an eminent citizen, he was forced to

leave. In 1839 he enlisted in the army, fell ill while on the way to his company in the Balkans, and he was discharged. With nowhere to go, he returned to his by now impoverished parents. His father urged him to learn a trade, but he joined a group of stalking actors for a season. In 1841, disillusioned with his rootless life, he resumed his academic studies in the town of Pápa. This was when his poems finally began to earn recognition, even acclaim. Unable to make a living, he resumed his wandering ways, but even in his footloose and always destitute condition he attracted the attention of important literary persons. It was not until 1844 that he was able to have a modest collection of his poems published. These represented a sharp departure from the formulaic, classicist style of poetry that the aristocracy, guardians of Hungarian literature, favored. Petőfi's poems were written in the accents of plebeian democracy, with powerful native motifs, and they incurred the hostility of much of the nobility. He became the target of venomous press attacks, especially after he published his naive but deeply moving epic poem *János Vitéz* (Hero John). By now, 1845, wherever he went he was received with great affection by the common folk and fellow literati alike. In an era of ever more assertive Hungarian nationalism, his interests became more political. He also began to read socialist authors, St. Simon in particular, and became convinced of the necessity of a revolution. In September 1846 he met a cultured young lady, Julia Szendrey, but it took a long and disheartening struggle for him to overcome her hesitations and her parents' opposition. Love conquered and in the happy early months of his marriage he produced some of the great love poems in world literature. When in March 1848, under the impact of the revolutions in Paris and then in VIENNA, BUDAPEST too rose in revolt, Petőfi was on the barricades. His *Nemzeti Dal* (Song of a nation), which on March 15 he read to a delirious reception from the steps of the National Museum, became the battle song of the revolution. But his politics were too radical, even to some of his admirers. He continued to write poems, pamphlets, and articles. In June 1848 he stood for election to parliament but was defeated. That same month he joined the rebel Hungarian army as a captain. His son, Zoltán, was born, on December 15 while he was stationed in the town of Debrecen. He asked for transfer to a battle unit and, in January 1849, he left his wife and newborn son and joined a revolutionary army corps under the command of Polish general Josef Bem, who was fighting with the Hungarian forces against the Habsburgs. He continued to move from place to place, had conflicts with the minister of war in the provisional capital of Debrecen, resigned his commission, and returned to Bem's army corps as a private. After the new Habsburg emperor, FRANCIS JOSEPH appealed to Russian czar Nicholas I to help put down the Hungarian revolt, Petőfi moved his family to a safe place and, urging his nation to resist to the last, went to the front. On July 31, 1849, after a battle near the town of

Segesvár, about six in the afternoon, he disappeared. What happened to him was never discovered. Legends arose and in later years many false Petofis appeared, but the fate of the real Petofi remains a mystery to this day.

Prague Spring

A major political crisis in Czechoslovakia in the spring and summer of 1968, pitting the reformist wing of the Communist Party against the old hard-line leadership, and eventually against the Soviet party. The crisis was symptomatic of the wider problem affecting all the countries in which Communists monopolized political power, of finding a formula for "communism without Stalin." Stalin had been dead for 15 years but for many of his erstwhile adherents the survival of Stalinism was a matter of political life or death in face of a reform movement rapidly gathering strength. In Czechoslovakia the leading Stalinist, Antonin Novotný, was clinging to power, though apart from attempting to silence and repress voices of opposition, he had no viable program and no solution for the country's accumulating ills, among which the growing rift between the Czech and the Slovak parties was probably the most serious. In the autumn of 1967 his position became so shaky that in December Soviet party chief Leonid Brezhnev paid a personal visit to Prague to assess the situation. Realizing that Novotný's position was practically untenable, but shrinking from the ouster of an old faithful, Brezhnev declared that the matter was for the Czechoslovak comrades to solve, which left the question open why his visit was at all necessary. The reformers at this point intended to move slowly and asked for no more than that Novotný resign one of the two key posts he held, namely, first secretary of the Communist Party while still retaining the presidency. This did happen early in January 1968, and the position of first secretary was taken by the Slovak Alexander Dubček. When on February 25, 1968, one of Novotný's closest associates, a chief official in the ministry of defense, Jan Šejna, privy to some of the most closely guarded military secrets, defected and subsequently turned up in the United States, Novotný had to resign even the presidency. His successor in that post was a man of uncertain political principles, who had played a key role in the coup of February 1968 that turned Czechoslovakia into a satellite state, Ludwik Swoboda. The key figure however was Alexander Dubček. While he in time came to be looked upon as the very epitome of a reformer, he was actually a compromise choice, with no substantial following and no clear program. He followed the lead of the reformists rather than defined their course. The Soviet leadership displayed early concern about the line he proposed to follow and when, on April 5, 1968, the party's Central Committee under his leadership approved an Action Program and published it a few days later, Dubček had fatally tipped his hand. The program proposed innovations practically unheard of in the Soviet sphere, including freedom of speech and the press, free trade unions, and, most dangerously, a Communist Party that, far from being the sole force in the politics of the nation, would be subject to the democratic process and might have to face opposition from other parties. While inside Czechoslovakia the program was received with almost delirious enthusiasm, Moscow and Soviet satellites ruled by Stalinists—and even by cautious post-Stalinists like JÁNOS KÁDÁR in Hungary—viewed it with extreme alarm. If the Czechoslovak experiment succeeded, if it met with wide popular approval and succeeded in revitalizing a stagnant economy, how could the continuation of rigid and repressive communist leadership be justified and preserved? In Stalin's time such questions did not have to be answered; they were silenced and the omniscience of the party was dogmatically affirmed. The new leadership in the various national parties was unable to silence the questions, but they still possessed the means of repression—that was the only surviving feature of the Stalinist past. In the last days of July the Soviet leadership met with the Czechoslovak party leaders for three days in the

Slovak village of Čierna. Apart from hurling insults at each other, little more was accomplished than that Dubček and his colleagues promised to take some corrective steps in their reform program. It was too little too late. Not only most of the Soviet leaders but also such satellite leaders as Walter Ulbricht in Germany and Wladislaw Gomulka in Poland were urging action to stop the reform program. On the night of August 20 to 21 military units of the Soviet Union, the German Democratic Republic, Hungary, Poland, and Bulgaria invaded Czechoslovakia. The force involved was stunningly, and probably needlessly, large—some half million military personnel, over 6,000 tanks, 800 planes, and even missile units.

On the political plane the Soviets hoped to apply the familiar formula of an appeal by "loyal" elements for intervention in order to overcome the threat to socialism that the current leadership posed. This expedient failed and the appeal was never published. The party Presidium in fact condemned the invasion. Another problem involved the formation of a new government acceptable to Moscow. There simply were not enough available candidates to fill the party and ministerial positions. Worse still, when a list for the new government was finally presented to President Swoboda, he refused to sign off on it. Meanwhile the population resorted to ingenious means of passive resistance: street signs, name plates, and a number of other identifying signs were removed, and the public, engaging in conversation with Soviet military personnel pointed out to them the discreditable nature of the invasion. The radio went underground and issued defiant broadcasts. The Soviets blamed it all on Dubček and his colleagues, who were arrested and taken first to Poland and then to the Ukraine. Left free was President Swoboda, who, at Soviet invitation, went to Moscow and on August 23 was received with full presidential honors. Aware of Swoboda's "principles," the Soviet leaders agreed to release the arrested Dubček group and to include them in the discussions. Long and tortuous negotiations followed. In the end the so-called Moscow Protocol provided for a new party leadership in Prague, headed by the Slovak Gustav Husák, and a cancellation of most of the reforms. Seeing no alternative, both Swoboda, and even Dubček, agreed to the protocol; both went on the radio in Prague and urged the populace to accept it.

Another challenge to Soviet leadership of the Communist bloc had been overcome, but it was once again apparent that the communism was unable to reform itself, that any attempt in that direction led to popular expectations that could not possibly be fitted into communism's mold. Repression, if necessary by military means, was then the only alternative.

Pressburg, Peace of (December 26, 1805)

Peace treaty signed between FRANCIS I of Austria and Napoleon I of France, following the momentous BATTLE OF AUSTERLITZ, which left the Austrian armies shattered and separated from their Russian allies. In the treaty Austria lost Venetia, which it had gained in the Peace of Campo Formio of October 1797, leaving the empire practically landlocked. Venetia was joined to the Kingdom of Italy of which Napoleon was to be king. Two states of the Holy Roman Empire, Bavaria and Württemberg, were raised to kingdoms and, together with the archduchy of Baden, made independent. Bavaria received the Austrian territories of Tyrol and Vorarlberg, as well as some rich bishoprics of the Holy Roman Empire. Austria accepted, as meager compensation for her losses, Salzburg and Berchtesgaden. Subsequently Napoleon created the Confederation of the Rhine, a new, secular, conglomeration of German states. In August 1806 Francis, recognizing the inevitable, abdicated as emperor of the Holy Roman Empire and released its rulers from any obligation to him.

Quadruple Alliance

One of the concluding acts of the CONGRESS OF VIENNA between Austria, Prussia, Russia, and Britain, following Napoleon's final defeat at Waterloo. The four powers had bound themselves earlier, while the war was still being waged, to fight for 20 years if necessary to force Napoleon's ouster and bring an end to French domination of the Continent. After Waterloo they renewed their association, this time principally to ensure that no new revolutionary uprisings would disturb the peace of Europe. They pledged, in case such uprisings did occur, to supply 60,000 troops each to help put down the disorders. They further undertook that no member of the Bonaparte family would ever be allowed to occupy the throne of France. Before disbanding they promised to hold periodic meetings to deal with such problems as could imperil the peace of Europe. This association was referred to as the Concert of EUROPE. It is interesting to note that all the undertakings were in time violated; Britain proved recalcitrant in supplying aid in helping to suppress what the other powers judged as threats to peace, and the periodic meetings were discontinued after the fourth, held in Verona. Revolutions did break out, in France, Belgium, and Poland in 1830, and across Europe in 1848, following which Napoleon I's nephew, Louis Napoleon, became the president of the Second French Republic, then emperor of the Second French Empire.

shared property, proved most popular. All three faiths produced many martyrs as neither the Roman Catholic Church nor the Holy Roman Emperor conceded to any Christian subject the free choice of his faith. However, persecution fortified the devotion of believers to the new teachings. Many noblemen sent their sons to study at Protestant institutions, mainly in northern Germany; the teachings they brought home were soon adopted by the whole family. In Austria the most illustrious early followers of Lutheranism were the Jörgers, the Starhembergs, the Polheims, the Ungnads, the Zinzendorfs, and others; in Hungary the first evangelical Lutheran was Mátyás Dévai Biró, who suffered many years in the prisons of two subsequent Habsburg rulers. Another Hungarian Lutheran, Imre Ozorai, published a widely read pamphlet, *Of Christ, His Church, and the Anti-Christ and His Church,* in which he attacked Catholic practices and defended Lutheranism. Still another Hungarian author, István Gálszécsi, published the first Lutheran Book of Psalms in Europe.

Lutheranism affected every sphere of public life, especially after Luther's chief spokesman, Philipp Melanchthon, in 1530 issued the so-called Augsburg Confession in which he clarified and systematized Lutheran teaching. When, for instance, at the end of 1541, Habsburg emperor FERDINAND I summoned to Prague an imperial congress of representatives from the provinces to discuss with them plans for a counterattack against the advancing Turks and means of financing the campaign, he was confronted with religious demands, such as the choice between the Catholic and the Lutheran prescription for communion. Such attempts to find common ground deepened rather than reconciled differences, and gave them a political character, because in the Austrian Empire it was not the Catholic Church but rather the emperor as *advocatus ecclesiae* who stood in the forefront of the fight against Protestantism. It was a losing battle: disturbingly, even Catholic congregations, especially in Carinthia and Styria, in explaining their position to synods, as to that in Salzburg in 1549, used Lutheran arguments. Nor was the new teaching confined to German- and Hungarian-speaking areas; by the 1560s it had made many converts in the southern Slav provinces. The Slovene theologian, Primus Trubert, translated the New Testament in the Lutheran spirit into his native tongue and was actively supported by the governor of Styria, Hans Ungnad von Sonneck.

Ferdinand I did try to find some formula by which Catholicism and Lutheranism in the empire could be reconciled and religious peace achieved, but the edicts of the COUNCIL OF TRENT, which was held between 1545 and 1562, so firmly reasserted Catholic dogma that all hope for a religious compromise was dashed.

In Hungary Calvinism was especially strong in Transylvania, benefiting from the isolation of that province from Austrian lands by Turkish occupation of central Hungary.

Renner, Karl (1870–1950)
Austrian Social Democratic politician, statesman, premier, president of parliament, president of Second Austrian Republic

Born on December 14, 1870, to a peasant couple in Unter-Tannowitz in Moravia, Renner was an example of how the peasant stock much despised over the centuries harbored a large reservoir of talent and ambition. The multilingual environment in which he grew up awakened his interest in the nationalities problem that plagued the Dual Monarchy in the closing years of its existence, and the endemic poverty of the people in the region sensitized him to the problems of the downtrodden.

His intellectual gifts were early discovered, and he was able to attend Vienna University to study law between 1890 and 1896. Through most of these years he earned his keep as a tutor, but in 1895 he was employed by the library of the Imperial Council, the central legislative body of Austrian lands, and his work there quickened his interest in the legislative side of the political process. He earned his doctorate in jurisprudence in 1898. The introduction of universal male franchise made it possible for him to win a seat in the lower house of the national legislature in 1907 from the Neunkirchen district of Lower Austria. From this time on he kept his mandate as a Social Democratic deputy uninterruptedly until parliamentarianism in the first Austrian Republic was extinguished in 1933. After the First World War, when socialism triumphed in Russia but failed in many other places, Renner had a sharp disagreement about tactics with another stalwart of the Social Democratic Party, OTTO BAUER. The latter felt that the party should depend on its own strength and not participate in a coalition government, whereas Renner, a moderate throughout his career, sensed a decline in the appeal of socialism and held that the party could best exert its influence in a coalition format. In 1919 he served briefly as interior minister, minister of education, minister of foreign affairs, and even as chancellor. He had the dubious honor of heading the Austrian peace delegation that traveled to Paris to receive the peace terms from the victorious Allies, and had to sign the Treaty of ST. GERMAIN. This fact proved to be a heavy political liability for him, especially among the German-Austrian nationals, who resigned from his cabinet *en bloc* in protest. Renner subsequently restricted his political activities, but he was a frequent speaker on behalf of Social Democratic causes.

Between 1930 and 1933 he served as president of the Parliament, at a time when the ravages of the Great Depression and the rise of ultranationalist sentiment greatly weakened the very foundations of democracy. When in February 1933 Chancellor Dollfuss effectively ended parliamentarianism in Austria, Renner's 26-year-long career as a legislator ended. He remained however a champion of an *Anschluss* with Germany, not on racial grounds, to be sure, but because he felt that a union of the Austrian and the German labor movements would produce a powerful force (although this motivation is more assumed than proven).

As the Second World War neared its end, Renner, well aware that the Soviet Union, as the geographically nearest victorious power, would have

a preponderant influence in Austrian affairs, turned directly to Stalin. His letter to "Most honored Comrade Stalin" earned him much criticism from many quarters, but it apparently impressed Stalin sufficiently to name Renner chancellor of the provisional government of the Second Austrian Republic and later its president. Once the four-power occupation of Austria was in place, the Western powers strenuously insisted that Renner broaden his political base with the inclusion of non-leftist ministers. He continued his practice of politics as the art of the possible, and it may have been in some measure due to his labors that Austria escaped the harshest features Germany had to suffer under four-power occupation.

Stalin's insistence that a German and an Austrian peace treaty be concluded simultaneously prevented the recovery of Austrian independence in Renner's lifetime. He did not live to see the happy day when Austria became its own master again (in October 1955). He died on New Year's Eve, 1950, at age 80. He was followed as president by another Social Democrat, Theodor Körner.

Rudolf I of the House of Habsburg
(1552–1612)

son of Austrian archduke and Holy Roman Emperor Maximilian II; Czech and Hungarian king between 1576 and 1608, Holy Roman Emperor until 1612

Mentally defective, he hardly visited his native Austria at all but spent most of his time in the Hradžin Castle in Prague, where he dabbled in astrology and alchemy, having such outstanding figures as Tycho Brahe and Johannes Kepler prepare horoscopes for him. A great admirer of Philip II of Spain, to whom he was in many ways related, it was probably under his influence that he developed his militant Catholicism, declaring that he would rather rule in a desert than be a king of heretics. In the 15-year war against the Turks that broke out in 1591 his forces fought with varying success; Rudolf saw a chance of restoring TRANSYLVANIA to his rule, thus putting irresistible pressure on the Turks in the middle, but he did not dare to take this course because the Transylvanian nobles whose cooperation he needed were Protestants and he would only have strengthened their hand by removing the Turkish danger. He sought to cover the expenses of the war by trying nobles on trumped-up charges of lèse-majesté and imposing heavy fines. His persecution of Protestants led to the outbreak of the rebellion by ISTVÁN BOCSKAI in 1604. In 1608, having proved himself totally incompetent, he was forced to abdicate in favor of his younger brother, Matthias.

S

St. Germain, Treaty of

Of all the peace treaties the victorious allies were called upon to construct after the Great War, the one with Austria was by far the most complicated. As an empire with a small Austro-German core, Austria had ruled over a number of nationalities ethnically foreign to it; some of these had in the final stages of the war, by declarations of independence, constituted themselves as separate states and made often exorbitant territorial demands. President Wilson in his Fourteen Points had called for the "autonomous development" of the people in the Austro-Hungarian Dual Monarchy, but by war's end that was a passé position. Independence had replaced autonomy and the newly emerged states, as well as Italy, which was on the victors' side, paid little attention to the "clearly recognizable lines of nationality" the Fourteen Points demanded. The Austrian Provisional National Assembly set up after the collapse of the monarchy placed itself in favor of the ethnic principle and in a pronouncement on November 22, 1918, laid claim to the German-inhabited territories of Brünn, Olmütz, and Iglau in BOHEMIA and Moravia, and to the South Tyrol, which Italian forces had occupied as far north as the Brenner Pass. The overwhelmingly German population of the South Tyrol sought to prevent incorporation by Italy by attempting to proclaim itself as a state separate from both Austria and Italy, but that scheme never materialized. Meanwhile troops of the recently proclaimed Czechoslovak republic by stages occupied all of Bohemia and Moravia and Austria was in no position to resist. Its newly formed government under the Social Democrat KARL RENNER could only hope that the peace conference would adopt Wilson's formula and overrule the forcible annexations of areas with a German-speaking population. A similar situation developed in the southeast, where the government of the newly established Serbo-Croatian state, in a manifesto at Laibach (Ljubljana), affirmed its right to all of Carinthia with no attempt to dispute its ethnic character but arguing that its German character was due largely to the systematic Germanizing policies of the Habsburg monarchy. Here too military power for the time being prevailed, and in the first half of December 1918 South Slav forces occupied several major towns in Carinthia and advanced on the provincial capital, Klagenfurt. An irregular Carinthian provincial militia launched a counterattack and reoccupied most of the towns the Yugoslavs had taken. Truce negotiations, attended by an American committee of the peace conference, followed; semiofficial plebiscites held in the disputed regions of South Carinthia showed that a majority of over 90 percent of the population opted for a unitary Carinthia within the Austrian state. This was what the committee duly reported to the peace conference. Finally there was the Burgenland question concerning the strip of land along Hungary's western border; here the population was heavily German but the land had belonged to Hungary since the THIRTY YEARS' WAR and had been integrated into the Hungarian Kingdom. The entire complex of problems was further complicated by the *ANSCHLUSS* question, which divided the peacemakers. President Wilson took the view that while he could not countenance a forcible German annexation of Austria, a voluntary association of the two states was another matter, but French premier Clemenceau vigorously opposed such a union.

The Austrian peace delegation headed by Premier Karl Renner received the draft of the peace treaty with Austria on June 2, 1919, and at once protested against the position whereby the Austrian republic would be regarded as the legal successor to the Habsburg empire and be saddled with such material and other obligations as should have been shouldered by all component parts of the old empire. The condescending manner in which the allies treated the Austrian delegation was an indicator of the consideration with which the protests would be treated. The draft ignored Austrian territorial claims in their entirety. It placed the German-inhabited territories of Bohemia-Moravia within Czechoslovakia, joined South Tyrol to Italy, southern Styria with Marburg to Yugoslavia, leaving the matter of southern Carinthia to future consideration, and making no mention of the Burgenland.

Subsequently, as had been the case with the German peace treaty, certain ameliorations were effected. As signed on September 11, 1919, the treaty was on the whole modeled on the Treaty of Versailles with Germany. Entire sections of the latter were verbatim incorporated into the Treaty of St. Germain. Austria was reduced to an all-German state, 33,000 square miles in extent. Burgenland was given to Hungary—although a subsequent modification following the collapse of the soviet regime in Hungary transferred it, with the exception of the city of Sopron, to Austria. All of Bohemia, Moravia, and Austrian Silesia went to Czechoslovakia. Italy received the South Tyrol, as well as Trieste and Istria. Bukovina was assigned to Romania. To Yugoslavia Austria ceded BOSNIA-HERCEGOVINA and Dalmatia, but Carinthia remained Austrian. By other terms the Austrian army was to be limited to a volunteer force of 30,000 men in units not larger than regiments. Austria was forbidden to build an air force, its seagoing ships were confiscated, and her "navy" was limited to three patrol boats on the Danube. Again as in the case of Germany, owing to Austria's destitute condition, the amount of

reparations to be paid was left for later determination, but Austria, like Germany, had to make payments in kind in the meantime. Amounts of livestock Austrians had presumably driven away from territories to be transferred to Italy, Yugoslavia, and Romania, were to be restored. Austrian objections that the principle of national self-determination had repeatedly been ignored fell on deaf ears, except in the above-mentioned case of the Burgenland.

Thus Austria, once the largest empire in Europe outside of Russia, was reduced to an impoverished core with no military capability and no international influence. The only viable future a realistic statesman could envision was union with Germany.

Schönerer, Georg von (1842–1921)
Austrian politician, advocate of the extreme pan-German orientation in Austrian politics, and a leading anti-Semite
Schönerer was a partisan of the Prussian Hohenzollern house over the Habsburgs and one of the most outspoken anti-Semites of his day in Austria. Son of a railroad magnate who was ennobled, Schönerer's early interest was in agriculture and he achieved modest fame by greatly improving the lot of the peasants on his estate. In 1873 he was elected to the Austrian parliament. At that point he represented the left-wing Radical Democratic Nationalists, but his fiery temperament and his demagogic bent inclined him to champion extremist causes. He was one of the leading pan-Germans of his time, openly contemptuous of the Habsburgs and their polyglot empire, spicing his speeches and comments with virulent anti-Semitic diatribes. He himself authored the slogan: *"Was der Jude glaubt, ist einerlei; in die Rasse liegt die Schweinerei."* (What a Jew believes in is one thing; in his race lies his swinishness.)

Interestingly, in 1881 he became one of the authors of the so-called LINZ PROGRAM together with two Jews, VICTOR ADLER and Heinrich Friedjung, advocating German domination within the empire and the separation of Slavs and Hungarians from the Germans. He soon adopted a more extremist line, however, which glorified the recently established German Empire and its architect, Otto von Bismarck, at the expense of Austria. As most extreme nationalists, Schönerer found it impossible to reconcile the universalism of the Roman Catholic Church with the German national ideal and he became a vocal advocate of the *Los von Rom* (Away from Rome) movement, something which was calculated to set him on a collision course with the devoutly Catholic Habsburgs. His narrow German nationalism, and the provocative terms in which he advertised it, also alienated the non-German elements in the empire. "I hold reconciliation with the Slavs to be a useless effort," he once proclaimed "One hears talk about the equality of Germans and Slavs. It is as if one compared a lion to a louse [only] because both are animals."

The Jews remained the favorite targets of his venom. His anti-capitalism was flavored with the conviction that the worst offenders were foreign Jews who had established themselves in Austria. When, in the wake of the assassination of Russian czar Alexander II, pogroms erupted in Russia and a number of Jews sought refuge within the Austrian Empire, Schönerer, in 1882, sponsored a bill in the Austrian Reichsrat (parliament), banning the entry of such refugees. Although the bill did not pass, it garnered 23 votes. And when the widely circulated *Neues Wiener Tageblatt,* in 1888, prematurely reported the death of German emperor William I, on March 8, with a number of drunken adherents Schönerer invaded the offices of the newspaper, which by his version was Jewish-owned. He was put on trial, sentenced to imprisonment, stripped of his noble title, and banned from parliament for five years. He returned only in 1897 when he and five pan-German supporters were reelected. The peak of his political success was reached in 1901 when 21 pan-Germans entered parliament. But his political support remained thin to the end. Apart from the non-Germans and Jews, he also turned much of the peasantry against him with his militant anti-Catholicism. His true influence, as it turned out, was exerted not in his own time, but on the Nazi movement in Germany years after his death. ADOLF HITLER embraced his *Völkische Weltanschauung,* which rated the worth of an individual or ethnic group on the basis of its race. After Nazi Germany's bloodless conquest of Austria in the 1938 ANSCHLUSS a street in the Jewish quarter of Vienna was named for Schönerer. During his active political career he may have served as an example of the truism that no man is a prophet in his own country.

Schuschnigg, Kurt von (1892–1977)
Austrian statesman and federal chancellor
Schuschnigg was a Christian Socialist politician, member of the federal parliament from 1927, minister of justice 1932–33, minister of education 1933–34, and finally federal chancellor 1934–38. Born in the Trentino to a deeply religious Catholic middle-class family, he studied law and practiced it in Innsbruck until his election to parliament. In October 1933, as minister of education, he was appointed by Chancellor ENGELBERT DOLLFUSS to negotiate with the German government conditions under which Austrian Nazis would be restrained from continuing their agitation for an ANSCHLUSS; the demands put forth by the German negotiator Rudolf Hess proved unacceptable. After Dollfuss's assassination by Austrian Nazis on July 25, 1934, Schuschnigg was named chancellor. He was as determined to keep Austria independent as Dollfuss had been and played a cagey game of granting domestic Nazis some concessions with one hand and taking them back with the other. Economic considerations (Hitler had imposed an effective ban on German tourism into Austria and high tariffs on Austrian exports to Germany) persuaded Schuschnigg to make another attempt at accommodation, and in this the German ambassador in Vienna, Franz von Papen, played a key role. It was he who, on July 11, 1936, appended his signature next to Schuschnigg's to an agreement whereby Germany recognized Austria's complete sovereignty and each side pledged to refrain from interfering in the inter-

nal affairs of the other. It also provided, however, for amnesty for political prisoners; under it over 17,000 Austrian Nazis were freed from prison. In the months that followed Schuschnigg watched warily as Austrian Nazis, for whose actions the Berlin government disclaimed any responsibility, increased their demonstrative and provocative activities. It was Papen again who, early in 1938, proposed to ADOLF HITLER and Schuschnigg a tete-à-tete at which they would discuss unresolved issues between their two countries. The meeting took place in Hitler's mountain retreat at Berchtesgaden on February 12. Although Papen had assured Schuschnigg that Hitler, owing to internal problems in Germany, wanted peace in his part of Europe, Hitler in an imperious tone of voice demanded essentially the installation of a Nazi regime in Vienna, a demand to which the cowed Austrian chancellor agreed. Upon his return home he began to implement the promised changes, then, in an abrupt volte face, he scheduled a referendum for March 13 asking voters to opt for a "Free, Christian and independent [i.e., from Germany] Austria." The outcome could not be in doubt and Hitler, to prevent an expression of national will rejecting union with Germany, on the 12th sent his troops across the Austrian border and on to Vienna, effecting an *Anschluss.*

Schuschnigg resigned on March 11 and was subsequently arrested by Nazi authorities. He remained a prisoner in the remaining year of peace and throughout the war. Freed in 1945, he emigrated to the United States in 1948, and became a university professor. In 1967, he returned to Austria. He published his first memoir, *Kampf gegen Hitler* (The struggle against Hitler), in 1969, and the second, *The Brutal Takeover,* in 1971. He died six years later at the age of 79.

Schutzbund

Paramilitary arm, between 1923 and 1934, of the Austrian Social Democratic Party. Organized in April 1923, largely in response to the ever more forceful actions of the HEIMWEHR, which represented the Catholic conservative forces in the

polarized constellation of Austrian politics, after the First World War it went into action only after the proposal in parliament by the Social Democratic deputy Julius Deutsch that the government disband all militias was voted down. From its very beginning the Schutzbund was on a collision course with the Heimwehr and with the political forces the latter represented. These groups accused the Schutzbund of seeking to plunge the country into civil war while the Social Democrats accused the Heimwehr of seeking to block the powerful forces that the Great War had unleashed, forces that strove to liberate the working man and institute long overdue social reforms. Although the Schutzbund was much more tightly organized than its adversary, fundamental differences on tactics in its leadership persisted. One faction, led by a former major in the army, Alexander Eifler, saw the task of the Schutzbund as defending social democracy on the barricades; only in an armed struggle could the working class triumph, he held. "Within 24 hours," he declared, "either we will be the masters of Vienna, or they will. . . . There will surely be street battles, and at first we will surely be in a difficult position, . . . but in face of a military attack we can defend ourselves only by military countermeasures."

The other faction was represented by a former general of the imperial army, Theodor Körner, who, after being pensioned off in 1924, devoted himself wholly to the buildup of the Schutzbund. He opposed the view that the future of the workers' cause could and should be entrusted to a paramilitary organization and advocated the primacy of political measures. In the end, albeit in a negative sense, he was proved right.

When, in January 1927, in the Burgenland village of Schattendorf, a peacefully marching unit of the Schutzbund was fired on by members of the rightist Front Soldiers' Union, and a child and an old man were killed, the struggle between the two paramilitary organizations burst into the open. A jury acquitted the assailants, an action that provoked large-scale demonstrations in VIENNA and the burning of the Palace of Justice, events that marked the beginning of the liquidation of the Schutzbund. In March 1933 Chancellor ENGELBERT DOLLFUSS suspended parliament and, in February 1934, largely at the behest of Mussolini, sent the army, supported by the Heimwehr, on a frontal assault against Vienna's workers' quarters; after four days of fighting the Schutzbund was liquidated by the very means its own chief tactician (Alexander Eifler) had advocated. Although after this it no longer existed as an organized unit, some of its members were in the aftermath of the ANSCHLUSS elevated by the Nazis into civilian leadership positions in the hope of winning the support of the working class. By then the goals the organization had fought for had been overwhelmed by the spectacular rise and success of the National Socialist Party, in Germany and subsequently in Austria.

Schwarzenberg, Prince Felix
(1800–1852)

Austrian statesman

He exchanged his military service in 1824 for a career in the diplomatic field. In 1826 he had to leave his post at the London embassy because of a scandal occasioned by his infidelity. Subsequently he served at several other embassies. In 1846 he became Austria's envoy in Naples, Italy. From here a revolution against the ruling house in March 1848 forced him to flee to escape an enraged crowd. During the revolutionary wars that followed he served as a general in northern Italy. After the defeat of the revolution, in VIENNA, on November 22, 1848, he was elevated to the post of head of the new, reactionary, government in which he also became foreign minister. He was one of the principal figures in arranging the abdication, on December 2, 1848, of the ruling Austrian emperor Ferdinand V and his succession by FRANCIS JOSEPH. He was also instrumental in the dismissal, on March 4, 1849, of the Bohemian assembly in Kremsier, which the previous emperor had convened under duress, and also in the proclamation of a new constitution that deprived Hungary of her independence. In May 1849 he accompanied Francis

Joseph to Warsaw, where the latter met Russian czar Nicholas I to plead for military help to put down Hungary's armed revolution against Habsburg rule. After the revolution was defeated, he labored with uncompromising rigor to create a united Austria in which a single political will prevailed, but he achieved only superficial success. In the German Confederation, of which Austria was the commanding member, he managed to prevent the secession of a number of states that wished to unite under Prussian leadership by having the Prussian king himself reject such a new arrangement, in the so-called humiliation of Olmütz; but his project of having the non-German parts of the Austrian Empire included in the German Confederation failed. In his program of introducing absolutism into Austria he could not have found a better partner than the new young emperor Francis Joseph, although in character they were very different. Francis Joseph's rigidity of principle stemmed from a straightforwardness that was free of ulterior motives. Schwarzenberg, who was a whole generation older than the emperor was entirely different. Although he regarded himself primarily as a soldier, he spent the majority of his life in the diplomatic service and deviousness was second nature to him. His youth was deeply influenced by the loss of his mother when he was 10 years old; she died tragically in a fire that broke out at a ball at the Austrian embassy in Paris. Another negative influence was that in his youth he never received a thorough education and only with the passage of time was he able to overcome the psychological effect that it left. Notwithstanding the quip applied to him that "in the army he was a diplomat, in the field of diplomacy he was a soldier" he did yeoman service in both fields. The foundation of his political conception was a hostility to every idea of freedom and every progressive system of government. In his view all conservative states opposed to revolution had to adopt such a philosophy. He nevertheless made the liberation of the serfs a part of his program and took important steps to limit the influence of the large landed aristocracy. He still intended the noble class to play an important part in the state system, manning the bureaucracy and the church, institutions that, he believed, should at the same time be financed by the rising wealthy middle class.

Seipel, Ignaz (1876–1932)
Austrian Christian-Socialist politician, chancellor from 1922 to 1924, and again from 1926 to 1929

A Jesuit prelate, he had been the father confessor of the royal family and had participated in composing the text of the abdication of the last Habsburg monarch; it was he who had suggested a wording whereby Charles pledged retirement from all affairs of state but did not actually renounce the throne. During the First World War, as the bonds holding the empire together weakened by the day, Seipel, in his book, *Nation und Staat,* decried the narrow nationalism of the parts that sought to negate the supranational ideal that the Habsburg Empire had represented. About Seipel's physical appearance a young contemporary author wrote: "Always and everywhere he wore the same tight black priestly garment. No one would have been surprised to hear that the man had no body. People remembered a head, a large, entirely barren ascetic head, with a narrow prominent nose, wearing wire-framed glasses, [and] narrow lips pressed together. His muffled voice sounded as if it issued from a crypt where the bones of the Habsburgs rested. In his reluctantly given speeches he often quoted Dante and St. Thomas Aquinas, [and] he never employed the tricks of a demagogue." (His asceticism, incidentally, was in good part due to his advanced diabetes, which limited him to a very spare diet.)

He first became chancellor in May 1922, after the resignation of Johannes Schober, of whom it was said, with some justification, that he became a victim of his own successes. During one year as head of the Austrian government Schober had been able to rescue the country from economic ruin, direct the attention of the League of Nations

to Austria's financial plight and thus began a process that resulted in substantial international loans being extended to the Austrian republic. He also concluded with Czechoslovakia the so-called Lana agreement, whereby Austria renounced any claim to the German-inhabited Sudeten regions of Czechoslovakia, pledged to cease agitation in that direction, and in exchange secured major credit for the delivery of coal and sugar, both in disastrously short supply in Austria at the time. It was mainly this agreement, which the Greater German party could not accept, that led to Schober's resignation when the latter party made common cause with the Christian Socialist Party, which then elevated Seipel to the chancellorship.

A monarchist by sentiment, he realistically accepted the republic, if only to avoid the condemnation of the major powers. His opposition to an *Anschluss* was due not to his hostility to Germany but to the fact that he perceived a better chance for the restoration of the monarchy if Austria remained independent. In his political pronouncements he eschewed long-term goals. He averred that the country was in too dire straits to make the pursuit of distant objectives possible. The economy was caught up in a catastrophic inflation and certain very basic necessities were out of the reach of ordinary men. Seipel, after allowing himself ample time to become familiar with every aspect of the problem, concluded that of all possible (as well as impossible, as an *Anschluss*) solutions a large loan by the League of Nations was the only viable one. In August of 1922 he visited three capitals, Prague, Berlin, and Rome, and gained support in principle for such a loan. At the League meeting in September his most potent argument was that the collapse of Austria's economic, and consequently political, system, would produce a power vacuum in the center of Europe with incalculable consequences. The major powers in the league agreed and, although their conditions for issuing the loan were severe (over 200,000 public officials had to be dismissed or summarily pensioned off), they also contained an essential remission of Austria's reparations obligations.

Seipel remained chancellor only long enough to ensure that the inflation was brought under control and Austria's economic restoration was accomplished; in November 1924 he resigned. However, his separation from the center of power lasted only two years. The visible growth of the Social Democratic Party produced unease in bourgeois and conservative circles, and these supported Seipel's assumption of his second chancellorship in October 1926. It was not a happy tenure. The rivalry between the political right and the left, and between their respective militias, the Heimwehr and the Schutzbund, had significantly sharpened, and on July 15, 1927, it culminated in mass demonstrations by leftist masses in VIENNA, in the course of which the Palace of Justice was set on fire. Seipel earned the unenviable epithet *Prälat ohne Milde* (prelate without mercy), when he announced that those who had participated in the disturbances could not count on mercy.

It was probably from this time on that Seipel's contacts with the right-wing militia, the Heimwehr, became closer, though they never crystallized in a clear-cut political alliance. When on October 7, 1928, the Heimwehr invaded the Social Democratic stronghold of Wiener Neustadt and large-scale disturbances broke out anew, Seipel used the occasion to propose numerous changes in the constitution that, if enacted, would have greatly strengthened rightist forces. But an element of mystery surrounded his every action. On April 3, 1929, he unexpectedly resigned as chancellor. There were many circumstances that could explain his decision. The economic situation had taken a sharp turn for the worse, unemployment was endemic with a quarter million out of work, and the debates surrounding the proposed changes in the constitution were vehement, but according to some he felt that he could pursue his political objectives more effectively out of office.

In fact his political career was at an end. He did have one last opportunity to influence Austrian politics, in the summer of 1932, when the new Austrian chancellor, Engelbert Dollfuss, fac-

ing still another economic crisis owing to the Great Depression that hit Austria exceptionally hard, once again turned to the League of Nations for financial aid. The league set conditions which the Austrian political right, specifically the Heimwehr, and its most conspicuous spokesman, the Prince von Starhemberg, judged incompatible with Austrian sovereignty. Seipel, though he may have agreed with the principles of the Heimwehr's reservations, persuaded Starhemberg that, in the interest of Austria's economic rescue, he place his influence behind Dollfuss's plan. Seipel died on August 2, 1932, leaving behind an Austria well on its way to ruin.

Seven Weeks' War (1866)

A war between Austria and Prussia, it was ostensibly fought over final dispositions concerning the Danish-German duchies of Schleswig-Holstein, but the true issue was mastery over the confederation of German states that had replaced the Holy Roman Empire in 1815. The Prussian statesman Otto von Bismarck had been convinced since his appointment as Prussian delegate to the Diet of the German Confederation in 1850 that the maturing unification of German lands could not be accomplished until Austria, which presided over the confederation, had been expelled. In 1864 he had involved Austria, as well as several other German states, in a war against Denmark, whose new king had incorporated the northern of the sister provinces of Schleswig-Holstein into Denmark, in violation of a centuries' old compact whereby the two were inseparable. The alliance between Austria and Prussia held firm only until Denmark was defeated and Schleswig and Holstein were occupied by Prussia and Austria, respectively. From then on Bismarck singlemindedly pursued a policy of confrontation with Austria. He allied Prussia with Italy, which aspired to regain Venetia, left in Austrian hands after the AUSTRO-FRENCH WAR OF 1859, and also assured French neutrality in exchange for vague promises of cessions to France of German lands along the Rhine. FRAN-

CIS JOSEPH of Austria sought to make his own deal with French emperor Napoleon III, promising *him* Venetia (in exchange for Austrian gains elsewhere) if he prevailed on Italy to stay out of the war, but the rapidly developing events overtook these attempts.

On April 21, 1866, at the insistence of the military, Austria's southern army was mobilized against Italy, and on the 27th the northern army was readied against Prussia. The Prussian army mobilized on May 3. Austrian attempts at seeking a political solution by referring the matter of the duchies to the Diet of the German Confederation were interrupted when Prussian troops moved into Holstein, formally under Austrian occupation. On June 14 a number of central German states rallied to Austria's side and Prussia withdrew from the Germanic Confederation. In the coming war Prussia was pitted against Austria and her allies, Bavaria, Württemberg, Baden, Saxony, Hesse, Nassau, and Hannover.

In Italy, the Austrian army of 75,000, under Archduke Albrecht, won a great victory at Custozza on June 24; a month later a fleet under Admiral Tegethoff destroyed the Italian navy at Lissa. In Germany, the Austrians disposed of an army of 238,000, joined by a Saxon contingent of 23,000. Emperor Francis Joseph, after much hesitation, placed this army under the command of General LUDWIG BENEDEK, who accepted the assignment with reluctance. Although in the battle of Königgrätz in BOHEMIA the Austrians had a slight advantage in manpower (220,000 against 215,000), they were grossly inferior in generalship, staff work, and weaponry (the Prussians used the new, breach-loading, "needle gun," over the old-fashioned Austrian muskets); the persistent disagreements between Benedek and his generals were undoubtedly also a factor in the crushing defeat Austria suffered. (Benedek had urged the emperor, as late as July 1, to seek a peaceful solution.)

Bismarck offered a generous peace: he demanded no territorial cessions, only that Austria agree to the dissolution of the German Confederation and allow Prussia to organize the north German states into a new conglomeration in which Prussia would play the same dominant role Austria had played in the former. In the south, Italy, despite her defeats on land and sea, gained Venetia.

Seyss-Inquart, Arthur (1892–1946)
National Socialist Austrian chancellor and later Reichskommissar for the Netherlands in the Second World War

Austrian lawyer and pro-Nazi politician, Arthur Seyss-Inquart was minister of interior in the days before the ANSCHLUSS and chancellor from March 12, 1938, until Austria's formal incorporation into the Reich. During the Second World War he served as Reichskommissar for the occupied Netherlands. After the war he was indicted as a war criminal, condemned, and hanged.

Dr. Arthur Seyss-Inquart delivering a speech, 1942 *(Hulton/Archive)*

In the turbulent 1920s and early 1930s Seyss-Inquart was one of those déclassé young men (as were ENGELBERT DOLLFUSS and Ernst Kaltenbrunner, among others), who were attracted by the ideas of the rising National Socialist Party in Germany and sought to secure for it a home in Austria. In the summer of 1937, Chancellor KURT VON SCHUSCHNIGG appointed Seyss-Inquart to head a Commission of Seven, whose task it was to integrate the Austrian Nazi Party into the single Fatherland Front. Not yet a Nazi Party member, Seyss-Inquart in time made the commission a center of Nazi propaganda and provocation. When Schuschnigg visited ADOLF HITLER at Berchtesgaden in February 1938, one of Hitler's key demands was that he name Seyss-Inquart minister of the interior, thus placing control of the national police in pro-Nazi hands. While Schuschnigg complied with this demand, in other ways he sought to prevent an impending *Anschluss,* and an enraged Hitler, on March 11, demanded that, in place of Schuschnigg, Seyss-Inquart be named chancellor. The next day Austrian president Wilhelm Miklas complied with the demand.

After Austria's incorporation into the Reich, Seyss-Inquart became a German Nazi official. Following the defeat of Poland in September 1939, he was briefly named deputy minister in that region of Poland not joined to Germany, called the Government General. After the conclusion of the campaign in the west, and the defeat and occupation of the Lowlands, Hitler named Seyss-Inquart Reichskommissar for Holland. As such, he superintended anti-Jewish legislation, the large-scale deportation of Jews, the brutal suppression of several strikes, and a growing resistance movement. He was one of those men who, while politically restrained at first, fell under Hitler's spell and assiduously tried to adopt "National-Socialist hardness." Hitler, just before he committed suicide, named him foreign minister of the Third Reich.

Arrested by Allied forces after the war, Seyss-Inquart was put on trial with 20 other war criminals at Nuremberg. The tribunal condemned him to death for crimes against humanity, and he was hanged on October 16, 1946.

Slánský, Rudolf (1901–1952)
Czechoslovak Communist politician

A confirmed Stalinist, Slánský as so many other faithful, fell victim to the hysteria in the Soviet bloc that followed the expulsion of the Yugoslav Communist Union from the COMINTERN. Son of a Jewish family and imbued with that revolutionary spirit so many young Jews in Europe adopted as their credo after the success of the Bolshevik revolution in Russia, he joined the party at age 20, and by age 28 became a member of the national party's Central Committee. In 1935 he was elected to the Czechoslovak National Assembly as a Communist deputy. When in March 1939 the Germans occupied what was left of Czechoslovakia after the cession of the Sudetenland according to the MUNICH AGREEMENT, he fled to the Soviet Union. During the war with Germany he fought with the Red Army on the Ukrainian front. In 1944 he made his way back into Slovakia and participated in the partisan rising against the occupying German army in that year. After the war he plunged into politics and was one of the most devoted and selfless stalwarts of his party. Elected secretary general in 1947, he worked hand in hand with Soviet agents who prepared the putsch of February 1948 that turned Czechoslovakia from a multiparty democratic state into a totalitarian society under Communist Party rule. In the more complacent days before Tito's treason such exemplary conduct ensured a lasting future for a member of the party. In 1951, on the occasion of his 50th birthday, Slánský was awarded the highest Czechoslovak decoration the state could bestow. But by now the hunt for Titoists had produced a network of complicities and Stalin had also become uneasy about the attraction the newly formed state of Israel had for many Jews in the Soviet orbit. Slánský was arrested in October 1952 on charges of treason, espionage, and sedition and, on November 27, was found guilty and sentenced to death with 11 other defendants. He was hanged on December 3 of that year. As happened with so many victims of the Stalinist purges, Slánský's case was subsequently reviewed. In 1963 he was declared innocent of the charges brought against him and rehabilitated and in 1968 his party membership was restored.

Spanish Succession, War of the

A war arising out of a most complex diplomatic imbroglio involving all the major powers of Europe, and for good reason, because the richest prize, the Spanish inheritance, involving immense territories in Europe and overseas, was at stake. The Spanish king, Charles II (1660–1700), of the House of Habsburg, feeble-minded, ill, and childless, was dying. By law as well as tradition the Habsburgs of Austria were the legitimate heirs to his throne, and this was the position the king in VIENNA and Holy Roman Emperor Leopold I took. He regarded the matter of succession a family affair to be settled within Habsburg councils. But King Louis XIV of France took a different view. There was Habsburg blood in his line on the maternal side and he himself had married a Spanish Habsburg woman, Maria Theresa, daughter of Philip IV. Earlier, during young Charles II's childhood, in 1668, as he lay gravely ill and was not expected to live, the two houses, the Habsburg and the Bourbon, did work out a plan of partition. By this Leopold of Austria would inherit Spain with the archduchy of Milan and the American colonies; Louis would receive the Netherlands, Franche-Comté, Naples-Sicily, and the Philippines. Charles, however, recovered and the agreements lapsed. By the time they became timely again, in the closing years of the 17th century, other powers had taken an interest in the matter of Spanish succession. Britain and the Netherlands having nibbled away at Spanish colonies in America, were now anxious to acquire more, and did not relish the prospect of the colonies falling to a major power. Of the prospective inheritors France was

the more powerful. As the British and Dutch saw it, the Spanish inheritance should fall to an heir without the military and naval muscle to defend its overseas possessions. In 1698 they agreed that the young son of the Bavarian elector, Joseph Ferdinand, would be a felicitous choice. By their plan, he would inherit Spain and the overseas colonies; Austria and France would be compensated by Milan and Naples, respectively. The dying Charles II, with no political will of his own, agreed. So did Austria and France to avoid what was certain to be a major European war. Louis XIV had already fought three exhausting wars over Spanish inheritance and Leopold I of Austria had just concluded a long war with the Ottoman Turks.

But in the following year the designated Bavarian heir, only six years old, died. The one plan that could have saved the peace became inoperative. The decision of who should inherit the crown of Spain once again reverted to the gravely ill Charles II, or rather his camarilla, and their dominant consideration was that the Spanish inheritance remain intact, in one hand. Considering power realities, only France would be able to defend it, and then only if the throne devolved on a Bourbon. In the end, this was the choice of the Spanish camarilla. Charles II signed his last will to this effect just before he died on November 1, 1700. When the will, whose provisions were secret, was read, the Austrian Habsburgs were stunned to learn that a crown that had sat on Habsburg heads for two centuries was lost to a rival house, personally to Louis XIV's grandson Philip. The Spanish population, long living in anxiety over the future of a sickly king and his crumbling empire, greeted the new monarch, healthy and vigorous, with enthusiasm. But Leopold of Austria was determined to defend his family's claim to Spain. He did not go so far as to propose to unite the crowns of Spain and Austria as they once had been, under CHARLES V, but planned to leave his own, Austrian, crown to his older son Joseph and have the crown of Spain inherited by his younger son, Charles (later Holy Roman Emperor Charles VI).

Charles, before he left for Spain to claim the crown, made a secret family compact whereby the Austrian branch of the family (Leopold and his older son Joseph) renounced all claims to the Spanish throne, and Charles any claim to the Austrian throne, with the exception that if the male line on either side died out, the other would inherit it and, failing a male heir, a female could inherit the throne. Charles then betook himself to Spain. With British help he twice occupied Madrid but was unable to hold on to it. Meanwhile the Austrian general Eugene of Savoy broke from the Tyrol into the Spanish Italian possessions and conquered large portions of them. Britain and the Netherlands at first supported the Bourbon claim to the Spanish throne but by 1702 reconsidered and entered the war against France. The ensuing conflict was a prolonged and fluctuating affair, and each fluctuation resulted in increased demands by the winning side, which lapsed when the tide of war turned again. A part of the German principalities sided with Louis, another part with Leopold; major battles were fought in the Netherlands and in Spain. The Anglo-Dutch side won significant victories at Blenheim in Bavaria in 1704, Ramillies in 1706, Oudenaarde in the Spanish Netherlands in 1708, and Malplaquet, also in the Spanish Netherlands, in 1709, where the French suffered a major defeat. Louis XIV did not, however, accept the heavy demands put to him. He was probably rescued from an imposed peace when, in Britain, the Tories gained a majority in Parliament and were disinclined to continue the costly struggle. Another decisive factor was the untimely death, in 1711, of Joseph I, Austrian king and Holy Roman Emperor, which left the highest German dignity vacant. The electors could only agree on one person, Joseph's younger brother, Charles, the very man who by the secret family agreement was to become king of Spain. The last time the king of Spain was also Holy Roman Emperor was in the reign of CHARLES V, and no repetition of such concentration of power was possible. By now Charles held only one Spanish town, Barcelona, and that was where the call to go to Germany to

be crowned emperor reached him. He answered the call, and the issue that had sparked the war was decided, by default as it were. The peace conference met in the Dutch city of Utrecht. It ruled that the Spanish throne and all Spanish overseas possessions would devolve on the Bourbon Philip V, with the proviso that the crowns of France and of Spain could never be united. Spain's European possessions—Belgium, Naples, Milan, Livorno, Sardinia, and northern Italy—fell to Charles of Austria. However, these terms were worked out by the maritime powers and presented to Charles for acceptance. At first he refused; he could not reconcile himself to seeing a foreign monarch sit on the throne that had for two centuries been a Habsburg possession. But the resumption of the war against a coalition of powers was not an option, and so on March 7, 1713, in Rastatt, he accepted the terms. The Habsburgs had no more overseas possessions remaining and were confined to their holdings in eastern Europe.

Stadion Constitution

Count Franz Seraphin Stadion-Werthausen (1806–53), when in November 1848 he was named minister of the interior in FELIX VON SCHWARZENBERG's cabinet, had since 1841 been the governor of the Austrian littoral on the Adriatic, and from 1847 governor of Galicia. As interior minister he had the unpleasant task of disbanding the Kremsier Assembly that the Vienna court had under revolutionary pressure allowed to convene but had no intention of allowing to finish its work, which would have introduced constitutional government into the empire. As it happened, the committee of that assembly charged with drafting the constitution finished its work on March 2, 1849, and was ready to submit it to the plenary assembly, with plans to proclaim the constitution on March 15, the first anniversary of the day on which it was promised.

On the evening of March 6 Stadion, just arrived in Kremsier, announced to the assembly that the emperor was about to proclaim a constitution of his own. On the next morning a pre-dated proclamation dissolved the assembly and those members of it who had not been fore-warned were arrested. Simultaneously, a new constitution from the emperor's hand was proclaimed. It tempered its absolutist character by requiring that the monarch take an oath to the document; it designated him as the supreme commander of the armed forces and the absolute master of foreign policy. He was given the right to declare war, conclude peace, and enter into treaties binding the whole empire. He was to appoint and dismiss ministers and civil servants, but as to decrees issued by him, they had to be countersigned by the responsible minister. He had legislative power "in unison with" an Imperial Council, the Reichstag, and the provincial Landtage, the former to be convoked yearly. He had an absolute veto over all legislative acts. He had the right to dissolve the Reichstag, but when he did so, another one had to be called within three months. In an emergency, when the Reichstag was not in session, he could legislate by Order of Council, but such acts he later had to justify before the Reichstag. The Reichstag was to be bicameral, with the lower house directly, the upper indirectly elected.

Judicially, Stadion's constitution guaranteed equality before the law to all citizens, as well as equality of opportunity to obtain public office.

Assumedly as a challenge to the Hungarians who were still waging a war of liberation against the Habsburgs, the constitution provided that there was only one citizenship (a separate Hungarian citizenship was a long-standing demand of the Hungarian estates); only one ruler, to be crowned only once (a weighty proviso, for another Hungarian condition of cooperation was that the monarch be crowned in Hungary separately); and only one central legislature, the imperial Reichstag. In a feeble and humiliating sop to the Hungarians, the proclamation stated that "the Constitution of Hungary remains in force, with the reservation that those of its provisions which are contrary to the present Imperial Constitution are abrogated."

It is unlikely that realists at the Vienna court expected the legal effects of this document to survive the great disturbances through which the empire was passing. But as an interim position it was a strong one and unmistakable in its intention to resist all attempts to infringe on the system of absolutism the Habsburgs had practiced, and intended to continue to practice.

Szakasits, Árpád (1888–1965)

outstanding figure in the Hungarian workers' movement, head of Social Democratic Party (SDP) until its merger with the Communist Party in 1948, president of the Hungarian republic

After finishing six elementary grades, he was apprenticed as a stonecutter. He joined the labor movement in 1903 and became an official functionary of the construction union in 1908, later editor at *Népszava,* the Social Democratic daily. In 1911 he married Terézia Schneider, from whom he had a son. After divorcing her, he married Emma Grosz, who gave him a son and a daughter. During the short reign of the Hungarian soviet republic he was a member of the government's executive committee. Following the fall of that regime he was imprisoned for some three years; in 1927–28 he was secretary of the SDP; from 1928 to 1938 he was president of the National Association of Hungarian Construction Workers. In November 1938 he became secretary general of the SDP and continued in that position until the German occupation of Hungary in March 1944. During the same time he was editor-in-chief of the party daily, *Népszava.*

Under German occupation he became a leading light in the National Front, a leftist political movement established to prepare the nation for a fresh political start after the war. In October 1944 he signed for the SDP an agreement providing for close cooperation and eventual union with the Hungarian Communist Party. After liberation he again became secretary general of the SDP, and for short periods he was minister of state and minister of industry. The merger in June 1948 of the SDP and the Communist Party into the Hungarian Workers' Party (MDP) was arranged while he was out of the country; he subsequently gave it his reluctant approval. In August 1948 he was named president of the Hungarian republic, a substanceless dignity. In May 1950 he was accused of having betrayed to the police a planned strike of construction workers while he was president of their association before the war; he was tried and sentenced to life in prison. Amnestied in March 1956 he was later rehabilitated. In October 1956 he placed himself in opposition to the revolution against the Communist regime and after the revolution was defeated he took active part in consolidating the position of the new Moscow-supported government. In 1958 he became president of the National Association of Hungarian Journalists; from 1959 he was a member of the Central Committee of the Hungarian Socialist Workers' Party, a successor to the defunct MDP. In 1960 he became president of the National Peace Council. He died on May 3, 1965.

Széchenyi, Count István

Hungarian politician and statesman, the chief reformer in the years preceding the revolution of 1848

Son of Count Ferenc Széchenyi, founder of the Hungarian National Museum. As a young soldier Széchenyi had participated in the campaigns against Napoleon I, fought in the Battle of Nations at Leipzig in 1813 and participated in the social whirl of the CONGRESS OF VIENNA in 1815. After the war he traveled widely and returned with the impression that his homeland was far behind west European states in culture and social development. He decided to devote himself to uplifting Hungary to a worthy place among European nations. He made his first public political appearance in 1825, when Emperor FRANCIS I reconvened the Hungarian Diet after an 11-year absence. The initiative for a cultural revival did not come from him; the noble estates of the Diet, in order to strengthen Hungarian national feeling and consciousness, urged the establishment of a scientific association, or, preferably, a national academy. The financial

means for such an undertaking were not readily available and Széchenyi volunteered to donate a year's income from his estates toward that end. Many others offered financial support and the academy became a reality. Széchenyi intended much more, however, than merely a cultural upswing. In a series of books (*Credit, World, Stadium*) he explored the reasons for Hungary's backward state.

He sent several reform proposals to the imperial chancellor KLEMENS VON METTERNICH, but the latter, in the grip of postrevolutionary conservatism, had little interest in reformist ideas. Széchenyi then launched his own initiatives, usually on the English model; he organized horse races, wrote a popular book about horses, established in Budapest a casino in which nobles of a progressive bent congregated, and soon casinos sprang up in many provincial cities.

The 1830 revolution in Paris and the Polish uprising against Russian rule of the same year deeply affected Széchenyi and gave impetus to his hitherto tentative ideas for the necessity for reform. He became ever more outspoken in his criticism of the feudal system, but his chief interest remained the promotion of native culture. He recognized that a national revival made the development of the Hungarian language, which had been losing ground to the Latin and the German, imperative, and he became a champion of neology, the Magyarization of foreign terms, the Hungarian version of which either did not exist or had fallen into disuse.

It was in 1830 that he published his book *Credit*, which attracted immediate attention. In 1828, he had applied for a bank loan to modernize his estate but was refused because of a hostile reaction from many conservative nobles to whom any measure curtailing feudal privilege, a measure Széchenyi advocated, was anathema. In his book he analyzed the adverse effects of the lack of investable capital for lack of credit. More progressive-minded landowners welcomed Széchenyi's ideas and some, especially the young Wesselényi, even proposed going beyond them, advocating, for instance, the involvement of peasants in the legislative process. Széchenyi, who above all wanted to avoid a confrontation with the government in VIENNA, turned his attention to politically less explosive activities. He planned, after sailing down the Danube as far as he could, to make Hungary the eastern end of a continuous waterway, connecting it to the west. It was at his legislative initiative that the first bridge between the cities of Buda and Pest, the Chain Bridge, was built and in the process he breached the nobility's freedom from all taxation by providing that nobles as well as commoners pay tolls when crossing the bridge. The Vienna government, honoring Széchenyi's moderate reforming activities, appointed him to various prestigious positions in the fields of transportation and communication. In the 1840s his political star began to sink as a much more radical reform movement, spearheaded largely by the gentry, began to gain ground and to attract to itself large numbers of the middle nobility.

The latter movement gained an exceptionally gifted and eloquent champion in the person of LOUIS KOSSUTH and for several years, until the outbreak of the revolution of 1848, the two men engaged in a spirited and not always friendly press debate over constitutional and other questions. One point of lively contention was that Széchenyi still trusted the high nobility to spearhead a gradual but persistent reform movement, whereas Kossuth regarded the aristocracy as hidebound and reactionary and put his faith in the lower nobility with whom the preservation of the old order never became an article of faith. Although it was Kossuth who dubbed Széchenyi "the greatest Hungarian," he also took issue with the latter's readiness to envision Hungary's future in close alliance with and under the aegis of the Habsburg monarchy. Kossuth mapped a far more independent course, and his bold visions culminated in Hungary's armed challenge to the Habsburgs in 1848 and 1849.

Széchenyi's role in the tumultuous March days of 1848 was an ambiguous one; although he championed a never clearly defined national independence, he was also ready to work to-

Count István Széchenyi *(Hungarian Museum of Photography)*

gether with Vienna and his vision of Hungary's future was within the imperial structure; had it not been for the presence of Kossuth and the radical elements around him, he may have had a salutary restraining influence on the headlong rush toward confrontation with the Habsburgs. In the short-lived Batthyány government of March 1848 Széchenyi was minister of finance. In September of that year he experienced an apparent mental collapse and was taken to the medical facilities at Döbling in Austria, where he remained for the next decade. In 1857 the interior minister ALEXANDER BACH, confident that imperial authority had been firmly reestablished, issued a pamphlet titled *Rückblick auf die jüngste Entwicklungsperiode Ungarns* (A retrospective glance at the most recent developmental phase of Hungary) Széchenyi responded to the pamphlet the next year with a pamphlet of his own, titled, *Ein Blick auf den Anonymen Rückblick* (A glance at the anonymous retrospective glance), assailing not only Bach but the person of the emperor as well. The writing was published in London. When it became known in Vienna, the government ordered a search of Széchenyi's house and, in the process, a good part of his papers were impounded. This action produced a new crisis in his mental and emotional condition. On April 8, 1860, he ended his life with a pistol shot in the head. The requiem for his salvation was attended by 80,000 people and was an occasion for new demonstrations against Habsburg rule. In death Széchenyi became a symbol of national independence.

Sztójay, Döme (1883–1946)

family name, Stojakovics. Hungarian military man and politician, ambassador to Berlin from December 1935 to March 1944, premier of Hungary under Nazi auspices from March 19 to August 29, 1944

His father was of Serb nationality, Greek Orthodox, and worked as an insurance agent. After graduating from military officer school and the Viennese military academy, Sztójay was assigned to the army general staff. In the First World War he served first as captain and then as major and later headed the operational section of the military command of BOSNIA-HERCEGOVINA. In the last two years of the war he headed the Balkan section of military intelligence. During the 1919 soviet regime he placed his services at its disposal in the belief that he was defending the country's territorial integrity against invading foreign armies. Between March and July 1919 he headed the intelligence and anti-espionage section of the Hungarian Red Army. After the collapse of the regime, he entered MIKLÓS HORTHY's "national army" and held several posts at the defense ministry. In 1925 he was assigned to the Berlin legation as military lecturer; from 1927 to 1933 he served as military attaché. In 1933, back in BUDAPEST, he became head of the defense ministry's presidential council. In December 1935 he was promoted to vice marshal and at the same time appointed minister to the Berlin legation. Despite his many promotions and responsible assignments, he was known to those around him as of mediocre abilities, but with a gift for ingratiating himself with superiors and subordinates alike. He was not a fanatic, had no great admiration for either Germans or Nazis, but, like so many others, was deeply impressed by ADOLF HITLER's spectacular successes. He sent perceptive and not overly biased reports to the foreign ministry in Budapest and he enjoyed the trust of the Nazi leadership in Germany. During the war he had unshakable faith in eventual German victory. When, in March 1944 Hitler decided to occupy Hungary to prevent her possible desertion from the common front, in agreement with the visiting Regent Horthy, he chose Sztójay to head a new government. As premier, Sztójay banned all opposition parties, introduced strict press censorship, and carried out a thorough purge in the state administration. With a series of new enlistments he raised the size of the Hungarian army fighting on the side of the Germans to 300,000. He presided over the deportation to Nazi death camps of some 600,000 Hungarian Jews. On August 29, 1944, Horthy, as a first step toward leaving the war, dismissed Sztójay and appointed a liberal-minded military man in his stead. After the war Sztójay was arrested as a war criminal, tried before a people's court, and condemned to death. He was executed by firing squad on August 22, 1946.

800,000. Similar devastations occurred elsewhere. Of the 40,000 inhabitants of the Protestant city of Magdeburg less than 5,000 remained alive after a siege and conquest by Catholic forces. The peace diminished both the possessions and the authority of the Habsburg monarch. The northern Netherlands, contested since the reign of Philip II (1556–98) became independent, and lands in Alsace, hitherto under Habsburg rule, were transferred to France. The peace also ended whatever significant authority the emperor had had in the Holy Roman Empire. It allowed each component to govern itself. In their own empire, however, the Habsburgs remained supreme. They had not been able to break Protestant power in Germany, but the Counter Reformation was largely triumphant in the Habsburg realm.

Tildy, Zoltán (1889–1961)

minister of the Calvinist Church in Hungary, politician, premier, president of the Hungarian republic

He studied theology at the University of Pápa, and also at the University of Belfast in Ireland. Returning to Hungary, he became a professor of theology, and subsequently a minister, in Pápa. During the First World War he entered politics, but in 1932 he returned to the ministry in the Calvinist Church. In 1930 he participated in the founding of the Independent Smallholders' Party. His 1931 run for a parliamentary seat was unsuccessful but he was elected in 1936 and retained his seat until 1944. In 1945 he was chosen president of the party. In the parliamentary elections of November in that year he was again elected to parliament as a Smallholder and, with his party having achieved an absolute majority at the polls, he was appointed premier. His political power, to be sure, was illusory, because by now the Communists, supported by the presence of a large Soviet occupation army, were in effective charge of affairs of state. In February 1946, when Hungary was proclaimed a republic, Tildy was chosen its first president. As such, reluctantly but with no recourse, he placed his

presidential powers at the disposal of the Communists. In July 1848 it proved convenient to use as a pretext the fact that his son-in-law, serving at the Cairo legation, had been found engaging in illegal activities, to ask for Tildy's resignation, which he duly tendered. He was placed under house arrest. During the short-lived Hungarian revolution of 1956, Tildy served as minister of state in the IMRE NAGY cabinet. For that "crime" he was later sentenced to a six-year prison term. He was pardoned in 1959 and lived in obscurity until his death two years later.

Tisza, Count István (1861–1918)

Hungarian politician, premier, one of the principal figures in the immediate pre-history of the First World War

Son of Premier Kálmán Tisza and of Ilona Degenfeld Schonburg, he had two brothers and a sister. In 1885 he married Ilona Tisza; they had a son and a daughter. He pursued his studies in law and economics at the universities of Berlin and Heidelberg. At the end of a one-year military service he was discharged as an officer; he decided on a career in the army, but his father vetoed the decision. For five years then he managed the family estate in Bihar County. From 1886 on he served in the lower house of parliament as a member of the Independence Party. In 1897 the emperor bestowed on him and his brothers the title of count. He became the president of a major bank and sat on the board of several corporations. His politics sought to promote an alliance between landed and financial wealth and he saw in the Dual Monarchy the most hospitable environment for such an alliance. He early perceived that the foreign policy of the monarchy, on a collision course with Russia, would eventually lead to war, and he urged timely preparations. As a parliamentary deputy he displayed his formidable debating skills in just such a debate when in 1889 a measure on the defense forces was being discussed. Until the turn of the 20th century his convictions were essentially liberal, but later he became a spokesman for conservative causes.

Count István Tisza *(Hungarian Museum of Photography)*

During his first premiership (November 1903 to June 1905) when his proposal for increasing enlistments ran into parliamentary obstructionism, he introduced a voting reform to prevent the delay of important measures. Firmly opposed to the nascent labor movement, in 1904 he crushed a railwaymen's strike. In January 1905 the legislative opposition to his policies formed a coalition and voted him no confidence. For months he remained acting premier nevertheless. In 1906 he disbanded his Independence Party and formed from its former stalwarts a new party, the Party of National Labor, which then earned a great victory at the polls. It was in these years that within Tisza's cherished economic alliance the balance of power shifted from the agrarian to the financial elite. He resisted attempts to undermine this new political force, as for instance a proposal to extend the franchise. In May 1912 he was elected president of the lower house with a mandate to implement military reforms. His

appointment was by no means consensual; there was vehement opposition to it from the benches as well as from the labor movement. He silenced both and put his program into place. He then forced a vote on special measures to be taken in case of war and carried it.

His second term as premier began in June 1913 and was marked by intense war preparations and the further curbing of liberal forces. Freedom of assembly and association were curtailed and the purview of juries was restricted. In October 1913, after the Second BALKAN WAR he advocated a strong stance against Serbia to restore the Dual Monarchy's damaged prestige. But when the war crisis of July 1914 erupted, he opposed hasty measures and an unduly harsh ultimatum to Serbia, as he judged international conditions unfavorable and feared a Romanian attack against TRANSYLVANIA while the Monarchy was engaged on other fronts. After sustained pressure from VIENNA and Berlin, at a cabinet meeting on July 19, he finally concurred with the decision to send Belgrade an exceptionally demanding ultimatum. War did ensue and no quick victory over Serbia was achieved. During the general war he urged close coordination of plans with Germany and the placing of the Dual Monarchy's internal forces on a complete war footing. But he was unwilling to make any concession to labor in order to gain its cooperation. The death of the aged emperor in November 1916 deprived him of his strongest support and the new king, Charles IV, looked on him with disfavor. Attacks on him within parliament and from the press became more numerous and when he refused to give up his opposition to the extension of the franchise he came in conflict with the sovereign and, on May 23, 1917, he had to resign. He had himself appointed commander of a cavalry regiment and went, first, to the Russian and, then, to the Italian front. On October 17, in parliament, he admitted that the war was lost; however, he did not foresee the outbreak of a revolution and resisted his family's urging to flee. On October 31, 1918, some soldiers, seeing in him the very symbol of the war and an enemy of all democratic reform, invaded his apartment and, in the course of an angry exchange, shot him to death.

Tito, Marshal (1892–1980)
(Josip Broz)

Yugoslav revolutionary politician, general secretary of the Yugoslav Communist Union and, after the Second World War, president of Yugoslavia

One of the most strong-willed, independent-minded, and durable national leaders in the post-1945 era, Josip Broz Tito was born on May 25, 1892, in a village in CROATIA, then part of the Austro-Hungarian Dual Monarchy. His parents, Franjo Broz, a Croatian, and Maria Javaršek, a Slovenian, had 15 children born to them, only seven of whom survived infancy. Josip was born seventh, into the straitened conditions of Balkan peasantry. He had to work on his father's farm from an early age but must have shown intellectual promise because he was allowed to attend primary school until age 12. Even after he was apprenticed, at age 15, in the locksmithing trade, he attended night school and took courses in history, geography, and foreign languages. After becoming a journeyman locksmith, he practiced his trade in various locations within the Dual Monarchy and even in Germany.

In 1913 he began his compulsory two-year military service, which, because of the outbreak of the Great War, was extended to 1916; but in that year he became a prisoner of war in Russia. After the Bolsheviks seized power, he joined the Red Guard and stayed within its ranks until his return to his homeland in September 1920. He joined what was then called the Yugoslav Communist Party and became an active trade unionist. For his role in organizing strikes and carrying out agitation, he was several times arrested and, in 1928, sentenced to five years in prison. After his release authorities confined him to his native village, but he defied the ban and, to be able to move about more freely, adopted a new name, Tito. In 1934, as a member of the Politburo of the Yugoslav Communist Party, he was sent to Moscow to work in the Yugoslav section of the Comintern. He returned home in 1936 and was elected secretary general of the party in 1937. He revitalized the upper echelons by appointing to key positions men "who had been hardened in the field of struggle," as he proudly asserted.

It was the Second World War and the invasion of Yugoslavia by Axis powers that marked the beginning of Tito's rise to political prominence. Resistance to German and Italian occupation forces began early but at first the illegal Četnik movement, organized and commanded by the royalist Mihailović Draža, was in the forefront of the struggle and had the backing of the Yugoslav government in exile in London, as well as London and Washington. Gradually a communist resistance movement, the National Liberation Partisan Detachments, commonly known as the Partisans, gained the upper hand in the fight against the German occupiers. When Yugoslavia was liberated by the advancing Red Army, Tito, by combining elements of both the Četniks and the Partisans, emerged as head of the provisional Yugoslav government. In the autumn of 1945, after the Communist Party earned a great victory at the polls and King Peter II, still in exile, abdicated, Tito became the effective head of a Yugoslavia under Communist Party control.

In the immediate postwar years Tito, as other satellite leaders in Eastern Europe, remained loyal and even subservient to Moscow's authority; he visited the USSR every year. The Yugoslav constitution was modeled on the Soviet constitution of 1936, industry was nationalized, and the government took energetic steps to exclude bourgeois elements from economic life. It closely coordinated its foreign policy with that of Moscow. Nevertheless, disagreements between the two governments developed early. They might conceivably have been adjusted had it not been for Stalin's tyrannical temperament and his determination to have absolute control in his newly gained Eastern European sphere. He expected satellite countries to organize their economies according to the needs of the Soviet Union and such an arrangement would have assigned to Yugoslavia essentially an agricultural status, something Tito was not ready to accept. He acted independently in Balkan affairs too, seeking to keep out Western influence according to his own prescription, and also aided Greek communist insurgents, though Stalin's infamous "percentage deal" with Churchill, concluded in October 1944, had assigned Greece into the British sphere and excluded interference by Communist states. In the fall of 1947, when the COMINFORM was formed under Soviet tutelage to coordinate the work of Communist parties in Europe, Tito still enjoyed the position of first among the non-Soviet Communist Party heads and the headquarters of the Cominform was placed in Belgrade. But in successive months exchanges between Tito and Stalin, the latter speaking largely through his foreign minister Molotov, grew ever more heated. After Tito gave Soviet advisers their walking papers, a rupture was inevitable. A special meeting of the Cominform in late June 1948 read the Yugoslav party out of its ranks and there began immediately the most vituperative campaign of denunciation by Moscow, and by satellites loyal to her, against the Yugoslav party and Tito personally. By standing his ground, and treating Stalinists in his party with the same merciless discrimination Stalin treated his own "unreliables," Tito was able to defy Stalin's worst threats; in fact, of the many fiascoes Stalin suffered in the closing years of his life—his inability to stymie the Marshall Plan and to prevent the regeneration of Western Europe, the failure of his Berlin blockade, his gross miscalculation in unleashing the Korean War—the futile campaign against Tito was probably the most humiliating. Stalin had boasted, "I shake a little finger and there will be no Tito," yet when he died in March 1953, Tito was more firmly entrenched than ever and had established profitable contacts with the West.

One of the first foreign policy moves on the part of the post-Stalin Soviet leadership was to seek rapprochement with the Yugoslav party. Tito responded slowly and it took two years before normal relations were resumed on the basis that the Soviet party recognized the equality of status of parties in other socialist states with that of the Soviet Union. But the brutal Soviet suppression of the Hungarian revolution

of 1956, although Tito had not expressly objected to it, led to a new worsening of relations, as Moscow blamed the Yugoslav party for fostering the spirit of defiance against the Soviet Union, and Tito on his part accused the Soviet leaders of violating their safe conduct promise to Hungarian "reform Communists" who had been active in the revolution and after its termination had taken refuge at the Yugoslav embassy. Also, Tito's "Yugoslav road to socialism" was not much more palatable to the post-Stalin Soviet leadership than it had been while the dictator was alive. In foreign policy, while Tito refused the Western offer that he join NATO, by 1953 he had become indirectly connected with it by an alliance, in 1953, with Turkey and Greece for mutual defense.

Tito sought to benefit from his country's relative independence from either bloc by proclaiming the virtues of "nonalignment," in defiance of the so-called Two Camps concept, proclaimed in the Stalin years by Andrey Zhdanov, which held that there was no third option between the "capitalist-imperialist," and the "socialist-democratic" camps. In 1954 he visited India, early in 1955 Burma, and in 1956 Egypt, to emphasize his affinity with countries not belonging to any power bloc.

Internally, he continued the economic model started in the 1950s, largely authored by his close political confidante Edward Kardelj, and referred to as self-management, the very feature the Soviets so objected to, marked by growing decentralization and the formation of workers' councils made responsible for production. After a decade of experimentation the system proved successful in the 1960s and 1970s, though a good part of the prosperity in the latter decade was due to heavy borrowing abroad.

Of Tito's personal life little is known. He was thrice married: during the Russian civil war to a 16-year-old Russian girl, Pelaghia Belousnova, who, after their return to Yugoslavia, bore him a son, Žarko; she died in 1938. In 1940 Tito married a Slovene woman, Berta Has, a marriage that ended in divorce after the Second World War, having produced another son, Miško. In

1952 he married a Serbian woman, Jovanka Budisavljević, to whom he was still married when he died on May 4, 1980.

Transylvania

At present the name refers to the province that Romania gained from Hungary in the TREATY OF TRIANON after the First World War. It covers a little over 100,000 square kilometers, but historically the name denotes a much smaller area (about 57,000 square kilometers), bounded by the eastern and southern Carpathians and a central mountain range. The root of its Hungarian name (Erdély) means, roughly, "beyond the forest," as does its Latin name, *Ultrasilvania terra.*

In ancient times the area was crisscrossed by nomadic tribes, each displacing the one before it; when in the second century A.D. the Roman emperor Traianus conquered it, he attached it to his empire under the name Dacia, derived from the name of its inhabitants at the time. After the collapse of the Roman Empire in the west, the movement of peoples through Transylvania continued, but only the Magyars (Hungarians), invading the CARPATHIAN BASIN in 896, were able to achieve its political organization. In time a coherent Hungarian population settled in central Transylvania; in its southeastern corner lived the Székelys, possibly remnants of the Hunnish host that in the fifth century A.D. populated the province and spoke a dialect similar to Hungarian. (The very name Hungarian is presumed to be a contraction of Hun-Ugrian). King St. Stephen in the year 1009 established a Transylvanian bishopric. In the 12th century large groups of Saxons loyal to the Hungarian crown were settled in the province. In order to tame the heathen Cumans in southern Transylvania, King András II in 1211 invited the Teutonic Knights, who were pursuing Christianizing missions, into the Barcza region; 13 years later he expelled them for acting too independently. The first written mention of Romanians in the province dates from 1166; from that time on they arrived in successive waves. Their chief occupation was the rearing and tending of sheep.

As early as 1479 Turks coming from the Balkans invaded Transylvania. They were at first beaten back and a number of towns and churches, anticipating further incursions, were fortified. Several religious orders, the Benedictines, the Dominicans, the Franciscans, established monasteries, which became centers of learning and culture.

After the BATTLE OF MOHÁCS in 1526 and the Turkish conquest of Buda in 1541, Hungary became divided into three parts: the western strip fell under the rule of the Habsburgs who had inherited the crown of Hungary (as well as of BOHEMIA, Moravia, and Silesia) when the young king LAJOS II died at Mohács; the central region became part of the Ottoman Empire; Transylvania achieved a precarious independence. The three Transylvanian nations (Hungarians, Saxons, Székelys), in 1542 elected one GEORGE MARTINUZZI their viceroy; he played a principal role in separating Transylvania from the Hungarian kingdom. With the concurrence of the Porte, under Martinuzzi's tutelage an infant king, John Sigismund, son of János Szapolyai, who had challenged the Habsburg succession to the Hungarian throne after the Battle of Mohács, became king. But by a later agreement at Speyer (1570), John Sigismund abdicated as king of Hungary and took the title, "Prince of Transylvania and of parts of Hungary by the Grace of God," on the understanding that, should he die without a male heir, Transylvania would revert to Hungary and be subject to the authority of its (Habsburg) kings. But upon John Sigismund's death the Transylvanian estates, in violation of the Speyer Agreement, elected another nobleman, ISTVÁN BÁTHORI, prince; supported by the Turks, he was subsequently (1575) elected king of Poland as well. He set up his court in that country and let his brother Kristof rule Transylvania. This was the time when the so-called Partium, the eastern counties of Hungary proper, was added to the territory of Transylvania. It was also the time when continuous migrations from Moldova beyond the Carpathians established a series of Romanian settlements. The rulers of the province were known for their great cultural, as well as religious, toleration. Four established religions (Catholic, Lutheran, Calvinist, Unitarian) enjoyed equal status and even Greek Catholicism, practiced by the Romanians, was accepted. Between 1593 (this date is uncertain because desultory warfare had gone on for some time), and 1610 renewed hostilities between the Habsburgs and the Turks engulfed Transylvania and brought bloody invasion by imperial forces as well as widespread pestilence. The realization took hold, with long-term historical consequences, that Austrian rule of Hungary must be counterbalanced by an area of Hungarian sovereignty, and in the circumstances Transylvania alone could fulfill that role. A series of Hungarian princes occupied the throne of the province and one of them, GÁBOR BETHLEN, fought against the Habsburgs in the THIRTY YEARS' WAR. But in the decades following that war, owing to adventurous policies by Prince György Rákoczi II, Transylvania once again became a battleground of contending forces from without and within. It took decades for the belligerents to become sufficiently exhausted for a measure of stability to return to the province.

After the Turks were by degrees expelled from Hungary, the title of prince of Transylvania was bestowed upon the Habsburg ruler. But early in 1704 the Transylvanian estates once again demonstrated their independence by electing FERENC RÁKOCZI II prince of Transylvania, and he became a standard-bearer of the Hungarian aspiration to be free of Habsburg domination. After initial successes Rákoczi's ill-equipped forces were overcome by superior imperial armies and the freedom fight ended in failure. From this time on the Habsburgs, presumably to limit Hungarian national aspirations, tried to endow Transylvania with special status. MARIA THERESA in 1765 elevated it to the rank of a principality, but she also brought the Catholic COUNTER REFORMATION to the province, without, however, breaching the legal equality of the four established religions.

By the end of the 18th century the Romanians were in the majority in Transylvania and, in 1791, demanded to be recognized as the fourth nation. JOSEPH II, in his reforming zeal, abolished the whole system of nations, divided Transylvania into counties for administrative purposes, and made German the sole official language. But before his death he canceled these measures and the competition of nations in Transylvania was resumed. The strong nationalistic tendencies in the first half of the 19th century strove to make Hungary one integrated nation, with Transylvania as an organic province and Magyar the official language. The effort met with the same lack of success as the Austrian initiatives. The revolutions of 1848 produced centrifugal tendencies: Hungarians, Saxons, Romanians were all seeking to achieve their own ends, and imperial troops struggled to ensure uniform Habsburg domination. With the defeat of the revolution, Hungarian parliamentary resolutions integrating Transylvania into the kingdom lost their validity; by order of the victorious Habsburgs Transylvania was administered separately from Hungary proper under a plenipotentiary governor appointed by Vienna.

The Great Compromise of 1867 changed this. Transylvania became an integral part of the Hungarian half of the Dual Monarchy. A parliamentary statute of 1868 spoke of a united Hungarian political nation while at the same time guaranteeing the freedom of the use of languages spoken in respective provinces. The idea of a united political nation remained a chimera, however. The chief political arm of the Romanians, the Romanian National Party, demanded autonomy, especially as the census of 1910 showed that of Transylvania's 5,260,382 inhabitants, 2,829,925, or 53.8 percent, spoke the Romanian language. In the First World War Romania, an independent state since 1878, comprised of the Trans-Carpathian provinces of Wallachia and Moldova, by a secret treaty of 1916, entered the war on the side of the Entente in full anticipation of gaining Transylvania in case of victory. Indeed the TREATY OF TRIANON of 1920 transferred all of Transylvania, as well as the Bánát of Temesvár, to Romania, which thereby nearly doubled its size. Hungary lost, to the Romanians alone, territory larger than the truncated central core that remained with postwar Hungary.

Trianon, Treaty of (June 4, 1920)

The formal treaty terminating Hungary's belligerence in the First World War and establishing her new, greatly diminished borders. At the time of its conclusion the ethnic minorities within "historic Hungary" had declared separation from the mother country: Slovaks had become part of the new Czechoslovak republic, Croatians had joined the United Kingdom of the Serbs, Slovenes, and Croats, and the victorious powers recognized the borders of these new states, thereby predetermining Hungary's frontiers in these directions. The TREATY OF ST. GERMAIN with Austria had decreed plebiscites in the Burgenland and eventually that strip of land of 4,000 square kilometers and a population of 292,000 went to Austria. Only the fate of Transylvania with its majority of Romanians was as yet undecided. The determination of that border in turn was influenced by the fact that in an attempt to overthrow the soviet government set up by the Hungarian Béla Kun, the Romanians, with Entente blessing, invaded Hungary in the spring of 1919, drove all the way to the Tisza River, and, for a brief while, occupied even BUDAPEST. Although they were forced to withdraw from that advanced line, the final frontier was drawn well beyond the perimeters of historic Transylvania. In the end, of the 282,000 square kilometers of Greater Hungary, in which 124,000 square kilometers were inhabited by ethnic Hungarians, only 93,000 square kilometers were left to newly independent Hungary. Hungarians numbering 3,200,000 found themselves in neighboring states. The Hungarian army was to be limited to 35,000 long-term volunteers.

Troppau, Congress of   See CONCERT OF EUROPE.

V

Verona, Congress of See CONCERT OF
EUROPE.

Vienna

Capital city of Austria; at the turn of the 20th
century the fifth-largest metropolis in the world.
Its development as a city began in the first century A.D. when it was a Celtic town called Vindobona (White Field); Roman conquerors
turned it into a garrison town. German, Avar,
and Magyar invaders followed in waves. The
town was part of Charlemagne's empire and the
area east of it served as an eastern march against
future invasions. A record from 881 refers to the
city as Wenia; a later one from 1030 as Wienis.
Ideally located at the intersection of trade routes
from east to west and south to north, the city
benefited from the continuous flow of trade,
especially after the Crusades. It was first selected
as the seat of government in 1146, and in 1189
it received a municipal charter granting it
administrative, judicial, and commercial rights.
The walling in of the city by fortifications, which
became its most conspicuous feature, began
early in the 13th century; tradition has it that it
was financed by the ransom extracted for the
release of King Richard I of England from Austrian captivity.

Although Vienna prospered conspicuously in
the Middle Ages, the peak of its affluence and
enlightenment was reached during the Renaissance; its university, founded in 1356, was a
center of Renaissance learning. Cultural development was interrupted and then halted by the
coming of the Reformation and the religious and
cultural intolerance that followed in its wake.

CHARLES V of the House of Habsburg, overwhelmed by his responsibilities as king of Spain
and the Americas, as well as of the Netherlands
and parts of Italy, ceded governance of Austria
to his brother FERDINAND I as regent. Vienna
looked unkindly at the rule of a perceived foreigner and sought to pursue its liberties in opposition to his edicts. In 1526 Ferdinand in an
ordinance deprived the city of much of its special rights. Soon he faced a greater crisis than
that of Viennese defiance. The Ottoman Turks,
having conquered Hungary, besieged the city in
1529. The fortifications proved too powerful for
the Turks to breach and they retreated with the
advent of winter. Walling in the city proved
providential after all.

When Ferdinand was elected Holy Roman
Emperor in 1558, Vienna regained many of its
prerogatives. However, the religious question
continued to rankle. Luther's Reformation had
attracted many Viennese, but the PEACE OF AUGS-
BURG of 1555, although it allowed Lutheranism in
some states of the Holy Roman Empire, left it to
the ruling prince to decide which of the two
authorized religions he wished to practice, by
himself and by his subjects. As the Austrian ruler
chose Catholicism, there was no place for Lutherans in Vienna and many had to leave.

The true development of the city began only
when the Turkish menace was finally lifted and
the Peace of Karlowitz of 1699 put Ottoman
power at a safe distance. In the opening decades
of the 18th century feverish construction began
outside the congested Innere Stadt, and, to protect these new suburbs, a second line of fortifications was erected. By now the Habsburg
Empire had been enlarged by the addition of

Hungary, BOHEMIA, Moravia, and Silesia, with Galicia soon to be added, and there was an influx of immigrants from these provinces to Vienna, many attracted by fledgling industries that found a home in the city.

At the end of the century the Austrian empire was the first to enter the war against revolutionary France and for the next two decades, with some interruptions, the state of war continued within successive coalitions. The protracted warfare brought a great deal of economic misery, partial bankruptcy, and inflation, but the commanding position of Vienna within the empire remained unchallenged. After the final defeat of France Vienna became the venue of the great gathering of crowned heads, the CONGRESS OF VIENNA, in September 1814, called to sort out the tangled affairs left by the French Revolutionary and Napoleonic Wars.

Despite the economic hardships, and despite the repressive regime instituted by imperial chancellor KLEMENS VON METTERNICH, Vienna remained a rich cultural center; its denizens had an affinity for esthetic appreciation, especially in music and art, and a boundless capacity to enjoy its pleasures. By 1845 the city had a population of 430,000 (the whole empire at the time had some 32 million inhabitants). But until the 1850s it was still hemmed in by its defensive walls, outside of which by royal edict no construction was permitted. The army insisted that the surrounding area, the Glacis, be preserved as a military assembly field. All this changed when in 1857 emperor FRANCIS JOSEPH I, in a rescript addressed to interior minister ALEXANDER BACH, stated that, "It is my will that the regions beyond the city walls be opened to construction." During this so-called *Gründerzeit* (foundation era) enormous architectural enterprises refashioned the face of the city. With the Ring, a huge boulevard, following the line of the demolished walls, the new bourgeoisie constructed a veritable *via triumphalis* for itself. The parliament building was erected in the style of ancient Greek temples, city hall in the Gothic style, the stock market and many banks in Italian Renaissance style. The employment of

new building techniques made possible a remarkably short period between the commencement and ending of construction, generally between six and eight years. In 1890 the recently built suburbs became integral parts of the city; then the area past the Danube was integrated, giving Vienna 21 districts. Outstanding merits in making Vienna a truly modern and yet esthetically pleasing city belonged to its mayor KARL LUEGER, who compensated for his many political follies by leaving a lasting memorial to the explosively creative *Gründerzeit*.

It was in Vienna that the fateful decision for war against Serbia was made in July 1914, unleashing the First World War. During the war refugees from all parts of the empire once again flooded the city and its population grew to over 2 million. It was also in Vienna that, in November 1918, after the fall of the House of Habsburg, the Austrian republic, shorn of all its non-German territories, was proclaimed. Under the guidance and leadership of an invigorated Social Democratic Party, numerous social and economic reforms were introduced. One result was that Vienna, whose population was almost one-third of that of the country, became ideologically separated from the countryside and came to be referred to as Red Vienna. As such, the city could not maintain itself against the overwhelmingly Catholic and conservative provinces, and Social Democratic strength was destroyed in February 1934 by then chancellor ENGELBERT DOLLFUSS. Four years later, as a result of Hitler's summary *Anschluss,* Vienna ceased to be the capital of an independent country and was but one of the metropolises of Greater Germany.

Vienna Awards

Two German-Italian arbitral awards that revised in Hungary's favor the borders drawn at Trianon with Czechoslovakia and Romania, respectively.

FIRST AWARD

The MUNICH AGREEMENT, whose primary disposition was the transfer of the Sudetenland from

Czechoslovakia to Germany, also stipulated that the four parties to the agreement arbitrate territorial disputes between Czechoslovakia and Poland, on the one hand, and Czechoslovakia and Hungary, on the other, if direct negotiations between the parties for border rectification did not produce agreement within three months. The Poles gained their claims to Teschen and Trans-Olza by way of an ultimatum in the days after Munich. Talks between the Hungarian and Czechoslovak delegations began on October 9, 1938, on a boat moored in the Danube. The Hungarians demanded 14,153 square kilometers, which the Czechs refused to grant. They offered 1,800 square kilometers; this they later increased to 5,405 square kilometers. Talks broke down on October 14. German foreign minister Ribbentrop tried to mediate and at his persuasion, on October 20, Czechoslovakia offered 11,300 square kilometers, with a population of 740,000, of whom 680,000 were Hungarians, but her map left a number of Hungarian-speaking cities within her borders. Hungary proposed plebiscites in the disputed areas, an offer the Czechoslovaks rejected. Thereupon the Hungarians asked for arbitration. Britain and France declared their disinterestedness and Hungary and Czechoslovakia agreed to request German-Italian arbitration. On November 2, in VIENNA, Hungarian foreign minister Kánya, Czechoslovak foreign minister Chvalkovsky, German foreign minister Ribbentrop, and Italian foreign minister Ciano met in the Golden Room of the Belvedere Palace. Ribbentrop and Ciano awarded to Hungary the southern strip of Slovakia and the southwestern portion of Ruthenia of Hungarian habitation. The grant comprised 11,927,000 square kilometers with 896,299 inhabitants. Later corrections increased the area to 12,012,000 square kilometers and 1,057,323,000 inhabitants, including refugees. On November 5 the Hungarian occupation of the ceded areas began. On November 18 the government announced its intention to retake all of Ruthenia, but Italian protests stopped the action.

SECOND AWARD

When France surrendered to Germany on June 22, 1940, Alsace-Lorraine again became a part of Germany. Four days later the Soviets, although they did not state a connection, demanded of Romania the session of Bessarabia and northern Bukovina, both of which had been part of Russia before the First World War. The Romanians, receiving no encouragement from the Germans to resist, yielded. Starting June 28, Soviet troops began their occupation of the provinces. The previous day the Hungarian cabinet had decided that if Romania complied with the Soviet demand, Hungary would insist on satisfying her own territorial demands. That day the supreme defense council mobilized the national forces, but the cabinet held back on military action before Germany's attitude was ascertained. On July 10, Premier PÁL TELEKI visited Hitler and asked him to support Hungary's claim to two-thirds of Transylvania. German pressure prevailed on the Romanians to start direct talks with Hungary; these began on August 16. The Hungarian delegation asked for a southern frontier that ran along the Maros River, with a southeastern protuberance to embrace the land of the Székelys, a tribe whose members spoke Hungarian. The Romanians refused and proposed a population exchange with small territorial concessions. On August 24 the talks broke down. Two days later the Hungarian government decided to attack Romania. Operations were to begin on the 28th, but on the 27th the Romanians asked for arbitration and the attack was canceled. The arbitration once again took place in Vienna. Hungary was represented by Premier Teleki, himself a Transylvanian, and Foreign Minister Csáky, Romania by its foreign minister Manoilescu. Ribbentrop and Ciano were the arbitrators. When the award was announced, on August 30, the land of the Székelys, northern Transylvania, and some other parts, altogether 43,104 square kilometers with 2,185,564 inhabitants, were transferred to Hungary. After border rectifications, 400 square kilometers were added. Neither side was happy, but repossession of the territories began on September 5. The Hungarian parliament enacted the annexation into law on October 8.

When in the autumn of 1944 Transylvania fell under Soviet occupation, it was again made part of Romania. The January 1945 armistice between Hungary and the Soviet Union, and the Paris Peace Treaty of 1947 between Hungary and the victorious powers declared the two Vienna Awards invalid and restored the TREATY OF TRIANON frontiers.

Vogelsang, Karl von (1818–1890)

principal founder of the Austrian Christian Socialist Party

A scion of a Mecklenburg Protestant family, Baron von Vogelsang converted to Catholicism and chose to spend his life in Austria. Appalled by the growing destitution of the lower classes that stood in such stark contrast to the prosperity of the middle class produced by the economic boom of the closing years of the 19th century, Vogelsang tried to counteract the appeal of the Social Democratic Party and marxism by advocating a state policy that, motivated by Christian charity, protected the poor from capitalist exploitation. Deeply hostile to capitalism, he condemned *Zinsknechtschaft* (slavery to interest on loans) and wanted the state actively to promote a social contract that would mitigate the gulf between the social classes. Under his influence, and under that of a group of aristocrats led by Prince Alois Liechtenstein, the government, between 1885 and 1887, enacted a number of reforms, limiting hours of work, prohibiting the employment of children under the age of 12, and reducing the hours of work for women to eight a day. Other reforms were largely modeled on German social legislation in the 1880s.

W

Waldheim, Kurt (1918–   )

Austrian politician and statesman, minister for foreign affairs (1968–70), Secretary General of the United Nations (1972–77), and president of Austria (1986–92)

An international figure of wide learning and respectful recognition, his notoriety in the end stemmed not from his accomplishments but from the controversy surrounding his activities in the Second World War, which served as evidence that no public figure can for long escape the shadow of any association with ADOLF HITLER's Third Reich.

He was born in Sankt Andra-Warden west of VIENNA on December 21, 1918. Following his graduation from high school, he entered the University of Vienna and earned a doctorate in jurisprudence in 1944. After the war he earned a second degree from the Consular Academy in Vienna.

Waldheim entered the diplomatic service in 1945, and in the years between 1948 and 1951 he served in Paris and later in Ottawa. From 1951 to 1955 he headed the personnel department of the Austrian Foreign Ministry in Vienna. When Austria was accepted into the United Nations in 1958, Waldheim was a member of its delegation, and between 1964 and 1968 he was his country's permanent representative. In 1968 he was appointed foreign minister of Austria. After a two-year tenure in that post, in 1970 he ran for the presidency of Austria but was defeated. In December 1971 he was appointed to a five-year term as Secretary General of the United Nations, a post to which, after the expiration of the term he was reelected in 1976, despite protests from developing coun-

tries. When he ran for a third term in 1981, a Chinese veto prevented his reelection.

Even though very much in the limelight, especially in the course of his many travels as Secretary General, trying to resolve persistent conflicts in places like South Africa, Cyprus, South Asia, and the Middle East, with more diligence than success to be sure, his past, especially during the Hitler years, remained unexplored, even though documents relating to it were readily available. By 1986, when he ran for the second time for the Austrian presidency, he was able to campaign on the slogan, "A man whom the world trusts." Possibly to present himself as a man of history, he had, in 1985, published his autobiography, *Im Glaspalast der Weltpolitik* (the English version titled *In the Eye of the Storm*), in which he glossed over his war years by asserting that after being wounded from shrapnel on the Russian front in 1942, he was allowed to return to his studies in law. "Following my study leave and the recuperation of my leg I was called up again for active duty. Shortly before the end of the war I was in the area of Trieste."

An Austrian boulevard journal reported in March 1986, two months before the scheduled presidential election was to take place on May 4, that Waldheim, upon being recalled to service, was posted in the Balkan region and served under General Alexander Löhr who, as commanding general for the region of Greece, Serbia, and Croatia, had warred on Serbian partisan units in the ruthless manner in which such conflicts were generally waged on both sides. He reportedly also supervised the deportation of over 40,000 Greek Jews to death camps to Germany. (Löhr, after escaping from the Balkans

AUSTRO-HUNGARIAN EMPIRE
1522–1918

August 1522

Treaty of Brussels. Emperor Charles V of the House of Habsburg, king of Spain, Austria, and several other countries, bestows upon his brother Ferdinand his Austrian lands, thus separating the Austrian from the Spanish line of Habsburgs.

August 1526

Battle of Mohács. Disastrous defeat of Hungarian forces by invading Turks. Death of Lajos II, king of Hungary and Bohemia.

October 1526

Bohemian estates elect Ferdinand of Habsburg, archduke of Austria, king of Czech lands.

November 1526

Hungarian estates elect János Szapolyai, prince of Transylvania, king of Hungary.

December 1526

Pro-Habsburg Hungarian estates, hoping for military help against Turks, elect Ferdinand of Habsburg king of Hungary.

1526–29

Repeated clashes between forces of Ferdinand and Szapolyai. Latter seeks and obtains Turkish support for his claim to the throne of Hungary.

September 1529

Sultan Suleiman II of Ottoman Empire besieges Vienna. Lifts siege a month later because of poor weather conditions and returns to Constantinople.

April 1532

Suleiman II leads new attack against Vienna, is held up by heroic defense of the Hungarian fortress of Kőszeg and abandons campaign.

February 1538

Ferdinand I and Szapolyai, still rivals for the Hungarian throne, conclude Peace of Várad, dividing Hungary between authority of the two, Szapolyai to rule the eastern part of the country (Transylvania) and Ferdinand the western. Agreement provides that upon death of Szapolyai, all Hungary passes to Ferdinand or his heir.

After years of sporadic fighting, mainly on Hungarian soil,

June 1547

Vienna and the Porte conclude five-year peace. Treaty formalizes trisection of Hungary, into self-governing Transylvania in the east, a Turkish-occupied center, and western strip of Transdanubia under Habsburg rule.

1564–76

Maximilian II of Habsburg takes throne of Austria and of Holy Roman Empire. Devoutly Catholic, he nevertheless shows marked tolerance toward Protestantism, which gains impetus under his reign.

May 1566
Suleiman II launches still another attack against Hungary.

September 5, 1566
Suleiman II dies.

February 1568
Maximilian II of Habsburg buys peace from the Porte on basis of territorial status quo, but he is obliged to pay heavy annual tribute.

1576–1612
Rudolf II of Habsburg succeeds Maximilian II. Ineffectual ruler and Holy Roman Emperor. Under his reign sharp resurgence of religious conflict in lands of the Austrian Empire.

1578–80
Start of Counter Reformation in Austrian, Hungarian, and Bohemian lands. Under Rudolf's protection and with his encouragement, intensive Jesuit influence in education. Large-scale Protestant emigration.

1593
New Turkish offensive, start of Fifteen Years' War.

May 1594 through 1597
Peasant revolts in Upper Austria, presumably in defense of Protestantism, but more likely in protest to feudal oppression. Severely put down. Hungarian estates, now largely Protestant, place themselves in open opposition to Rudolf II and his militant Counter Reformation. They find a gifted leader in Transylvanian prince István Bocskai, who organizes an army of *hajduk,* shiftless but ferocious peasants and shepherds, and earns numerous victories.

June 1606
Peace of Vienna between Rudolf II and Bocskai. It guarantees free religious exercise to Protestants and concessions to Hungarian self-rule.

November 1606
With Bocskai's good offices, Vienna and the Porte conclude Peace of Zsitvatorok, ending Fifteen Years' War.

June 25, 1608
Rudolf forced to abdicate in favor of his brother Matthias.

July 1615
Peace of Vienna, extending the Peace of Zsitvatorok by 20 years.

May 23, 1618
Revolt of Czech estates in Prague. Habsburg representatives, seeking to bring Hussite Bohemian nobles to heel, thrown out of window of Hradčany Palace. Thirty-member council set up to conduct Bohemian affairs of state. Jesuits expelled. Beginning of Thirty Years' War.

March 20, 1619
Death of Matthias. He is succeeded by a cousin. Ferdinand II.

August 1619
Czech estates declare their Austrian king, Ferdinand II, deposed and elect Frederick of the Palatinate, son-in-law of James I of England, king.

November 8, 1620
Battle of White Mountain. Austrian imperial forces decisively defeat Czech insurrectionists, putting drastic end to Bohemian bid for independence.

1627
Vernewerte Decree. Deprives Bohemian estates of right to elect sovereign unless current (Habsburg) ruling line, on male *or* female side, becomes extinct.

May 1635
Jesuit Péter Pázmány founds school in Nagyszombat, in western Hungary. It later becomes a university named for him.

December 16, 1645

Peace of Linz, between Transylvanian prince György Rákóczi and Austrian emperor Leopold II. Concluded after protracted fighting between Rákóczi's Protestant forces supported by the Porte on one hand and Austrian imperial forces on the other. It assures religious freedom to Protestants, extending that freedom to areas previously excluded from such guarantee, agricultural towns, and villages.

October 1648

Peace of Westphalia ends Thirty Years' War.

1660s

These years are marked by growing Hungarian antagonism to Habsburg rule, in part because of resentment over the lackadaisical Austrian conduct of the war against the Turks, a war fought almost exclusively on Hungarian soil; but increasing royal demands for taxes, as well as religious conflicts, also play a part.

June 1663

Renewed Turkish campaign against Hungarian territory. By year's end a number of forts and towns in northern Hungary fall to invaders.

August 1664

Leopold I, even though he had just inflicted great defeat on Turkish army, in the Peace of Vasvár allows Turks to keep all their recent conquests and concedes Turkish dominion over Transylvania. During the rest of the year many Hungarian nobles begin to organize under leadership of Ferenc Wesselényi, and after his death in March 1667, of Péter Zrinyi. They seek Turkish support for their cause of depriving the Habsburgs of sovereignty over Hungary.

1665

For the first time in Austrian history all the diverse provinces under the Habsburg crown, hitherto ruled by different members of the family, placed under single authority of emperor.

April–December 1671

Vastly superior imperial forces crush Hungarian uprising and execute leaders. This marks beginning of grassroots resistance to Habsburgs. Hungarian escapees from imperial revenge roam countryside and wage guerrilla warfare.

The Porte, encouraged by the sporadic success of the insurrectionists, which it interprets as Vienna's inability to wage major military operations, decides on a new challenge to Austrian power.

June 1683

Turkish forces besiege and encircle Vienna. Leopold and his court flee to Linz. Leopold is able, however, to secure alliance of Polish king John III Sobieski and Bavarian elector Maximilian, both of whom send troops to relieve Vienna. Pope Innocent XI provides diplomatic support.

September 1, 1683

Decisive battle under walls of Vienna between Turkish and united Christian forces. Latter earn great victory. A slow steady retreat of Turkish power from Austrian and Hungarian soil begins. But Hungarian defiance of Habsburgs continues.

January 1684

Leopold I offers amnesty to Hungarian rebels who take oath of loyalty to him. Many counties and free cities accept the offer.

March 1684

Holy League of Leopold I, Pope Innocent XI, Polish king John III Sobieski, and the State of Venice against the Turks is formed.

September 1684

Buda Castle, center of Hungarian political authority, held by Turks, falls to forces of Holy League.

September 1697

Battle of Zenta. Forces of imperial general Eugene of Savoy surprise and massacre Turkish forces at the latter cross Tisza River.

September 1698

Emperor Leopold I summons to Vienna the secular and ecclesiastical lords of Hungary to announce to them that annual taxes are increased from 2 million to 4 million, two-thirds to be paid by serfs, one-third by nobles.

January 26, 1699

Peace of Karlowitz between Porte and Holy League concluded. Hungary, except for Temesköz, an enclave in the south, evacuated by Turkish forces. The Porte for the first time recognizes Habsburg sovereignty over Transylvania, but the province continues self-governing.

During last phases of war against Turkey, then following the Treaty of Karlowitz, Vienna, relieved of worry over Hungarian resistance, begins to lay heavy burdens on the population, nobles and commoners alike. Thousands of soldiers, demobilized after the deactivation of border forts, are cast adrift. The peasantry, bonded and free, is charged with billeting and feeding imperial soldiery and their horses (*oralis et equilis portio*).

On the theory that a nation is governed best when of a single religion, Habsburgs in many areas confiscate Protestant places of worship and ban Protestantism. These measures give rise to new discontent and resistance under leadership of a Transylvanian noble, Ferenc Rákóczi II.

May 29, 1701

Rákóczi, seeking French aid for his struggle against Habsburgs, is betrayed by his French liaison, arrested, and taken to Vienna to stand trial for his life.

September 1701

Outbreak of War of the Spanish Succession, greatly affecting the position of Rákóczi's forces, as Austria has to deploy bulk of her fighting forces in the west.

November 8, 1701

Rákóczi escapes from Vienna and finds refuge in Poland.

May 6, 1703

Rákóczi issues manifesto to Hungarian nobles and commoners, calling on them to fight "against illegal and insufferable yoke" imposed by Habsburgs.

Summer 1703

Rákóczi's ragtag forces break out of Tisza highlands and advance into Great Plains. Noble apprehensions of the plundering and violence of peasant "*kuruc*" forces is allayed by Rákóczi's warning of strict punishments for such acts.

1703–11

Hungarian war of independence against Habsburgs, with many changes of fortune.

May 1711

Peace of Szatmár. Leopold I offers general amnesty to those who lay down arms and pledge loyalty to him. Now all of Hungary, including Transylvania, under Habsburg sovereignty. Leopold promises to respect laws of Hungary and offers freedom of worship to Protestants. He dies that same year.

1711–40

Reign of Charles VI as Holy Roman Emperor; Charles III as archduke of Austria, king of Hungary and Bohemia.

1713

Opening acts of Pragmatic Sanction. Charles VI declares the process of royal succession identical in all Habsburg lands (ensuring that individual lands will not, upon his death, choose monarchs of their own) and that in the absence of a male heir a female can inherit the throne. (According to family compact concluded in 1703, throne would pass to daughters of Joseph I, Leopold II, and Charles in that order; Charles now amends this, placing his own daughter, Maria Theresa, first in line of succession.)

March 1714

Peace of Rastatt. Charles VI accepts terms of Peace of Utrecht of previous year, ending War of the

Spanish Succession. This marks end of Habsburg rule in Spain and vests the crown of Spain with its overseas possessions in House of Bourbon. Austria however gains Belgium (Austrian Netherlands), and retains Naples, Sardinia, and Lombardy.

1715 and 1717

Census in Hungary, including Transylvania, but excluding Croatia, shows total population of about 4.5 million and catastrophic depopulation in areas that had been under Turkish occupation: ca. 7–10 souls per square kilometer.

March 21, 1731

Carolina Resolution, regulating position of Protestants in Hungary. Public worship permitted only in specified towns and areas; in these Protestants are allowed to build churches and employ ministers. In all other locations they can worship only at home and cannot invite outsiders. Protestant clergy placed under supervision of Catholic bishops. Mixed marriages must be officiated by Catholic clergy and children born from them must be raised Catholic.

1736

Crown princess Maria Theresa marries Francis of Lorraine.

1738–42

Last great epidemic of plague in eastern part of the Austrian Empire.

October 20, 1740

Death of Charles VI. His daughter Maria Theresa succeeds him on thrones of Habsburg possessions; her husband, Francis of Lorraine, is elected Holy Roman Emperor.

1740–48

War of the Austrian Succession. Following seizure of rich Austrian province of Silesia by Frederick II of Prussia, in violation of Pragmatic Sanction his father had signed, Austria goes to war for its recovery. France and several other states fight on Frederick's side, Britain on Austria's.

October 23, 1748

Peace of Aix-la-Chapelle ends War of the Austrian Succession. Austria retains most of her possessions but Prussia is confirmed in her possession of Silesia.

1756–63

Seven Years' War. The basic issue is once again the possession of Silesia but there has been, thanks to the labors of Austrian foreign minister Count Kaunitz, a complete reversal of alliances. The Austrian side possesses great advantages in material and manpower but Frederick's tenacity and generalship prevail in the end.

February 15, 1763

Peace of Hubertsburg, ending Seven Years' War. Territorially inconclusive, but Prussia retains Silesia.

November 1772

First partition of Poland between Russia, Prussia, and Austria. Austria gains Galicia.

November 29, 1780

Maria Theresa dies. Her oldest son Joseph (Holy Roman Emperor since his father's death in 1765) succeeds her. In order that conservative privileged estates would not frustrate his plans for liberal reforms in the empire, he does not call them into session as is customary upon an accession and does not have himself crowned, earning the moniker "king in a hat." With a minimum of delay he begins to issue his imperial edicts.

March 1781

By decree of this month papal encyclicals can be published in Austria only with sovereign's permission. Catholic religious orders severed from Rome's authority.

May 1781

Existing civil disabilities on Jews removed.

June 1781
Catholic Church deprived of right of censorship.

October 1781
Patent of Toleration guarantees freedom of worship to all non-Catholics, who can now also hold public office. Pro-Catholic bias in marriages removed.

January 1782
All religious orders not engaged in education or in care of the sick are disbanded.

1785
Feudal reform. The term "serf" can no longer be used. Peasants are allowed to move freely, marry freely, and choose their trade; they cannot be expelled from their plots without legal reasons, but their basic obligations to landlords remain.

February 1888
War against Turkey in alliance with Russia declared. A series of military reverses follow.

October 1789
On his deathbed, Joseph II pledges restoration of (unwritten) Hungarian constitution and the calling of estates.

January 28, 1790
Joseph, seeing his reforms had failed, cancels them except for Patent of Toleration and decrees affecting serfs.

February 1790
In response to challenge posed to royal authority by revolution in France, Austria and Prussia enter into formal alliance.

February 20, 1790
Joseph II dies. He is succeeded by his brother, Leopold II.

August 27, 1791
Leopold II and Prussian king Frederick William IV jointly issue the Declaration of Pillnitz, intended to assuage the misgivings of the French revolutionary government, stating that the two sovereigns would not intervene in French affairs except with the consent of other powers. It nevertheless vitiates Austria's relations with France.

March 1, 1792
Leopold II dies. Is succeeded by son, Francis I.

April 20, 1792
Legislative Assembly in France declares war on "king of Hungary and Bohemia." (Francis has not yet been crowned Holy Roman Emperor.)

September 20, 1792
Prussian army invading France under the duke of Brunswick, after initial successes meets great defeat near French town of Valmy.

November 6, 1792
Austrian army is also defeated at Jemappes. French occupy Austrian Netherlands.

1793–95
In Hungary a series of "Jacobin" conspiracies under the spiritual guidance of one Ignaz Martinovics, a Franciscan friar and former police informer, is discovered. In time the major participants are seized, tried, and executed.

1792–96
Austria, as a member of the First Coalition against France, fights with changing fortunes and inconclusive results.

May 1796
French Army of the South under Bonaparte invades northern Italy, seizes Milan, and detaches Lombardy from Austrian Empire.

October 17, 1797
Following new military reverses, Austria in the Treaty of Campo Formio cedes to France its Belgian provinces, receives in compensation Venetia, Istria, and Dalmatia, although Bonaparte has to conquer these before disposing of them.

December 1798

Austria adheres to Anglo-Russian alliance against France, thus forming Second Coalition. While Bonaparte is tied down in Egypt, the Austrians, as well as Russians, earn several major victories against French forces in Italy and on the Rhine.

April–December 1800

A series of battles between Austrian and French forces in Italy and on the Danube; the French advance into the Tyrol and to Linz.

February 9, 1801

Treaty of Lunéville. France gains the left bank of the Rhine. It is the first step toward liquidation of Holy Roman Empire.

April 1805

In France Napoleon had crowned himself emperor and Austria joins Britain and Russia in Third Coalition.

December 2, 1805

Battle of Austerlitz. Disastrous defeat of Austro-Russian army by Napoleon in Bohemia.

December 26, 1805

Peace of Pressburg. Austria recognizes Napoleon as king of Italy and cedes to that kingdom all she had gained at Campo Formio: Venetia, Istria, and Dalmatia. In Germany Austria cedes to Bavaria Vorarlberg, the Tyrol, and several bishoprics. Austria receives Salzburg and Berchtesgaden.

August 6, 1806

Emperor Francis II (Francis I of Austria) formally declares Holy Roman Empire at an end.

April 1809

Archduke Charles, commander in chief of Austrian armies, issues call to all German people to enter a war of liberation against French occupiers. Only the Tyrol answers appeal and Charles meets several defeats, after which,

May 13, 1809

The French enter Vienna.

Napoleon, in an attempt to weaken Austria, issues proclamation to Hungarians, promising them independence. But Hungarian nobility, in fear of Jacobin ideas as well as integrity of Hungarian frontiers, rejects the offer.

October 1809

Francis I appoints Klemens von Metternich foreign minister.

April 1810

Marriage of Napoleon to 18-year-old daughter of Francis I, Marie Louise.

August 12, 1813

Austria, encouraged by Napoleon's disastrous defeat in the Russian campaign in 1812, and by the formation of a new coalition against him, again declares war on France.

September 9, 1813

Treaty of Teplitz. Austria joins alliance of Russia and Prussia; the parties guarantee one another's territorial integrity and pledge not to conclude separate peace until France is defeated.

October 16–19, 1813

Battle of Nations near Leipzig. Napoleon defeated.

March 31, 1814

Paris falls to allies; effective end of Napoleonic France.

April 11, 1814

At Fontainebleau Napoleon abdicates unconditionally, is exiled to island of Elba.

September 1814–June 1815

Congress of Vienna under informal presidency of Prince Metternich of Austria. Territorially, Austria receives Lombardy and Venetia, Dalmatia, Galicia, but loses Belgium, which is united with the Netherlands in one kingdom.

1814–1848

Age of Metternich. In Austria, as well as Hungary and Bohemia, referred to as Age of Stagnation, as Metternich has a neurotic fear of all novelty and social change.

Summer 1822

Hungary regains Adriatic shoreline lost during Napoleonic Wars.

July 1825

Emperor Francis I recalls the Hungarian Diet after a 13-year absence. It meets in Pressburg on September 11.

October 22, 1825

Hungarian Diet issues a list of grievances. Calls on king to summon it at least once every three years, to take an oath to Hungarian constitution, and recognize that only the Diet can authorize new taxes and military conscription.

November 2, 1825

Diet takes up defense of Hungarian language in reaction to royal edict issued by Joseph II stating that German must be the language of all official contacts within the empire. Count Széchenyi, a member of the Diet, pledges a year's income toward establishment of Academy of Sciences for the cultivation of learning in Hungary.

1831

Cholera epidemic in Hungary spreads to Austria, Epidemic is fought by adding bizmuth to the well waters; overdoses cause many deaths, leading to rumor that the lords are trying to poison their serfs.

July 1831

Great peasant uprising in eastern Hungary. Ignited by the devastating cholera epidemic, it also highlights the crisis of the feudal system.

August 1831

Uprising crushed by the military. Usual reprisals follow.

March 2, 1835

Death of Francis I. He is succeeded by his weak-minded older son, Ferdinand. Francis instructs him in his will: "Displace none of the foundations of the edifice of state. Rule and change nothing."

Under Ferdinand's rule, despite strict censorship, many liberal writings from abroad find their way into Austria and there is increasing agitation for constitutional change. In Hungary, in 1833, Széchenyi publishes *Stadium*, a book advocating emancipation of serfs and complete equality before the law.

April 1840

Hungarian Diet passes a series of laws, greatly affecting the feudal system. Serfs can, with landlord's consent, buy their freedom. When having enough capital, they can buy or establish a workshop or a factory—a grievous blow to the outdated system of guilds. As to child labor: until age 12 a child can engage only in work not injurious to its health; between ages 12 and 16 can work no more than nine hours a day.

January 1841

Lajos Kossuth, a fiery reformist politician, launches his oppositionist newspaper, *Pesti Hirlap*. It soon becomes the powerful voice of liberal reform in the empire. It argues that feudal system is terminally outdated; it demands unconditional right for serfs to buy their freedom and the granting of state loans for that purpose. Kossuth is also severely critical of Austria, fans the flames of Hungarian chauvinism while conceding no rights to Hungary's own subject nationalities.

In the quarter century before the 1848 revolution, industrialism gains ground in the empire. In 1816 the first steam engine is put in use. Coal production increases ninefold, textile production sixfold. Steam boats appear on the Danube; in 1828 the Danubian Steam Ship Company is founded.

November 1847

Hungarian Diet, elected pursuant to royal proclamation of September, contains a majority of liberals. The leading spirit, Francis Deák, a jurist of a cool head and a keen intellect, proposes his Ten Points, which contain most of the demands put forth by liberals in the past decade.

February 1848

News of the overthrow of French king Louis-Philippe galvanizes liberals all over Europe into action.

March 3, 1848

Kossuth in a major speech in Diet demands liquidation of absolutism, a responsible ministry, constitution for Austria as well as Hungary.

March 11, 1848

Members of the Young Hungarian Radicals, with the poet Sándor Petofi their leading light, compile demands in Twelve Points, going much further than the parliamentary opposition. The Twelve Points contain demands for free press, annual meeting of the Diet—not in Pressburg but in Pest—equality before the law, a national militia, cessation of feudal obligations, jury trials, a Hungarian national army, and release of political prisoners.

March 11, 1848

A national assembly in Prague demands autonomy for Bohemia-Moravia and the right to work, among others.

March 13, 1848

Disorders in Vienna, the crowd demanding a constitution and Metternich's resignation. The latter at first refuses, but royal princes persuade him to resign as chancellor. He departs for Britain. To quiet the temper of demonstrators, the crown promises press freedom, a constitution, and a national guard organized from the ranks of the demonstrators

March 15, 1848

The news of Vienna uprising occasions solemn demonstrations in Budapest. Petofi reads to the crowd the Twelve Points and recites his stirring poem, the National Song. In Pressburg the Diet adopts measures that in effect liquidate the feudal system. These are presented to Vienna court, which, in fear of revolutionary crowd, sanctions them.

March 17–31, 1848

Angry reaction on part of privileged estates (clergy and nobility) opposed to emancipation of serfs. But the revolutionary movement has gone too far to be reversed. In Galicia the Austrian viceroy himself announces freeing of serfs. In Zagreb, the new Croatian *bán*, Josip Jelačić, proclaims emancipation independently of the Hungarian Diet, placing Croatia under Vienna's authority.

March 28, 1848

Vienna court, encouraged by the fact that Hungary and Croatia are at loggerheads, seeks to dilute March reforms. Among others, it seeks to postpone the effective date of emancipation of the serfs.

Now the Slovaks are heard from. At a county assembly they demand use of the Slovak language in law courts and in county assemblies. Vienna court refuses.

March 31, 1848

Budapest revolutionary council, upon hearing of Vienna's breach of faith in downgrading promised reforms, issues call to country to resist. The imperial government thereupon retracts its reservations.

April 8, 1848

Demonstrations in Prague and elsewhere impel Vienna to promise convocation of constituent assembly for Bohemia.

April 25, 1848

Emperor promulgates constitution for Austria.

May 17, 1848

Continuing disorders in Vienna force imperial government to flee to the safer city of Innsbruck.

June 1848

A pan-Slav congress, mainly of Czech delegates, meets in Prague. Its purpose is to demonstrate solidarity of Slavic people in empire against Germans.

June 12, 1848

In a clash between demonstrators and the imperial military in Prague the wife of military governor General Windischgrätz is killed.

June 17, 1848

Windischgrätz bombards Prague and crushes Czech uprising.

June 22, 1848

Constituent assembly meets in Vienna and enacts, among other things, the emancipation of serfs.

July 1848

Marshal Radetzky, commander in chief of imperial forces in Italy, overcomes insurrections against Austrian rule in Lombardy and Piedmont. Now Hungary alone in the empire continues to defy Vienna.

Meanwhile Croatians have denounced Hungarian sovereignty and now, in September 1848 a Croatian army under *bán* Josip Jelačić invades Hungary with full approval of Vienna.

October 1848

Hungarians repel Croatian forces and drive to the very gates of Vienna. The news creates consternation in the Austrian constituent assembly where a small radical group opposed to oppression of nationalities is now in charge.

October 31, 1848

Windischgrätz brings his forces to the gates of Vienna and bombards the rebellious city into submission.

December 2, 1848

The effete emperor, Ferdinand, abdicates. His brother is the legitimate heir to the throne but he yields his claim to his son, Francis Joseph, 18.

April 1849

Windischgrätz's forces, having invaded Hungary and occupied Budapest, are driven back by the armies of General Artur Görgey, they hold on to Buda only.

April 13, 1849

After imperial general and premier Felix von Schwarzenberg dismissed Austrian constituent assembly and promulgated a centralized constitution for all Austrian lands, Hungarian Diet, which had retreated to town of Debrecen, proclaims a Hungarian republic. Lajos Kossuth is elected president.

April–May, 1849

Hungarian forces earn many victories over imperial armies.

May 21, 1849

Francis Joseph meets in Warsaw with Czar Nicholas I of Russia. Latter promises an army of 200,000 against Hungarian insurrectionists. That same day Görgey's forces retake Buda, which the Austrians had held since their invasion.

June 1849

Russian forces invade Hungary.

June 27, 1849

Hungarian government calls for a national uprising against Austria and Russia. But because it has not initiated social adjustments, and has taken no effective steps toward land reform, and because many high nobles fear just such reforms and actually side with Russians, response to appeal is meager. After several defeats in course of the summer.

August 3, 1849

Near the town of Világos, Görgey surrenders. Four days later Kossuth and members of his government flee to Turkey.

Commanding generals of Hungarian armies are arrested and held for trial. Görgey, at czar's intervention, is given clemency and is exiled to Klagenfurt in Austria.

September 1, 1849

Julius Haynau, Hungary's recently appointed military governor, orders all those in the military, the legislature, and the judiciary who had participated in the revolution to report to military tribunals.

October 6, 1849

Thirteen Hungarian military commanders are executed in Arad. First premier of revolutionary government, Lajos Batthyány, is shot in Budapest.

1849–1867

The age of neoabsolutism in Austrian lands.

July 1850

Vienna court, moved by international outrage over executions and harsh oppression of Hungarian people, and confident that the spirit of revolution had been crushed, relieves Haynau as military governor and announces wide amnesty.

August 1849–August 1859

The age of Bach, so named for Austrian interior minister Alexander Bach, known for his dull, oppressive, bureaucratic rule.

August 1851

Emperor discontinues practice of a ministry responsible to legislature and makes it responsible to him alone.

1852

A number of conspiracies against Habsburg rule are discovered in Hungary. Principal organizers are arrested.

June–August 1852

Francis Joseph makes extended tour of Hungary. Following his visit the laws of Austria are declared to apply to Hungary too.

February 1853

Revolt in Milan against Austrian rule.

February 18, 1853

Attempt at Francis Joseph's life in Hungary. New wave of terror follows.

June–November 1854

Kossuth, in Britain after a brief stay in the United States, organizes Hungarian emigrants to lobby British government. But the government, anxious to preserve the Austrian empire, is unresponsive.

November 5, 1855

Concordat with Holy See concluded. It ends imperial veto on papal pronouncements, assures free communication of Austrian clergy with Vatican, confirms church's possession of ecclesiastical lands, makes lower clergy subject to dispositions by the higher, and places education under church jurisdiction.

April 1859

Start of Austria's war against Piedmont allied with France.

June 1859

Austrian forces defeated by French at Magenta and Solferino.

July 11, 1859

Armistice of Villafranca, Austria cedes Lombardy, long a center of Italian resistance, to Piedmont.

August 22, 1859

Emperor relieves Bach from his office of interior minister.

September 11, 1859

Protestant Imperial Patent. It places the governance of Protestant churches entirely under state authority. The decree provokes widespread protests in Hungary, which give rise to nationalist demonstrations.

March 15, 1860

Hungarian university youths hold great demonstration on anniversary of 1848 uprising. Police shoot at demonstrators. Funeral of one of the victims occasions fresh disorders.

April 8, 1860

István Széchenyi, a national hero, commits suicide. Protracted period of mourning, lasting into the fall.

October 20, 1860

Emperor Francis Joseph issues October Diploma. It provides for a federal constitution granting wide autonomy to the lands of the empire, which would in effect become internally self-governing. Hungarian public expresses dissatisfaction and demands restoration of Hungary's own constitution.

December 27, 1860

Francis Joseph, in an attempt to disarm Hungarian objections, invites Francis Deák and Joseph Eötvös, two prominent Hungarian politicians, to join imperial government. Both decline.

February 20, 1861

February Patent. Issued as a conciliatory follow-up to October Diploma. It provides for delegates from non-Austrian lands to participate in Imperial Council that legislates for the entire empire, and provides for distribution of seats for each land. Two days later the emperor states that the February Patent represents the limit of his concessions, and that furthermore the Imperial Council will have no say in military and foreign affairs. Hungarian public rejects February Patent as it had rejected the October Diploma. Legislative bodies pass resolutions branding all those who answer their invitations to the Imperial Council traitors.

April 15, 1861

Croatian provincial assembly also rejects February Patent and at the same time declares its separation from Hungary.

May 15, 1861

In Transylvania a popular assembly in a town with Romanian majority raises demand for separation from Hungary.

June 1861

Slovaks in a town meeting voice similar demands.

April 16, 1865

In an open Easter Letter to the emperor, Francis Deák, by now the most weighty voice in the Hungarian Diet, writes, in a voice of moderation that is his hallmark, that Hungary does not intend to separate itself from Austria and is ready to bring its laws into harmony with the interests of the empire. In later articles he outlines his plan for a federal government.

December 1865

Hungarian Diet meets. It insists on reinstatement of laws of 1848, which effectively made Hungary a separate state. Emperor, while not opposed in principle to compromise with Hungary, would not do so on the basis of laws of 1848. The parliament is divided over the question of how far to accommodate the emperor, but in the end refuses to abjure 1848 laws. Deák continues to work for compromise. He proposes a "'67 Committee" to decide which matters of state should be handled by joint ministries.

June 25, 1866

Outbreak of Austro-Prussian War.

July 3 1866

In battle of Sadowa Austria suffers defeat at the hands of Prussian army. Hungary is passive. The lost war compels Vienna court to take a more flexible attitude toward Hungary, and toward Deák's compromise plan.

July 5, 1914
German emperor William II assures Francis Joseph of Germany's unconditional support should Dual Monarchy wage war against Serbia—the "Blank Check."

July 18, 1914
Tisza abandons his opposition to presenting an unacceptable ultimatum to Serbia.

July 19, 1914
Ultimatum to Serbia is composed in Vienna.

July 23, 1914
Presentation of ultimatum in Belgrade.

July 25, 1914
Serbian reply to ultimatum received. Vienna deems it unsatisfactory and severs relations.

July 28, 1914
Dual Monarchy declares war on Serbia.

July 30, 1914
Russia mobilizes against Dual Monarchy.

July 31, 1914
Francis Joseph orders full mobilization of Dual Monarchy's armed forces.

August 1, 1914
Germany declares war on Russia.

August 3, 1914
Germany declares war on France.

August 4, 1914
Britain declares war on Germany.

August 5, 1914
Dual Monarchy declares war on Russia.

August 12, 1914
Britain and France declare war on Dual Monarchy.

May 4, 1915
Italy renounces its membership in Triple Alliance.

May 23, 1915
Italy declares war on Dual Monarchy.

October 14, 1915
Bulgaria enters war on side of Central Powers.

February 1916
Formation of Czechoslovak National Council under leadership of Masaryk, Beneš, and Štefanik.

June 1916
Brussilov offensive on Galician front virtually destroys Dual Monarchy's position in that sector.

August 17, 1916
Romania and Entente sign Treaty of Bucharest. In return for joining the war, Romania is promised Transylvania, the Bánát, Bukovina, and a part of East Hungary proper. By the end of month Romanian troops breach the Carpathians.

November 21, 1916
Death of Emperor Francis Joseph. Accession of Charles IV.

December 12, 1916
Charles, in concert with German government, addresses note to the Entente inquiring about possibility of peace.

December 30, 1916
Charles is crowned king of Hungary.

December 31, 1916
Entente's reply to Charles's note is negative.

January 10, 1917
Entente's note to Germany states as one of the war aims the reorganization of Dual Monarchy on the basis of nationalities.

March 24, 1917
Charles, through his brother-in-law Sixtus, prince of Parma, approaches Entente about

possibility of separate peace. The approach is rejected.

July 20, 1917
Corfu Declaration by South Slav nations demands creation of a kingdom of Serbs, Croats, and Slovenes under Karageorgević dynasty.

November 7, 1917
Bolshevik seizure of power in Petrograd.

December 5, 1917
Bolshevik government of Russia concludes armistice with Central Powers.

December 7, 1917
United States declares war on Dual Monarchy.

January 8, 1918
Wilson states his Fourteen Points before Congress.

March 3, 1918
Russia on one hand and Central Powers and Turkey on other conclude the peace treaty of Brest Litovsk.

April 8, 1918
Meeting in Rome of leaders of nationalities within Austria-Hungary. They declare in unison that they do not wish to remain within the Dual Monarchy.

May 7, 1918
Peace of Bucharest imposed on Romania by Central Powers. Romania cedes Dobrudja to Bulgaria, Carpathian passes to Dual Monarchy.

July 13, 1918
Pittsburgh Agreement. Czech and Slovak emigrant politicians agree that in a future Czechoslovak state Slovaks will have equality of rights with Czechs.

August 18, 1918
Formation of Yugoslav National Council.

September 14, 1918
Dual Monarchy's joint foreign minister Burián inquires of Entente powers about armistice terms.

September 16, 1918
Reply to above received. Before any negotiations are undertaken, Central Powers must relinquish their conquests.

October 17, 1918
Hungarian parliament declares Hungary's independence from Austria.

October 27, 1918
Dual Monarchy sends note, this time to Wilson, requesting separate peace.

October 28, 1918
In Prague, Czechoslovak National Council proclaims itself government of newly formed Czechoslovakia.

October 30, 1918
Slovakian National Council affirms the merging of Slovakia with Czech lands in unitary Czechoslovakia.

AUSTRIA
First Republic
1918–1938

November 3, 1918

Austrian Communist Party founded.

November 11, 1918

Emperor Charles announces his withdrawal from public affairs. He does not however expressly abdicate the throne.

November 12, 1918

A provisional national assembly proclaims Austria a republic. Name of the state is German Austria. Social Democrat Karl Renner elected chancellor.

March 2, 1919

Austrian foreign minister Otto Bauer and German foreign minister Ulrich von Brockdorff-Rantzau work out in Berlin secret plan for Austro-German union.

February 16, 1919

Election of constituent assembly. Social Democrats get 72 seats, clerical-agrarian Christian Socialists 69, German nationalists in favor of union with Germany 26.

March 24, 1919

Emperor Charles in Feldkirch, Vorarlberg, issues declaration stating he does not regard his abdication as final but will await suitable moment for reclaiming throne.

June 2, 1919

Government receives draft of peace treaty. Objects to Austrian republic being regarded as direct successor to imperial Austria. Also objects to several territorial provisions.

September 10, 1919

Peace treaty signed at St. Germain. All non-German lands separated from former empire. Treaty furthermore forbids union with Germany. Name of state changed from German Austria to Republic of Austria.

June 11, 1920

Renner government resigns, followed by that of Christian Socialist Michael Mayr.

October 1, 1920

Provisional National Assembly adopts new federal constitution for an Austria composed of nine provinces, including Vienna.

October 10, 1920

Plebiscite in disputed Austrian province of Carinthia, claimed by new Kingdom of Serbs, Croats, and Slovenes. Great majority votes for remaining with Austria.

October 17, 1920

New national elections. Social Democrats are great gainers.

April–May 1921

Plebiscites in the Tyrol and Salzburg result in majority vote for union with Germany. Foreign protests, especially from France, negate the results.

June 21, 1921

Mayr, unable to secure foreign aid for the country's faltering economy, resigns. Succeeded by nonparty candidate Johannes Schober, former police officer.

Autumn 1921

Burgenland imbroglio with Hungary. Although peace treaties assigned that strip of land to Austria, Hungarian irregular troops refuse to evacuate it. Finally a plebiscite in December 1921 results in Austria gaining most of the region, but the city of Sopron and environs remain with Hungary.

April 1, 1922

Former emperor Charles of Habsburg dies.

May 31, 1922

Chancellor Schober is forced to resign. His economic agreement with Czechoslovakia, the latter granting Austria major credit for coal and sugar, angers German nationals who look on Czechs as despoilers of the empire. Schober is succeeded by Ignaz Seipel, Christian Socialist, a Jesuit clergyman.

October 4, 1922

Because of catastrophic economic conditions, League of Nations grants Austria emergency financial assistance with strict controls over finances. Seipel makes rounds of European capitals with requests of long-term aid for Austrian reconstruction.

November 17, 1924

Seipel, ill with diabetes and suffering from a shot wound he had sustained in summer, resigns. However, he returns to office on October 15, 1925.

During 1926

Sharpening antagonism between Social Democrats and Christian Socialists. Each in time organizes its armed militia, the Schutzbund and the Heimwehr, respectively.

July 1926

When two National Socialists who had fired on a Socialist parade and killed an old man and a boy are acquitted, mob violence erupts in Vienna and the Palace of Justice is set on fire.

Early 1928

Deteriorating relations between Austria and Italy when Italian government orders that, in the South Tyrol, language of religious education must be Italian. Tense diplomatic impasse ensues.

December 5, 1928

Wilhelm Miklas elected president of republic.

February 6, 1930

After Hungarian premier István Bethlen has mediated Austro-Italian dispute in the interest of a desired tripartite agreement, friendship treaty between Austria and Italy is signed.

November 4, 1930

In national elections Social Democrats win 72 seats against 66 for Christian Socialists.

March 20, 1931

Economic crisis in both Austria and Germany impels the two states to agree to form a customs union. Sharp objections from France, Italy, and Czechoslovakia lead to cancellation of the scheme.

May 11, 1931

Failure of Austria's largest bank, the Kredit Anstalt intensifies economic crisis.

September 13, 1931

Encouraged by Nazi electoral successes in Germany, Austrian stalwart of Greater Germany cause, Walter Pfrimer, carries out a putsch in Styria, announcing he has taken over dictatorial powers in Austria. Heimwehr is sympathetic, authorities are slow to take action, but the attempt is eventually suppressed.

May 30, 1932

Christian Socialist Engelbert Dollfuss named chancellor. Although of fascist leanings, he is determined to stem Nazi tide.

July 15, 1932

League of Nations loan of 300 million schillings on condition that Austria pledges not to enter into political or economic union with Germany.

October 9, 1932

President Miklas is reelected.

January 30, 1933

In Germany, Hitler is named chancellor.

February 13, 1933

Austrian Nazis celebrate Hitler's appointment by mass demonstrations in Vienna.

March 4, 1933

Disturbed by growing pro-Nazi agitation, Dollfuss suspends parliament, prohibits assemblies, and curtails freedom of the press.

Easter 1933

Dollfuss seeking support against German encroachments, confers with Mussolini in Rome. Mussolini assures him that preservation of Austrian independence is a pillar of Italian foreign policy. Austria has to reciprocate by breaking the back of the political left.

June 19, 1933

In retaliation for a series of outrages by thugs, Nazi party in Austria is outlawed.

February 11–15, 1934

Following a decree dissolving all political parties except the Fatherland Front, Dollfuss, pursuant to his promise to Mussolini, sends government troops, supported by Heimwehr units, to bomb Socialist housing in Vienna. It in effect destroys Social Democratic strength in Austria.

March 18, 1934

Rome Protocols, signed by heads of government of Austria, Hungary, and Italy, create close political and commercial relations among the three.

July 10, 1934

Under a hastily drafted new constitution, Dollfuss reorganizes his government along fascistic lines.

May 1, 1934

A new concordat with Vatican grants Catholic Church increased power over education.

July 25, 1934

Nazi coup attempt in Vienna. A band of conspirators invades chancellor's office, shoots Dollfuss and allows him to bleed to death. Over the radio, which the group has seized, it announces Dollfuss' resignation. Government and Heimwehr units disarm and arrest the conspirators. Italy and Yugoslavia rush troops to the Austrian border; Hitler, unprepared for decisive action, disavows the coup.

July 30, 1934

Christian Socialist Kurt Schuschnigg named chancellor. He seeks to intensify cooperation with Hungary and Italy; domestically he continues Dollfuss's policies, even though after the failed Nazi coup he had an opportunity to return to democratic parliamentary government.

July 11, 1935

Austro-German Agreement. Hitler pledges to respect Austrian independence; Schuschnigg pledges to conduct Austrian foreign policy in the spirit of a German state.

October 10, 1935

Schuchnigg places Heimwehr outside the law and includes its members in the Fatherland Front militia.

February 1937

Schuschnigg, to create a counterweight to Nazi agitation, raises the question of Habsburg restoration; on February 14, 1937, declares that it is for him to decide on such a step.

April 22, 1937

Schuschnigg visits Mussolini in Venice. Mussolini, who has since concluded with Hitler the so-called Axis pact, coordinating the two nations' foreign policies, warns Schuschnigg not to count on Italian military intervention in case of a German move against Austria. Alarmed, Schuschnigg attempts rapprochement to Little Entente states in hope of French protection of Austrian independence.

February 12, 1938

At initiative of German ambassador to Vienna, Franz von Papen, Hitler and Schuschnigg meet at Berchtesgaden. Hitler makes demands of amnesty for arrested Nazis and inclusion of pro-Nazi persons in Austrian government. Schuschnigg, under severe pressure, agrees.

February 20, 1938

Hitler makes speech in Reichstag, pointedly referring to 10 million Germans living outside the Reich to whose fate the Reich cannot be indifferent.

February 24, 1938

Schuschnigg makes speech, affirming independence of Austria.

March 1, 1938

A series of demonstrations by Nazis in Styria in favor of an *Anschluss.*

March 9, 1938

Schuschnigg schedules referendum for March 12 on question of Austrian independence.

March 11, 1938

German ultimatum demanding cancellation of referendum and resignation of Schuschnigg.

March 12, 1938

German troops invade and occupy Austria without resistance.

March 13, 1938

New chancellor, Arthur Seyss-Inquart, proclaims Austria's union with Germany.

March 14, 1938

Hitler arrives in Vienna to general acclamation.

April 10, 1938

National plebiscite produces overwhelming vote in favor of *Anschluss.* Austria becomes organic part of Third Reich.

AUSTRIA
Second Republic
1945–2000

April 15, 1945

With Germany's military collapse impending, Karl Renner, first president of First Austrian Republic is selected by Soviets to head provisional government of liberated Austria. He pledges to cooperate loyally with Soviet Union.

April 25, 1945

Second Austrian Republic proclaimed in Soviet-occupied Vienna. Western powers, however, do not recognize Renner government.

May 9, 1945

All of Austria liberated from German rule and occupied by victorious powers along previously determined lines of demarcation.

July 17–August 2, 1945

Conference in Potsdam of United States, Britain, and Soviet Union decides that in Austria, as in Germany, four-power military control commission will exercise supreme political power.

September 11, 1945

First session in Vienna of four-power control commission.

September 24, 1945

Meeting of delegates from all nine Austrian provinces agree on enlargement of Renner government with members of nonworkers' parties.

November 25, 1945

In national elections Austrian National Party (Volkspartei) garners 1,602,227 votes, the Socialist Democrats 1,434,898 votes, the Communists 174,275 votes. Elections for provincial assemblies yield similar results.

December 1945

Government, with Leopold Figl of Volkspartei chancellor, is formed.

June 28, 1946

Control Commission grants Austrian government broader authority, limiting its own competence only to constitutional changes and international treaties.

Summer 1947

Austria is allowed to participate in Marshall Plan. In the following 10 years receives over $1 billion in aid.

April 1948

Political rights of some 482,000 former Nazis restored. As this amounts to a new voting bloc, a new party, the Union of Independents is formed.

October 9, 1949

New parliamentary elections. Volkspartei loses its absolute majority but is still the largest party. Figl remains chancellor.

April 1950

By now military occupying forces, originally numbering 700,000, have been reduced to less than 70,000. Control Commission is composed of civilians.

December 31, 1950

Karl Renner dies. Leaves behind recording, pleading for restoration of Austrian independence.

February 22, 1953

Parliamentary elections. In part because of worsening economic conditions (Korean War has caused great reduction in foreign aid) Socialists are the greatest gainers. But gerrymandering gives Volkspartei majority in parliament. Julius Raab named chancellor.

Summer 1953

Foreign minister Gruber visits Indian premier J. Nehru vacationing in Switzerland and asks him to intervene with Soviets in the interest of a peace treaty with Austria. That item had been on the great power agenda since the end of the war but has never moved forward, mainly because of Stalin's insistence that German and Austrian peace treaties must be concluded simultaneously. Stalin has died March 5, 1953.

Fall 1953

Indian ambassador to Moscow, Krishna Menon, presents Austrian request to foreign minister Molotov, who receives it sympathetically.

February 1954

Foreign ministers' council meeting in Berlin. Molotov presents Soviet conditions for peace treaty with Austria, the principal one being that Austria remain permanently neutral and not join any military bloc.

April 11, 1955

Austrian governmental delegation in Moscow finds understanding for its desire for a peace treaty.

May 2–13, 1955

Ambassadors of four great powers complete text of projected peace treaty with Austria.

May 15, 1955

Foreign ministers of four great powers sign peace treaty in Vienna. Austria, independent and neutral, will never join a military alliance or make any agreement with Germany that may, directly or indirectly, lead to a new union between the two states.

May 13, 1956

First parliamentary elections in independent Austria. Proportion of votes among parties remains essentially unchanged, Volkspartei in first place, Socialists in second. Julius Raab, first appointed chancellor in April 1953, will continue in that position until April 1961. The presidency will at the same time be held by Socialists, Theodor Körner until 1957, then for two terms (1957–65) by Adolf Schärf, and another two terms (1965–74) by Franz Jonas.

June 1961

Vienna is the venue for the historic meeting between recently elected American president John F. Kennedy and Soviet premier Nikita S. Khrushchev.

March 1966

With Volkspartei gaining absolute majority at the polls, coalition with Socialists is dissolved and latter retreat into opposition. Josef Klaus chancellor.

October 1971

This time elections produce an absolute majority for the Socialists and they form a one-party cabinet with Bruno Kreisky chancellor.

1986

Kurt Waldheim is elected president, despite allegations of war crimes during Second World War. This leads to some diplomatic isolation until Waldheim's replacement by Thomas Klestil in 1992.

1995

Austria becomes a full member of the European Union (EU) Community.

1998

NATO membership is ruled out.

2000

A new coalition government is elected, made up of the conservative People's Party and the far-right Freedom Party, led by Jörg Haider.

HUNGARY
The Regency
1918–2000

October 30, 1918

Start of revolution in Hungary against union with Austria. Political prisoners are freed and a large crowd in Budapest takes oath to Hungarian National Council. Habsburg monarchy is, however, retained.

October 31, 1918

King Charles names Count Mihály Károlyi, a reformist nobleman, premier. Károlyi forms a cabinet, which declares Hungary's independence, but offers its oath to the king.

November 3, 1918

Austria-Hungary and Italy sign armistice in Padua.

November 16, 1918

Hungary declared a republic.

December 1918

Acute political crisis. Government is unable to cope with crowding economic difficulties, exacerbated by masses of returning soldiers. Growing fear of leftist tendencies represented by communists.

January 11, 1919

Mihály Károlyi named president of Hungarian republic.

March 21, 1919

Károlyi, upon receiving demand from victorious powers that Hungarian troops withdraw from buffer zone designated by powers between Hungary and Romania, finds conditions unacceptable and resigns. On the same day a government formed from the fused Communist and Social Democratic parties takes power in Hungary. Its president is Sándor Garbai, but foreign commissar Béla Kun holds real power.

April 10, 1919

Romanian government authorizes invasion of Hungary. Its forces receive full support from Entente troops in the Balkans.

April 27, 1919

Czechoslovak forces invade Hungary and in short order establish contact with Romanian units.

April 27–August 1, 1919

Hungarian Soviet Republic. The political conditions for its survival are never present but its demise is accelerated by foreign invasions and by great power hostility to it at peace conference.

May 1919

Successful counterattacks by government's "Red Army" against Czechoslovak invaders.

May 8, 1919
Peace conference in Paris draws new Hungarian-Czechoslovak and Hungarian-Romanian borders.

May 20, 1919
A counterrevolutionary government is formed in Szeged in southeastern Hungary under former imperial admiral Miklós Horthy.

June 7, 1919
Peace conference, concerned about Hungarian military gains against Czechoslovaks, demands end to attacks and in conciliatory move hints that it might invite Garbai's government to peace conference.

July 1919
Great Romanian gains against Hungarian forces in eastern Hungary; peace conference demands resignation of soviet regime before it orders halt to attacks.

August 1, 1919
Garbai-Kun government resigns, its members flee.

November 16, 1919
After several short-lived and unstable governments, and after withdrawal of Romanian troops from Budapest and eastern part of the country, Miklós Horthy enters the capital as head of a new government.

Autumn 1919
White Terror. Many adherents of soviet regime, even simple workers and a number of Jews, are lynched.

November 25, 1919
Paris peace conference invites Hungarian government to send a delegation to Paris. Members of the delegation are named on December 20.

June 4, 1920
Hungarian delegation, after repeated futile protests against conditions, signs peace treaty at Trianon. Hungary loses two-thirds of her territory and population.

July–December 1920
Pál Teleki forms two successive governments.

March 26, 1921
Charles IV of Habsburg arrives in Szombathely to reclaim his throne. At Horthy's insistence he leaves country.

April 14, 1921
István Bethlen of National Unity Party forms government; with periodic personnel changes it stays in office for 10 years.

October 23, 1921
Second unsuccessful attempt by Charles to reclaim his crown.

September 18, 1922
Hungary is admitted to League of Nations.

August 2, 1923
Several members of the government's Unity Party secede to form the extreme right Party for Racial Protection.

July 1, 1924
After four years of economic hardship and rampant inflation, new currency is stabilized and conditions for economic growth are achieved with help of foreign loan.

April 5, 1927
Signing of "eternal friendship" treaty between Hungary and Italy. Among its secret provisions is Hungary's planned rearmament in violation of peace treaty.

1931
New, severe, economic crisis due to Great Depression; another appeal to the League of Nations. Fear of leftist demonstrations impels government on September 19, 1931 to institute summary administration of justice.

August 19, 1931
Bethlen resigns, Gyula Károlyi is new premier. During his tenure of one year economy takes another downward turn.

October 1, 1932
Gyula Gömbös becomes premier. On

October 25, 1932
he announces his National Work Plan of 95 points: bank reform, land reform, tax reform, low interest credit, acquisition of foreign agrarian markets, secret ballot. His strategic goal is creation of fascist corporative state.

November 10–13, 1932
Gömbös visits Mussolini, ostensibly to augment commercial relations between Hungary and Italy.

November 20–21, 1932
Austrian chancellor Dollfuss visits Hungary.

March 17, 1933
Gömbös holds new talks with Mussolini in Rome, seeking firm Italian support for his government program.

June 17–18, 1933
Gömbös has talks with Hitler in Erfurt, Germany. The result is the strengthening of Hungary's relations with fascist states.

March 17, 1934
Austro-Italian-Hungarian pact signed for closer commercial and trade relations.

November 7, 1934
Rome Protocols between Austria, Hungary, and Italy pronounce in favor of closer commercial relations among the three and also affirms commitment to Austrian independence (in face of rising fear of an *Anschluss* with Germany).

October 9, 1935
In League of Nations Assembly Hungary refuses to support sanctions against Italy imposed for her invasion of Ethiopia.

October 6, 1936
Gömbös, officially on sick leave, dies in Munich. He is succeeded as premier by Kálmán Darányi.

1936
Rising National Socialist tendencies in Hungary. Premier Darányi firmly and openly opposes them.

November 29, 1937
Visit to Germany of Darányi and foreign minister Kánya. They are informed of Hitlers's acquisitive plans regarding Austria and subsequently Czechoslovakia, and given vague promises of support for Hungary's revisionist aspirations.

April 3, 1938
Government, to take wind from sails of fascist agitation, introduces in parliament Jewish Law; it is enacted on May 24, providing that not more than 20 percent of the medical, judicial, engineering, and press chambers can be Jewish.

May 13, 1938
Darányi resigns, succeeded by Béla Imrédy. Latter announces that his government stands on a nationalist, Christian, rightist platform, but issues warning to extreme right to abstain from agitation.

August 20–29, 1938
Horthy, Imrédy, and Kánya visit Germany; and are received with reserve because Hungary has just concluded the Bled Agreement with Little Entente (including Czechoslovakia) when Germany is about to proceed against Czechoslovakia in pursuit of claims for Sudetenland.

September 29, 1938
Munich Agreement. Apart from losing all of the Sudetenland, Czechoslovakia is advised to

settle her territorial disputes with Poland and Hungary within three months.

November 2, 1938
First Vienna Award, assigning to Hungary southern Slovakia and a slice of Ruthenia.

First quarter of 1939
Under influence of events in Germany, strong Nazi-type organizations appear in Hungary; they are opposed by conservative elements, Regent Horthy included. On February 3 the recently formed extreme right Arrowcross Party throws a bomb at Central Synagogue in Budapest.

February 14, 1939
At Horthy's insistence, Imrédy resigns as premier and is replaced by Pál Teleki.

February 23, 1939
Hungary joins Anti-Comintern Pact, thereby committing herself to Axis side.

March 15, 1939
In line with Hitler's dispositions, while German troops occupy Bohemia-Moravia and Slovakia declares her independence, Hungarian troops take possession of Ruthenia.

April 11, 1939
Hungary, in another bow to Hitler, leaves the League of Nations.

April 1939
While in foreign policy the government forges closer ties with Axis, internally it takes determined action against extreme rightist parties.

May 1939
Second Jewish Law passed. It defines Jewishness on a racial, not religious, basis, further restricts Jewish participation in the professions and greatly limits the number of Jews who can be employed in the civil service.

July 1939
Premier Pál Teleki, himself a Transylvanian, seeks Axis support for territorial revision at expense of Romania while curbing extreme rightist parties within country. In his letter to Hitler he stresses Hungary's inviolable sovereignty.

September 1, 1939
The day Germany attacks Poland, Teleki announces assumption of extraordinary powers to control internal dissent and ensure economic stability.

September 10, 1939
Teleki refuses German request for troop transport across Hungarian territory for deployment against Poland.

Autumn 1939–Spring 1940
Even though Hungary is not at war, sundry economic restrictions and food rationing are introduced.

July 20, 1940
By economic agreement Hungary obligates herself to sell Germany 200,000 tons of grain, 200,000 tons of corn, and 100,000 tons of other produce.

August 30, 1940
Second Vienna Award. Arbitration by German foreign minister Ribbentrop and Italian foreign minister Ciano awards Hungary northern Transylvania and Székely enclave in the east.

November 20, 1940
Hungary joins Tripartite Pact of Germany, Italy, and Japan. Alignment with Axis is complete. Teleki government allows German troops to cross Hungarian territory into Romania. (Start of German preparations for campaign against Soviet Union.)

December 12, 1940
Signing of Hungarian-Yugoslav "eternal friendship" treaty.

March 28, 1941

Following coup in Yugoslavia in protest against friendship treaty with Germany, Hungarian council of ministers authorizes armed attack on Yugoslavia, if (1) Yugoslavia as a state disintegrates; (2) Hungarian minority is persecuted; (3) as a result of German attack on Yugoslavia a power vacuum arises in Hungarian-inhabited regions.

April 3, 1941

Premier Teleki commits suicide in protest against betrayal of friendship treaty with Yugoslavia. He is replaced by László Bárdossy.

April 10, 1941

Hungarian troops enter Bačka province of Yugoslavia in alliance with Germany.

Early June 1941

Chief of general staff urges that Hungary offer its participation in impending attack against Soviet Union. Council of ministers refuses.

June 22, 1941

Germany attacks Soviet Union.

June 23, 1941

Council of ministers resolves to break diplomatic relations with Soviet Union.

June 26, 1941

Hungarian town of Kassa is bombed by unidentified aircraft.

June 27, 1941

Hungary declares war on Soviet Union.

December 7, 1941

Britain declares war on Hungary.

January 4–23, 1942

Unauthorized massacre of several hundred persons, mainly Jews, in city of Ujvidék, recently recovered from Yugoslavia.

January 1942

German demands for large-scale military participation by Hungary in war against Soviet Union. Regent Horthy under pressure agrees.

March 9, 1942

Miklós Kállay, in outlook favoring the western Allies, forms new government.

April 12, 1942

First units of Hungarian Second Army leave for Russian front.

June 29, 1942

New economic restrictions are introduced in the country.

August 20, 1942

Younger son of Regent Horthy, recently designated as his father's successor, is killed in an airplane accident in Russia.

January 1943

Destruction of Hungarian Second Army on the Don. Attempts begin through a special bureau to establish contact with London and Washington with a view to making a separate peace with them.

April 17–18, 1943

Horthy visits Hitler; refuses latter's request to dismiss Kállay.

March 18, 1944

Horthy visits Hitler at latter's invitation, only to be informed that next day German military forces will enter Hungary.

March 19, 1944

At four in the morning occupation of country begins. Kállay resigns as premier. Consultations at German embassy regarding composition of new government.

March 22, 1944

New government formed under Döme Sztójay, former Hungarian ambassador to Berlin.

June 16, 1989
Solemn reburial of Imre Nagy and codefendants. Also of the Unknown Revolutionary of 1956.

September 10, 1989
Hungarian government, in violation of standing agreement with socialists states, opens borders to Austria to a group of East German tourists, allowing them to depart. Collapse of communism in East Europe commences.

March 25, 1990
First round of democratic elections in Hungary.

April 8, 1990
Second round of democratic elections in Hungary.

May 22, 1990
Hungary's first freely elected government since 1948 installed.

1991
The withdrawal of Soviet forces is completed.

1996
A friendship treaty with the Slovak republic is signed, as is a cooperation treaty with Romania.

1997
Hungary is invited to join NATO and to begin negotiations for membership in the European Union. A referendum shows clear support in favor of joining NATO.

1998
Viktor Orbán, leader of right-of-center Fidesz, becomes prime minister after the general election.

1999
Hungary becomes a full member of NATO.

2000
Ferenc Mádl elected president.

CZECHOSLOVAKIA
First Republic
1918–1938

November 14, 1918

A Czech-Slovak national assembly in Prague confirms establishment of Czechoslovakia as a republic and elects Tomáš Masaryk president.

January 1919

Dispute arises with Poland over possession of town of Teschen. Armed clashes occur.

April 16, 1919

Enactment of major land reform. Large estates are broken up and divided into lots of about 25 acres each for distribution among poor peasants.

February 29, 1920

Republican constitution, closely modeled on American, is adopted.

April 18, 1920

Parliamentary elections reveal bewildering array of parties, largely on ethnic basis; coalition governments must be formed.

August 24, 1920

Treaty with Yugoslavia, pledging to fight Hungarian revisionism and Habsburg restoration. It is the first installment of what is to become the Little Entente.

April 23, 1921

Treaty with Romania on same conditions as with Yugoslavia the year before. Although these bilateral agreements tie the three countries together to the same end, the final tripartite agreement is signed only on February 16, 1933.

January 25, 1924

Treaty of mutual defense alliance with France.

July 6, 1925

Decision to commemorate the 510th anniversary of Jan Hus's death as a heretic leads to rupture of relations with Vatican.

October 16, 1925

Within framework of Locarno Treaties, Germany concludes arbitration treaty with Czechoslovakia (as well as Poland), foreswearing any intention of solving outstanding disputes by force.

May 27, 1927

Reelection of Tomáš Masaryk to the presidency.

July 1, 1927

In an attempt to meet Slovak and Ruthenian complaints about Czech domination of republic, Prague grants greater autonomy to the provinces.

1930–1934

Severe economic crisis as Great Depression engulfs the country. Industrial production falls to 60 percent of 1927 level.

April 6–8, 1932

International economic conference in London discusses plan of French premier André Tardieu for closer economic cooperation among Danubian states. Plan fails because of German and Italian opposition.

April 26, 1934

Visit to Prague of French foreign minister Louis Barthou. He seeks a fresh review of possible Danubian economic cooperation after failure of Tardieu Plan and the conclusion of Rome Protocols between Austria, Hungary, and Italy.

May 24, 1934

Tomáš Masaryk is elected president of the republic for third time.

May 16, 1935

As a follow-up to military convention with France, Czechoslovakia concludes a similar pact of mutual assistance with Soviet Union. The latter is to come to the aid of Czechoslovakia if she were attacked, but only if France fulfills her obligation under the Franco-Czechoslovak treaty of January 1924 first.

May 19, 1935

General elections, marked by great surge of the Sudetendeutsche Partei (SdP), which wins in the largely German-inhabited Sudetenland by landslide.

November 5, 1935

New cabinet is formed under Slovak Agrarian Milan Hodža.

December 13, 1935

President Masaryk, 85 years of age, resigns. He is succeeded by Edvard Beneš.

September 14, 1937

Death of former president Masaryk.

October 1937

Escalation of crisis between Prague government and Sudeten Germans. Konrad Henlein, head of SdP, demands full autonomy for Germans in Sudetenland. Because of growing tension government cancels elections scheduled for November.

November 29, 1937

Sudeten deputies walk out of parliament.

March 12, 1938

German occupation and subsequent annexation of Austria jeopardizes position of Czechoslovakia, strategically because the Czech lands are surrounded on three sides by an enlarged Germany, politically because it encourages Sudeten Germans in the republic to increase their agitation for self-determination.

April 24, 1938

Sudeten leader Konrad Henlein in a speech at Karslbad demands clear delimitation of German areas in republic, full autonomy for Germans, free adhesion to the "idea of Germanism," pro-German revision of Czechoslovak foreign policy.

May 19–21, 1938

German military maneuvers near Czechoslovak border prompt President Beneš to alert France and Britain to a possible German strike against the republic. Both powers warn Germany of consequences of such a step. The provocation impels Hitler to decide upon the military destruction of Czechoslovakia in near future.

Summer 1938

Repeated clashes in Sudetenland between Germans and Czech authorities. Intemperate outbursts in German press against Czechoslovakia and against President Beneš.

Early August 1938

Runciman Mission. British prime minister Chamberlain sends one of his confidants, a wealthy businessman and ship owner, Lord Walter Runciman, to Czechoslovakia to assess the magnitude and respective merits of the Sudeten crisis.

September 12, 1938

In a speech at the end of Nazi Party rally in Nuremberg, Hitler for the first time demands that Sudeten Germans be given right of self-determination.

September 15, 1938

Chamberlain, determined to find peaceful solution for Sudeten crisis, pays personal visit to Hitler at latter's Berchtesgaden retreat. Hitler demands annexation of Sudeten areas on basis of self-determination.

September 18–21, 1938

French and English pressure Prague government to agree to German demands. Beneš at last capitulates.

September 23–24, 1938

Chamberlain's second visit to Hitler at Godesberg. Hitler increases his demands to immediate entry into Sudetenland, with plebiscites to follow.

September 25–28, 1938

War crisis of first magnitude. Both British cabinet and the French resist Hitler's latest demands and war preparations ensue.

September 29, 1938

Four-power conference in Munich (Britain, France, Germany, Italy). Soviet Union is excluded. All of German demands are met. Czechoslovaks are to evacuate Sudeten areas between October 1 and 10 under conditions determined by an international commission. That commission is also to delineate plebiscite areas. Czechoslovaks do not participate in discussions and are informed of decisions at end of conference.

October 1–10, 1938

German troops march into Sudetenland in stages, occupy about 10,000 square miles with 3.5 million inhabitants. Plebiscites are in the end dispensed with. Germany is given right to use highways across Moravia for transports between Germany and Vienna. Hungary's, as well as Poland's, territorial claims on Czechoslovakia are to be settled within three months, after which Munich powers would guarantee what was left of republic.

October 2, 1938

Poland, by way of an ultimatum, acquires from Czechoslovakia the city of Teschen and region of Trans-Olza.

October 9, 1938

Talks between Czechoslovakia and Hungary get under way. As the two sides are unable to agree on the extent of territorial cessions, Hungary invites arbitration by Munich powers. Britain and France beg off.

November 2, 1938

In First Vienna Award German foreign minister Ribbentrop and Italian foreign minister Ciano, meeting in Vienna, determine the territory in southern Slovakia that Czechoslovakia is to cede to Hungary.

October 5, 1938

President Beneš resigns and soon leaves country.

October 6, 1938

At so-called Žilina Congress Slovakia gains full autonomy. Name of republic is hyphenated to Czecho-Slovakia. Monsignor Tiso is chosen premier of Slovakia.

October 8, 1938

Ruthenia likewise gains autonomy. Renamed Carpatho-Ukraine.

November 30, 1938
Emil Hácha, a high court judge, is named president.

March 15, 1938
Extinction of Czechoslovakia as an independent state. Concerned about virtual bankruptcy of Slovakia and its renewed dependence on the Czech parts, Hitler decides to liquidate the rump republic. Bohemia and Moravia are incorporated into the Reich as protectorates, Slovakia becomes "independent," Hungary annexes Carpatho-Ukraine.

CZECHOSLOVAKIA
People's Republic
1943–1993

December 1943

Edvard Beneš, president of Czechoslovak government in exile, visits Moscow and concludes Treaty of Friendship and Mutual Assistance with Soviet Union.

April 5, 1945

Promulgation of Košice Program by Communist functionary Klement Gottwald. Announces provisional political grouping, the National Front, embracing several "democratic" parties. Hints at expulsion of hostile minorities, that is, Germans and Hungarians.

October 28, 1945

Nationalization Decree. All enterprises employing more than 500 workers are nationalized.

February 27, 1946

Prague and Budapest governments agree on population exchange. An equal number of persons from each country volunteering for settlement in the other country is given opportunity to do so.

May 26, 1946

General elections for National Assembly (parliament). With 2.7 million votes (38.7 percent of the total), the Communists emerge as the strongest party in coalition. Klement Gottwald, hitherto vice premier, is named premier.

June 7, 1947

Government signals acceptance of Marshall Plan aid. Stalin summons a delegation to Moscow and in effect vetoes participation. The government accordingly reverses its position.

Autumn 1947

Clandestine preparations by Communists for seizure of power at first suitable opportunity.

February 20, 1948

Cabinet crisis. A number of ministers resign in protest against the purging of police of noncommunists, expecting that Gottwald, heading a defunct cabinet, will also resign. But Gottwald quickly fills vacancies with Communists or their sympathizers. Street demonstrations in favor of Communist takeover. Visiting Soviet deputy foreign minister Valerian Zorin coordinates transfer of power.

March 10, 1948

Foreign minister Jan Masaryk an apparent suicide as his body is found under a bathroom window in Czernin Palace.

March 10, 1948

All industrial firms are nationalized.

April 1948

Gottwald's government presents National Assembly with draft of new constitution on

Soviet model. Assembly passes it on May 9, but President Beneš refuses to endorse it and resigns. He is succeeded as president by Gottwald, with Antonin Zápotocký premier and Rudolf Slanský first secretary of Communist Party.

May 30, 1948

New national elections produce great victory for Communist-dominated National Front. Encouraged by popular mandate, government begins purge of "unreliable" elements, intellectuals, noncommunist police and military officers, and "reactionaries."

June 7, 1948

Social Democratic Party is forced to merge with Communist Party.

1950–1951

In wake of Tito affair a series of political purges sweep satellite states. Most victims are Communists, charged with "bourgeois nationalism" or Titoism. Prominent victims in Czechoslovakia are foreign minister Vladimir Clementis and first party secretary Rudolf Slanský.

March 5, 1953

Stalin dies.

March 17, 1953

Klement Gottwald, who had caught a chill at Stalin's funeral, dies. Zápotocký succeeds him as president. Endeavors to ease repressive regime.

May 1953

Monetary "reforms" that have effect of wiping out savings of many workers and middle class individuals lead to riots and disturbances. These give a group of party hard-liners under Antonin Novotný the pretext to return to Stalinist methods.

September 1953

Novotný named first secretary of Communist Party. His long tenure witnesses economic and cultural stagnation, and the repression of all dissent with police methods. He manages to stay in power largely because of his close personal relations with Kremlin bosses, especially Khrushchev, with whom he differs only in his displeasure with Khrushchev's famous de-Stalinization speech and denunciation of Stalinist methods. At a time of growing liberalization in satellite states, even in Hungary after the bloody repressions following the defeat of the revolution in 1956, Novotný clings to principle and practice of a police state.

October 1964

When Khrushchev is removed as first secretary of the CPSU, Novotný is the only satellite leader to lodge a protest against his friend's ouster in Moscow.

January 5, 1968

With reform-minded Communists in the ascendancy, Novotný is forced to resign as party secretary. He is succeeded by a Slovak, Alexander Dubček, one of the leading reformists. Novotný still remains president, a largely ceremonial position, but two months later he is removed from that post too.

April 8, 1968

A new cabinet devoted to economic and political reform takes office in Prague.

June 15, 1968

Possibly as a warning to the reformists not to go too far, Soviets decide to hold Warsaw Pact maneuvers in Czechoslovakia.

June 27, 1968

Publication of an open letter, titled "Two Thousand Words," by intellectuals sharply critical of the policies of government.

July 14–15, 1968

Five governments of Warsaw Pact nations, clearly at Moscow's behest, warn the Prague government not to stray from Marxist-Leninist principles.

August 20, 1968
Soviet troops, supported by small contingents of satellite armed forces enter Czechoslovakia, occupy Prague, put an end to the period of reform communism that had been dubbed the "Prague Spring." Possibly to lessen resistance, the Soviets allow Dubček to remain first secretary, but they back another Slovak, a hardline Communist, Gustav Husák, as the true possessor of political power.

September 11, 1968
Soviet troops evacuate Prague.

September 12, 1968
In first outside protest against intervention in Czechoslovakia, Albania announces its withdrawal from Warsaw Pact.

October 16, 1968
New Czechoslovak government signs treaty with Moscow providing for permanent stationing of Soviet troops in Czechoslovakia.

October 30, 1968
Czechoslovakia is transformed into a federation of two states: the Czech lands and Slovakia.

November 12, 1968
Speaking to Polish Party Congress, Leonid Brezhnev, in what becomes known as Brezhnev Doctrine, affirms right of the Soviet Union to intervene in any state where socialism is threatened on the principle that "a threat to one socialist country is a threat to all socialist countries."

April 17, 1969
Gustav Husák replaces Alexander Dubček as first secretary of the Czechoslovak Communist Party.

January 1, 1977
About 250 civil rights activists sign a manifesto termed *Charter 77*, calling the government to task for failing to abide by its own pledges of respect for human rights, even such as are guaranteed by the constitution and in international undertakings. This charter gives rise to a creeping movement for general liberalization later referred to as the Velvet Revolution.

December 17, 1987
Gustav Husák, by now with no support within or without the party, is forced to resign as general secretary of the Czechoslovak Communist Party. He does retain however his post as president of Czechoslovakia, and his membership on the presidium of the party. As general secretary he is replaced by Miloš Jakeš.

November 17, 1989
Peaceful prodemocracy demonstration by students is brutally put down by political police. Subsequently *Charter 77* signatories embrace these prodemocracy demonstrations, thus creating a loose umbrella organization called in Czech lands Civic Forum and in Slovakia Public against Violence.

December 27, 1989
Gustav Husák resigns as president and Miloš Jakeš resigns as general secretary of the Communist Party. The party is in a virtual state of collapse.

December 29, 1989
Leader of the Civic Forum, playwright Václav Havel elected president of Czechoslovakia. A coalition government, in which Communists play minor role, is formed.

June 1990
First free elections in Czechoslovakia since 1946. Civic Forum in Czech lands and Public against Violence in Slovakia win landslide victories.

1991

Increasing Slovak demands for greater autonomy within republic.

June 1992

In national elections distinct division between returns in Czech lands, where Civil Democratic Party headed by Václav Klaus, dedicated to economic reform is big winner, whereas in Slovakia Movement for Democracy, headed by Vladimir Meciar, on a separatist platform, sweeps to victory. President Havel tries to halt movement toward separatism, but fails.

July 1992

Václav Havel resigns as president.

August–December, 1992

Václav Havel and Vladimir Meciar work out a formula for separation of Czech and Slovak lands.

December 27, 1992

Law to this effect is passed in federal parliament.

January 1, 1993

A separate Czech republic and a separate Slovakia are peacefully founded.

YUGOSLAVIA
The Monarchy
1917–1944

July 20, 1917

Declaration of Corfu. Leading political and military personages from Serbia, Croatia, Slovenia, and Montenegro agree to form single nation under Serbian Karageorgević dynasty.

April 10, 1918

At conclusion of Congress of Oppressed Nations held in Rome, Italy recognizes the independence of unitary Yugoslav nation.

October 19, 1918

South Slav National Council sitting in Zagreb declares itself competent body to speak for South Slavs to be united in one state.

December 1, 1918

United Kingdom of Serbs, Croats, and Slovenes proclaimed. Prince Alexander Karageorgević named regent for his ailing father King Peter.

January–February 1919

Government issues series of decrees on administrative, fiscal, and tax matters, as well as land reform.

1919

Formation and crystallization of political parties: Serbian People's Radical Party, aiming for a centralized kingdom, Independent Demo-crats, of more liberal bent, Croatian Democratic Peasant Party favoring federal structure, and Communist Party.

May 1, 1919

At Paris Peace Conference Entente Powers recognize new kingdom.

September 10, 1919

New state signs Treaty of St. Germain with Austria.

November 27, 1919

New state signs Treaty of Neuilly with Bulgaria.

June 4, 1920

New state signs Treaty of Trianon with Hungary.

August 14, 1920

Defensive treaty with Czechoslovakia, first in series of bilateral pacts by states that had gained territory from the Dual Monarchy.

October 10, 1920

Plebiscite in southern Carinthia. Vote heavily in favor of Austria.

November 12, 1920

Treaty of Rapallo with Italy over the disputed city of Fiume. The two powers divided the territory but leave Fiume itself a free city.

November 29, 1920
National elections for constituent assembly. Majority of votes go to centralist Radical Party, with strong showing by Croatian Peasant Party.

December 30, 1920
Communist Party and revolutionary labor unions banned.

January 1, 1921
Provisional constitution provides for a centralized government. Nicola Pašić named premier.

June 7, 1921
Mutual defense treaty with Romania.

June 21, 1921
So-called Vidovdan constitution voted. Of somewhat dubious legitimacy, as Croatian Peasant Party delegates did not take their seats and abstained from voting. Of elected 419 delegates only 258 cast ballots, of these 233 vote for constitution. State is renamed United Kingdom of Serbs, Croats, and Slovenes.

August 16, 1921
King Peter dies. His son Alexander succeeds him.

1921
Census shows that 14.5 percent of population not of South Slav ethnicity. Mainly Hungarian, German, Albanian.

December 5, 1921
Yugoslav state subscribes to ethnic minority protection clauses of League of Nations Covenant.

April 28, 1922
Administrative reforms introduced, aimed at greater centralization.

March 18, 1923
Parliamentary elections result in victory for government party, the Serbian Radicals.

January 27, 1924
Signing of Adriatic Treaty of Friendship with Italy.

July 1924
Long-simmering conflict between central government under Nicola Pašić and Croatian Peasant Party under Stjepan Radić comes to a hed when Peasant Party candidates return to parliament with obstructionist tactics. Pašić resigns, then forms new cabinet.

December 24, 1924
The Peasant Party is outlawed and Radić is imprisoned.

March 27, 1925
Chastened, the Peasant Party accepts the Vidovdan constitution from which it had withheld its vote and joins government of Pašić.

November 18, 1926
Kingdom enters into friendship treaty with Poland.

February 24, 1927
Peasant Party leaves cabinet and enters into Peasant-Democratic Coalition with Independent Democrats.

September 11, 1927
Parliamentary elections bring victory to government party.

November 11, 1927
Treaty of Friendship with France.

June 20, 1928
Peasant Party head Stjepan Radić and several others of his party are shot in parliament by a Serbian deputy. Protest demonstrations in Croatia. (Radić dies of his wounds August 8.)

January 6, 1929
King Alexander, seeing no prospect of orderly parliamentary government, suspends consti-

tution, dissolves parliament, and introduces virtual dictatorship.

February 17, 1929
In place of parliament, legislative council is set up, but is given only advisory powers.

June 1929
Sharply rising tensions with Bulgaria over Macedonia as Macedonian rebels cross border into Yugoslavia.

October 3, 1929
Name of country changed to Kingdom of Yugoslavia. Historic provinces are reduced to mere administrative districts, banats.

September 3, 1931
Introduction of a new constitution by royal fiat: bicameral legislature, open voting for candidates, party that receives a plurality of votes gets two-thirds of the seats in legislature.

November 8, 1931
Parliamentary elections boycotted by opposition parties.

1931
Deepening economic crisis. Within two years gross national product falls to one half of that in 1927.

November 14, 1932
Following arrest of Croat leader Vlasko Maček (successor of Stjepan Radić), Peasant Party denounces king's dictatorship.

February 16, 1933
Signing of so-called Little Entente treaty binding Czechoslovakia, Romania, and Yugoslavia against any Hungarian attempt at territorial revision or Habsburg restoration.

December 10–13, 1933
King Boris of Bulgaria visits Belgrade. Beginning of reconciliation after Macedonian troubles.

February 8, 1934
Balkan Pact between Yugoslavia, Romania, Greece, and Turkey concluded, aimed largely at prevention of German penetration. Bulgaria, still dissatisfied with Macedonian border, refuses to join.

May 1, 1934
Yugoslav-German commercial agreement. Beginning of Yugoslavia's economic orientation toward Germany.

June 25, 1934
French foreign minister Barthou's visit to Belgrade.

October 9, 1934
King Alexander, visiting France, is assassinated by Macedonian terrorist in league with Croat ustaša terrorist organization. Twelve-year-old Peter king. Prince Pavel, a cousin of his father's, is regent.

November 22, 1934
Yugoslavia, in League of Nations, accuses Hungary of being accessory to king's murder and of harboring ustaša leader Ante Pavelić.

May 5, 1935
Parliamentary elections. Despite sundry government pressures, Croatian Peasant Party garners two-fifths of vote.

June 20, 1935
Milan Stojadinović of Serbian Radical Party forms government. Forecasts phasing out of dictatorial regime and easing of restrictions.

July 25, 1935
Concordat with Vatican grants Catholics special privileges. Protests from Eastern Orthodox force effective cancellation.

August 19, 1935
In attempt to frustrate continued federalist pressures from Croatia, Stojadinović forms Radical Union of Serbians, Slovenians, and Bosnians (Muslims).

September 23–24, 1987
Plenary session of Central Committee of Serbian Communist Union. Slobodan Milošević emerges as commanding figure.

January 1989
Disorders and demonstrations in Montenegro, bringing Milošević's partisans to power.

February 27, 1989 '
Albanian protests against Serbian policies in Kosovo lead to the proclamation of a state of emergency in that province.

March 28, 1989
Amendment to Serbian constitution provides for greater (Serbian-dominated) centralization.

September 27, 1989
Slovenia amends her constitution for broader sovereignty of the republic within Yugoslavia. Disintegration of federal structure underway.

January 20–22, 1990
Last congress of Yugoslav Communist Union; because of sharp divisions disbands before conclusion.

1990
In course of the year individual republics choose new constitutions, in December Slovenia votes itself independent; on May 19, 1991, Croatia follows suit.

June 27–July 7, 1991
"Ten-Day War" between Serbian People's Army on one hand and Slovene militia on other. At its conclusion Serbians withdraw from Slovenia.

July 1991–January 1992
Serbian-Croatian war fought on Croatian territory. Serb forces occupy approximately one-third of Croatia.

April 27, 1992
New Federal Republic of Yugoslavia, comprising only Serbia and Montenegro, with capital in Belgrade, proclaimed. It is in a practical state of war with Bosnia and Croatia. United Nations, charged with mediating the conflict, imposes strict economic sanctions on Serbia.

September 8, 1992
Plebiscite in Macedonia.

September 26–30, 1992
Plebiscite by Albanians in Kosovo, resulting in proclamation of independent Kosovan Republic.

November 20, 1992
Macedonia proclaims her independence.

October 15, 1992
Proclamation of Bosnian independence.

1993
Pro-Milošević Zoran Lilic becomes Yugoslav president. There is antigovernment rioting in Belgrade. Macedonia is recognized as independent under the name of the Former Yugoslav Republic of Macedonia. The economy is severely damaged by international sanctions.

1994
A border blockade is imposed by Yugoslavia against Bosnian Serbs; sanctions are eased as a result.

1995
Serbia plays a key role in the U.S.–brokered Dayton peace accord for Bosnia-Hercegovina and accepts the separate existence of Bosnia and Croatia.

1996
Diplomatic relations are restored between Serbia and Croatia, and UN sanctions against Serbia are lifted. Allies of Milošević are successful in

parliamentary elections. Diplomatic relations are established with Bosnia-Hercegovina. There is mounting opposition to Milošević's government following its refusal to accept opposition victories in municipal elections.

1997

Milošević is elected president and the prodemocracy mayor of Belgrade is ousted. The validity of Serbian presidential elections continues to be questioned. The anti-Milošević candidate is elected president of Montenegro.

1998

A Serb military offensive against ethnic Albanian separatists in Kosovo leads to a refugee and humanitarian crisis. The offensive against the Kosovo Liberation Army (KLA) is condemned by the international community and NATO military intervention is threatened. President Milošević appoints Momir Bulatović as prime minister.

1999

Fighting continues between Serbians and Albanian separatists in Kosovo. In March, following the failure of efforts to reach a negotiated settlement, NATO begins a bombing campaign against the Serbs; the ethnic cleansing of Kosovars by Serbs intensifies and the refugee crisis in neighboring countries worsens as hundreds of thousands of ethnic Albanians flee Kosovo. In May President Milošević is indicted for crimes against humanity by the International War Crimes Tribunal in the Hague. A peace is agreed on NATO terms in June. Refugees began returning to Kosovo.

2000

Presidential elections are held in September in which opposition candidate Vojislav Kostunica claims outright victory against President Slobodan Milošević, but the federal election commission orders second round of voting to be held. The opposition claims ballot-rigging and organizes mass demonstrations throughout Yugoslavia, in the face of which Milošević concedes defeat. Zoran Djindjic is appointed prime minister. The UN reinstates Yugoslavia's membership, which had been suspended in 1992, in October. There are clashes with Albanian guerrillas on the border between Serbia and Kosovo in November. Parliamentary elections held in December gives a majority to Kostunica's party.

2001

Former president Milošević is arrested and charged with abuse of power, corruption, and fraud.

APPENDIXES

APPENDIX I
Rulers and Statesmen

APPENDIX II
Maps

APPENDIX I

RULERS AND STATESMEN
Austria

Margraveship since 960, Duchy 1156, Archduchy 1453, Empire 1804, 1st Republic 1918, part of the German Reich 1938, 2nd Republic 1945

MARGRAVES/DUKES/ARCHDUKES/EMPERORS	
Name	**Reign**
Burchard (–980)	960–976
Luitpold I (–994)	976–994
Heinrich I (–1018)	994–1018
Adalbert (–1055)	1018–1055
Ernst the Brave (–1075)	1055–1075
Luitpold II (–1095)	1075–1095
Luitpold (or Leopold) III the Saint (–1136)	1095–1136
Luitpold (or Leopold) IV (–1141)	1136–1141
Heinrich II Jasomirgott (duke since 08.09.1156) (–1176)	1141–1176
Luitpold (or Leopold) V (–1194)	1176–1194
Friedrich I (–1198)	1195–1198
Luitpold (or Leopold) VI (–1230)	1198–1230
Friedrich II the Pugnacious (1210–1246)	1230–1246
Hermann (VI of Zähringen) (–1250)	1248–1250
Friedrich (I of Zähringen) (1249–1268)	1250–1268
Ottokar (II House of Przemysl) (1233–1278)	1251–1276
Albrecht I (1255–1308)	1282–1308
Rudolf II (1271–1290)	1282–1283
Rudolf III (1282–1307)	1298–1307
Friedrich the Beautiful (1289–1320)	1298–1320

MARGRAVES/DUKES/ARCHDUKES/EMPERORS (continued)

Name	Reign
Leopold I (1290–1326)	1298–1326
Albrecht II (1298–1358)	1330–1358
Otto (1301–1339)	1330–1339
Rudolf IV The Founder (1339–1365)	1358–1365
Albrecht III (1349–1395)	1365–1395
Leopold III (1351–1386)	1365–1386
Albrecht IV (1377–1404)	1395–1404
Albrecht V (1397–1439)	1404–1439
Ladislaus Postumus (1440–1457) (Archduke 06.01.1453)	1440–1457
Friedrich V (1415–1493)	1458–1493
Albrecht VI (1418–1463)	1453–1463
Sigismund (1427–1496)	1475–1490
Maximilian I (1459–1519)	1493–1519
Karl (1500–1558)	1519–1521
Ferdinand I (1503–1564)	1521–1564
Maximilian II (1527–1576)	1564–1576
Rudolf II (1552–1612)	1576–1608
Matthias (1557–1619)	1608–1619
Ferdinand II (1529–1595)	1619–1637
Ferdinand III (1608–1657)	1637–1657
Leopold I (1640–1705)	1657–1705
Joseph I (1678–1711)	1705–1711
Karl III (1685–1740)	1711–1740
Maria Theresia (1717–1780)	1740–1780
Joseph II (1741–1790)	1780–1790
Leopold II (1747–1792)	1790–1792
Franz I (1768–1835) (Emperor of Austria 14.08.1804)	1792–1835
Ferdinand I (1793–1875)	1835–1848
Franz Joseph I (1830–1916)	1848–1916
Karl I (1887–1922)	1916–1918

PRESIDENTS

Name	Term
Karl Seitz (1869–1950)	1919–1920
Michael Hainisch (1858–1940)	1920–1928
Wilhelm Miklas (1872–1956)	1928–1938
Karl Renner (1870–1950)	1945–1950
Theodor Körner (1873–1957)	1951–1957
Adolf Schärf (1890–1965)	1957–1965
Franz Jonas (1899–1974)	1965–1974
Rudolf Kirchschläger (1915–2000)	1974–1986
Kurt Waldheim (1918)	1986–1992
Thomas Klestil (1932)	1992–

PRIME MINISTERS

Name	Term
Johann Christoph, Baron von Bartenstein (1690–1767)	1727–1753
Anton Corfiz, Count Ulefeld (1699–1760)	1742–1753
Wenzel Anton, Count Kaunitz (1711–1794)	1753–1792
Johann Philipp, Count von Cobenzl (1741–1810)	1792–1793
Johann Amadeus Franz de Paula, Baron von Thugut (1736–1818)	1793–1800
Johann Ludwig, Count von Cobenzl (1753–1809)	1800–1805
Johann Philipp Karl, Count von Stadion-Warthausen (1763–1824)	1805–1809
Klemens Wenzel Lothar, Prince von Metternich (1773–1859)	1809–1848
Alfred C. Ferdinand, Prince zu Windischgrätz (1787–1862)	1848
Franz Anton, Count von Kolowrat-Liebsteinsky (1778–1861)	1848
Karl Ludwig, Count von Fiquelmont (1777–1857)	1848
Franz, Baron von Pillersdorf (1786–1862)	1848
Anton, Baron von Doblhoff-Dier (1800–1872)	1848
Johann, Baron von Wessenberg (1773–1858)	1848
Felix, Prince zu Schwarzenberg (1800–1852)	1848–1852
Karl Ferdinand, Count von Buol-Schauenstein (1797–1865)	1852–1859
Johann Bernhard, Count von Rechberg (1806–1899)	1859–1861
Archduke Rainer of Austria (1827–1913)	1861–1865

PRIME MINISTERS (*continued*)

Name	Term
Alexander, Count Mensdorff-Pouilly (1813–1871)	1865
Richard, Count Belcredi (1823–1902)	1865–1867
Ferdinand, Baron von Beust (1809–1886)	1867
Karl, Prince Auersperg (1814–1890)	1867–1868
Eduard, Count Taaffe (1833–1895)	1868–1870
Ignaz, Lord von Plener (1810–1908)	1870
Leopold, Sir Hasner von Artha (1818–1891)	1870
Alfred, Count Potocki (1822–1889)	1870–1871
Karl, Count von Hohenwart (1824–1899)	1871
Ludwig, Baron von Holzgethan (1810–1892)	1871
Adolf, Prince Auersperg (1821–1885)	1871–1879
Karl von Stremayr (1823–1904)	1879–1879
Eduard, Count Taaffe (2nd term)	1879–1893
Alfred, Count von Windischgrätz (1851–1927)	1893–1895
Erich, Count von Kielmannsegg (1847–1923)	1895
Kasimir, Count Badeni (1846–1909)	1895–1897
Paul, Baron Gautsch (1851–1918)	1897–1898
Franz, Count von Thun und Hohenstein (1847–1916)	1898–1899
Manfred, Count von Clary und Aldringen (1852–1928)	1899
Heinrich, Sir von Wittek (1834–1903)	1899–1900
Ernst von Körber (1850–1919)	1900–1904
Paul, Baron Gautsch (2nd term)	1905–1906
Konrad, Prince von Hohenlohe-Waldenburg (1863–1918)	1906
Max Wladimir, Baron von Beck (1854–1943)	1906–1908
Richard, Baron von Bienerth (1863–1918)	1908–1911
Paul, Baron Gautsch (3rd term)	1911
Karl, Imperial Count von Stürgkh (1859–1916)	1911–1916
Ernst von Körber (2nd term)	1916
Heinrich, Count von Clam-Martiniz (1863–1932)	1916–1917
Ernst, Sir Seidler von Feuchtenegg (1862–1931)	1917–1918
Max, Baron Hussarek von Heinlein (1865–1935)	1919–1918
Heinrich Lammasch (1853–1920)	1918–1918
Karl Renner (1870–1950)	1918–1920
Michael Mayr (1864–1922)	1920–1921

Johann Schober (1874–1932)	1921–1922
Ignaz Seipel (1876–1932)	1922–1924
Rudolf Ramek (1881–1941)	1924–1926
Ignaz Seipel (2nd term)	1926–1929
Ernst Streeruwitz (1874–1952)	1929
Johann Schober (2nd term)	1929–1930
Karl Vaugoin (1873–1949)	1930
Otto Ender (1875–1960)	1930–1931
Karl Buresch (1878–1936)	1931–1932
Engelbert Dollfuss (1892–1934)	1932–1934
Kurt Schuschnigg (1897–1977)	1934–1938
Arthur Seyss-Inquart (1892–1946)	1938
Karl Renner (2nd term)	1945
Leopold Figl (1902–1965)	1945–1953
Julius Raab (1891–1964)	1953–1961
Alfons Gorbach (1898–1972)	1961–1964
Josef Klaus (1910–2001)	1964–1970
Bruno Kreisky (1911–1990)	1970–1983
Fred Sinowatz (1929)	1983–1986
Franz Vranitzky (1937)	1986–1997
Viktor Klima (1947)	1997–2000
Wolfgang Schüssel (1945)	04.02.2000–

Hungary

Principality in the 9th century, Kingdom 1000 (personal union with Austria 1438–1457, 1526–1918), Republic 16.11.1918, Kingdom again 1920, Republic 1946, People's Republic 1949, Republic again 1989

PRINCES, KINGS

Name	Reign
Árpád (–907) (chieftain)	886–907
Zoltan (896–950) (chieftain)	907–946
Taksony (931–972) (chieftain)	946–972
Géza (940–997) (prince)	972–01.02.997
Stephen (István) I (Saint Stephen) (975–1038) (prince, king since 25.12.1000)	01.02.997–15.08.1038

PRINCES, KINGS *(continued)*

Name	Reign
Peter (1011–1059)	1038–1041
Aba Samuel (1010–after 1044)	1041–1044
Peter (2nd time)	1044–1046
Andreas I (1013–1060)	1046–1060
Bela I (1016–1063)	1060–1063
Salomon (1051–1087)	1063–1074
Geza I (1040–1077)	1074–1077
László I the Saint (1040–1095)	1077–1095
Koloman (1074–1116)	1095–1116
Stephan II (1100)	1116–1131
Bela II the Blind (1108–1141)	1131–1141
Geza II (1130–1162)	1141–1162
László II (1131–1163)	1162–1163
Stephan III (1147–1172)	1162–1172
Stephan IV (1133–1165)	1163–1163
Bela III (1148–1196)	1172–1196
Imre (1174–1204)	1196–1204
László III (1199–1205)	1204–1205
Andreas II (1176–1235)	1205–1235
Bela IV (1206–1270)	1235–1270
Stephan V (1240–1272)	1270–1272
László IV (1262–1290)	1272–1290
Andreas III (1265–1301)	1290–1301
Wenzel (1289–1306)	1301–1305
Otto (1261–1312)	1306–1307/08
Karl I Robert (1288–1342)	1310–1342
Lajos I the Great (1326–1382)	1342–1382
Maria (1370–1395)	1382–1395
Karl II of Durazzo (1345–1386)	1385–1386
Sigismund (1368–1437)	1387–1437
Albrecht V (1397–1439)	1438–1439
László Postumus (1440–1457)	1440–1457
Matthias I Corvinus (1443–1490)	1458–1490

Vladislav (1456–1516)	1490–1516
Lajos II (1506–1526)	1516–1526
Ferdinand I (1503–1564)	1526–1564
Maximilian (1527–1576)	1563–1576
Rudolf (1552–1612)	1572–1608
Matthias II (1557–1619)	1608–1619
Ferdinand II (1529–1595)	1619–1637
Ferdinand III (1608–1657)	1625–1657
Ferdinand IV (1633–1654)	1647–1654
Leopold I (1640–1705)	1655–1705
Joseph I (1678–1711)	1687–1711
Karl III (1685–1740)	1712–1740
Maria Theresa (1717–1780)	1741–1780
Joseph II (1741–1790)	1780–1790
Leopold II (1747–1792)	1790–1792
Franz I (1768–1835)	1792–1835
Ferdinand I (1793–1875)	1835–1848
Franz Joseph I (1830–1916)	1848–1916
Karl IV (1887–1922)	1916–1918

PRESIDENTS

Name	Term
Mihály, Count Károlyi (1875–1955)	1919
Sándor Garbai (1879–1947)	1919

REGENTS

Name	Term
Archduke Joseph of Austria (1872–?)	1919
Miklós Horthy de Nagybánya (1868–1957)	1920–1944
Ferenc Szálasi (1897–1945)	1944–1945

PRESIDENTS

Name	Term
Zoltán Tildy (1889–1961)	1946–1948
Arpád Szakasits (1888–1965)	1948–1950

PRESIDENTS *(continued)*

Name	Term
Sándor Ronai (1892–1965)	1950–1952
István Dobi (1898–1968)	1952–1967
Pál Losonczi (1919)	1967–1987
Károly Nemeth (1922)	1987–1988
Bruno Straub (1914–1996)	1988–1989
Mátyás Szürös	1989–1990
Árpád Gőncz (1922)	1990–2000
Ferenc Mádl (1931)	2000–

PRIME MINISTERS

Name	Term
Lajos, Count of Batthányi (1809–1849)	1849
Bartholomäus Szemere (1812–1869)	1849
Julius, Count Andrássy de Csik Szent-Király (1823–1890)	1867–1871
Melchior, Count Lónyay (1822–1894)	1871–1872
Josef Szávy (1818–1900)	1872–1874
István of Bittó (1822–1903)	1874–1875
Adalbert of Wenckheim (1811–1879)	1875
Koloman Tisza of Borosjenö (1830–1902)	1875–1890
Julius, Count Szapáry (1832–1905)	1890–1892
Sándor Wekerle (1848–1921)	1892–1894
Desider de Bánffy de Losonez (1843–1911)	1895–1899
Koloman of Szell (1843–1915)	1899–1903
Karl, Count de Khuen-Héderváry (1849–1918)	1903
István, Count Tisza de Borosjenö (1861–1918)	1903–1905
Geza de Fejérváry (1833–1914)	1905–1906
Sándor Wekerle (2nd time)	1906–1910
Karl, Count of Khuen-Héderváry (2nd time)	1910–1912
László of Lukács (1850–1932)	1912–1913
István, Count Tisza de Borosjenö (2nd time)	1913–1917
Moritz, Count Esterházy de Galántha (1881–?)	1917
Sándor Wekerle (3rd time)	1917–1918
Johann, Count Hadik de Futak (1863–1933)	1918

Michael, Count Károlyi de Nagykároly (1875–?)	1918–1919
Desiderius Berinkey	1919–1919
Sándor Garbai (1875–1947)	1919
Sándor Dovesak	1919
Julius Peidl (1873–?)	1919
István Friedrich (1883–?)	1919
Karl Huszar (1892–?)	1919–1920
Sándor Simonyi-Semedan	1920
Pál, Count Teleki de Szek (1879–1941)	1920–1921
István, Count Bethlen de Bethlen (1874–1950?)	1921–1931
Gyula, Count Károlyi (1871–?)	1931
Gyula Vitéz Gömbös (1886–1936)	1932–1936
Kálmán Darányi de Pusztaszentgyörgy et Tetétlen (1886–1939)	1936–1938
Béla Imrédy (1891–1946)	1938–1939
Pál, Count Teleki de Szek (2nd time) (1879–1941)	1939–1941
László of Bárdossy (1890–1946)	1941–1942
Miklós Kállay de Nagy-Kálló (1887–1967)	1942–1944
Döme Sztójay (1883–1946)	1944
Géza Lakatos (1890–1967)	1944
Ferenc Szálasi (1897–1946)	1944–1945
Béla Dálnoki-Miklós (1890–1948)	1944–1945
Zoltán Tildy (1889–1961)	1945–1946
Ferenc Nagy (1903–1979)	1946–1947
Lajos Dinnyés (1900–1961)	1947–1948
István Dobi (1898–1968)	1948–1952
Mátyás Rákosi (1892–1971)	1952–1953
Imre Nagy (1896–1958)	1953–1955
András Hegedűs (1922–1999)	1955–1956
Imre Nagy (2nd time)	1956
János Kádár (1912–1989)	1956–1958
Ferenc Münnich (1886–1967)	1958–1961
János Kádár (2nd time)	1961–1965
Gyula Kállai (1910)	1965–1967
Jenö Fock (1916–2001)	1967–1975
György Lázár (1924)	1975–1987

PRIME MINISTERS *(continued)*

Name	Term
Károly Grösz (1930)	1987–1988
Miklós Nemeth (1948)	1988–1990
József Antall (1932–1993)	1990–1993
Péter Boross (1928)	1993–1994
Gyula Horn (1932)	1994–1998
Viktor Orbán (1963)	1998–2002
Péter Medgyessy (1942)	2002–

Czechoslovakia (Czech Republic)

Independent Republic 1918, Protectorate of the German Reich as "Bohemia and Moravia" and Secession of Slovakia 1939, united and independent again 1945, Czech Republic after Independence of Slovakia 1993.

PRESIDENTS

Name	Term
Tomáš Garrigue Masaryk (1850–1937)	1918–1935
Edvard Beneš (1884–1948)	1935–1938
Jan Syrový (1888–?)	1938
Emil Hácha (1872–1945)	1938–1945
Edvard Beneš (2nd term)	1945–1948
Klement Gottwald (1896–1953)	1948–1953
Antonin Zápotocký (1884–1957)	1953–1957
Antonín Novotný (1904–1975)	1957–1968
Ludvig Svoboda (1895–1979)	1968–1975
Gustav Husák (1913–1991)	1975–1989
Václav Havel (1936)	1989–1992
Václav Havel (2nd term)	1993–

PRIME MINISTERS

Name	Term
Karel Kramař (1860–1937)	1918–1919
Vlastimil Tusar (1880–1924)	1919–1920
Jan Cerny (1877–1959)	1921

Edvard Benés (1884–1948)	1921–1922
Anton Svehla (1873–1933)	1922–1926
Jan Cerny (2nd term)	1926
Anton Svehla (2nd term)	1926–1929
Frantisek Udrzal (1866–1938)	1929–1932
Jan Malypetr (1873–1947)	1932–1935
Milan Hodza (1878–1944)	1935–1938
Jan Syrový (1888–?)	1938
Rudolf Beran (1887–1953)	1938–1939
Alois Elias (1890–1942)	1939–1941
Jaroslav Krejci (1892–?)	1942–1945
Zdenek Fierlinger (1891–1976)	1945–1946
Klement Gottwald (1896–1953)	1946–1948
Antonin Zápotocký (1884–1957)	1948–1953
Villem Sirocký (1902–1971)	1953–1963
Jozef Lenárt (1923)	1963–1968
Oldrich Cernik (1921–1994)	1968–1970
Lubomir Strougal (1924)	1970–1988
Ladislav Adamec (1926)	1988–1989
Marian Calfa (1946)	1989–1992
Jan Straský (1940)	1992
Václav Klaus (1941)	1993–1997
Jozef Tosovský (1950)	1997–1998
Milos Zeman (1944)	1998–2002
Vladimír Spidla (1951)	2002–

Slovakia

Part of Czechoslovakia 1918, independent Republic 1939, re-united with Czechoslovakia 1945, independent Republic again 1993

PRESIDENTS

Name	Term
Josef Tiso (1881–1947)	1939–1945
Michal Kovac (1930)	1993–1998
Rudolf Schuster (1934)	1999–

PRIME MINISTERS	
Name	**Term**
Josef Tiso (1881–1947)	1938–1939
Adalbert Tuka (1660–1946)	1939–1944
Stefan Tiso	1944–1945
Vladimir Meciar (1942)	1992–1994
Jozef Moravcik	1994–1994
Vladimir Meciar (2nd time)	1994–1998
Mikuláš Dzurinda (1955)	1998–

Yugoslavia

United Kingdom of Serbs, Croats and Slovenians 01.12.1918, Kingdom of "Yugoslavia" 03.10.1929, German Occupation 1941–1945, Federal Republic 29.11.1945, Separation of Slovenia, Croatia and Bosnia-Herzgovina 1991/1992, founded again (only Serbia and Montenegro) 27.04.1992

KINGS	
Name	**Reign**
Peter I Karajordjević (1844–1921)	1918–1921
Alexander I (1888–1934)	1921–1934
Peter II (1923–1970)	1934–1945
Paul (1893–1976) (Regent)	1934–1941

PRESIDENTS	
Name	**Term**
Ivan Ribar (1881–1968)	1945–1953
Josip Broz, Marshal Tito (1892–1980)	1953–1980
Lazar Koliševski (1914–2000)	1980
Cvijetin Mijatović (1913)	1980–1981
Sergej Kraiger (1914–2001)	1981–1982
Petar Stambolić (1912)	1982–1983
Mika Spiljak (1916)	1983–1984
Veselin Duranović (1925)	1984–1985
Radovan Vlaiković (1922)	1985–1986
Sinan Hasani (1922)	1986–1987

Lazar Mojsov (1920)	1987–1988
Raif Dizdarević (1926)	1988–1989
Janez Drnovšek (1950)	1989–1990
Borisav Jović (1926)	1990–1991
Stjepan Mesić (1934) (since 10.1991 de iure)	1991
Branko Kostić (de facto until 12.1991)	1991
Dobrica Cosić (1921)	1992–1993
Zoran Lilić (1953)	1993–1997
Slobodan Milošević (1941)	1997–2000
Vojislav Kostunica (1944)	2000–

PRIME MINISTERS

Name	Term
Mika Pašić (1846–1926)	1918
Stojan Protić (1857–1923)	1918–1919
Ljubomir Davidivić (1863–?)	1919–1920
Stojan Protić (2nd time)	1920
Milenko Vesnić (1862–1921)	1920–1921
Mika Pašić (2nd time)	1921–1924
Ljubomir Davidović (2nd time)	1924
Mika Pašić (3rd time)	1924–1926
Mika Usunović (1879–1954)	1926–1927
Velja Vucicević (1871–1930)	1927–1928
Anton Korošeć (1872–1940)	1928–1929
Petar Živković (1879–1947)	1929–1932
Vojeslav Marincović (1876–1935)	1932
Milan Srškić (1880–?)	1932–1934
Mika Usunović (4th time)	1934
Boguljub Jevtić (1886–1960)	1934–1935
Milan Stojadinović (1888–1961)	1935–1939
Dragisha Cvetković (1892–?)	1939–1941
Duschan Simović (1882–1962)	1941
Milan Nedić (1882–1946)	1941–1944
Josip Broz, Marshal Tito (1892–1980)	1945–1963

PRIME MINISTERS

Name	Term
Petar Stambolić (1912)	1963–1967
Mika Spiljak (1916)	1967–1969

PRESIDENTS

Name	Term
Mizja Ribicić (1919)	1969–1971
Demal Bijedić (1917–1977)	1971–1977
Veselin Duranović (1925)	1977–1982
Milka Planinć (1924)	1982–1986
Branko Mikulić (1928)	1986–1988
Ante Marković (1925)	1989–1991
Milan Panić (1929)	1992
Radoje Kontić (1937)	1993–1998
Momir Bulatović (1956)	1998–2000
Zoran Zizić (1951)	2000–2001
Dragisa Pesić (1954)	2001–

APPENDIX II

MAPS

Empire of Charles V, 1506–1519

Habsburgs in Central Europe, 1618–1700

Habsburg Expansion and Contraction, 1700–1814

Europe after Congress of Vienna, 1815

Revolutions in the Austrian Empire, 1848–1849

The Austro-Hungarian Ausgleich, 1867

Balkan Peninsula after the Treaty of Berlin, 1878

Habsburg Territories, 1814–1914

Eastern Europe during World War I

Hungary after Trianon, 1920–1939

Yugoslavia, 1921–1941

Czechoslovakia and Germany, 1920–1939

Eastern Europe during World War II, 1938–1944

Eastern Europe, 1948–1991

Wars of Yugoslav Succession, 1991–1995

Dayton Accord Settlement, 1995

The Kosovo Crisis, 1999

Austria, 2000

Hungary, 2000

Yugloslavia, 2000

Czech Republic, 2000

Slovakia, 2000

REVOLUTIONS IN THE AUSTRIAN EMPIRE, 1848–1849

PRUSSIA

RUSSIA

Sadova

Prague

Silesia

Krakow

Galicia

Bohemia

BAVARIA

Olmütz

Vác

HUNGARY

Danube R.

Munich

Pressburg
(Bratislava)

Bukovina

Vienna

Buda ● ● Pest

Debrecen

Innsbruck

AUSTRIAN

Pákozd

EMPIRE

Cluj

SWITZER-
LAND

Graz

Transylvania

Venetia

Ljubljana

Világos ● Arad

Lombardy

Zagreb Slavonia

Timişoara

WALLACHIA

Po R.

Venice

Croatia

Tuscany

Zadar

Dalmatia

Bosnia

Belgrade

Danube R.

Sarajevo

SERBIA

N

PAPAL
STATES

Adriatic
Sea

Split

OTTOMAN

0   100 miles

MONTENEGRO

EMPIRE

0   100 km

Dubrovnik

—— Austrian Empire	➤ Main Austrian military operations, 1848–1849
– – – Border between Austria and Hungary	➤ Operations of Jelačić, 1848

⇨ Russian interventionist forces, 1849

THE AUSTRO-HUNGARIAN AUSGLEICH, 1867

THURINGIA

SAXONY

PRUSSIA

RUSSIA

Sadova

Prague

Silesia

Krakow

Galicia

Bohemia

Olmütz

BAVARIA

Slovakia

Danube R.

Munich

Pressburg
(Bratislava)

HUNGARY

Bukovina

Vienna

AUSTRIA

Buda Pest

Debrecen

SWITZER-
LAND

Innsbruck

Pákozd

Cluj

Transylvania

Graz

Arad

Slovenia

Ljubljana

Po R.

Zagreb

Croatia

Timişoara

Venice

ROMANIA

Bosnia

Belgrade

Danube R.

ITALY

Zadar

Dalmatia

Sarajevo

SERBIA

N

Adriatic
Sea

Split

Mostàr

Bulgaria

0   100 miles

Herze-
govina

MONTE-
NEGRO

Sandjak of
Novi Pazar

OTTOMAN

EMPIRE

0   100 km

Dubrovnik

Austrian lands   Border of Austria-Hungary

Hungarian lands   Border between Austria and Hungary

Border between regions

BALKAN PENINSULA AFTER THE TREATY OF BERLIN, 1878

Budapest

AUSTRO-HUNGARIAN
EMPIRE

RUSSIA

Danube R.

Drava R.

Sava R.

Prut R.

Dniester R.

land gained
by Russia

BOSNIA-
HERZEGOVINA

Belgrade

ROMANIA

Bucharest

land gained
by Romania

Sarajevo

Morava R.

SERBIA

Mostar

Danube R.

Black
Sea

*Adriatic
Sea*

land gained
by Serbia

BULGARIA
(autonomous
principality)

MONTENEGRO

Mitrovica

Sofia

Eastern
Rumelia

Cetinje

Podgorica

Philippopolis
(Plovdiv)

land gained
by Montenegro

Shkodër

Skopje

O T T O M A N

Constantinople

Tirane

Vardar R.

Salonika

E M P I R E

Corfu

*Aegean
Sea*

G R E E C E

Smyrna

Athens

	Newly independent from Ottoman Empire
	Autonomous areas within Ottoman Empire
	Relinquished by Ottoman Empire and placed under Austro-Hungarian administration
	Land gained under Treaty of Berlin

Rhodes

N

Crete

Mediterranean Sea

0   100 miles
0   100 km

HABSBURG TERRITORIES, 1814–1914

REPUBLIC OF KRAKOW

Krakow

Bohemia

• Prague

Moravia

Galicia and Lodomeria

Dniester R.

ARCHDUCHY OF AUSTRIA

Bukovina

Lake Constance

Vienna •

Danube R.

Salzburg

Tyrol

Budapest •

KINGDOM OF HUNGARY

Lake Como

Sava R.

Lombardy

Venetia

Drava R.

Transylvania

• Milan

Venice •

• Trieste

Croatia

Slavonia

Banat

Lake Garda

Po R.

Bucharest •

• Genoa

MODENA

BOSNIA
(Protectorate, 1878; annexed 1908)

Belgrade •

Danube R.

Sarajevo •

SANJAK OF NOVIPAZAR
(Occupied, 1878–1909)

Adriatic Sea

• Mitrovica

Corsica

Lake Scutari

Sardinia

N

Tyrrhenian Sea

Ionian Sea

	Habsburg territory, 1814
	Territory regained after Congress of Vienna, 1815
	Territory acquired, 1815–1914
	Austro-Hungarian Empire, 1914
	Kingdom of Hungary, 1866

0   100 miles
0   100 km

Sicily

EASTERN EUROPE DURING WORLD WAR II, 1938–1944

North Sea

Baltic Sea

Lithuania
• Vilnius

• Minsk

Danzig

EAST PRUSSIA

Belorussia

• Berlin

GERMANY

Warsaw

POLAND

SOVIET UNION

Silesia

• Prague

• Krakow

• Lviv

Kiev

BOHEMIA AND MORAVIA

Danube R.

Galicia

Ukraine

Slovakia

Munich

Bratislava

Trans-Dniestria

Vienna

SWITZER-LAND

AUSTRIA

Budapest

HUNGARY

Szeged

Bessarabia

Venice

Ljubljana

Zagreb

Timişoara

Transylvania

Odessa

Rijeka

Croatia

• Brasov

Sarajevo

Banat

ROMANIA

Zadar

Bosnia-Herzegovina

Serbia

Bucharest

ITALY

Split

Danube R.

Constanţa

• Rome

Adriatic Sea

Dubrovnik

Sofia

Varna

Black Sea

BULGARIA

Skopje

ALBANIA

Istanbul

N

GREECE

TURKEY

Athens

Mediterranean Sea

Legend:

— Greater Germany
–·– 1938 Borders
- - - 1943 Borders
Axis powers
States aligned with Axis powers
States annexed or occupied by Axis powers

0   200 miles
0   200 km

EASTERN EUROPE, 1948–1991

NORWAY

FINLAND
Helsinki

Leningrad

Stockholm

Tallinn
Estonia

SWEDEN

DENMARK

Baltic Sea

Riga
Latvia

North
Sea

Copenhagen

Kaliningrad

Lithuania
Vilnius

UNION OF
SOVIET SOCIALIST
REPUBLICS

Berlin

EAST
GERMANY

POLAND

Warsaw

WEST
GERMANY

Prague

CZECHOSLOVAKIA

Vienna

MOLDAVIA

SWITZ.

AUSTRIA

Budapest

HUNGARY

Kishinev
Odessa

ROMANIA

ITALY

Danube R.

Belgrade

Bucharest

YUGOSLAVIA

Black Sea

BULGARIA

Sofia

Adriatic Sea

Tirana

Istanbul

ALBANIA

TURKEY

GREECE

Independent communist state

Soviet intervention, 1956

Soviet intervention, 1968

Strong Soviet influence

Western boundary of the
Warsaw Pact states, 1955–1991
(Iron Curtain)

0   200 miles

0   200 km

N

WARS OF YUGOSLAV SUCCESSION, 1991–1995

DAYTON ACCORD SETTLEMENT, 1995

AUSTRIA

SLOVENIA

HUNGARY

Varaždin

Ljubljana

Zagreb

CROATIA

Vojvodina

Drava R.

Danube R.

Rijeka

Glina

Okučani

Osijek

Vukovar

Novi Sad

Slavonia

Sava R.

Sava R.

Krk

Bihać

Banja Luca

Brčko

Danube R.

Cres

Rab

Tuzla

Belgrade

Pag

Jajce

Maglaj

Knin

Zadar

BOSNIA

Srebrenica

Žepa

Dalmatia

Sarajevo

Pale

SERBIA

Split

Goražde

Mostar

YUGOSLAVIA

MONTENEGRO

Kosovo

Dubrovnik

Podgorica

Adriatic Sea

ALBANIA

Muslim-Croat federation

Serbian republic

UN presence in eastern Slavonia

Bosnian border

MONTENEGRO Republic

0   50 miles

0   50 km

N

KOSOVO CRISIS, 1999

Raška

Niš

YUGOSLAVIA

Morava R.

Novi Pazar

Kuršumilja

SERBIA

Leposavić

MONTENEGRO

Leskovac

Ibar R.

Mitrovica

Podujevo

Plav

Peć

Sitnica R.

Priština

Pristina

Kosovo Polje

Novo Brdo

Beli Drin R.

KOSOVO

Gračanica

Dečani

Kamenica

Vranja

Gnjilane

Morava R.

Dakovica

Bajram Curri

Preševo

Kačanik

Drin R.

Lake Fierzës

Prizren

Blače

Kumanovo

Kukës

ALBANIA

Skopje

N

Tetevo

Drin i Zi R.

Vardar R.

MACEDONIA

Gostivar

Veles

NATO peacekeeping sectors

——— Border of Kosovo province, Serbia

French

German

– – – NATO peacekeeping sector boundaries

Italian

U.S.

British

| 0 | 300 miles |
| 0 | 300 km |

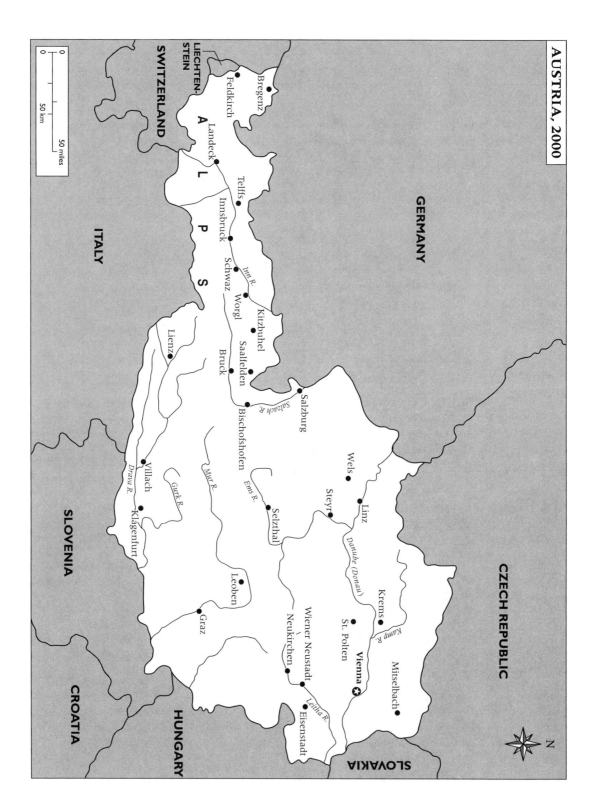

AUSTRIA, 2000

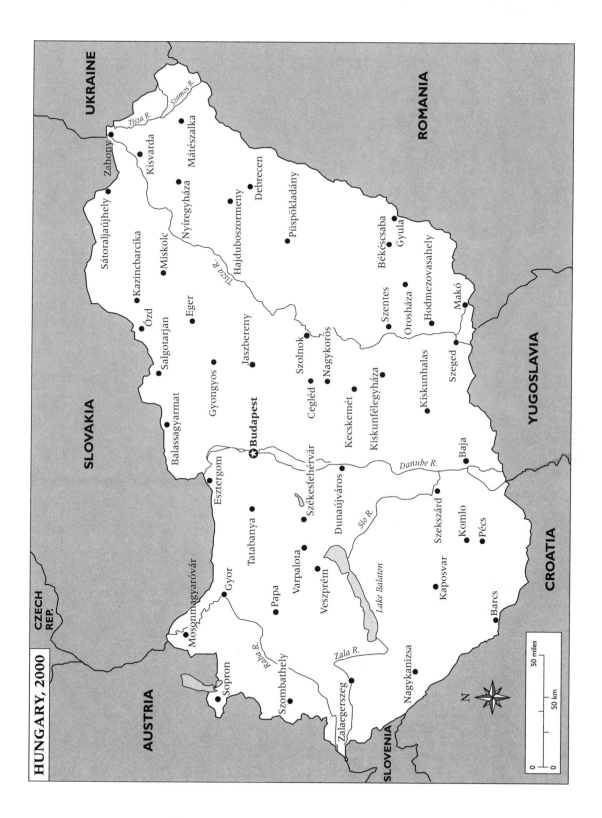

HUNGARY, 2000

CZECH REP.

UKRAINE

ROMANIA

SLOVAKIA

YUGOSLAVIA

AUSTRIA

CROATIA

SLOVENIA

Tisza R.

Szamos R.

Zahony

Kisvarda

Mátészalka

Sátoraljaújhely

Nyíregyháza

Debrecen

Hajduboszormeny

Püspökladány

Kazincbarcika

Miskolc

Békéscsaba

Gyula

Ózd

Eger

Tisza R.

Szentes

Hodmezovasahely

Makó

Salgotarjan

Jaszbereny

Orosháza

Gyongyos

Szolnok

Nagykorös

Balassagyarmat

Cegléd

Kecskemét

Kiskunfélegyháza

Kiskunhalas

Szeged

Budapest

Esztergom

Székesfehérvár

Dunaújváros

Danube R.

Baja

Tatabanya

Varpalota

Veszprém

Sio R.

Szekszárd

Komlo

Pécs

Mosonmagyaróvár

Gyor

Papa

Lake Balaton

Kaposvar

Barcs

Sopron

Szombathely

Raba R.

Zala R.

Zalaegerszeg

Nagykanizsa

N

50 miles

50 km

0

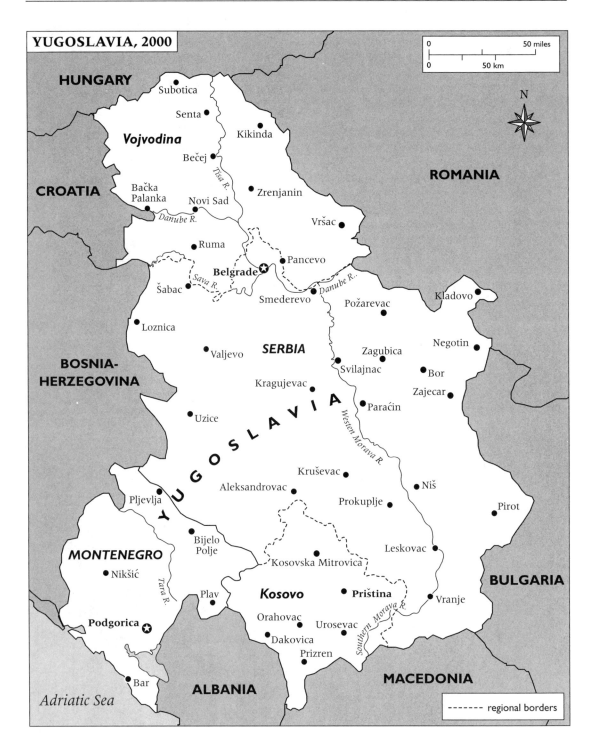

YUGOSLAVIA, 2000

HUNGARY

Subotica

Senta

Vojvodina

Kikinda

Bečej

Bačka
Palanka

Novi Sad

Tisa R.

Zrenjanin

CROATIA

Danube R.

Ruma

ROMANIA

Vršac

Pancevo

Belgrade

Šabac

Sava R.

Smederevo

Danube R.

Kladovo

Požarevac

Loznica

SERBIA

Zagubica

Negotin

Valjevo

Svilajnac

Bor

BOSNIA-
HERZEGOVINA

Kragujevac

Paraćin

Zajecar

Uzice

Western Morava R.

Y U G O S L A V I A

Kruševac

Niš

Aleksandrovac

Prokuplje

Pirot

Pljevlja

Bijelo
Polje

Leskovac

MONTENEGRO

Kosovska Mitrovica

Nikšić

BULGARIA

Tara R.

Plav

Kosovo

Priština

Vranje

Orahovac

Urosevac

Southern Morava R.

Podgorica

Dakovica

Prizren

Bar

ALBANIA

MACEDONIA

Adriatic Sea

N

0   50 miles

0   50 km

------- regional borders

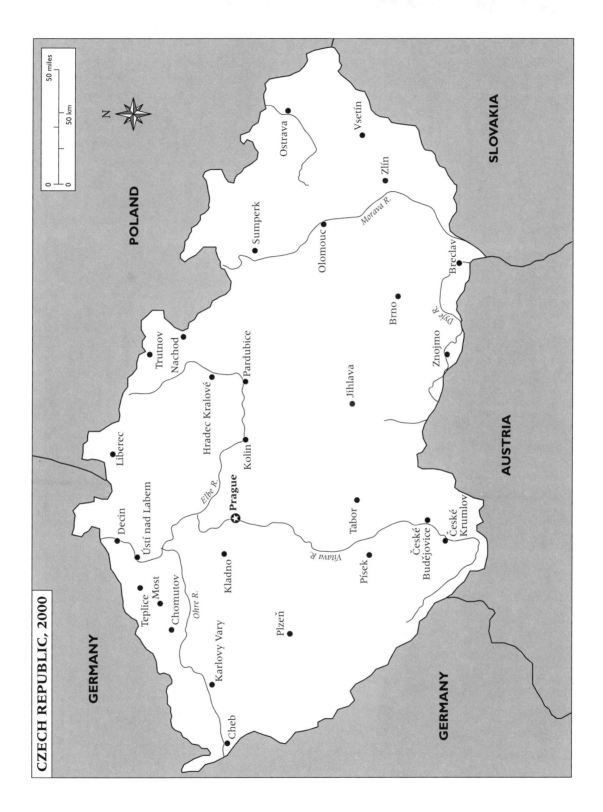

CZECH REPUBLIC, 2000

POLAND

SLOVAKIA

GERMANY

AUSTRIA

GERMANY

Ostrava

Vsetín

Zlín

Šumperk

Olomouc

Morava R.

Brno

Břeclav

Trutnov

Náchod

Pardubice

Znojmo

Dyje R.

Hradec Kralové

Jihlava

Liberec

Kolín

Děčín

Elbe R.

Prague

Ústí nad Labem

Tabor

České
Krumlov

Most

Kladno

Písek

České
Budějovice

Teplice

Chomutov

Ohře R.

Vltava R.

Karlovy Vary

Plzeň

Cheb

50 miles

50 km

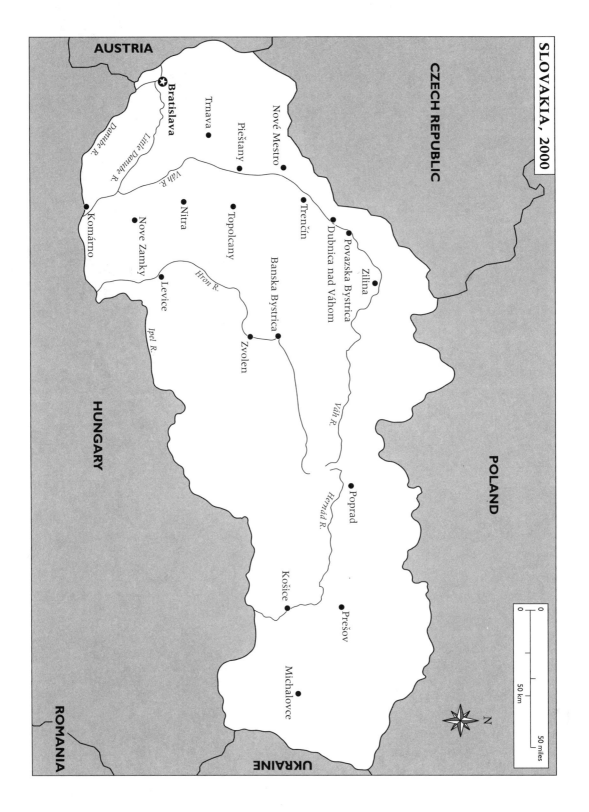

SLOVAKIA, 2000

SELECTED BIBLIOGRAPHY

Ádám, Magda. *Magyarország és a kisantant a harmincas években* (Hungary and the Little Entente in the 1930s). Budapest: Akadémiai Kiadó, 1968.

Autry, Phyllis. *Tito: A Biography.* New York: McGraw-Hill, 1970.

Balogh, Sándor, and Jakab Sándor. *A Magyar Népidemokrácia története* (History of the Hungarian people's democracy). Budapest: Kossuth Kiadó, 1978.

Barsányi György. *A válságévek kronikája, 1929–1933* (Chronicles of the years of crisis, 1929–1933). Budapest: Kossuth Kiadó, 1986.

Beales, Derek. *Joseph II.* 2 Vols. Cambridge: Cambridge University Press, 1987.

Beneš, Edvard. *Memoirs of Dr. Eduard Beneš, From Munich to New War and New Victory.* Trans. by Godfrey Lias. London: Allen & Unwin, 1954.

———. Tr. Paul Selver, trans. *My War Memoirs.* New York, Arno Press, 1971.

Bertényi, Iván, and Gyapay Gábor. *Magyarország rövid története* (Brief history of Hungary). Budapest: Maecenas Könyvek, 1992.

Bukey, Evan Burr. *Hitler's Austria, Popular Sentiment in the Nazi Era, 1938–1945.* Chapel Hill: University of North Carolina Press, 2000.

Crankshaw, Edward. *The Fall of the House of Habsburg.* New York: Viking Press, 1963.

Djilas, Milovan. *Tito: The Story from Inside.* New York: Harcourt Brace & Jovanovich, 1980.

Gonda, Imre, and Emil Niederhauser. *A Habsburgok; Egy europai jelenség* (The Habsburgs: A European phenomenon). Budapest: Gondolat, 1978.

Hanák Péter, ed. *Egy ezredév, Magyarország rövid története* (A thousand years; A brief history of Hungary). Budapest: Gondolat, 1956.

Held, Joseph, ed. *The Columbia History of Eastern Europe in the Twentieth Century.* New York: Columbia University Press, 1992.

Jelavich, Barbara. *Modern Austria, Empire and Republic, 1815–1986.* Cambridge: Cambridge University Press, 1987.

Juhász, Gyula. *A Teleki kormány külpolitikája* (Foreign policy of the Teleki government). Budapest: Acádémiai Kiadó, 1964.

Juhász, József. *Volt egyszer egy Jugoszlávia, A délszláv állam törénete* (Once upon a Yugoslavia; History of the South Slav state). Budepest: Aula, 1999.

Kann, Robert A. *History of the Habsburg Empire, 1526–1918.* Berkeley: University of California Press, 1974.

Kerekes, Lajos. *Ausztria hatvan éve. 1918–1978* (Sixty years of Austria, 1918–1978). Budapest: Gondolat, 1984

Kerner, Robert, ed. *Czechoslovakia.* Los Angeles: University of California Press, 1949.

Klemperer, Klemens von. *Ignaz Seipel, Christian Statesman in a Time of Crisis.* Princeton, N.J.: Princeton University Press, 1972.

Leff, Carol S. *The Czech and Slovak Republics.* Boulder, Colo.: Westview Press, 1997.

Legters, Lyman, H. *Eastern Europe; Tranformation and Revolution, 1945–1991.* Lexington, Mass.: D.C. Heath & Co., 1992.

Low, Alfred D. *The Anschluss Movement and the Paris Peace Conference.* Philadelphia, Pa.: American Philosophical Society, 1974.

MacCartney, C.A. *The Habsburg Empire, 1790–1918.* New York: Macmillan, 1969.

Masaryk, Tomas Garrigue. *President Masaryk Tells His Story.* New York: G.P. Putnam's, 1935.

May, Arthur J. *The Habsburg Monarchy, 1967–1914.* Cambridge, Mass.: Harvard University Press, 1951, 1968.

McLean, Fitzroy. *The Heretic: The Life and Times of Josip Broz Tito.* New York: Harper & Brothers, 1957.

Morris, Constance Lily. *Maria Theresa, The Last Conservative*. New York: Alfred A. Knopf, 1937.

Pavlowitch, Stevan. *Tito: Yugoslavia's Great Dictator*. Columbus: Ohio State University Press, 1992.

Plaschka, Richard G., ed. *Nationale Frage and Vertreibung in der Tswchechoslovakei* (The nationality question and expulsion in Czechoslovakia). Vienna: Verlag der Österreichischen Akademie, 1997.

Portisch, Hugo. *Österreich; Der lange Weg zur Freiheit* (Austria; The long road to freedom). Vienna: Kremayr & Scheviau, 1986.

Prague Spring, 1968: A National Security Archive Document Reader.

Rákosi Mátyás. *Viszszaemlékezések* (Memoirs). 2 vols. Budapest: Napvilág Kiadó, 1997.

Remer, Hans. *A History of Czechoslovakia since 1945*. Trans. by Evelien Hurst-Buist. London & New York: Routledge, 1996.

Roman, Eric. *Hungary and the Victor Powers, 1945–1945*. New York: St. Martin's Press, 1996.

———. *The Stalin Years in Hungary*. Lewiston, N.Y.: Edwin Mellen Press, 1999.

Sandgruber, Roman. *Illustrierte Geschichte Österreichs; Epochen, Menschen, Leistungen* (Austria's illustrated history; Epochs, men, accomplishments). Vienna: Pickler Verlag, 2000.

Sára János. *A Habsburgok és Magyarország* (The Habsburgs and Hungary). Budapest: Atheneum, 2000 and Kiadó, 2001.

Schuschnigg, Kurt. *My Austria*. New York: Alfred A. Knopf, 1938.

Shandor, Vikentii. *Carpatho-Ukraine in the Twentieth Century; A Political and Legal Crisis*. Cambridge, Mass.: Harvard University Press, 1997.

Suval, Stanley. *The Anschluss Question in the Weimar Era; A Study of Nationalism in Germany and Austria, 1918–1932*. Baltimore: Johns Hopkins University Press, 1974.

Szinai, Miklós, and László Szücs., eds. *Horthy Miklós, titkos iratai* (Secret papers of Miklós Horthy). Budapest: Kossuth Kiadó, 1962.

Thomson, Samuel H. *Czechoslovakia in European History*. Princeton, N.J.: Princeton University Press, 1953.

Vajda, Stephan. *Felix Austria, Eine Geschichte Österreichs* (Felix Austria; A history of Austria). Vienna: Ueberreuter, 1980.

West, Richard. *Tito and the Rise and Fall of Yugoslavia*. New York: Carroll & Graf, 1995.

White, Leign. *Balkan Caesar: Tito versus Stalin*. New York: Scribners, 1951.

Williams, Kieran. *Prague Spring and Its Aftermath*. New York: Cambridge University Press, 1997.

Williamson, Samuel R. Jr. *Austria-Hungary and the Origins of the First World War*. New York: St. Martin's Press, 1991.

Wilson, Duncan. *Tito's Yugoslavia*. New York: Cambridge University Press, 1979.

Zöllner, Erich. *Geschichte Österreichs von den Anfängen zum Gegenwart* (History of Austria from its beginnings to the present). Munich: R. Oldenburg, 1974.

INDEX